SECOND IN LINE SECOND TO NONE

A Photographic History of the 2nd Air Division

Ron Mackay
with Mike Bailey & Steve Adams

Schiffer Publishing Ltd
4880 Lower Valley Road • Atglen, PA 19310

-MIKE BAILEY-
2012

Library of Congress Control Number: 2014933266

Type set in Tasse & Georgia

ISBN: 978-0-7643-4382-7
Printed in Hong Kong

Published by Schiffer Publishing, Ltd.
4880 Lower Valley Road
Atglen, PA 19310
Phone: (610) 593-1777; Fax: (610) 593-2002
E-mail: Info@schifferbooks.com

Table of Contents

4 **Chapter One**
The B-17—Partner or Competitor?

10 **Chapter Two**
Girding up for Combat

19 **Chapter Three**
Parlous times for the 44BG

33 **Chapter Four**
"Ted's Circus" Travels

42 **Chapter Five**
Ploesti—Nightmare at Zero Feet

56 **Chapter Six**
From Wing to Division Status

67 **Chapter Seven**
Belated Expansion

84 **Chapter Eight**
Slugging it Out

100 **Chapter Nine**
Operation "Argument"

112 **Chapter Ten**
"Bearding the Nazis" in their Den

131 **Chapter Eleven**
D-Day Beckons

154 **Chapter Twelve**
A Plane a Day has Flown Away

165 **Chapter Thirteen**
Focus on Normandy

190 **Chapter Fourteen**
Stranglehold on Oil and Transportation

213 **Chapter Fifteen**
Strategic Priorities Regained

233 **Chapter Sixteen**
Martyrdom at Kassel

246 **Chapter Seventeen**
Last Rites

266 **Chapter Eighteen**
Nailing down the Coffin

Addendum (1) Field Order No.28, October 10-11, 1944 282
Adendum (2) Keeping the Memory Alive 283
Addendum (3) B-24 Armament 284
Appendix Listings 285
Color Gallery 288
Index 304

Chapter One

The B-17—Partner or Competitor?

The USAAF's strategic Bombing Offensive, launched in August 1942 and spanning the ensuing 32 months of WWII, depended upon twin, four-engine designs for its prosecution; predecessors were the Boeing B-17 Flying Fortress and the Consolidated B-24 Liberator. Between them, they brought home to the Nazi leadership the horrendous material and human cost of waging war upon what was primarily a democratic-based group of united nations. Air Chief Marshal "Butch" Harris, C-in-C RAF Bomber Command, had stated, following his appointment to command that mighty force in February 1942, "The Nazis have sown the Wind, and now they are going to reap the Whirlwind." A mere three years later, the Anglo-American heavy bombers had brought a stark prophecy to its terrible, but logical, fruition.

However, the ensuing seven decades since that comprehensive and ghastly conflict was concluded have witnessed the continuation of an imbalanced concentration upon, as well as praise directed towards, the B-17 and converse diminished recognition in a similar degree for the B-24. That the B-24, therefore, tends to sit firmly in the shadow of its WWII contemporary can be traced back to the wartime media. It is a fact that during the first winter of the Bombing Offensive, four "Pioneer" Groups carried the bulk of the assault upon the industrial and military infrastructure of the Third Reich. In the same period of operations, the two B-24 Groups saw their overall effort diluted by the lengthy detachment to North Africa of the 93BG, leaving the 44BG to soldier on.

As the campaign intensified during 1943, the build-up of what was initially the 2nd Bomb Wing (later the 2nd Bomb, and finally Air, Division) proceeded at a far slower pace compared to the 1st and 4th Bomb Wings. The evermore costly air battles over Northwest Europe, culminating in October's "Black Week," were ultimately prosecuted by no less than ten B-17-equipped Groups. By this latter stage of 1943, a mere four units comprised the now re-titled 2nd Bomb Division (BD).

This logistical factor in itself did not justify the over-concentration by reporters and cameramen upon the perceived exploits of the B-17 crews. The fact that the 91BG was based at Bassingbourn—a Permanent RAF airfield with brick-built structures and proper heating, which was also located within easy distance of London—presumably played no part in this unit's continuing prominent image within postwar publishing and film circles! It cannot be denied that the B-17's overall structural outline, especially on the ground, was aesthetically superior to its more bulky and elephantine-proportioned partner, the B-24. The fact that the former design was four years older and could not fly as fast or

The relative aerodynamic inelegance provided by the XB-24 prototype's slab-sided fuselage and foreshortened nose section is added to by the lowered landing gear. The first flight was completed on 29 December 1939, and nearly 19,000 airframes would be constructed over the ensuing six years.

A second view of the prototype, from a higher angle with the landing gear out of sight, gives a somewhat enhanced aerodynamic presence. The slim Davis wings possessed advanced flight characteristics, but were to prove particularly vulnerable to battle damage.

as far and with as large a bomb load, as the B-24 weighed little in the eyes and minds of the Public Relations staff. "Blitz Week," the first Schweinfurt mission, and "Black Week," which encompassed the second Schweinfurt mission within its four-mission sequence that furthermore cost 148 bombers and crew MIA. All these operations witnessed the almost total exclusion of the B-24 in terms of direct participation. That the B-24 crews had bled equally over the Ploesti oil complex tended to be virtually pushed into the background, not least because the attack was mounted from North Africa, far away from the U.S. publicity mills based in Britain!

Technical Comparisons—the B-17

The emergence of the B-17 prototype in 1935 witnessed a leap forward in military design for the United States Army Air Corps (USAAC). The ability (at least in theory) of a bomber that could safely operate at over 30,000ft and do so at speeds exceeding 300mph was greeted with delight. The high-altitude performance owed a deal to the introduction of turbo-supercharger gear for the Wright Cyclone engines. By the late 1930s, Carl Norden's precision bombsight had come into service. Along with the sight's (sadly mis-quoted, as well as hopelessly optimistic) ability to drop bombs "into a pickle barrel"—WWII experience would regard a strike within 1,000 feet of the Mean Point of Impact (MPI) on any target as a sound result—went the defensive qualities of what had been labelled the "Flying Fortress."

Ever since then, the term Flying Fortress has tended to be misused. Granted, the five .5 machine guns, albeit all flexible and single mounted, formed a solid weapons array in terms of 1930s developments. On the other hand, the RAF by the decade's end featured power turrets with two or four machine guns on its Wellington and Whitley bombers. In fact, it is likely the "Flying Fortress" tag that was credited to a reporter attending the aircraft's official unveiling could have related to his anticipating the bomber being developed as an aerial version of the military forts straddling the American frontiers in the eighteenth and nineteenth centuries. In other words, the aircraft's use was perceived as being couched in a defensive rather than an offensive manner, such as attacking an invasion force approaching from seaward. (Its use in bombing operations over another country would seem to have been remote, given America's huge geographic isolation from any potential adversary at this point.)

The Fortress was to prove a relatively stable base, both for flying in formation and as a bombing platform, although its pedestrian speed over targets, usually made around 150-160mph, turned the bomb run into an eternity for the crews. A climb rate of approximately 300ft per minute under full load conditions meant that assembly into Group, Wing, and finally bomber stream formation ate up between one and two hours before departure for the enemy hinterland could be launched; this factor in turn ate into the fuel reserves.

The B-17E, F, and G variants with which the 8USAAF conducted the Daylight Offensive over Europe sported between eleven and thirteen machine guns, a quantum leap from the original model. Top and ball power turrets (and the Bendix chin turret on the B-17G) were supplemented by a flexible pair in the tail, with single weapons in the nose compartment, waist, and radio room, the latter being deleted on later G variants. The original range of 1,300 miles was theoretically extended to 2,200 miles with the addition of outer-wing fuel cells known as "Tokyo Tanks."

The B-17 was no exception to vulnerability in the face of fighter and flak opposition. The toxic mix of fuel, bombs, and ammunition, along with inflammable properties within the very metal skin was to bring disaster to countless airframes and their hapless crews. On the other hand, degrees of battle damage ranging from heavily shot-up airframes to the loss of wing, stabilizer, and tail sections regularly witnessed the B-17 concerned being brought back home.

Technical comparisons—the B-24

The Consolidated Co., based in San Diego, CA, was approached by the USAAC at the beginning of 1939 in terms of constructing a four-engine bomber. The bulk of the company's design experience had hitherto involved seaplanes, but this proved no real impediment in a switch to land-based aircraft. A major innovation that was on hand for installation into Consolidated's latest intended seaplane was now to become part of the new specification. This was the Davis Wing, a slim, high-aspect aerofoil that, when fitted to the XB-24 prototype, provided a wingspan of 110ft. The fuselage was slung beneath the wings that were in a "shoulder" position when viewed from a fore and aft angle; this configuration was to cast up serious and often lethal flaws when combat operations were subsequently flown. The stabilizers were mounted along the top of the fuselage and provided with twin fins and rudders.

The overall visual effect was of a lumbering, "ground-hugging" machine, especially when given the tricycle landing gear provided. The main wheels were too long to retract into the inner engine nacelles and swung up into the wing instead. On the other hand, the engine nacelle pattern was aerodynamically slim and neat compared to the B-17, which had to accommodate the landing gear within its bulk. Power was provided by four Pratt and Whitney Twin Wasps with the same total output of 4,800hp as the B-17's Cyclones. Both engine designs were to prove very reliable in the midst of combat operations, their air-cooled structures proving more resistant to battle damage compared to their oil-cooled contemporaries.

The XB-24 was aloft by year's end, at which point sizeable orders split between the USAAC and the French government had already been placed. (The latter supply would be diverted to the RAF following the fall of France in June 1940.) The overall performance in terms of maximum speed, climb rate, and range was to prove equal to, if not distinctly ahead of its Boeing contemporary, as was its bomb load capacity, while attained altitude was around the same thanks to the turbo-supercharger facility.

The B-24's Operational Pros . . . .

When the B-24 was flown on solo operations, the pilot's task was relatively comfortable. Granted, the control responses on any WWII bomber were none too immediate, while the physical pressures in operating the control column, and particularly the rudder pedals, absorbed a fair proportion of individual strength. The function of the Liberators by No. 120 Squadron operating out of Iceland in the winter of 1942/43 proved absolutely vital. The region in the central North Atlantic had hitherto been dubbed "the Gap" or "Black Hole." These terms referred to the ability of U-boat "wolf packs" to operate against Allied merchant convoys with complete immunity from aerial assault. Now, the presence of even one Liberator circling a convoy in this zone had an effect out of all proportion to its solitary presence. U-boat commanders became ever more cautious in their maneuvers. More than one report radioed back to Doenitz's HQ in France, or uttered on return from a patrol, spoke of enemy aircraft in much greater

The power turret provision for the bulk of B-24D production batches was limited to the top- and rear-fuselage locations. Flexible armament was mounted in the nose compartment and also placed in the waist hatches with their detachable panels that can be discerned directly behind the National insignia.

A production B-24D airframe demonstrates two alterations compared to the prototype and early production batches. First of all, the nose compartment has been lengthened; second, the "stepped-up" stabilizer's union with the fuselage has now been lowered to leave a "flush" visual outline. Aircraft is the 93BG's **Teggie Ann** seen at Alconbury.

A frontal view of **Teggie Ann** picks out the high wing position of the B-24 and the outward-retracting landing gear. This construction layout presented major problems in maintaining the airframe's integrity in cases of either crash landings or even more so during a "ditching" action.

numbers than previously had been the case!

An equally important solo use of the B-24 was in the field of supply, or more precisely, in supporting resistance activities, primarily within Nazi-occupied countries in Europe and to a lesser degree in the Far East. The capacious fuselage interior of the Consolidated aircraft allowed for the carriage of a sizeable quantity of supplies along with the "Joes" (slang for the agents of the Special Operations Executive [SOE] and Office of Strategic Services [OSS]), whose function it was to direct sabotage operations and, in Churchill's words, "to set Europe ablaze" from within.

The RAF's use of the Liberator extended to the Mediterranean and the Far East. In the latter instance, several squadrons based in India in 1944/45 carried out attacks on Japanese-occupied Burma and Siam. Although the aircraft flew as a formation, the relative absence of fighter opposition and flak meant that a spread-out pattern could be maintained as opposed to the tight, serried ranks of bombers required over the hotly-contested skies of Europe. The former scenario, therefore, allowed for less physical effort from the pilots. Another advantage gained in Far East operations was that operations could be conducted from much lower altitudes, thereby leading to more generous fuel reserves, compared to the heavy initial drain experienced during Assembly in the European Theater of Operations (ETO).

The clear maximum speed advantage the B-24 enjoyed over the B-17 extended anything up to 30mph, with the original camouflaged production batches; when camouflage was dispensed with, the weight loss in paint added at least another five mile per hour advantage. It was all the more ironic that the inclusion of both designs in the same bomber stream during 1942, and particularly during 1943, pulled the B-24's performance downward in this respect. However, once the 8AF went over to attacking multiple targets in 1944, the B-24 units could then be separately assigned, in which case the speed benefit could at last be applied.

.... and Cons

The B-24's armored seat layout for both pilots, from the B-24H onwards, was very uncomfortable compared to the B-17. The seat-back was fixed vertically, while movement into and particularly out of the positions during an emergency was badly inhibited by the close-up presence of the controls pedestal. Visibility out of the cockpit windows was not good directly ahead and the wing layout ensured that the wingtips could not be seen by the pilots—hence, the manifold pictures of crewmen with their heads out the escape hatch directly behind the pilot, advising on the aircraft's correct alignment on the perimeter track while it was being taxied out of or back to its dispersal.

The problem of efficient control while aloft truly manifested itself when flying tight formation. For a start, the bomber had to be brought into and maintained at a marginally nose-down angle. Any other configuration generally resulted in inordinate physical strain being placed upon the pilots. The Davis Wing's high-aspect ratio was a factor in this issue and compared poorly with the more generous wing area of the B-17. Although aesthetic in appearance, the Davis wing proved dangerously susceptible to icing-up when the aircraft was flown at high altitude for prolonged periods—the very scenario facing the VIII BC fliers; the grim jest going the rounds was that the wing could not safely support enough ice to fill a drink glass!

The bomb bay doors that slid up the fuselage sides, as opposed to being hinged and opening out into the slipstream, provided another source of complaint. The frames could easily distort and either refuse to open or conversely jam in the full or partially open position, should battle damage warp the fuselage and/or jam the fragile operating mechanism. The flimsy nature of the doors often tempted the bombardiers to release in circumstances where these refused to open, trusting on the bomb weight to smash a way through.

It was in respect of battle damage that the B-24's structure showed up as a serious liability, particularly within the ranks of the strategic bomber forces in Europe. The Davis Wing was very prone to fatal damage, and not only from opposition sources. On one occasion, an airman bailing out of a higher-flying

B-24 impacted with the outer wing section of a fellow aircraft, resulting in the complete sub-unit snapping off under the man's weight, which had acted, in effect, as a human "missile," equivalent to a small bomb. (The absence of a wing spar structure on the outer wing section probably contributed to incidents such as this.)

The fuel lines interconnecting the wing tanks ran through the upper fuselage, so any puncture resulted in the saturation of the interior as well as the crew with what was the already high fire hazard hugely increased. The twin fin arrangement rendered itself much more susceptible to fragmentation, leading to irrecoverable loss of control should material damage be suffered; this contrasted with the B-17, where more than once the loss of a sizeable section of fin and rudder or stabilizer still left the aircraft maintaining its flight path and capable of at least regaining friendly territory for either a bail out or even a safe landing.

The structural limitations of the B-24's high-wing configuration really came into play in the case of a forced landing. The B-17's low wing position meant that the main shock on contact with land or water was absorbed without too much strain to the fuselage. Not so with the B-24. Not only was there no main spar in a similar position, the fuselage directly beneath the wings contained the bomb bays, whose "roller blind" doors coupled with the thin metal frame at the base, providing crew access between the front and rear compartments constituted no real strength factor.

In the case of impact with the ground, the tendency was for the fuselage either to twist as it slid along or literally give way and grind itself downwards. Twisting usually saw the fuselage break up directly behind the cockpit; this had the effect of dislodging the top turret, whose weight could and regularly did crush any crewmen unfortunate enough to be there at the time. Secondary fractures usually occurred directly behind the wing trailing edge. The weak lower fuselage structure more than once resulted in the overall frame being reduced to anything up to half its normal height in a forced landing, with serious injury or death claiming anyone on board.

As if forced landing on the ground was risky enough, the action promised even more potentially lethal consequences when carrying out a "ditching." The general tendency for a B-24 fuselage to fracture on either side of the wing area came into play in many instances. Even should the airframe hold together upon impact, the high-wing configuration almost always ensured that the crew were swamped by the inrush as the aircraft sank into the water and thus experienced much greater difficulty exiting the interior. (The B-17's low wing layout and even the mid-wing locations on RAF Lancasters and Halifaxes provided a potentially superior "ditching" platform, although the fact that the action naturally could not be practiced made it a "hit or miss" maneuver on the part of the pilots.)

The B-24 presented problems not only for the combat crews, but also for the ground crews. The loading of bombs was a particular source of complaint, given the low-slung profile of the airframe. The movement of bombs into the fuselage was a much more protracted duty compared to the B-17, whose angled-up fuselage allowed for instant and easy access. Carrying out maintenance work on the B-24's upper surfaces posed a clear physical risk, given the height of between ten and twelve feet. This was particularly the case with the narrow and sharp-cambered wing surfaces, off which it was easy to slip even in dry conditions, let alone when the wings were wet or ice- and snow-bedecked. A fall onto the concrete surface of a dispersal area could result in severe injury or even death.

The foregoing negative comments would seem to leave little option for even the most die-hard former Liberator crewman to argue to the contrary.

The armorers' duties were arduous enough in respect of any USAAF bomber, but were arguably worse when dealing with the B-24. The minimal degree of clearance with the ground compared to the B-17, for example, clearly added to the physically cramping handling of the bomb load either into or away from the bomber's racks.

The B-24's contemporary was a more aesthetically pleasing airframe as exemplified by a B-17F on a test flight. Abilities to hold formation more easily, as well as absorb greater degrees of battle damage compared to the B-24 were to its advantage. Conversely, the Boeing bomber's maximum bomb load was smaller, while the B-24 enjoyed greater maximum speed and range operational factors.

A Ford-built B-24J demonstrates the ultimate armament provision for the Consolidated design. The nose compartment now possesses an Emerson power turret in place of the flexible weapons and a ball turret has taken the place of the original and highly-unsatisfactory single flexible "tunnel" gun under the rear fuselage.

This picture confirms the inherent weakness of the B-24 in attempting crash landings. Lacking any material support from the wing-spar, the fuselage on **Shack Rat** (466BG) has twisted and fractured, leaving the Engineering staff with little choice but to apply "salvage" action. This incident occurred at Attlebridge while landing back off a mission on 19 April 1944.

However, for every individual who would support such a contention, there are more who genuinely appreciate the qualities of the aircraft that took them into battle and more importantly delivered them safely through their combat tours. The average pilot, as did all other crewmen, certainly lost weight during his combat tour, but unlike the others, would have ended it with a stronger pair of arms after wrestling with the controls. Navigators in the early models might easily have developed a permanent stoop, thanks to the unbelievable fact that no seating was provided. The remaining personnel were accommodated in a more reasonably comfortable manner, although bombardiers on later Models equipped with power turrets would have preferred the roomier upright clearance provided on the turret-less B-24D's nose compartment.

The jibes about the B-24 being a "banana boat" and "the crate the B-17 arrived in" were regularly countered by the counter-retort that the B-17 was "that four-engined medium bomber." This utterance was with regard to its inferior internal bomb weight capacity. The theoretical imbalance in favor of the B-24 did not work out so greatly in practice, however. Whereas the Boeing bomber's maximum load was 6,000lbs within its 11-ft, single-cell compartment, this figure was rarely exceeded by more than 2,000lbs on the B-24, despite its 17-ft, twin cell equivalent length. On numerous occasions, B-24 loads could be as low as 5,200lbs when carrying incendiary weapons, while standard bomb loads of 6,000lbs were another regular feature. (The maximum individual bomb weight that both designs could accommodate internally was 2,000lbs, since the central walkway divided the bomb bay width, creating this limitation.)

Given the perceived manifold difficulties surrounding the B-24's use as a strategic bomber, it begs the question of whether or not the aircraft should have been persisted with as a strategic bomber. The bald truth is that there was no realistic alternative. The withdrawal of hundreds of the design from this specific duty could not realistically have been made up from alternative sources. More pertinently, it should be realized that the overall loss rate in relation to total numbers of B-24s deployed within the 8th and 15th USAAF was materially no higher than in the case of the B-17. The majority of aircraft and crews survived operations, and that was the most effective, if crude, logistic yardstick justifying the B-24's continued service in this specific and key role. (A similar situation applied to Allied tank designs, which, in general, were inferior, both in armor and firepower to the Germans. The Sherman tank was a classic example, suffering a kill/loss rate of 1/6 in Normandy, with little better odds enjoyed throughout WWII. But its production rate *vis-à-vis* the enemy was such that the Allies could absorb such loss rates and still come out ahead in the long run in terms of intact numbers of units on hand. The striking power of the Sherman only approached that of its adversaries when numbers of British tanks were equipped with the 76-mm (17-pounder) weapon, but the hull frame remained dangerously vulnerable to destruction through blast and/or fire effect.)

Chapter Two

Girding up for Combat

Several weeks following Pearl Harbor, there occurred the initiation of what would, in time, become known as the "Mighty Eighth," when the U.S. Eighth Army Air Force was officially established in Savannah, GA, 28 January 1942. However, its subsequent presence in Britain was not an automatic fact at this point. It was only when M/Gen. Carl Spaatz, the officer selected to command USAAF forces in Britain, recommended to Gen Arnold (CG, USAAF) that it be deployed in this manner in order to operate in a strategic bombing role that the die was cast. An overall force of 60 Groups was projected, consisting of 17 Heavy, 10 Medium, and 6 Light bomber units, 12 Fighter units, and 8 Transport and 6 Observation units, all to be in place by mid-1943. In fact, the pace of this build-up would extend into early 1944, regarding the Heavy bomber and Fighter Groups. In addition, the Medium and Light units—those that did not suffer swift redeployment to North Africa in late 1942 and who functioned from British shores—would be transferred out in late 1943 to form the nucleus of the 9USAAF. A similar hiving-off of the other two categories of sub-forces would also occur, with the North African Campaign's expansion in November 1942 also causing redeployment of Transport Groups.

The bomber elements were gathered under the generic title of VIII Bomber Command and the fighters similarly assigned to the VIII Fighter Command. In the case of the former sub-force, four Bombardment Wings (BWs) were projected, but only the first two were to be given practical effect during 1942. The 1BW was assigned to the B-17 Groups, the 2BW to those operating the B-24, and the 3BW was intended to cover Medium and Light Groups. The 4BW was intended as a B-17 operating force, but its practical creation would be delayed until 1943.

2BW

The 2nd Bombardment Wing was officially created at Derrick Field, Maryland, on 7 June 1942, with B/Gen James P. Hodges as its Commanding General. At this stage in its history, there were just two Groups that fell within its purview: the 44BG and 93BG. The former unit had been activated nearly 18 months before, on 15 January 1941, while the 93BG was a more recently-activated unit, having commenced life 15 March 1942.

Although what was to be known as the "Flying Eight Balls" was to be the longest-lived Group operating in the B-24, its progress towards active combat operations was to prove particularly staccato, if not extremely frustrating in evolution. McDill Field in Florida was the chosen location, with an initial cadre of four officers and ten enlisted men being drawn from the ranks of the 2BG and 79BG. At this stage of USAAC existence, all groups possessed three

The magnificent splendor of Ketteringham Hall, which was sequestered as the Headquarters for the 2nd Bomb Wing, is apparent in this angled view; the living premises form the bulk of the property, with a large chapel adjoining at the front right. The building was located in between Norwich and Wymondham.

squadrons; in this instance, the numbers allocated to the 44BG were 66BS, 67BS, and 68BS. One of the squadron COs was a Maj. Ted Timberlake, but his tenure of office with the group would end in March 1942, when he was assigned to the command of the 93BG.

America was neutral at this point in WWII (January 1941), but the impetus to expand its military strength as quickly as possible was to bear particular "poisonous" fruit for the 44BG in the months ahead. A more immediate problem in group development was not just the lack of personnel, but also the fact that McDill was in the initial stages of construction and therefore unable to handle their numbers. The first two weeks involved the men on hand living in tents at Drew Field, after which sufficient proper accommodation was on hand. The relative luxury of these facilities with air conditioning, proper washrooms, and screened windows would be recalled with true regret when the personnel then at Drew finally arrived at their Norfolk-based operational airfield (Shipdham), whose facilities were very Spartan by comparison.

Equipment, both as regards aircraft and maintenance back-up, proved to be sparse, at least during the first half of 1941. One ground crew witness arriving in May recalled that the Group, far from possessing any B-24s, held a trio of machines: a PT-17, a B-18 and, horror of horrors, a YB-17 Fortress! Nevertheless, within these tight logistical limits, a constant degree of cross-country flying and navigational exercise and gunnery practice was indulged in.

The first B-24s were received towards the end of 1941, by which time America had been brutally thrust into the global conflict. The reaction of most personnel to the events in Hawaii can be summarized by Sgt. Arthur Harvey's recollection: "I had been to the Base Cinema where I had seen 'Target for Tonight,' a film based on RAF Bomber Command's operations. When I emerged from the building, I encountered a colleague who asked if I had heard the news that the Japs had bombed Pearl Harbor. I asked him, 'Who's she?'—so much for geography lessons."

A move to Barksdale. Louisiana, in February, would normally have seen the Group further expanding and extending its training patterns in readiness for combat assignment well within the year. Unfortunately, the authorities now decided that the 44BG would become an Operational Training Unit (OTU) source for cadres of personnel that would form the nucleus of newly-appointed Groups! The first such body of officers and men was assigned to the 98BG between February and March, with another large party dispatched to the 92BG around the same time (despite the latter unit being intended to operate the B-17). On 26 March, yet another cadre of personnel were transferred to the newly-created 93BG, while a fourth and fifth dilution of overall Group strength occurred in May, when over 600 were sent to the 90BG and 319BG.

Senior Appointment

It was during the Group's time at Barksdale that the latest CO was appointed. He was Col. Frank H. Robinson, who would be the third of nine officers to assume this post by VE-Day. However, his time in charge would end on a sour note on 4 January 1943, following an unfortunate end to the mission flown the day previous. He was also to be credited with the "*Flying Eight-ball*" term borne ever after by Group personnel. While at Will Rogers Field, and discussing the prospects of the Group ever going overseas, he said: "I cannot understand how the Air Force could ever think of my going into combat with these misfits, ninety-day wonders and odd-balls," further adding, "I have never seen such a bunch of eight-balls in my military career!" The ensuing weeks and months certainly saw him undergo a dramatic switch in his opinion, while the crews had a "Flying Eight-ball" painted on the forward fuselages, with the appropriate color for each squadron applied to the artwork noses.

The maritime crisis across the North Atlantic, and particularly off America's eastern seaboard and down into the Gulf of Mexico, caused by the depredations of the U-boats, called for every countermeasure by the Allied Naval and Air Forces. The "Rattlesnakes of the Ocean," as President Roosevelt had aptly tagged them, were having a field day, given the absence of proper escorts for the merchant vessels in what was America's back yard. The 44BG was in position to carry out patrols, in addition to which the B-24's extended endurance made it an eminently suitable design for this vital task.

The initial period of these operations between April and July cast up little positive in the way of sightings and/or attacks on a U-boat. In fact, the single incident was tragic in nature. On 9 May, B-24D/41-1117, bearing Lt. Herbert Frawley and eight crewmen (66BS), had barely cleared the airfield when it was seen to inexorably fall out of the sky. The resulting crash and explosion of the over-laden machine left nobody alive. In contrast, the next day, Lt. Norson (68BS) ultimately experienced a positive aspect to his patrol. His bombardier had initially directed him towards a dark patch of water onto which a 300-lb bomb was dropped, only to discover that the effect was caused by nothing other than a shoal of fish. The patrol was in its final stages when Lt. Diehl (CP) sighted what he described as a submarine off to starboard. By the time the B-24 was homing in on the vessel it had submerged, but the release and detonation of the four demolition bombs and single depth charge still on hand produced a welter of debris and a very dark oil patch.

A very different and "passive" role for the Group involved the detachment of three 67BS crews to Boling Field, Washington, D.C. They were attached to the Pentagon's 1st Photo Group and were tasked with photographing eastern Canada's region between Hudson Bay and the North Pole, the Canada/U.S. border zone, and areas of Greenland and Iceland. During this time, a specific search mission involved the successful tracking down of the crews on two B-17s acting as navigation leaders for eight P-38s heading for Europe. All ten aircraft had crash-landed on Greenland's icy wastes and their location was followed by an equally successful retrieval of all the airmen involved in the incident.

93BG Fortunes

The group that was destined to share the burden of early 2BW operations over the coming autumn and winter was one of those units that had in effect been "fostered" by its already long-established 44BG contemporary, still in seeming stagnation at Barksdale. Activation had occurred at the Field on 1 March, and it was here that First Phase training would take place. The Group CO was Ted Timberlake, who as a Maj. had originally been the CO of the 44BG's 66BS before first transferring to the 98BG, from where he was reassigned 26 March. His tenure of office over the 328BS, 329BS, 330BS, and 409BS—

The first Commanding General of what evolved from the 2nd Bomb Wing into its final form as an Air Division was Gen. James Hodges. He is seen here with the twin stars of a Major-General. His tenure of office extended to the middle of 1944, when Major-Gen. William Kepner assumed command.

The second overseas CO of the 44BG was Col. Leon Johnson, whose command of his personnel was firm but personable, as seen in this picture along with several combat crewmen. He was in charge of the Group between January 1943 and the following September, when he was promoted to Major-General and took charge of the 14 CBW.

The early-morning sun shot clouds form a backcloth for an anonymous B-24D as it lifts off on a mission with the landing gear's nose wheel already retracting. The airman in the left foreground waves to the crew in an apparent act of encouragement for their safe return—one that all too often was never fulfilled.

A four-ship formation of 93BG B-24Ds display minimal individual markings, other than their aircraft letters on the fin; two of **Joisey Bounces's** fellow aircraft are **Bomerang** and **The Duchess**. The former-named bomber finally went down on 13 November 1943, along with Lt. Loren J. Koon's crew, the pilot, and five others having formerly been part of Capt. Walter Stewart's team.

forming the Hardwick-bound unit—would last until 17 May 1943, when he would be replaced by Col. Addison Baker, a future posthumous winner of the Congressional Medal of Honor. However, long before then he had left his mark on the unit.

In sharp contrast to the protracted development of the 44BG, the 93BG's progress toward ultimate entry into combat was to follow the standard pattern for all ensuing Groups. By 15 May, it had completed its initial training and transferred to Fort Myers. In common with the 44BG, operations against the current U-boat threat in the Gulf of Mexico were added to the basic training schedule, during which operational activity no less than three successful attacks against U-boats were claimed.

On 2 August, the initial moves to England were initiated. A protracted journey by rail extending over 13 days resulted in the Ground Echelon arriving at Fort Dix. Here the personnel languished for just over two weeks, when the personnel were directed to board the Royal Mail Steamer (RMS) *Queen Elizabeth*. Any anticipation of a comfortable trans-Atlantic crossing was swiftly dispelled. The average carrying capacity of the *Queen Elizabeth* and its sister vessel, *Queen Mary*, was to be grossly exceeded several times over; no less than 15,000 to 17,000 servicemen would be packed onto either vessel. Such numbers would ensure that the cabins would be shared day-by-day, meals would be served as and when available, and individuals would have to have recourse to relaxing and even sleeping on alternate days. Both vessels were destined to trans-ship vast numbers of personnel across the Atlantic between 1942 and 1945, with each voyage completed in a matter of days, but it was axiomatic that personnel comfort had to be sacrificed in the process.

The transit of the Air Echelon was swifter, commencing from Fort Dix and up to Fort Grenier, NH. Here the Group transferred onto new B-24D models and prepared for the crossing of the North Atlantic. The transfer was commenced in early September and successfully achieved, which proved a credit to the navigators, for whom such an extended passage over featureless water stretches was a stiff navigational test. The initial element of the 2BW had arrived on British soil and was ready to add its weight to the admittedly limited effort that could currently be put forward by the VIII Bomber Command. George M Cohan's script to his WWI song "Over There" contained the line "The Yanks are coming," but initially only in small, scattered numbers on this occasion.

44BG Developments

The fortunes of the 44BG, as July was about to give way to August, now took a positive turn in terms of personnel integrity. The days of transfer-out under OTU constraints were finally over and the training schedule now steadily directed towards graduation for combat operations. During July, the four-squadron structure (66Bs, 67BS, 68BS, and HQ) was reduced to three, with the latter listed sub-unit disbanded.

The latest transfer was to Will Rogers Field, Oklahoma, and spanned the period 19 to 26 July. Here, intensive close-formation flying, with cross-country sorties honing navigational and bombing skills also thoroughly examined, was the regular Order of the Day. However, at this point, the Group was still seriously short in terms of numbers of Navigators, Bombardiers, Engineers, and Radio Operators—all key posts in ensuring the full efficiency of a crew under operational conditions.

A final transfer for the Air Echelon to Grenier Field, NH, was effected 29 August. Here, the inclement weather conditions did not provide a sound background for further honing the combat crews' skills; a number of the bombers originally received at Barksdale were not fully equipped for high-altitude flying. A further technical hindrance affected some of the most recently-assigned aircraft, since specific equipment items were missing. Return to Wright Field and Middleton Airport for the necessary updating had to be made in view of Grenier's Sub-depot proving not to be up to the task. The assignment of sufficient numbers within the four crew categories mentioned in the previous paragraph was being made here, but a question mark hung over how soon the Group could attain 100% combat status.

The combat crews responded well to this challenge and worked up to the required levels demanded by the authorities by the middle of September, with the Order for Overseas Movement anticipating the 26th as the date it would be put into effect. On that day, the first aircraft took off for Gandar Lake, in Canada's Newfoundland territory. A four-day stopover for the nine-strong B-24 force assembled there ended with the departure of the 66BS—destination Britain and assignment to the VIII Bomber Command.

Capt. Howard Adams maintained a diary and recorded the following notes on the crossing:

> I had originally taken off from Manchester, NH, for Lake Gander. A more miserable and bleak place is hard to imagine. No towns or roads, few people, but much wind and bitter cold. With 3,145 gallons of gas and a mess of baggage and equipment, my *Maisie* (B-24D/41-23777/H) was rather sluggish on take-off. On board were my eight crew and T/Sgt. Cotterman. [Cotterman recalled that the delay was due to a 500-mile cold front; the men were further informed that the first snowfall was already two weeks behind schedule and expected any time, so the sooner the crews departed the better!]
>
> We took off near midnight; it was black as pitch as we pulled up and turned on course, but the full moon soon came out to shine beautifully through the clouds. Flying at 500ft, we maintained this altitude for several hours to avoid icing up. We then climbed up through the overcast, picking up a little icing on the wings, but this melted around 7,000ft, which made us feel better.
>
> Only occasionally did we sight the cold Atlantic. Every hour, Lt. Gotke (N) would call up to provide an approximate position and a course change. All worked smoothly, as we had engaged the autopilot, so I could sit and watch the compass while making adjustments to maintain a correct course. The light in the east gradually improved to be followed by one of the most beautiful and breath-taking sunrises I have ever seen, with everything painted a golden color.
>
> Soon after, Gokte said we should sight land, so I started a gradual let-down; we hit solid cloud which persisted down to 1,000ft. The cold, grey water soon cast up a mountain mass, whereupon I climbed back up through the overcast to pass over the radio beacon on Dernacross, directing us to alter course for Prestwick, Scotland. We now sighted Bob Miller, who had departed several minutes before us, so we flew formation into Prestwick, where we made a landing at 1100GMT, exhausted but happy. Following dinner, we went to our quarters and fell into bed, not wakening until 0900!" [Howard's lease on life had less than five months to run.]

The other two squadrons suffered a similar weather-restricted delay in crossing the North Atlantic. The 68BS

The B-24D, which was the 2BD's operational variant until the autumn of 1943, possessed only flexible defensive armament in the nose compartment. The weapons mounted on either side behind the nose Plexiglas frame are backed by twin centrally-mounted guns; these in turn have displaced the single mounting located in the lower nose frame. The amount of firepower rendered even when both bombardier and navigator could get into action was barely adequate against the concentrated and often cannon-based fighter gunfire.

Lts. Llewellyn Brown (P) and Robert Quinliven (CP) are posed by the artwork on **Flying Cock**. The B-24's slab-sided fuselage skin was naturally made for depicting both detailed and large-scale paintings, of which this is an early example, both in terms of theme and size. Both these officers are believed to have completed their combat tours.

Jerks Natural, along with its crew, displays a U-boat outline on its nose to denote a measure of fame for both bomber and crew even before deploying overseas with the 93BG. During a flight over the Gulf of Mexico, the crew sighted one of Hitler's "Rattlesnakes of the Ocean" and were given credit for dispatching it to a permanent place on the sea bed! Medium Green blotching is evident in the shot of the B-24D.

arrived at Gander Lake 2 October, but commenced their overseas movement only on the 8th. The weather conditions en route were far worse than for the 66BS; in fact, crews landed at airfields spread between Northern Ireland, Scotland, and Wales. Only eight B-24s were involved; the ninth, held over due to a ruptured fuel, tank saw Lt. Chester R. Phillips and crew only reaching Shipdham in mid-October.

The Orders that dispatched the 67BS were issued on the 5th, but executed four days later. All but one reached the planned destination of Prestwick. In contrast, Lt. Bill Cameron's navigator could not pick up the necessary coordinates and the crew was grateful to manage a diversion into Ballyhalbert, Northern Ireland, where two of the 68BS teams had previously landed.

Cheddington, west of London, was the temporary destination for the group prior to final dispatch to Shipdham—the latter airfield was currently deemed unsuitable for heavy aircraft operations, and the runways, perimeter tracks, and dispersals were being accordingly strengthened—but the patchwork British countryside did not make an easy introduction for the navigators, who had to search somewhat before locating the airfield.

44BG Ground Echelon

The group support echelon's progress into combat was inevitably more protracted, since movement was by train and ship. A three-day train journey from Will Rogers Field ended at Fort Dix, NJ. Over the ensuing week, the personnel were subjected to all kinds of processes, including the replacement of summer clothing for ODs, an indication that Europe was their probable destination. On 4 September, the men were taken by train to a quayside, along which lay the RMS Liner *Queen Mary*, and one among their number said gloomily, "What a big f...... target!" This natural sentiment would fortunately never bear fruit up to VE-Day, however.

The number of men in relation to the accommodations, which saw on average eight bunks packed into a space normally occupied by two, ensured that individuals would have to spend alternate nights sleeping out on the open decks, while meals were served only twice daily. The seven-day voyage culminated in Scotland's Clyde Estuary, from where the hours-long debarkation and loading into trains was the start of the extended journey down to Cheddington.

Cheddington's facilities were basic, to the extent that it possessed no proper sewage system; the regular emptying of the "honey buckets" (naturally) became the task of lower-ranked personnel. In the month's stay there, the men had ample time to become acquainted with the local population, particularly in the "pubs." Exposure to British food was not so pleasant, but proved necessary with the current dearth of U.S.-produced supplies. One shining exception was the availability of that classic British meal fish and chips, especially when served up in a paper wrapping and liberally sprinkled with salt and vinegar—and a welcome substitute for Brussels sprouts, mutton, and so forth.

The Ground echelon transferred by train to Shipdham 9 October, and one man recorded that as they were approaching the railway station in Norfolk, he looked out of the carriage window to see the 67th and 68th BS bombers in the circuit, having completed their transit flight from Prestwick.

Flight Line "Rough Living"

The four-week period between the 44BG's full assembly at Shipdham and being placed on operational status was utilized to the maximum. This onrush of effort on what was a typical "utility" airfield resulted in a great deal of physical discomfort, particularly for the ground crews. They not only faced the ever-perverse Anglian climate that is primarily damp in nature, but were forced to live and work "out in the open," as it were, thanks to a current lack of construction material with which to fashion huts, as opposed to making the long-winded hike to and from the regular living sites. Heating and lighting was nonexistent within the aircraft, making flashlights a necessity once the shortening hours of daylight had gone.

The foregoing weather conditions often resulted in hands and limbs becoming stiff and frozen, thus creating problems when conducting intricate mechanical checks of engines, landing gear, and other external equipment that prevented the wearing of gloves. It was not uncommon for the personnel to work in successive short spells. Having been relieved, but with no buildings available for shelter, each airman would use every physical means to restore some degree of warmth to his chilled frame: running, stamping his feet, thrashing his arms, etc. The dearth of building material would extend over several months, as the American military effort during the first winter of WWII was painfully expanded and the liberal appearance of "line shacks" at Shipdham would be similarly inhibited until the Spring of 1943.

The Grim Task Ahead

In the superb 1949 film "Command Decision," which focused on the strategic aspects of the Daylight Offensive, there is a scene involving Clark Gable—himself a former USAAF officer who flew five missions in spite of being 43 years old—whose words aptly encapsulate the ever-contradictory as well as frighteningly variable atmosphere surrounding the combat crewmembers. Gable, as Division CG, is on the control tower balcony, watching the bombers assembling for a mission; alongside him is one of a party of visiting U.S. Congressmen who, gazing upon the scenario above, says to Gable, "I suppose nobody ever gets used to this?" In response Gable says, "The weirdest kind of war, Mr. Stone. A few hours from now, they'll be fighting on oxygen, five miles over Germany; tonight, some of them will be dining at the Savoy...and some of them will still be in Germany."

This conversation provides an accurate summation of what (along with their RAF contemporaries by night) was to be the common experience of any American airman destined to prosecute the Daylight Offensive. The majority of their time would be passed in the almost normal world of war-time Britain. In what was a frighteningly stark contrast, once committed to the several hours constituting a mission, they would forsake that hitherto mundane lifestyle for the very real chance of facing death, mutilation, or if fortunate, a POW's fate; a few would have the greater fortune of evading capture. This "never-never-land" existence would place an inordinate psychological strain upon everybody and the wonder was that so relatively few would break under the pressure.

First into Combat

The advance towards full combat status for the 93BG began to gather momentum around the time when its future 2BW partner's Air Echelon was still anchored in the USA and its Ground Echelon was being transported across the Atlantic. In fact, the 93BG's Ground Echelon had only arrived in Scotland a mere six days ahead of the 44BG party. However, the almost simultaneous arrival of the Air Echelon in Britain was coupled to the group's overall assembly at Alconbury. Unlike the 44BG's temporary and non-operational deployment at Cheddington, Col. Timberlake's crews were destined to actually commence operations from what was also a source of "temporary" deployment.

One 1,000-lb bomb from a load of four has been repositioned on a more mobile trolley for transfer into **Eager Beaver's** bomb bay. The 93BG B-24D is fitted with "needle"-bladed propellers that would be displaced on later production B-24s by broader and more efficient "paddle"-bladed units. This bomber became the 446BG Assembly ship following retirement from combat operations.

Five 1,000-lb bombs are displayed alongside **Katy Bug**, with the weapon closest to the bomber having both nose and tail fuses fitted in place. This, and the **Eager Beaver** picture were taken at Alconbury prior to the 93BG's transfer to its permanent base at Hardwick on 6 December 1942.Note the original nose gun position that proved to be useless in combating fighter attacks from higher angles.

The first VIII BC mission had been launched 17 August by B-17s of the 97BG and the 301BG, and the 92BG had also commenced operations within the 1BW on 5 and 6 September. These initial forays into Nazi-occupied Europe totalling thirteen credited missions by 2 October were conducted over France, Belgium, and Holland, and largely at ranges that ensured escort cover by RAF Spitfires. Only two B-17s had been declared MIA, although the average operating force was less than 30 and targets were a mix of ship building and marshalling yards, as well as Luftwaffe fighter airfields.

"The Wild Blue Yonder" Beckons

The second heavy bomber mission on 9 October would witness the expansion of bomber numbers exceeding three figures for the first, and very temporary, occasion within the Command's initial operational life span. On hand with the three "pioneer" B-17 groups would be the 303BG, with 24 B-17s standing ready at their Molesworth airfield. Further added to mission numbers would be 24 crews of the 93BG, and all five groups were briefed to attack aviation industry factories at Lille, in NE France. (It should be mentioned that at this stage in its operational career, the 93BG was officially operating within the 1BW; it would not be transferred to the 2BW until 6 December, and its first recorded mission within this structure would be on 27 January.)

Although the city lay barely 70 miles inside enemy territory, the 79 crews gaining mission credit out of 108 dispatched faced determined Luftwaffe opposition from the Fw190s of JG26. Four crews were lost, including one from the 93BG, while this figure also included a 303BG bomber—a sharp and painful initiation into the "Big League of Sky Fighting" for each Group. On the way in, Capt. Alexander Simpson's B-24D-1-CO/41-23678/330BS **Bathtub Bessie/Big Eagle** was summarily dispatched by Maj. "Pips" Priller, a leading JG26 *Experte* (Ace) and *Geschwader Kommodore*, crashing NE of the target at Roubaix-Wevelgham; six of the ten-man crew became the first group and 2BW combat fatalities. Out of the four survivors, only Sgt. A Cox (Eng.) evaded capture to eventually return to Britain via Spain.

The original 24-strong Group formation had fallen to ten at "bombs away" thanks to technical failures, in addition to which the overall bombing effort was generally abysmal. Battle damage was widespread, with 41-23722/(328BS) so battered that the initial reaction was to consider her for cannibalization as a spare parts hulk—a tempting remedy in light of a serious dearth in equipment availability. The airframe was instead repaired and **Bomerang** went on to fly many more missions, and indeed became the first 2BW bomber to complete 50 missions; she was finally flown back to the States in April 1944.

There could easily have been a more painful combat introduction for the group. An Fw190's gunfire struck home on 41-23667 **Ball of Fire**, flown by Lt. Joe Tate. Oxygen lines were severed, with recourse to walk-around bottles having to be made, while a ruptured fuel line soon drenched the bomb bay with the volatile fluid that very fortuitously did not ignite. The latter condition was only discovered after clearing the coast and T/Sgt. Aaron Moses (TG) managed to staunch the flow with a finger, but not before being liberally sprayed and suffering a frozen hand in the process. The pilots diverted into RAF Northolt, outside London. (This B-24D would survive combat operations before being ultimately salvaged in May 1945; Lt. Tate would not.)

A full twelve days now elapsed before the next mission was briefed, which was also the sole other October example. Once again, a three-figure number of aircraft (107) were sent out between the five groups, but to no real effect, because cloud cover prevented all but eight crews from bombing Cherbourg airfield instead of the Primary, which was Lorient's U-boat pens. Not only was this occasion the final mission for the 97BG prior to reassignment for Operation *Torch* (the projected Allied Invasion of NW Africa) and permanent deployment in the Mediterranean Theater of

Operations (MTO); it was the last occasion for several months when a three-figure number of bombers would be dispatched. The locust period for VIII Bomber Command material and human logistics was now at hand.

Tactical Disadvantage

When the defensive provision for the B-24 was set up, little thought appears to have been given to attacks initiated from a forward angle; a similar lack of consideration applied to the B-17. Whereas both designs featured power turrets behind the pilots and below the fuselage on both bomber types (albeit only first appearing on final B-24D production airframes), all weaponry in the nose compartment was single and flexible in nature up to 1943. On the B-24D currently in use, one was located to the right of the center nose Plexiglas frame, with one mounted centrally at the base. A third machine gun was mounted in the port-side window directly behind the nose frame.

This apparent sufficiency of forward firepower concealed the fact that (a) only the navigator and bombardier were "up front" and able to handle two at most, and (b) one or both could not always perform this vital function if they were involved in doing their respective duties. A further limitation lay in either officer being unable to bring the weapons into a fully forward direction other than for the central example, which also had a limited degree of elevation. This latter machine gun was subsequently repositioned higher up the frame, while some units placed two .5s in that location.

The top turret did provide a solid weight of fire, even though it held just two .5 machine guns, but the high closure rate of the *Jagdwaffe* fighters at best provided a fleeting chance to get the gun sight in operation. The absence of a ball turret on early and interim B-24D airframes was another disability, although the chances of picking up a fighter shooting past at a combined pace of anything up to 450/500mph was equally marginal in terms of sighting and firing. The bald truth was that the Germans were to hold the advantage over the *Big Friends* regarding overall firepower and ability to make effective strikes. The best that could be hoped for was for the USAAF gunners to ward off the worst effects of the aerial assaults. Even when nose-positioned power turrets were introduced on the B-24H and B-17G, the odds were still basically pitched in favor of the *Jagdwaffe* pilots.

At this stage of the Daylight Offensive, the proponents of the "self-defending bomber" theory were still in the ascendancy. The need for efficient long-range escort fighters was seemingly not considered paramount; only the P-38 possessed the ability to go deep into central Europe, but these were not yet on hand and would only arrive the following autumn. The few P-47 groups operating from March 1943 onward were found to be incapable of providing cover beyond the Low Countries; in time, the fitting of drop tanks would extend their range, but incredibly, these were not on hand to any extent and it would fall to the British Bowater concern to manufacture the initial batches in the latter half of 1943. As for the P-51, the marriage of the Rolls-Royce Merlin 61 Series engine with its two-stage supercharger to the North American airframe was also destined to be initiated on the company's production lines during the latter half of 1943.

Chapter Three

Parlous Times for the 44BG

The 44BG's initial months in combat were to prove extremely testing for all three available squadrons and particularly painful for the 67BS, whose original strength in bombers and crews would be virtually wiped out. The current absence of the fourth squadron was explained by the fact that the aircraft and personnel intended for the Group had been diverted into the Aleutian Islands in anticipation of a Japanese encroachment within the region, and the time interval between this act and the Group's departure overseas reportedly did not permit time for a replacement sub-unit to be created and trained. The situation would be rectified by the following March with the arrival of the 506BS.

The Ground Echelon's spell at Cheddington ended 9 October, when the move by train to Shipdham was made. The city of Norwich, which would be the social epicenter for the Groups of the ultimately-titled 2 Air Division, lay 15 miles to the east. The airfield onto which the combat and ground personnel descended was still a veritable mud heap thanks to the barely completed strengthening work on the runways and perimeter track. Over the next 27 days, the final polish was applied to operational procedures by the fliers, while the ground crews made similar strenuous efforts to maintain the bombers on the top line. The latter were literally exposed to the damp climatic conditions that made intricate mechanical work a nightmare, especially at night.

Come the evening of 6 November, and with final clearance for combat having been announced, the combat crews retired to bed to sleep as soundly or fitfully as they could. These young, brash, energetic Americans were representative of any party of USAAF personnel facing an uncertain immediate future. They were a long way from home; "school" was over and aerial combat with all its vagaries and attendant threats to life and limb was about to envelope them in its grim fold.

Operational Debut

The existence of several key U-boat bases on the western French coast had provided a deadly barb in the side of the Allied merchant fleets over the past two years, so any measure, however effective, to inhibit their function was to be called upon. The heavily reinforced concrete pens sheltering the "Grey Wolves" was to prove impervious to any material damage that even a 2,000-lb weapon, the largest in the USAAF's standard range, could inflict. Bombing of the surrounding building complexes was somewhat more rewarding.

The Kriegsmarine facilities at Brest were targeted 7 November by 1BW, but the seven 44BG crews were briefed to carry out a diversion to Cap de La Hague. This debut mission proved to

An Element from Shipdham is holding a tight formation, a basic requirement in both combating fighter assaults and providing a concentrated bomb pattern. Aircraft are reportedly (top to bottom) **Fascinating Witch** (41-23811/K), **Avenger** (41-23788/H), and **Sure Shot**, all "original" 66BS bombers; the first two-named bombers would be lost on 1 October and 16 December 1943, respectively, but **Avenger** would by then be a 68BS assignee.

be uneventful compared to the equivalent introduction for the 93BG, but the lack of fighter escort for the formation fortunately did not prove deadly, since no Luftwaffe opposition was encountered. Two days later, a six-strong formation participated in an attack on St. Nazaire's pens; the location was known as "Flak city" with good reason, since its gunners were top of their deadly trade. The three B-17s culled out of the force could have been more, since the bombers had gone in at a potentially suicidal 8,000 feet with enhanced bomb concentration the hoped-for result—an experiment not repeated to all-round relief!

The third group mission resurrected the "diversion" theme for the five crews dispatched to the Cherbourg Peninsula, this time under solid fighter cover. Next day, six crews headed for Maupertuis airfield at Cherbourg, but solid cloud allied to restrictions on "blind bombing" over Nazi-occupied Europe caused the five bombardiers still on hand to bring back their loads. Only two more November missions would be briefed, the first (15th) being diversionary in nature by six crews spread between the 67BS and 68BS. By the time the final mission was briefed (26th), the 66BS had returned to Shipdham, but its operational debut this day was denied, since adverse weather forced a "scrubbing."

Langford Lodge

The current availability of aircraft during most of November had dropped to 18, since the 66BS contingent had been dispatched to Langford Lodge, Northern Ireland, for operational modifications at the Depot sited there. One of the most basic was replacement of the ventral armament fired through a hatch by one placed further aft with scanning side windows in the fuselage. A more practical adjustment affected the nose-mounted weapon, which was raised higher to provide a greater degree of azimuth scanning. A VHF Command radio was installed, a fixed aerial replaced its trailing predecessor, and an updated IFF system was installed. Finally, protective armor placed in the bombardier's section of the nose doubled as a counter-weight to the ventral armament. In the months ahead, the modification list would rise to 40+.

The Blues Begin

To date, the 44BG had been briefed for or flown six missions with no casualties. This comfortable situation was sadly deceptive, as events in the weeks and months ahead were to reveal. Three of the briefings for missions in the first week of December were all "scrubbed" prior to take-off thanks to weather conditions. The fourth, on 6 December, saw the "recall" signal issued after the 44BG was crossing the English Channel with a nineteen-strong formation, the target being Abbeville/Drucat airfield.

The city of Norwich became the epicenter for 2BD personnel in the same manner as Cambridge did for the 1BD. It was rich in medieval churches, but this cultural aspect was probably not so much engraved upon the airmen's minds as the plethora of public houses and dance halls on hand! The city was particular host to the 458BG, since the Group's airfield impinged upon its northern fringes.

The flat fields of East Anglia, whose openness is scarcely embellished by any tree life, forms an unattractive backcloth to two 44BG B-24s; lower bomber is **Black Jack**, while its companion is **Suzy Q**. This picture is probably one of a sequence being shot from the accompanying bomber as it banks to starboard.

Rugged Buggy displays the "Flying 8-Ball" logo bestowed upon the Group by Col. Frank Robinson, who trained and brought the unit overseas. This "original" B-24D belonging to the 68BS survived until 14 May 1943; it was then one of five bombers MIA off the disastrous mission to Kiel and was being flown by recently-promoted Maj. O'Brien (Squadron CO), who survived as a POW.

SNAFU (40-2354), the oldest B-24D in the 2BW, was used to test a non-standard gun mount aft of the bomb bay. The original pitot mast location seen here was repositioned further back and up to permit the fitting of a gun-bearing window on the port side. Initials stand for the terse Service expression "Situation normal—all F....D up!"

Worse still was the fact that two of the three squadrons responded positively, leaving the 68BS in Lead position to continue on. The six crews managed to drop their bombs and turn for home unmolested, but as they approached the coast their luck ran out.

The recently introduced Luftwaffe tactic of head-on assault had soon found a basic weakness in current B-17 and B-24 defensive firepower. Apart from the power turret directly behind the pilots, all other guns were flexible, single items manned by the navigator and bombardier. The weight of firepower compared to the fixed batteries of machine gun and cannon-caliber weapons on the enemy fighters was miniscule. In addition, strikes on the forward fuselage regularly disabled or killed the crews positioned therein.

Lt. Dubard's B-24D-5-CO/41-23786/B lost power completely on No. 4 and partially on No. 3 engine from one such assault, whereupon the crippled bomber inexorably fell behind. Continued assault, particularly from behind and below the straggler, saw all return fire cease before it began to droop down towards the Channel waters. The pilots appeared to momentarily arrest the descent at minimum altitude, but then the nose again dropped and the aircraft sliced into and below the surface, leaving no survivors. Uffz. Schnell from 3/JG26 *Schlageter* was adjudged to have finished off the bomber. A measure of revenge was exacted by the B-24 gunners, whose fire brought down Ogfr. Eschke, serving with 1 *Staffel*, after he ill-advisedly attacked from behind; he went in with

Col. Frank Robinson (44BG CO) is flanked by actresses Martha Ray (right) and Kay Francis. The two actresses, along with a third individual, visited Shipdham on 15 December 1942. Sadly, within three weeks of this pleasant social occasion Robinson, would be supplanted by Col. Leon Johnson in questionable circumstances following a disastrous mission on 3 January.

his Fw190 near Ault. Shipdham's particular blood debt had commenced, although the full measure of sacrifice still lay in the weeks ahead.

Abbeville /Drucat featured on the Group maps (12) but only as a diversion for the main force, as cloud prevented bombing of the Primary. Ten days later, the Command's crews attacked Romilly-sur-Seine airfield and encountered strong opposition that downed six of the 76 attackers, none from Shipdham.

Capt. Adams (68BS) noted in his diary:

> The enemy fighters shot by so close that the pilots and their aircrafts' camouflage was clearly discernible. Our waist gunners were having a hell of a time with freezing hands and oxygen masks. The Spitfire escorts gave good support, but I felt it was an eternity before we re-crossed the Channel. Soon we lost altitude and began to pass the B-17s as we chattered over the interphone like silly schoolboys; what we said seemed funny, although we sobered up on hearing that Maj. Key's ROG had been wounded. At Interrogation everyone was polite as the questions flowed: How many planes did you see?; where did your bombs drop?; where did you meet flak?; did you see any bombers go down? We answered as best we could, although tired and strained, since food and sleep were our natural priorities. So ended our first real raid.

The reference to "silly schoolboys" must be put in context, since many of the combat crew were barely out of high school. Seemingly aimless chatter in reality was far from "silly," as it was a natural if not necessary psychological response to the dreadful pressures of combat flying by boys doing a man's job, all too many of whom would never survive to be on hand when victory was ultimately achieved.

Getting to know you - Well....?

As soon as the chance arose, many group personnel seized on the opportunity to travel further than the immediate area around Shipdham, with the city of Norwich, some fifteen miles to the east, proving to be a natural attraction. One airman recalled the initial confusion in the Americans establishing themselves with the citizens:

> I caught the Liberty Run, whose terminal was the Cattle Market. We wandered down the hill and questioned some people, "Where is downtown?" - "Down-town, what's that?" We explained that was where the main sources of entertainment would be. When that matter was settled, we asked, "How many blocks is it!" - "Blocks?.... Blocks?" We had received our first painful lesson regarding the common language that keeps us apart!
>
> Almost as frustrating as the weather was the British currency, at least on initial encounter. The multitude of denominations from farthings to half-crown coins, as well as the bank notes, was illogical and arithmetically confusing compared to the equivalent U.S. currency system. As for the commodity sold *en masse* in the pubs—beer it might be in name, but to most Americans, beer it was not! Nevertheless, the liquid's flat and warm nature did not prevent its wholesale consumption by me and other Trans-Atlantic "cousins" in indulging our thirst, in spite of our initial negative reaction!

Bad Start to 1943

The minimal ranks of the VIIII BC had been barely increased by year's end. Although 1BW witnessed the arrival of the 91BG, 303BG, and 305BG, this logistical advance had been trimmed back by the permanent departure for North Africa of the 97BG and 301BG. The situation for the even more minimal resources of 2BW became even bleaker as December commenced because the 93BG was also sent on detached duty to North Africa, leaving the 44BG as the sole Wing representative until late February.

The pounding of U-boat bases in France involved the first mission of the New Year, one that would end disastrously for Col. Robinson, as well as the Group. The (unlucky) thirteen crews briefed for St. Nazaire were led by Maj. Key (66BS CO), and their specific target was buildings reported to hold torpedoes. "Aborts" due to technical failures affected five B-24s, but the truncated formation held course behind the 1BW formations to deliver a strike assessed as "fair." So far, so good.

On the way back, landfall over the extreme SW English coast was anticipated but did not occur, since the Lead Group had reportedly gone off course. Lt. Bartmess (N) suggested to Lt. W. Cameron (P) that it was his estimation the formations were heading up the Irish Sea; the situation was worsened by the reduced fuel loads previously loaded. With this in mind, the Group turned to starboard and the crews were advised to seek suitable landing sources—none too easy, given the hill and mountain terrain of large areas of Western England, as well as Wales.

In any event, all but three of the B-24s managed to land on airfields, at least one of which was a small grass strip from which Lt. Cameron would be hard-pressed to subsequently take off. Lt. J. B. Long (67BS) and crew, having suffered progressive loss of power, survived a heavy crash in 41-23808/P **Texan** following the loss of their last engine as they approached an airfield at Aberporth, South Wales. Their good fortune was not matched by four airmen on the remaining two bombers. First, Lt. R. L. Hilliard, piloting 41-23771 (66BS), and finding no suitable source as his fuel was running out, settled his charge down into a Welsh field bordered by what he assumed were hedges, but were actually lichen-covered dry-wall dykes; impact with a dyke wrecked the aircraft and fatally injured Lt. D K Canfield (CP). The other three fatalities were borne on 41-23806/Z **Bat out of Hell** (68BS), another B-24D-5-C. Lts. Roy B. Erwin (P), Clark E. Swanson (CP), and Tom G. Deavonport (N) either were killed or fatally injured when the B-24 went out of control following loss of all power on landing approach to an airfield, again in South Wales.

The repercussions from this seemingly avoidable incident (at least according to the authorities) extended to Col. Robinson. It was several days before the scattered remnants could find their way back to Shipdham. Bill Cameron was among other pilots who were dumbfounded when they were not greeted by Col. Robinson, but his successor, Col. Leon Johnson. The new CO would probably have elicited a range of negative reactions from the personnel during his initial spell of command, since Robinson had been very popular. In time, this West Point graduate would gain equal unconditional respect and later move up to General status and command of the 14CBW following eight months in charge at Shipdham.

The adverse winter weather conditions interceded in launching missions during January. Up to the 18th, seven out of eight briefings had resulted in a "scrub" for the 44BG. The exception (13th) saw the crews heading out towards the Dutch coast in a "diversion" run while 1BW went into NE France. It was ten days after this run that seventeen B-24s took off for Lorient. Five bombers failed to make assembly and the reduced formation, having failed to link up with 1BW, initially headed for the Secondary at Brest; Col. Johnson finally decided that the risk to the Group from fighter interception was too great and all turned for home.

Into Germany at last....

To date, VIII BC's operations had been conducted outside Hitler's homeland, but the final completed January mission would commence ringing the changes to that hitherto frustrating scenario. Wilhelmshaven, in NW Germany, was a major naval base that was briefed for assault on the 27th. Although the 44BG was to provide the majority of the 2BW's effort (20), a further six crews from the 93BG would also participate.

Although the B-24s got off in good order, ever-more cloud cover over the North Sea and uncertain navigation intruded to separate the formations from contact with the 1BW. The undercast finally broke sufficiently for Col. Johnson to establish the B-24s were

Ms. Francis (right) and Raye in turn flank Mitzi Mayfair as the former-named actress samples an offering from one of Shipdham's cook houses. The trio had appeared in the Hollywood film "Four girls and a Jeep"; the picture provides a good indication of their interest in the overall running of a Group as opposed to restricting their visit to socializing in "Officer Country."

A line of Shipdham B-24s led by **Fascinatin Witch** (whose rear fuselage bears a myriad of flak patches) is taxiing out. The thunderous roar of the 1200-hp Pratt and Witney engines, accompanied by squealing brakes as the stream bobs its way towards the runway end will signal to the civilian population that a mission is "on."

Space was ever at a premium inside any bomber, with the B-24 no exception. Here, the waist gunners have a marginal opportunity to avoid bumping into each other as they wield their bulky 65-lb machine guns, while attempting to maintain balance in their often-swaying and undulating bomber—all under imminent threat of injury or death from fighter assaults.

over the Ijsselmeer water stretch of Holland and a Target of Opportunity (TOO) was picked out in Lemmer. Turning for home, the bombers were intercepted by a mixed pack of Bf109s and Fw190s striking mainly from ahead. One of the latter, flown by Fw. Koch of 3/JG1, failed to complete a safe breakaway and rammed the port wing on Lt. Nolan B. Cargile's 41-23690 (68BS). A progressive disintegration of the bomber immediately ensued and the sections tumbled into the Waddenzee, leaving no survivors among the ten-man crew.

The 68BS's woes were doubled with the loss of Lt. Max W. Sullivan's 41-23775 **Spirit of 76**. The No. 3 engine was set ablaze by gunfire from several Fw190s and the B-24D-5-CO fell out of formation to almost immediately break apart and crash close to or in Terschelling's harbor. Three parachutes were reported prior to the explosion, but only Lt. Albert W. Glass (B) survived; as it was, he was very fortunate to be plucked from the frigid waters, although the subsequent amputation of one leg led to his ultimate repatriation to the States. Today's mission thereby signalled the start of what would arguably be the darkest period in the Group's existence.

Broken Taboo

A key principle in flying formation was that any aircraft finding itself out of position for whatever reason was expected to seek its own salvation. In no circumstances were other bombers to come to its assistance, because not only did the "helper" risk annihilation from the defenders, but the absence of such aircraft reduced the overall defensive firepower of the formation. A court martial was the threatened outcome for any offenders, assuming that they survived the incident.

Capt. J. O'Brien's 41-23819 **Rugged Buggy** sustained fighter strikes that killed two gunners, as well as disabling the nose and tail armament, followed by the B-24 dropping several thousand feet and being ripe for individual dispatch. Lt. J. Diehl, Jr. (also a 68BS "original"), flying in 41-23816 **Black Jack**, took it upon himself to drop out and down in what transpired as a successful effort to both "beef up" defensive firepower and finally win through; Diehl's navigator, Lt. Kelley, also functioned for both crews, since O'Brien's navigator had been seriously wounded, and both aircraft landed back at base. Far from suffering any official sanction, Lt. Diehl would carry on until February 1944, by which time he had attained L/Col. status and was regularly flying as a Command Pilot!

Torrid February

The first part of February 1943 produced nothing in the way of combat experience for the Group or the 2BW. One mission was commenced (4th) to Hamm's marshalling yards. So many among the fifteen-strong Shipdham formation, further reinforced by six 93BG bombers, reportedly suffered technical malfunction that the mission was abandoned as the Dutch coast loomed up; an alternative account of VIII BC operations asserts that extreme minus temperatures forced the abandonment. One recurring problem lay in the oil used on machine guns freezing up. Dispatching such a small force well into enemy territory seemed rash, to say the least; it was difficult enough for a large-scale VIII BC force to make a positive attempt in terms of bombing results and nil or low losses, let alone this minimal force. (One calendar month later, the 91BG penetrated to the same target, but only because their Leader purported not to receive the "recall" signal to which the other 1BW Groups responded. The facts were not officially announced until after VE-Day, the inference being that USAAF hierarchy did not want to encourage similar acts during the course of the Conflict.)

"Milk-run" Debacle

The morning of the 15th, the crews at Shipdham and Hardwick called to the Briefing Rooms saw the map ribbons stretching no further than to Dunkirk, on the NE French coast; this in turn promised a short-duration mission with marginal flak and fighter interference—in effect, a "milk-run." The more experienced airmen would not have been too relaxed, since no such guarantee of a risk-free mission could arise. Nevertheless, the few minutes over enemy soil did promise an easy-paced sortie—in theory.

The *Togo* was originally a merchant vessel that had been converted to a mobile aerial radar platform. Normally based in the Baltic, it had been dispatched to Dunkirk for re-fitting and anticipated anchoring in the Helgoland Bight, off the NW German coastline. Here, its long-range *Freya* and *Wuerzburg-Riese* sets, functioning as part of the *Nachtjagd's* defensive system, would pick up and track the RAF bomber formations well before they crossed the night-shrouded North Sea.

Seventeen and six B-24s, respectively, rose up from Shipdham and Hardwick and headed SSE, where less than 100 miles distant lay their maritime target. The weather conditions were clear as the bomb run commenced, with Maj. Don W. McDonald and Capt. Arthur V. Cullen in the latter officer's 41-23783/M **BettyAnne/Gallopin' Ghost** (67BS) as the formation Lead. The flak gunners speckled the sky around the bombers, but the bomb run proceeded with no adverse effect up to "bombs away," other than an engine strike on Capt. Cramer's bomber.

Cullen later recalled that the "bomb release" light in the cockpit confirming Lt. Caldwell (B) had operated his bomb sight had just blinked when he was rendered temporarily unconscious by a tremendous explosion under the B-24's nose. On recovering his senses, he was astounded to find himself in a roofless cockpit with nothing but the instrument bulkhead remaining, the nose compartment having been totally excised by the flak shell!

Maj. McDonald had suffered a serious stomach wound, but was conscious enough to indicate that Cullen bail out as the bomber began to fall into a steady dive with heavily smoking engines. Despite a broken leg, Cullen assisted his fellow pilot to unstrap before both airmen jumped—but not before Cullen sustained further fractures to the other leg and an arm by impacting with a vertical fin. His luck was still in, since he managed to deploy his parachute and land safely, as did McDonald. Unfortunately, the Major's injuries proved fatal, even though he ended up on the operating table of a German hospital after being apprehended. Only four of the eleven airmen on board survived the bizarre demise of their bomber.

An even worse casualty rate (100%) involved the eleven men on board Lt. Rufus A. Oliphant's **Railway Express** (41-23794, 67BS). Flak had inflicted heavy damage which, allied to fighter assault, ultimately ended with the B-24D-5-CO plunging into the English Channel close to Dunkirk. Nor was the pressure eased for Capt. Thomas R. Cramer's 41-23800/Y **Captain and his Kids** (68BS). A number of Fw190s appeared out of the sun as the bombers turned back. The Oliphant and Cramer-led B-24s were out on their own, accompanied by Lt. Diehl, again acting as a straggler "protector." The swift dispatch of Oliphant's aircraft, which sustained fatal engine and fuselage damage before exploding on impact with the water, was followed by Cramer having a second engine disabled and a third set ablaze. The situation was made even worse by failure to release the bombs due to release mechanism damage on the bomb run. Fortunately, Lt. Bob K. Flynn (B) did carry out a manual jettisoning as the English coast loomed up. Cramer elected to make a crash landing on the sand- strewn Sandwich Flats adjoining the current world-famous golf course. Sadly Flynn, Lt. William A. Poole (N), and T/St. John W. Crump (Eng.) took up Cramer's advice to jump prior to this action, but died in the process—all the more tragic, in that the remaining seven

Lt. John Diehl (standing on the right) is posed with his 68BS crew against the neat artwork on 41-23 816/X **Black Jack**. Diehl ultimately completed his combat tour as a L/Col. on 21 February 1944. **Black Jack** was not so fortunate, being lost over Wiener-Neustadt on 1 October 1943, with Lt. Whittaker and four of the five Enlisted men going down with her.

The scavenged inner wing surface on **Black Jack** is clear evidence of how the ravages of the weather as well as combat operations soon left their effect upon the camouflage paint. Medium Green blotching stands out on the aileron surfaces. Absence of leaves on the trees confirm this as a 1942/43 winter shot.

Two 44 BG bombers are snapped on 15 February 1943 as they overfly Dunkirk. The Channel port was current home to the **Togo**, a night fighter radar platform, but the vessel remained unscathed, despite the welter of bomb strikes. A third Group B-24 out of frame being flown by Maj. McDonald (KIA) and Capt. Cullen (POW) is in the process of falling to the flak gunners.

A major weakness with the original B-24D's forward defensive armament was the positioning of a single machine gun at the base of the Plexiglas frame; the result was an inability to engage attackers approaching from above a horizontal level. The raising of the weapon to the revised position along with a doubling up of firepower as shown here alleviated the situation to some degree.

crewmembers came through the subsequent crash landing with slight injuries at most.

The Grim Reaper struck again within 24 hours of the Dunkirk mission, with the twin casualties a self-inflicted loss. Formation flying required a high concentration in skills from the pilots; in addition, the unpredictable air conditions had to be added to the equation when maintaining proper station. The mission to St. Nazaire was being led by Maj. McDonald's successor, Maj. "Pappy" Moore. Also on hand was Lt. Long, whose crew had survived a crash landing on 3 January. The English coast was just being cleared when the 66BS aircraft 42-40354/C **Snafu**, flown by Lt. J. R. Billings, dropped sharply down to the left. Lt. Long, in 41-23818/R **Texan II**, was behind Billings and opened his throttles to bypass his faltering companion; for whatever reason, he chose to go below, rather than above **Snafu**, whose title now became tragically appropriate.

Billings, upon noting Long's approach, reportedly swung to starboard, but in doing so his port wing tip made contact with the other B-24's fuselage to throw both aircraft out of control. Mere seconds passed before the volatile mix of bombs, ammunition, and fuel caused both airframes to erupt into massive balloons of flame and smoke. Reports of up to four parachutes, even if true, provided no salvation for the airmen concerned, and twenty more names on Madingley Military Cemetery's "Wall of the Missing" would be their stark corporate epitaph.

One of the most arduous, as well as dangerous ground crew functions was that allotted to the armorers. In this picture, the exposed nature of Shipdham's bomb dump is shown as three airmen begin to move one from a pile of 1,000-lb bombs, with their distinctive "hogshead," using a mobile crane. Death or serious injury through accidental explosions or bomb release consumed a fair number of 8AF personnel's lives

The shattered top turret frame and massive destruction around the copilot's position bears apparent mute testimony to the fate of the gunner T/Sgt John Crump, along with Lts. William Poole (N) and Robert Flynn (B) on 41-23800/Y **Captain and the Kids** (68BS) over Dunkirk. The three deaths were actually caused by bailing out too low prior to Capt. Cramer "bellying in" when the fuselage most likely split open on impact; the copilot would have been fortunate to emerge unscathed, however.

Capt. William McCoy (66BS) was known as "Wild Bill," but this title was a misnomer; far from being reckless, the six-foot, sturdy-framed pilot was admired for his flying skills. On 20 February, he was "shooting" a series of "circuits and bumps" (RAF slang for "touch and go" maneuvers) with Col. Snavely on board. Howard Adams's diary notes take up the details on the ensuing tragic incident:

> Following several sessions, the Col. got out to be replaced by Lt. Brown (B), acting as stand-in copilot. Some 20 minutes later, we heard the aircraft had crashed; I hoped against hope it wasn't serious, but on rushing into Operations I was crushed by the news that Bill and crew were dead. All were swell fellows, but Bill's loss was the hardest individual blow yet suffered, as he was liked by all, from Colonel to Private. He could put a B-24 through its paces and had led the Group many times, being far the best at it. Apparently, the whole tail assembly fell off and the B-24 went into a flat spin. (Howard had unknowingly made his last diary entry, with his equally young and vibrant life six days from running its final course.)

The B-24D-1-CO in question was 41-23703/A. On one of the seven missions it had flown to date, it had apparently been dived to half its original 28,000-ft altitude while still bearing its 6,000-lb bomb load. The clear inference is that the fuselage had been strained beyond safe limits and ultimately failed. Suggestions that the pilot had added to the disaster by heavy maneuvering during this terminal flight were firmly rebutted. None of the eight airmen came through alive, all doubtless being held in position by centrifugal forces.

Unpublished Endeavors

One 44BG bomber (41-23784/T **Miss Dianne** (67BS)) had survived on 16 February, but was badly shot up in the process. The endeavors of the ground crew to bring her back into commission were typical of the "ground-pounders'" zeal during WWII. The port wing had been liberally shredded with holes and the punctured fuel cells had to be replaced. This seemingly simple task was nothing of the sort. First, hundreds of panel screws on the 3ft x 5ft aluminium plate beneath the cells that also formed the wing skinning had to be detached. The physical effort of working at arm's length while standing on boxes and ladders was arduous; it was also prolonged, because screws would regularly fracture and have to be drilled out. Finally, the damaged cells were released and replacements inserted.

In all, the entire task absorbed nearly 24 hours of the mechanics' time. The No. 3 engine was also shot-up and its detachment revealed an equally damaged supercharger, a second duty that took up most of a second 24-hour period. M/Sgt. Baccath's team, by then almost reduced to a zombie-like state, had fulfilled their basic brief to "keep em' flying" by returning their charge to full combat condition. Countless achievements of this nature not only kept the American bombers aloft, but also ensured that maximum pressure was maintained upon the enemy's resources. Sadly, anecdotes of this nature were rarely if ever deemed worthy of the media's attention.

End of the Road

The Writing 69th was a tongue-in-cheek title for a group of U.S. newspaper journalists serving as War Correspondents. On 26 February, VIII BC launched its penultimate monthly strike, this time at Bremen. The total 2BW force was seventeen, with eleven from Shipdham. This day, several of the correspondents had elected to join in the mission, all but one opting for positions on 1BW bombers. The exception was a *New York Times* representative, named Robert Perkins Post, who elected to go with the 44BG.

Post was assigned to Capt. Adams's crew operating 41-23777/H **Maisey** (66BS). The formations tracked out over the North Sea towards the Frisian Island chain, skirting the North Holland coastline. Fighter attacks began to mount over the Dutch landscape, but the B-24 force stationed at the rear of the bomber stream remained relatively unscathed at first. The situation altered sharply as the B-24s made the final run-up to the Primary. Following several fighter passes, in particular those by Oblt. Heinz Knoke of JG11, Capt. Adams's aircraft absorbed strikes that set first the lower fuselage and then No. 3 and 4 engines on fire. The B-24 veered out of formation and finally exploded to leave two out of the eleven-man crew alive—Bob Post was not one of them and his body was never found, while Howard Adams was also counted among the dead.

Lt. Gotke (N) did survive, and his last recollection while still on board was of somebody pushing at his back, after which he lost consciousness. He recovered in midair, only to find his ripcord would not operate; a desperate recourse to pulling off his pack's cover and feeding the parachute folds out into the air very fortunately worked. Even then his troubles were not over, because on landing, the canopy fouled in the tops of trees to leave him some 20 feet above the ground before his captors assisted him down.

Knoke provided a vivid postwar account of the incident in his book *I Flew for the Fuehrer*. His first approach landed strikes on **Maisey's** starboard wing as he barrel rolled and barely missed colliding with the B-24. A second approach was more deadly, when cannon shells set the fuselage on fire. His vision registered the bomber veering right in a wide sweep to become a victim of *Heraus-schuss*—a term translating as "shooting out of position"; this was the next best action to destroying an opponent, since the aircraft so affected was ripe for terminal treatment, having lost the protective fire of the formation.

Two more passes were made, the final one from above and behind, but still met with strong return fire. Then:

> I watch the shells burst and rake the fuselage top and the right wing. Fire spreads along the wing, which then breaks off. The body of the stricken monster plunges vertically, spinning into the depths. A crewmember attempts to bail out but his parachute is in flames; he somersaults and falls like a stone. At 3,000ft there is a tremendous explosion, causing the spinning fuselage to disintegrate. Flaming fragments fall on a farm close to Zwischenahn airfield that sets buildings on fire. I land and run over to the scene, where the wreckage lies strewn over the field. The explosion threw the crew out in midair and their bodies lie beside the smoking remains. One hundred yards away I find the captain's seat and nose wheel. A little doll, evidently a mascot, sits undamaged between the cabin's shattered windows. I cannot help thinking about the Americans. When will our turn come? These airmen share in common with us the great adventure of flying. Separated for the moment by the barriers of war, we shall be reunited.

Although the latter sentiment seems mawkish in tone, and Knoke has to be regarded as defending an extremely autocratic political and military system, it cannot be denied that there has always been a degree of common respect, if not appreciation between most aerial combatants ever since WWI witnessed military conflict expanding into the skies. "The Knights of the Sky" may not all have fought under the Geneva Convention and "The clean Air War" was far from being so, bringing death and injury in often horrifying circumstances. Nevertheless, aerial

A mixed party of 44BG personnel and British firemen stand back from the shattered remnants of B-24D 41-23703/A **Scrappys Pappy** straddling a country road adjoining Clarmont Hall, near Watton. The 66BS bomber was conducting test flights in the hands of Capt. "Wild Bill" McCoy when it went out of control and slammed into the ground, killing all on board. The incident occurred on 20 February 1943.

Three Elements of 44BG aircraft are tracking over a more geographically attractive area of Norfolk, whose tree foliage indicates a date no earlier than May. The lower sub-formation has not formed up in similar closed fashion to its two contemporaries. Relatively low altitude suggests the flight was a practice for the forthcoming Ploesti mission.

conflict in comparison with the soldiers' lot on a battlefield has probably been regarded as a somewhat more sanitized and impersonal way of carrying out the act of combat.

A second 66BS crew was taken down around the same time. With two engines on fire and the bomb bay sheathed in flames, Lt. Robert H. McPhillamy had little choice but to order a bail out, to which all but Lt. Rexford W. Lippert responded, the navigator having already been killed. **Sad Sack** (41-23804/J) finally crashed outside the western fringes of Oldenburg. The squadron contingent of three faced total annihilation when 41-23811/K **Fascinating Witch** began to straggle, but two other pilots, seeing her plight, took it upon themselves to take up close position, an act that fortunately paid off for all three crews.

March

The pattern of operations in March would witness a marked increase in the number of missions flown—nine compared to five—while the attrition rate for the Group would drop noticeably, at least for March. Diversions (4th, 12th, and 13th) and runs to bomb Brest's U-boat pens (6th) and marshalling yards at Rouen two days later took up the first half of the month. The numbers of crews dispatched between the 44BG and 93BG were still small, averaging fifteen per mission. Although the Rouen mission was briefed for the city's marshalling yards, it was apparently regarded as a "diversion" effort for the 1BW heading for Rennes, even though the 2BW would be encroaching on enemy territory as opposed to making a feint.

Lying just inland on the river Seine, there was hope that a "milk run" could be in the cards, but as with Dunkirk, such a prospect was to be in vain. The region possessed the elements of JG2 *Richthofen*, a battle-tested *Geschwader* extending back to the Battle of Britain and tasked with covering Western France. The escort cover of P-47s and Spitfires was largely drawn off as the bombers approached the target, an act that permitted almost unfettered access to the sixteen-strong B-24 formation for up to forty Fw190s. Maj. Clyde E. Price was Lead in 41-23784/T **Miss Dianne** (67BS), having displaced Maj. O'Brien; the latter had aborted during assembly, and although taking off in another B-24 was unable to catch up. On the way over, Lt. Robert W. Blaine had moved up from the formation rear into the Lead element No. 2 slot—an act that would be tragically counterproductive.

A devastating burst of fire blasted the Lead B-24's fuselage and the aircraft went out of control. Although the bail out bell was sounded, just four out of eleven crewmembers got clear. This survival rate was reduced by one when Lt. Morton P. Gross (B), having suffered a severe stomach wound, expired on the ground in the arms of Sgt. Ken L. Erhard (WG). The same firing pass fatally crippled 41-23988/E **Emma Lou/ Double Playmate** (67BS), reportedly killing Blaine in the process. Once again, although the bail out bell was rung, only Lt. Leo O. Frazier (N) safely exited the doomed bomber that piled in north of Rouen. Today's squadron cull had reduced the original nine-aircraft complement to four. Postwar records indicate Hptm. "Wutz" Galland (II/ JG26 *Kommandeur*) and Ofw. Roth (4/ JG26) were granted credit for these *Abschuesse* (Kills).

The Vegesack mission (18th) was the first that the 93BG again flew in group strength, having returned from its North African detachment, in addition to which the 44BG was in the minority for crews dispatched (9 compared to 18). Group losses were confined to the fatal wounding of S/Sgt. L. M. Balsley (66BS), who died 72 hours later.

The 506BS had recently arrived at Shipdham and dispatched its first crews to Wilhelmshaven on the 22nd, one of whom commenced the sub-unit's MIA count. Out over the North Sea during approach to the Dutch coast, Lt. V. R. Fouts, piloting 41-24191/X **Cactus**, steadily fell behind and finally disappeared; aircraft and crew were never seen again. During the mission, the 67BS' 41-23832/N **Maggie** was badly shot-up, first by flak and then by fighter gunfire. Capt. "Bucky" Warne's efforts to maintain his lagging B-24 in flight finally ended with a desperate call for all to bail out, although the bomber was out over the sea. It was never established how many of the eleven airmen did take to their parachutes, but the sad outcome was that a mere two—Lt. Robert K. Walker (N) and Sgt. Lester G. Klug (WG)—were fortunate enough to be plucked out of the remorseless North Sea by a ship in passage to Helgoland. The group's blood debt for March was over

April

The Daylight Offensive during April demonstrated a frustrating relapse into mission "scrubbing," as well as by far the worst punishment handed out on a single mission. Only four missions were completed, with the all-1BW force on 17 April losing sixteen out of 115 B-17s over Bremen. The 2BW went out on the 4th, 5th, and 16th, and it was the 93BG that suffered all the losses over this operational period, with three downed on the Brest mission dispatched on the latter date. The respite from similar sufferings was doubtless welcomed within the 44BG, but there could be no guarantee of its extension, as events in May would cast up.

A Briton's View of his Ally

It was around this time that a Mr. Lee, reporting for the *Norfolk News*, put into more positive perspective the manner in which the Americans conducted themselves; in effect, what he recorded balanced out the "Over-paid, over-sexed, over-here" image the British were generally expressing about their Ally:

> For some months, the sight of officers and men of the USAAF has been a familiar feature across Norfolk; so familiar that it has long ceased to be a matter of curiosity. Now we accept them—almost, for we are still East Anglian—as part of our community. How did this happen in a country that is traditionally slow to talk to "foreigners?" Part, I think, because we have been quick to realize that these Americans are as much a part of Great Britain. Partly, because an innate hospitality instinct has been quickened by the thought they are in a way our relations, albeit distantly removed! Mainly, I believe, because so many have proved eager to fit in with our ways, and are delighted when an "Englishman" gives the slightest of chances to show what good "mixers" they are.
>
> I visited a Norfolk base where on the outside of a hedge was a farmer drilling barley; on the other side was the USA. The accents I heard would make a hardened film fan realize the Hollywood accent I knew so well was as foreign and affected to an American as an Oxford accent was to a blunt Yorkshire-man. My turn of speech did not prevent my being made very much at home.
>
> Rumors about their lavish lifestyle had previously made my mouth water. Well, this is one item that proves the saying "Believe nothing you hear." I saw no luxury, and if USAAF rules approximate to our Navy's "hard living" allowance, the personnel earn it—they work and live hard! The officers and men have a narrower distinction in their conditions, and the former have no servants. There are no "passengers," each man doing his job. All of them—outside of administration, office, and cooking staff—are contributing to flight operations.
>
> One thing pleased me. I saw several RAF airmen, and knowing we formerly occupied the Base, remarked upon this to my guide. "Yes, but they'll be going soon. We have to stand on our own feet and these are the last of a grand bunch of guys who have taught us a lot. In fact, all we know about air tactics and operations over here has been taught by your RAF boys."
>
> The blunt, uncomplimentary comments made by the same guide about my first Link Trainer "flight" made me realize that Americans say what they mean and mean what they say. I therefore accepted the compliment to the RAF as one that was completely sincere. I departed with a wholesale regard for their efficiency; no "spit and polish" and a military discipline lax compared to ours, but actions bypassing what they regard as unessential. It does not apply to their keenness in the big job they do as part of the Allied Air Offensive over Europe.

Variations in Fortune

As May was entered, the VIII BC was about to see a steady upsurge in its strength. The arrival of the 351BG in April saw this unit ready to commence operations, along with the 379BG and 384BG that had arrived in Britain around the same time. Also on hand during the month were the 94BG and 96BG, while the 95BG Air Echelon was already on hand and waiting for the Ground Echelon. These three units would form the basis for the 4BW. There was no similar increase in 2BW strength, however.

Disaster over Kiel

May would witness a dramatic switch in fortune for the 44BG, all within a 72-hour period. The perennial "diversion" mission was allotted the Wing on 1 and 4 May, while three days later, Maj. O'Brien was given command of the 68BS, a duty that would soon lapse a mere seven days further. On 14 May, the crews were briefed to attack Kiel Naval Base, which possessed U-boat construction yards among its industrial facilities. The Battle of the Atlantic was still in a critical state of balance, hence the perceived importance of this particular target. The plan of attack was for the 1BW to drop high explosives with the 2BW in train, releasing incendiaries—a fine theory, but one that would rebound drastically upon the 44BG.

The 0500 hours awakening of the assigned crews was later than usual, but

The disastrous Kiel mission of 14 May is over, with the 44BG short five crews. Group personnel are milling around **Victory Ship**, which has incurred casualties among the crew as attested to by the waiting "meat wagon." Lt. Tommy Holmes (P) was struck by a flak fragment, but his injuries were thankfully light.

Sir Anthony Eden, Britain's Foreign Secretary, visited Shipdham on 25 June 1943 and is seen with Gen. Jacob Devers (directly behind); Lt. Robert E Miller (P) is at the extreme left, lined up with his crew. **Fascinatin' Witch** (41-23811/K), a 66BS "original," forms the backcloth to the occasion; it would be lost on the Wiener Neustadt mission of 1 October, although most of Lt. Bridges' crew would survive as POWs, with the pilot escaping in May 1944 and regaining Allied lines in August.

was also a time too late for Bill Cameron and "Pappy" Hughes to participate, even though they were on hand at the briefing after arriving back from London. Bill, having been copilot to Capt. Chester Phillips, was now an Airplane Commander, but the link between these three "original" pilots was to be cruelly eclipsed this day.

Maj. James E. O'Brien, with Lt. Malcolm C. "Mac" Howell, had the lead for the eighteen-strong force in 41-23819/Bar-A **Rugged Buggy** (68BS); Assembly was made, but combat altitude was not completed until the aircraft were well out over the North Sea. Navigational error placed the formation over the Frisian Islands and flak from there landed strikes on the Lead B-24, resulting in manifold pressure loss on No. 1 and 2 engines. The bomb run was commenced, but the poor trajectory performance of the incendiary loads forced the Group to proceed beyond the briefed bomb release point for the 1BW. A further problem arose at "bombs away," because the unpredictable flight path of the incendiaries caused many to form a vertical spread that in turn forced pilots to open up the formation in a prearranged manner. Unfortunately, it was right at this stage that the Luftwaffe intervened.

The formation was turning for home at this time, but at least three B-24s were straggling and therefore particularly ripe for enemy attention. One was **Rugged Buggy**, which now had a punctured fuel tank whose content vaporized within the bomb bay and inevitably ignited thanks to fighter strikes. T/Sgt. Ralph C. Ernst (ROG) tried to batter a gap in the forward bomb bay doors to allow an emergency exit for crewmembers, and in fact eight of the ten on board bailed out safely. Following Maj. O'Brien's capture and custody, one of his interrogator's asked: "Do you know a little man in a yellow suit? He is *Tot* (dead)." This turned out to be Lt. Howell, who was believed to have suffered a ripped parachute. The other fatality was Sgt. Harold D Van Oyen (BT), who was picked up already dead from Kiel harbor.

The Lead bomber's loss was paralleled by four others. The 67BS had three aircraft on hand, with Capt. Chester Phillips flying **Little Beaver** (41-23807/U). Flak struck home to set the fuselage on fire, after which the B-24 fell into a flat spin with the pilot already dead and Lt. Everett W. Wilborn (CP) either killed at his post or subsequently. A particularly cruel fate awaited Lt. Thomas E. Bartmess (N), a 22-mission veteran, who drowned in Kiel Bay. Lt. William E. Hill (B) delayed his jump and floated safely down onto land, while three gunners further made up the survivor element out of eleven on board.

Lt. William A. Roach in 42-40126/T **Annie Oakley** was taking his crew on their baptismal and (unknowingly) final mission. The team was the first squadron replacement, but their operational career was cruelly eclipsed at the first hurdle; only Lt. Louis I. Kissinger (N) of the two airmen reported as bailing out ended up as a POW, while the B-24 came down west of Neumunster.

The attrition continued apace with the final 67BS casualty. Lt. Robert I. Brown's 41-24278/Q **Miss Delores** was fatally crippled by flak after losing one engine and dropping behind, allowing fighters to latch onto its tail. Three gunners, out of the ten airmen on board, lost their lives, with Capt. Robert H. Bishop (N) being fortunate to be fished out of the water. T/Sgt. John L. Susan was even more fortunate to survive a similar immersion. He misjudged his height when releasing the parachute harness and was initially smothered by the spreading canopy; a fisherman with a gaff pole proved to be the airman's salvation, as he hooked him out from underneath the potentially deadly material.

The latest group torment was completed by another straggler, 41-24295/J **Wicked Witch**. A head-on assault set an engine on fire and damaged the cockpit while the formation was still out over the Baltic waters. A turn towards land was made and the bail out order given by Capt. John W. Swanson, but only the four officers ultimately survived; the five enlisted men came down in the sea, four of whose bodies subsequently washed ashore. Lts. Richard L. Schieffelbusch (N) and Sidney W. Bank (B) nearly shared their fate, as they also descended into the sea, but the fortuitous presence of a fishing boat proved to be their salvation.

Lucky Exception

The 44BG's latest reverse could have been intensified by what happened to the 66BS' **Scrappy** (41-23014/P) in Lt. John Y. Reed's hands. According to the pilot, the formation had experienced a number of bombs released from the preceding 1BW group that fell within its ranks, fortunately without lethal effect—other than to thoroughly frighten those who also viewed the incident. Then a burst of fire shattered the top turret and severely injured T/ Sgt. Adam C. Wygonik (Eng.). First aid was given by Sgt. Alan T Perry, who also snapped on his colleague's parachute pack, ready for bail out. Finding himself going dizzy, he took a few seconds to inhale oxygen from his detached mask before turning back to Wygonik—only to find him absent! A. natural concern was that the Sgt., having fallen out of the open bomb bay, might have passed out and never recovered in time to deploy his parachute; this would only be eased in the fullness of time, when word of Wygonik's POW status was received. (He was hospitalized after being picked up, but his head injuries resulted in the removal of one eye.) Orbiting over Shipdham, Reed discovered that the landing gear would only partially lower, leaving him with little safe option for even a grass landing, since the gear might "dig in" with probable fatal results. He and Lt. Winger bailed out the crew before heading towards the coast; applying the Automatic Pilot, both pilots jumped to leave the B-24 flying to destruction, a fate that was accelerated by a group of Polish fighter pilots who shot the bomber out of the sky.

Ruthless (506BS) had been heavily damaged; however, instead of landing at Shipdham, Lt. Slough was directed to head northwest to Northern Ireland in 41-24282/Y and land at Langford Lodge Depot for repairs. A second badly damaged aircraft, 41-24009/W **Margaret Ann**, flown by Lt. Jansen (68BS), was bearing four seriously wounded gunners, one of whom (S/Sgt. Leo V. McGrady Jr.) lost his hold on life the next day.

Shipdham's experience up to now had been particularly traumatic within the VIII BC structure, and the 67BS had borne a virtual 100% loss. The day following Kiel, just 41-23817/L **Susy-Q**, along with Bill Cameron, Howard Moore, and a handful of other personnel formed the remnants of nine aircraft and—more relevant as well as tragic—over 100 combat crew who, so full of spirit, had set out across the Atlantic the previous October. The locust days of material and human logistics were on the point of being permanently buried, while just three days later the Group fortunes would take an upward turn.

Bordeaux "Bullseye"

The port of Bordeaux lies well down on the Bay of Biscay coast and adjacent to the Spanish border. Among its facilities was a repair depot for U-boats, while the docks served as a staging post for Axis blockade-running merchantmen. On 17 May, while the 1BW was assigned Lorient, the 2BW was briefed for Bordeaux. The chosen route would place a special onus upon the Lead navigator, since the approach took the form of a huge curve out into the Bay of Biscay. In addition, the crews would not set off from Norfolk, but stage down to Davidstow Moor, in SW England. Here, they would top up their fuel tanks before take-off. The transit flight was made the previous evening and all was ready for the mission.

Thirty-nine crews from both groups departed with the 44BG as Lead. Maj. Howard Moore and Gen. Hodges (CG, 2BW) headed twenty other Shipdham crews, with Lt. Ed Mikolowski navigating the projected 700-mile route. His D/R skills were such that the target finally loomed ahead, precisely in line with the briefed ETA. Lt. DeVinney (B) now displayed his equal Norden operating skills, with the bomb loads blowing in the main entrance lock-gates as well as damaging an aero-engine plant.

Thirty-eight crews duly headed for home, with the exception taking up a southern course. Lt. Ray L. Hilliard (66BS) had suffered "runaway" propellers on two engines on the way over and the chances of regaining friendly shores were deemed highly problematical, not to say very fraught with risk, especially since the formations were retracing their steps over the sea. B-24D-30-CO/42-40130/H **Avenger II** finally crossed into Spain and set down safely on an airfield. All ten airmen were subsequently repatriated via Gibraltar. An eleventh crewmember suffered a particularly cruel fate; he was a waist gunner whose parachute inadvertently opened, drawing him out through the gunnery hatch and down into the pitiless Atlantic ocean wastes.

Chapter Four

"Ted's Circus" Travels

The 93BG's direct participation in the USAAF's Daylight Offensive was to be limited during its first winter in England. Not only would two of its squadrons serve a several-week detachment to SW England and participate in anti-submarine patrols, but by the end of November, the major part of the Group would be facing a prolonged three-month detachment to North Africa. At the same time, the 329BS would be training in a specialist electronic role involving the RAF's *Gee* navigation system.

Diversion (1)

This convoluted existence did not immediately commence within the Group's initial operational period spanning October to November. However, during the latter part of October, two squadrons instead found their services redirected towards anti-submarine duties. The 330BS flew to Holmsley South and the 409BS to St. Eval, in SW England, on the 25th. The crucial Battle of the Atlantic was still tilted in the German submariners' favor, so constant pressure against the U-boats was necessary not only as they transited the Bay of Biscay to and from the main convoy routes; there was also a current need to provide maximum supporting cover to the convoys of men and material heading for NW Africa and the *Torch* Invasion.

The two squadrons were subordinated to RAF Coastal Command's control and the B-24's great range capability ensured a steady flow of 12-hour sorties, commencing 25 October. All passed off uneventfully up to 29 October, when the latest patrol was dispatched. Capt. William J. Williams had charge of B-24D-1-CO/41-23712/R **Ambros**, based at Holmsley South. The bomber took off in the mid-afternoon, but shortly after it came down at Porlock Bay, killing all but one of the twelve-man crew. A more positive if not surprising result occurred 21 November, when Maj. Ramsey Potts's B-24 was intercepted by a number of Ju88s, probably from V/KG40. The outcome of what should have been an easy *Abschuess* (Kill) for the fighters was that following a furious air battle, the bomber's gunners were given credit for two Ju88s and a third damaged, while the B-24 came through in basic order!

During November, the 328BS and 329BS were available for the six missions flown from Alconbury. All were directed against the U-boat pens in Brest, Lorient, or St. Nazaire, with an average of twelve crews per mission dispatched. No bomber losses were incurred in direct combat, but there was one serious incident on 18 November. An "abortive" landing attempt at Alconbury was followed by the two port engines failing on 41-23745 **Katy Bug** as Lt. Alfred Asch was again orbiting the circuit. A desperate attempt to set

Katy Bug, a 93BG "original" bomber, is snapped in two greatly contrasting circumstances. The first shows the aircraft in pristine condition as armorers prepare her intended bomb load. The second was taken on 18 November, when with two engines "out" an attempted crash landing ended violently after the B-24D plunged into a deep ditch adjoining the airfield; four of Lt. Alfred Asch's team were killed in the process.

the B-24 down for a crash landing nearly succeeded, but unfortunately, on the final approach one wing impacted with a tree. The skidding aircraft then careened into a deep ditch that had the effect of grinding down the forward fuselage almost to wing level, as well as separating the rear fuselage behind the wing trailing edge. One officer and three Enlisted men were killed in the incident.

Diversion (2)

The spell of detachment from the Group's perceived function within the strategic bombing campaign lasted a bare month, but was also to prove far from the last. The 330BS and 409BS returned to Alconbury at the end of November. Their return was in process when the 329BS was ordered to Hardwick, the Group's future permanent base. Once there, the aircraft were fitted out with the RAF's navigation sets codenamed "Gee" and the crews began to train with a view to conducting "intruder" operations (codenamed "Moling") in adverse weather conditions. (Within seven days, a further move was made to Bungay.) The thought of single B-24s penetrating Europe even when the weather conditions might provide concealment from fighters could not have sat well with the personnel. After all, the basic concept of USAAF heavy bomber operations was to rely upon unit "integrity"—that is, holding tight formation and depending on the multitude of .5 machine guns to ward off the Luftwaffe.

This first use of electronic equipment could also be construed as the initial step in the degradation of American hopes of conducting their bombing campaign against military and industrial targets and simultaneously avoiding large-scale civilian casualties. "Area precision bombing" would inevitably become more of the norm from late 1943 onwards, as Europe's perverse weather patterns, especially during winter, regularly cast a visual veil across the Continent, as well as the British Isles.

However, the current aim was not an "active" one, but was rather "passive" in nature. Once the crews were deemed operational, the intention was to dispatch single aircraft across a wide geographic spread, with the industrial Ruehr as a prime example. Their intrusion was expected to create large-scale movements of industrial workers away from their workplaces and into shelters; their absence would in turn adversely reflect on overall output rates. Between 3 January and 28 March, seven separate missions were flown, none of which succeeded. This failure lay not with the crews, but with Mother Nature, who on every occasion perversely cast up steadily diminishing cloud or even virtually clear sky conditions over the Continent that mitigated against any chance of success—or survival!

Diversion (3)

The largest and longest-term detachment from VIIIBC operations for the 93BG to date conversely did *not* result in duties other than bombing, although a large degree of tactical as opposed to strategic operations would be involved. Operation *Torch*, the Invasion of NW Africa, had got off to a

Three Hardwick-based B-24Ds are photographed low down over the Mediterranean during one of the Group's 1942/43 detachments to North Africa. The bomber closest to the camera is **Bomerang**, which would cap a long combat career by returning Stateside during early 1944 for the purpose of being a centerpiece for a War Bonds drive.

sound start. However, the need to hinder supplies reaching Gen. Rommel's *Deutsches Afrika Korps* (DAK) via seaports further along the Mediterranean coastline resulted in the Group being detached to the region in order to bolster the efforts of the heavy and medium RAF/USAAF units currently on hand. The period of detachment was officially estimated at less than two weeks—a hopelessly optimistic assessment in the event, since nearly three months was to elapse before the combat crews would cast off the dust of Africa, and not for the last time either.

The Air Echelon, other than the 329BS, was alerted following the 5 December call from Gen. Eaker (CG, VIII BC) to Ted Timberlake, informing him of the operation. Within 24 hours, the 24 crews assigned were flying their aircraft to Portreath, in SW England, the staging point for the protracted overseas flight to Oran. Algeria. A small element of ground personnel went along as maintenance men, the majority remaining at Alconbury and being tasked with the imminent transfer to Hardwick.

The transit flight to Oran commenced in the early dawn of 7 December, and although the crews were never free of possible intervention by the Luftwaffe, especially as the Bay of Biscay was being skirted, the 328BS and 409BS contingents finally arrived in sound order on Tafaroui's airfield. The experience of the 330BS was more fraught, because it was one B-24 short after landing. The aircraft in question was 41-23707, flown by Lt. Robert A. Johnson and bearing thirteen other combat and ground personnel. The Atlas Mountain chain extends along and close to the western Mediterranean seaboard of North Africa; on approach to Tafaroui, the bomber impacted with high ground and left nobody alive out of its complement. In addition, several other squadron crews, when bypassing Gibraltar, had gone off course to starboard and strayed over Neutral Spanish Morocco, whose AA batteries threw up an explosive "welcome," fortunately with no real effect.

The anticipated sunshine and clear skies over Africa were totally absent during the group's first few days at their new base. Indeed, the current occupants had made up a ditty about conditions that began, "We are here in Tafaroui, where the mud is thick and gooey!" Apart from this, the facilities at Alconbury might have been regarded as fairly Spartan, whereas Tafaroui's were almost nonexistent, especially in terms of technical backup. Another limitation related to the runway lengths, which were regarded as dangerously marginal for permitting safe take-offs and landings.

The Group was subordinated to XII BC, whose hierarchy was understandably anxious to deploy the B-24s as soon as possible. Successive daily briefings up to the 12th either resulted in a "scrub" before start-up or, on the latter date, a cancellation after the Lead bomber's nose-wheel became firmly embedded in the muddy soil as it commenced take-off. The next day witnessed the start of a dry period that swiftly dried out the airfield surface to a safe level. Bizerte, on the northern tip of Tunis and some 500 miles distant, was a key Axis harbor facility and was duly briefed on this and the following day. The first loss in combat was borne this day by Lt. John Roche's 41-23009 **Ambrose II** (330BS). What was listed as a "dead stick" landing at Bone culminated in the aircraft breaking its back, with three crewmembers killed in the process.

Thwarted Expectations

Come the 15th, which marked the supposed end of the Group's detachment period, Orders were received to move—not back to England, but eastwards, in this case to Gambut-Main, near Benghazi, in what is now part of Libya, but was then the Italian colony of Cyrenaica. Here the group's operational supervision was transferred to IX BC, which held sway in the region.

The geographic conditions in what has always been regarded as part of the North Africa Desert were arguably much harsher than in Algeria. Here the sunshine was generally unremitting, with temperatures soaring almost to an unbearable level; once darkness

The perceived "glamor" of combat operations—other than in the minds of the crews—is fully dispelled in this photograph of a Hardwick crew just returned from a mission. The dreary British weather, coupled with the mud-stained road and surrounds, just adds to the weariness of the men heading for debriefing in their sweat-soaked flight clothing.

descended, the temperature drop was swift and almost equally extreme. The dry, arid atmosphere over what was as much scrub bush and stone as sand cast up veils of dust at regular intervals; the effect on the airframes, and particularly the engines, was bad, and merited constant counter-attention from the ground personnel in order to ensure safe operation for the combat crews. This task was made even harder by the fact that no hangar facilities were on hand.

By now, the British and Commonwealth troops within Gen. Montgomery's 8th Army were pushing on towards Tunisia and the emphasis on bombing operations, although basically still concentrating on Axis supply conduits, was to primarily shift across the Mediterranean to Italy in particular. It was inevitable that casualties would be incurred, but the first aircraft loss seems to have been non-operational in nature. Capt. Owen L. Kunze was in charge of 41-23665 **Big Dealer** (330BS), which came down in Egypt while returning to Gambut-Main on 10 January; the pilot and three of the other eight airmen were killed. The same bomber had suffered over 300 holes on a run to Bizerte when the flak barrage had reached an intensity almost matching that of "Flak City" (St. Nazaire), but her luck had now run out.

A total of 22 missions would be flown during the spell of detachment, a rate that would have been regarded with envy by VIII BC-operating crews, whose equivalent operational progress was far more stretched out in time. Equally important from a personal security angle was the relatively low loss rate of aircraft and crews. The first four personnel losses were incurred in a rather cruel manner, since the enemy did not intervene directly. B-24D-1-CO/41-23724 (409BS) was reportedly participating in a mission to Naples (15th) when it suffered flak strikes. Four of the airmen took to their parachutes, but seemingly drifted down into the sea to either drown or die from exposure.

Four days later, during a run to Sousse, Tunisia, Capt. Benjamin F. Riggs' 41-23672 **Double Trouble** (328BS) was shot out of the sky and crashed off the coast, leaving two officers out of ten crew on board alive but facing captivity. The run to Naples on 15 February resulted in the latest MIA statistic. **Celhalopdos** (41-23675/330BS) failed to return and almost certainly descended into the Mediterranean, since neither Capt. Charles T. Moore nor any of his nine-man team was ever recovered. The previous day, and over the same target, flak almost brought about the demise of the 328BS' 41-23729/D **Shoot Luke**. Capt. John Murphy and his copilot fought to maintain the bomber in flight, but matters seemed terminal when fire broke out and persisted in one engine. The B-24 had several crewmembers wounded as course was held for the Island of Malta, scant miles SW of Sicily, where a safe landing was made.

The 22 February mission was preceded on the 18th by the issue of Orders dispatching the Group back—not to Alconbury but to Hardwick. The positive side of operations was the dropping of over 500 tons of bombs and incendiaries during the 22-mission sequence that witnessed an average air time of around 9 ½ hours. A total of eight B-24s were either MIA, lost in non-operational crashes, or in one instance (the 328BS' 41-23744 **Geronimo**) "written off" following a ground incident. One senior Group HQ officer remained behind; L/Col Keith K Compton was subsequently assigned to command the 376BG, a B-24 unit. (On 1 August 1943, he would also play an unfortunate part in the chaos that ensued from his decision to direct the Force heading for Ploesti onto a premature and therefore wrong target approach.)

A final loss occurred during the Group's return to Hardwick. The proximity of Spanish Morocco to the Straits of Gibraltar provided a very narrow navigational gap through which Allied aircraft had to channel their flight paths. Adverse weather conditions were faced by Lt. Jacob Epting as he hauled 41-23740 **Red Ass** (409BS) off the runway at Gambut-Main on 25 February. Many hours later, the bomber and its 14 occupants were again on the ground—but this time on neutral soil at Villasicneros, Spanish Morocco! Aircraft and crew were duly interned, and although records indicate the B-24 was later transferred north to Spain, no clear evidence of whether or not the airmen were released prior to VE-Day appears to be on hand.

"Normal" Service Resumed—in Full

The Air Echelon now assembled at its future permanent airfield as February ran out was still short of the 329BS, whose return from Bungay would not occur before mid-March. As it was, a small element of group strength had been on hand to participate in seven VIII BC missions between 27 January and 27 February; the average-sized force was six, and it flew alongside the larger 44BG formations. One aircraft loss was incurred on 26 February; battle-damaged 41-23734 **Night Raider** (409BS) was brought back to Norfolk for a crash landing at Ludham airfield, from which seven on Capt. Beattie H. Fleenor's crew walked away unscathed, the other three suffering wounds. The extent of the damage was such that "Category E" (salvage) action was deemed necessary.

The third month of 1943 promised little in the way of improvement in VIII BC logistics, whether material or human. The six heavy Groups on hand would still face a frustratingly slow advance in terms of mission completion that totalled a mere nine and involved three-figure numbers in strength only on the final four runs. Nor were the majority of attacks mounted against German-based targets (four in all). This locust period of VIII BC operations was beginning to fade by April, however.

The 2BW's initial contribution to March operations (4th) involved that old stand-by for the Wing, a diversion. The 93BG contributed five to the small overall figure of eleven, whose exact flight path is unclear; the fact that the 1BW was heading out to Hamm's marshalling yards NE of the Ruehr confirms a track to the north or south of the Main Force's route, especially since the B-24s were briefed to attack any shipping sighted. The U-boat threat was still absorbing the Command's regular attention, as evidenced two days later. The B-17 groups headed for Lorient, while the 2BW sent fifteen crews to Brest on what was again listed as a "diversionary" mission. It was just as well the Luftwaffe did not take the bait, given that the 2BW formation was almost miniscule in terms of defensive firepower, while the flak battery strength at this port was far from light.

The inordinate number of ground personnel clustered around the starboard flank of **Shoot Luke** would suggest this picture was one within a publicity sequence, an assertion reinforced by the absence of bomb fins anywhere in the vicinity. The national insignia is "dulled down" and bears the thin surround, originally yellow at the request of the RAF during North African operations, but now similarly darkened.

The run to Rouen (8th) was the penultimate example of single-figure numbers dispatched by Hardwick, whose crews had suffered no MIA losses to date. However, 41-23658/R **Thar She Blows** (329BS) was "written off" after crash landing in Kent on return from Rouen, though none of Maj. Bill Cowart's crew seems to have been adversely affected. This happy, if ever temporary, situation continued on the 12th and 13th, when "diversion" missions were launched, followed five days later by the mission to bomb U-boat construction yards at Vegesack, adjoining Bremen, when good fortune finally deserted the group. Then, all but one on Lt. Howard E. Kleinstuber's team went down in 41-23666/ S **Hot Freight**, with the 330BS bomber crashing near Oldenburg. The final two missions on the 22nd and 28th passed off uneventfully, although the latter run to Rouen saw the Wing recalled thanks to poor weather conditions.

The 328BS' 41-23729/D **Shoot Luke** had already survived the mission of 19 February, when Capt. J. Murphy brought his badly shot-up charge into Malta. Now, both aircraft and crew would face a second test, with one airman coming through a horrendous physical ordeal. One B-24 was seen to be lagging behind and Murphy took it upon himself to drop back as cover in the event of any recurring fighter assault, the sky being currently clear. A single Fw190 did loom up to commence a pass not at the laggard, but at **Shoot Luke**. Strikes along the fuselage wounded several crewmembers, the worst affected being Sgt. Paul Slankard (TG).

The blast of the shell impacting below his seat threw him halfway through the turret front's shattered Plexiglas, as well as opening dreadful wounds in his left leg and hip. After Sgt. Floyd Mabee succeeded in pulling the gunner back into the fuselage, Lt. E. Janic (B), who was tasked with providing emergency aid, regarded the leg as being incapable

A second view of **Shoot Luke** from a forward angle shows several mechanics hard at work on the No. 3 engine. The number of personnel has lessened, but is still too many for a standard maintenance crew. A triangular wooden trestle appears to be inserted tight against the rear fuselage.

of other than amputation—assuming that Slankard did not succumb to his condition prior to hospitalization. Attempts to staunch the blood flow through medical means appeared impossible; instead, the wounds were exposed to the sub-zero atmosphere, with the desired effect being achieved. The B-24 landed several hours later and Slankard was rushed to hospital, with the medics echoing Janic's opinion of a likely fatal outcome. Amazingly, the doctors succeeded in saving the airman's life, although his combat career was certainly at an end.

Rotterdam, a key Dutch seaport, was briefed on the 31st and twelve-strong forces from both 2BW Groups took off to join in an assault on the city's shipyards. Although the range permitted P-47 cover, there was still the promise of solid defensive opposition. In the event, two of the three 1BW losses involved a mid-air collision. The mission proved both frustrating and sad for the 93BG. Not only did cloud intrude to prevent bombing, but the run of loss-free missions was concluded. On the way out, 41-24025 **Satan's Chariot** (409BS) was observed to develop a fire in one engine as it disappeared going back to Hardwick. Nothing further was ever seen or heard from Lt. William F. Williams's ten-man team and the North Sea almost certainly consumed both they and their bomber on what cruelly was to have been their 25th and final mission.

The Nissen Hut - All the Comforts of Home?

The majority of USAAF airfields in East Anglia were utility in nature, having been carved out of the countryside in relative haste. Accommodation in particular was basic, in the form of the Nissen hut, and the following account by an officer probably sums up the general reaction among the personnel:

> The truck came out and took us to the Operations block, then on to the Billeting Office, where we were assigned our permanent quarters. Our four officers were placed in a Quonset hut that had eight beds; a twelve-man hut housed our Enlisted men, along with another crew's complement. The hut was a galvanized steel structure like a tomato can cut in half and laid on its side. There were doors and windows at either end. In the center was a coke-burning stove with a cast-iron pipe extending up through the roof. This cement-floored building was now our "home," although it never became "homey" or merited such treatment in our eyes. In fact, we felt it was a chore just to sweep the floor of its stark interior—on a windy day we just opened the doors and hoped some of the dust and cigarette and stove odor would blow out!
>
> The stove had been invented by some fiend to aggravate us. The weekly coke ration was not enough to keep this "tin monster" hut warm. Nobody had ever previously tried to light coke, which is the residue after coal had been heated and distillates have been drawn off. Paper and cardboard as fire lighters failed, so we picked up twigs and even branches, but this didn't always work. Finally, we used lighter fluid and even oil residue after an engine change. Even when finally lit, it just smoldered and emitted a foul smell.
>
> The discovery of a coal pile behind the Mess-hall kitchen saw us sneak out every night and utilize the mosquito nets (part of our survival gear) to haul some away; this worked fine until authority got wise and fenced the compound off. A Notice board missive said anyone caught stealing would face court martial, the penalty usually being about $75 and 30 days confinement to base.
>
> Another justified source of complaint involved the mattress provision. This was not a single item, but three sub-units. The resultant gaps that occurred whenever one moved in one's sleep not only interfered with overall comfort, but also let in the draught. Attempts to tie them together or enclose them in a blanket usually met with little or no more than moderate success. Bed sheets were at a premium for the first few weeks but then became available.

The following poem sums up the general attitude towards the Nissen hut's designer:

Say, you don't know
what you're missin',
till you've lived in huts by Nissen
Who has built them
by the thousands for GIs,
Shaped like half a jelly roll,
Black as famed Calcutta's Hole
One can hold from ten
to twenty any size.
Well, the inside's tin that's bent,
while the back and front's cement,
With three holes for doors and
windows at each end.
Double-deckers of the sort,
you can sleep in—if you're short,
In the center there's a
stove we have to tend.
Our mattress is in threes,
and it buckles at the knees.
Yes, these houses sure have brought
this fellow fame,
You may build huts,
Mr Nissen,
but you ought to sleep in this'n
Then you'd surely hang
your head in abject shame!!

April Deceleration in Operations

The expansion of the 2BW, in contrast to a confirmed increase in 1BW strength flowing into Britain during April, still lay several months ahead, with the arrival of the 389BG at Hethel. In the meantime, the twin lobes of the B-24 force had to soldier on, along with their equally-tested B-17 contemporaries. The pace of operations during this latest month fell away to a level barely exceeding that produced during the initial months in combat—four completed runs in all—with Mother Nature playing her ever-perverse part in restricting activities. April would also bring the hardest rebuff to the Hardwick fliers experienced to date on a single mission.

The first mission (4th) was diversionary in nature for the B-24 crews, but the next day, both Wings linked up to bomb aviation production facilities in Antwerp. Unfortunately, a high proportion of the bomb loads fell well outside the MPI, causing hundreds of deaths among the civilian population and natural friction between Americans and the exiled Belgian government. There now ensued well over one week before the latest attack was launched. On the 16th, the twin targets of Lorient and Brest appeared on the 1BW and 2BW briefing maps, respectively, but whereas the last time the 93BG had ventured in this direction with impunity, today's sortie would sadly prove very costly.

Thirteen crews took off from Hardwick and joined up with twelve Shipdham B-24s. By the day's end, only one B-17 out of 59 gaining mission "credit" was MIA. This was in sharp contrast to the 2BW, which suffered three MIA losses out of nineteen going over the target—all three being from the 93BG. (Only eight crews out of the thirteen were credited with bombing.)

The formations encountered fighter opposition to add to the flak barrage. Lt. Franklin D. Lown, whose lagging B-24 was successfully "escorted" by

Col. Timberlake (93BG CO) stands second from right as he explains a point to Sir Hugh "Boom" Trenchard (right). The latter was known as the "Father of the Royal Air Force" and gained his nickname thanks to the deep and rich pitch of his voice. He was also a firm advocate of the principle of Strategic Bombardment.

T/Sgt Ben Kuroki was a Nisei-American citizen and a top turret/engineer with the 93BG. The Martin turret Plexiglas frame he is supporting has a huge hole in the center, almost certainly resulting from combat damage. The complete absence of metal inserts compared to the B-17's equivalent fitting left the occupant with little chance of avoiding injury or death in such circumstances.

Col. Timberlake is addressing his staff during a briefing session sometime during April 1943. He was originally a squadron CO with the 44BG in the States, but was then transferred out, first to the 98BG and then to the 93BG as its CO. His sound leadership witnessed his promotion to B/Gen and command of the 20CBW; prior to this he had handed over the Group to L/Col. Addison Baker on 17 May 1943.

Geronimo has nosed over, and her nose wheel has become firmly embedded in the soil of Tafaroui airfield in Algeria. The incident occurred on 20 December, during the Group's first North African detachment, and although the damage seems marginal, salvage action was subsequently initiated.

Shoot Luke on the 31 March mission to Rotterdam, was to experience no such luck over Brest, although he did end up a POW. Fighter attacks inflicted so much damage prior to and during the bomb run on his B-24D-15-CO/41-23983 that the 328BS bomber finally dropped out. Bail out was being made by some of the crew when the B-24 exploded. Amazingly, just three of the ten still alive at this time died; Lt. Hal J. Tannenbaum slipped out of his parachute, while T/Sgt. Herbert B. Daly (Eng.) and probably Lt. Thaddeus I. Hawkins (B) were killed at their posts.

Capt. Beattie H. Fleenor brought his badly-damaged B-24 back for a crash landing 26 February, but his luck also ran out over Brest; unlike Lt. Lown, he did not escape with his life, nor did any of the other nine on 41-24122 **Missouri Sue** (409BS). Severe damage, including the excision of the left rudder and an engine fire, forced it out of formation. The pilots headed for home and picked up cover from Spitfires. Sadly, the ailing bomber slipped inexorably down towards the sea and fatally "ditched" north of the Brittany coastline.

The final MIA loss concerned a second 328BS aircraft, 41-23732/B **Liberty Lass**, in the hands of Lt. Frank R. Hodges (POW). This bomber's time of loss indicated that it was downed before completing its bomb run; it came down in the sea west of the target, along with three of the ten on board. By the mission's completion, the five surviving B-24s credited with bombing ended up one short, albeit not right away. Capt. Leon C. Packer, piloting the 329BS's 41-23874, got his battle-damaged bomber back as far as RAF St. Eval, in SW England. Lt. Parkman W. Davis (B) had bailed out over the French coast to become an MIA statistic, but the other nine airmen survived the crash landing. Not so their bomber, which was subsequently salvaged.

The events of 16 April must have sat badly with the Hardwick personnel, but in the fullness of time would be regarded as no more or less an inevitable downturn in operational fortune. The Group would be able to lick its wounds and recover over the rest of April, especially since no further missions would be dispatched by the 2BW. (In crude terms, the punishment inflicted upon the 93BG was eclipsed within 24 hours at Molesworth, whose 303BG ranks were shorn of ten B-17s during the Bremen mission! Most if not all USAAF bomber units would bear such a degree of suffering more than once.)

Summer Beckons

An even stranger division of Wing effort seemingly occurred during May. Whereas the 1BW flew all nine and the recently established 4BW operated on seven occasions, the 2BW was dispatched on only five missions, with the 93BG restricted to three. In addition, the Group strength for the first mission (1st) was limited to six crews, although the diversionary run to the Brittany coast was secondary to the 1BW's attack on St. Nazaire. A full sixteen days elapsed before the call came for Hardwick crews to again take to the air. However, the result must have been pleasing, since the port of Bordeaux was well struck by both Wing units. Almost the same time span extended between this run and the attack on a naval storage depot at Rennes (29th), when U-boat facilities at La Pallice were assaulted by seventeen Group aircraft.

Plans were well in process for a daring mass assault upon a key oil production complex in Romania. This target of prime strategic importance located north of the Rumanian Capital Bucharest was currently nestling in complete security from aerial assault—a cosy assumption at least within the Nazi hierarchy, although a senior military official was building up the area defenses in anticipation of a raid. The several production plants at Ploesti provided a major source of supply for the Nazi war effort. The target's production-restriction, or even better its destruction,

A close-up of a 93BG formation on a pre-Ploesti flight demonstrates the simple national insignia, added to by RAF fin flashes, the latter an aspect of 1942/43 North African operations. **Jerks Natural** (41-23711) is seen nearest to the camera; **Heinie Hunter** (41-23980) leads the sub-formation. Both were MIA by the autumn, the former on 1 October and its companion on 19 August.

The B-24's dorsal defense was provided by a power turret positioned behind the cockpit. The twin machine guns were mounted in a Martin Company-produced unit whose clear-piece Plexiglas cover provided superb visibility; on the other hand, the complete absence of any support framing meant that there was little chance of the occupant escaping injury or death. T/Sgt Al Lee (93BG) is the turret operator here, although just the gun cooling barrels are on hand.

Ball of Fire has just exchanged the relatively pleasant and simple surroundings of its Norfolk habitat for the decidedly spartan and very harsh desert landscape of North Africa. The crew are loading the lorry with various items of gear and equipment, and are likely reflecting upon the chances of departing the Theater as quickly as possible!

would inflict a grievous blow upon the enemy's capacity to prosecute the conflict. The B-24's superior range capacity over the B-17 made it a suitable candidate. Deployment to North Africa was necessary in order to penetrate to the target, which was not far short of even the B-24's flight endurance.

The staccato operational involvement of the 2BW during May was probably a misnomer. The 44BG's and 93BG's absence from regular combat might be explained by the introduction of an unusual training schedule that involved the crews practicing low-level formation flights. On the other hand, most accounts of the Ploesti mission indicate that it was early June before the low formation flying practice was initiated. Whatever the facts, only Col. Timberlake, among either group's hierarchy, was aware of a likely deployment to North Africa.

Chapter Five

Ploesti—Nightmare at Zero Feet

Industrial "Achilles Heel"

During WWII, the Allied military planners endeavored to seek out and give priority to the dislocation of the Axis Powers' industrial "bottlenecks." Among the categories, few loomed larger than oil, although the enemy's transportation system gradually began to assume almost similar importance. The fixation with ball bearings production as a vulnerable product extended throughout late 1943 early 1944 USAAF operations, but the availability of third country supply sources indicated that production dislocation within Germany, or even Nazi-occupied Europe, would not necessarily be fatal. This was not so much the case with oil, of which Germany had no natural resources; synthetic manufactured substitutes were available from a number of plants, but not in overwhelming quantities.

By 1943, the gigantic oil production complex at Ploesti, Rumania, was assuming an ever greater importance to Germany's war effort, especially with the failure to comprehensively over-run Russian resources in the Caucasus the previous year, and then a burgeoning threat of permanent ejection from that region that was to be realized by the current and critical year's midpoint.

The standard high-level approach to USAAF targets was regarded as providing the enemy defenses with far too much leeway in time with which to marshal its fighter strength, in particular. Col. Jacob Smart has since been credited with suggesting an alternative approach to be flown at minimum altitude. In this manner, the radar warning system was likely to be bypassed, while the flak batteries surrounding Ploesti would be provided with much less time to focus on the bombers than would otherwise be the case. In fact, the defenders would be alerted even before the formations transited the Mediterranean thanks to monitoring of Allied radio traffic, but this was a factor that either never entered the overall planning equation or was disregarded if the matter was raised.

Another reason for the low-level approach was in respect of anticipated losses. The final availability of five groups provided an overall force of around 200-250. If more than one high-level mission had to be launched, which seemed likely, then there was a great risk that overall strength would be so weakened by cumulative losses as well as unserviceable bombers that a sufficient degree of destruction would not be achieved. Compared to this scenario, one concerted strike delivered at minimum altitude was confidently expected to achieve the desired effect—in theory, at least.

Two B-24 Groups were currently operating with the IX BC: the 98BG "Pyramidiers" and 376BG "Liberandos." The recent deployment of the 93BG to

What is clearly a well-assembled and spaced-out Group formation is traversing the East Anglian skies during yet another practice flight for **Tidal Wave**. The altitude shown here—relatively close as it is to the ground—would be drastically lowered during the Ploesti mission, especially on the bomb run and also during the withdrawal stage over the Continent.

Suzy Q, one of the nine "original" 67BS B-24Ds, was the sole survivor from that cadre by the time the 44BG decamped to North Africa for Operation **Tidal Wave**. Her already well-scarred airframe will receive further abrasive punishment from the sand-strewn landscape. She will never return to England, as she will be lost fifteen days after coming through the mission to Ploesti.

North Africa made it a natural candidate for inclusion in the plan codenamed "Soapsuds." Also allocated to the Force was the 44BG and the 389BG; the latter unit, although assigned to the VIII BC and arriving at Hethel, south of Norwich, would fly its initial run of missions out of North Africa after it too was dispatched to the Mediterranean.

The first indication that something significant was brewing came with the order for both Shipdham and Hardwick crews to commence formation flying at well below 1,000 ft. "Buzzing," or low flying as it was officially titled, was never tolerated and invited severe censure and punishment if the perpetrators were identified. Now, official sanction was being granted to carry out this normally heinous act, although the altitudes involved were not quite "down on the deck," as it were. The regular sight of B-24 formations criss-crossing the countryside would bring surprise to the civilian population in general and fury among many in the farming community at the disturbance to their livestock created by the multi-thousand horsepower din emitted by the Pratt and Whitneys!

The "Sky Scorpions" Arrive

The ranks of the 2BW were increased during June by Col. Jack Wood's 389BG, with the Air Echelon commencing arrival at Hethel on the 11th and making completion by the 25th. The B-24s they had brought over were a mix of later-production D Models that were partially equipped with Sperry ball turrets, while fuel capacity was increased with the addition of "Tokyo" tanks in the outer wing sections that held 550 gallons. Unbeknownst to the combat crews was that within a matter of weeks, they would add to their protracted flight across the North Atlantic a second extended flight south, then east to Cyrenaica, in North Africa.

The low-flying program that must have come as an operational culture shock to the crews naturally anticipating high-altitude missions was soon commenced, with one flight producing a near disaster. On 25 June, Lt. E. Fowble's 42-40687 (565BS), flying No. 3 to Lt. H. James's 42-40774 (566BS), came together; both port wing propellers were dislodged from James's B-24 and a wide gash was cut into the waist that left both waist gunners severely injured, but the pilots were able to bring off a crash landing at the conveniently adjacent airfield of Seething (446BG). Unfortunately, the nose section was mangled in the process, with one of the two occupants still in position there (Lt. C. B. Quantrell, navigator) killed. Sgt. Earl Zimmerman (ROG) was fortunate to escape with just a leg injury after he was crushed by the dislodged top turret. After completing his combat tour, which included an internment spell in Turkey off the Ploesti mission, he would be even luckier to survive the 1944 crash of a 458BG bomber right by the house he was visiting in Norwich. Fowble's B-24 was landed back at Hethel, and though less damaged still joined its companion in misfortune and was scrapped.

In the meantime, the Ground Echelon, having trained equally rigorously since the unit's inception at Davis-Monthan airfield on 24 December, was still sitting around at Camp Kilmer, NJ, awaiting Orders to ship out by sea; they boarded the **Queen Elizabeth** on 1 July, but their reaction on arriving six days later and viewing an airfield bereft of the majority of the Group's B-24 strength must have been one of stark astonishment.

On their Way

The last week in June witnessed the transfer of all three B-24 groups beginning on the 26th, when the 44BG and 93BG took off and headed for what was a familiar location for the latter unit (SW England), in this instance RAF Portreath. Four days later, the 389BG followed suit. The first leg of the overseas flight was a novelty for the 44BG and

T/Sgt Harold Kretzer was Engineer to Lt. George Winger and is photographed at Shipdham on a bleak winter day. On 1 August, the nine-man crew's regular mount B-24D-15-CO 41-24015/R **Wing Dinger** was downed. Only two airmen survived and Kretzer's body was one of five from the remaining seven never recovered from the blazing wreckage.

The citizens of Attleborough, in Norfolk, will surely be startled by the dinning roar emanating from a 44BG formation's engines as the crews practice for Ploesti. The currently anonymous B-24D in the foreground will evolve into **Flak Alley** and bear the WQ codes of the 68BS, as well as a rather suggestive form of female artwork. She will finally go MIA on 24 February 1944 during "Big Week."

Lt. Bill Cameron adopts a casual pose alongside his regular B-24D 41-24229 **Buzzin Bear**—both are "original" members of the 67BS. Bill will survive his combat tour, as well as attaining L/Col. rank, but his charge will suffer a fiery fate on an Italian beach during the same mission that will also claim **Suzy Q**.

Sgt. Frank Maruszckski, tail gunner on Lt. Cameron's team, smiles confidently while perched on his A6A turret that forms his operational "perch." A point of interest is the staggered nature of the twin machine guns. Also of note is the double-entendre meaning of the statement applied below the turret ring.

389BG personnel, as well as nerve-wracking for the navigators in particular, since the entire route was over the featureless Atlantic. All arrived safely at Oran, Algeria, but accommodation for all proved to be "out" and the unlucky element had to sleep inside or under their aircraft. Twenty-four hours later, the crews were ensconced upon their IX BC airfields around Benghazi.

B/Gen. Uzal Ent had been assigned to command the Force for what had been retitled Operation *Tidal Wave*, so it was ironic that he held strong reservations about the feasibility of a successful strike going in at minimum altitude. Furthermore, he regarded the available numbers of B-24s as basically inadequate for achieving a one-off positive result. It took a good degree of persuasion from Gen. Louis Brereton (CG, IX BC) to convince Ent to carry on.

The arid conditions of the desert were familiar to the 93BG veterans, but nonetheless unpleasant. Engine life was eroded by anything up to or even more than half of the 300-hour rating for European operations. Sensitive mechanisms were prone to jamming and failure from the fine dust and grit, while Plexiglas was inclined to craze under the same influence. The heat was almost unbearable, added to which flies, locusts, desert rats, and even snakes and scorpions were on hand to increase the discomfort. In essence, the "Desert Song" image was a million miles distant from the truth. In spite of this, the 2BW personnel buckled down to the task at hand, while regarding the erstwhile Spartan conditions of East Anglia as a relative paradise compared to their current situation!

Ante-Ploesti

A full calendar month lay ahead of the groups before they would venture towards Rumania. In the meantime, combat operations, as well as low-level practice, would absorb their attention. On 2 July, a mission was dispatched to Lecce, Italy, from which two "Eightball" crews were MIA. Engine damage to 42-40094/E **Miss Virginia** (68BS) finally forced Lt. W. J. Garrett into a "ditching" from which only six of the eleven on board emerged alive. A worse casualty rate affected Lt. R. E. Peterson's crew of ten on 42-40745 (also 68BS). Fighter gunfire raked the fuselage, whereupon the B-24 inverted and almost immediately exploded, killing all the crew. Much further to the northwest, a 389BG crew in 42-40783/K **Pistol Packin' Mama** (566BS) was suffering the indignity of being interned after going off course and landing in Portugal.

Seven days later, separate losses from the 93BG and 389BG were recorded. The former incident, although not so bad, still held similarly cruel overtones to the loss of the IX BC's **Lady be Good**. In both instances, the bombers survived the mission, but flew on into the African hinterland. Although both crews initially survived, not all came through the experience alive. F/O W. M. McKelvey's 42-40627 **Big Job** (330BS) was finally abandoned over Sudanese territory and all ten airmen got together on the ground. The pilot linked up with one other at the wrecked aircraft and headed off north, according to the note left there and read by some or all of the other eight. This assembly then split into a six/two pairing to search for water, but Sgts. Gomez and Wilson were never seen again, as was the McKelvey-led duo. The survivors were lucky to be found by a combined RAF/USAAF search team of aircraft two days later with supplies and water dropped to them, but six more days elapsed before RAF trucks rendezvoused with the exhausted airmen.

The 389BG loss was incurred in what was regarded as an "easy" mission to the Island of Crete for the acolyte unit. Maleme airfield was the target, but the Luftwaffe made a sharp series of interceptions from head-on, an angle that exposed the B-24's defensive firepower to serious limitations. As it was, only Lt. A J. Scates and crew experienced the terminal effect of gunfire. Fire caught hold immediately on 42-40779 (567BS) and several crew bailed out to float down into the Mediterranean. The tail section snapped off to bear all still on board to their deaths; one body was subsequently washed ashore and none of the other nine airmen survived. The 389BG's combat blood debt had begun.

By coincidence, the vital briefing material for *Tidal Wave* was on its way from England the same day. It was borne in one of the five B-24s making the journey, piloted by Lt. Hugh Roper (93BG), who was nearing the end of his combat tour—and who would perish in the most needless manner, coming off Ploesti on what was the final mission. Thermite sticks were attached to the documents to ensure their total destruction should there be the slightest risk of the material falling into enemy hands.

The "Conscience" Mission

The Vatican, located in Rome, was the religious epicenter for the Catholic faith. Therefore, on 19 July, when the Briefing maps for all five groups cast up the city's marshalling yards as the target, special dispensation was offered to all Catholic-raised personnel not to participate in the mission. How many took advantage of the offer is unknown, but the Holy City remained unscathed and most if not all bomb loads impacted around the MPI.

One 389BG aircraft did not return, but its crew did. Lt. H. Ben Walsh found his 42-40665/A **Ten High** (564BS) having fuel transfer problems that forced him to turn back en route to Rome. Fighter attacks ensued and the aircraft was finally abandoned on approach to Malta. Eight of the ten landed on the island, but the pilots were particularly fortunate to survive. Walsh recalled his parlous and almost terminal experience:

> A 20mm exploded in the cockpit, with fragments striking my neck and shoulders; I knew I was hit but felt no immediate pain, since we were busy holding the aircraft at wave-top height. When bail out was called the crew had to go back and jump via the camera hatch due to the jammed bomb doors. I knew my chances of getting out the same way were slim, so I asked Lt. Spelling (CP) to take my pack and place it by the hatch; I then trimmed the bomber to fly level and dashed back, attaching the pack and jumping—so far, so good!
>
> I knew I was some distance from the island, but naturally unaware that the sea current was not in my favor; worse still, my *Mae West* was shot full of holes. Consequently, I spent the rest of the afternoon swimming and floating on my back, hoping against hope I could make landfall before dark. As the sun was lowering, I realized time was running out; fatigue was setting in. Then, as my hopes were fading, I saw a ship on the horizon that I thought in my eternal optimism was looking for me. I soon noticed its course was not in my direction,

Forky II, from the 68BS, squats on her Shipdham dispersal, bathed in the sunlight of an English summer day. These surroundings will ultimately be exchanged for a Rumanian cornfield south of Ploesti on 1 August, into which she will descend on fire; only Sgt. Charley Bridges (WG), out of Lt. Gentry's (66BS) nine-man crew, will stagger clear before a violent explosion consumes the others.

Storage facilities in the North African Theater of Operations were minimal, with very few structures on hand compared to those in Britain. Fuel drums are laid out in the open at Oudna, in Tunisia, temporary home for the 44BG during its second north African detachment. Two of the B-24Ds in the background are 41-23779/G **4-0-2** (67BS) and 42-40764/M **Helen Be Happy** (66BS).

and realizing this was my final opportunity, I literally tried to leap out of the water while frantically waving my arms.

A combination of Fortune and God's Grace worked for me, as the reflection caused by my watch-class caught the eye of someone on the bridge and the Royal Navy ship swung towards me. On heaving-to, a sailor with a grappling hook pulled me out like a drowned rat and the Captain handed me a large measure of rum that rendered me docile as a lamb. He then proceeded to try to extract the shell fragments from my neck and shoulders; although I could feel him working me over, I was beyond pain.

We docked in the black-out at Malta, where a small quayside crowd called out, "Well done, Yank!" as I was carried to an ambulance. Around midnight, as I lay in bed, hoping the day would soon end and I could enjoy a little rest, the Luftwaffe arrived overhead to administer a pounding to the island!

Lt. Spelling (CP) spent upwards of three hours immersed and was equally fortunate to be plucked out.

Preparing for the "Big One"

The Rome mission rung down the curtain on standard operations. Next day, all five Group COs were briefed on *Tidal Wave*, the Operation's revised title. Feasibility tests on fuel consumption were carried out and aircraft were stripped of all extraneous equipment. Conversely, nose armament was "beefed up" and extra fuel tanks installed in the forward bomb bays. Actual practice flights commenced not *en masse*, but with single elements that gradually linked up into Group strength. Although the 2BW units had flown formation in England, the heights flown were well above the ground-hugging levels now flown—hence the need to work up to full Group numbers. More than one crew scared themselves witless by nearly striking the ground, or in one case doing so and literally scraping the paint off the underside before regaining full flight, while another hazard encountered was bird strikes. A model of Ploesti was painstakingly laid out in the desert soil and the initial practice flights involved individual Groups completing attack approaches. Finally, with just one day to go, the final practice mission now flown by all five turned out to be a complete success. Naturally, there was no flak or fighter opposition, but hopes remained high for success on the day.

The Attack Plan

The outward route would be directly northward as far as the Island of Corfu, straddling the Albanian/Greece border zone and then approximately NNE to the target area. Three pin-points on the final approach were Pitesti, Targovisti, and Floresti. The first location was where the 389BG would angle off to port and head for its specific target of Steaua Romana, at Campina, some 18 miles NW of Ploesti. The other four groups would maintain course until Floresti, where a turn to starboard would be made in the following order:

- The first 44BG sub-formation to Creditul Minier (Blue), five miles SW of Ploesti
- The second 44BG sub-formation to Columbia Aquila (White V)
- The 98BG to Astra Romana (White IV)
- The first 93BG sub-formation to Concordia Vega (White III)
- The second 93BG sub-formation to Unirea Sperantza (White II)
- The 376BG to Romana Americana (White I)

The route back would basically be south of the inward route during the initial portion to Corfu, but narrowing all the way to the island pin-point, after which it would be virtually the same track to Benghazi. That was the plan in theory, but sadly, it was not destined to be realized in most of its detail on 1 August.

The Mission

The Ploesti mission's manifold failures have been well documented over the years; in addition, the following account of the mission will primarily deal with the experiences of the three VIII BC Groups. The radio traffic advising Allied sources of a large formation movement was picked up by Axis monitoring stations, while an observer on Corfu, as well as a radar station at Sofia, Bulgaria, provided indications of the route following a direction that could threaten Ploesti, in particular. Differing opinions between VIIIBC and IX BC operational procedures concerning power settings and whether to climb above or directly penetrate the cloud formations encountered en route resulted in the 376BG and 93BG gradually widening the gap with the following three groups. A strong tailwind affecting the front units only further added to the separation factor.

A measure of counter-confusion arose among the defenders when radar contact was lost as the bombers gradually descended from their hitherto varying 10,000 to 15,000-ft altitudes necessary to clear the mountainous hinterland of Albania and descended over the Danube Plain. At this stage, Gen. Ent and Col. Compton in the 376BG Lead B-24 would still be optimistic about achieving some form of surprise assault.

The 93BG's Target Experience

Col. Addison Baker was Lead pilot for the group and also headed the twenty-four B-24s tasked with striking Concordia Vega (White III). He had sworn beforehand to get the formation over the target regardless of what might transpire with his aircraft and crew. In the event, neither his twelve-strong sub-force nor L/Col. G. S. Brown's similar contingent would hit the briefed target. Nor would Maj. Ramsey Potts get his twelve-strong sub-force through to Unirea Sperantza (White II).

The second approach pin-point at Targovisti was looming up when, to the horror of the Hardwick fliers, the 376BG was observed to bank to starboard—a mal-action that would take them directly to the city of Bucharest, lying well south of Ploesti. Baker had little option but to follow into the turn to avoid collisions occurring between the two Groups. Once straightened out, however, it was not long before he initiated a reverse turn to port. The drastic course alterations meant that a precise strike on the briefed refinery was virtually impossible, but at least some measure of destruction could be dealt out. However, a deadly flak ambuscade now awaited the Group; an attack approach from this very angle had been predicted by Gen. Gerstenberg, the officer responsible for protecting the refinery complex, and the defenses had accordingly been built up.

The flashes from the initial flak onslaught represented the first shocking indication of looming disaster. Almost immediately, Baker's **Hell's Wench** (42-40994/D) absorbed the first of three devastating strikes that set the 328BS bomber on fire and spelled its imminent doom. Baker's resolve to lead his men over the target never wavered, although he still had the opportunity to "belly in" onto the flat countryside stretching back from the looming White V. refinery that was actually assigned to the 44BG. (The approach path for the Baker/Brown formations would have taken them directly over the Creditul Minier refinery at Brazi, which was also assigned to the 44BG, but it was either ignored in favor of White V. or not picked up.)

The refinery was almost within reach when **Hell's Wench** took another strike and began to ease into a shallow climb before the now flame-engulfed aircraft dropped inexorably away and crashed into a railroad siding; all ten airmen died, even the ones seen to bail out. Baker and Maj. John Jerstad (CP) were subsequently awarded posthumous Medals of Honor. The Colonel had kept his word "even unto death."

42-40612/K **Euroclydon**, in Lt. Enoch M Porter's hands, was Baker's No. 2 and had also been set on fire during the run-up; it too came down before bombing, with two gunners and the navigator miraculously surviving bail out at less than 300ft. The crews were flying into a veritable maelstrom of smoke, fire, and debris cast up by preceding bomb explosions. Storage tanks were exploding and threatening to immolate any bomber unlucky enough to stray into the resultant

Two waves of B-24s are demonstrating the low-level approach to the "dummy" target of Ploesti laid out in the North African landscape. The air turbulence left in the wake of the bombers blew down numerous of the tented structures seen here, an act that did not sit well with the ground personnel!

Col. Johnson (44BG CO) is now fully attired in a lightweight uniform for operations in the MTO. He is destined to lead the Group on 1 August while flying right seat for Lt. William H. Brandon in **Suzy Q**, as well as be awarded the Congressional Medal of Honor for his leadership, one of five awarded to personnel off the Ploesti mission.

Capt. John Jerstad is photographed during a briefing session at Hardwick. He too will be awarded the CMH, but his will be tragically posthumous in nature as copilot to Col. Addison Baker (93BG CO); Baker will be similarly honored, but share Jerstad's fate in **Hells Wench** after the blazing B-24D crashes shortly after "bombs away" over a Ploesti refinery.

Three of the five Congressional Medals of Honor earned over Ploesti went to members of the 2BW, of which two were posthumous awards. Lt. Lloyd Hughes (389BG) was one of the unlucky duo; he bombed the target, but fuel from his B-24's already-punctured fuel tanks ignited and the subsequent attempt to crash land his doomed charge ended in failure, although two crewmembers did survive the tragic incident.

The 44BG is destined to lose eleven aircraft during *Tidal Wave*, one of which is 42-40780/H **Available Jones**; its pilot, Lt. Fred H Jones, stands by her artwork. The damaged B-24D was finally "ditched" off the island of Corfu during the return leg thanks to fighter-inflicted damage; all nine airmen survived the ever-fraught experience, albeit as POWs following their pick-up by an Italian boat crew.

fireball. As it was, no further loss to Baker's sub-force would occur over the refinery, but not all of the remaining ten crews would come back to Benghazi.

Lt. N. Stampolis and crew, flying No. 3 in Col. Brown's third element, were on their first mission in **Jose Carioca** (42-40617/N). Flak had set the bomber on fire around five miles out, but they managed to bomb before gravity bore the aircraft and its ten-man team to a terminal conclusion within the town of Ploesti; adding to the tragedy was the fact that the B-24 finally impacted with a women's prison structure, resulting in numerous deaths among the inmates.

Another casualty was **Honky Tonk Gal** (42-40265/W), flying as No. 2 in Col. Brown's last element. The No. 3 and 4 engines were disabled during the run-up, but the bombs were released before further flak strikes knocked out a third motor, leaving the pilots with no choice other than to belly in. Lt. H. Womble (P) unknowingly had one foot severed by a shell and had to be assisted out via the top hatch after the bomber skidded to a halt; Lt. W. H. Little (B) was trapped in the nose, and although extracted, he died of his injuries 8 August, the sole fatality among ten.

Another Displaced Strike

Maj. Ramsey Potts had swung his Force to port shortly after Baker and Brown, and was now angling in upon Astra Romana (White IV), allocated to the 98BG. His No. 2 was Lt. Worthy A. Long piloting **Jersey Bounce** (42-40609/I), who had already lost S/Sgt. L. Havens (TG) to a shell burst, while Lt. D. Lipton (B) was mortally wounded during the fusillade of gunfire that afflicted the bomber. Barely had the bombs gone when a crash landing had to be considered. Fortunately, the aircraft was again over open country and was put down, but the force crushed the bomb bay and the extra fuel tanks caught fire. As the flames spread forward, Lt. Long found himself caught up by his harness; he managed to free himself, but suffered burns in the process. Lt. N. Adams (N) was even luckier; he was still in the nose section when it was severed by the impact and rolled to one side, leaving its occupant unharmed.

Neither of the two-plane element flying behind Potts cleared the target. The No. 2 was Lt. Roy C. Harms's **Hell's Angels** (42-40781/U), which was shot up and ablaze even before "bombs away." With little prospect of even reaching the target, the pilots broke away to port in a desperate bid to give the crew a chance to jump. The aircraft barely attained several hundred feet altitude before beginning to descend; Sgt. J. J. Read (Eng.) was the only member to get out alive, and even he was badly burnt in the process. No. 3 was **Bertha** (2-40804/X, also a 329BS machine), piloted by Lt. William E. Meehan, which was similarly flak-stricken; her condition forced a swift crash landing upon the pilots, but the wheat field into which she slid saw the airframe disintegrate. Once again, there was a tithe of one survivor (Sgt. L. Yates), and he had scarcely scrambled clear of the wreckage when it was totally consumed in an explosion along with the other nine crew.

44BG's Perfect Strike

The disastrous navigational failure at Targovisti involving the 376BG and 93BG was not repeated by the remainder of the *Tidal Wave* groups. The 44BG had 36 crews split into two formations. Col. Leon Johnson (Group CO) headed sixteen B-24s assigned to bomb Columbia Aquila (White V), with twenty still heading for Creditul Minier (Blue); one from the latter sub-force led by Col. Jim Posey had already "aborted." Posey's target, being SW of Ploesti, meant his crews were probably the first to turn and prepare for their bomb run. The bombers were aligned in successive M-pattern Elements of five, a layout that was expected to bring about a maximum bomb load spread that in turn would create overall havoc among the refinery's variegated structures.

The flak defenses were ready to take on this formation during the five-minute period to "bombs away." Although strikes were borne by a number of bombers, none were taken down, although injuries and at least one fatality were borne prior to bombing commencing. The initial bomb loads began to leave their mark in exploding tanks and specialist mechanisms, such as cracking plants. The fire and smoke thus generated made problems for succeeding waves, as these crews attempted to avoid chimneys and other taller units.

It was a surprisingly still-intact group of B-24s that emerged from this inferno with its crematorium-like atmosphere. This positive scenario was soon to lapse with the appearance of several Bf109s from I/JG4 led by Hptm. W. Steinmann (*Gruppen Kommandeur*). He latched onto 42-40995/C **Satan's Hellcat**, flown by Capt. Rowland B. Houston and trailing smoke from an engine. The Luftwaffe pilot laced the B-24 with fire as he ran in from behind but received hits in turn. Worse still, he had come in too close and had no room to maneuver out of the dying bomber's downward motion. In a reflexive action, he jettisoned the canopy and literally flew the fighter into the ground. The very good fortune that saw him come through the incident alive and unscathed did not extend to the nine young Americans who perished in their aircraft's shattered wreck.

Only one other crew would fail to get back, led by Lt. E. Rainhart in 42-40371/Q **G. I. Girl**. Flak-inflicted damage on the bomb run and coming off the target left the bomber in a parlous state. The pilots held course for home, but some 80 miles on from Ploesti the aircraft was abandoned; F/O C. L. Starr (CP) lost his life thanks to a partially deployed parachute that presumably resulted in fatal contact with the ground, but the other eight ended up as POWs. This specific strike would prove to be one of the most positive aspects of *Tidal Wave*'s generally ill-starred outcome, one that moreover incurred the lowest loss rate between the seven sub-forces.

An arguably even more tragic loss for the 93BG concerned Capt. Hugh R. Roper, who is seen earlier in England pointing out some aspect of a just-completed mission. His B-24D-1-CO **Exterminator** (41-23717/H) was bearing Roper's crew back from Ploesti on what was their final mission when it was involved in a mid-air collision that cruelly took the lives of all eleven airmen.

The 389BG's **Chattanooga Choo Choo** ended her combat career a crumpled wreck in a Rumanian dry riverbed shortly after releasing her load over Ploesti. Lt. O'Reilly's attempted crash landing went awry and T/Sgt. Frank Kees (Eng.) proved to be the single fatality after being crushed by the dislodged top turret.

44BG's "Flawed" Strike

Col. Johnson's formation was unknowingly heading into an already-punished Columbia Aquila refinery, in addition to which one-third of the crews would be flying their final mission. The 98BG was paralleling the 44BG off to port as they homed in on Astra Romana (White IV). As the bomb run was being initiated, flak started to rise from railroad flat-beds hauled by a locomotive running on a track parallel to and "formating" with the 44BG! Although some of the guns targeted the "Eightball" formation, it was the 98BG that reportedly absorbed the bulk of this unexpected mobile barrage.

An arguably greater shock to the crews would arise with their first sight of White V. In place of a pristine, undisturbed complex there emerged the stunning vision of a smoke and flame-shrouded zone in which colossal gouts of oil-fired flame from ruptured storage tanks added to the hellish scene that the low-flying bombers would have to attempt to successfully traverse.

Johnson's Lead element headed for an area that was relatively visible and untouched; a distillation plant and a boiler house took the impact of the Lead B-24's bombs and the wingmen's loads added to the destruction. The second Element also got their loads off and followed Johnson safely out of the target area, although damage to at least two aircraft was quite severe. Fortune was not to spread its favor among the remaining three Elements, however.

Lt. W. Weaver was leading the third element in **Lil' Abner** (42-40761/D) as he plunged into the smoke cloud. Already nursing a sick No. 2 engine, the bomber's woes increased with further flak damage that reduced power to one-third as it cleared the refinery. It nevertheless staggered on for around ten minutes before the pilots were forced into a crash landing that fractured the fuselage behind the cockpit and left Sgt. W. Schettler dead in his top turret. Fire caught hold and Weaver, Lt. R. Snyder (CP), and Lt. W. Sorenson (N) were particularly fortunate to scramble clear.

Scrappy II (42-40375/G) was untouched as the fourth element penetrated the target area, but apparently was "torched" by an exploding storage tank's eruption, since it emerged sheathed in flames. Lts. T. Scrivener and E. Anderson were seen to ease the B-24 down in a bid to crash land; the bomber did make a sliding contact, but had barely halted when it exploded, killing all nine airmen.

Lt. Lasco was No. 3 in Scrivenor's element and his aircraft had already lost one crewmember to flak, as well as bearing heavy damage before "bombs away." Just after bombing fighter attacks added to the damage, as well as causing two more fatalities and badly wounding Lasco and Lt. J. Kill (CP), **Sad Sack II** (41-24153/L) finally struck the ground and ground to a mangled halt. Fire was threatening to immolate the pilots; Kill was trapped by the legs, but Lasco managed to free him and drag him out.

The quartet making up the final element surrendered half its number. Capt. Rowland M. Gentry, flying Lead in 42-40182/A **Forky II**, cleared the target with two engines on fire and two dead crewmembers. Fighters closed in on the cripple and Gentry attempted to carry off a crash landing; he basically succeeded in his endeavors, which sadly only left Sgt. C. Bridges to stagger clear before the B-24 exploded. Over on the right, Lt. G. Winger was in charge of 41-24015/R **Wing Dinger**, which probably suffered the same experience as the Scrivenor B-24 by running into a fireball and emerging on fire. The doomed bomber was seen to fly straight and level for a short time before torturously rising up several hundred feet. Both waist gunners proved to be the sole survivors out of nine on board, the others failing to clear the B-24 as it stalled and crashed to the ground. Seven 44BG bombers had gone down in the target area, but further losses would occur on the way back, not all with an unhappy conclusion.

"Sting in the Tail" Success

The third England-based Group's experience over Ploesti, while proving relatively costly, was to produce bombing results deemed good to excellent. In addition, the bomb run would be conducted in a novel manner. Whereas the other formations were to make a single mass run-up while crews maintained their individual station, the 389BG *Sky Scorpions* would break into three distinct factions. The center sub-force of fifteen B-24s headed by Capt. K. Caldwell, with Col. J. Wood (Group CO) in the right seat, would assume a straight approach on 143 degrees. Nine of the other sub-force flying on the left flank were to angle out to 129 degrees for one minute before banking to starboard on a 170-degree heading. Finally, the five crews over to starboard of Caldwell's five Elements were to angle out to 168 degrees for 45 seconds, then turn onto the same heading as the other flanking formation. In this way, the flight path of each sub-force would be guaranteed to be within the 500ft lateral spread of the Steaua Romana refinery, a situation not to be realized if the overall formation had remained in its original layout.

Matters could have been fouled up in the same manner as for the 376BG and 93BG. A map reading error by Col. Wood had the Lead bomber banking to starboard prior to the correct final turning point. The mistake was immediately brought to the pilot's attention by both Lt. Meador (the Lead navigator) and Maj. Brooks (Deputy Lead), and the correct course was resumed. The Attack Plan had anticipated that the first bombs would only explode after the entire Force had cleared the target. However, there was an unavoidable technical "fly in the ointment" that could and did subvert this desired aim. To the volatile nature of storage tanks was added the equally fragile nature of some of the plant equipment, such as gas pipes. The impetus of a missile of any size impacting with such units could easily cause an explosion, and this situation was to be visited upon the 389BG attackers, as undoubtedly proved to be the case at the other target locations.

Lt. John Fino (Lead bombardier) in 42-40629/N—appropriately named **The Scorpion**—picked out his allotted boiler house target and the four 1,000-lb bombs shattered the structure, while a cracking plant to starboard was similarly "blitzed" by Lt. Tolleson's bombardier. Sure enough, violent explosions began to erupt from fractured pipes, with the smoke-shrouded flames swiftly limiting visibility for the following waves of B-24s.

A combination of already punctured fuel tanks and the need to fly at low level through a fire-stricken zone was to lead to tragedy for one crew. Lt. Lloyd Hughes was No. 2 in Caldwell's second element, but when his perilous situation was called to his attention by Capt. P. Ardery (564BS CO) as Lead, Hughes tersely replied, "OK—but I gotta get the bombs on target." He achieved his goal, but emerged from the inferno with a solid banner of flame licking the port wing of 42-40753/J **Eager Eagle**. Hughes and Lt. R. H. Helder (CP) held position for several miles as they sought out a suitable crash landing site. A dry creek bed was chosen, but just after the B-24 was eased up over a bridge, the starboard wing dropped and struck the ground, throwing the aircraft into a violent cartwheel. Two gunners and an officer did survive the crash, but the latter succumbed to his terrible burns within 48 hours. The dedication to duty exemplified by Lt. Hughes' action would culminate in his receiving the third of five Medals of Honor awarded to Ploesti participants.

The entire Force crossed over the refinery without any loss, but three further crews were to taste the bitter seeds of failure, with nine of the thirty-one airmen concerned forfeiting their lives. The worst affected in terms of human loss was Lt. Robert W. Horton's 42-40735/C **Sand-Witch** (566BS). A shell impacting with the bomb bay set the overload tanks ablaze and a resultant crash landing attempt went tragically awry when one wing struck a tree and the fuselage broke into sections before exploding. Amazingly, the sole survivor was Sgt. Zerrill J. Steen (Eng.), who was in his top turret at this point; the turret was probably cast out of the airframe by the blast, but Steen somehow emerged alive!

Target flak also left **Chattanooga Choo Choo** (42-40782/X), piloted by Lt. Robert J. O'Reilly, Jr. thoroughly shot up. The prospect of carrying out a successful crash landing was almost nullified by the existence of one "hung up" bomb, but desperate attempts to get it free finally succeeded. As with Hughes and Horton, a dry riverbed was the platform for a "belly in" action. The B-24's airframe did not hold up under the impact and the result was a shattered nose section and fractures on either side of the wing roots. Sgt. F. Kees (Eng.) was crushed by the dislodged top turret, but the other nine got out alive, although Lt. Richard W. Britt (N) was trapped in the nose and was ultimately freed—not by the crew, who thought the Lt. was dead and had then commenced their bid for freedom, but by local Rumanian citizens.

The final MIA loss for the group's own Force was four. Lt. Melvin E. Neef had charge of a B-24 on loan from one of the IX BC groups (42-40115/A **Boomerang**). The crew included Maj. William H. Yeager, Jr. (566BS CO), who was now about to involuntarily relinquish his post. Total power loss on the starboard wing left the wallowing bomber in no position to maintain formation, although the pilots desperately held course for North Africa. Finally, it was decided to crash land in what appeared to be the suitable side of a cornfield; unfortunately, the bank of an unseen stream connected with the onrushing B-24, tearing off the nose section and dislodging the top turret. Lt. C. V. Ferguson (N) and Lt. C. N. Wallace (B) were cut free from the nose after several hours, while T/Sgt. H. T. Godwin (Eng.) was very fortunate to avoid being crushed by the turret's fall.

Detachment Fortunes

Seven 389BG crews had been assigned to Col. J. Kane's 98BG, but the fortunes of war would ensure a positive outcome to the mission for just three among this number. The *Pyramiders* had a 46-strong Force aligned in four ten-strong waves, with seven making up the fifth. (The first wave was reduced to nine due to one B-24 suffering a fatal crash landing after aborting over its airfield.) The target was Astra Romana (White IV), lying on the western fringe of the overall complex, but already struck by the second sub-force of the 93BG. This fact became all too apparent as the IX BC group made its final approach.

The 389BG crews were spread throughout the group ranks, with Lt. Andy Opsata's 41-11817/H **The Stinger** on the extreme left of the first wave, while fourth from left in the second wave was Lt. L. N. Ellis flying 41-11815/G **Daisy Mae**. Finally, 41-11774/O held Lt. T. P. Fravega's crew. All three bombers would regain North African shores, with only four wounded members from among the twenty-nine airmen.

Lt. Charles A. Salyer penetrated as far as the target, but observers reported on return that **Battleaxe** (42-40973/X) came out of the smoke cover out on its own and blazing fiercely; for whatever reason, the bombs were only released at this point, after which the B-24 nosed down and crashed. Lt. Julian Darlington's 41-11840/P **The Witch** was on the right of the third wave and directly ahead of Salyer. He placed his bombs into a power plant and headed away, but fate was not finished with him.

The last 389BG crew to go down at this stage was led by Lt. John J. McGraw, whose nine-man crew were on their first mission. Flak struck home as 41-11776/O **Jersey Jackass** left the target and an immediate decision was made to crash land. After the bomber lurched to a flame-encased halt, the pilot got hung up by his harness; fortunately, Lt. C. Cavit (CP) got his badly-burnt colleague free. The sole other survivor was Sgt. John R. Ross.

Heading for Home—Maybe

The tattered remnants of the 376BG and 93BG were streaming away from Ploesti, even as the other three groups were lining up for their bomb runs. This was evident in the reports by many of the 44BG and 98BG crews, who could not understand why both Olive Drab and Desert Pink B-24s were observed cutting across their inward course, or why there were sightings of crashed or crash-landed aircraft.

The 93BG had already lost seven crews over the target area and the defenders were unknowingly far from finished with the battered formation. Both the Baker and Brown-led formations had lost two crews, but the former assembly was now separated into smaller groups. The White II formation led by Maj. Potts was reduced to the same overall number, but ten became nine not long after "bombs away." **Pudgy** (42-40613/E) was off Pott's left wing with Lt. Milton Teltser in charge. Battle damage was such that the pilot decided to take up a heading to port for neutral Turkey.

The arrival of two Bf109s sealed the bomber's fate, as fire took hold; with both port engines out. the wing drooped and the pilots had barely raised it again before the B-24 sliced into a cornfield. The port wing broke off and up over the fuselage; the bombardier and navigator were killed in the telescoped nose section, and the final death toll was six out of eleven. Several of the survivors were badly burnt and all five were fortunate to escape alive after being threatened by a pitchfork-bearing group of civilians, whose obvious intentions were thankfully thwarted by the arrival of what was described as a "local official"!

The third Element from Baker's force had held together and steadily maintained course for home. Luck was seemingly on their side as they climbed for altitude to clear the looming mountain barrier. In the Lead was Lt. Hugh Roper's 41-23717/H, bearing the (unconsciously-cruel) title **Exterminator**. No. 2 was Lt. Vic Olliffe in 41-24121/J **Let er Rip**, while Lt. Russell Longnecker held the left position with 42-40246/T **Thundermug**. Roper and crew were heading for the States on their return, since this was their final mission—but fate would intervene to lethally cast their aircraft's name back at them. A solid if brief cloud bank in the bombers' path caused Longnecker to ease off to port, but when he emerged into the clear he was stunned to find himself alone. The other two B-24s had come together and gone down, leaving none of **Exterminator's** eleven-man team alive, while eight out of eleven was the fatality figure on **Let er Rip**.

Internment Option

Two group crews were to face the shadowy fate of internment. Lt. C. Turner was flying No. 3 in Col. Brown's second element and had lost an engine on 42-40608/M **The Urgin Virgin** (328BS) during the bomb run, as well as having three gunners wounded. Fortune was on the crew's side, as they avoided interception to finally land at an unspecified Turkish airfield.

No. 3 position in Col. Baker's last Element had been occupied by 42-40754/U **Little Lady** (409BS), flown by Lt. R. L. Wilkinson with eleven others on board. Luck was really on the side of this crew, especially since it was straggling for the bulk of the return route, as well as being fortunate to thread its way through valleys in the hill and mountain zones barring the bombers' path. The route diversions so created threw them off course for North Africa and forced the navigator to head for Turkey. There was now every chance that fuel reserves would run out if this neutral refuge was not found within 60 minutes at most. An airfield at Corlin was thankfully found within this time span, but its runways appeared too

Lt. Robert C. Peterson (N) is seen in the cockpit of **Avenger**; this was the B-24D in which his crew, led by Lt. William D. Hughes, came through the holocaust of Ploesti. His Spaniel, dubbed "Pilot Officer Rusty," reportedly accompanied his owner on the mission, as well as several others.

The problems associated with operating aircraft in a desert scenario are further exemplified by this taxiing 44BG B-24. The abrasive effect of the sand and dirt particles upon the airframe, both on this aircraft and any following machine, is clear; the blinding cloud would not assist pilots directly behind in wending a safe path over the airfield surface. British weather did not seem so bad in these circumstances.

short, as the now-laboring B-24 was eased in for a safe if brake-burning landing. Barely had the crew emerged when the port wing collapsed at the wing root—a double dose of luck!

The final MIA figure for those 93BG crews getting through to Ploesti would be twelve, but the overall figure would rise to thirteen. Maj. Ralph J. McBride was to have led the second element of White II's force behind Maj. Potts. The MACR states that he took off late but never managed to join up; at some point, 41-24230/Z **Jo Jo's Special Delivery** was felled by fighters over the sea, leaving eleven names destined for a postwar "Wall of the Missing."

The Cost Mounts

The USAAF Force's untidy retreat from Ploesti was adding to the cost for all five groups in terms of bombers and their crews. In the case of the 44BG, luck would be on the side of two crews who took up a heading for Turkey thanks to the serious condition of their B-24s. The first was led by Lt. Edward R. Mitchell in 42-40267/N **Horse Fly (**67BS), while Lt. Charles E. Hughes was in charge of 42-40777/N **Flossie Flirt** (66BS). A total of nineteen airmen were duly interned, some of whom subsequently returned to England; Lt. Mitchell was one, but he was on borrowed time, since he was lost the following November.

The group's final loss involved Lts. Fred H. Jones and Reginald L. Carpenter and their crews, both of whose bombers ended up in the Mediterranean. In the case of Jones, his nine-man team survived 42-40780/H **Available Jones's** "ditching" south of Brindisi, although put "in the bag" after rescue by an Italian float plane. The same number of crewmembers was on board 41-24024 **Bewitching Witch**. The aircraft had survived flak and fighter damage, but its demise was ultimately brought about by diminishing power and fuel reserves. Unfortunately, two individuals never got out of the bomber, while the other seven spent an uncomfortable night afloat in dinghies before being sighted by an RAF Wellington that circled the area until an RAF Air-Sea Rescue (ASR) Launch hove in sight.

Terminal Gallantry

To the six 389BG B-24s lost over Ploesti or after "bombs away" would be added four more. Lt. Darlington's 41-11840/P **The Witch**, on loan from the 98BG, had cleared the target, but as the bombers commenced the climb ahead of the mountains further fighter attacks developed. A strike on No. 4 engine caused the propeller to "runaway" and the B-24D began to fall back. On being informed of the fact by Sgt. Stanley Horine (TG), Lt. James Gunn, piloting 42-40364/Y **Prince Charming**, elected to drop back as "escort." This breaking of the rules proved both unavailing and tragic. By the time Gunn had reduced the distance, Darlington's B-24 was already doomed, while the fighters had latched onto Gunn's bomber and set it ablaze; only Horine got out and he was badly burned. Meanwhile, **The Witch**, although fatally crippled, was finally brought in for a successful crash landing with seven of the ten airmen still on board; four of them managed to evade capture and link up with the Yugoslavian Partisans.

The two 44BG "Internees" were joined by two from the 389BG. Lt. Harold James was piloting 42-40744/S, but critical fuel levels was the reason why the B-24 finally ended up landing at Izmir, Turkey. Capt. Robert C. Mooney, in charge of 42-40544/R **Hitler's Hearse**, had been fatally wounded by a flak burst. Lt. J. F. Gerrits (CP) was assisted by T/Sgt. C. E. Garrett (Eng.), and although they finally crossed into Turkish territory, a crash landing had to be carried out that left the nine survivors alive.

The nightmare of the *Tidal Wave* mission will still be very fresh in the minds of these surviving combat crewmembers from an unidentified Group. Some are seated with others milling around, with most or all talking out or reflecting upon every aspect of a mission that cost the Force of 177 almost one-third of that figure in bombers and their crews.

T/Sgt Ben Kuroki, a Nisei-American, completed his combat tour over Ploesti as a member of Lt. Kenneth Desert's crew in 41-24105/Q **Tupelo Lass**. He is seen here shaking hands with a S/Sgt. from among a quartet of ground personnel who are probably **Lass**'s maintenance crew.

Summation

The Ploesti mission, as with Schweinfurt on 17 August and 14 October the same year, would take its place in USAAF history as a gallant but costly foray deep into Hitler's European domain. The mission also has distinct overtones of the British Army's "Charge of the Light Brigade" during the 1850s Crimean War. Two of the seven sub-forces never struck their assigned targets of Unirea Sperantza (White III) and Romana Americana (White I), which part of the 93BG and all of the 376BG would have respectively homed-in upon had the mission gone as planned.

The damage inflicted varied from very severe—particularly at Creditul Minier (Blue), where the facilities for producing aviation fuel were permanently crippled—to a disappointingly low degree of punishment at Concordia Vega (White II) and full production recovery by September, while the 50% drop at Astra Romana (White IV) was reversed and indeed exceeded within several months. In between, in terms of effect, was an immediate total loss of production for several months at Steaua Romana (Red) and for a longer period at Columbia Aquila (White V).

Of the 178 crews dispatched, 53 (almost 30%) had not regained their North African airfields. Of that melancholy figure, no less than 35 had come from the ranks of the 44th, 93rd, and 389th BGs. The mission's savage intensity was recognized by the award of five Medals of Honor, four of which went to the VIII BC groups. Added to those CMHs earned by Col. Baker, Maj. Jerstad, and Lt. Hughes was that of Col. Leon Johnson (44BG CO), who was the sole living recipient.

2BW's Extended Sojourn

The bulk of the two weeks following Ploesti involved no missions for the 2BW Groups, although there was still no indication of when the period of detachment would be concluded. Recovery from the 1 August operation was adjudged sufficient for the crews to be briefed on the 13th for a relatively lengthy run to Wiener Neustadt, Austria. Although the Luftwaffe had ample warning of the bombers' approach, their presence was gratifyingly sparse. There were no direct losses to flak and fighters, but three crews in all did not return to their airfields. Lt. Alva J. Geron had suffered an engine loss on 42-40611/W **Death Dealer** on the way up and a second crippled by target flak. The relative proximity of Switzerland induced him to head there and land at Thurau, where the B-24 was set on fire and the ten airmen were interned. The USAAF's presence in that country accordingly commenced this day.

Lt. Robert Lehnhausen had already survived a Mediterranean "ditching" on 2 July. Now the former 68BS co-pilot had charge of 41-24211/U **Wing and a Prayer**. The bomber was dangerously short of fuel as Sicily was looming up; worse still was the small airfield he had found whose runway was smothered in shell holes. A parallel area of grass seemed to offer a limited clear space, but the progressive loss of power forced a once-only landing approach. The recently replaced nose wheel collapsed on landing, but the undignified forward momentum ended safely. A second unlisted group crew landed elsewhere on the island.

Mutual Trust?

On one occasion, Sgt. Jack Cox (566BS) was walking back to Benghazi airfield when he met up with an Arab selling chickens. Jack bought one of the fowls—or rather, he handed over a "packet" of cigarettes that in reality only contained a handful of the sticks, as opposed to its normal complement of twenty. His "red rooster" was rather skinny, so he decided to head for the Mess tent for a loaf of bread and some marmalade; the latter item attracted all the bugs around, which suited the bird perfectly, adding them to his diet. However, the bird did not increase in bulk, although his crowing ability remained undiminished, especially at night. Every time someone turned on a light—a regular act with personnel coming and going—he would hold forth from the foot of Jack's bed!

This nocturnal cacophony finally proved too much and the bird was dispatched by Jack's revolver. The rooster was plucked and cooked, but even after three days, the anticipated meal failed to materialize; the skin withstood every attempt at penetration with a fork, so it was disgustedly cast out. On examination, it emerged Jack's prize was a fighting cock and therefore highly inedible, so neither vendor nor purchaser gained much from the transaction—although the Arab was ahead by five cigarettes in the long run!

Costly "Milk Run"

Foggia, in southern Italy, promised a fairly easy-paced mission on the 16th, especially since the one dispatched one month previous had fallen into the "milk run" category. A very different experience would befall the 44BG in particular this time round, however. The briefed target was Foggia North airfield and all three 2BW units were again involved. The Shipdham ranks included several "rookie" crews, given the (sadly inaccurate) expectation of a trouble-free mission. In fact, 38 of the 70 airmen fated to go down would never witness another dawn.

Nothing untoward occurred until after the bomb run was completed and the twenty-three strong formation had turned for home. Then "peace and quiet went to Hell," as a pack of Bf109s and Fw190s harshly intervened. All four squadrons were involved in the carnage, with the often luckless 67BS the worst affected. The first of three losses involved the veteran **Buzzin' Bear** (41-24229/P), bearing Lt. James F. DeVinney, Lt. Cameron's regular bombardier. Fighter assaults knocked the bomber out of formation and she finally broke in two; Lt. Leighton C. Smith (P), DeVinney, and four others bailed out, while the remaining four, all gunners, lost their lives.

Suzy Q (41-23817/L) was the sole squadron "original" aircraft, but she also succumbed; her reported fiery end on an Italian beach seems odd, since all ten on Lt. W. R. Bateman's crew ended up as names on a "Wall of the Missing," so suggesting that their mount came down in the sea. The trio of losses was completed by Lt. Hager's 42-41021/T **Black Sheep**; the badly damaged aircraft was headed for Sicily, but an engine fire forced the pilots into a crash landing on Italian soil. Five of the crew escaped from the B-24, although Hager was badly burnt on his face and arms, but the other four were trapped and consumed in the resultant explosion shortly after the B-24 ground to a halt.

The 506BS surrendered two aircraft, its first since arrival in North Africa. Lt. Charles A. Whitlock was "Tail-end Charlie" in 42-40606/X **Timba-a-ah!**, which had survived two fighter passes but not the third. Once again, half the ten-man crew escaped by parachute after the bomber went into a terminal dive. Its companion in death was 42-40778/T **Southern Comfort**, which had two engines and the bomb bay set on fire. Although all ten crewmembers did bail out, two officers reportedly suffered partial parachute failure and were killed.

Lt. R. A Curelli's 41-23778/F **Lady Luck** (66BS) was already straggling with one engine "out"; both bomber and all but one of the ten airmen were granted no quarter, as enemy gunfire induced a violent explosion. The melancholy loss tally was completed by the 68BS' 42-40373 /Z **Natchez Belle**, which had fallen behind and was duly hammered by the fighters. Fire took hold in two engines and a bail out was called for, an action that all but three airmen managed to carry out. Lt. E. M. Shannon (P) and the other six were soon captured, but no less than five of this group later escaped and regained Allied lines.

Running Down the Clock

A return to Foggia on the 19th must have led to a very muted mood among the 44BG crews assigned to go; serviceability levels were sufficient for only ten bombers to be dispatched, of which four subsequently "aborted." In fact, a good bomb run on marshalling yards was attained while the some thirty-strong enemy fighter force left the now miniscule group formation alone. A further 48 hours elapsed before what would be the final mission for the 2BW Force was called. Cancello airfield, north of Naples, was assaulted without loss, the second mission in succession with this fortunate conclusion.

Temporary Homecoming

The Orders for a return to East Anglia were issued right after the latest mission, and in the case of the 389BG were acted upon beginning the 25th, with all but two of the crews landing back at Hethel. Lt. D. C. Lighter had refused to fly the Ploesti mission, but was ironically destined to end up in enemy hands. His 42-40767 (564BS) was bearing ten combat and five 44BG, 93BG, and 389BG ground crew. It was within 30 minutes of SW England when the Luftwaffe struck, sending the B-24 into the sea; only the pilot and two other personnel were very fortunate to survive as POWs. A second 564BS crew led by Lt. J. T Blackis in 42-40772/C **Scheherazade**, as well as five ground crew suffered a kinder if frustrating fate when they ended up on a Portuguese airfield and were interned—the second group team to do so within two months. The sole other loss suffered by the other two groups involved three of the five ground crew lost on Lt. Lighter's B-24. The final aircraft movements were completed by month's end—but North Africa was not yet finished with the 2BW.

Chapter Six

From Wing to Division Status

Key Structural Alteration

The basic sea change from Bomb Wing to Division status occurred 13 September, when the concept of the Combat Bomb Wing (CBW) was first initiated. The intention was to bring three groups within each CBW entity, a task that was already in process within the 1BW, with its nine current serving groups. In the case of the 2BW, with just four groups on hand, the process was naturally still fractured. On 2 September, the 44BG and 392BG were reassigned to the 202 PCBW, which on the 13th became the 14CBW. In the case of the 93BG, it became the founding unit of the 20CBW and the 389BG became the equivalent founder of the 2CBW. In time, no less than five CBWs would exist within what was now the 2BD, but this expansion was still several months distant from its ultimate fulfilment.

New Kids on the Block

A further albeit limited expansion in the ranks of the still-titled 2BW had occurred during the initial detachment to North Africa; the arrival of the 392BG additionally heralded the introduction into combat of the B-24H variant. A principle external difference from its B-24D predecessor was the displacement of the "birdcage" nose canopy frame by a power turret mounted above a revised triangular Plexiglas panel for the bombardier. The ball turret introduced on the final B-24D production run, with some of these airframes allotted to the 389BG, was to become a standard production item.

The acolyte Group had been activated at Davis-Monthan, AZ, on 26 January 1943, and its development and advance to operational status had followed a similar pattern to its Hardwick and Hethel predecessors. Over the following five months, moves were made first to Biggs Field, TX, then to Alamogordo, NM. The Ground echelon had made the Trans-Atlantic transfer during the second half of July; the Air echelon's equivalent movement was effected during the first half of August, with arrival at Wendling (Station 118) commencing on the 15th. The airfield lay approximately 30 miles WNW of Norwich and was wartime utility in layout, just like the other three B-24 bases.

The absence of the bulk of 2BW bombers and crews in North Africa until late August was the basic reason why the 392BG fliers had to wait almost two months before being blooded in combat. That call came in the early hours of 6 September, but the mission proved passive in nature, being yet another diversion in which all four Groups participated without incident. Not so the main 1BW Force, which went to Stuttgart and ended up 45 B-17s short by the day's end. Nor was there much more excitement three days later, when

Each USAAF airfield in Britain was technically leased and officially handed over following the arrival of each Group. In this instance, the official ceremony of hand-over is being performed at Hethel. "Old Glory" flapping from a long pole oversees events with the 389BG Guard of Honor to the left on what is a pleasant if cloudy day. Date is 23 August 1943.

Four members of the crew manning the 389BG's **Little Gramper** have discarded their upper clothing as a counter to the searing heat of North Africa. Their return from a mission occurred during the Group's second deployment to the MTO in early September.

airfields in NE France were attacked without loss.

Unbeknownst to the Wendling airmen, they had now flown their last full mission in September. (On the 23rd, 26th, and 27th they would fly three more diversion missions, the first on their own and the other two supported by single figures of 44BG bombers totalling three and two, respectively.) Chartres airfield was focused upon by the three veteran 2BW Groups on the 15th with the loss of one crew. Lt. William Loveday's 42-40938/K (330BS) was culled from the 93BG formation by fighters and crashed SW of Dieppe with the loss of four out of ten, including the pilot.

Back to the Desert

The normal post-mission procedure on all three airfields was rudely dispelled when the announcement was made of a second trip to savor the delights of North Africa. The regularly-stated reason for the move has been ascribed to the critical situation facing the troops involved in the seaborne landing at Salerno, south of Naples. The invasion had commenced 10 September, and the 5th U.S. Army troops appeared under real threat of expulsion, at least for the first 24 hours; the twin bombardments made by the Allied Air Forces, and even more directly gunfire from supporting Royal and U.S. Navy warships, had stabilized the overall situation by D+2/3. In spite of this recovery, the 2BW was still being called upon in a broader sense by adding its weight to the overall campaign.

The detachment of the three Groups to the Mediterranean would extend over a far shorter period compared to the high summer experience; in fact, the resumption of operations from East Anglia would occur 8 October for Hardwick and Hethel and the following day for the Shipdham fliers. The crews did not have so far to travel to their temporary bases this time, since Tunisia was now in Allied hands, and the airfield to which they were directed was at Oudna. Enough aircraft were on hand by the 21st to merit dispatching a mission that was to focus on the docks at Leghorn. In the event, only the 44BG managed to make Assembly and carried out their bomb runs as well as returning, albeit minus two B-24s that had "aborted" due to technical failure. Marshalling yards at Pisa (24th) and an airfield at Lucca the next day were on the target list for the 44BG, although not for the 389BG on the 25th. (A "recall" signal was issued on the latter date.) Diversions were flown on the 27th and 29th, again without apparent participation by the Hethel airmen. Records for the 93BG are equally vague over this whole operational spell, although it is most unlikely that Shipdham would have borne the entire weight of assault.

Lt. Dout's Diary (1)

Personal diaries were completed by numerous combat crewmen, and the surviving examples provide a wealth of material for authors and historians. Unfortunately, not all diarists completed their combat tours, with death and captivity intervening with distressing frequency. Lt. Boyd Dout was a 567BS pilot who kept his log between joining the 389BG and going MIA the following January. Excerpts from his diary will feature in subsequent chapters and commence here with an entry for 21 September:

> Bastia (Corsica). The crew's first raid with Lt. Nading in the left seat and me as copilot. The mission lasted six hours. We passed over Leghorn after weather split up the groups. Flak was moderate and we had one hole in the port wing. After passing twice over the Primary, we struck the harbor at Bastia, on Corsica, with a good pattern. Left the formation on the way back due to a gas shortage. Threw stuff overboard. Finally landed at Bizerte with just 15 minutes to spare. One ship landed with two engines "out."

Mayhem over Wiener-Neustadt

Wiener-Neustadt's aircraft production facilities in Austria had already been attacked by the B-24s on 13 August with amazingly minimal flak or fighter interference. The previous 15 July over Foggia, the 44BG had enjoyed almost complete immunity from casualties; on 16 August, no less than seven Group B-24s were lost when the bombers were again dispatched to Foggia. As with this target, so the same stark contrast was to arise between the first and second runs to the Austrian target.

Hellsadroppin II is "flaring out" prior to completing a smooth landing at Hardwick. Red surround to the "dulled down" national insignia was officially superseded by blue in September 1943. Note the Lorenz blind landing aerial behind the nose wheel. The 329BS bomber was later transferred out to the 448BG.

The return mission was laid for 1 October, and the 44BG was chosen as Lead, with Gen. Hodges (CG, 2BD) as Command pilot with 26 Group aircraft. Weather conditions increasingly deteriorated in terms of cloud cover and bombing results assessed as "poor." On the other hand, opposition was building up, especially in terms of fighter numbers. Among the ranks were eight 67BS crews. Several hours later, the squadron was short three MIA from among this figure, with at least two more having diverted elsewhere—the latest setback since the group had commenced operations.

The first of the 67BS B-24s to go down was incurred during the bomb run. The Low squadron had been forced out of position and coincidentally now suffered a head-on assault. Lt. Charles P. Henderson, Jr.'s 42-72853 lost both starboard motors and the B-24 assumed a steep spiralling maneuver; the bail out signal was successfully responded to by just three airmen. Henderson was among the dead, while Lt. Greyhosky (CP) was very fortunate to get out; he was knocked out as he went to jump and only recovered his full senses when already on the ground, having no idea what transpired, other than that he had come through alive.

The second loss occurred almost at "bombs away." Lt. Reginald L. Carpenter was piloting 42-41017/L, which also had two engines set on fire, followed quickly by a third. The 25th mission for S/Sgt. F. Paliga (Eng.) was his last, but in a harsh if not terminal manner. In the tail was S/Sgt. E. B. Bryl, an RAF veteran with 60 operations behind him; he would not share Paliga's relative good fortune as a POW, being killed when he was blown out of his turret. Bryl's fate was shared by four of the ten on board, but Carpenter got out alive, although it is believed he was still at the controls when his B-24 disintegrated. The circumstances in which Lt. G. Bronstein's 41-23918/O **Bela** met its fate are unclear, since its absence was not noted by anybody. Suffice to say, the pilot and all but two of his nine-man crew died, with several bodies, including Bronstein's, never being found, suggesting a very violent end to the aircraft's progress.

Fascinatin' Witch (41-23811/K), a 66BS "original," should not have participated, as both inboard engines had already been diagnosed as unfit for operations due to excessive oil consumption. It had been "cleared" this day on the very dubious grounds that the mission duration, assessed at less

The ever-hostile reaches of the North Sea are slipping by beneath **Dorothy** as the 389BG climbs out towards the Continent. Two important field modifications seen here are the doubling-up of the forward-firing guns and the slab of armor sheeting bolted under each cockpit frame; the latter measure became a standard feature on B-24s.

than ten hours, would be sufficient for the motors to hold out—a decision based on Lt. Richard W. Bridge's (P) plea! However, both engines were again playing up and losing power after the group ascended to bombing altitude; although failing to climb initially, Bridges somehow coaxed his charge back into formation. The bomb run had just been completed when a fighter pass completely disabled Nos. 2 and 3, as well as firing the overload fuel tanks in the forward bomb bay. Three gunners were killed at this time, but the other seven bailed out. (Bridges was originally imprisoned in Hungary and then Yugoslavia before escaping in May 1944 and managing to link up with Tito's Partisans.)

Also downed from the 66BS was 42-72877/A, flown by Lt. Tom B. Hobson. No. 4 engine was fired during the initial fighter pass and the controls were adversely affected. Further damage was borne, after which the B-24 began to spin, an action only partially corrected by lowering the flaps and "feathering" all functioning engines. The reduced centrifugal force permitted the pilot and five others to get out alive before the bomber finally went out of control. Hobson, after landing close to the wreckage, noted that the starboard control surfaces on the tail plane were almost wholly excised, confirming the loss of control experienced by both pilots following the first fighter pass.

The other two squadrons each contributed a single aircraft to the MIA tally. Lt. Coleman S. Whitaker's 41-23816/X **Black Jack** had been assigned on 20 September 1942, but now was last reported as falling away and on fire in the bomb bay just after leaving the target. Parachutes were reported at debriefing, but Whitaker and four of the ten-man team did not survive after the bomber split in two. S/Sgt. Robert J. Reasoner (TG) was the sole survivor from among the Enlisted man complement, and he received such serious burns about his head that he was later repatriated. The 506BS loss involved 42-72857/X, which caught fire in the bomb bay and peeled off to starboard with the bomb load being jettisoned. Lt. Stanley F. Olsen got all his crew out safely, but sacrificed his life in doing so; his body was never found after the B-24 reportedly blew up and crashed near Bad Voeslau, SW of Vienna—"Greater love hath no man than this...."

Single crews were lost from the 93BG and 389BG. Flying within the Hardwick formation was yet another "original" bomber, 41-23711/B **Jerk's Natural**; it had flown the first Group mission on 9 October 1942 and survived Ploesti. The 328BS veteran must have suffered heavy damage, since she was out of formation on the return leg when set upon by several fighters. Lt. William F. Stein managed to survive the assault, but the crew's luck finally ran out as the pilots were attempting a crash landing in hill-strewn territory; the aircraft developed a spinning action and only Lt. William W. Sykes (N) got clear prior to a terminal impact with the ground. Lt. Kenneth N. Matson was piloting 42-40775/Y **Wolf Waggin** (565BS), which absorbed a flak strike sufficient to blow the top turret out of the airframe, along with T/Sgt. Stanton A. Earley, while five other crewmembers ended up dead. Despite being wounded, Matson managed to bail out to become the sole officer survivor.

The greatly reduced 44BG formation arriving back at Oudna gave a false impression of overall losses, even if seven MIA crews was a bad result. In actual fact, no less than seven crews had diverted into Allied airfields or territory in Italy and Sicily. Three B-24s from among this figure would not return to the group, however. Lt. Butler's 42-72860/N **Emmy Lou** was so badly shot up that it was finally "written off" the following month; the pilots were lucky to get her down safely after suffering right flap retraction and the other deploying in the fully-down position, an aerodynamic imbalance that was only promptly countered by applying full right rudder and advancing the throttles! Also declared "Category E" was 41-23235/P **Earthquake McGoon** (67BS), which Lt. Aldridge was forced to land on a beach near Salerno. The third "write off" was 41-23769/B **Princess Charlotte/ Sure**

Shot (66BS), which landed at an airfield at Salerno. (**Margaret Ann** - 41-24009/W - was a fourth B-24 that did not remain with the group after Lt. Kessler landed his shot up charge at Bari; however, it remained in service after being transferred to the 98BG.)

Wiener-Neustadt had provided a painful rebuff to the American fliers, but it also signalled the end of what would be the last period of Mediterranean service for what was now the 2nd Bomb Division (BD). This title would be the penultimate example in the evolution of the 8USAAF. In the case of the B-24 units, the original two units had comprised the 201 Provisional Combat Bomb Wing (PCBW) from 25 March. The 389BG had joined this structure 11 June, while the 392BG had been assigned the title of 202 PCBW on 2 September.

Yankee Know-How?

The endearing impression that still exists among the British population in general about WWII American servicemen is that they were largely "men of the world" from the big cities, free with their favors and money-wise. The bald truth is that far from falling into this corporate category of "Street-wise City Slickers," thousands among their number were not raised in these conditions, but rather evolved into Service life from small towns and settlements in the wide open expanses of their nation's rural expanses. Exposure to the big, wide world only commenced after they had enlisted or were drafted.

A simple example of putting one's trust in a fellow individual concerned two 389BG airmen: Harold Brown and Richard Corner. A three-day break between operations saw several of their crew heading into Norwich. While strolling around the city, they encountered an elderly lady and asked from where they could obtain a bottle of spirits. She responded by saying that by coincidence she possessed a spirit ration card.

After accepting a princely sum of £6 ($24 in equivalent U.S. currency), she requested that the men remain where they were while she did the purchasing, adding that any inkling on the shop staff's part that the bottle was for the Americans would jeopardize matters. Some 20 minutes duly elapsed before the party decided to look for her and/or the shop concerned—only to discover (surprise, surprise) that neither was anywhere to be found! Although this case could be regarded as simple naivety, there can be little doubt that it was repeated elsewhere, at least during the initial period of the Americans' presence in Britain.

Another instance of naivety, or rather genuine ignorance, lay in coming to terms with British currency—a structure that was confusing enough for the indigenous population. (Remember farthings, florins, half-crowns and guineas, for all of us Britons of pre-1971 vintage?) One U.S. Serviceman still possesses the Bill of Sale given him for the purchase of a bicycle from a Norfolk native - £24! Once again, this act of gross over-charging was not an isolated example. It was also not uncommon for a Serviceman to hold out a selection of British coins and ask the vendor to extract the requisite figure, an action that more unscrupulous persons surely did take advantage of. However, most personnel quickly or at least gradually came to terms with their Ally's financial structure.

Lt. Walter Bunker's crew are more than relieved to be back from the Group's second detachment to North Africa. He stands on the left, while his copilot, Lt. Dick Butler, is fourth from the left. The latter was subsequently granted his own crew, but was seriously injured following a failed crash landing on 20 December, an incident that effectively ended his combat career.

Back to the "Big League"

The USAAF Bombing Offensive conducted from British shores against the Nazi empire has gone down in American military annuls as "The Big League of Sky Fighting." This title in no real way denigrates the effort of the 15USAAF in simultaneously prosecuting the overall campaign to shatter the enemy's industrial infrastructure. It simply indicates that the main logistical thrust logically emanated from East Anglia, since the bulk of Germany's landscape, along with the Northern reaches of its conquered territories, could be more comprehensively covered from this sector of operations.

The three 2BD Groups transferred back during the first week of October just in time for the final series of deep-penetration missions into Germany before winter weather conditions, along with the lack of long-range escorts, put

The 392BG was the first 2BD unit to operate the B-24H, a variant that bore power-operated nose and ball turrets. The H variant was constructed at Ford's Willow Run plant and the distinctly scalloped camouflage separation line was a visual feature as demonstrated here by **Axis Grinder**.

Hethel's **Missouri Mauler** also bears the red surround insignia, albeit on a smaller scale to **Hellsadroppin II**. Her forward-facing gun is still awkwardly positioned to counter "twelve o'clock high" assaults. The "tunnel" gun under the rear fuselage provides an even poorer return in defensive effectiveness, to be replaced by the ball turret.

a halt to matters. However, the latter consideration was probably still not exercising the minds of Gen. Eaker and his senior staff. In spite of increasingly unsustainable loss levels suffered over the past several months, the USAAF authorities were seemingly still clinging to the hope that the B-17s and B-24s could penetrate to and accurately bomb their targets with an acceptable loss factor. The encroaching operational spell would finally subvert that prospect and earn the unenviable sobriquet of *Black Week*, as the death knell of the "self-defending bomber" theory was sounded.

"Black Week"

Black Week commenced 8 October, and signalled the first of four concentrated assaults on German industry. Five days prior to this, the North African units were heading back. Among their number was 42-40773 (564BS) from Hethel, piloted by Capt. Ed. L. Fowble and bearing fifteen combat and ground crew. The B-24 originally took off from its airfield, but then returned to reportedly fuel up, this despite having 2,300 gallons, which was more than sufficient to reach Marrakech. On approach to its destination, the sole survivor, T/Sgt. Kenneth A. Mike, recalled that the personnel were told to don parachutes, followed by progressive loss of all power. The bomber crash landed several miles north of Marrakech and subsequently caught fire. Mike was fortunate enough to be dragged clear, along with T/Sgt. E. G. Le Jeune, who later succumbed to his injuries. Fowble's luck in surviving a midair collision during training for Ploesti had sadly run out here.

They also Serve

While the combat crews' experience created an emotional roller coaster ride in psychological terms, the pressures on the ground crews, although much reduced in comparison, provided a constant test of physical stamina. Unlike their airborne colleagues, who could gain some relaxation during missions, the "ground pounders" had to expect to be called upon round the clock in order to ensure 100% aircraft availability.

Will Lundy was stationed at Shipdham from the onset and recalls how the airmen often had to walk to their far-flung dispersals in the early weeks of combat operations. Then, having traversed the east end of the main runway, he further recalled:

> And there she was, **Miss Diane**, up by the fence. We climbed up through the rear hatch, went forward, and opened the bomb bay doors. Next step was to clamber up onto the wings, being careful not to slip on the narrow and sharply cambered surfaces, which was ever a risk, especially in wet or frosty conditions. One by one the canvas covers on the Pratt and Whitney motors were removed.
>
> Our Crew Chief (Sgt. Baccash) and I took up the pilot and copilot positions as Stoddard and Bailey "pulled through" the propellers in order to ensure the engine cylinders were free of oil; this had to be done carefully, as the 450-lb propellers could "kick back," delivering a nasty physical blow to the unwary!
>
> Having completed this duty, Bailey turned to the Auxiliary Power Unit (APU) that provided an external source to operate the aircraft's various systems, in this case the engines. We fired up the four engines and tested them for power settings, magneto drop, etc. This was an aspect of servicing that no matter how many times I was involved, it gave me a great charge; however, the test was carried out as quickly as possible, because fuel was a precious commodity.
>
> With these primary tasks completed, all we would do was wait. Elsewhere, other crews were attending to bomb loading, last-

minute repairs, etc.; these activities were hidden by the darkness, but the occasional carelessly exposed flashlight provided a visible indication of somebody's labor. Time hung in the air, as there was nothing to do and nowhere to go. The chill air entered one's bones and each man slapped his hands, jogging up and down the dispersal in a basically vain attempt to restore some body warmth. At long last, the jeeps and trucks transporting the combat crews from Briefing would roll along the perimeter track and we could put the discomfort behind us—the business of getting the mission under way once again consumed our minds.

Diversion Misfortune

Involvement in diversion missions generally engendered the anticipation of a boring exercise that was expected to be free of enemy opposition. From time to time, the intention of a Group so involved in pulling enemy attention away from the Main Force was to rebound on the units concerned; such a grim situation was visited upon the 392BG on 4 October. Frankfurt was the target for the major assault, and with this in mind, the 392BG were briefed and dispatched over the North Sea towards the Frisian Island chain, skirting Northern Holland.

Thirty-two crews from Wendling were briefed for what was the fourth in a succession of diversion sorties over the past eleven days. A further six crews on hand there were dispatched from Shipdham. The combat "blooding" of the 392BG was imminent, but nobody could have foreseen this in these seemingly easy-paced circumstances. The 38-strong formation split between two sub-forces assembled and headed out over the North Sea; the approach to the island chain was made without event, but the relative calm of the mission was shockingly interrupted as the Luftwaffe appeared on the scene to join battle.

Three bombers—all from the 579BS—were to be culled from the ranks, the first apparently 42-7474/ M-bar **Satan's Flame**. At least one engine was seen on fire as the bomber fell inexorably behind and below the formation, a victim of fighter strikes. Lt. Brian T. Smith and nine crewmembers were never seen again, having died in the frigid waters of the North Sea. This 100% human loss was sadly realized on the other two MIA aircraft. Lt. Orval S. Morphew controlled 42-7471/ G-bar **Filthy Annie**, which was finally reported in a spin following collision with a fellow bomber and pursuit by several fighters. Nor did anyone emerge alive from Lt. James A. Feuerstacke's 42-7481/ J-bar **Ole Whiskers**, which also bore the 579BS CO, Maj. Donald A. Appert; this bomber, that was Lead for the second sub-force's High squadron, had already been badly damaged through collision with a fighter that in turn appeared out of control thanks to accurate fire from other bombers. The death tally here was eleven, making a figure of 31 empty places in the mess halls and billets that evening

The generally tight formation flown by VIIIBC groups invited the reverse risk of collision, either from within or without the formation. The latter threat was naturally posed by the Luftwaffe, especially now that the "Twelve o-clock high" approach was currently the norm. The 44BG's 42-40989/B-Bar **Holiday Mess** (506BS) was holding position when a Bf109 made lethal contact; whether this was a deliberate act by the pilot, or whether he or his aircraft had been disabled by return gunfire would never be determined. Whatever the reason, the incident condemned ten more Americans, led by Lt. Fred V. Johnston, to a watery fate and to their names being listed on a "Wall of the

The electrically-powered Emerson nose turrets installed in the B-24H provided a much-needed boost in frontal defensive firepower compared to the manual layout on the B-24D. A further refinement on the H-variant was the Sperry/Briggs ball turret, which became standard from this point in WWII. **Poop Deck Pappy** demonstrates both fittings; this Wendling-based bomber later served with three other Groups.

Col. Leon Johnson is shaking hands with Col. James T. Posey following the latter's return from a mission in **Flak Alley**. Full Colonel rank badge on his left shoulder indicates this picture is taken after 3 September, when Posey assumed 44BG command from Johnson; he held the post until the following 3 December.

The Enlisted man element of a 93BG crew are about to mount their bicycles with apparent varying degrees of skill and/or confidence. The ubiquitous form of transport was British in design and tended to cause problems, especially with its braking system, which was at odds with the U.S. bicycle design—numerous airmen received injuries from being unseated when overlooking this basic point!

Sharkmouth artwork on B-24Ds and subsequent variants' nose compartments would be regularly seen during WWII; this fairly basic example is applied to B-24H-1-FO/42-7549/K, which arrived at Shipdham from the 392BG in September or early October and served with the 66BS.

Four Shipdham mechanics are clustered around a No. 1 Pratt and Whitney engine, whose oil-stained propeller blades are placed in the "feathered" position. Servicing of this regular nature was conducted outdoors in one of the most variable and unpredictable range of weather conditions faced by the USAAF personnel during WWII.

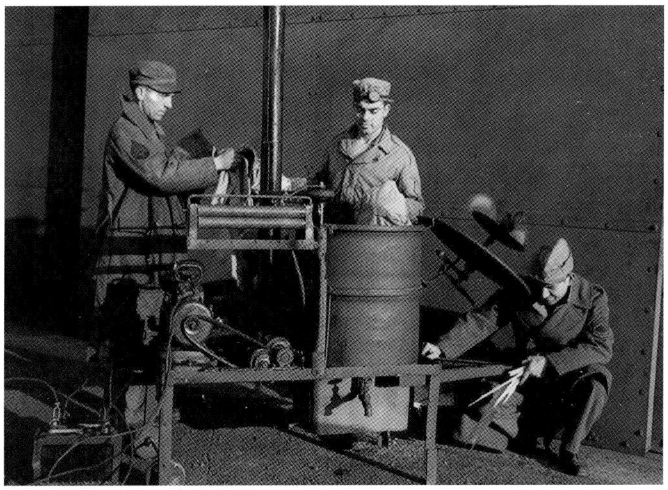

The regular laundering of clothing was a constant bugbear among 8AF units, given the circumstances in which ground personnel worked. This trio of airmen are operating a home-made washing apparatus, although where the picture was taken is unclear—or indeed whether any patent was indented for by the designer!

Missing." They were joined in death by two members of Lt. Stamos's crew on 42-72873/ B. (67BS). The pilot had called for a bail out after head-on attacks had cast the B-24D into a spin, a situation that was corrected by use of the automatic pilot, but not before Lts. John A. Must (N) and Donald G. Campbell (B) had tragically responded to the order

Purple Heart—the Hard Way

Sgt. "Red" McLachlan was a 565BS waist gunner and "original" member of Lt. O'Reilly's crew. He had been too ill to fly on the Ploesti mission, a fact that saved him from a POW camp after O'Reilly's B-24 was downed in the target area 1 August 1943, and he was reassigned to Lt. Green's crew. He was noted for his laconic sense of humor, as the following incident confirms.

On return from a mission over Germany, "Red" went up to the Flight Surgeon's office and asked him to examine what was a rather nasty wound on one of his buttocks. When asked how this was incurred, he informed the officer so. "Red" possessed a three-tooth denture that he very sensibly removed and placed in his flight suit's hip pocket. The Group had flown through high turbulence over the target, during the course of which the Sgt. had been thrown to the fuselage floor. The resultant impact had broken the denture set and the fractured unit had literally given him a "bite on the ass." On ending his account, he looked the Surgeon straight in the eye and enquired if the incident qualified him for the Purple Heart!

"Black Week" Beckons

The first of four major missions to be dispatched in October's second full week was directed at the important industrial city of Bremen, which possessed aircraft plants, as well as ship and U-boat construction yards. The latter target category was concentrated at Vegesack, bounding on Bremen's western fringes, and was assigned to the 2BD. Only the 44BG was left off the operational roster, but it would be in action within 24 hours.

Fifty-five crews took off, of which 43 finally made bomb runs. However, this figure was further reduced by 14, regarding strikes over the Primary. Emden received one 93BG bomb load, while the entire 13-strong 392BG element had recourse to dropping on Targets of Opportunity. (An alternative and responsible narrative states *fifteen* of the *seventeen* aircraft dispatched from Wendling bombed the Primary—so illustrating the manifold problems of postwar research!) The defenses were in their usual spirited mood and all four sub-forces felt their malign effect. In the case of the 2BD, three crews were destined to fall.

The first of a pair from Wendling was taken out by fighter strikes as at least part of the bomber stream was describing a right-hand curve for home. Oerdingen lies directly south of Bremen and became the grave for the shattered remains of 42-7488/S **Hellsadroppin** (758BS); eight of the ten on Lt. John B. Buschman's crew received the gift of life. No such measure of survival was granted Lt. William W. Clifford's crew on 42-7470/ F-bar **Exterminator** (579BS), which lived up to its grisly name. The B-24 was last reported flying NE of the city when it exploded. None of the airmen survived the 579BS bomber's loss, nor were their bodies ever recovered. The Bay of Wilhelmshaven lies some 30 miles from Bremen, so both aircraft and its human load could have descended into the waters; alternately, the explosion could have been so violent that complete evisceration of both could easily have taken place.

The report on the single loss suffered by the 389BG states that Lt. Michael J. Fuerst managed to hold 42-63958/-R **Lucky Tiger** (565BS) in formation until completion of the bomb run. The B-24 then lost position before cutting underneath and to one side of the

The 392BG was the first 8AF Group to equip with the B-24H, whose electrically-operated Emerson A-15 power turret provided the first potentially effective answer to head-on fighter assaults. The overall visibility factor, especially in terms of lateral viewing, was good, with the only marginal obstruction being posed by frames flanking the gun barrels. This turret later became standard on the B-24J as seen here.

The use of smoke markers with which to supplement the Lead bomber's release of its bomb load is well illustrated here. The five 44BG aircraft are acting on one fully- and two imminent-igniting flares; bomb loads vary between six 1000-lb and twelve 500-lb bombs, with the example on the right salvoed in a tight pattern. One B-24 appears to be in trouble with smoke exuding from behind its No. 2 engine.

formation as it was heading up towards the coast, all the time harried by fighters. The coast was passing below as the final *coup de grace* was given by Ju88s, and the now-burning bomber went into a spiral to descend into the sea, along with seven airmen. Lt. Reino E. Hockert (CP) alone survived; two other parachutists were reported on return, but even if they survived their bomber's loss, drowning or death by exposure was their fate.

Marginally "In on the Act"

The participation of the 2BD at the beginning of this negatively momentous period for the Daylight Offensive was destined to be cut short during the penultimate and final missions. Of course, the experienced combat crews would not be too exercised at having to fly diversion runs as opposed to flying into the enemy's firing zones! A. more important strategic factor was the loss of bomb tonnage resulting from this passive if also valuable operational aspect that was carried out in order to draw the *Jagdwaffe* away from the main striking force.

The 9 October mission was firmly in the "deep penetration" category. All four briefed targets were located on the Baltic coast within the German/Polish border: Danzig and Gydnia's shipping facilities, Anklam's industrial plants, and perhaps most relevant to the bomber crews, the newly-built FW construction factory at Marienburg were the Primaries. All four 2BD Groups were finally on hand and between them would dispatch a surprisingly limited force of 51 bombers, which in the 44BG's case only came to eight. Thirty VIII BC crews had been lost over Bremen and this figure would also be equalled today. The defenses appear to have been taken by surprise, at least during the bombers' ingress, but a steady increase in interception occurred from then on.

The Anklam sub-force would take the brunt of the punishment (18), but the 2BD contingent, tasked with assaulting Danzig and Gydnia, was lightly punished to the tune of two, both from the 93BG. However, good fortune came to the fore for all but two of the 21 airmen concerned. The progress of Lt. Tom W. Atkinson's 41-24111/P **Piccadilly Filly** (329BS) towards the target was abruptly terminated when the bomber, appearing to have no problems, turned back. This usually fatal course of action ended happily for all but one of the crew after they headed north and finally landed in neutral Sweden. The sole unfortunate loss was Lt. F. F. Shafer (N), who bailed out when the aircraft momentarily lost power and floated down to an inevitable death in the Baltic.

Soon after, ten more group members out of eleven were enjoying the fruits of neutral soil. No. 2 engine on the 409BS' 42-40610/Y **Death Dealer** was disabled over the target and Lt. Miles R. League's crew was soon watching their fellow airmen advancing evermore in the distance. The pilots nevertheless held apparent course for home, as the ailing B-24 was observed to be still in sight as Bornholm Island was skirted. It was then that the cripple turned to starboard in a successful bid for Sweden. Once there, the bomber was set on fire at Ringoby airfield. S/Sgt. Richard C. Hurlburt (TG) was the unlucky exception not to survive the mission.

The Danzig/Gydnia mission unknowingly spelled *finis* for the 2BD's direct involvement in *Black Week*. The two B-17 Divisions were briefed for a deceptively medium-range mission to Muenster, NW of the Ruehr (10th). The 13CBW's experience was horrendous, because it lost no less than 25 of the 30 MIA bombers, while all but one of the remaining five came from the 3BD. While this aerial holocaust was in progress, 39 crews from the 44th, 93rd, and 389th BGs were up over the North

The standard tail turret on the B-24D and H variants was the hydraulically-operated A6A, which was also adopted for the nose location on the B-24J; this latest Consolidated variant entered 8AF service in the autumn of 1943. Comparison with its Emerson contemporary demonstrates the restricted all-round view, with the lateral restriction due to the bulky gun barrel fairing covers intended to smooth out the airflow.

The Motor Products Company's A6B turret, displacing the A6A as the rear form of B-24 defense during 1944, had its guns properly aligned, compared to its predecessor's staggered layout. Note the improvement in lateral vision on the A6B, as well as the circular streamlined fairings, which in truth were more relevant "up front," where slipstream drag effect really merited their inclusion.

A vital improvement in defensive firepower to combat assault from below was provided by the Briggs/Sperry ball turret, which displaced the single "tunnel" gun on later B-24D production batches onwards. The turret provided 360-degree cover compared to the extremely limited visual scan afforded by its flexible predecessor.

The distinctive circular discs with a specific Group letter applied to the outer fins and starboard wing on 2BG bombers was introduced in September 1943. The letter D was allocated to the 392BG, as seen on these two B-24Hs; the aircraft in the left background is from the 44BG, as confirmed by its letter A.

Sea on their latest diversion exercise.

On 14 October, a return to direct operations was in prospect for all three Divisions, although the 2BD's contribution still remained proportionally restricted in numbers; a figure of sixty crews is quoted, but even this was to be cut in half. The reasons why only the 93rd and 392nd BG sub-forces managed Assembly were ascribed to poor weather conditions, but the neighboring 3BD was not similarly inhibited. The overall situation deteriorated further when the 2BD's reduced force of 29 was either unable to join up within the bomber stream or was directed to carry out a diversionary sweep towards the Frisian Islands. Whether the Germans would have taken much notice on their radar screens of such a miniscule force is very debatable, but it is unlikely that any sizeable or even marginal dilution in *Jagdwaffe* strength away from the main VIII BC thrust directed at Schweinfurt would have occurred. The crews landed back at Hardwick and Wendling without incident. Meanwhile, an even greater aerial holocaust destined to be commemorated as *Black Thursday* was being enacted over Central Europe, with sixty B-17s due to be culled by the day's end and a further eight "written off" after staggering home in varying states of distress.

Operational Diminuendo

The 14 October disaster put a practical end to regular long-range missions almost to the year's end. Dueren lies between Aachen and Koeln and was selected for assault on 17 and 18 October; the 2BD was yet again called upon to fly diversions up to the North Sea zone between Britain and Northern Holland. However, the main mission was recalled on both occasions before penetration of enemy territory thanks to adverse weather. On the latter occasion, the 93BG came back one crew light. A number of Bf109s had intercepted the bombers and 41-23729/D **Shoot Luke** (328BS) was unfortunate enough to be cut out of the formation. It was last seen under heavy attack, after which Lt. Charles R. Hutchens and nine others disappeared without trace, doubtless under the remorseless waters. A rather kinder fate was met by the group's 42-63974/U and its crew of six. Dispatched on a round trip to pick up a crew at Watton. a combination of a grass airfield surface that was wet and a landing too far along for a safe halt saw the B-24 overshooting and incurring sufficient damage for Category E. action to be applied to the 409BS airframe; Lt. J. M. Thomas (P) bore responsibility for the accident.

Dueren was to prove an elusive target, at least at this time; a third mission attempt on the 20th was carried out, but with the use of the RAF's "Oboe" blind bombing equipment. Cloud tops up to 29,000ft were encountered and bombing results were far from good; compounding this relative failure were the nine B-17s declared MIA. Seventy 2BD crews went out on a diversion that passed off in order. This mission was the last destined to be completed by the VIII BC before the month's end; one was launched on the 30th but was abandoned after some formations had already taken off. The generally gloomy weather conditions as winter approached were surely matched by similar strata of gloom among the Command's senior echelons. The prospects for striking effectively at German industry in a cost effective manner appeared to be fast receding, unless the *Jagdwaffe's* strength could be diminished, let alone brought to a point of permanent exhaustion.

Chapter Seven

Belated Expansion

Transiting Dangers

By 1 November 1943, the CBW structure within the Command was still much more expanded within the 1BD and 3BD compared to the 2BD. The nine groups currently comprising the first-named body were now formed into the 1st, 40th, and 45th CBWs. Six of the 3BD Force were spread between the 13th and 45th CBWs, with the 94BG the sole representative of the 4th CBW. In contrast, only the 44BG and 392BGs were linked together in the 14th CBW, while the 93rd (20CBW) and 389th (2CBW) BGs were in a similar solo position to the 94BG. However, expansion to a level commensurate with the other Divisions was imminent, with two groups being on the point of arrival and a third due at month's end. The Ground echelons for the 445BG and 446BG were wending their way across the Atlantic in late October, while their Air elements were in transit via the Southern route of Puerto Rico, Brazil, West Africa, and Morocco, due to reach Tibenham and Bungay from 4 November onwards. The 448BG's Overseas Movement was commenced on the 3rd (Air echelon) and 26th (Ground echelon), with both in place at Seething at the beginning of December. The 445BG would be assigned to the 2CBW, with the other two Groups joining the 93BG to complete the 20CBW structure.

The four groups currently on hand had all flown the Northern route to Britain, but from now on, the B-24 units would be directed to fly the Southern route. This flight path was well over twice as long compared to its Northern equivalent, while the stretch between Brazil and West Africa was no shorter than that between Gandar and the British Isles; equally forbidding was the initial flight stages that largely over-flew dense jungle and had no place within which to attempt a forced landing.

It was asking a great deal for still rather inexperienced crews to fly either route in security, and a number were destined to go missing or suffer some form of fatal contact with the sea or terrain. This was the sad fate visited upon two 448BG teams and a single 445BG crew, with two more Seething B-24s "written off" en route. On 15 November, Lt. Albert A. Poor departed Puerto Rico with twelve combat and ground crew on board 42-7617 (703BS), but never arrived at Trinidad; wreckage was sighted in the sea by search aircraft, but that was all. Four days later, Lt. Carroll C. Key's 42-52128 (712BS) was "written off" due to a poor landing effort at Waller Field, Trinidad.

On 23 November, Lt. Joseph W. Shank's crew lifted off from Marrakech in 42-52108 (714BS), but turned back with engine problems; the airfield was unfortunately over-flown and the Atlas Mountain range gave no quarter when the B-24 blundered into its undulating surfaces. The second 448BG fatal loss occurred 7 December and involved Lt.

The patchwork nature of the British landscape provided a stark and confusing scenario for USAAF pilots and navigators, in particular. They had trained-up under immeasurably better weather and geographic conditions regarding navigation—only to be confronted with this distinctly unstructured layout as viewed by the crews flying in the 392BG's **El Lobo** and **Georgia Peach**!

The high-kicking animal seen here adorns the nose of B-24D-95-CO/42-40769, based at Hardwick. She would bear her oil- and dirt-stained airframe aloft into combat until 1 December; then she would fall to fighter assault south of Euskirchen, leaving all but one of Lt. Horace R. Ketchum's crew to face captivity.

John P. Rhodes, along with thirteen others in 42-7681 **Fink's Jinks** (713BS). The pilots had safely negotiated the protracted route as far as the last stage at Marrakech, Morocco. After eight days there the B-24 took off, but several minutes into the flight, it apparently lost power and stalled, killing all on board. Among the twenty aircraft heading up to Britain the same day was 42-52135 (also 713BS). Lt. Lawrence T. Crepeau successfully completed the flight, but for whatever reason, he had to crash land in South Wales, fortunately without injury to himself or any of the thirteen personnel.

Laki-Nuki (42-7733/712BS) was in the hands of Lt. R. Ayerst, and bomber and crew were very fortunate to arrive in Britain on the 12th, although the B-24 ended up another "write-off." A combination of bad weather and false German radio signals probably combined to leave the bomber's navigator searching for an airfield over what was taken to be SW England but was in fact NW France. To their horror, as they entered an airfield circuit the airmen gazed down upon black crosses in place of roundels, and before the pilots could clear the area flak had severely crippled the desperately weaving aircraft. Flak ships added further damage as a westerly course was taken up, but fuel reserves were almost exhausted before RAF Predannack loomed up. Their difficulties were not over, because the flaps and landing gear would not extend, so the pilots had to "belly in" at high speed; the B-24 caught fire, which rapidly spread, but all fourteen personnel evacuated safely.

Several other 448BG crews were fortunate to transit unscathed. One team turned back over the Atlantic thanks to an inability to transfer fuel from the Tokyo tanks when already past the "point of no return," but were lucky to find the island of San Fernando de Noronha, out from the Brazilian coast. A second crew must have suffered collective heart failure when all four motors ground to a halt due to vapor lock in the fuel lines, but prompt action using booster pumps swiftly resurrected the situation. Luckiest of all was a third crew who landed at Marrakech after breaking through the clouds to find themselves flying through a valley in the Atlas Mountains. Later they realized that the calculated mountain tops' altitude was not 4,000ft but actually 4,000 meters!

Operational Slow-down

The staccato operational pattern for the 2BD would continue into November. Although eleven VIII BC missions were completed, four did not involve the 2BD; on the other hand, the Division did fly one of its seven missions (19th) as a solo effort. The month commenced with an uneventful run to Wilhelmshaven, when all crews returned. Bombing was conducted using *H2X,* the American adaptation of the RAF's *H2S*, but refined from the original 10-centimeter wavelength to a sharper three centimeters. The resultant bomb pattern was "blind" in nature and was a further necessary corruption of the precision bombardment theory, seeing as it was vital to keep pressure applied to the enemy's industrial potential in any manner possible.

Muenster was a name that had loomed large and ugly within the ranks of the 3BD scarcely four weeks past; now, on 5 November, the city's marshalling yards were again targeted, this time by the 2BD. The 118-strong Force was reduced to 104 by the stage of bomb run completion, but three of the four groups returned unscathed regarding losses. The unfortunate exception was the 392BG, whose ranks were shorn of three crews.

The group's progress towards Muenster had reached the Dutch/German border before the first loss occurred. **Big Ass Bird** (42-7490/U /578BS) descended at Uedem, SE of Kleve, and all ten of Lt. Douglas R. Steinmetz's team shared its fate. The MIA list was added to over the target by 42-7543/B **Georgia Belle** (579BS), which had suffered a combination of flak and fighter damage. The bomber's final impact with the ground thankfully occurred minus all ten on Lt. William P. Nicholson's crew, who floated down to "Kriegydom." The group cull was culminated on the way back, with the 579BS' 42-7477/K **The Drip** being struck both by flak and fighter fire and gradually falling back and down to finally crash adjacent to Bergen-op-Zoom, in SW Holland. All four officers, headed by Lt. Wallace W. D'Aoust (P), and one gunner were instantly killed, with the B-24H piling in at Domburg; five reached the ground alive, but Sgt. C. D. O'Neill (G) died of his wounds 6 November.

The Bremen "Jinx"

Bremen, in NW Germany, had already been struck several times over the past seven months, but had generally proved to be a ferociously defended location. It was destined to be assaulted five more times before year's end, during which time double figures of losses varying between 10 and 29 would be suffered by the attackers. The first mission in this sequence was launched on 13 November, and all the bad luck associated with this date-number would almost exclusively rebound upon the 2BD. The fact that the majority of losses were incurred other than over Bremen was of little consolation to the personnel.

All four groups would absorb punishment, with the overall MIA total adding up to thirteen. In addition, the bulk of the punishment appears to have been inflicted during the outward route, while four B-24s were self-inflicted casualties thanks to that recurring bugbear of close formation flying, midair collision. The 93BG had departed with 25 bombers, of which a sizeable number must have "aborted," since only eight gained mission "credit." As it was, one-fifth of the dispatched total became casualties. The *Jagdwaffe* was up and on hand, even as the formations were heading in towards the Continent.

All four squadrons featured in the MIA figure, with the 328BS' 42-63988, piloted by Lt. Claude A. Turner, probably being the first to succumb. The group was NW of Texel when the bomber faded out of sight to become an anonymous tomb for its eleven-man crew. Capt. Ralph P. Gewehr had Capt. John P. Bowman in the right seat as Command pilot in 41-24298/V **Queenie** (409BS). The fighters latched onto and dispatched the B-24 into the sea, along with all eleven on board. The last sighting of 42-41004/O **The Urgin' Virgin** (329BS) was north of Wilhelmshaven, curving off to starboard; sadly, whatever the intentions of Lt. Floyd F. Ramsey, nothing positive evolved, since another eleven names on a "Wall of the Missing" was to be the crew's stark postwar epitaph.

Three Hardwick crews had gone down to the enemy, but the final pair of losses involved collision. **Utah Man** (41-24226/L) had been the regular 330BS mount for Capt. Walter Stewart's crew. He was now tour-expired, but on board her were six "original" crewmembers, including Lt. Loren I. Koon (former CP). The bomber came together with 42-40765/T **Valiant Virgin** (329BS). **Utah Man** fell close to Husum, almost 100 miles due north of the target, to leave two of the ten crewmembers alive; the three survivors out of ten on **Valiant Virgin** came down near Kielsburg, where the B-24 crashed. The 93BG's blood debt for the day was now closed, along with a shocking mortality figure of 47 out of 53 airmen.

Shared Misery

The second 14CBW group suffered almost as much, with four crews declared MIA from Wendling; this statistic was again shared between the squadrons. Lt. John D. Harris never got to Bremen, having failed to form up, even though persisting in doing so until well out over the North Sea. He finally turned for home in 42-7540/A **Crew Chief** (576BS), but after letting down through the persistent undercast found himself over Rotterdam, whose flak batteries administered a pasting that knocked out two engines and killed Lt. James L. Ryan (N). The bail out order was responded to by the other seven; Harris and Lt. L. I. Kearns (CP) remained on board and brought off a safe crash landing at Willemsdorp. Lt. Ralph E. Lamma got as far as the target area before the 577BS' 42-7561/A **Mac's Sack II** finally succumbed to fighter assault near Ahlhorn, SW of Bremen. Half the crew, including the pilot, forfeited their lives.

Big Dog (42-7483/R), of the 578BS, also reached the target area as well as

Leland G. Fiegel was originally assigned to the 381BG as Deputy Group CO to Joe Nazarro. On 9 August 1943, he assumed command of the 93BG following the death over Ploesti of Col. Addison Baker, retaining the post until 27 September 1944. He is seated in a P-47 that is likely a Group "hack" used for formation monitoring, among other non-combat duties.

Dry Run, from the 446BG, is a Consolidated Fort Worth (CF) B-24H that bears a regular camouflage separation line. This contrasts with B-24Hs turned out by Douglas Tulsa (DT), whose staff applied a shallow scalloped separation line demonstrated by a 453BG aircraft. This in turn contrasted with a deeper variation of scallop as seen on Ford-produced B-24Hs!

keeping station for home, but was subsequently finished off by fighters after first suffering flak damage. Not only did all of Lt. Isaac S. Marx's ten-man crew survive, but two were able to evade capture and finally win through to Spain following bail out over Dutch soil; a third member also evaded, but was later captured when attempting the crossing into Spain. The bomber came down at Zwartsluis, on the western fringe of the Zuiderzee, with its final destruction being claimed by Ofw. Heitmann from 4/JG26. Finally, the 577BS surrendered 42-7503/V **Miss America** to the North Sea. Fuel shortage forced Lt. Frank Marfia and crew into a "ditching" shortly before sighting the English coast, but all ten airmen ended up on the MIA list; even if anyone had survived the impact, the frigid waters would soon have taken their lethal toll.

The first mission for the 67BS' Lt. Leroy M. Hansen and crew did extend to the target, but the return leg ended in Holland. The No. 4 engine had been disabled by fighter gunfire en route and further damage to two other engines was inflicted by flak. **Ole Miss** (42-7650/J) did cross out over the Dutch coast, but when the bomber's already parlous state deteriorated further, with more power loss, the pilots turned back and finally "bellied in" near Lemmer, leaving ten more for the Germans to round up. (In fact, the B-24 had one main landing gear descend and refuse to re-deploy seconds prior to landing, whereupon the pilots deliberately lowered the wing so that the unit impacted with a canal bank to be torn off, so allowing a successful touch-down!) Lt. Harlan C. Almlie was still within the 44BG ranks as the formation was approaching or was over the Ijsselmeer. Then, 42-40973/D **Battleaxe** (66BS) was observed to start into a glide and finally disappeared out of sight. What actually transpired was never confirmed, but several bodies were recovered from the sea in early 1944; Sgt. John V. Lundstrom (WG) did survive either by parachuting or getting out of the B-24 after it "ditched," but he died soon afterwards in hospital, taking the grim facts of the incident to the grave.

The second midair collision involved the 389BG and occurred in the same small air space as the 93BG incident. Lt. Leroy R. Bosetti banked **Liberty Lady** (42-72875 /K/564BS) to starboard, passing over another B-24. Almost simultaneously, Lt. Sam R. Connelly, Jr. maneuvered 42-72868/N **Tinker Toy** (565BS), an action that saw his No. 4 engine bite into the other bomber behind its No. 1 engine. Bosetti's aircraft immediately suffered a progressive disintegration, out of which none of the crew escaped alive. Little better fortune attended the Connelly team, although two Enlisted men parachuted safely; both bombers came down between Husum and Flensburg, according to MACR documents.

"Operational" Extras

Thirteen Division B-24s were on the MIA list, but three more would be "written off," with the 44BG doubling its losses in aircraft and losing two more airmen in the case of Lt. W. H. Hart's crew on 42-7647/R **Sabrina**. The 506BS bomber was circling Shipdham when it either faltered or lost position on the landing approach, striking some trees in the process. Sgts. Clifford C. Hurst (WG) and George E. Olsen (TG) were killed; several of the survivors were already wounded, while S/Sgt. W. Procyszyn (Eng.) was absent, having bailed out over Germany. The 66BS' 41-29168 /F was already a wrecked airframe, having crash landed NW of Norwich at North Repps, a victim of power loss. None of the ten airmen led by Lt. Robert G. Bickerstaff died, but Lt. F. L. Jope (N) was trapped in the distorted nose compartment for several hours, and it was only the arrival of a mobile crane from RAF Coltishall that enabled the officer's extraction. The arrival of 42-40604/I **Satan's Angels** at RAF Lympne, on whose surface it over-shot, seems strange, since the airfield is on the Channel coast, many miles south of the return track from Bremen. Nobody was injured and all ten later returned to Hardwick, but the 328BS bomber was subsequently salvaged.

The 93BG's **The Urgin Virgin**, displaying its bomb-straddling nude female, is photographed inside a hangar not at Hardwick, but rather at Watton's Air Repair Depot, to which this B-24D was reportedly the first dispatched there. She survived operations until 13 November, when she delivered herself and all eleven on Lt. Floyd R. Ramsey's team to a North Sea grave.

The 389BG's **Nana** is seen with Lt. "Rut" Laurens's crew. His nickname did not refer to any amorous intention similar to a stag, but was more prosaic, being a contraction of his first name, Rutledge. He, along with Lts. John L. McClellan (N), Charles O. Rogers (B), and T/Sgt. Dan "Gluck" Gardner (Eng.), whose names are also seen on the fuselage skin, became POWs off the 20 December mission to Bremen while manning B-24H-1-DT/41-28589/RR: J **Old Ironsides**.

Norwegian Rebuff

Mid-November saw the VIII BC taking up a northerly route on the 16th and 18th to attack targets in southern Norway. The first (16th) involved all three Divisions in what turned out to be an unsuccessful bid to bomb industrial facilities at Knaben and Rjukan. Only two B-17s were MIA out of 388 crews; the reason why only seven crews were dispatched by the 44th and 389th BGs between them is not known, especially since the other two groups sent up a total of 32. At least no losses were borne, but it was a false dawn in terms of a respite from this ever-sad aspect of operations. The next mission would prove to be a point in case.

Rebuff over Jkeller

Oslo/Jkeller airfield was selected for assault by the 2BD on the 18th, with the Division operating alone. Although the *Jagdwaffe* had elements stationed in southern Norway, there was a good chance that the formations could strike and clear the area before full interception was initiated. Thirty-four of the 102 crews setting off came from Shipdham; a few hours later, the returning personnel were mourning the loss of five crews. Four more crews were absent from the other three airfields.

Unfortunately, the Luftwaffe did intervene on both the approach and return portions of the mission. The depredations wrought upon the 44BG were only realized on the way home in the case of four crews, but this was of no consolation to the airmen concerned. Lt. Ed Dobson, flying 42-7603/L-Bar **Raggedy Ann**, and Lt. Earl T. Johnson in 42-7545/D **Touch of Venus** went down into the North Sea, along with eighteen other hapless souls. The third 67BS crew lost nearly made it back, but 20 miles off the coast Lt. Joseph L. Houle's severely damaged 41-29164/I was eased into the sea. Capt. Butler orbited the scene and had several one-man dinghies cast out and down to the wallowing B-24, which had broken in two. Although ASR facilities were called for there was little likelihood of any survivors, since none had been seen emerging from the wreckage and shortage of fuel finally forced Butler to depart the area. None of the thirty personnel on these B-24s were ever found.

A fourth crew from the 68BS was lost in similar fashion. Capt. Edward R. Mitchell ended up in Turkey off the Ploesti mission but had been repatriated.

On 13 November 1943, B-24D-75-CO/42-40604/O was badly damaged and diverted southwards from Bremen, where a landing at RAF Lympne, on the Channel coast, resulted in an overshoot. This was her final combat mission, as she was declared "Category E" several days later. The two officers examining the nose are unidentified, but are most likely the pilots.

The 18 November run to Jkaller, in Norway, cost the 44BG five crews MIA. Lt. Rockford Griffith's damaged B-24J was brought in for a one main wheel landing due to a badly-wounded crewmember being unable to bail out. The bomber inevitably ground-looped as speed fell away, but the airframe remained intact, albeit thoroughly battered.

Today he was flying 41-29139/E, but the bomber never turned up at Shipdham, having almost certainly deposited itself along with its human cargo beneath the waves. In sharp contrast, the final loss involved an act of internment. Capt. W. Baxter Weant's 42-63971/W **Helen Hywater** (also 68BS) had absorbed so much damage that the chances of surviving a North Sea crossing were minimal. The close proximity of Sweden encouraged the pilots to head east, where they made a good landing at Trollhattan. Their attempt to set the aircraft on fire was successful.

A fourth 67BS bomber was destined to provide one of the most dramatic crash landings ever captured on film, that of 41-29161/H. Lt. Rockford C. Griffith had brought his shot up bomber back to Shipdham, but not before circling a "ditched" B-24 while calling up ASR facilities. On entering the airfield circuit, he discovered his starboard main wheel only partially deployed and it defied all efforts to bring it back up into the wing well. He had all crew members bail out apart from Sgt. William T. Kuban (BT), who had been seriously injured and was in no state to jump.

Griffith and Lt. Lawrence W. Grono (CP) then made a steady landing approach to the main runway and gently eased the bomber down on the two deployed wheels while holding a level configuration as long as possible. When gravity inevitably took hold to drop the starboard wing, the resultant contact with the concrete surface threw showers of sparks from the No. 3 and 4 propeller blades and swung the errant aircraft round in a full semi-circle before it ground to a halt. Both starboard propellers were snapped off at their base, No. 1 and 3 engines were partially dislodged, and the port landing gear almost fully collapsed, but the overall airframe remained intact. Several minutes ensued before the pilots clambered out and summoned assistance for Sgt. Kuban. The Silver Star was later bestowed upon Lt. Griffith.

Capt. John B. McCormack and crew had come through the Ploesti run in their Hethel-based 42-40787/V **Vagabond King** (565BS), but their luck finally ran out this day while flying the same B-24. Fw190s struck to cripple both port engines and set the starboard inner fuel tank ablaze as the formation was heading for home. The doomed bomber fell behind, then fell away down to port before striking the sea, taking all ten airmen to their deaths off the North Danish coastline.

The loss tally was completed by a duo of Wendling crews and one from Hardwick, although only one of the trio was directly shot down. The 578BS' 42-7486/V was finally "ditched" off the Danish coast, but the desperate bid for survival was denied to all ten on Lt. Ted Dudziak's crew. The other 392BG crew managed to head into Sweden after Lt. David N. Fogarty radioed in this intention, having discovered that fuel reserves were not sufficient to regain England; 42-7502/X **Bakadori** from the same squadron was the B-24 concerned, which landed at Orebro. (Following full crew repatriation in 1944, four members who resumed combat operations were tragically lost thanks to an Assembly collision over Norfolk in March 1945.) Similar good fortune was granted Lt. Frank Kilcheski's team flying in 42-40128/J **War Baby** (328BS) out of Hardwick; the shot up bomber joined its 392BG companion in internment at Orebro airfield, along with its crew.

CMH Ceremony

The undoubtedly subdued mood of the personnel at Shipdham following the Oslo mission was somewhat lightened four days later, when a specific ceremony took place. One of the five CMH awards resulting from the Ploesti mission had gone to the former Group CO, then Col. but now B/Gen. Leon Johnson. Gens. Ira C. Eaker (CG VIII BC) and Jacob Devers were on Station in order to bestow America's supreme decoration upon Johnson. The ceremony took place in front of the control tower with 41-23813, an untitled survivor of the costly run to Rumania, parked in the background. The ever-modest senior officer, who was now the CG for the 14CBW, later stated: "I have no particular ownership on this medal, but accept it for all who took part. I didn't do anything that every man behind me didn't do—the higher the rank, the easier it is to get a medal."

Back to Bremen

The lethal blow administered to the "Self Defending bomber" theory did not seemingly deter the U.S. authorities from considering a strike against one very emotive target that moreover fell well within the "deep penetration" category—Berlin. The Nazi capital was briefed on 25 November, and the reaction of the VIII BC crews when the curtains were pulled from the Briefing hut maps must have been one of extreme nervousness. As it was, and despite several similar briefings during the ensuing midwinter spell, the mission remained in the "suspended, not cancelled" category until the beginning of March. On the other hand, Bremen was already a very familiar target, and the latest mission was launched 24 hours later.

Full Division participation was made, with 80% of the 101 crews sent out granted mission credit; single losses were borne by three groups, one of these being self-inflicted. While heading in towards Bremen, 41-24234/N **Mr. 5 by 5** was reported as flying into propeller wash that caused it to lift up below and to starboard of Lt. Cary's 42-7501/P **Bing's Big Box**. The latter bomber's propellers cut through the rear fuselage on Lt. Alex Trolese's 66BS bomber and the truncated remains tumbled down to crash at Brual, leaving no survivors. Cary's aircraft was thrown out of control by the impact but was mercifully stabilized, albeit with a loss of 14,000 feet in altitude. The bomb load was jettisoned and the resultant and successful homeward path remained free of all but some coastal flak.

Four members on Lt. Roy E. Braley's 565BS crew from Hethel were granted the gift of life, with Lt. Melvin H. Verberg (B) evading capture. Flak had already disabled one engine when fighters added lethal damage to 42-40749/P **Sack Time Sally** over NW Holland. The crash site was at Drachten, near Leeuwarden. and one of the six corpses was only discovered within the smashed airframe on the 30th. The sole 392BG crew to go down were on board the 577BS' 42-7493/S **Gregory the Great**. A combination of fighters and naval flak at Cuxhaven, due north of Bremen, brought the B-24 down to destruction on mud flats on the northern bank of the Elbe estuary. Lt. Henry P. Bolick (P) and ten other airmen were killed.

Lt. Dout's Diary (2)

The Lt's diary entry for 26 November was particularly detailed in view of several problems with the B-24:

> Takeoff delayed by vapor lock in No. 2 carburetor. Ailerons badly affected by frost. Met tail-end of B-17s and horsed around, waiting for our group to turn up. Formation was SNAFU, so we picked a likely spot and hung on. No. 3 propeller governor stuck at 2,300 revs. as we crossed the enemy coast. Temp. -45 degrees at 23,000ft, but everyone OK thanks to new electric heated suits. Contrails up to 10 miles long. The 93BG passed through our

The second view of the Griffith-piloted aircraft shows the ground personnel in the process of hosing down the area under the engines where fuel from fractured lines had impregnated the ground. The No. 1 engine is partially dislodged after impact with the airfield surface and 4129161/H will be declared worthy only of salvage days later.

A damp and cloud-clamped Shipdham is the scene for a CMH award ceremony on 22 November. The recipient will be the former Group CO (now CG, 14CBW) Leon W. Johnson for his perceived leadership skills over Ploesti. The B-24D with the blanked-out "Flying 8-Ball" logo is 41-23813/V **Victory Ship** (68BS), destined to be one of five aircraft MIA 21 January 1944 over France.

formation just before bomb doors were opened.

Our group was "Alphabet Soup" (code for a poor bombing pattern). Saw target was smokescreen covered, but high winds made this ineffective. Bombed by sections on PFF flares. Flak heavy and accurate. After leaving target, we saw a prop come floating past our right wing, followed by a 44BG bomber turning on its back, split-essing with tail surfaces coming off—saw nobody get out. Evidently two ships collided. [This was the Trolese B-24 run into by Lt. Cary's bomber.]

Now everyone was calling in flak and suddenly something jarred us. Two Fw190s passed to port and I only had time to yell "Fighters!" Gilow called the waist for a damage report and S/Sgt. Kuehler replied that he and Sgt. Cashman had both received head injuries. I had them use oxygen on "emergency" to keep going and once over the sea I dived and levelled off at 3,000ft. Hess [Lt. Lowell K. Hess, CP] went back and found the bomb bay full of gas. Gilow administered First aid. No. 2 prop began running away, so we feathered it and got home on 35"Hg on the other three. Got QDM on VHF to field and received permission to make an emergency landing.

Landed long and stopped right by the ambulance. Kuehler walked away OK, but Cashman was vomiting while they were trying to get him out; he will pull through, but he'll be blind. Neither would have been hurt had they worn their steel helmets. Only 50 gallons left in No. 2 tanks. A 20mm shell went into the left wing root and another struck the top of the waist, injuring both gunners. Getting armor plate on pilot's and co-pilot's sides. I will also wear a flak helmet and flak suit from now on, as will everyone else.

This was Kuehler's second exposure to danger within two weeks that left him intact, but his and his pilot's luck would run out within two months. It is also illuminating that Dout rightly criticized both gunners for their lapse in not donning flak helmets—yet he was not similarly protected, although promising to take the requisite countermeasure in the future!

Into "Flak Valley"

The Ruehr industrial region known to the RAF and USAAF as "Happy Valley" or "Flak Valley," respectively, was rich in suitable targets, but also well protected not only by technical but also natural means—the latter in the form of persistent haze caused by industrial smoke. Solingen lies close to Koln, on the region's southern fringes, and was picked for attack on the 30th. Nearly 400 bombers were dispatched, but only a small proportion bombed; large-scale abandonment spread between the 1st and 2nd BDs occurred as a result of heavy cloud. The four B-24 groups dispatched 101 crews, of which 77 made effective sorties.

No Division losses had been incurred on the first Solingen run, but the Grim Reaper was ever looming in the shadows and swung his scythe selectively on 1 December, when the twin locations of Leverkusen and Solingen were briefed; only the 1st and 2nd BDs got through this time round and were destined to suffer an overall 8% loss factor. The 3BD had abandoned their effort thanks to the weather conditions. The 2BD was fully present, with 69 of the 78 crews sent out making their bomb runs over the former listed target.

The first of two Hardwick losses occurred during approach to the target. Turning back over enemy territory was a desperate course of action, given the high chances of fighter interception or even over-flying flak concentrations. When close to Dueren, SW of Koln, Lt. Horace R. Ketchum's 42-40769/X **Iron Ass** reversed course for home with one engine smoking heavily. Its progress was brutally cut short within minutes after fighters picked up the isolated aircraft and dispatched it north of Euskirchen; only Sgt. Harry E. Byerman (TG) failed to parachute to safety, having been killed by the gunfire. The other group loss was initiated during the bomb run when flak struck home. However, Lt. Joseph M. Wurzer held course for home and had reached the region of the German/Belgian border when a pair of Bf110 fighters reportedly administered the fatal blow. B-24D/42-63987 (409BS) was down to 4,000ft when it exploded, with the remnants landing NE of St. Vith, Belgium. The pilot and three out of the other nine survived as POWs.

Three more crews would be lost on the return leg, including two from the 389BG. One Hethel bomber was bearing two brothers among its crew complement: Lt. Thomas P. Fravega (P) and his brother Anthony (ROG). The brothers, along with five others on board, had gone over Ploesti, but the Fates were now to act against the pilot and three other crewmembers. The 566BS bomber (42-72876/E) fell behind near Aachen under fighter attack and fire took hold in the bomb bay. The bail out signal was probably given before Tom Fravega exited via the cockpit top hatch—only for his parachute to fail. The uneven contest lasted as far as the area around Louvain, which was where the B-24 finally crashed. Anthony Fravega was one of the six airmen ending up as POWs. The other 389BG crew, flying in 42-72856/H **Nana** (567BS), was similarly afflicted by fighter gunfire that finally caused the bomber to explode and fall SW of Bonn, with Lt. Marion E. Fletcher (P) as one of six fatalities.

The 18-strong Shipdham formation was still intact as it crossed out over the coastline, but B-24H/42-7544/C **Seed of Satan** (67BS) was observed by then to be on half power. Shortly after this the bomber turned back, and once over land Lt. Edward F. Taylor gave the bail out signal, to which all ten responded and parachuted safely. Sgt. Miles J. McCue (WG) said he noted a conversation between the pilot and engineer regarding whether or not the necessary switching procedure for the fuel tanks had been completed. The

MACR document states the aircraft did not have enough fuel to guarantee reaching friendly shores, so the loss could perhaps be put down to human error as much as enemy action. The aircraft crashed in Belgium near Paschendaele, epicenter for the infamous WWI battle in 1917.

December 1943

December's operational pattern would see the USAAF crews largely attacking targets on the western coastal fringes of Europe, with late-month lunges well into mainland Germany on the 22nd and 30th. The availability of the 55FG—a P-38 unit soon to be joined by the similarly-equipped 20FG—along with enhanced drop tank capacity for the seven P-47 units within VIII Fighter Command (FC), meant that the NW German coastal zone could now be covered in terms of escort provision. Also coming "on stream" was the pioneer P-51 group, the 354FG. This superb Anglo-American hybrid design was destined to be the principle harbinger of doom for its *Jagdwaffe* adversaries, although the other pair of USAAF fighters would add their weight to the burgeoning air battles that would cast the Luftwaffe onto a permanent back foot. All of this was still no guaranteed promise for the future.

One in Ten Odds

The second of eleven monthly missions went out on the 5th; the 1BD struck at targets in central France and the other two Divisions endured an extended flight to that country's SW coast to attack two airfields at Bordeaux and Cognac. The latter target was allotted the 2BD, with 96 B-24s sent out; the mission was weather disrupted to the extent that only two crews bombed St. Nazaire's U-boat pens as a Target of Opportunity. Added to the frustration—for the 389BG at least—was the loss of one crew in cruelly spectacular fashion. The group, if not the entire Force, was heading back above a solid cloud pattern, but unfortunately navigational errors caused the bombers to over-fly St. Nazaire—not known as "Flak City" for nothing. Lt. Harley Mason was in charge of 42-40738/J **The Oklahoman** (566BS), positioned to starboard of the group Lead. A photographer in the High squadron pointed his camera at the Lead elements and fired just as the flak pattern was developing. When his film was developed, it contained a dreadful image sequence showing Mason's bomber disintegrating from a direct flak strike. The dismembered and flaming state of the airframe provided no prospect that any of the veteran crew—who were nearly tour-expired—could have survived.

Given the degree of destruction, it was amazing that the pilot was the sole member to escape death; he naturally had no memory of the aircraft exploding, and having regained consciousness in midair had barely pulled his ripcord before the canopy delivered him into the frigid coastal waters. Having divested himself of his harness with difficulty, he then fought an apparently uphill battle to prevent the onset of hypothermia; fortunately, the swift appearance of a German patrol vessel that just beat a French civilian-manned boat to the scene hauled him out. (In 1999, a memorial commemorating the event was unveiled in St. Brevin les Fins, a town close to where Harley descended; he was by then too physically handicapped to attend, but a cousin represented him at the ceremony.)

Incident at Wendling

Although the 392BG returned intact from Cognac, it nevertheless was short one B-24 even before takeoff. Mission preparation was in full swing in the early hours with 42-7556 on its 579BS hardstand recently delivered of its bomb load, which was placed on either side of the bomb bay exterior. Sgt. Wyllie, Cpl. Ottenstein, and one other airman were loading the guns. Ottenstein then went to the next hardstand to collect fuel for the Auxiliary Power Unit (APU), which was filled up and started.

This busy but normal scenario became violently transformed at 0130, when the starboard wing tanks burst into flames, followed quickly by bullets "cooking off" as the fire reached the fuselage; a fuel servicing unit close by was also ignited by the ammunition. Sgt. Shockley was in the bomb bay and was set on fire by the spurting fuel; as he ran frantically out and away he was grabbed by Cpl. AC Jacobs, who smothered the flames with his jacket.

The efforts of the fire crash crew to extinguish the blaze proved in vain and priority was given to confining it. A principal concern, apart from the adjacent B-24s, was a fuel dump none too distant, but all became really threatened when eleven of the stacked 500-lb bombs erupted. The crash crew, who were now spraying a burning refuelling truck, were very lucky to escape injury as a hail of shrapnel whistled past; a crewmember named Sgt. L. A Doolittle recalled being thrown bodily onto the muddy ground.

A second explosion ignited a fuel trailer and the debris effect was to damage two other B-24s. Doolittle noticed that another bomber seemed to be about to catch fire. He immediately sprinted to it, entered the cockpit, and got the inboard engines started. A squadron pilot named Lt. R. E. Fletcher then joined him and together they taxied the B-24 away to a safer location. Both would receive one out of the eleven Soldier's Medals subsequently awarded this day.

Two further explosions occurred, the latter at 0220, after which the men turned their hands to quenching the several fires while Lt. W. Giesecke (Engineering Officer) carried out inspections of the damaged B-24s. He concluded that in spite of fuselage warping and twisted tail assembly structures, both 42-7510 and 42-7529 were capable of restoration to combat status; by the year's end that prophecy was proven correct.

Suspicion as to the cause of the explosion pointed to the APU. Cpl. Ottenstein stated that no fuel had been spilled during filling up, while two M/Sgts. said they had smelled no fumes

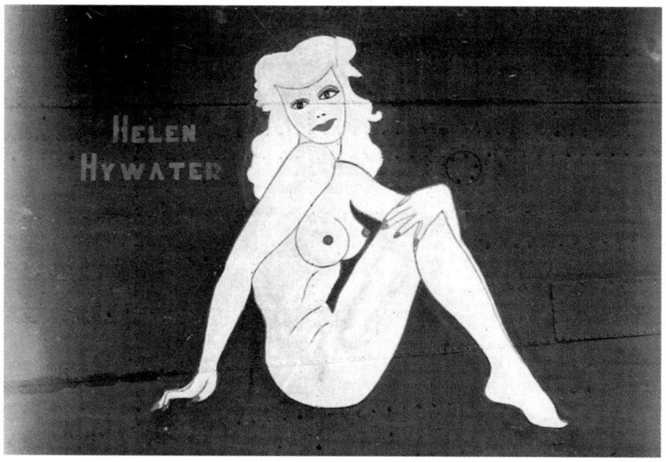

The beautiful, if also blatantly nude figure painted on 42-63971/E/W-bar saw just over one month's service at Shipdham. The B-24D-15-CF was assigned on 5 October 1943, but was diverted into Trollhatten, in Sweden, by Capt. Baxter W. Weant the following 18 November; the ten-man crew was interned, but the bomber was reduced to ashes after being deliberately set on fire.

Ford-built B-24H-1/42-7507/X joined the 44BG from Wendling in early 1944 and flew with the 68BS until the following 12 March. A mission to Siracourt on that date culminated with a crash landing at Friston, on the English Channel coast, that left Lt. Bowman's crew alive but saw their bomber consumed by fire.

while entering and exiting -556 several times. The recommendation for future APU operation was that should spillage occur, the machine must not be started up until thoroughly dried and with a fire extinguisher on hand—very sound, logical advice.

Structural Sea Change

A full five days elapsed until the latest call to action came for the 2BD; in addition, the run to Emden (11th) would signal the end of the first phase of the Division's development into a Force, ultimately matching its contemporaries in overall strength. By month's end, seven groups would be operational, with the 20CBW at full establishment and the 2nd and 14th CBWs two-thirds complete.

Emden cost the 44th and 392nd BGs one crew each, with the Shipdham experience a tragic "own goal." Lt. Richard F. O'Neill (67BS) had a reputation for taking evasive action during the bomb run, and today such maneuvering would cost his crew dearly. Just as the bombs were released from 41-24232/M **Calaban** and the B-24 was swinging to one side, bombs from another aircraft struck the starboard wing outboard of No. 4 engine, as well as the tail section, severing both sub-sections and casting the aircraft into a spin from which it never recovered before impacting west of the target at Wybelsum; Sgt. Robert C. McAdams somehow fought off the centrifugal forces to bail out, but his nine companions were not so fortunate. Wendling's 42-7506/C **Southern Comfort** (576BS) brought no such cheer to eight on Lt. Milford O. Bingham's crew; fighters downed the bomber near Barkholt, with only Lt. George T. Schutz (N) and Sgt. Melvin C. Harris (WG) surviving. Structural damage to the nose section had left a large gap through which Lt. Schutz made an involuntary exit by falling out, while Harris jumped out of his waist window.

Kiel's port facilities were briefed on the 13th, when the Division ranks were amplified by the presence of the Tibenham-based 445BG for its inaugural mission, having been assigned to partner the 389BG in the 2CBW. Fifteen crews, of which eleven bombed and returned safely, were part of the 111 dispatched. Wendling bore the single 2BD MIA loss, this time the 578BS' 42-7626/B **Liberty Belle**. Lt. Douglas S. Rogillo, Jr.'s charge had suffered heavy fighter-inflicted damage on either side of the target and No. 3 and 4 engines went "out" shortly after the bomb run was completed. Cloud cover was entered around 8,000ft with the crew alerted for a possible "ditching," but when the cloud cover cleared the bomber was almost at sea level and the pilots barely had enough time to turn into wind before the initial impact. All but three gunners survived the ever-risky experience that saw the impact cast the pilot out through the windshield, but he was able to recover and clamber onto one of the lift rafts; unfortunately, their rescuers turned out to be German, who brought them back to Holland. Particularly unlucky was Sgt. Walter F. Bryan (WG); having initially moved forward, he had then taken the prior advice of an airman involved with maritime patrol flying that he would be better off positioning himself in the waist section, where he became one of the fatalities, along with the other waist and tail gunners.

The dreaded name "Bremen" was again uttered by the Briefing officers on 16 December, when the second of the new groups joined in the Offensive. Bungay was home for the 446BG, which was linked up to the 93BG within the 20CBW. Over 600 bombers went out, of which 235 were B-24s, but this particular target's well-deserved reputation as a hard nut to crack was largely absent this day, with just ten crews going down and none of them from the 2BD. However, the city's flak defenses, along with the *Jagdwaffe,* would strike back in their normal vitriolic manner 96 hours later.

"The Joes" – The Men behind the Men

This finely-pitched and heartfelt tribute summation of "The Men behind the Men who made the Headlines in WWII" was put together by Bob Stone, a 389BG combat crewmember:

> Two of the four propellers are "feathered" and a third is smoking. The brakes are gone, two gunners are wounded, and flak holes make the B-24 look like a piece of Swiss cheese. The bomber sets down, but overruns onto the rough ground beyond before its momentum is fully spent and comes to an easy halt. Lucky! The smoking engine is doused by the crash crew as medics attend to the wounded.
>
> Five days later the B-24 is back, fully gassed and bombed up, the shattered top turret Plexiglas, three engines, brake lines, and the port wing tip all replaced. The patched flak holes show up since the crew insisted a patchwork quilt in loud colors be applied over each skin graft. The whole process of rescuing the bomber—from the moment the control tower staff spotted its dead engines and red flares to its departure on its next mission—was taken over by ground-bound airmen whose work seldom appears in the papers and by extension can hardly arouse the awareness of war-conscious Americans...
>
> The first *Joe* was the control tower airman who cleared the airfield to ensure no traffic problems could add to the already serious problem of getting the bomber settled down safely. The next *Joes* were the crash and "meat wagon" drivers and crews on hand to squelch any fires and aid the wounded; also in attendance were the *Joes* who drove the towing tractors with which to drag the aircraft clear.
>
> Next, a whole crew of *Joes* went to work on the hangared B-24: armament *Joes* who repaired the top turret and replaced the ball turret; warehouse *Joes* who wrestled the replacement engines and wing tip section out of their crates so the hangar *Joes* could install them; and *Joes* from the sheet metal and hydraulic shops who worked on the airframe. Meanwhile, and almost forgotten, were the *Joes* who filled the fuel and oil tanks, as well as loading up the bomb bay.
>
> These then are the *Joes* that strove to put and keep us in the air. They were present in a ratio of five-to-one compared to the combat crews. Among their ranks were also the *Joes* of the Intelligence, Photographic, and Mess Hall staff, as well as the *Joes* manning the telephone and radio/radar systems. Don't forget the chaplains, military police, and numerous other tradesmen—all were necessary elements to ensuring an efficient group structure. While not bearing the glamor of the 'fly-boy" image, they nevertheless accomplished a tremendous mission with both feet on the ground!

Bremen – Again

The two latest operational additions to the 2BD had enjoyed three cost-free missions between them, but the first installment in their particular blood debt would emerge on the 20th over Bremen. Bungay's 42-7494/ **Bums Away** never came back after Lt. Tom B. Long (704BS) indicated he was

Peep-sight (41-24225/T) is fortunate to have returned to Shipdham after suffering a severe battering, as shown on her rear fuselage. The waist gunners in particular, having little protection from the thin fuselage skin, would have been fortunate to avoid serious injury or death. The parachute backpack on the airman second from right indicates he is one of the pilots.

EL Lobo (42-7510/C) was very fortunate to survive this scale of damage after an errant B-24 made contact with one of its propellers. Sgt. Donald S. Pippert (TG) was not so lucky, since he was discovered in the excised rear turret after it plummeted down onto one of the islands in the Frisian chain. The 392BG bomber was involved in the 20 December run to Bremen.

turning back, followed by a call that the B-24 was under fighter assault. The same anonymous fate affected the 445BG's 42-7534/U **Good Nuff** (700BS), flown by Lt. Milton A. Patterson. A total of 21 airmen were subsequently named on Cambridge's "Wall of the Missing." The 20CBW's loss scale was raised to three when two Hardwick crews out of 26 were absent from debriefing. Both portside engines were disabled on 42-40133/ (328BS) as Capt. Cleveland H. Hickman's crew vainly fought off fighter attacks in the target area. Yet again, the North Sea appears to have swallowed up bomber and crew, since no wreckage or bodies were ever found. The same nine-man complement on 42-63964/ (329BS) enjoyed an almost diametrically opposite fate, since they survived as POWs. Their B-24 was reportedly seen to angle off in a SW direction after the formation had barely crossed in over northern Holland, according to the MACR, but the exact crash site was undetermined. (Two crewmembers were captured at Delmenhorst, close to Bremen, which seems to indicate that Lt. J. F. Cosgrove altered course back towards the target before the bomber was finally abandoned.)

All six participating groups suffered losses, with single crews declared MIA from the remaining three. Lt. William M. Maynor's crew had flown ten missions to date, but their progress towards tour completion was halted today. Fighter-inflicted damage as Bremen appeared had knocked their B-24H out of formation and further damage was inflicted while heading for home. The 44BG bomber was down to 9,000ft, proving difficult to hold aloft, and rapidly running out of fuel by the time the coast near Wilhelmshaven had just been left behind. The pilots reluctantly decided to turn 42-7630/P+ (506BS) back to land and abandon their charge, which crashed on one of the Frisian Island chain. Six of the crew drifted down onto solid land, but Sgts. Augustus Aho (listed as Bombardier on the MACR) and Glenn C. Stoffel (WG) were unfortunate enough to float down into the sea, from where their bodies were never recovered. Two other gunners also experienced immersion, but were fished out by the crew of a seaplane.

Shipdham's CBW companion unit from Wendling bore the loss of 42-7500/D **Sky Queen** (576BS). The precise circumstances of its demise are unclear, other than the crew bailed out as the bomber steadily descended and finally piled in at Lehnstedt, NW of Bremen. Lt. Henry C. Lo Presto and five others ended as POWs, but the other four did not survive. Hethel completed the ever-dismal tally with 41-28589/J. The area around Aurich, west of Wilhelmshaven, was where the flak-stricken 566BS B-24H crashed during the return leg, but by then it was minus all ten on Lt. Rutledge Laurens' team. The "Battle of Bremen" had run its course, but it would leave its mark upon many of the 1943 Class of USAAF combat crews, similar to the effect that their 1944/45 successors would experience over the equally bombarded and fiercely defended capital Berlin, or the synthetic oil complex at Merseburg.

Hard Knocks Ahead

The last of the acolyte units within the 2BD was geared up for combat by 13 December, but the crews sent out next morning only got as far as the Dutch coast before (according to a 448BG history) a "recall" signal was responded to. No official VIII BC mission was launched on this date, however. Two days later 18 crews were again recalled, while a third briefing (20th) culminated in a diversionary action. The 448BG had missed out on the final Bremen missions, but its introduction to operations during the last eleven days of 1943 would be painful.

Combat's Cruel Twists

S/Sgt. Donald D. Pippert was manning his tail turret on 42-7510/C **El Lobo** (579BS) as the Division stream was crossing in near Texel Island when a 446BG bomber (recorded as 42-7494) flying in close proximity to the 392BG suddenly absorbed a flak burst on No. 4 engine that tore the propeller off. Tragically, the airscrew's errant path coincided with **El Lobo's** tail section. The hapless gunner could have known little, as his turret was totally excised and thrown out into mid-air; up front, the pilots later said they felt just a light jar from the impact, but were quickly appraised by the Engineer of the potentially lethal damage that had also removed the lower segment of the starboard rudder and bitten chunks out of both elevators. Although the controls acted sluggishly according to Lt. Peyton (P), he experienced little problem in guiding his charge through the remainder of the mission—but he did express surprise on inspecting the damage that control problems had not arisen. The turret, with S/Sgt. Pippert's body still inside, was later discovered in Texel's sand dune fringes. As for the B-24H, it was repaired and returned to operational duties, but finally went down on 29 April 1944 with all ten on Lt. Wyatt's crew.

Last Frontier (41-29135/GC: A-bar) was in a parlous state, heavily damaged and down to two functioning engines as Lt. Everhart circled Wendling at a low altitude. T/Sgt. T. E. Johnson (Eng.) was attempting to lower the nose wheel when all remaining power was abruptly lost and the crew were told to prepare for crash landing. Realizing that the nose gunner had not received the information, Johnson unhesitatingly pulled his fellow airman out of the turret, but by the time both had clambered back to the bomb bay the B-24 was virtually on the ground. Johnson literally threw the gunner up onto the flight deck but was unable to follow suit before the impact with the ground twisted and crushed in the lower fuselage, killing him in the process. His selfless courage was later recognized by the award of a Distinguished Service Cross.

Twin Strike

The twin cities of Osnabrueck and Muenster were targeted the 22nd; the 2BD force was split, with five groups going to Osnabrueck and the 14CBW assigned to the latter target. One hundred sixty-two crews went out, but only 148 landed back. Most of the fourteen MIA B-24s had come from the ranks of the Osnabrueck strike force, with the 93BG again punished to the tune of five out of nine 20CBW crews lost.

The run in was over northern Holland and angling SE to Osnabrueck, but 42-63982 **El Toro** (328BS) never got through. The group was turning at the IP when the bomb bay and flight deck on Lt. Luther S. Bird's bomber erupted in flames from reported air rocket strikes, before exploding and falling near Quakenbrueck. The pilot was one of four killed, while three of the five survivors were fortunate, being blown out into mid-air following the airframe's disintegration.

A second CBW loss was initiated around this stage when heavy damage forced Lt. Sydney C. Jacobson to fall out in his 42-7613/H (706BS). The 446BG bomber staggered back over the inward route, but after the bulk of the crew had bailed out the aircraft exploded and descended at Noordwijk, SW of Groningen, Holland, along with the pilot, bombardier, and engineer. **Silver Dollar** (42-7611/704BS) was fatally crippled by a bomb released from another aircraft that removed part of one wing, whereupon the aircraft reportedly spun to its destruction. However, the listed crash site near Menslage is some 20 miles NW of the target, so indicating that some measure of control must have been re-established before the final impact; F/O Joseph M. Smith (P) was one of eight fatalities.

Expensive Withdrawal

The bulk of the losses appear to have been incurred after the formations were just clear of the target area. Persistent fighter and flak attention ultimately caused the 93BG Lead aircraft to take sharp evasive action that in turn broke up formation integrity. The Lead bomber was 42-41002/O (409BS), flown by Lt. Richard B. Mays with L/Col. Joseph S. Tate—another Ploesti veteran—as Command pilot. The B-24 was lost sight of prior to the Dutch border and was later assumed to have come down in the North Sea. A fellow squadron machine (42-40974/R **Boomerang II**) progressed as far as the North Dutch coast before Lt. Harry A. Daywalt, Jr. bailed the nine-man crew out over Texel Island; the vagaries of high-altitude wind cruelly worked against the pilot and four crewmembers to deliver them into the sea, while the remaining four were more fortunate and ended up on enemy-occupied soil.

On 1 December, Lt. Russell S. Unangst (B), on Lt. Krause's crew, had got rid of two "hung up" bombs before taking the place of badly wounded Lt. Carter (CP); he and Krause then brought the B-24 in for a forced landing near Tilbury, on the Thames Estuary. The result of his action earned him a DFC. Now today, having been keen to get on with his combat tour while his crew were hospitalized, he had been flying with Lt. Daywalt, but had no idea how he got out of the doomed machine, having recovered consciousness on a Texel sand dune with his ripcord clutched in one hand. A similar fate to that of Lt.

A Group of 389BG ground personnel is clustered around a barrel of beer as they celebrate Christmas 1943, their first of three that will be spent in England. The airmen sitting on the right bears a reflective look his face; whether he has indulged a little too freely or is thinking of his family and friends an ocean away is unclear. Sgt. Gerald Opitz is the pipe-smoking individual standing on the left.

Rose Of Juarez has overshot the runway at Watton and suffered a collapsed nose wheel in the process. Repairs will be effected and B-24H-1-FO/42-7469 will be brought back to combat status. The 392BG bomber will then operate until 10 April 1944 when, now marked as GC: E, it will face salvage action after making a wheels-up landing at Wendling the previous day.

42-7537/CI: Jungle Princess looms over a farmhouse near Swanton Morley, Lt. R Berger (P) having seen his 392BG charge nose to a very scarifying halt following a crash landing attempt off the 31 December mission to St. Jean/D'Angely airfield in France.

The sizeable crater caused by the explosion of bombs stacked by and intended for 42-7556/GC: G on 5 December 1943 has left little evidence of the B-24 for whom the weapons were intended. The sole indication of a multi-ton aircraft are the two shattered engine mounts in the background. And the B-24H's name?—Exterminator II!

Daywalt overtook all nine on Lt. Grady G. Hunt's 42-63969/H (330BS) and the same complement on 42-41015/(328BS), flown by Capt. Herrell E. Ford. The sea had clearly swallowed up both B-24s and only four bodies were subsequently recovered out of this overall figure.

Seething was short two crews by the day's end, both of which had gone down in the North Sea, killing 19 out of 21 airmen. Lt. Edward D. Hughey, Jr. was flying an element Lead in 41-28609 of the 714BS, which was seen to explode as the group crossed out over the Frisian Island chain; there were two survivors, with Sgt. James G. Hicks (WG) being blown out. A second squadron bomber left nobody alive after suffering flak and then fighter damage; Lt. David E. Manning in 42-52105 had been in the same element as Lt. Hughey, but the aircraft's descent into the sea bore all eleven souls to their deaths, although five bodies later drifted ashore. This was a hard manner in which to commence the group's combat operations and matters would not improve over the coming weeks.

The 445BG's share in the carnage was also incurred on the way back. Target flak had already damaged 42-7554/(702BS), and by the time the formations were approaching the Dutch coast, Lt. John H. Allen was believed to have been attempting a crash landing or "ditching," but the bomber crashed fatally on the northern fringe of the Ijsselmeer; one man had already bailed out but drowned, while one of the three survivors ended up in Resistance hands. The second loss occurred almost simultaneously around the same region; fighters latched onto 42-64438 (also 702BS) and brought it down at Bolsward, leaving no survivors among Lt. Norman M. Nelson's ten-man crew. The third 2CBW casualty was from Hethel, being 42-40706/F+ **Tondelayo**, a 566BS bomber. Fighter-inflicted damage in the target area forced the crippled aircraft ever lower, and when bail out was considered the ground was too close for other than a crash landing near Mettingen. All but one on Lt. Paul J. Lambert's crew survived the incident.

Muenster Strike

Muenster was attacked simultaneously with Osnabrueck and 30 out of 43 crews dispatched dropped their bombs and headed back still intact. Flak had inflicted some damage and was probably the indirect cause for the two 66BS losses. F/O Kent Miller (P) and Lt. Charles Taylor held course for home above the solid cloud patterns in 42-7638/B **Lili Marlene/Big Banner**, but inexorably lost height and distance from the formation, finally disappearing over the Dutch border. Power fell steadily away to a 50% level and finally the bail out order was given, to be promptly cancelled when a break in the clouds revealed water below; unfortunately, two airmen had already jumped.

The decision was then taken to "ditch," and this action duly occurred within the southern boundary of the Ijsselmeer. Taylor managed to get out before extracting one of the lift rafts from its hatch; he clung desperately to the raft, having exhausted himself in inflating it and was accordingly unable to clamber in. He later recollected seeing two other airmen floating, supported by their 'Mae Wests," but sadly, he was destined to be the sole survivor, having been rescued by a Dutch-crewed vessel before being overcome by exposure to the freezing waters.

Taylor returned to the scene in the early 1970s to participate in a TV documentary, "Some of our Airmen are no longer Missing." It dealt primarily with WWII aircraft hitherto declared MIA along with their crews who had been discovered during land reclamation within the Ijsselmeer. In this way, the MIA tag formerly attached to the dead airmen—a situation generally causing even more anguish to their kin than knowing they were definitely dead—

could finally be removed and their bodies be granted proper Christian burial.

The other Shipdham loss involved Lt. Warren W. Oakley's 42-7533/E **Holiday Mess II**. Battle damage had disabled three engine superchargers and worse still was an inability to release the bomb load. The bomber was last seen spiralling down around the same time as **Big Banner's** disappearance. Lt. Frank D. Power (N) and two Enlisted men barely managed to bail out before the B-24, whose spinning motion was by now converted into a shallow dive, finally ploughed into the Dutch soil; a farmer whose barn had just been missed by the B-24 was yelled at by Lt. Powers to throw himself down; scarcely had both men done so when the aircraft erupted in a massive explosion, killing anybody still alive within the fuselage. Powers and Sgt. Abel Fleischmann (ROG) were soon apprehended, but Sgt. John F. Byers (Eng.) evaded capture for some time. (Fleischmann was doubly lucky, because he had originally trained with F/O Miller's crew.)

The loss of two crews on its combat initiation was not peculiar to the 448BG alone, but the Osnabrueck mission was the start of a fifteen-day spell during which no less than eleven crews would go MIA. A Christmas Eve "milk run" to bomb *No-Ball* sites in the Pas de Calais nearly brought about two additions to this figure. Capt. W. Blum (712BS Ops. Officer) was piloting a bomber (believed to be 42-7591) when it received serious damage to the port rudder and main wing after being run into by a fellow bomber—42-52118 **Piccadilly Pete**, in Lt. Teague's hands—which also sustained notable damage. The proximity of the English coast to the target area permitted a safe if shaky return for both crews, but Teague bailed out his crew prior to landing.

Closing Out the Year

Operations on Christmas Day and Boxing Day were suspended, a situation probably created by weather, rather than any religious consideration, although 44BG records report a "stand down" was declared. In fact, it was the penultimate day of December before the next call to arms happened, with the first of two consecutive daily runs. Ludwigshafen, situated opposite Mannheim on the Rhine, possessed chemical production plants to which over 700 bombers were sent. This was no shallow penetration mission, given that the city lay just over 300 miles distant from the North Sea coast. Fighter opposition could be anticipated as sizable and sustained, which proved to be the case. All three Divisions shared in the 23 MIA figure, with nine coming from the 2BD. The 20CBW's share was one-third, all sustained by the 448BG.

A recurring problem for the group, at least during the initial operational period, was a distinct tendency towards indifferent to poor formation retention. Adverse weather on this day did hinder proper Assembly, as did one bomber going off the perimeter track and holding proceedings up for ten minutes. Twenty-one crews made Assembly, but once over enemy air space, the formation began to fall back from the CBW ranks. The Luftwaffe was up and pecking away at the bomber stream, despite the presence of P-47s, but matters for the 448BG remained stable until "bombs away," when the situation steadily deteriorated.

The first 448BG crew to probably feel the *Jagdwaffe's* effect was on board 41-28599 (714BS). Two engines were disabled and the B-24 steadily lost altitude around the French/Belgian border. Cul-des-Sarts, south of Charleroi, was where the aircraft finally descended, with Lt. Abraham J. Kittredge and two others still in position and destined to die, the other seven having bailed out when ordered. Lt. Thomas A. E. Foster's 42-64444 **Consolidated Mess** (715BS) suffered a punishing fighter pass that set the bomber on fire and fatally wounded the pilot; the blazing B-24 ultimately exploded SSW of Soissons, killing seven of the other nine airmen and blowing the survivors out. Finally, the formation was bypassing Paris when Lt. Ray G. Gelling's 41-28588/D, another 714BS aircraft, was culled from the ranks. Grisey-les-Platres, a few miles NW of the metropolis, accommodated the shattered airframe from which all but one among the crew complement jumped safely, Sgt. Harold J. Lane (ROG) having suffered parachute failure.

The other two CBWs completed the overall loss figure. The veteran 44BG added one more crew to its casualty figure. On the 22nd, Lt. Don J. Heskett (66BS) had pulled alongside Lt. Oakley's ailing and ultimately doomed B-24, but had been waved forward. Now he too would taste the bitter seeds of combat failure, although in far more positive fashion compared to Oakley's crew. The pilot had maneuvered 42-7548/T **Bull O' the Woods** in order to replace an "aborting" B-24, but was caught in an exposed position by the fighters. Lt. James R. Billings (CP) and Sgt. Aulus L. Blitz (WG) were killed and the now-battered bomber began to descend and crash at a location north of Soissons.

Bail out was ordered, but proved to be particularly fraught with problems for Lt. William A. Rendall (N). First, his clothing snagged a snap hook on a dinghy lying stowed in the access tunnel, but he disengaged the equipment from its location before exiting via the nose wheel doors with the dinghy in tow. On opening his parachute, the dinghy fell clear, but his escape kit went with it; the dinghy snap hook was attached to the pocket containing the gear and ripped open under the force of the dinghy's departure! Both pilot and navigator evaded capture, but whereas Heskett made a quick "home run," Rendall was either caught by or betrayed to the Germans in June. Five of the other six also got into friendly hands.

Wendling also gave up one B-24 as the formations were approaching the French coast near Dieppe on the way back. Both port engines had been progressively disabled as a result of target flak, but Lt. James M. Sibley still managed to keep 42-7588/R **Mah Ideel** (578BS) on a crabbing course for home. Although the Channel was

One of the eleven Soldier's Medal awards arising out of the violent demise of Exterminator II went to Sgt Lee A Doolittle, a member of the crash crew. He is seen receiving the medal on 22 February 1944, but by then he had transferred to the 453BG.

Prior to the introduction of fuselage code letters, the 448BG utilized a squadron markings variation with their aircraft that took the form of geometric shapes applied around the aircraft letter. The square on the nearside B-24 denotes the 714BS; triangles, circles, and diamond pattern were used by the 712th, 713rd, and 715th BS, respectively.

tantalizingly within reach, altitude was by then being lost at 500ft a minute, and with power failing on the two operating engines the pilot reluctantly gave the order to jump. All the crew floated down north of Evreux, with four gaining access to Resistance sources and ultimate return into Allied hands.

A double loss was incurred by Hethel, beginning with 42-7766/H+ from the 566BS. Power was reduced by half thanks to fighter-inflicted strikes and a bail out called for near Charleville. Lt. Eldon N. Colby (P) was one of seven POWs, while of the other three, two evaded and Lt. Roger R. Taylor (CP) was the sole fatality. Five of Lt. Richard F. Schafer's nine-man complement, including the pilot, were evaders, while the others became POWs following 42-63973/G's (564BS) demise SE of Soissons.

The same MIA loss scale affected the 445BG, with a third later declared "Category E" during landing. Both MIA crews were from the 703BS, one of which came down on enemy soil SSW of Sedan, another fighter victim. Lt. Oliver J. Saunders (P) and three crewmembers survived 42-7508 **Liberty Belle's** destruction, which was paralleled by the deaths of the other six airmen. F/O William P. Kane and Charles H. Clemmons fought to keep 41-29123 **Big Joe** aloft and nearly made it to land. Sadly, their fight ended with a "ditching" in the Channel a mere three miles south of Beachy Head, from which only Kane and five others were picked up by a fishing boat. Clemmons was not among this fortunate group. On landing back at Tibenham, Lt. Bernard C. Avery landed too far down the runway and ran 42-64436 **Two Gun Flossie** into its companion 701BS bomber 41-29130, piloted by Lt. Lawrence F. Melby, who was not yet clear of the runway's end. The errant pilot was treated as wholly to blame and reduced to copilot, while his B-24 was subsequently "written off."

Costly Reminder

The final VIII BC mission for 1943 involved an even more extended run for the majority of the combat crews, as well as a second split-mission pattern for the 2BD. The 20CBW was dispatched, along with elements of the other two Divisions, to bomb airfields on France's SW coastal zone, being allotted La Rochelle as its specific target. The 2nd and 14th CBWs headed for St. Jean D'Angely, situated a short distance inland from La Rochelle.

Although the bomber stream could take advantage of a seaward approach to and from the region, there was to be no immunity from Luftwaffe intervention, as 26 crews out of 464 were to discover. In addition—and as on the 5 December mission to the same area—the 20CBW Primary remained untouched, with the Secondary at Cognac/ Chateaubernard to the SW unloaded upon and further struck by a good proportion of the B-17 formations that had Bordeaux/Merignac as their Primary. The bulk of fighter opposition also appears to have challenged this section of the overall bomber force that absorbed 23 of the MIA losses.

The day before, the 20CBW had suffered one loss, compared to six from the other CBWs; now these figures were to be virtually reversed at five to one. The 93BG had a single B-24 tacked on to its current monthly MIA loss tally of seven, with two more "written off." Lt. Edwin J. Todd's crew made it to the Secondary, but suffered battle damage or technical problems on the return flight. When almost within sight of the English coast, 42-64433 (330BS) was set down into the Channel, an action that left only four out of ten airmen alive. Todd was among the rescued, but tragically died in a car accident Stateside in 1945, shortly after being physically cleared for duty. The 448BG's 41-29248 (713BS) was struck by flak during bomb run completion. The tail section and part of one wing became detached and none of Lt. Max R. Jordan's crew survived the terminal descent near La

Rochelle. **Harmful Little Armfull** (42-7754/715BS) cleared the target, but was last seen on fire. It came down near the Gironde estuary, midway between Cognac and Bordeaux; Fate decreed that Lt. Philip J. Chase would face "Kriegydom," as did four others: two would evade and two paid the supreme price.

The 446BG's sixth mission pushed its losses in direct combat up from three to five. A 100% mortality rate occurred on 42-7577 **Buzz Buggy** (704BS), which disappeared out of sight shortly after bombing; five bodies were recovered from the Bay of Biscay, including that of Lt. Lee V. Allen (P). In the lottery that was aerial combat, Lt. Charles V. Frascati, Jr. got all but one of his crew out and down safely after fighters knocked 42-7581/ **Flak Bait** (706BS) out of formation around the same time as **Buzz Buggy**. Sgt. Edwin R. Ashworth (WG) was wounded but did jump clear, so his death was probably due to parachute failure.

Better overall fortune attended the St. Jean D'Angely attackers, with a single Wendling crew lost out of 87 completing their bomb runs. However, the report that 42-7605/T (578BS) exploded came from a 445BG crew, and this, along with the reported map coordinates and crash site at Montlieu-la-Garde—with Cognac in between there and the group's Primary target—has the MACR compiler suggesting the bomber had linked up with the 20CBW. (The sole survivor, S/Sgt. Anthony J. Malavasic (TG), stated the bomber did leave the 392BG formation in the target area.) Whatever the precise facts, the human cost was nine out of ten airmen on Lt. Thomas R. McKee's team.

To the six MIA casualties would be added another five bombers "written off." Hardwick gave up 42-7597, while Tibenham's 42-7568 overshot the runway after diverting to Gosfield. The 448BG's 41-28601 **Crazy Mary** (715BS) landed with gear up at Yeovilton, a Royal Navy Base in SW England. A pair of Hethel bombers completed the figure. The 564BS' **Unstable Mabel** (42-63957/E) was flying over Sussex when all four engines ran out of fuel; the crash landing east of Hastings by Capt. Frank Ellis was safely carried out for the crew,but not their mount. Further north another squadron bomber, 42-63967/J **Stork Club**, was similarly affected; the fortunate proximity of Birch, a proposed USAAF airfield in Essex, provided landing facilities. Unfortunately, Lt. Fred Sayre was unable to prevent his powerless B-24 from overshooting and being sufficiently "bent" for "write-off" action to be recommended.

Lt. R Berger's charge 42-7537/ (392BG) was forced to land in open country near Swanton Morley, but its momentum threatened to run it right into a looming farmhouse. He recalled the crew yelling "St-o-p-p-p!" to their mount, which finally obliged, albeit with its left wing over-hanging the property's front door. One crewmember clambered out and knocked on the door, and when it was answered by an elderly lady he apologized for the bomber's "intrusion." Then, after rendering he and his fellow airmen's relief that no harm had been visited on her, he assured her that "somebody would be along to collect the machine."

Comment

The first full year of VIII BC's campaign was now at an end. The hoped-for advance in terms of applying inexorable pressure upon the Axis Powers' ability to sustain their overall war effort had fallen far short of such a laudable intention. The skies over central Europe still belonged to the *Jagdwaffe* and its ground-based flak and electronic surveillance apparatus. The long-planned invasion of Western Europe by the Anglo-American military was primarily dependent upon aerial supremacy being in permanent place so that the land armies could function in relative comfort, if not total security. The coming initial period of 1944 air operations would accordingly determine the fate of the Western military powers and by extension that of future democratic rule within the European Continent.

Ed and Larry

"This is London" was the telling opening announcement with which Edward R. Murrow used to begin his broadcasts from Britain to America from 1940 onwards. Along with Quentin Reynolds, this duo of fine journalists was instrumental in regularly bringing home to their fellow citizens the direct threat to Britain's survival and by extension the latent threat to their nation's very existence that was posed by Hitler and Mussolini prior to Pearl Harbor.

Hethel's Red Cross chief decided he was going to put the group on the map, having requested CBS Corporation to send a leading personality to interview personnel for a Christmas Day broadcast home. Gwen Jones was delighted to discover one of the two guests was to be Murrow, having rubbed shoulders with him in the same Madison Avenue building; she also knew Larry LeSeur.

Both men arrived Christmas Morning and were taken to the Aero Club for the interviews. The Christmas dinners were scheduled for 1300 hours, but the guests were not officially invited, so Gwen took the initiative by offering places in the Enlisted Men's Combat Mess hall. That they would have to stand in line compared to the Officer's Club, to which their official hosts had clearly not arranged an invitation, caused no comment. When they eventually reached the serving tables, the ladled-out mix of turkey, cranberry sauce, and mushy vegetables must have been regarded as a world away from the refined dining facilities in New York!

Chapter Eight

Slugging it Out

Higher Echelon Changes

The first week of 1944 wrought important structural changes within the Allied High Command, beginning with the transfer from the Mediterranean to Britain of Four-Star Gen. Dwight D. Eisenhower as Supreme Allied Commander for the forthcoming Operation *Overlord*, a superbly emotive title for the projected invasion of Western Europe. In turn, "Ike" had brought with him several Allied Senior staff from his former Theater of Operations; among them was M/Gen. James H. "Jimmy" Doolittle, who was to take over the former VIII BC (now re-titled 8th Air Force) from Gen. Ira C. Eaker. Lt/Gen. "Tooey" Spaatz was appointed to command all USAAF European-based Forces under the umbrella title of United States Strategic and Tactical Air Forces (USSTAF). His Deputy charged with supervising operations was M/Gen. Fred Anderson.

The new 8AF "Boss" was an individual who although standing no nonsense from his subordinates could still take a poke at himself whenever put on the back foot. An example of this occurred during a visit to an airfield where the crews had just completed a mission. Doolittle and his entourage went to one dispersal where a bomber was newly-parked with the crew still milling around. One turret had been particularly shot up and on approaching its recent occupant Doolittle asked, "Were you in there when it happened?" The clearly irritated Sgt. tersely answered him in the affirmative, but barely had the Gen. moved away when the gunner turned to one of his colleagues and blurted out, "Where the Hell did he think I was—out buying a ham sandwich?" When his shocked fellow airmen said, "Keep your voice down; do you know who that is?" he responded, "Yes, and it's still a damn-fool question!" Far from turning on the gunner, Doolittle walked away and later acknowledged the gauche nature of his enquiry, especially given the feral circumstances recently faced by the airman in question.

"Bombers as Bait" Misnomer?

In recent years, a number of spokespersons on film documentaries about the 8th USAAF have concentrated upon what is perceived as a cold-blooded operational decision that is credited to Doolittle. He had soon gone about altering the current use of the P-38, P-47, and now P-51 escorts. The fighter pilots had acted in a natural if unconscious passive manner; that is, they saw their duty as ensuring that the *Big Friends* were provided with the means to survive each mission. This attitude was embodied in a poster that stated in effect, "The fighters' primary duty is to ensure the survival of the bombers." Doolittle, while making a visit to a fighter base with B/Gen. Bill Kepner (CG 8th Fighter Command), is quoted as reacting thus; on studying the poster's central tenet regarding 8FC combat functions he said to Kepner, "The fighters' primary duty is to destroy enemy fighters." In his opinion, the breaking of *Jagdwaffe* strength was primarily dependent not on warding off their forays against the bombers, but rather on bringing them to battle away from the bomber stream and reducing both their quantitative and qualitative resources in the process.

Doolittle has been presented as a cold-blooded individual who was quite prepared to detach his fighter Groups from direct bomber support; by doing so, so runs the criticism, he was hoping that the apparent lack of direct escort cover would entice the Luftwaffe into mass forays against their strategic bomber prey, whose defensive provisions to date had proven dangerously inadequate. Such a move would conversely lay the Luftwaffe open to effective countermeasures by the 8FC formations, who would spread out well clear of the bombers and pounce upon the enemy formations as they strove to gain the necessary altitude—a variation of the *Freie Jagd* (free hunt) tactic used effectively against RAF Fighter Command in the early stages of the Battle of Britain. The "bombers as bait" canard had accordingly been raised and would be reiterated in postwar broadcasts.

The bald truth is that constant close escort of the B-17s and B-24s over the course of an entire mission was never remotely possible. The flight duration of even the P-51, arguably the USAAF escort design with the greatest range potential, was not equal to that of a four-engine bomber, meaning that a relay system of at least two P-51s to one bomber would have been necessary as the bombers pushed ever deeper into Hitler's *Festung Europa*. Such a goal might have been basically achieved, had the Mustang been able to regularly fly entire missions under normal non-combat conditions, but once engaged in combat, this cosy theory became badly blunted, as fuel reserves were noticeably eaten into. This prime logistical factor was far ahead of fighter to bomber numbers in practical terms within the ETO at any stage of the Daylight Campaign. Instead, the fighters were disposed in a relay system of support, with units briefed to fly to specific coordinates, where they would pick up their particular portion of the bomber stream and simultaneously relieve the fighter cover currently on hand.

The operational hiatus within the B-24's development is basically encapsulated here with the presence of the B-24D and H variants in this 1943/44 shot. Two of the fully-visible earlier variants include **Princ-Ass** (left foreground), while one of the duo of H-models is unidentified (lower center). The latter, along with the J-Model in particular, will be in the ascendancy of numbers by mid-1944.

Also problematical was the visual positioning of fighters in relation to the bombers—very comforting to the bomber crews, but of doubtful benefit in terms of effective cover, since it could permit the enemy fighters to approach within range before being challenged. Added to this limitation was the loss of airspeed and with it equally vital maneuverability required for the fighters to station themselves within the immediate vicinity of the bomber formations that were flying at a measurably more pedestrian pace.

Another potential inhibition with engaging the Luftwaffe in sight of the bomber stream was the inherent danger of "friendly fire" incidents. Bomber gunners had instilled in them the principle "fire first, identify later"; any fighter vs. fighter melee occurring within range of the B-17 and B-24 defenders could and often did draw fire. This was hardly surprising in view of the closing speeds involved in aerial combat, as well as the difficulty of identifying one's own fighters from those of the enemy in such feral circumstances. For these reasons, it was far better for the 8FC pilots to intercept the Germans well before they got within range of their lumbering prey.

Doolittle's premise meant in practice that there would inevitably be occasions when the *Jagdwaffe* pilots would gain access to a bomber formation currently bereft of cover. However, the bombers were going to be engaged regardless of the disposition of escort fighters, so the "bombers as bait" blanket assertion becomes capable of challenge. The back of the *Jagdwaffe* would not be broken by allowing its personnel access to the bomber stream—the Bf109s and Fw190s and their Bf110 and Me410 contemporaries had to be taken on and dispersed beforehand, and the basic manner of achieving this laudable, not to say vitally necessary, measure was to hunt them down, not draw them on.

Shipdham's B-24H-5-CF 41-29231/J **The Impatient Virgin** is a 67BS assigned aircraft. This picture was taken prior to the application of Group code letters in March/April 1944. This bomber was "written off" following a crash landing on 25 February 1944 by Lt. Keith Cookus—in the same southern English county (Kent) where he had crash landed another B-24 off the 21 January mission!

Bomerang (41-23722) A B-24D-1-CO was to prove more fortunate than was the case with many of its contemporaries; it was the first 2BD bomber to complete 50 missions and was flown home by Capt. Walter Stewart in April 1944. It underwent numerous engine changes, of which this is the 16th; the smiling mechanic is M/Sgt. George E. Ewald, her Crew Chief.

Comment

Regardless of whether the bombers were to be regarded as "bait," the current strength of the *Jagdwaffe* was one to be respected, since it was a still-formidable barrier to the advancement of daylight offensive operations. The theoretical establishment was one of over 1,100 day fighters for utilization by *Luftflotte Reich* and nearly 400 for *Luftflotte* 3, covering France and Belgium. This was reduced in practice to available strength figures of just over 750 and nearly 240 with an operationally-serviceable percentage of 70% and 60%, respectively. This factor, when allied to the current quality of pilots within the *Jagdwaffe* ranks, was a clear indication that the struggle to break this battle-tested organization could not only be protracted, but might cost the 8FC dearly in the process.

Another Winter of Discontent?

The prospects of surviving a combat tour had ever been poor since the beginning of the Daylight Offensive, with an approximate one in three chance of achieving this precious goal the norm. The current state of affairs did not bode well for the foreseeable future, given the strength of enemy fighter and even flak opposition. The bomber crews just had to buckle down to their physical and psychologically onerous duty and hope good fortune was on their side. The ensuing three or four months would evolve into an aerial "slugging match" that neither opponent could afford to lose.

The first mission of 1944 was also the penultimate one to be launched under the current VIIIBC title. The bulk of the 569 crews dispatched on the 4th to Kiel (486) completed their bombing runs, with the 2BD figures being 130 and 115, respectively. The overcast conditions merited the use of PFF equipment in achieving a strike. The target's distance from East Anglia limited escort provision to the P-38s of the 20th and 55th FGs and the 354FG' P-51s. Bomber losses were limited to seventeen overall, six of which were B-24s. However, for at least the third occasion, the 392BG was punished to the tune of five crews MIA and a sixth "written off" on return.

The extended North Sea crossing was ever fraught with risk should "ditching" have to be considered; this was especially so with the B-24, whose record in bringing crews to a safe entry into the sea would remain very poor compared to the B-17 and even its RAF contemporaries. Only six Wendling airmen out of forty were left alive, with the sea apparently claiming three of the B-24s. One was 42-7482/P+ **Shack Rat**, one of three 577BS losses that was deemed to have been dispatched off the Frisian Island chain by a fighter, leaving no survivors among Lt. Raymond P. Lambert's crew. The circumstances of Lt. Clyde W. Rigby and his crew's death in 42-7479/O+ **Ole War Horse** were never established, since the bomber disappeared, having likely been claimed by the sea. No doubt existed as to why all ten on Lt. Robert L. Hull's team were killed; an attempted landing in a meadow near Bredstedt during a snowstorm went tragically wrong when 42-52083/H-bar **Out House Mouse** (579BS) immediately inverted on contact with the ground and exploded.

The grim death tally was completed by the 576BS' **Million $ Baby** (42-7487/B). The aircraft was set on fire, but three of Lt. John R. Becker's crew were found in the wreckage strewing the ground NE of Bredstedt; one of the seven jumping out also did not survive. Becker's MACR report stated that strikes just after bombing set his bomber ablaze, and in his opinion the three

Enlisted men whose bodies were later discovered in the wreckage had probably been trapped and overcome by the flames and smoke. The final MIA bomber brought herself and her crew through, although its problems were self-imposed, rather than thanks to enemy action. Barely had the bomb run been completed when all four engines cut out before recovering for a few minutes when this pattern was repeated. The risk of ultimate failure over the North Sea and the relative proximity of Sweden to Kiel coupled to what thankfully became steady cloud cover induced Lt. Leander Page, Jr. to redirect his ironically-titled mount (42-7637/ S+ **The Queen of Peace** [577BS]) northward, even though no maps of the Baltic region were on hand for the navigator's benefit. Luck was on their side, however, and an emergency wheels-down landing was finally made at Smedstorp, where the ten airmen surely anticipated the relaxing pleasures of their surroundings.

The 20CBW lost the remaining crew flying in 41-23810/S **TARFU**. The exact circumstances of its loss are again undetermined, but its crash south of Flensburg left only Lt. Andrew M. Reynolds (P) and two of the nine-man crew alive. Wendling's woes were not ended with the group's return over Norfolk. An emergency landing was attempted by Lt. Colby A. Waugh in 42-7485/O **Alfred**, but the 578BS bomber ended up crashing at Sheringham, on the Norfolk coast; an eyewitness stated that the B-24 was coming in low with two engines "out" and had just cleared the unforgiving North Sea when it turned sharply to port and impacted with rising ground. Waugh and three crewmembers were instantly killed and a fifth died in hospital to leave four survivors. Ironically, the tenth crewmember was already absent, having bailed out over enemy territory to end up a POW—a relative measure of luck in these circumstances.

A second "Category E" incident had occurred during take-off at Shipdham. Lt. Richard E. Harleman had attempted to "abort" his run in 42-7476/H **Nice N' Naughty**, but the 66BS aircraft's forward motion was not yet spent when it ran off the runway's end and through a ditch that ripped off the landing gear; all ten airmen remained uninjured. Sadly, the pilot's luck, along with that of Lt. William E. Cobana (N), was to run out on 27 March 1944. (Lt. T. F. McNichol's crew returned to Wendling in 41-29174/DC: R. **Amblin' Okie**, which was bearing the body of S/St. Albert J. McPherson (G), a KIA victim.)

Piling on the Torment

So far, the 448BG had lost seven MIA crews during the four missions commencing 22 December. Its sixth venture into hostile airspace was on 5 January and was destined to be the most painful experience to date; four of the 20CBW losses would emanate from its ranks, with the 445BG providing the sole other Division loss. Kiel's submarine construction yards and port facilities were again selected for assault, with upwards of 600 tons of bombs and incendiaries from 215 bomb bays cascading onto the target.

The Seething contingent appears to have penetrated as far as the target area before matters began to deteriorate. One crew led by Lt. William F. Ferguson in 42-7709/ **Maid of Tin** (715BS) were last observed over Kiel; also lost sight of at this stage was 42-7722/ (714BS), flown by Lt. Walter A. Yuengert. Both bombers and their 10-man crews were almost certainly the latest Division casualties claimed by the North Sea. A second 715BS crew led by Lt. Graham G. Guyton in 41-29234/ was taken down by fighter attack and the final crash site at Horstheide, NE of Hamburg, killed the pilot and seven out of the other nine. The same region claimed the shattered fragments of 42-7712/ from the 712BS, although its problems had commenced over Kiel. Flak blew off the nose turret and fire took hold within the fuselage. The B-24's final explosion near Itzehoe, NE of Hamburg, blew Lt. James E. Curtis and his copilot and navigator out into mid-air, allowing them to deploy their backpack parachutes; the other seven were either killed instantly or unable to don their chest packs even if still conscious.

The single Tibenham crew declared MIA was in 42-7512 **Gremlin's Roost/** (703BS). The loss of an engine en route caused height to be lost, but it was only after bombing that fighters picked up the straggling bomber. Strikes set the rear fuselage so fiercely ablaze that just one Enlisted man (Sgt. E. A Fippinger, ROG) managed to bail out. Lt. W. L. Yerkes, Jr. (B) completed the fatality figure of six, with the bomber blowing up and distributing its remains near Brunsbuettel, on the northern shore of the Elbe estuary; Lt. Victor I. Smith (P) and the other two officers were the remaining survivors.

Back at Seething, a fifth B-24 was laying off the end of a runway. Maj. Robert L. Campbell had "aborted" the mission at a stage where the majority of the fuel load was still not spent. This factor, along with the retained bomb load, should have indicated to him that he should orbit and "burn off" enough fuel to lighten the bomber for a safe landing. Instead, he elected to fly straight back and land immediately, a feat he only achieved after three overshoots. Unfortunately, the combination of an icy runway and a landing made too far along the runway caused 42-64451 (712BS) to careen off the end and strike a hedge with enough force to cause major damage and a "write-off" action. (Campbell was the squadron CO, whose lease on life would end on 18 March.)

Tibenham also added a "Category E" to its loss tally. Lt. Alvin L. Owen lost an engine shortly after take-off in 41-29116/ (700BS), but had scarcely decided to "abort" when a second engine suffered a "runaway" propeller. Poor visibility on his landing approach threw the B-24 off to one side of the runway alignment, and to increase his problems, Owen had the starboard rudder cable snap. A second approach was even further off to one side, and with the landing gear refusing to retract the time was deemed ripe for abandoning his

A basic structural weakness on all B-24 fuselages was the lack of wing spar support that left it ill-fitted for holding out against heavy contact with land and especially water. B-24H-1-FO/42-7578 /FL: N **Hula Wahine's** underside is well-crumpled and the supporting tractor unit is one of two tasked with moving her either for repair or, following inspection, for salvage.

Blunder Bus is B-24H- 1 -FO/42-7593/P of the 565BS from Hethel. The current absence of Group codes must have caused some problems in forming up at least with the correct squadron when attempting Assembly in adverse weather conditions. The bomber was one of four MIA on 7 January 1944 with Lt. Royce E. Smith's (POW) eleven-man crew.

charge. All ten airmen exited in good order, leaving the bomber to impact on open farmland at Fritton, Norfolk.

Comment

As in the foregoing instance of today's Seething casualty, there were to be a number of occasions during the bombing offensive where the pilots would be the sole survivors on a crew. The constant wearing of the normal chest pack by the other crewmembers generally proved impractical. This was caused either by their being unable to work and/or move freely at their stations, in the case of radio or radar operators, while the weight of a back pack borne by the gunners (or on early B-24 variants where the navigator had to stand) would be an energy-sapping factor; the pilots in contrast were normally immobile for the entire mission and so could avail themselves of the backpack equipment

Ludwigshafen Revisited

The Grim Reaper was ever selective in wielding his scythe within the combat crew ranks, and on 7 January he took a sharp tilt at the 389BG in particular. The normal seven-group participation by the 2BD was reduced to five when the 44th and 448th BGs, having both lost distance with and failed to gain Divisional altitude by the time the Dutch coast was looming up, decided to turn back. The reduced sub-Force pressed on for Ludwigshafen and duly added its bomb loads to the destruction before taking up a similar route to that flown on 30 December.

Although defensive opposition was sharp as ever, the 2BD appears to have staved off any losses until approaching the region south of Paris. It was at this stage of the mission that Maj. James Stewart, leading the 445BG behind the 389BG, noticed that the Hethel fliers were veering dangerously off to the left. On calling up the Hethel Lead bomber to inform them of this, he was told that he was wrong. Stewart agonized over whether to allow his fellow fliers to head off on their own or to add his Group's weight of defensive firepower to the errant unit, neither choice being easy to make. Within seconds, he chose the latter course of action.

The two French-based *Jagdgeschwadern* were JG26, responsible for the eastern zone, and JG2 covering the central and western zone of operations. The latter was led by Maj. Egon Mayer, the airman credited with initiating the "12 O'clock high" attack approach upon the USAAF bombers. Elements of his *Geschwader* with him in the Lead were up and heading for an interception with the 2BD. The first sight of the B-24s from the 2CBW was gained as the two Groups were tracking west between Paris and Orleans.

The quartet of Hethel losses were incurred between Orleans and Chartres, some 40 miles further to the NW. In Lead position was Capt. David L. Wilhite with Maj. Kenneth M. Caldwell as Command Pilot flying in 42-41013/K+ **Trouble N' Mind**. The 566BS bomber was engaged by Mayer and thoroughly shot up, as well as being set on fire. It then went into a steep almost inverted dive for 10,000ft before breaking apart near Bouville, south of Chartres. Only Sgt. Robert Sweatt (BT) came through the experience alive out of eleven on board. Mayer reportedly took out all four B-24s, the first probably being 42-63977/Z **Los Angeles City Limits** (567BS), since its crash site at Trainou, NNE of Orleans, is the furthest to the east. Lt. Earl T. Cooper forfeited his life along with five others, whereas the surviving four all evaded capture.

Down at Vrigny, close to the Cooper crash site, was Lt. Carl A. Mattson's 42-40747/S **Heavy Date**, also a 567BS machine. Fighter strikes swiftly sent the B-24 into a spin, followed shortly by an explosive disintegration that killed the pilot; four others also died, but no less than four of the remaining five slipped out of the grasp of their potential captors. **Blunder Bus** (42-7593/-P, a 565BS aircraft) probably fell almost simultaneously with the Lead bomber; Lt. Royce E. Smith would be the only airplane commander to survive, while his ten colleagues suffered various fates: two were killed, seven ended up as POWs, and two evaded capture. However, one of the latter (Lt. Francis J. Thackeray) was cruelly denied his life. While traversing the Pyrenees, he and four others were buried by a snow slide; when later dug out, his was the sole death from suffocation. Orgeres-en-Beauce, where the aircraft came to earth, is close to where the Lead B-24 descended.

20CBW

The 20CBW was short one group, but whether the absent defensive firepower of the 448BG would have made any material difference to the situation was academic. The 93BG had already struck off one crew that was now residing in Switzerland. An engine loss on 42-7519/D **Ole King Cole** of the 328BS caused Lt. David M. Richardson's machine to drop back and finally descend below the cloud layers; luck was on the crew's side, since their southward route was unchallenged and they landed without incident at Duebendorf.

The other two crews failing to get back would not fully share their colleague's collective good fortune, with five out of the nineteen losing their lives. Two in this tragic category were on board 42-7614, another 328BS machine. The 20CBW had already come under fighter attack SE of Paris, although the identity of the attackers was not stated. With one engine on fire and two others disabled, Lt. James R. Carnahan had little option but to ring the bail out bell. The two fatalities were adjudged to have "frozen" at the thought of jumping and probably went in with the bomber, which crashed near Melun, SE of Paris.

The third squadron loss was suffered further on when 42-40990/L **On the Ball** had two engines and its bomb bay set on fire. Lt. C. W. Walters bailed out to become one of four evaders, of whom one—Lt. J. D George (B) - unluckily was later apprehended; two others also survived, albeit as POWs, while the remaining trio of airmen were killed. Their B-24 reportedly exploded in mid-air with the shattered remnants falling close to Unverre, 20 miles SW of Chartres.

The 445BG remained free of loss during the mission, but suffered one while heading in for Tibenham. The reason for 41-29119 (701BS) ending up crashing in a Suffolk field is not stated. Three on Lt. Lester I. Eike's crew were trapped in the nose section and burned to death after the bomber caught fire. A group of British farm workers rushed to the scene and attempted to rescue the seven other airmen, six of whom ultimately survived; the tenth member was only discovered under the wreckage a full week later. A much more positive result in terms of personal salvation was earlier achieved by the 392BG crew of Lt. Rex L. Johnson after they "aborted" the mission in 42-7596/U **Sheila** (578BS). The long runway was out of commission and the pilots made contact on their landing run far too late to prevent an overshoot into a ditch that collapsed the starboard main landing gear. The control tower staff, having judged the bomber's approach as being too high and fast, had issued an instruction to go round again, but this had not been picked up; at least all ten airmen walked away unscathed, although the group CO would have been rather unhappy with the pilots' wrongful action. **Sheila** was less lucky, since the damage scale merited a "Category E" fate.

Oschersleben

Oschersleben lies some 80 miles SW of Berlin and was therefore "deep in there" in terms of both mission duration and likely Luftwaffe opposition. The town possessed a large Fw190 production plant whose destruction was expected to put a noticeable dent in the provision of this key design to the *Reichsverteidigung* (Home Defence Command). Just as the Luftwaffe had set out to destroy RAF Fighter Command's aerial and ground support structure in the Battle of Britain, so now the *Jagdwaffe* was similarly to be brought to book in the air and on the ground, although the latter intention was directed more at the enemy's production lines as opposed to his airfields, as happened in 1940; Oschersleben was an early example falling into this first-mentioned category.

The mission was dispatched 11 January, although Oschersleben was just one of three aircraft production sources briefed for assault. The 1BD was assigned the Fw190 plant and a second factory at Halberstadt, while the 2nd and 3rd BDs headed for a plant in Brunswick. However, Mother Nature cast a large meteorological spanner into the operational works. The clear conditions forecast for Germany held out, but deteriorating conditions over East Anglia persuaded Doolittle into issuing a general "recall." A confused operational position turned into a disaster, especially for the 1BD and less so for the 3BD, as some of their ranks held course for their Primaries. The round number of sixty crews finally chalked off the 8AF's inventory as MIA was equal to that incurred during *Black Thursday*.

Of the 2BD' 66 crews gaining mission credit, none struck the Primary. On the other hand, just two crews were added to the overall MIA figure; unfortunately for the 448BG, both were borne by the Group. What was later credited to indifferent formation keeping—a basic operational factor that had plagued and was to plague the Seething fliers for several more weeks—led to one-third of the 24 bombers dispatched ending up isolated as the Group was heading back and subsequently being engaged by a pack of Bf109s. The Dutch/German border was below as 42-52123 **Thirty Day Furlough** absorbed terminal strikes. It sagged out of formation and

Victory Ship, from the 68BS at Shipdham, demonstrates the acute degree of dihedral exerted upon the wings of a fully-loaded B-24. Assigned to the 68BS on 20 September 1942, this Group "original" survived Ploesti, but finally met her end on 21 January 1944; Lt. Starring (P) was one of five fatalities when fighter strikes brought her down near Auffray, in NE France.

then reportedly exploded over Odoorn, 10 miles inside Holland, expunging the lives of all ten on Lt. James E. Urban's crew; a memorial was erected on the crash site in 1990. Dwingerloo lies 10 miles directly west of Odoorn, and this was where 41-28593 **Prodigal Son** (712BS) crashed. Lt. Donald G. Schuman (P) and five others bailed out, but Lt. H. E. White (CP) did so too low for his parachute to deploy and he joined the remainder of the crew in death.

It was to be almost two weeks before a mission of any geographic depth was launched, although several "scrubbed" efforts would occur in that period. The single briefed and completed run occurred on the 14th, when all three Divisions were sent to bomb *No-Ball* sites mainly located in the Pas de Calais, but also sited on the Cherbourg Peninsula. The full 2BD strength was sent, with all but three of the 178 briefed crews dropping their loads. The sole Division loss out of three in all came from the 44BG. At least one of a handful of enemy fighters challenging the bombers' progress reportedly landed strikes on the No. 2 engine of 41-23779/G **4-Q-2**. The former 66BS machine, and now with the 67BS, assumed a gliding attitude. Lt. Henry C. Goodwin, Jr. punched the bail out bell, but only two gunners out of the ten crewmembers got out alive; the others were probably killed outright when the B-24 exploded, distributing its remains at Lillebonne, in between Rouen and Le Havre.

Control Tower Duties

The control tower was a visual and aural epicenter for the combat crews, from where its staff provided often vital guidance instructions, especially when weather conditions were marginal. A 448BG member provides his impressions:

> The tower consisted of two sections, and my initial duty was to act as watch Airman. I manned a desk equipped with two telephones. When a mission was planned, the officer in charge would present me with the relevant paperwork. One sheet contained the formation layout; although the actual target was not included, a bit of ferreting work could reveal this, too. Also on hand was a huge flight board on which we entered each aircraft's detail and its pilot, the estimated and actual take-off time, and the same split details for the Group's return. Thus was created an overall picture of each bomber's movements or sadly their loss, although examples initially placed in the latter category later arrived, having diverted for a number of pressing reasons.
>
> The air traffic control duty was carried out either from the "greenhouse" extension on the tower's flat roof or from the Air Traffic Control (ATC) caravan at the operational runway's end. This specific function was far from easy; the need for general radio silence other than to issue brief instructions, coupled to the sizeable numbers of bombers maneuvering over the packed airspace of East Anglia—particularly on mission return, when damaged aircraft were often on hand within the bomber stream—made for much expenditure of nervous energy by the staff concerned. They were well aware that the lives of the airmen hung on their skills in verbal guidance, as well as the correct use of flares and signal-lamps.

"Milk-Run" Myth

The 44BG was a seasoned combat unit that was well acquainted with operational reverses over its 14-month spell in England. The 67BS in particular had accommodated a good deal of the Group's losses, but on 21 January, it would be the 68BS that would be left reeling. The rebuff administered by the defenders was all the more painful because the mission was of the "milk run" variety, being the latest cross-Channel foray against the Pas de Calais region.

Two sub-formations were sent out, but were thwarted from making their bomb run by clouds. The formations continued to seek out a suitable target, but all the time both fighter and flak-based opposition were building up. JG26 was in on the hunt in the form of Hptm. Borris's *I Gruppe* based at Florennes; in this case, it was 1/JG26 led by Oblt. Beese (*Staffelkapitaen*) who made the interception of the Shipdham sub-Force, comprising the 66th and 68th BS. There are conflicting reports between JG26 records and those of the five MACR forms. The former states that all five B-24s were downed simultaneously at 1530 in the immediate area around Poix, whereas four of the MACR crash sites are ranged westwards from Poix, with the furthest example being located up to fifty miles distant on the Channel coast between Dieppe and Le Havre.

It appears that the bombers were tracking away from having delivered their bomb loads when the first interceptions came in from six o'clock. Probably the first B-24 downed was 42-72813/L **Queen Marlene** (66BS), which disintegrated under one or more Fw190 fusillades to crash at Equines, two miles SW of Poix; Sgt. Richard A. Mayhew was doubly fortunate in being the sole survivor, who furthermore evaded capture.

The first 68BS loss involved Lt. Frank W. Sobotka's (KIA) 42-7501/P, which had both port engines knocked out, an act that precipitated a sharp roll over onto its back. The pilots brought their charge out of this parlous situation but could not prevent the flat spin that had developed. Lt. Milton Rosenblatt (CP) carried out a frantic but successful retrieval of both his and his pilot's chute packs before both bailed out. Rosenblatt and Lt. Teitel (B) evaded capture from among the six survivors. The crash site was at Grattenoix, which appears to have been close to Poix, since two of the dead were initially interred at Poix de La Somme cemetery.

Next on the execution list appears to have been Lt. Gary M. Mathisen's veteran crew, which was on its 18th mission; fate was not kind to the pilot nor six others, as fire took hold and 42-7514/O became the second squadron victim. The B-24 exploded and Lts. Cleary (N) and Hoeltke (B), along with Sgt. Allen (ROG) survived as the shattered airframe descended at Neuville-Ferrirers, SE of Dieppe.

Scant minutes later, the third squadron bomber crashed at Bosmelet, due south of Dieppe. Both port engines were fired before 41-23813/V **Victory Ship** went into a spin. Six of Lt. Alfred A. Starring's (KIA) crew, flying their first mission, got out, but Lt. Weldon H. Maneval (N) struck the ground before his parachute opened fully. The depredations wrought upon the 68BS continued with the demise of **Ram It—Dam It!** (42-7635/Q). A head-on attack landed a devastating burst that either killed or fatally injured Lt. Hartwell R. Howington and his three fellow officers. Among the other seven on board was St. Ray P. Reeves, an ROG functioning as a cameraman while reportedly recovering from nose and ear problems sustained during his combat tour. Whatever the truth behind this rather contradictory status, he and the other six successfully evacuated their doomed aircraft, which expended itself at Lignieres-Chatelain, 56 miles from Poix. Five among this fortunate number also managed to evade capture.

Bucking the Odds

The other two 44BG squadrons would not feature on the MIA list, but one among their number would barely make it back to England. In Lead position was Lt. Keith Cookus's 67BS crew with Maj. William N. Anderson as Command Pilot flying 42-299970/M **Liberty Belle**. Having been thwarted in completing five bomb runs against the assigned target located in the Calais region, the Major finally elected to "abort" and started back on what was to be his 25th and final mission. Scarcely had the course been taken up when a fierce flak barrage swallowed up the formation, which was operating at a meager 12,000ft. **Belle's** port engines were disabled and No. 3 set on fire, while the right landing gear was torn off and the hydraulic system was crippled. In a matter of seconds, a fully functioning bomber had been converted into an airborne wreck.

Anderson had received fatal wounds and St. Richard J. Treichel (ROG), blown into mid-air, miraculously survived to parachute into captivity. Capt. Henry A. Weiser (Group Bombardier) and Capt. Robert L. Ager (Gunnery Officer) bailed out to join the Sgt. as POWs. Meanwhile, Cookus resisted the natural temptation to switch off No. 3, since the result would have seen the aircraft failing to remain airborne. As it was, 4,000 feet of altitude was lost before the bomber was stabilized in level flight. Lt. Woodrow W. Cole (B) was virtually ripping his hands to shreds attempting to free some of the bomb load, but finally collapsed after barely managing to crawl back into the nose compartment—an act that unknowingly sealed his fate.

The woman with see-through clothing and a dog lead wrapped around her shapely frame belongs to B-24D-125-CO/42-41013/K (566BS). The full title is **Trouble n' Mind**, which tragically came her way on 7 January, along with the 389BG Lead crew led by Maj. Kenneth M. Caldwell. A fighter pass south of Paris sent her out of control and only Sgt. Robert H. Sweatt (BT) out of the eleven airmen escaped her violent demise.

The English coast was no more than minutes distant across the Channel, but just as it loomed the No. 3 engine finally blew up. The bomber was by now "down on the deck," with Cookus frantically seeking out a suitable crash landing site. The final location near Wingham was

The social pleasures for the ground crew while on the airfield were relatively few, especially within their sparsely-equipped Nissen huts. This group of Hethel personnel are engaged in a card game while their colleague in the background performs what appears to be basic calisthenics—either that or he has trapped his feet in the bed frame. The "pot belly" stove on the left was ever a notoriously wayward vehicle in heating provision.

barely attained, because just after switching off all available power a house inconveniently appeared dead ahead; fortunately there was sufficient air speed for the pilot to swerve his charge to one side, after which he set it down in a field, but its momentum was not yet spent when it ran into a ditch that crushed the nose compartment. Lt. Cole was trapped with two others, but by the time all three had been freed the bombardier who had been doubled up and pinned down had suffocated.

Meanwhile, the No. 3 engine's persistent burning condition was frantically but successfully extinguished. Several of the eleven survivors required hospital treatment that was non-fatal in nature. (The return flight path of the 67/506BS formation was clearly in a diametrically opposite direction compared to the other group elements; the flak barrage was suspected as being delivered by the port of Calais, to which the bombers had probably strayed too close; on the other hand, flak provision within the area occupied by the *No-Ball* sites was being strengthened in the face of the increasing frequency of RAF and USAAF assaults, so it was more likely that the bombers had over-flown one such concentration.)

Evasion

No less than five members of Lt. Howington's crew would savor the joy of returning to Allied soil. T/Sgt. Archie R. Barlow (Eng.) had landed near a village and was met by a woman. Meanwhile, St. Charles W. Blakely (WG), who had landed near a wood, concealed himself therein. Shortly after, he heard Barlow and the woman coming along the adjoining road, and as they drew level he whispered his presence, upon which he was joined by the Engineer. The woman left and later fulfilled her promise to return and take them to her house, which already held Sgts. Alfred M. Klein (WG) and Alvin A. Rosenblatt (ROG). After three days the quartet, fitted out in appropriate clothes, travelled from Poix to Paris, where they were separated.

A further movement south was begun on 1 March, but the party left the train at Foix, south of Toulouse, some 30 miles short of the Franco/Spanish border. Here five guides were on hand to escort a fourteen-strong group of evaders. The trek's initial stage ended at a barn, where all languished for five days thanks to heavy snowstorm conditions. The party then recommenced its journey, but Sgt. Barlow was now displaying signs of physical distress and he was reluctantly left behind. He would also win through, but in an extended and incredible manner. Sgt. Reeves' passage to ultimate freedom would entail a similar period of time. The others were lucky to evade a German patrol as well as managing to forge a path through heavy snow, but on 13 March the guides led the men through a passageway to an aqueduct that permitted access to the Principality of Andorra; two days rest here was followed by a nighttime movement onto Spanish soil.

A British Embassy representative arrived in a car, after which the men were transported to Barcelona. Here they were medically examined and provided with proper civilian clothing. The next stage of their journey was to Madrid and on to Gibraltar. Once there the clothing was exchanged for military attire, after which a further transfer was made to Casablanca. Finally, a C-87 transport variant of the B-24 was available to fly them back to Britain almost three months after they had faced the real prospect of captivity or worse.

T/Sgt. Ray P. Reeves' journey towards freedom would parallel that of Sgt. Barlow in terms of time. He had barely escaped being detected by the Germans during his time in Paris, but finally got as far as the Franco/Spanish border using a combination of bus and train. His particular piece of good luck occurred when he was abandoned by his guide while traversing the Pyrenean mountain range; he struggled on through the deep snowfields with their attendant frigid temperatures to finally achieve his goal of entering neutral Spain; final repatriation to Britain occurred in early June.

This still-anonymous B-24J-75-CO/42-100146 was assigned to the 389BG in the autumn of 1943. She is seen when assigned to the 564BS, but later transferred to the 567BS as HP: U, where she was named **Mistah Chick**. Poelitz, on 20 June 1944, proved to be its final mission, but Lt. Ralph P. Leslie succeeded in reaching Halmstad, in Sweden, where the eleven crewmembers were interned.

With the type of artwork applied to her lower nose section, is it surprising that B-24H-1-FO bore the title **The Shark**? The 67BS aircraft was originally assigned to the 392BG, but transferred to Shipdham around October 1943. She flew missions until 16 March 1944, when a crash landing at the hands of Lt. Scarborough culminated with her being declared "salvage."

Torturous Advance

The desired return to deep penetration missions was still proceeding at a very staccato pace and events on 24 January did not improve the situation. Frankfurt's industrial facilities and marshalling yards were laid on with all three Divisions rostered; however, just seven 3BD groups and the 1CBW for the 1BD were actually dispatched, the 2BD contingent not even getting airborne. The weather conditions over East Anglia were poor and caused difficulties in forming up. Finally, a general recall was issued as the formations were approaching the German borders, although one element of the 3BD did bomb a Target of Opportunity at Eschweiler.

This being the second occasion in thirteen days that a mission recall had been issued by Gen. Doolittle was a prime matter that did not sit at all well with his superior Spaatz, who did not mince his words in suggesting that his subordinate was not seemingly up to the job. As it was, the next few weeks would begin to see a marked improvement at striking into the enemy hinterland and doing so in a steady but increasingly effective manner. (Today reportedly witnessed the implementation of Doolittle's revised use of his fighters in "relay" operations as opposed to the former constant close support.)

Several missions over the next four days were briefed and then "scrubbed" before two of the final days in January witnessed the beginning of a positive operational trend. Nearly 95% of the 860 crews sent on the 29th duly carried out the strike originally intended for the 24th, making effective runs over Frankfurt through heavy cloud. The 8FC pilots also left their mark to the tune of 47 "kills" for fifteen losses. However, twenty-nine bombers went down, five of them B-24s split between the 2nd and 14th CBWs.

Shipdham added two to its already sizeable blood debt. A fighter attack over France on the way in knocked out No. 4 engine and damaged the tail plane controls on 41-29157/J (66BS). Lt. George H. Maynard elected to head for Switzerland. The MACR statement that the bomber was last seen on fire in the bomb bay and with two parachutes issuing forth was incorrect, since all ten airmen were still on board when neutral soil loomed. Matters went tragically wrong at this point, however. By then down to 1,000ft, the aircraft was an easy target for flak that knocked out No. 2 engine; Maynard and Lt. John E. Norquist (CP) began to circle as bail out commenced, but only three airmen got out before the B-24 crashed SW of Mulhouse.

When a B-24 or any heavy or even medium bomber adopted the steeply twisting maneuver demonstrated by a stricken 392BG bomber, the outcome was usually fatal. Either the aircraft went into an uncontrollable spin or alternately the tremendous pressures exerted upon the airframe tore it apart, leaving the hapless crew dead or unconscious and unable to open their parachutes—assuming these could be attached in the first place.

The light layer of snow forms a pleasing backcloth for B-24H-1-FO 42-7546/DC: P **Alfred II**, but the ground crew will be less enamored of the frosty atmosphere as they attempt delicate repairs and adjustments with equally frozen hands. The impressive bomb log was extended as far as 29 April, when the badly-damaged bomber was abandoned to crash at Walcot, in Norfolk; Lt. John W Reed (P) was the sole fatality.

The IP for the IG Farben und VDM plant was just ahead when an Fw190 landed fatal strikes on Lt. Hal. H. Pinder's 42-7547/X **Sky Queen**. No. 4 engine was disabled and the wing was set on fire while control cables were severed. In spite of this, the pilots managed to stagger back as far as Houffalize, Belgium, where the B-24 finally succumbed. The various fates borne by the crew highlighted the unpredictable nature of combat flying. Sgt. Green (LWG) was in shock from leg wounds and Sgt. Robinson (RWG) assisted him to don a parachute pack before pulling the ripcord as he pushed Green out. Robinson was not so fortunate, having reportedly given up his own pack to Green or one of the other airmen. Sgt. Abe Sofferman (Eng.) got out and evaded capture along with Lt. Pinder until 1 April; they were then intercepted by German police and in the ensuing gun battle Sofferman was killed. Lt. Grono (CP) had partnered Lt. Griffith in the spectacular crash landing off the 18 November run to Jkeller, Norway. He ended up a POW, but any prospect of living out a full life was cruelly eclipsed when he developed tuberculosis and died the following August.

The 392BG lost the CBW's third crew when flak or fighter gunfire damaged the starboard wing and worse still ignited leaking fuel in the bomb bay. Lt. John Stukas, in charge of 42-7484/L-bar **Sally Ann** (579BS), cleared the way for a bail out that was effectively carried out by nine airmen, including himself, and a figure that included no less than six evaders. The two fatalities involved the navigator and bombardier, who came down with the B-24's remnants just south of Waterloo, Belgium, following the aircraft's mid-air disintegration.

Hethel accommodated the pair of 2CBW MIA casualties, whose crews suffered diametrically opposite fates. Capt. Stanislas J. Podolak's 42-40795/-X (565BS) was last seen SW of Frankfurt and steadily losing height, but his complete crew bailed out. Lt. Boyd L. Dout was maintaining a detailed diary of his combat tour commenced on 21 September, with today's mission marking his and the crew's near-halfway point on the road to permanent salvation. Whatever damage had been suffered left the B-24 trailing the homeward-bound formation as far as the North Sea. Then, with altitude down

This picture of a 453BG element was taken prior to 25 February 1944, when 42-52302E3: C **Ken-O-Kay II** (at top) was MIA. Lead 732BS machine is 42-52201/ L **Battle Package**, which lasted until 11 July, when it went down during a Munich mission. Nor was 42-64469/I (foreground) any luckier; she was blown in half on what was her 78th mission. The first two mentioned aircraft are H-10-FO airframes, with **El Flako** an H-10-CF example.

All USAAF units included one or more Chaplains in their establishment of personnel. Apart from administering to the airmen's spiritual needs, these non-combatants carried out a range of secular duties described in the book *Target Germany* as "extending from running errands for pipe tobacco to sitting beside a dying airman in a hospital plane." Capt. Leonard P. Edwards was the Protestant Chaplain who served with the 458BG over its period of operations at Horsham St. Faith.

to around 4,000ft, the pilot called up Channel D and was given a course of 305 degrees to steer. The Group's position at this time was 51.42N, 01.19E—less than 50 miles from the Essex coast—but all subsequent efforts by the ASR Service to locate 42-72833/ Y- (567BS) were in vain. The Grim Reaper had clearly scythed down all ten airmen.

The 392BG actually lost the bulk of two further crews in a tragically self-imposed manner. The mass of aircraft forming up in the restricted airspace over East Anglia invited the constant risk of collision. In this case 42-7669/, a 482BG PFF aircraft flown by Maj. Clyde T. Gray (Mission Command Pilot) and a 576BS crew led by Lt. James N. Taylor was orbiting at 14,000ft when it impacted with 42-100005/P+ **Old Man Boston Marclar** (577BS), in Lt. William F. Usry, Jr.'s hands. Gissing and Tivetshall, in Norfolk, was where both bombers impacted, along with all ten on Ursy's machine and seven out of eleven on board its companion Group machine. A kinder fate awaited all ten on the 446BG's 42-7578/N **Hula Wahine** (704BS) after it lost all four superchargers at "bombs away." Lt. Ernest W. Bruce held his ailing bomber aloft as it straggled homewards; RAF Detling, on the SE coast, was reached and a forced landing made that left all eleven Bungay airmen intact but rendered their B-24 liable to "write-off" treatment.

Brunswick provided the aerial battleground for the month's final "deep" assault on the 30th. While nearly all of the 777 crews mustered for the mission bombed, the B-17 Divisions' loads went down on the city center thanks to cloud blanketing the aviation plants forming the Primaries; the six groups forming the 2BD sub-force that were split between the three CBWs did no better, having to settle for Targets of Opportunity in Hannover. On the other hand, the 8FC pilots again bit firmly into the *Jagdwaffe's* ranks by downing 45 for the loss of four. Twenty crews were culled from the bomber stream, of which just two involved B-24 personnel. On the way over one engine was observed to be smoking on 42-7565 **Turd Bird** of the 703BS; Lt. Tom B. Connor, Jr. elected to turn back near Osnabrueck, but his luck in avoiding fighters and flak availed the crew naught, because the B-24 never arrived back at Tibenham, having presumably gone down in the North Sea. In contrast, the fickle finger of Fate blessed all on 42-7507 with life, although the four that did not evade capture would have to sweat out over one year's incarceration in a POW camp. Lt. H. J. Killian left the formation between Hannover and the Duemmersee (Lake Dummer, a prominent geographic feature and navigation checkpoint some 50 miles west of the city). The 328BS bomber then progressed as far as Amersfoort, SE of Amsterdam, where the pilots made a perfect crash landing north of the town.

January 1944 concluded with a reduced-size 2BD sortie against Pas de Calais *No Ball* sites at St. Pol/Siracourt. One of the four groups involved turned back after failing to catch up to its companion units, having been delayed during take-off by a blocked runway. The others delivered their loads on the Primary and returned without loss. However, one 93BG crew had never cleared the area around Hardwick. A failure to reduce the No. 2 engine revolutions was followed by this and No. 3 over-speeding, while manifold

A pair of waist gunners are manning their positions; picture gives a clear impression of the swivel frames supporting the machine guns. The hatches being opposite each other on the B-24 (as compared to the staggered waist windows on most B-17Gs) inevitably led to the duo knocking into each other during a running and/or protracted air battle with the *Jagdwaffe*.

pressure was also incapable of reduction via closing of the supercharger controls. Lt. Richard J. Pettit was advised to point 42-63970/J **Heavenly Daze** seawards after bailing out the crew; all on board having safely evacuated their errant 330BS bomber, it flew eastwards into imminent oblivion, but was apparently dispatched by fighter gunfire.

Sex Was Not Always fun!

During WWII, the American servicemen in Britain were regarded with great favor by many among the indigenous female population. However, one of the less welcome aspects of this international "liaison" was the general upsurge in venereal disease that caused U.S. authorities to issue stern-pitched reminders—both verbal and written—about the danger to health accruing from "catching a dose," as the condition was crudely if accurately described among the ranks.

The Hethel records make the following remarks in respect of one of its squadrons: "the Adjutant called for a squadron meeting. Proceedings were opened with a sex/morality lecture followed by the Adjutant, who read out the semi-annual resumé of the Articles of War. The squadron CO then thanked the personnel for their good work during his reign—and drew their attention to a 'few shortcomings....!'" What appears to have been a hard-headed/soft approach to the main subject of discussion may have well brought a wry smile on some individuals' faces. However, VD was no joke, given that the infection could result in serious consequences not only for the airmen's health, but also for those around them, who could easily be infected in turn by a casual attitude towards the sexual act. (One group recorded two Divisional "firsts": one was to do with military combat operations—and the other was the unit's corporate degree of VD cases incurred during social "combat"!)

All the Comforts of Home - Almost!

The ninth group to join the 2BD was the 458BG, whose crews traversed the Atlantic via the southern route to arrive early in February at Horsham St. Faith, located on the northern outskirts of Norwich. Of greater significance than the proximity of Norfolk's capital was the fact that the airfield was one of the RAF's prewar "permanent" structures. The general physical lot of most 8th AF personnel was not enhanced by the facilities at their assigned airfields. The majority of bases had been hastily created under the urgent demands of the conflict, with metal-sided T2 hangars and similar basic support structures the norm. Living quarters for combat and ground crews alike were equally basic, with the dreaded corrugated-iron Nissen Hut another regular feature; cold and damp with pot-bellied stoves as the prime and barely adequate heating source.

The number of groups who were assigned to an established prewar RAF airfield could be counted on one hand. These locations featured proper working facilities, while better still were the brick-constructed barracks equipped with steam heating. Drawing this "jackpot" in terms of individual and corporate comfort was a very welcome bonus in comparison to the other 2BD groups languishing in discomfort and doubtless envy in their "tin shack" facilities.

The fact that the Horsham-based airmen had arrived in the middle of an English winter only enhanced the bonus factor. The weather existing over the British Isles cast up a pattern system that was simply perverse in its lack of predictability. Hail stones in the summer, prolonged clear and warm spells in winter, heavy and persistent rain at any stage of the year—all these variables presented by Mother Nature caused the average G.I. to constantly grumble at his lot. In the words of one: "Why don't they just cut the barrage balloon cables and let the god-dammed island sink!"

The saving grace for the men in the 458BG's specific case meant that they could rest and sleep in comfort during this normally frigid season. Of course, once the ground crews in particular went out onto the open airfield spaces, they encountered the full effect of the local climate, in particular the almost permanently damp atmosphere that cut through even heavy clothing and literally chilled the hapless individuals to the bone. It speaks volumes for the support personnel's overall service that the bombers were largely kept in top-line condition despite the numbed fingers (and probably even some minds) that posed a severe challenge in carrying out often intricate mechanical and electrical equipment tasks.

Retrenchment

The first nineteen days of February 1944 provided little indication, at least for the 2BD, of a looming large-scale assault upon German industry, with Nazi aviation production located across the length and breadth of Germany and Austria (the latter country in the case of the Italian-based 15USAAF) as its epicenter. Indeed, even the 2nd and 3rd BDs were to be limited in striking regularly into the enemy hinterland. Missions were completed on eleven days within this timespan, with just three runs by the B-17 Divisions to Frankfurt (4th, 8th, and 11th) and one to Brunswick (10th) falling into the long-range category. The 2BD joined in on the first occasion only.

The initial pace of operations was almost constant between 2 and 6 February, although the 2BD's inaugural run was not cost-free, despite the targets being at St. Pol/Siracourt and Watten. Five groups participated and came back short two crews, with a third lost on return. Bombing was conducted through the heavy cloud cover using *G-H*, a special RAF device. The circumstances under which the two MIA crews were lost were never established, although the fact that two bodies from Wendling's 42-7570/GC: A-bar **Our Baby** subsequently washed ashore clearly suggests the B-24 ended up in the North Sea with Lt. James N. Stewart and the other six on his crew. A similar lack of detail for 42-7523's demise was recorded, but it appears that the sea also claimed the Tibenham-based bomber, since none of Lt. E. G. Metcalf's team were ever found.

Lt. James O. Bolin and crew (44BG) had come through the bomb run in 41-24282/Y **Ruthless**, a Ploesti veteran originally in Lt. Slough's regular charge. The group's return to base was minus the aircraft, but shortly after came the chilling news that it was now a charred wreck near Eastbourne, on the Channel coast. Eyewitnesses had seen the B-24 at roof-top height just before the impact, so it appears the pilots were seeking out an airfield amid the zero altitude cloud condition. All ten airmen lost their lives, although either one or two were extracted alive by rescuers but died later in hospital.

The next day was free of loss for the Division, although only 53 of the 193 briefed crews actually got airborne; the Primary at Wilhelmshaven was not reached by even the reduced formation, since the mission was abandoned over the Ijsselmeer region in the face of ever-mounting cloud formations. The first run to Frankfurt ended up with marshalling yards being targeted through heavy cloud. Only four of the assigned groups were on hand, the 14CBW having previously "aborted" through failure to link up with the bomber stream. The two Division losses seem to have both occurred on the return leg. Trier lies close to the border with Luxembourg, and it was around this region where flak put paid to 41-29133/ (328BS), although Lt. Kelly Ritter got all but one crewmember safely out prior to the Hardwick B-24's final crash at Daufenbach. The 446BG's 42-7542/ 707BS **Black Widow** held off from unconsciously devouring some of her 707BS crew until the group was fast heading towards the Channel coast around Amiens. Fighter passes had set the bomb bay on fire and probably killed at least one airman when bail out was finally ordered by Lt. M. W. Garber; only Lt. F. J. Hinton (CP) survived out of the officer complement, while two of the six Enlisted men also perished. **Black Widow** ended up a shattered wreck five miles SE of Albert.

The same loss scale was suffered 24 hours later, when 90 out of 101 Division crews dropped on Tours/Parcay/Mesley airfield, one of a clutch of similar locations spread in an arc SW of Paris. Although far from being a short-range mission in geographic terms, only two of the 452 crews gaining mission credit went down—both from the 2BD. The fifteen-strong Shipdham contingent was targeted by fighters whose fire excised part of one wing on 42-100181/Z **Star Valley**. The 68BS bomber instantly fell into a spinning motion that carried all but one of Lt. Carl A. Bohnisch's crew to their deaths 15 miles north of Blois, with Sgt. Warren E. Klein (WG) being the very lucky exception. A second bomber from the 67BS was fortunate to survive its battering and diverted into a Kent airfield. The 93BG was again in the firing line when 41-28626/P **Thunderbird** (328BS) failed to return. However, the reason why Lt. A B. Austin's crew bailed out to leave their aircraft to crash SSW of the target at Chateaudun remains unclear.

The rash of MIA losses up to now virtually ended for the Division in the course of the ensuing two weeks, although what were euphemistically named "operational casualties" were incurred. *No-Ball* sites were attacked without loss on the 6th and 8th, and the same applied to an attack on Gilze-Rijen airfield, Holland. The 453BG incurred its first loss (6th) at the runway end on what was its second mission. **Little Agnes** (42-52178/) was in Lt. Alfred A. Voskian's charge, and what transpired is recalled by him, after spending almost a week unconscious in a hospital bed, having suffered serious burns and a fractured spine, the sole other survivor being T/Sgt. Archie J. Bloodworth (Eng.):

> We started our take-off run and got off the ground in normal fashion. However, after gaining an altitude of about 75-80 feet we stopped climbing and began to settle. I do not remember hitting the ground, but thought my wheels should have been halfway up when we did hit. Major Sears, our squadron commander, confirmed that when he visited me in the hospital. We

> had ten 500-lb bombs on board. He told me that after we hit the ground we were sliding well, until we reached the end of the runway, where there was a ditch about ten feet wide and six feet deep. At that point the ship broke up; one bomb exploded and one bomb broke in half, and the powder was burning. They salvaged the other eight bombs.

Four further *No-Ball* sites were assaulted on the 11th, 12th, 13th, and 15th, but the 93BG suffered its latest MIA statistic on the former occasion when heading for Siracourt. A flak shell impacted with the rear fuselage on 42-63978/E (330BS) and excised it completely. The dramatic aerodynamic imbalance pitched the B-24 onto its nose and gave little or no chance for Capt. Omar A. Turner and crew to bail out; one crewmember was reported impacting with another B-24's wing trailing edge, which probably killed him even if he was still alive at this point. The aircraft descended just south of Dieppe, which was a heavily defended seaport.

"Non-Operational" Casualties

It was hard enough to bear any loss of a bomber and/or crew to flak or fighters, but death could and did strike regularly other than in these sadly anticipated and realized circumstances. Take-off and landing crashes, whether on a mission or for practice, that resulted in injury or death left as bitter a taste in the mouths of colleagues as any MIA incident, especially since hostile intervention had not brought about such casualties. In the period between the 9th and 15th, where just a single crew had gone MIA, the 2BD suffered three fatal incidents, with six further operational crash landings recorded. The formerly mentioned incidents all occurred on the 10th, with two of these involving 448BG crews. The first affected crew came from Hethel, however. Icing conditions were in evidence as a prime hazard to what were often grossly over-laden bombers. The 565BS' 42-100046/Y **Patsy Ann**, flown by Lt. Herbert Loebs, was climbing up around 11,000ft close to Norwich when it went out of control; none of the eleven airmen survived its lethal descent at Taverham, NW of the city, but it is likely that icing of the flight surfaces could have finally stalled out the machine. (Eyewitnesses asserted that the B-24 had been heading for the village when a measure of control was re-established around 1,000ft and the pilots then appeared to be seeking out a crash landing site when the bomber suddenly exploded.)

One of the Seething losses occurred close to Tibenham and was rumored to have been initiated by a collision with a P-47, although no confirmation was ever made. Suffice to record that only one officer and two gunners from Lt. R. C. Ayerst's crew on 42-52132/ **The Boomerang** escaped the Grim Reaper's grasp. The pilots had been directing the 712BS bomber in an attempt to pinpoint the group formation when it suddenly dipped down sharply before being pulled back into level flight—too abruptly as it happened, because the aerodynamic forces caused the tail section to snap off; the B-24 promptly stalled and entered a terminal spin. Sgt. Ed Schroeder (WG) had been pinned down by centrifugal forces that suddenly released their lethal hold, whereupon the gunner was pitched backwards and out through the now-absent rear section. Even then, he was fortunate to drift just inshore from the water stretch over which he initially pulled his ripcord.

Around the same time, 42-52115/ **Hells Belle** (714BS) in Lt. Edward A. Markiewicz's charge was up at 18,000ft when the first intimation of trouble arose with the airframe beginning to shake. Lt. Richard Nardi (B) later recalled:

> I clipped on my parachute pack and disconnected all leads. Lt. Harry J. Oppelt (N) seemed to be frozen, so I thought to open the emergency exit and push him out. As I went under his table the plane must have flipped over and I found myself in the access tunnel. I managed to get back to the emergency handle, but the doors remained in position. I then thought to exit via the bomb bay, but halfway along the tunnel a blast of flame greeted me. The plane must have flipped again, as I wound up on my back, tangled in wires. I freed myself, and having ended up at the emergency exit noted the open doors. My chute harness got caught up to leave me hanging head first. I was initially unable to get free and nearly gave up, but a final effort was successful and I got clear.

The other survivor, Sgt, James S. Whyte (WG), said he called the navigator for the altitude and immediately after the aircraft vibrated violently, throwing the men about. Then:

> We put on our chutes, expecting to use them. After this vibrating we seemed to fall off on the right wing, straighten out, and go into a power dive with engines screaming. When we fell off, I was thrown against the fuselage side and believe this is how I dislocated my shoulder. The pilots appeared to be trying to pull the plane out of the dive, but in vain. Then the right wing broke off and immediately after an orange sheet of flame that struck my face blew the door to the bomb bay open. This is all I recall until regaining consciousness in mid-air; I believe I was blown out, because I did not jump. I pulled the ripcord and while floating down saw pieces of the plane falling past me. I lost consciousness before landing.

Nardi later stated in a letter: "The shock of the loss of those wonderful companions in our crew, I cannot get out of my mind... Their screams still echo in my ears." The area around Badingham, Suffolk, accommodated the wreckage that included a complete fin; this item lay hooked into a hedge until 1968, when it was removed to an aviation museum.

The PX staff at Hethel used to play a rather underhand trick upon the combat crews. Whenever a particularly desirous range of products were received they would post a sign "Closed for inventory"—only for the facility to open again when the fliers were aloft on a mission! (The staff's view was probably that their airborne colleagues gained more than their share of "perks" and the foregoing action was a way of balancing the situation for the ground support staff.)

Mother Nature had been in her most maligned mood, and a mere five out of the 31 airmen involved had survived this crop of incidents that furthermore happened without any intervention on the part of the enemy. A fourth crew flying out of Old Buckenham was immeasurably more favored after failing to find their group and suffering a radio compass failure that in turn prevented the pilots from homing in on the Buncher. Once down out of the broken cloud layers and scattered snow showers, Lt. Robert B. Bickerstaff started looking for a landing site. The airfield he found was under construction, so an alternative approach was made to a field at Hilgay, Norfolk. The "wheels down" landing was smooth, but the soft nature of the soil combined with heavy braking caused the nose wheel to collapse. Some of the ten airmen were injured but not seriously, whereas 41-29254/(734BS) was later deemed too damaged to be repaired.

Mother Nature Relents

The onset of a period of high pressure out in the Atlantic and spreading eastwards was the signal for the USSTAF authorities to initiate a sustained campaign against the German aero industry. The hoped-for results from this would be a sharp reduction in the provision of fighters for the *Jagdwaffe*. To this would hopefully be added an equal reduction in available pilot manpower, particularly among the top echelons of commanding staff from *Staffelkapitaen* to *Kommodore*; many of these were veteran combat fliers and *Experten* whose loss at the hands of the 8FC units would be crucial to the Allies achieving ultimate domination of the skies above *Festung Europa*. As the evening of 19 February was drawing in, the combat crews who had been ground-bound for the previous 96 hours had no way of knowing that the battle lines had been drawn ready for the morn—Operation *Argument* was on!

Jagdwaffe Tactical Changes

In early 1944, the *Reichsverteidigung* (Home Defense) structure had been amended in recognition of the burgeoning power of the 8AF, both in terms of the bombers' potential striking ability and the parallel threat posed by their escorts. The deployment of fighters in Holland and Belgium (*Jagddivision 3*) with which to mount early challenges was reduced in order to have the redundant units bolster up the resources based further within the national hinterland.

The concept of the *Gefechtsverband*, consisting of anything up to four *Gruppen* under a single leader, was also gaining favor by February; these sub-forces were primarily formed from single-engine fighters. However, the use of the twin-engine Bf110G and Me410 was still a factor in *Reichsverteidigung* operations, although their heightened vulnerability to the American escorts was recognized by their being granted escort cover. (ZG26's "twins," for example, were linked with I/JG11 in the *Gefechtsverband* operating under *Jagddivision* 1 control.)

The perceived intention of meeting mass with mass was fine in theory but far from perfect. First, these sub-forces took time to assemble, and worse still, were liable to suffer being "bounced," with the attendant effect of dispersing or negating any effort at bringing heavy punishment to bear upon the *Big Friends*. In addition, the geographic scale of potential cover was simply too great for the available number of such sub-forces on hand. However, the "heavies" would suffer on the occasions when their currently unescorted portion of the bomber stream were unfortunate enough to be intercepted by a *Gefechtsverband*.

Chapter Nine

Operation "Argument"

Background

The "Point Blank" Agreement listing the target category priorities for the Anglo-American strategic bomber forces had been created in May 1943, with the first and third categories relating to the *Jagdwaffe* and the aircraft production industry, respectively. However, it was the following November when a more specific plan was formulated that concentrated on aircraft production, with those plants turning out fighters as its kernel. The timing would appear to be rather belated, as well as ironic, since the VIII BC "heavies" had just been placed firmly on the operational back foot with their current inability to penetrate into the Nazi hinterland without suffering unacceptable losses. With one or two exceptions—Bremen being the most obvious source—the bulk of fighter production was adjudged to be located well within Germany and consequently immune from regular assault. A swathe of locations lay in a huge geographic triangle roughly bounded by Hannover, Berlin, and Leipzig, but factories could be found in other regions.

The basic intention was not only to bomb the plants, but also to do so in a concentrated period of time lasting upwards of one week. To the obvious pressure of even attaining the targets was the question of the 8AF being capable of doing so with sufficient logistical strength, both technical and human. An even more insidious potential blockage to the scheme was the weather conditions, which were perverse at most times of the year, let alone during the winter months. The first seven weeks of 1944 had reinforced this ever-frustrating operational factor. Then, as the weekend of 19/20 February came to hand, Mother Nature appeared to be making an unbelievably accommodating gesture. The Meteorology staff had noted a high-pressure system over the Atlantic with an eastward-flowing pattern that held the necessary operational conditions. Were Gen. Spaatz and his immediate circle of Field Commanders going to grasp the nettle and launch Operation *Argument*?

"Let's Go!"

Although the skies over central Europe were confirmed as clear on Sunday the 20th, the weather conditions greeting the crews as they rose, breakfasted, and went for briefing were depressingly familiar. Lowering cloud and scattered snow showers dominated the East Anglian region, providing potentially dangerous conditions in which to even attempt Assembly. The overall force of bombers numbered 1,003, split between 314 (3BD) and 869 (1st and 2nd BDs). The first-listed force was to head northeast towards the Danish/German border, then east to attack three plants on the Baltic coast; the other two

Divisions would assume a course into central Germany, but would divide into sub-forces assigned to at least six locations; reassembly for withdrawal would be commenced SE of Kassel before proceeding home south of the Ruehr. The protracted distances to be flown and the fact that the 3BD force would be dependent upon the defenses directing their attention towards its much larger contemporary—no escorts being assigned for any cover—had led to the USAAF authorities anticipating a horrendous loss rate extending to *Black Thursday* proportions.

Several hours later, as the shadows lengthened over eastern England, the burgeoning roar of the returning formations filled the air. When the last aircraft was down and parked a head count elicited an astonishing but gratifying result; a mere 21 B-17s and B-24s were missing, along with two fighters; the latter had been part of a 835-strong force that had added a further 61 *Jagdwaffe* "scalps" to its belt! Operation *Argument* was off to a solid start.

2BD Fortunes

The B-24 crews were briefed to attack three targets at Brunswick, Halberstadt, and Gotha. All eight groups were sent and put up a total of 272 bombers, with the great majority striking either a Primary or a Target of Opportunity; Halberstadt remained unblemished, however, as cloud intervened and the assigned PFF aircraft suffered technical failure of its equipment.

The 2CBW was assigned to attack a plant at Brunswick as the Division swung in from the NW; then, after "bombs away," it would arc round to the SW for the link-up SE of Kassel for all Main force elements. Six of the eight Division losses would come from the Wing, as it was intercepted by fighters that gained unencumbered assess thanks to a gap in escort cover. The first was during target approach, when 42-7569 (701BS) was culled from Tibenham's complement. The B-24's end must have been violent, since the wreckage was recorded as widely scattered north of Endmissen, along with the nine bodies of Lt. Stanley R. Neal's crew.

A clutch of four bombers were taken down between the target and approach to the link-up point. The 389BG crew led by Lt. Robert J. Wozniak, flying in 42-100352/I **Swamp Angel** (565BS), had barely cleared the target when the latest fighter pass by a *Schwarm* (four-plane formation) from a 2 o'clock angle left the bomber floundering; it exploded shortly after and the remains fell at Sillium, eighteen miles SW of the target. Sgt. W. M. Anderson (TG) was killed at his post, but the other nine airmen managed to bail out. Two aircraft were lost almost immediately after. The second Hethel loss involved Lt. Warren R. Blakeman's crew in 42-100085/ (564BS), after the bomber was observed peeling off with a large hole in the port wing. Eight parachutes blossomed out before the bomber disintegrated, but only seven crewmembers survived, the pilot being one of the three fatalities.

Lamspringe/Heuhof was **Angel's** crash site area, just north of Bad Gandersheim, and Greene, southwest of the latter town, was where 42-64433 (700BS) descended, the latest fighter victim. This time round the ten-man team led by Lt. Alvin L. Owen, Jr. successfully cleared their doomed 445BG charge. The fourth loss occurred NW of Goettingen, when 42-52139 (734BS) became the sole Old Buckenham casualty. The bomber had suffered strikes that set the forward and center fuselage on fire, as well as killing two of the four crewmembers on Lt. Albert L. Lane, Jr.'s crew.

The martyrdom of the third 445BG aircraft to go down was seemingly extended over a much longer time period. The Wing had turned west after reaching the link-up point and was almost 100 miles further into the homeward leg was rapidly approaching the Rhine north of Koblenz when a fighter attack caused 42-64439 (703BS) to explode and fall at Sessenhausen, taking Lt. Robert NQ Kiser and eight other crewmembers to their deaths.

14 CBW

The precise target for the 14CBW on the first day of *Argument* seems unclear. The sole other listed Primary for the 2BD is Gotha, around 100 miles SE of Brunswick and soon to be the epicenter for a major Division defeat. As it was, the PFF equipment on the Lead and Deputy aircraft failed and recourse was to seek out Targets of Opportunity; these evolved as the AGO plant at Oschersleben, as well as an unstated facility to the NW at Helmstedt (itself a road/rail "flash point" in postwar years, as it was a major crossing point into Communist East Germany).

The Wing had completed its bomb runs and was heading home south of Kassel when 42-100373/Y, bearing a first-mission crew, finally gave up; flak had previously struck the 68BS bomber, knocking out an engine and starting a fire in the tail. Lagging ever further behind, it was finally given the *coup de grace* by fighters and tumbled to destruction north of Marburg/Lahn. Lt. Fred H. Rawson jumped clear, but only after Lt. James R. Lewis (CP) helped him to release his flak suit covering his pack hooks. At least five others bailed out, but Lt. William P. Johnson (N) suffered a failed canopy. Having had his pack destroyed and being unable to find a spare, Sgt. Wapensky's (TG) last desperate gambit at surviving by clinging to Lt. Lewis's harness failed as the opening shock of the canopy shook him off, whereupon he fell to his death.

The 66BS' 42-64166/A **Big Fat Butterfly** was similarly assailed by fighters just after "bombs away" and was unable to maintain the briefed 18,000-ft altitude. It nevertheless was kept on course for some time before being encountered by Hptm. Lange, commanding 6/JG26 near Charleroi, Belgium; the straggling B-24 was summarily dispatched, along with Lt. Donald R. Decker's entire crew. (Lange's claim to this aircraft is not confirmed, according to a detailed history of the *Geschwader*.)

Two Group crews had been lost, but a third B-24 failed at Holbrook, near Ipswich, fortunately without any

M/Sgt. Dick Williamson (left) and S/Sgt. Larry Billemay delve into the innards of the No. 3 engine on **Flak Alley**; the late autumn or early winter weather is casting up a clear if perhaps chilly condition. On 24 February, they would wait in vain for their 66BS (41-24225/T) bomber to return from Gotha, one of two Group casualties.

Three 448BG bombers seen over a virtually solid undercast include two B-24Js and a single B-24-H-5-FO **Bag O Bolts** in the foreground. The latter lived up to its title after suffering over 400 flak- and fighter-inflicted holes during the second "Big Week" mission (21 February 1944). Lt. Harvey E. Broxton brought his charge and eight out of the nine crew back to Seething, but the B-24 was deemed fit only for salvage.

fatalities among Lt. David R. Talbot's team. All fuel reserves ran out on 42-100285/J (66BS) and the attempted crash landing ended disastrously—at least for the aircraft—when it struck some trees and an electricity pylon that thoroughly wrecked the airframe; two airmen were seriously injured but ultimately recovered. Further south at RAF Manston, the Grim Reaper collected another tithe of ten, this time from Wendling. Lt. John B. Payton was bringing his shot-up 42-7529/D **Coral Princess** in on its landing approach when the 579BS machine was seen to explode. Two further Group bombers were "written off" on return, albeit with no recorded fatalities from among Lts. C. E. Jones's and R. K. Goodwin's crews; the B-24s in question were 42-99938 **Dixie Thumper** (576BS) and 42-100340/Q (578BS), respectively.

Survivor's Reaction

Lt. Harold Gnong was Lt. Wozniak's bombardier on the 389BG's **Swamp Angel**, whose crew were on their 19th and final mission. Having delivered the B-24's bomb load, he climbed into the nose turret as the formation headed homeward from the Rally Point so that he could better observe the results of the strike and therefore deliver a more comprehensive debriefing report. What then transpired provides a good picture of a combat crewman's reactions to imminent disaster:

> Straining my eyes through the sun glare and icy perspiration, I was startled by the sight of Fw190s diving on us from ahead and above; right now, our P-38 escorts were absent, leaving us in a vulnerable position. With no time to yell a warning, I pressed the gun triggers and directed a stream of fire right at the Lead fighter, whose shells were shredding our starboard wing's leading edge. I swung the turret as he shot by, seemingly unscathed, and I lined up on the next Fw190, but before I could pick him up his shells smashed into us, shattering No. 3 into a thousand fragments and setting it ablaze. We tilted down and in an instant, from thoughts of relief at heading home, we were suddenly faced with escape from the deadly spiral into which our bomber had fallen!
>
> I ripped off my oxygen mask and intercom lead before throwing myself violently backwards; Lt. Wyman quickly handed my chest pack over before opening the escape hatch doors and effortlessly bailing out. No. 4's "runaway" propeller was screeching like a banshee, and as we plunged ever faster I was forced to clamber up towards the

Col. James Isbell took over command of the 458BG from Col. Hardy while still stateside at Tonopah, UT. The tall, rangy officer was a West Point graduate and became the Academy's heavyweight boxing champion. He led the Group until early 1945 and proved to be a firm-minded but amenable leader at Horsham St. Faith.

B/Gen. Walter R Peck assumed command of the 96CBW, of which the 458BG was a component. His physical build caused Col. Isbell to comment: "He was the only man who could pat me on the back and knock me down!" He suffered the personal loss of a son who survived his combat tour, only to be killed in a Stateside flying accident.

hatch. When nearly there, a violent explosion tossed me back and I was jammed between the bombsight and turret base.

My mind was temporarily fuddled and I floated in a euphoric state, just like a boxer who has taken a left hook. Fortunately, a stronger sense of self preservation overcame this mind set and almost numbly I again scrambled upward to the open hatch, through which the sky was beckoning temptingly. I grasped the edges and heaved myself into open space.

No training had been imparted to us on how a parachute functioned or what was the procedure when faced with such an emergency as bailing out. Therefore, my initial reaction after the parachute deployed was surprise at seeing the red metal ripcord still clutched in my hand, followed by pure gratification on looking up and seeing the gorgeous white nylon canopy under which one battered Bombardier, now totally disarmed and helpless, was wholly dependent for his survival!

The startling and almost shocking contrast between the feral noise and images of combat and the eerie silence enveloping his descent would become a permanent memory of that day's traumatic events for Harold. His sense of tranquillity was momentarily threatened when an Fw190 loomed up to initiate what he took to be a firing pass, but which evolved into a wing-waggling salute as the fighter shot by. He finally landed in two feet of snow and bare minutes later was apprehended by a Wehrmacht squad, and in his words, "several less than hospitable natives." Fifteen months incarceration at *Stalag-Luft I*, Barth now awaited him.

Piling it On

The second of *Big Week's* five-mission tally went out bare hours after the weary survivors of the first assault had crawled into their beds. This time round airfields provided the Primaries, with Achmer and Lippstadt assigned to the B-24

This is a pleasing close-up of **Satan's Mate**, a B-24J-95-CO belonging to the 753BS, as confirmed by the J4 code letters, a practice finally if belatedly adopted by most 2BD Groups in March/April 1944. The 458BG bomber was lost on 11 July 1944, along with five members on Lt. J. Jones, Jr.'s crew when it crashed on Walcheren island, in the Scheldt estuary.

This view of two Wendling B-24s is believed to have been taken over the Continental coastline, with few geographic features to identity the exact location. **Rose of Juarez** (right) is a B-24H-1-FO/ 42-7469 with **Short Snorter** 42-99990/H (579BS) behind; **Rose** was salvaged on 10 April, while its companion soldiered on until it crashed on 2 August.

groups. In the event, the majority of locations bombed constituted Targets of Opportunity thanks to adverse weather conditions. Of the 244 briefed and dispatched 2BD crews, a mere handful delivered onto Achmer, with three airfields and the town of Lingen absorbing over 200 bomb loads between them. Overall MIA losses were very low at seven, including three B-24s (two from Seething).

The 20CBW was engaged in a second bomb run upon either Achmer or Hesepe while under steady fighter and flak attack. The ground gunners struck home on 42-100178 **Carry Me Back**, causing the 715BS machine to falter and begin to drop away. Nine airmen jumped, but Lt. W. V. Helvey (CP) suffered parachute failure, leaving their bomber to crash near Westerkappeln with Sgt. Nickerson (WG) slumped dead at his post. Several Fw190s then delivered a concerted barrage of gunfire on 42-7768/**The Proud Wanderlost** (714BS), killing Sgt. R. H. Yarnell (BT); Lt. C. W. Cline called for a bail out to which all nine survivors responded, but tragically the ninth, Sgt. Ira C. Lloyd, was reportedly found minus his parachute pack. The B-24 finally plunged into the ground at Tecklenburg. Elsewhere, the 14CBW surrendered 42-64435, a 579BS bomber from Wendling, over the North Sea. Lt. Herman H. Miller turned for home over Holland after fire developed in No. 3 engine; the two escorting P-38 pilots later reported that the bomber exploded, an action that none of its ten occupants survived.

Survival Against the Odds

There should have been a third crew failing to regain Seething this day. Lt. Harvey E. Broxton's 42-7764/B **Bag O' Bolts** was flying within the High squadron when a flak burst disabled No. 3 engine, leaving a "windmilling" propeller that inevitably caused the aircraft to fall behind. Barely had "bombs away" been signalled when a bunch of Fw190s latched onto the straggler. Broxton and Lt. Dwight W. Cowell (CP) desperately maneuvered their lumbering charge as best they could as they dived for cloud cover; Sgt. Henry Kubinsky (G) apparently thought all was lost, since he bailed out, but instead of a POW camp, he encountered only death after descending into a river in Holland.

The cloud bank soon dispersed and further gunfire knocked out No. 4 engine, as well as thoroughly riddling the airframe, leaving several crewmembers wounded, with Sgt. Robert E. Hudson (LWG) the most seriously affected. Then hydraulic fluid in the bomb bay ignited, but Lt. C. E. Sharp (B) managed to extinguish the flames. By now low down over Holland, the end seemed in sight, especially as the fighters were still milling around and coastal flak added its weight of punishment. Still, the crippled B-24 was held aloft with both functioning engines pushed to maximum power and both pilots pushing the rudder pedals in order to maintain level flight against the asymmetric power imbalance.

The Dutch coast finally cleared and the bomber was held on course for home, a goal that was ultimately achieved. The landing gear had to be hand-cranked down and a final desperate lunge upon the rudder pedals made in order to maintain a straight landing approach. Without hydraulic fluid the brakes were "out" and the 715BS B-24H over-shot the runway. Later examination revealed some 400 holes, a severed right rudder cable, and an unexploded cannon shell in a fuel tank. DFCs were awarded to the pilot and two others; in sad contrast, Sgt. Hudson fought an extended but ultimately vain battle against death, succumbing the following 10 January.

The Accelerating Cost

To date, *Argument* had largely belied the 8AF senior staff's fears regarding the likely casualty rate in pursuing this specific campaign. Not only had the overall MIA rate been a mere 37 crews out of 1,642 granted mission "credit," but the 8FC's pilots had added to the *Jagdwaffe's* woes by downing close to 100 of its fighter strength at minimal cost to their own numbers. However, the Germans were far from beaten, as events over the ensuing 72 hours would reveal. The third day's sustained effort witnessed a sharp upsurge in bomber losses, with 41 crews declared MIA out of 799 dispatched, while roughly 30% actually bombed. (The 3BD's 333 crews never entered enemy airspace due to problems in forming up.)

On the other hand, the 2BD was regarded as being too far inside Europe to merit being recalled; its seven-unit-strong force of 177 crews sought out Targets of Opportunity that were believed to be on the German side of its border with Holland, but unfortunately resolved themselves as four Dutch sources, with heavy civilian casualties at Nijmegen in particular. The 448BG records state that on further investigation, its 36-strong formation was deemed to have released its incendiary loads over Enschede.

The briefed target for the 44BG was Gotha, but it was not reached, in addition to which two crews never returned. Lt. Mercer (67BS) was leading one element, but on emerging from a solid cloud bank he found himself alone. One wingman was Lt. Earl A. Evans flying 42-72865/F **F For Freddie**. The 67BS B-24D was taken out by fighters and came down near Wesel, although all but one of the ten airmen bailed out into captivity; Lt. Harold E. Flaugh (B) was the unlucky exception. The other crew, headed by Lt. George E. Fish in 42-100402/M, remain missing to this day, having presumably come down in the ever-remorseless North Sea along with their 67BS bomber. Sharing their fate was Lt. R. M. Ingram's team on board Old Buckenham's 41-28615 /733BS. Fighters brought the bomber down into Holland's southwestern estuarial waters, where it reportedly exploded on contact.

Downturn in Fortune

The first three missions of *Argument* had left the Division relatively unscathed regarding losses, but this cozy situation would sharply deteriorate on the 24th, with the 2CBW particularly stricken. Gotha was the briefed target, which was duly hammered by nearly 80% of the actual attacking force; a further 44 crews headed towards and bombed Eisenach, mistakenly acknowledged as the Primary. Several hours later, no less than 33 crews were missing from among the ranks of the 213 granted mission "credit." The 2CBW's share was nearly two-thirds of this melancholy statistic, with the 445BG landing back thirteen short to add to the 389BG's tithe of seven.

The 389BG was selected as Lead both for the CBW and the Division, which placed an extra responsibility upon the Lead crew in ensuring an accurate strike. During the bomb run, a potential disaster was largely averted after the bombardier in question became anoxic and accidentally tripped the bomb release switch. Fortunately, only the Lead squadron acted upon the error; the remaining elements held on for the Bf110 production plant and made a solid strike that was basically repeated by the following groups.

The Luftwaffe was still a potent force, despite the depredations being wrought upon its strength, as were the flak defenses, a fact the survivors on seven Hethel crews would have attested to this day. Two crews appears to have been culled around Gotha, one being Lt. Donald R. Nowalk's on board 42-109828/M+ (566BS). Loss of power on No. 4 had caused the bomber to lag, but it was closing the gap when fighters intervened to knock out No. 2; the fatally damaged machine was abandoned by

The waist gun windows on both the B-17 and B-24 designs up to early 1944 were wide open to the elements. The sub-zero atmosphere, whose extreme discomfort was added to by the high-speed slipstream from the aircraft's forward motion, made the gunner's life a constant misery as they operated their single machine guns. The flexible hatch cover was retained above the aperture when the guns were deployed.

This is a detailed view of the forward nose area on Shipdham's Assembly ship; she is **Lemon Drop** (B24D-1-CO/41-23699), an "original" 68BS combat veteran. Black/yellow vertical stripes adorn her fuselage and upper wings; her impressive mission and "kills" tally are retained along with the Group "Flying 8-Ball" insignia.

This Group of B-24s based at Wendling are probably part of a formation returning from a mission. However, normal altitude when entering an airfield circuit was usually noticeably higher at around 1,000ft, to allow for a cleaner break up and extended landing approach.

The inevitable ravages of combat operations are evident on most of this sub-formation of 446BG bombers. B-24H-1-FO/42-7505/H **Old Faithful** (706BS) in the foreground flew on until salvaged on 26 August. **Lazy Lou** (top right) is B-24H-1-FO/42-7609/D (also 706BS), which lasted nearly four months longer (18 December) before following **Old Faithful** into the "salvage" register.

six of the eleven crewmembers, with Brotterode, SW of Gotha, being where it crashed. Lt. Alton C. Belanger's 42-73504/ Y- came down not far distant at Finsterbergen. Lt. Keeffe (CP), on another crew, reported that as it banked left fire took hold in the waist while the bomb bay doors were blown off. One of two crewmembers bailing out was seen with his parachute ablaze, followed shortly after by the rear fuselage snapping off; this violent aerodynamic failure ended with but two out of the eleven airmen managing to end up as POWs.

The 567BS was destined to lose three further crews, beginning with 42-100338/W-, flown by Lt. Claud E. White. Fire took hold within the fuselage and then the B-24 went into a flat spin; three officers and two Enlisted men jumped, but Sgt. Mario Pellegrino (NG) died after landing, having suffered head injuries during the fighter attacks. The other two aircraft descended around Bad Salzungen. Stadtlengfeld was the crash site for 42-40733/Y- **Tourney**, out of which all but Lt. James O. McMullin, Jr. (P) escaped by parachute, while Dermbach, to the southwest, absorbed the remains of 42-40619, along with three crewmembers off Lt. Freelin A. Carlton's ten-man team. Mansbach, several miles west of these crash sites, was where 42-40807 (566BS) spun and tumbled to its destruction, taking Lt. John E. Gold and five of the remaining nine crewmembers to their deaths.

The final group loss did not occur until the formation was over Belgium on the homeward leg. Lt. Marion E. Brown in 42-100280 **Little Audrey** (565BS**)** had experienced technical problems before fighters engaged their prey, which had finally drifted out of the ranks. Strikes shot away the starboard wing flap, disabled the hydraulic system, and riddled the fuselage, but a descending course for home was held until near Liege. At this stage, a bail out was ordered to which all ten airmen responded; in addition, Brown received a bonus in evading capture and finally regaining his freedom during September.

Tibenham's Nightmare

The punishment inflicted upon the 389BG was severe enough, but as it transpired, it was barely half that suffered by its fellow unit, the 445BG. Nor was the current beating destined to be the heaviest borne by Tibenham's fliers; the following 27 September would witness the worst-ever percentage loss by any group within the 8AF's ranks during WWII.

The thirteen losses were spread between all four squadrons, with the 701st and 702nd BS the worst affected (four each): three from the 703rd BS and a pair from the 700BS. The earliest casualty seems to have been 42-7567/: **Black Dog** (700BS), which progressed no further than Baalder, in Holland; the fighter attacks that brought it down resulted in five of Lt. Robert A. Blomberg's (KIA) crew losing their lives. The second bomber down was probably 42-64440/701BS, which was downed by fighters at Drohne, south of Diepholz and close to the Duemmersee (Lake Duemmer), a prominent navigation landmark. Two-thirds of Lt. William J. Desmond's (KIA) crew failed to get out before the final impact. A third loss on the inward route affected Lt. Sidney D. Swanson's 41-29130/ (also 701BS) as the group was skirting SE of Osnabrueck. Strikes set the bomb bay on fire and the B-24 peeled off and down to impact near Vlotho. Half the ten-man crew, including the pilot, failed to survive as POWs.

Continuing Torment

The attrition rate seems to have commenced its grim acceleration for the 445BG on the return leg, with the second 700BS crew led by Lt. Philip M. Costain to be lost (41-29149/IS:)

recorded as exploding and crashing at Brotterode, close to where one of Hethel's bombers had crashed. Only T/Sgt. Elroy R. Enlow (Eng.) was granted the gift of life from among the ten souls on board.

Bad Salzungen formed the epicenter for two losses. First, 42-100312/ (703BS) exploded violently under the impact of fighter gunfire, killing all but two of Lt. David P. Skjeie's crew, one of whom—Sgt. Dunster (ROG)—was miraculously blown clear. The wreckage fell near Leimbach. Then a third 701BS aircraft— 42-52364/, in Lt. John S. Constable's charge—was culled to fall at Steinach, leaving Sgt. Lawrence C. Nichols (WG) as the sole survivor.

At this stage the 702BS was still intact, but the first split in its ranks was already developing, with 42-7579/:, flown by Lt. Alfred J. Looney, down to half power shortly after bombing. Course for home was doggedly held, but fire finally caught hold as the group was near Herborn; the pilot was one of three fatalities among the nine-man crew following their B-24's terminal descent at Driedorf.

Herbstein, further east and close to Fulda, formed the final resting place for the other two 703BS losses. Lt. John J. Suitch did not survive the explosion and splitting in two of 42-100374/:, but six of the other eight nevertheless got out alive. The equally flak- and fighter-battered 42-100335/: had staggered on from the target but finally expired, although not before eight on Lt. Peter T. Abell's crew jumped clear.

The *Jagdwaffe* pilots kept up a steady pressure on the Division as it tracked homeward, with a further three Tibenham crews downed between Bad Hersfeld and the Giessen/Wetzlar area. The final 701BS crew taken down belonged to Lt. Fred Malen, piloting 42-7515/. A rocket that demolished one rudder also killed Sgt. William H. Steinmann (TG), but the other eight cleared their aircraft prior to its crash SE of Bad Hersfeld. The other two crews belonged to the 702BS: B-24H/42-7517/, in Lt. Thomas Gray's hands, came down west of Giessen, its terminal fate being shared by all nine airmen on board. Five of the nine on 42-7566/, flown by Lt. William E. Shurtz (KIA), were also lost following the bomber's crash NW of Wetzlar.

There is confusion regarding the thirteenth Group casualty's demise. The crash site of Unterreit and time of loss (1400) has been ascribed to German records. However, the time detail is exactly the same as the two foregoing losses that occurred upwards of 100 miles west of Erfurt! Unterreit is one of two such towns, both being close to Munich and over 200 miles SE of the target. It is not unfeasible that Capt. Henry G. Bussing had directed his B-24 in the direction of Switzerland; in the event, he and eight of the ten-man crew survived as POWs. If this is a correct assumption, it could explain the time discrepancy stated above.

14CBW Travails

The brutal punishment inflicted upon the 2CBW was to be reflected to a lesser, albeit still painful extent within the following 14th and 20th CBW formations. The 392BG contingent was leading the 14CBW and Lt./Col. Johnson was Command Pilot. Noting that the 2CBW up ahead was diverging from the correct course to the target, Johnson held the correct 85-degree heading to ensure that both his and the following 20CBW would deliver their loads on the Primary. The *Jagdwaffe* had been assailing the Wing since crossing into Holland, but the first Wendling casualty was only suffered as the IP was being left behind. Lt. Thomas J. Cox's 42-100102/N **Texas Refugees** (576BS) was taken out and finally impacted at Ruhla, south of Eisenach, leaving six survivors out of ten; two engines had been disabled and fire had caught hold before the bail out signal was given.

Next down was believed to be Lt. John V. Johnson's 42-7658/O **Poco Loco** (577BS). The pilot had probably exposed his aircraft to extra attention, as he was reportedly taking evasive action against flak during the bomb run and found himself marginally out of formation. The straggling B-24 was set upon by several fighters whose strikes set the center fuselage on fire. All too soon the crew had little option but to jump, leaving the pilot, Lt. Daniel P. Kelleher (CP), and Sgt. John P. Right (ROG) dead at their posts. The fourth fatality was probably caused by a failed parachute, although Sgt. Mitchell A. Walla's body was never found to confirm his exact fate; Woltershausen, scant miles SW of Gotha, was where the bomber's remains fell. **Black Widow** 42-7527/F (576BS) was taken out at this stage according to its pilot, Lt. Joseph B. Patterson, succumbing to a head-on assault and coming down to the west of Woltershausen; Patterson was one of the five survivors that constituted half the crew strength and was the sole survivor to officially report the circumstances affecting his B-24's demise.

The target had been struck and the formation was rallying for home when the attrition rate accelerated. Lt. Robert K. White and all but one of the other nine jumped clear after 41-29192/X (578BS) was fatally crippled; the bomb bay erupted in fire, a blaze that probably cost Sgt. Richard W. Wenzlaff (ROG) his life, since he was last observed attempting to extinguish the flames and never got out. By grim coincidence, the bomber's crash site was the same as for the Johnson-piloted B-24. Next down appears to have been 42-7511/L, another 576BS machine. It was last seen with both inboard engines ablaze and despite all ten on Lt. Mervyn T. Johns's team being reported as bailing out, only eight ultimately survived, leaving their aircraft to descend SW of Bad Hersfeld. (Sgt. Felix A. Zeranque was listed as dying on 30 March, but the exact circumstances leading to this unhappy conclusion remain unknown.) A second loss around this time appears to have involved 42-7496/U+ **The Jinx**, another 577BS aircraft. One rudder had been shot off and fire had taken hold in the fuselage. In the event, only seven airmen got out alive: Lts. Joseph C. Barnett (P) and Charles C. Doyle (CP) died, along with T/Sgt. Joseph B. Payton (Eng.). The River Rhine, between Koblenz and Bonn, was looming up

Flak Alley's original artwork did not include clothing applied to the lewdly-arranged figure; that situation has been at least partially attended to in this picture. B-24D-25-CO had an extended operational career from November 1942 until 24 February 1944. Then, while returning from Gotha, she was taken down by fighter strikes, along with six from Lt. Phillip W. Bell's (POW) crew.

Lt. Fish's crew comprises (standing, L-R) Lts. Robert H. Jeffs (B), Fish, Simon (CP), and Henry T. Staib (N); next to Staib is Sgt. Gordon L. May (Eng.). (Front row, L-R) Sgts. Fred B. Rogers (LWG), Paul A. Szabo (TG), Gene Corsilli (BT), Peter J. Masci (ROG), and William M. Swetlik. However, Lt. Simon was replaced by Lt. Charles M Sheridan. Ten more sacrifices to the Gods of War.

when the fighters downed the final Wendling crew, although fortune favored all ten airmen led by Lt. Marvin E. Schlossberg. The exact crash site for the 577BS' 42-100344 /W+ was never determined, but was believed to be near the Rhine's east bank, roughly in line with Koenigswinter.

Two more Wing crews were culled from Shipdham's ranks. Flak had disabled two engines on 41-29148/B (66BS) during the bomb run and to add to matters, the load could not be released. Fighters soon picked out the now straggling aircraft, and as Lt. Harold E. Etheridge was taking evasive action part of the bomb load broke free. Altitude was steadily lost until the pilot, realizing all was lost, rang the bail out bell, an action that only Lt. John L. Buechenstein (N) failed to survive.

Minutes previous, a veteran B-24D from the 68BS ended her operational career of 42 missions at Pferdsdorf, SW of Eisenach. This was 41-24225/T **Flak Alley**, which had earlier been caught out of formation just after "bombs away" and fatally crippled. Most of the crew had jumped before the bomber exploded, but Sgt. Antonio Milillo (ROG) suffered parachute failure. Lt. James I. King (CP) expired from his wounds shortly after landing, as did Sgts. Kenneth E. Sullivan and Wiley W. Haynes (WGs); two further Enlisted men lost their lives, leaving Lt. Phillip W. Bell (P) and three other airmen as survivors.

20CBW

The three units forming the 20CBW were least affected by enemy action, losing just four crews in all. Wuerzburg lies over 100 miles SSW of Gotha and Bad Kitzingen close by received the remains of 42-100236 from Hardwick's 409BS. F/O Rodolph Case's bomber had previously abandoned the mission and was clearly being steered towards Switzerland, given the flight direction, when it was finally and successfully evacuated by all the crew.

One of a duo of 446BG losses, 42-99978/H- **Lady Barbara** was abandoned by Lt. Charles E. Suprenant's crew prior to the 706BS machine breaking up and depositing itself some 20 miles south of Gotha. The other MIA crew progressed homeward as far as Belgium, despite 42-100282 (704BS) having suffered flak damage over Gotha; fighter gunfire finally took out Lt. Carl J. Kroells's aircraft that finally impacted north of Brussels; out of the ten-man team only the waist gunners failed to survive.

The final CBW loss involved Seething's 42-7606 **Abie's Irish Rose** from the 714BS, which was mortally affected by flak impacting around the cockpit when the formation unfortunately over-flew Brussels. The aircraft went into an increasingly spiralling descent that probably pinned Lt. Roland D. Warnock (P) and most on the flight deck in position until final impact, assuming they had not already been killed; all but one of the six Enlisted men did get clear before the bomber slammed into the soil near Woluwe-St. Etienne. Gotha's ghastly rebuff in respect of the Division was thus completed, but the sense of shock surely affecting the survivors as well as the personnel at Hethel, Wendling, and above all Tibenham must have lingered for several days afterwards.

Closing Off *Big Week*

All three Bomb Divisions had borne notable losses during *Argument*, with the 1BD losing 38 (22nd) and the 2BD's severe punishment over Gotha the two most prominent examples. Now, on 25 February, came the culminating mission, with strikes against targets deep in southern Germany on the agenda. Fuerth, outside Nuermburg, was assigned to the B-24s, with eight Groups participating. By the day's end, only six of the 172 crews coursing over the Primary or attacking Targets of Opportunity were left behind on the

Continent, along with 25 of their B-17 contemporaries.

Fighter opposition appears to have been much more sporadic on this occasion, and in fact flak proved to be the major cause for Division losses. The duo of losses borne by the 93BG occurred south of Kaiserslautern and west of the Rhine. Lt. David W. Thompson's 41-24147 **The Duchess** (330BS), flying deputy Lead, had suffered problems with two engines on the way. Target flak added to its problems by damaging one of the two fully functioning engines, resulting in total loss of formation position. A bid to make a run to Switzerland was soon brutally ended near Baden-Baden, when the latest of a number of fighter passes set the port wing on fire; following the bail out order all but two crewmembers managed to jump before their aircraft exploded and fell at Herxheim. The B-24D was a veteran bomber that had flown the Ploesti mission and had completed 53 missions prior to today. Flak batteries at Karlsruhe had already crippled 42-100323 (also 330BS), piloted by Lt. Walter W. McCartie, before fighters swept in to finish the B-24 off. The pilot and one other crewmember lost their lives, after which the bomber came down some 20 miles NW of Karlsruhe.

The other two 20CBW Groups lost one crew each. **Rigor Mortis** (42-7589) lived up to its sardonic title after flak strikes caused it to lag behind with at least one engine "out." Lt. William A. Hockensmith steered his dying 446BG bomber as far as French territory before all ten airmen successfully bailed out into captivity. A diametrically opposite fate awaited all ten on board Lt. Lawrence M. Edman's 42-52100 **The Lady from Bristol**. This 448BG bomber had similarly lost distance with the formation after suffering the loss of one engine that was subsequently fired up again. The aircraft never arrived back at Seething and it was only the subsequent drifting ashore of Sgt. Ghormley's (ROG) corpse onto the French coast that ultimately confirmed all but one of the ten airmen's watery fates. The apparent exception was Sgt. Harold L. De Lay (WG), whose parents were allegedly informed that he had survived following the receipt of a letter smuggled out of France by the Resistance; even if true, he never did subsequently surface alive, so cruelly intensifying the trauma suffered by his kin for the remainder of their lives.

The day's losses were completed by single crews from the 2CBW. Flak damage over Fuerth induced Lt. Lowell K. Hess to head further south for Switzerland, but 42-100368/-Z's progress towards that goal was ended at Goeppingen, SE of Stuttgart, where the 565BS machine came to earth. The 453BG surrendered 52-52302 (733BS) to a terminal flak burst that excised the starboard wing. The vicious aerodynamic imbalance that ensued would have provided little or no opportunity for any of Lt. Paul E. Koeppel's team to bail out before the aircraft crashed at Buch, on the northern outskirts of Fuerth.

Lt. K. Cookus and crew had already survived a heavy crash landing off the 44BG's 21 January 1944 mission. Now they were bringing back an equally damaged bomber, 41-29231/J **Impatient Virgin**, which had No. 3 engine's propeller "feathered" and another engine functioning on partial power. Fuel shortage forced the pilots to divert into Lymnpe, on the SE Channel coastline; however, the rest of the crew were ordered out prior to the 67BS bomber being brought in for a crash landing that led to the airframe fracturing from the impact. The scale of damage was enough for "Category E" treatment.

Summing Up

Big Week had witnessed the bringing about of regular fighter *vs.* fighter combat with the *Jagdwaffe*, as well as a general blitzing of the Nazi aircraft

B-24J-100-CO/42-100402/M holds station with the Assembly ship from which the picture was taken. The 67BS bomber lasted barely one month at Shipdham before going MIA on the Gotha mission of 22 February. Its remains, along with Lt. George E. Fish's crew, were never discovered and their most likely eternal resting place is either the Ijsselmeer or the dark maw of the North Sea.

The standard expression for personnel awaiting the return of their Group—known as "sweating out the mission"—has an ironic ring to it in this scene shot at Wendling, given the frigid nature of the weather. The large Group clustered around the control tower includes one harness-clad airman who may have been a member of the crew assigned to fly the 392BG's Assembly ship, or alternately has recently completed a test flight.

Aerial assaults upon USAAF airfields were to be few and far between, but the necessary deployment of AA defenses was naturally attended to. This single weapon is mounted on a trailer as part of the 458BG's Mobile Defense system. The large ammunition drums were awkward to handle, but contained enough rounds for prolonged bursts of fire.

Unlike the majority of 2BD Assembly ships, whose color scheme never varied, that of the 93BG underwent a three-stage process. Her original stripe pattern seen here was olive drab/white/yellow. This was first altered to red/white/yellow and finally to a narrow red/white stripe pattern. The wing stripes were angled out on the original version but revised to a fore and aft variation, at least on the interim version

The permanently-positioned Plexiglas frame for the B-17 and B-24 that first appeared in April 1944 proved a blessing for the previously physically challenged gunners. The example applied to the 458BG's B-24H-25-FO **Bombs Away** also incorporated a covered mount for the machine gun at the forward base of the Plexiglas panel.

A pair of radar-equipped B-24s at the top right are heading a 446BG formation; the "dustbin" shape of the H2S pod lowered by the left-hand aircraft is clearly depicted. **Kill-Joy** (foreground) is an H-1-CF (41-29141) assigned to the 706BS. **Werewolf** (top left) was B-24H-15-CF/42-7572/HN: M, which finally fell in battle on 11 April, but with none of Lt. Sterling L Tuck's crew sharing her fate.

production and distribution industry. As with the attacks on other industries, such as ball bearings manufacture, the immediate feeling that the 8AF had dealt a severe if not fatal blow to aircraft production was not basically realized. Although the bomb patterns had in many cases shattered buildings, material destruction had not been wrought among the key equipment element, namely the heavy plant machinery. The explosive content of even the biggest bomb capable of being borne by a B-17 or B-24—the 2,000-lb M34—was barely up to the task of disintegrating the massive dye presses, lathes, and similar solid manufacturing sets. In addition, the Germans undertook a swift process of dispersal to alternate sites, some of which, such as the SS-supervised factory at Nordhausen, were actually underground and therefore totally immune to aerial assault.

This apparent rebuff to the efficacy of the bombing campaign has to be seen in the light of short-sighted *Luftwaffe* policy regarding production priorities. Production levels did continually expand over the months ahead. On the other hand, the intention to phase out a range of already proven but increasingly performance-inhibited designs, such as the Bf110, Ju88, and Me410 was not being fulfilled even by mid-1944; a similar situation existed with the Bf109 and even the current versions of the Fw190. Distinctly superior replacement designs, such as the Fw190D-9, Ta-152, He219, and Me262 were desperately needed, but relatively few were yet appearing. In essence, "quantity over quality" still appeared to be the norm that moreover handed an ever-extending advantage to the Allies.

Another positive benefit to the Allied Air Forces arose from the loss of experienced *Jagdwaffe* pilots that had occurred during the week of intensive combat operations and was destined to open up a logistical wound in human resources that would never be closed up. In turn, the future ability of the heavy bombers to penetrate to and return from their targets with ever-increasing impunity from fighter attack would be a direct result of the 8th Fighter Command's burgeoning dominance over its opponent in the weeks and months ahead.

Jagdwaffe Tactical Changes

In early 1944, the *Reichsverteidigung* (Home Defense) structure had been amended in recognition of the burgeoning power of the 8AF, both in terms of the bombers' striking ability and the parallel threat posed by their escorts. The deployment of fighters in Holland and Belgium (*Jagddivision 3*) with which to mount early challenges was accordingly reduced in order to have the redundant units bolster up the resources based further within the national hinterland.

The *Sturmgruppe* adaptation of the *Gefechtsverband* tactic consisted of heavily armed and armored Fw190s provided with a high escort cover sweeping in upon a formation from behind.

The first such unit from a final figure of three was *IV (Sturm) JG3*, which was about to be conceived during March 1944, although the practical introduction of the concept only occurred in early July. The Fw190s were given heavier firepower in the form of two MK108 30mm cannon and two MG151 20mm cannon. However, the extra armor weight incurred a serious performance penalty if the pilots were forced to defend themselves, hence the need for a top cover escort.

The use of twin-engine fighters was still regarded as a viable element of *Reichsvertedigung* operations, even though the steady spread of 8FC activities over central Europe was making their use evermore hazardous. II/ZG26 (Me410s) and III/ZG26 (Bf110Gs) were stationed within JD1 and ZG76 (Me410s and Bf110Gs) as an element within JD7/8. However, by mid-1944, the depredations wrought upon all three *Zerstoerer* units would see their conversion to single-engine fighters and/or their disbandment.

ATC Caravan Duties (448BG)

As an airfield controller, most of our time was in the control caravan towards the active runway end. The requirement for radio silence meant that we operated with Aldis lamps and Verey pistol flares and kept contact with the tower. Refusing aircraft with wheels up or in danger of colliding to proceed with landing was one duty. Another was denying landing, should the approach be obstructed in any manner. Conversely, any B-24 in dispersal or at the runway end was held if its forward motion could hinder another's landing approach. A third involved reporting airfield light failure, while a fourth concerned the monitoring of vehicle movement in relation to their traversing the runways and perimeter track when flying was in progress.

Nocturnal activity largely involved the RAF; the safe landing of its aircraft usually involved the same flare gun and Aldis lamp usage, although sometimes two men standing on either side of the runway would form a visual arc with their gun. After our bombers were launched there was often little to do until their return, unless any "aborted." The 24-hour shift every alternate day was our basic duty that saw us sleep in the control tower on quiet nights. (Cpl. Ray Schwartz)

All the Comforts of Home

The often lengthy trek from their billets to the assigned dispersals on which sat their aircraft soon proved to be a handicap in more ways than one. Not only did it take up valuable time as well as leaving the men having to brave the wayward English weather, but their presence in the billets meant they were under constant disciplinary scrutiny.

The more enterprising airmen took to scavenging available building material with which to create huts alongside the dispersals into which were constructed not only sleeping and basic cooking facilities, but heating systems, the latter created and operating under conditions that would have seen them condemned by technical inspectors in peacetime. The other more subtle advantage with these alternative "billets" was that the men were now well removed from disciplinary staff inspections!

Packing cases formed a regular source for construction material, but at Shipdham, one 67BS team went a stage further by adapting a bomb shelter. These were open to the skies and naturally had a tendency to become waterlogged. The top was covered over and a wooden frame with a door attached placed at the entrance. Lighting consisted of a line extending from the nearby sheet metal shop, but the central core of physical comfort was the modified "heater."

A 50-gallon drum was situated at the shelter's vent and contained a mix of 100-octane fuel and motor oil. A fuel line to the stove was fitted with a hand-regulated valve with which a steady room temperature could be achieved. An aluminium tubing coil was placed around the stove jacket through which water could be heated; the heat induced spurts of the water to surge up into a discarded oxygen tank acting as a storage facility. A further refinement in this instance was a toaster.

Chapter Ten

"Bearding the Nazis" in their Den

Big B Beckons

Following the wholesale engagement of the 8AF's resources against the enemy's aviation industry, the die was now clearly cast in terms of continued aerial pressure against the Nazis' overall industrial fabric. While regions such as the Ruehr possessed much in the way of suitable targets, these were spread across an extended geographic manner. Major cities provided a more concentrated target, none more so than the German capital Berlin, which contained a plethora of military production plants, railroad facilities, and canals, as well as housing many government and military HQ locations within its massive boundaries.

Berlin had figured in the USAAF planners' minds for months and several potential missions against *Big B* had advanced as far as being briefed before cancellation. As March was entered, the situation assumed a more positive stance commencing on the 3rd. However, the month's inaugural mission (2nd) saw two Divisions dispatched and heading on an already well-trodden route to Frankfurt to bomb marshalling yards. Six 2BD groups were part of the overall Force, with 82 of the 154 crews striking the Primary or Targets of Opportunity. Only one B-24 remained MIA out of nine overall losses, but a further three Division bombers were lost over friendly skies, two in "operational" circumstances. Flak dealt the mortal blow to 42-100345 from Hardwick; the 409BS bomber lost two engines and finally began to spin as it descended before exploding in mid-air near Albert, in France. Lt. Charles W. Mankin, Jr. (P) was the sole fatality, while four of the other nine crewmembers evaded capture.

The 389BG had not been assigned to the mission, but later in the day sent up a practice formation. Flying the high right Element Lead was Lt. Gregory H. Perron in 42-100369/ (567BS), with Lt. John H. Kurtz as No. 3 in 42-100281/ K+ (566BS). While circling Hethel at 5,000ft, the Kurtz-piloted aircraft dipped sharply down before pulling up sharply to avoid a lower element, only to impact with Lt. Perron's aircraft under its port wing. At nearby Bungay, the personnel were amazed to watch the Kurtz B-24 with its partially excised starboard wing section describing no less than three complete circuits above their heads before diving into the ground at Swainsthorpe to the northwest. Tragically, and in spite of this protracted period of maneuvering, none of Lt. Kurtz's six-man crew survived, probably because the pilots were attempting to get their aircraft back down on the ground. Two airmen did jump at the last moment, but their parachutes did not deploy in time.

Only one out of the eleven on board the other bomber failed to survive the bail out, with Lt. Hatton (B) dying in hospital next day, while the abandoned

B-24 piled-in at Ilkeshall St. Margaret. Elsewhere, Lt. Hubert Cripe undershot the runway at Old Buckenham in 41-28642 **Libby Raider** (734BS); all ten crewmembers survived the incident, but the pilot and five others were fated to go down just four days later when only Cripe and Lts. Russell A. Anderson (CP) and Homer W. Alachua (N) would survive bailing out into the frigid waters forming Holland's Ijsselmeer.

During take-off at Horsham St. Faith, 41-28669/G **Ginny** (752BS), piloted by Lt. Kenneth M. Gorrell, faltered in flight and came to earth at Hellesdon, demolishing or badly damaging several buildings and killing seven of the ten on board. Gorrell was the sole officer survivor, and moreover was destined to have at least one other close shave with death or injury during his combat tour, which he successfully completed the following summer. However, he was held principally to blame for the crash, although iced-up flight surfaces were stated by the accident investigators to be a contributory factor.

The 8AF bore the loss of 69 bombers MIA off the first completed Berlin mission (6 March), but several among this figure managed to run the defensive gauntlet and reach Sweden. The "feathered" propeller and fuel loss from flak strikes confirm Lt. Charles C. York's emergency action in directing his Seething-based B-24H-5-CF/41-29191 **Hello Natural** in that neutral direction as justified.

Wallowing Wilbert arrived at Rackheath on 10 March and is now depicted in a currently non-operational state, with No. 1 engine detached. B-24H-15-CF/41-29421 would serve within the 791BS until 6 August, when it would be MIA with Lt. George Kotrabra's crew; a flak strike on one wing sent her out of control with just three of the ten crew getting out alive prior to her disintegration.

Schmid Assessment of *Big Week*

Gen. "Beppo" Schmid's (the CG of *I Fliegerkorps*) assessment of 8AF tactics immediately following *Big Week* not only acknowledged the ominous signs of the air war over Europe switching in the Allies' favor from a point of view of fighter *vs.* fighter combat, but he also pointed out that the switch from single to multiple target strikes by the 8AF "heavies" indulged in during the month's end and likely to be expanded in the future further inhibited the *Jagdwaffe's* efforts by dissipating its overall strength, which was already dangerously inferior in numbers needed for national defense. The technical superiority of the USAAF fighters, in his view further, diluted his fighter pilots' countermeasures, while the American numerical superiority of between three and four to one in terms of individual fighter sorties during February (10,452 to 2,861) was brutally emphasized by the equivalent loss percentages (299 to 310)—the point being that the latter statistic represented a reverse factor of 2.9% to 10.3%! If continued (and there was no immediate indication of even a marginal, let alone significant improvement in fortunes), then Schmid's overall opinion was that the *Jagdwaffe* would literally bleed to death in terms of both material and human resources.

"The Big One!"

The 748 B-17 and B-24 crews, rousted out of their beds and assembled in their Briefing rooms in the night-shrouded early hours of 3 March, would have reacted with a mix of profanity, resignation, and apprehension when the map curtains were drawn back to

Lt. Jewell's 44BG bomber is describing a dramatic sliding motion across Shipdham following the nose wheel's failure. The landing off the third Berlin mission (9 March) was primarily made by Lt. Koontz on what was his first mission after a flak fragment almost severed one of the pilot's legs. The B-24 was later salvaged; by contrast, and in spite of this severe injury scale, Jewell not only recovered, but subsequently returned to operational flying!

reveal the target: *Big B*. The Primaries involved aviation and ball bearing production plants in or on the periphery of the city boundaries. An average of 24 crews per group was the Division's share in proceedings, but the hoped-for hammering of the allotted targets would not be realized today. Instead, steadily deteriorating weather conditions, with visibility further badly compromised by dense condensation patterns, witnessed no progress beyond the NW German coastal fringe. A mere four B-24s unloaded on Targets of Opportunity and all but two crews returned to their airfields. Both teams remained permanently MIA and were presumed to have fallen into the sea. Wendling lost 42-7491/R **Pregnant Peg** (578BS), flown by Lt. Richard E. Smith, and the 458BG's 41-29298/G **Ole Satan** (755BS) bore Lt. Frank W. Herzik's ten-man crew to their deaths. In addition, three members on a second 93BG bomber were killed following the failure of 42-99939 **Big Fat Butterfly** to lift off due to jammed controls; Lt. Gomer J. Sneddon's effort to halt his charge's errant progress by ground looping failed, leaving the aircraft to smash through trees and halt close to the bomb dump. The resultant fire and explosion left only seven survivors.

Carol-N-Chick (42-63981) was reported as lost by returning 448BG crews, having been seen to adopt a "falling leaf" motion before flipping onto its back, spinning and disappearing into the clouds over the North Sea. Lts. Bill Brown and Kenneth Barnett fought their errant and seemingly doomed bomber's gyrations down to half the 20,000-ft operational height before pulling it out. Nothing daunted, they then proceeded to unload on the Island of Helgoland before coming home under escort by two P-51s! This B-24D-20-CF would soldier on until 13 February 1945, when it would be salvaged.

Any sense of even a temporary reprieve from striking Berlin was swiftly dispelled the following morning when it was again assigned for attack. Once again, weather conditions played a key part in frustrating all but a handful of 3BD bombers from penetrating to the city. The 2BD never even advanced as far as the enemy coast, since problems in Assembly led to a "cancellation" signal being issued. So far, it was a case of "two strikes and almost out" in launching a successful sortie, but the Nazi capital's fate was unknowingly only held in abeyance for a mere forty-eight hours.

Airfields in SW France were on the target menu for the 5th, but only the 2BD was briefed for the locations at Mont de Marsan, Cayeux, and Bordeaux/ Merignac. All nine groups were involved, with 164 of the 219 crews being granted mission credit, although none of the Primaries were bombed. Instead, several other airfields listed as Secondary or chosen as Targets of Opportunity were struck. The tithe of four MIA crews formed an "acceptable" loss factor in crude operational terms.

The 448BG suffered its latest pair of casualties. The group's bomb run upon Bergerac was totally disrupted by its fellow unit from Bungay intruding across its path, forcing part of the formation to retain its loads for fear of the bombs overshooting onto the adjacent town. Lts. Robert A. Martin and Lawson D. Campbell strained with the controls on their flak-afflicted 42-100414 (714BS) as it drifted back to become an easy target for fighter attack. One crewmember bailed out, but the other nine remained aboard after the fighters were eluded thanks to cloud cover and a crash landing site was sought out. This turned out to be a wheat field NE of Cognac, whose crop was so high that the Germans only discovered the B-24 three days later. The crew were spirited away by the population and five among their number would gain access to neutral Spain; Campbell progressed to within sight of the Franco/Spanish border before unluckily falling foul of a German patrol.

Lt. William O. Ross lost T/Sgt. A. F. Mied (Eng.) as fighter gunfire riddled the fuselage and wings of 42-100430 (715BS), knocking out No. 3 engine. The bomber was observed to describe a rolling action that just cleared a fellow B-24, at which point four parachutes emerged before it descended into the clouds still under fighter assault. In fact, all ten airmen managed to jump, of which no less than seven were destined to make a "home run." Mied was alive at this point, but although found and hospitalized, his lease on life expired two days later.

Fighters also put paid to the 389BG's 42-100421/Y (565BS), flown by Lt. Elbert F. Tucker. Once again, only S/ Sgt. James J. D'Amore (ROG) was the unlucky exception among the ten-man crew, who otherwise successfully abandoned the bomber, which crashed north of Mont-de-Marsan. The same total of evaders (seven) emerged here. Wendling's 42-7489/DC: Q+ almost made it back, but not long after crossing the French coast had to switch off No. 2 and 4 engines due to fuel shortage. An SOS was sent, since the chances of reaching England were now rapidly receding; the resultant "ditching" proved fatal for Lt. C. J. Hunter (P) and three others, the six survivors being fished out thanks to the combination of an RAF ASR launch and a "Walrus" amphibian.

"Three down—and Go!"

For the third occasion in four days, the Briefing maps on 6 March displayed locations within or on the southern outskirts of Berlin. The Daimler-Benz aviation plant at Genshagen allotted to the 2BD fell into this latter category. This time around, the three Divisions, who between them were dispatching over 800 crews, would gain partial access to their targets. In turn, and in concert with the flak gunners, the *Jagdwaffe* pilots, although now under regular pressure from the 8FC, would inflict the worst MIA figure borne by the "heavies" to date.

Whereas the routes on the previous two missions had angled up towards the Danish/German border and down towards the Bonn/Koblenz region, respectively, before heading for *Big B*, today's outward route would see the Divisions linking up in train over the Dutch coast at Egmond before heading directly east. When roughly at 10 degrees east and just beyond Celle, the Divisions would angle marginally southwards to their respective IPs south of the city and turn almost due north to the selected Primaries. Extended angular turns would see the Divisions that were formerly in train join up to the northwest of Berlin, there to assume a parallel course to one another; a slightly southwesterly course was to be maintained as far as a point between eight and nine degrees east, where a due west course would be adopted.

The original approach to Berlin had been from the northwest, in order to accommodate the current wind direction from the southeast; in the 2BD's case, it was to have assaulted the Heinkel plant at Oranienburg, on the city's northern fringe. The day's revised wind direction from the northeast would have required the B-24 Force to head across the city, whose flak batteries were deemed to have presented a lethally protracted barrier. As a result, a switch to Genshagen was initiated. As matters transpired, many groups would end up tracking over the center of the city in search of Targets of Opportunity after their Primary became obscured by cloud, so inviting the very opposition the planners had arranged for the 2BD to avoid. Also, the Division's alternate target was Tempelhof airfield, located well within the city, thus further contradicting the reason for the Primary switch!

The Division was to bring up the rear of the bomber stream, with the 2CBW in the Lead position, followed by a combined 14/96CBW sub-Force and the 20CBW last. The three CBWs, comprising 243 bombers overall, were separated by six miles from one another and positioned twelve miles back from the 3BD, holding the bomber stream's central status.

A 458BG formation presents a deceptively smooth aerial passage. In fact, the pilots will be working the control columns, rudder pedals, and throttles in order to avoid either bunching up to one another or alternately falling out of position. The physically draining labor is due to combating the air currents with their unpredictable up and down drafts added to by the malign effect of propeller "wash."

On Their Way

The daylight was just seeping in from the east as the first bombers commenced take-off in visibility conditions of between one and two miles and a solid cloud layer at lower altitude that became steadily more patchy as the bombers climbed. All but one crew safely cleared their airfields. The exception was 42-7473/J-bar **Jawja Girl** from Wendling, where misty conditions dictated an instrument take-off. The B-24 lifted off, but had progressed scant seconds distant from the airfield when it faltered before impacting with a tree and striking the ground at Great Dunham. It instantly exploded, obliterating the lives of all ten airmen led by Lt. Paul F. Shea.

The ever-tedious process of Group, Wing, and Division assembly was conducted with no further incident and the formations tracked out over the cold wastes of the North Sea to reach the enemy coastline between 1100 and 1130 hours. The 2CBW featured either the

The precise duplication of the female form has been applied to B-24J-70-CO/42-100100, based at Wendling. Points of note are the large "horn pattern" pitot mast structure and the armored-glass insert in the cockpit sliding panel. All but two on Lt. Gerald E. Roger's (KIA) crew were consumed in her loss off the 29 April Berlin mission; the exact reason for her final demise SE of Celle is unclear.

445th or 453rd BG as Lead, with the 389BG flying in the High position. "Aborting" a mission when well within enemy territory was inviting disaster, as Lt. Ned Serkland was sadly to discover. His 445BG bomber suffered technical problems that disabled No. 2 engine and prevented "feathering" of the propeller. The resultant drag caused 42-100796/ **Balls of Fire** (700BS) to lag behind, forcing the pilots to jettison the bombs and turn for home. With the errant propeller threatening to detach and smash into the fuselage, Serkland throttled back in a bid to prevent this happening; the propeller slipped back into position, but at the cost of increasing the time over hostile territory, as the bomber labored onwards at around 130 mph.

Altitude was steadily lost to around 12,000ft and more damage was inflicted by flak before the ailing aircraft was intercepted by fighters. The bail out order was given, but as the bomber was being held in level flight the errant propeller finally came off and smashed into the cockpit, striking Serkland on one leg, but amazingly without inflicting serious or fatal injury. Shortly after the B-24 exploded, the blast throwing the pilot clear but unharmed to float down towards captivity—this despite the entire nose section initially coming down directly above him! Three of the ten airmen lost their lives: Lt. Lyle E. De Kalb (B) had his parachute set on fire by burning debris, and Cpl. Chester F. Skalski (TG), whose left leg had nearly been shot off, bled to death after his canopy hooked up in a tree. This loss was the first of seven emanating from the ranks of the 2CBW.

Up ahead, the 13CBW was enduring its martyrdom over Hasseluenne, while further in towards Berlin, an equally torrid time was being experienced by two CBWs from the 1BD. In contrast, serious and sustained opposition to the B-24 formations appeared to have been reserved for *Big B* and the return route. The run-up to the Daimler-Benz plant was initiated around 1320 hours and partial cloud cover over the Primary did not prevent the 389BG, 44BG, and 392BG from delivering their loads thereon. The other six groups were thwarted in following suit and sought out Targets of Opportunity within the city. The next recorded casualty occurred as the 93BG was tracking over the Humbolthain district; Heavy Flak Abteilung 123 possessed eight 128-mm caliber guns, and these duly engaged the 20CBW as it angled from a SSW to a westerly course. The specific B-24 on whom such attention became lethally directed was 42-109832 **De-Icer** (330BS). Heavy damage to the forward fuselage was followed by a propeller detaching and smashing into the cockpit, whereupon the aircraft entered into a spin, followed shortly by its disintegration. Lt. Jack D. Harris (P) was killed, as were seven of the other ten airmen; Lt. Leland Walzel (B) attempted to extract S/Sgt. Hyman Waxler from the nose turret, but both ended up on the fatality list. The bomber's wreckage sprinkled the ground in the city district of Spandau.

Flak had punctured fuel tanks on the 448BG's 41-29191/E **Hello Natural** as the group was heading for the Rally Point and Lt. Charles C. York decided upon the potentially suicidal option of banking northwards in a bid to reach Sweden. Luck was on the crew's side, however, when their run ended in a landing at Bulltofta, next to Malmo. In contrast, luck was definitely out for eight airmen on the 458BG's 42-52515/H; the city's flak gunners' efforts culminated in the 754BS B-24 exploding to leave Lts. Guy C. Rogers (P) and Frank O. Proteau (CP) the sole very fortunate survivors. (The pilot later stated in a letter to the mother of a crewmember that the cockpit was set on fire and he had got out of his seat to seek a fire extinguisher, but fell onto the floor bare seconds before the bomber disintegrated; he sustained a broken leg whose condition subsequently deteriorated to the extent that it had to be amputated.)

Homeward Attrition

The defenses cut into the Division ranks as the groups began the homeward leg

The mangled airframe belongs to the 445BG's 42-100353, which bears no codes other than the aircraft letter L on the fin. The severe damage to the port wing and to a lesser extent the vertical fin was caused by impact with a tree, and salvage action will clearly be the fate of this machine. The date of the incident was 8 March 1944, with the crash site at Fressingfield, in Suffolk.

Switzerland became a second neutral haven for USAAF crews when making deep-penetration runs into southern Germany. On 18 March, this Wendling B-24H-1-CF/41-29127, a 579BS aircraft, won through to Duebendorf with Lt. William A. Kale and crew; it was one of only two out of fourteen MIA Group crews to enjoy this much more pleasant if physically restricting fate.

of the mission. Lt. George H. Lymburn's 42-7586/Q **God Bless our Ship** was barely clear of the city boundary when the flak-afflicted 445BG bomber began to rapidly lose height with one engine on fire. A German observer saw the aircraft with only the port main landing gear deployed make a partially successful landing on open ground at Wall, near Neuruppin. Of the eight crew who had previously bailed out, only Lt. Frank R. Serpico failed to survive after striking his head on a tree stump. The first of four 453BG losses occurred as the formation was passing south of Oldenburg. A final fighter thrust sent 42-64460/ (733BS) totally out of control and the bomber exploded to kill the six crewmembers of Lt. Patrick T. Tobin, Jr. (KIA), who were still on board at this point. A second 458BG crew fell around the same time north of Celle; the crew were unfortunate to be intercepted by Oblt. Greiner, a night-fighter *Experte* (Ace) with NJG1. The enemy pilot, in his Bf110G-4, made short work of his prey, killing Lt. Jesse L. McMains (P) and two of his nine crew on 42-52306/ J4: I; Greiner's latest "kill" was his second this day, as he had previously downed a B-17 that unfortunately was over-flying Quakenbrueck airfield, from which he had just become airborne.

The Division's passage over Holland would see a further six crews going down over its territory. The single Wendling MIA loss involved 42-7598/ CI: E. **Flak Ducker** (576BS), which had fallen behind thanks to one engine failing and was forced to drop its load in order to rejoin the group. Lt. Erling A. Hestad held his position almost up to the Dutch border, but oil loss from a second engine led to an inexorable detachment from the ranks. Overberg was where the pilots pulled off an almost perfect landing in a field; the nose wheel collapsed, but all seven airmen still on board (three having bailed out over the town) got out safely. Hethel's 42-100424/V- **Roll Call** (567BS) had taken a battering from flak at Vechta and staggered on as far as the region around Hoogeveen, where the crew jumped. Lt. Kenneth C. Griesel (P) and Alvis D. Roberts (B) evaded capture to begin a protracted wait under Resistance auspices until September, when the British Army liberated the area in Belgium where they were currently ensconced.

The 458BG was destined to suffer its worst mission loss today (five), the latest victim being 41-29286/R (753BS), with Capt. Jack L. Bogusch (KIA) in charge. A combination of heavy and light flak located on the Dutch/German border administered the death blow and the B-24 descended at Tubbergen, just inside Dutch soil north of Enschede, leaving six crewmembers alive out of ten. Next down was probably 41-29299 /M **Roll Call** (754BS), which had also

Naughty Nan, a B-24J-55-CO, bears freshly-applied squadron code letters, but her fin-mounted aircraft letter is almost invisible. This picture was taken in the spring of 1944, with the aircraft continuing on operations until 21 September. A landing on the Continent that day reportedly saw her languishing there until salvage action was declared in mid-November.

suffered a combination of flak and fighter damage. Eight of Lt. Thayer Hopkins's crew bailed out between Appeldoorn and Amersfoort, but the pilot and Lt. Samuel W. Roberts (N) remained to bring off a perfect crash landing at Jisp, close to Nijkerk. Pumerend lies some distance north of Amsterdam, and it was close to there that 42-52450/G's fight for survival came to an end. The 754BS aircraft had suffered flak damage over Berlin and came down in a spinning attitude along with three of her crew, but Lt. Beverley E. Ballard (P) was one of seven survivors, with Sgt. Victor W. Kreuger (BT) avoiding the "Kriegie" fate now awaiting his companions.

"The Sea Shall Have Them"

Four days previous, Lt. Hubert P. Cripe's crew had walked away from an over-shoot at their Old Buckenham airfield that "wrote off" the B-24, but now a far worse fate awaited three of those involved in that incident. Cripe's 42-52226/E8: E. (734BS) had been straggling for some time and was accompanied by a fellow-suffering B-24 when the duo was attacked by fighters. An urgent call for fighter cover elicited an anonymous Texan voice informing Cripe not to get excited, as "Poppa was coming." Unfortunately, the port wing now caught fire and the pilot called for a bail out. All on board responded to float down through the undercast—right into the waters of the Ijsselmeer. Cripe went right under the surface of the freezing water, but after popping up like a cork managed to divest himself of his parachute, as well as inflate his Mae West. He still faced the threat of a lingering death by hypothermia, but was very fortunate to be fished out by a Dutch fishing boat, as were just two others out of nine fellow airmen.

The act of "ditching" could never be practiced, and even if attempted would provide little or no guarantee that the crews concerned would survive the experience. Single 446th and 453rd BG bombers would be tested in this manner with an outcome fatal for all but four of the twenty airmen involved. Old Buckenham's 42-52191/ (735BS) was brought in for a "ditching," but by the time an RAF Walrus amphibian called to the scene had arrived only Lt. Joe G. Cyr (B) out of Lt. Herman J. Meek's crew was destined to survive. The RAF crew attempted to haul out the several airmen still alive at this time, but one stiffened and died as he was about to be extracted from the sea, while a second "froze" as he grasped a wing strut and could not initially be induced to let go; it was several minutes before his grasp was slackened enough for him to be hauled aboard. Both survivors were flown back to Martlesham, but Cyr's companion later succumbed in hospital. Removal of wet clothing and their replacement with warm blankets, followed by hospitalization, still did not guarantee that hypothermia would release its terminal hold. Joe later recalled how he had inflated his *Mae West* just prior to the "ditching" and his next memory was of coming to in the water and grasping a floating oxygen bottle with S/St. Donald G. Wright frantically doing the same. S/Sgt. William J. Gricas (BT) was floating nearby, but Joe's next memory was of both airmen's *Mae Wests* being the only visible objects.

The survival rate on Lt. Robert E. Paltz's crew was little better at three out of ten following 42-100288 **Major Hoopoo's** easing into the sea. The pilots had previously "aborted" the mission after losing an engine to fighter gunfire and kept the riddled bomber on course at minimum altitude. Now, the initial impact bounced the B-24 into the air with the second and final contact snapping the airframe in two directly at the wing trailing edges. Lt. Paltz nevertheless managed to scramble clear despite suffering two broken legs; he was assisted into one of the rafts by St. Richard Denton (TG), as was T/Sgt. Alva L. Songer (Eng.) with his injured shoulder. The trio of soaked survivors settled uncertainly down to await rescue as a P-47 circled overhead before heading home; 90 minutes later their relief when a ASR launch hove in sight must have been evident.

A third crew facing the life threatening peril of the North Sea were manning yet another 453BG aircraft; 42-64457 (733BS) was a flak victim heading back on its own under diminishing power until just a single engine was somehow keeping it aloft as the Dutch coast receded. Then, under fighter escort and with the English coastline at Great Yarmouth visible, the situation deteriorated sufficiently for Lt. Elmer B. Crockett and crew to take to their parachutes, an act that provided an immediate but not longer-term guarantee of survival. The airmen drifted down to wait being picked up by a Walrus amphibian and several vessels. Unfortunately, the spread-out nature of the ten airmen meant the time taken to complete the rescue bid proved lethal for half their number. Lt. Orvis G. Martin (B) later recalled that he was given a large measure of brandy that simply "went down like water" and how he shivered uncontrollably during the night despite being hospitalized, such was the traumatic effect of immersion upon his body. (The heading to this account is a sardonic version of the ASR Service's motto, "The Sea shall not have them"; on this, as on many occasions during WWII, the North Sea waters would claim their victims and thwart the ASR crews' gallant efforts in so doing.)

Summary

The 6 March inaugural run and full-scale strike upon *Big B* proved to be far from successful in terms of bombing results. Only the 2BD had gained partial access to its Primary, cloud cover having totally thwarted the other Divisions' efforts in this respect, forcing them to assault suitable Targets of Opportunity either within the city or elsewhere. Sixty-nine crews—sixteen from the 2BD—had paid the full price of operational "entry" to the Nazi capital. The 8FC pilots had enjoyed a much better result, knocking down 82 opponents at a cost of eleven of their own.

Second Strike

Forty-eight hours elapsed before the second mission to *Big B* was laid out. This time around, all three Divisions were to make a combined assault upon the major ball bearing plant at Erkner, on the city's SE fringe. The inward route was almost a duplicate of the 6 March mission, but the bomber stream would form a single stream from the English coast, while the final approach to the Primary would be made from an ENE angle. The homeward route would initially cross from north to south of its inward equivalent until north of Hannover, after which a reciprocal course to the Dutch coast would be assumed.

An overall figure of 623 crews included 209 from the 2BD, with all nine groups again engaged. Once again, the 3BD led the way in MIA casualties (23), compared to five (1AD) and nine (2BD), but four more B-24s were among the additional figure comprised of crashes and crash landings on British soil.

The 20CBW bore the brunt of the losses, with five crews removed from the ranks of the Bungay and Seething-based Groups. One B-24 from the former unit never got as far as the target. After becoming a straggler for unstated reasons, 42-7595 (706BS) was pounced upon by fighters, whose gunfire resulted in the starboard wing being set on fire, leading to the entire sub-unit snapping off to send the bomber into a vicious spin. In spite of this, Lt. Herbert F. Bohnet, Jr. and three other crewmembers survived after reportedly being blown out into mid-air; the shattered remnants of **Schif'lus Skunk** tumbled to earth near Zieckau.

Another pre-target loss occurred earlier, when the 453BG's **Portland Annie** (42-52175/P) had been turned for home near Celle after No. 1 engine was knocked out and No. 3 emitted smoke. Although spared the attention of the *Jagdwaffe*, the bomber only held itself aloft until Dutch soil was being over-flown. Then, Lt. Everett G. Ehrmann (POW) brought off a successful crash landing near Den Osterhuis after bailing out the crew; all ten airmen survived, but T/Sgt. Donald E. Anderson (ROG) was hospitalized for non-life threatening injuries. Ehrmann was also one of three initial evaders, but he and Lt. Walter H. Kendall (B) were subsequently captured.

Lt. John D. Adamson's 41-28720/J3: N's crash site was near Finsterwalde, 20 miles due south of Zieckau. Flak had administered punishment after the bomber fell out of formation and a twin-engine fighter administered the final fatal blow. The pilot was one of five fatalities that included one airman who tragically pulled his ripcord too soon and was dragged to his death after the canopy became wrapped around the rear fuselage; a second died from his injuries following hospitalization.

The flak barrage experienced over the target area, as well as the peninsula-

Although the American Red Cross provided large numbers of the mobile vans from which to dispense drinks and snacks, several British organizations were also involved. The Group of officers, along with a few Enlisted men, are clustered by a church Army vehicle at Seething sometime during 1944.

shaped segment of the city that the formations traversed after bombing, did not directly bring down any Division bombers, but in several cases caused a mechanical hemorrhage that was never staunched. One such case involved Hethel's 42-100375/F+ (566BS), which lost its No. 3 engine and began to straggle. A second flak strike over Osnabrueck disabled No. 2 and killed Sgt. Kenneth J. Miller (RW). The jettisoning of equipment did not halt a steady altitude loss, although the region around Rotterdam was attained before Lt. James B. McArthur finally gave the bail out signal before bringing off a crash landing SE of the city. **Yankee Rebel Harmony/The Latrine Rumor** (42-99975/D) was similarly affected and was guided as far as Eernewoude, in Holland's Friesland Province, where a heavy crash landing crushed the nose and fatally injured Lt. Stephen P. Judd (CP). F/O John M. Kendrick, Jr. (P) was so severely injured that amputation of both legs above the knee was carried out at a Leeuwarden hospital. The other nine crewmembers had provided immediate first aid to the pilots before dispersing into the countryside, with at least four gaining access to Resistance sources, but all were subsequently apprehended by August. Seething's 42-100342 suffered the loss of No. 1 engine, causing the 715BS machine to head on a downward path; Lt. John R. Bringardner still managed to keep heading westwards for a considerable distance before the eleven occupants abandoned their mount, which crashed southwest of Brunswick.

The stretch between Brunswick and Hannover added two further Division casualties to the overall tally, both 446BG aircraft. Fuhrberg claimed the remains of 42-100231 (707BS), although whether flak or fighters brought about the demise of the B-24, along with all ten members on Lt. Clifton F. Helfer's team, is undetermined. The same location is listed for 41-29292 (705BS), flown by Lt. James A. Merriman. Fighters hacked the bomber out of the sky and its terminal fate was the same for its ten hapless occupants.

The giant maw of the North Sea awaited its latest Division victim in the form of 42-100122 **Twin Tails** from the 448BG. Punctured fuel tanks ensured the ailing B-24's homeward progress was ended roughly 25 miles short of friendly soil. Any "ditching" attempt was fraught with risk, but the rough sea surface on 8 March further added to the danger. Sure enough, when the B-24 was set down into the sea east of Great Yarmouth it broke up on impact; it is amazing that anybody survived the disintegration, as well as immersion in the chilled conditions, but T/Sgts. James H. Hood (Eng.) and James T. Nugent, Jr. (ROG) were two of the fortunate exceptions out of Lt. John Daley's crew, who were subsequently recovered; Lt. Aaron Bramhall (N) was alive at this stage, but later died as the ASR launch was heading back. The fact that the vessel reached the crash location within 15 minutes of the "ditching" was a major factor in ensuring the two Sergeants' survival.

"Category E" Postscript

The B-24s returning home but ending up on the salvage list belonged to the 44th, 389th, 445th, and 458th BGs. Lt. Kenneth G. Jewell had his left leg almost severed following a flak strike over Berlin that wrecked the radio and forward oxygen systems and disabled No. 3 engine on 42-99980/QK: H. **E. Z. Duzit**. Lt. Harold L. Koontz (CP), who was on his first mission, was now tasked with the job of bringing the crippled 66BS B-24 back home and landing it. The nose wheel had been wrecked, so the bomber's nose-down progress along the Shipdham runway was eventful but successful. The dramatic landing was recorded on film by a Movietone cameraman and has featured in numerous postwar documentaries. Jewell's eventual recovery and fitting with an artificial leg culminated in his return to combat operations in February 1945!

The Hethel-based example was 42-100167/RR: L+ **Yours Truly**, which limped into Woodbridge Emergency airfield, where a heavy crash landing that extensively damaged the forward fuselage area earned the bomber "Category E" treatment. There are no details on who "bellied in" Tibenham's 42-100353 (703BS) at Fressingham, in Suffolk, other than that all ten airmen emerged intact. Finally, Lt. George N. Spaven had already lost one engine on 41-28729/J4: G as he broke through the low cloud over Watton, rather than Horsham St. Faith. He entered the circuit and was well into his final approach when No. 4 cut out; the swing to starboard saw the errant bomber heading for the hangars, whereupon Spaven pulled the nose up in a bid to clear the structures, an act that only stalled the aircraft. The resultant impact with the ground tore off the starboard landing gear and thoroughly mangled the engine cowlings and wing area. Once again, all ten airmen got out safely.

Today's combat debut for Lt. John D Ellis's 579BS team was eventful, to say the least. Their badly shot up bomber 42-7469/GC: E **Rose of Juarez**, which also contained S/Sgt. J. E. McGee (BT), who had been badly wounded, ended up being "bellied in," such was its overall condition. The other crewmembers emerged intact, but McGee's scale of injury ensured that his first mission would be his last, this 8 March 1944.

Immeasurably better bombing results had emerged compared to the first *Big B* strike. The damage at the Erkner plant was severe enough to cause a noticeable downturn in ball bearings output. The fighter *vs.* fighter combat also tuned out in the 8FC's favor at 79 to 18, yet another human as well as technical barb in the *Jagdwaffe's* ranks, even if one particular mass attack on the 45CBW had whittled down its strength by sixteen B-17s. However, the 8AF was not yet finished with Berlin, as two more major strikes during the month would attest—one of which would occur within 24 hours, as well as bringing an unexpected degree of relief from comprehensive punishment, whether fighter or flak-originated.

Gallopin Katie, a 566BS B-24J, flies off the wing of B-24D **Jackass Male** from the 565BS. Both Hethel aircraft were gone by 1 April, when the latter (42-72866/EE: Q) was claimed in combat. By then **Katie** (42-100332/RR: E+) was a Swiss internee off the 16 March run to Friedrichshafen, along with Lt. Miles Snyder's crew.

The second completed Berlin mission (8 March) culled 37 crews MIA, including two from Seething. Lt. John R. Bringardner's B-24J-95-CO/42-100342 was flak-stricken, with No. 1 engine largely excised; almost immediately following this shot, the eleven-man crew commenced a successful bail out, leaving the bomber to fall to earth south of Brunswick.

9 March

Berlin was destined to be given no respite, nor were many of the 8AF crews, since a bare 24 hours elapsed between the second and third missions. However, there would be a very welcome respite from the enemy's ever-lethal attention for the vast majority of the American participants. This situation would ironically come about thanks to Mother Nature.

As it transpired, the twin Primaries were located outside the city: the Heinkel plant at Oranienburg, just to the north; and the Arado plant at Brandenburg, some 20 miles from Berlin's southwestern fringe. Solid cloud patterns induced the use of H2X, but problems with the equipment dictated that the B-17 Divisions released upon the city as the Secondary. The 2BD did not even achieve this degree of intention and ended up picking out Targets of Opportunity at Hannover, Brunswick, and Nienburg, roughly 100 miles to the west, as opposed to their Brandenburg Primary.

If the 8AF crews were frustrated in their bid to strike the Primaries, the defenders were even more inhibited in their overall counterstrikes. Fighter sightings by the bomber crews did not exceed single figures and the 837 Allied fighters escorting the 490 bombers granted mission "credit" came home with equally minimal contact, as well as natural frustration at not tangling with the opposition. The Division lost a mere two crews out of eight overall. The latest 445BG casualty was 42-7604 (702BS), whose crew, under Lt. Norman Menacker's command, bailed out, leaving the B-24H with a burning engine to plough itself in near Hannover. Also lost from Seething was 41-28611 (712BS), which was last observed crossing the coast but in fact crashed at Arendonk, Belgium; by then it was bereft of all on Lt. Everett P. Musselman's crew, three of whom evaded capture.

Crews were only really safe from injury or death when well away from their bomber on either side of a mission or operational flight. Today, the 93BG's 42-100320/G (328BS) was put down in a field near Attleborough by Lt. Dwight Heming, but the bomber was very badly damaged in so doing. Thankfully, none of the eleven airmen were killed, although several were injured. Elsewhere, battle damage to Wendling's 42-7624/Z (578BS) culminated in a non-fatal crash on Beccles airfield. A further ten combat crewmembers led by Lt. James E. Muldoon were spared their lives, but both aircraft were later salvaged.

Operational activity for the 2BD for nearly one week following the latest

The expansion of combat operations deeper into southern Germany during March witnessed the tally of crippled bombers diverting into Switzerland increasing; two 2BD bombers succeeded on 16 March, one of which was **Big Noise** (B-24D-70-CO 42-40969, a 330BS aircraft). Lt. Richard J. Pettit brought her into Duebendorf, where she is seen parked on the lightly snow-bedecked airfield surface.

Berlin run proved to be virtually nil in terms of overall strength. Two groups bombed *No-Ball* sites in the Pas de Calais (11th) and three units went out the next day to the same region, both missions being cost-free, both in technical and human respects. The 2nd and 20th CBWs were dispatched to the same region 24 hours later, but none of the crews actually bombed, thanks to solid cloud cover. This time round the 93BG lost one B-24 during Assembly. The potentially malign effect of propeller wash, especially while in cloud, acted adversely upon 42-100363/YM: N. Lt. Alfred C. Chamberlain's (Killed) aircraft nosed up marginally before abruptly dipping down into a steep dive that was followed by its going into a spin almost immediately after it had been pulled out. The inordinate strain upon the overladen airframe caused the tail section to break off. In such circumstances, it was surprising that any of the four survivors managed to get clear, although one or more may have been thrown out.

The day before and during the latest Group's overseas transfer to join the 2BD (467BG), one crew was tragically written off its strength in North Africa. Lt. Edward J. Mosser, in charge of 42-52554/M **Rangoon Rambler II**, had taken off from Dakar, in Senegal, and headed north to Marrakech, a flight that was the penultimate leg before arrival in Britain. It never arrived, having probably impacted on the extreme southern fringe of the Atlas Mountain chain, killing all ten airmen. This was the latest but far from the last victim of the anonymous and extended geographic feature.

Brunswick was a regular feature on the USAAF planners' menu and was attacked 15 March by a reduced force of 2nd and 3rd BD groups, six of which were from the former organization. All but a handful of the 344 crews bombed, albeit with the city's aero production plants as the briefed Secondary. One of the two losses involved the 44BG's 42-52332/QK: K **My Ass'am Dragon**. The bomber had developed supercharger problems that were only partially solved by manipulating the supercharger and throttle controls. The return flight saw Lt. David R. Talbott's charge beginning to lag behind and ripe for fighter attention; sure enough, several Fw190s appeared and made firing passes. Fuel leaked into the bomb bay and fire took hold as the B-24 was thoroughly riddled; St. H. C. Gasser's (LW) flak vest proved his savior from the fusillade.

A bail out was called for, but as Talbott prepared to do so he was knocked unconscious when the aircraft went out of control. He somehow found himself out in mid-air and either regained sufficient consciousness to pull his ripcord or alternately his pack was ripped open; full awareness of his situation only returned after reaching the ground near Niue Leusen, in Holland. Having released his harness, he was approached by a civilian, the first of three whose advice over the next few hours led to his being concealed in a house—and the start of months of evasion before Allied troops liberated the region. All but two of the crew got out alive, while T/Sgt. Ray E. Swick (ROG) also gained access to Resistance sources that sheltered him until liberation occurred.

Nobody escaped alive from the 392BG's 42-99976/CI: D **Pocatello Chief**; flak damage finally forced the bomber out of formation after "bombs away" and fighter gunfire caused the aircraft to explode near Wuppertal, in the eastern Ruehr, killing Lt. Bert D. Miller and the other nine on board.

Friedrichshafen

Friedrichshafen lies on Lake Constance (*Bodensee*), linking Germany and Switzerland, so entailing an extended run for the 8AF; the Dornier production plant located there was a prime target that was attacked twice in 48 hours—16/18 March—by the 2BD. On both occasions, other targets in southern Germany were allotted the B-17 Divisions and much punishment was inflicted upon all the locations involved. On the other hand, no less than 66 bombers were MIA between the two missions, of which exactly half were borne by the 2BD.

The first Divisional foray involved 239 crews, the majority of whom struck the Primary at a cost of five MIA aircraft spread between four groups. Hardwick came home two light, although eleven

The 392BG lost fifteen out of 29 Division crews MIA on 18 March 1944. Lt. Rex L. Johnson was piloting B-24H-15-FO/42-52465/EC: X, which was claimed by fighters, along with the pilot and seven out of his nine-man crew. The burned-out wreckage of the 392BG bomber is being examined by local people at Mariazell, near Schramberg.

of the nineteen airmen involved were by then sitting in relative comfort in Switzerland. The luckier team was led by Lt. R. J. Pettit in 42-40969/AG: H. **Big Noise**. This B-24D fell out after bombing and crossed into Switzerland. In contrast, just two out of Lt. Secar J. Harris's ten-man crew on 42-100116/ enjoyed the same good fortune. Having made the bomb run on two still-sound engines after target flak knocked out the second motor a heading was made for neutral territory, but an absence of maps for the area caused the pilots to wander aimlessly. As it so happened, when the crew finally bailed out after fire developed in one engine their bomber came down in Switzerland, but the other eight unfortunate airmen parachuted down onto Austrian soil!

Galloping Katie (42-100332/RR: E+) also diverted into Duebendorf following engine problems to add Lt. Myles A. Synder's ten-man crew to the internment figure. The last two losses were incurred on the way home over France. Tibenham's 42-7643/IS: (700BS) had returned on its own and came down NE of Troyes, along with half of Lt. Richard A. Raroha's (KIA) crew. The 458BG casualty actually cleared the French coast, but came down in the English Channel. Lt. Neil J. Peters (P) was one of eight fatalities on 41-29331/J3: F **Blondie's Folly**; Sgt. Richard G Lowry (Eng.) was rescued alive, but later died in Dover Hospital.

Southern "Blues"

Whereas the 3BD had absorbed the greatest punishment on the 16th, the return to southern Germany on the 18th would switch the defender's attention to the 2BD, although the situation in terms of human casualties would be alleviated by those airmen winning through to neutral Swiss territory. Two groups in particular would feel the enemy's sting: the 44th and 392nd BGs, both veteran units and already well "blooded" in combat. However, and not for the last occasion, the Wing's exposure to severe punishment would be enhanced by its becoming separated from the Division bomber stream through adopting a wrong homeward heading. The initial interceptions by the JG11-based *Verband* would then be taken up around the Strasbourg region by II and III/JG2.

The 44BG was already on the bomb run when it was diverted off course by an errant B-17 cutting across the formation. A second run was in progress when 41-29431/GJ: Q-bar **Shoo Shoo Baby** lost two engines, as well as fuel loss from the starboard fuel tanks. Lt. William C. Irwin felt he had no option but to head for Switzerland. Also heading for neutral soil was Lt. Robert R. Lucas's 42-100400/GJ: Y-bar. The same corporate fortune did not favor a second pair of squadron crews. **I'll be Back** (42-52305/GJ: P-bar) failed to live up to its title after No. 4 engine was set on fire and Lt. Frank L. Albert was seen slumped over his controls by Lt. Edmund H. Donnelly (N). Two parachutes emerged before the port wing became detached and the blazing remnants fell to earth at Wintersulgen, leaving Donnelly and three Enlisted men as the sole survivors.

Better fortune attended the final 506BS loss. Despite the proximity of Switzerland, Lt. Raymond C. Houghtby decided to head for home, but the need to conserve fuel left the veteran B-24 out on its own on its 45th mission. Nevertheless, 41-29172/GJ: T **Lucky Strike** progressed as far as the Pas de Calais, but by now at an 11,000ft, which made it fair game for the flak gunners. Sure enough, the first salvoes damaged the controls; lowering the landing gear stopped the barrage, but the pilot, realizing the situation was terminal, ordered a bail out that was successful for all ten airmen, even if Houghtby broke a foot on landing.

A third interned crew belonged to the 66BS, being Lt. George D Telford's in 42-7618/QK: C. **Scourge of the Skies**. The airmen were on their last mission, whose conclusion was to be frustratingly incomplete. Two engines had lost oil pressure and this, along with fuel loss, had persuaded the pilot that a return home was highly problematical, whereupon he swung his B-24 southward; the fighter escort, on reaching Switzerland, was comprised of that nation's Bf109s. Neutral soil was a preferred option to captivity, but not so satisfactory as a return passage to the USA! A single loss was borne by the 67BS when flak crippled 42-100073/ NB: H. **Sack Artists**, flown by Lt.

More fortunate than its 14CBW fellow bomber was Shipdham's 42-7618/QK: C **Scourge of the Skies**, a Ford-built example assigned to the 68BS. It was one of two Group aircraft diverting into Switzerland to land at Duebendorf. Lt. Telford and his crew's relief at achieving this refuge would have been tempered by the fact that they had been engaged on the final mission of their combat tour!

Raymond J. Lacombe during the second bomb run. Two engines were set ablaze and a course promptly and successfully set for Switzerland, where all twelve airmen, including Capt. Robert L. Cardenas (Command Pilot), bailed out.

It fell to the 68BS to bear the final two unit losses, beginning with Lt. Eugene N. Dyer in charge of 42-109800/WQ: T, who also headed into neutral territory, seeking sanctuary at Duebendorf. The other squadron loss involved 42-100112/WQ: Q **Paper Doll/Lady Dot**, flown by Lt. Hollis R. Nichols. This was yet another B-24 that had experienced engine problems on the way in, added to which target flak knocked out a second engine. The pilot headed south across the Bodensee and bailed out his crew. However, after leaving his seat he hesitated to jump, thinking that the now-lightened bomber might be capable of being landed. Just as he got back to the cockpit the No. 2 propeller became detached, crashing into the fuselage and biting into his seat. Taking this as a clear omen, Dyer wasted no time in following his crew out into mid-air!

Wendling's Woes

Ten crews had been lost from Wendling on 24 February, signifying the Group's greatest rebuff to date. However, this scale of punishment, severe as it had been, was now to be exceeded by four on the Friedrichshafen run; a smaller measure of comfort compared to Shipdham lay in the fact that three crews did divert into Switzerland.

Once again, the losses were spread between all four squadrons, with the 578BS and 578Bs leading the way at four each, along with three from the other two sub-units. Two bombers were lost on the way over thanks to a mid-air collision. The invisible but ever-malign effect of propeller wash was the cause of 41-28651/CI:, flown by Lt. John E. Feran, making lethal contact with Lt. Gerald M. Dalton's 41-29174/DC: R+. Both B-24Hs suffered major airframe dislocation. Dalton's aircraft lost part of the starboard wing section and part of the tail assembly, while Feran's machine suffered even greater destruction when both wings and the port tail plane were excised. S/Sgt. Charles F. Payne (WG) from Dalton's crew only survived due to his wearing a backpack parachute, but the other nineteen airmen died and both B-24s crashed SE of Amiens in France. (Payne recalled that Feran's bomber, flying in the rear position, eased back and Lt. Dalton, as squadron "spare," was moving into the vacant slot when its companion in fate veered left and impacted.)

This unfortunate start to the mission was but the harbinger of much worse to come as the group bore ever-deeper into Germany. The *Jagdwaffe* was alerted and over the ensuing few hours would hack no less than twelve crews from the 392BG's formation. An unfortunate over-shoot of a course turning point over the French/German border and subsequent isolation from the bomber stream left the group wide open to assault by a massive *Jagdwaffe* formation. The resultant carnage was primarily incurred from this stage of the mission, being achieved by an estimated 60 to 75 Bf109s and Fw190s and spread over approximately 35 minutes before P-38s intervened to bring much-needed relief to the hard-pressed formation.

The unequal air battle reached its peak of ferocity between Rottweil, Freiburg, and extending up almost to Strasbourg. The bomber gunners' firepower, although formidable in theory, could not match the concentration of firepower put out by the *Jagdwaffe* fighters. Several crews did not long survive the bomb run, one of whom was led by Lt. Walter C. Raschke flying in 42-7518/EC: S **Hard to Get**; flak damage was believed to be the reason why the bomber fell out to come under instant fighter assault. The mid-air explosion that swiftly occurred expunged the lives of all but S/Sgts. Jack H. Rankin (WG) and Roy W. Davis (BT), although the latter subsequently died in a *Stalag* hospital.

Hard to Get's crash site west of Rottweil was several miles distant from where 42-100824/DC: W+ **Arsenal**'s shattered airframe descended after the aircraft was abandoned; this time around just three on Lt. Ellsworth F. Anderson's (POW) team survived. The pilot recalled that several crewmembers' parachutes caught fire, while Lt. Jack F. Maben (CP) was thought to have struck the top turret or tail plane after exiting via the cockpit hatch, since the parachute pack was unopened when the

Germans found his body. Also downed around this stage of the mission was 41-28742/GC:, out of which one of the ten in Lt. Dallas O. Books's (KIA) team survived their bomber's final crash west of Rottweil. Mariazell, also located west of Rottweil, claimed the remains of 42-52465/EC: X, along with all but two on Lt. Rex L. Johnson's (KIA) ten-man crew, the duo of survivors having jumped clear before the bomber "pancaked" into a field and burst into flames. Muehlenbach, NE of Freiberg, formed the crash site for yet another 578BS aircraft (42-99945/EC: Q **Pink Lady**), although Fate was kind to Lt. Bruce L. Sooy's entire crew, who all bailed out.

A second clutch of losses occurred further west. Ettenheinmuenster/Lahr, close to the border with France, was where 42-100117/GC: L-bar **Delayed Action/ Sinister Mister**, in the hands of Lt. William G. Sharpe, came to earth; Sharpe was one of seven fatalities within his crew, one of whom—T/Sgt. Frank C. Wallace (ROG)—reportedly died after capture. The same location was where 42-99981 /EC: U **BTU**, piloted by Lt. Clifford L. Peterson, crashed with just Peterson and four others surviving their bomber's demise.

One of the last crews to be culled at this frenetic stage of the mission was on board 42-52411/CI: B, which was set on fire, causing Lt. Donald K. Clover and crew to bail out and float down near Colmar, just over the French border with Germany. The fact that Colmar is well south of the main NW homeward track for the group suggests the pilots may have been attempting a run into Switzerland. The pattern of very severe attrition was probably completed by a crew from the 577BS in 42-7497/DC: N **Old Daddy**, which was last seen circling left with an engine on fire before spinning in with a total of seven parachutes observed. Lts Lynn C. Peterson and Willard V. Lidgard (CP) sacrificed their lives, along with S/Sgt. Bernard F Dinda (TG) out of the ten-man crew. (The MACR crash site at Kestenholz is not recorded on modern maps.)

Lt. Myers Wahnee, a native-American, examines the artwork on the 448BG aircraft whose title directly relates to his ethnic background. What is B-24H-5-CF/42-64447 /EI: would fly he and his crew into captivity on 20 March, although all ten airmen would take to their parachutes before their mount slammed into the ground SE of Dieppe.

A semi-somnolent aviator on a mattress probably sums up the feelings of the crew, who would prefer even the discomfort of a "biscuit" bed to flying combat. Former F/O (now Lt.) Raymond J. LaCombe, whose combat career stretched back to mid-1943, brought B-24J65-CO/42-100073/NB: H into Swiss airspace on 18 March before all twelve bailed out, with the aircraft crashing at Fehraltdorf.

Relative Luck

Further back along the Swiss/German border near Schaffhausen, Lt. Don H. McMullen (CP), on 41-109826 /DC: U+ **Late Date II**, had crash landed the bomber at Diessenhofen, in Switzerland, and set it on fire. Prior to this, Lt. George T. Haffermehl (P) had given the bail out order, to which he and four others responded, resulting in their descending onto German soil—fatally for S/Sgt. F. Y. Wagner, whose parachute failed.

The six gunners on a crew just returned from a mission on **Pallas Athene** (B-24J-80-CO/42-100187/ EV: V) are in active discussion. What is reportedly the pilot (far left) from among the other three crewmembers, judging from his backpack parachute, is signing the Report Form for the Crew Chief.

Pregnant Peg—whose title was later added to with **II**—has ground to an undignified if intact halt, having suffered what was a regular failing on B-24s, a collapsed nose wheel. The B-24H-1-FO served first with the 577th and then the 576th BS; her final fate is unclear.

McMullen had resisted the order on the (correct) assumption that the fighter-stricken B-24 was still capable of being controlled long enough to seek neutral territory. Also diverting into Switzerland was 41-28692/CI: J, flown by Lt. Walter T. Hebron, whose eleven-man crew was duly interned following the landing at Duebendorf. The third group casualty to seek neutral refuge was a 579BS aircraft flown by Lt. William A. Kale, whose 4-29127/GC; G-Bar **Lil' Gypsy** had lost an engine to fighter gunfire with a second "running away," after which the bomb load was salvoed and a southerly heading adopted. A total of 31 airmen were involved in these incidents.

Lt. James E. Muldoon had taken off with ten on board 42-100100/EC: T **Double Trouble**, but returned to Wendling with eight. Over the French/German border a 20mm shell had struck the B-24, setting the fuselage on fire; the flames in turn probably initiated a short circuit of the bail out bell, to which Lts. Frank T. Walsh (N) and Charles C. Savage (B) promptly reacted—naturally but precipitately as it transpired. The aircraft's title was an ironic commentary on the duo's action, which witnessed them now facing at least a year's unnecessary incarceration within a *Stalag*. To the personnel waiting on the 392BG's airfield that March day, as the late afternoon light gave way to the evening, the truncated ranks of the Group formation must have numbed their very senses. The losses had been almost equally spread, with two squadrons losing three and two surrendering four crews. Varied degrees of heavy battle damage had been sustained by nine of the other fourteen B-24s, one of which diverted into Gravesend with two dead crewmembers.

Spreading the Cost

Pairs of crews were lost from Tibenham and Seething. The 445BG's 41-28666/RN: lost a wing to unknown causes and tumbled to earth near Rouen, in France, with Lt. Gordon B. Parker (P) being one of four fatalities. The other group B-24, 42-7513/WV: T **Pistol Packin' Mama**, suffered a failure of No. 2 engine but held position until a flak barrage disabled No. 3. The steady but inexorable loss of altitude left Lt. Jean H. Sefton with little choice but to adopt a heading for Switzerland. The enemy defenses were thankfully evaded and a landing was made at Dubendorf to deposit ten more U.S. internees upon the Swiss authorities—but not before the bomber impacted with and destroyed overhead railroad cables during its approach run. Sadly, the MACR mentions that two children were killed in this incident.

The 446th and 448th BG's tithe of one B-24 each witnessed a happy if constrained ending for eighteen out of the twenty airmen. Lt. Edward J. Jennings had lost No. 4 engine on the way over but completed his bomb run in 42-7625/B **Happy Go Lucky** before diverting into Duebendorf; the crew's attempts to set the bomber on fire were thwarted. His crew remained intact, unlike Lt. Robert W. Carroll's flying in 42-100284/EI: L. Flak had struck home following the bomb run, but the severe injuries borne by S/Sgt. Robert F. Miltner and Lt. Castleton D. Smith (N) saw the others preferring to stay on board the B-24J that was now losing fuel at a rapid rate and head for Switzerland, where a crash landing at Duebendorf was carried off successfully. Sadly, both injured airmen expired within days and during July, respectively.

Old Buckenham's Lead bomber was its sole loss thanks to fuel starvation. Col. Joseph A. Miller was Command Pilot with Capt. Phillip A. Stock the crew commander; their 41-28649/F8: J+ **Little Bryan** was abandoned by all twelve airmen and finally descended at Vernon/Seine, south of Rouen. The other single group loss came from Hardwick during the mission's return leg, being Lt. Robert M. White's 42-99974/AG: L; a flak strike on the port wing killed the pilot and his crew abandoned the crippled bomber, which crashed near Abbeville.

Two further bomber losses occurred over England on return. The 392BG's 42-99989/DC: V+ crashed at RAF Gravesend, killing two of Lt. Tiefenthal's crew. A 453BG bomber flown by Lt. Stanley D. Kelly suffered a similar fate at Goudhurst, in Kent, but this time around only six out of ten on board 42-52218/F8: O outlived the incident.

The bulk of the 8AF bomber crews were rested on the 19th, with ten B-17 Groups amongst the 1st and 3rd BDs dispatching a total of less than 200 bombers in all to attack *No-Ball* sites in NE France. Frankfurt, another key industrial city, was briefed (20th), and the Division's contribution involved six groups sending out a surprisingly low average of fifteen crews. A few hours later, they were back minus two from Seething's original 25-strong formation.

It was ironic that both losses occurred after Maj. Robert L. Campbell, Jr. (712BS CO), acting as Command Pilot, decided to "abort" the mission. The group had become detached from the stream while forming up and was crossing the French coast near Dieppe when the foregoing decision was taken. The formation swung to port for the briefed exit point near Abbeville, but encountered flak as the turn was made. The Lead B-24 was 42-109808/ CT, and it was struck squarely by one or more bursts. An eyewitness in the Deputy Lead B-24 reported a large flash erupting around the cockpit and the metal skin above the bomb bay seeming to melt as the aircraft fell off and down for some 2,000ft. At this point, structural failure of the tail and outer wing sections occurred. He also saw three airmen emerge from the waist and nose but no parachutes were seen. In fact, Campbell, Lt. Robert O. Voight (P), Capt. F. S. Phillips (B), and Lt. W. Edwards (CP, but occupying the top turret) were thrown clear, despite the aircraft exploding violently; only the two Lieutenants survived, with the other duo subsequently dying from their injuries, a fate shared immediately by the remaining seven airmen on board.

Far better luck attended all ten of Lt. Myers Wahnee's team. Their B-24H was 42-64447/EI: **The Commanche**—a clear reference to the pilot's Native American background—which was similarly dispatched by flak. Not only did they all bail out prior to the bomber's mid-air explosion, but S/Sgt. Richard H. Elliot (WG) evaded and won through to freedom. (A group history states two officers also evaded, with one emulating Elliot's experience and the other subsequently betrayed during his evasion attempt.)

The concept of "war weary" B-24Ds being utilized as Assembly ships was brought to fruition during February 1944. In the case of the 458BG, it was assigned 42-40127 **Bucket of Bolts**, which was formerly with the 93BG as **Thar She Blows again**. The first stage of repainting involves a white coat applied to the fuselage from the middle of the bomb bay forward and the upper wing surfaces.

Back to *Big B*—by Accident!

On 22 March, the map ribbons ended at Oranienburg and Basdorf, both possessing aviation production facilities and both positioned close to Berlin's northern outskirts. Eight of the 2BD's nine regular units would participate in the mission, but they would be joined by the latest addition to Division ranks in the form of the Attlebridge-based 466BG. However, the acolyte group's initiation into combat would be a painful experience and partially self imposed in terms of loss.

The ever-perverse weather patterns over northern Europe kicked in today to subvert any attempt at striking either Primary, so recourse was to bomb the Nazi metropolis as the largest entity

The final stage of color presentation on what would be christened **First Sergeant** was the series of polka dots sprayed over the wing and stabilizer surfaces, as well as the entire fuselage; the colors were red, blue, and yellow. The aircraft's new career was fairly brief; on 27 May, she caught fire thanks to a carelessly discharged flare and, despite quick Fire Section attention, was totally burned out.

containing locations falling into the Target of Opportunity category, this despite the 8/10 to 10/10 cloud cover shrouding the entire region. While on the bomb run, a direct flak strike cast Lt. Gilley T. Brand's (KIA) 41-29416/ U8:—flying the No. 6 slot—into fatal contact with 41-29434/U8: **Terry and the Pirates**, flown by Lt. William J. Terry (KIA) in the No. 3 slot of the same Lead element. Only seven of the twenty airmen survived, five of these from the latter bomber.

The respective crash sites are listed as Malz, on Oranienburg's NE fringe, and Friedrichsfelde, in Berlin's SE suburbs, a distance of nearly 30 miles between the locations—yet both MACRs cite 1,330 hours as the crash time! What also appears uncertain is where the group actually released its loads. It is sufficient to state that the group's inaugural mission was far from happy. Debriefing reports by other crews added to the confusion. Some indicate that Terry's aircraft, after being struck by flak, rolled over and into the other B-24.

Attlebridge's CBW companion unit came home to Horsham St. Faith one crew light. The 96CBW was trailing the Division formation, and while crossing in over the enemy coast, the No. 2 propeller on Lt. Malcolm W. Dunlevie's 41-28678/J3: M "ran away," but an inward course was held; further east, Sgt. John C. Miller (TG) called in several "bogies" that he was unable to identify when requested from "up front"—whereupon the bail out bell was rung! Lt. Leonard W. Blednick (B) tragically found he had the wrong type of pack attachment on his harness and never located a pack that accommodated his harness fittings before the abandoned B-24 finally crashed in the area around Lueneburg; he was the sole fatality.

The two remaining MIA casualties involved the 446BG, both of which made the northern run towards Sweden. Lt. Guy L. Shafer had suffered engine problems with 42-100306/FL: **War Goddess** and his bid for the neutral haven saw the B-24J finally and successfully directed to Visby airfield and internment for the ten airmen. Lt. Julius C. Jaslofsky's similar bid with his 41-29151/HN: **Joker** was finally thwarted when the solo aircraft was intercepted and downed near Guestrow, south of Rostock. Lt. Foster P. Harbin, Jr. (N) was the unlucky exception from among the ten airmen, the reason for his demise being unstated.

Running Down March

The Division would go aloft six times during the remaining nine days of March and lose 10 MIA crews, plus several more in operational incidents during this period. The mission on the 23rd for most if not all the 2BD appears to have been Achmer/Handorf airfield. The previous day's unfortunate collision within the 466BG ranks was to be repeated today. In this instance, the Group had almost traversed Holland's Ijsselmeer when 41-29466 /2U: A+ **Dark Rhapsody** in Lt. Donald G. Griffen's (KIA) charge and 42-52587/2U: K+ flown by Lt. Robert L. Garrett came together in a deadly embrace. All nine on Griffen's B-24H perished, although one had a temporary lease on life after being pulled out of the lake near Vollenhove, into which the aircraft had descended. The other B-24 crashed nearby with six airmen still on board, but the remaining four, including Lt. Garrett, parachuted down; all evaded capture, but Garrett lost his life the following September while concealed at a Belgian location. This was not the last time the Attlebridge fliers would be so afflicted.

F/O Harold W. Hetzler's B-24H 41-29329/7V: L. **Fritzi** was struck squarely in the still-open bomb bay. A fire was started that spread rapidly as the 458BG bomber retained level flight for about one minute. Then it fell away and shortly after the tail section twisted off, followed by a rapid break-up of the rest of the airframe. The number of parachutes sighted ranged from "some seen" to "two seen," but neither statement proved to be completely accurate, since none of the ten airmen survived their aircraft's demise at Warendorf.

Flak was the executioner for the remaining three 2BD losses. Tibenham's 42-7590/WV**: Paper Doll**, flown by Lt. Francis E. Torr, lost two engines and had a wing set on fire, whereupon all ten crewmembers took to their parachutes, leaving the aircraft to descend near Wildeshausen. Lt. James W. Hamilton (P) was one of two fatalities on 42-52277/F8: Q+ which was flak-afflicted in one wing and finally came down on Dutch soil. Seething's **Maid of Orleans** (42-7739/IO:) was departing the target area at Muenster when the bomber began lagging behind. Fire caught hold in the bomb bay and Lt. Robert F. Pinkus ordered a bail out; he apparently got out, but then suffered parachute failure to become the sole fatal casualty.

St. Dizier and Nancy/Essay airfields in France were attacked without loss by 181 B-24s (24rd), but two days later, a single Division crew from Wendling was the sole MIA casualty during a mission to strike *No-Ball* sites in the Pas de Calais. The inherently weak wing structure on the Consolidated design provided little resistance to a direct flak strike on 42-109814/GC: D-bar **Jive Bomber**; the entire starboard wing was chopped off and the resultant spinning action induced by the aerodynamic imbalance held all ten on Lt. Walter F. Lowry's team in place all the way down near St. Pol.

The 27 March mission to assault airfields in SW France got off to a bad start at Attlebridge, with the loss of two crews. Shortly after take-off **Star Dust** (41-29364 /T9: H) crashed, killing all of Lt. Robert J. Mogford's crew in the process. Several minutes previous, 42-52562/2U: F: had lifted off in Lt. Prosper F. Pinto's hands, but this bomber crashed at Hoe, close to where its group companion in misfortune had descended. Rumors that both losses were due to a mid-air collision were never to become substantiated, as nobody survived from Pinto's crew, either.

The 44BG were assigned Mont-de-Marsan airfield and surrendered two bombers to flak. The first was 41-29554/NB: J- **Texas Rose**, which suffered flak damage over the target. Lt. Harold F. Hess decided to head south for Spain, where all ten bailed out near San Sebastian. Such corporate luck did not come the way of six on Lt. Richard E. Harleman's crew after the pilots took up the same course of action with their flak-affected 42-100836/QK: B. A second flak barrage on the way south set the bomb bay on fire and as a last resort the B-24 was "ditched"—unsuccessfully for four in the cockpit after the fuselage split on impact and the nose section immediately sank. Lt. Paul F. Baum (B) survived, but later drowned after he elected to swim ashore. A French fisherman picked up the other four crewmembers for (reluctant) handing over to the Germans.

A third crew from Tibenham joined the MIA list over the group's airfield target at Pau. The flak barrage was weak, but unfortunately one shell impacted against 42-64478/H6: **Cabin in the Sky**. Maj. Curtis H. Cofield (HQ, 732BS) and Capt. Alvin Lien (P), along with their nine-man crew, stood little chance, as their charge descended into the Bay of Biscay. Up to seven parachutes were reported, but it appears that the deployed canopies only provided a short lease of life to their users, since there were no survivors.

March's final mission (30th) resulted in nil MIA losses, but did involve a particularly heavy casualty list incurred during Assembly by the 20CBW for a short hop across the Channel to attack *No-Ball* sites. Hardwick's 41-28950/GO:, flown by Lt. Robert L. McFetrich and 42-110033/AG:, bearing Lt. Chester D. Mackinster and crew collided over Suffolk. Of the nineteen crewmembers involved, just two and one Enlisted men

The almost total excision of the starboard rudder and at least the visible part of the elevator on an anonymous B-24 from the 453BG is under examination by three of her crew, surely thankful at having made it back to Old Buckenham. The loss of these control surfaces would have rendered the pilots' task of even remaining airborne, let alone holding course, extremely difficult

respectively parachuted to safety before the bombers piled in at Henham. For whatever reason, some of the bomb load on one or the other aircraft did not immediately explode; this was to prove tragically unfortunate for some among a sizeable party of personnel from the nearby USAAF airfield at Halesworth dispatched to the crash sites to attend to various matters. Suddenly at least one bomb exploded, further adding to the disaster by killing six airmen and four civilians, as well as injuring many more on the scene.

Precision "Blind Bombing"?

The contrary weather conditions over NW Europe that regularly militated against visual target sighting for the 8AF persuaded the USAAF hierarchy to turn to the RAF for assistance beginning in late 1943 through the use of *H2S*, followed successively by *Oboe* and *G-H*. The former listed device was a basic form of Position Plan Indicator (PPI) whose scope screens displayed a light impression for land and a dark one for water stretches, with built up areas also capable of being identified by more experienced operators on the Pathfinder Force (PFF) B17s and B-24s bearing the sets.

These aircraft were initially concentrated within one group based at Alconbury (482BG), but by March 1944, a single squadron from one group in each Bomb Division was selected for training and was allocated twelve of these specialist aircraft. In the 2BD's case this was Hethel's 564BS, which was allocated B-24Hs and commenced operations on 22 March. At this stage of WWII two crews would fly to the airfield whose group was leading the Division. (As 1944 progressed, the provision of *H2X*-equipped bombers—*H2X* being an American adaptation operating on a more precise 3cm wavelength compared to the 10cm system with the original H2S—was steadily expanded until each unit had its own allocation of PFF aircraft by the year's end.)

There was an inevitable penalty inherent in the use of this equipment, since it clearly eroded the chances of carrying out the precision strikes that were central to the Daylight Bombing Campaign's prosecution as originally conceived. In effect, it was a case of saturating a target area with the hope that a degree of punishment would be visited upon the industrial or military facilities below. It was not basically different from the RAF policy of "Area Bombing" that had been forced upon its Bomber Command ever since the mandatory switch from daylight to nocturnal assault in the face of swinging losses during 1939/1940.

Jagdwaffe Reorganization

The *Jagdwaffe's* establishment figures at the end of 1943 totalled 1,108 (*Luftflotte Reich*) and 388 (*Luftflotte* 3), with an available strength of 758/237 in practical terms and an operational percentage of 548/148, respectively. By the end of March 1944, the equivalent figures read: Establishment 1,308/364; available strength 949/134; and operational strength 643/92. The latter set of figures were indeed marginally higher, but now the clear emphasis was on providing more cover over Germany with a notable reduction in *Luftflotte 3's* strength. The German fighter pilots' ability to dominate the total airspace over western and central Europe was steadily contracting as the Allied escorts continued their expansion in numbers, to which was added a technical superiority over their adversaries.

The Pending Plan

As March faded into April, a temporary, albeit significant, sea change in operations for both the RAF and 8th Bomber Commands was being decided. The need to isolate the proposed Normandy Landing Zone from prompt and surely lethal countermeasures from the Wehrmacht/SS forces stationed outside the region was of paramount importance in ensuring the success of operation *Overlord*. The Transportation Plan, already drawn up by the Allied High Command, had the intention of bringing to bear an overwhelming weight of assault upon the enemy's communications, particularly throughout eastern France, Belgium, and Luxembourg by the use of the Anglo/American air forces. Railroads, airfields, roads, and canals were all to be subjected to regular attack. In addition, emphasis would be placed upon an apparent isolation of the Pas de Calais region in NE France, whose flat coastal strips were already feeding Hitler's conviction that the Allied Landings would be focused on there.

To date, the RAF and USAAF "heavies" had fully indulged in their brief of attacking strategic type targets. In recent weeks, however, pressure had been brought to bear upon ACM Harris and Gen. Spaatz to divert their resources in order to supplement the efforts of the 9USAAF and RAF's 2nd Tactical Air Force (2TAF) medium- and fighter-bombers in implementing the Plan. The protests of the "Bomber Barons" that a switch would dilute their crews' efforts to hammer Germany's industrial base had been basically dismissed, although a total commitment to the Plan would never fully emerge between April and August before full strategic missions were resumed.

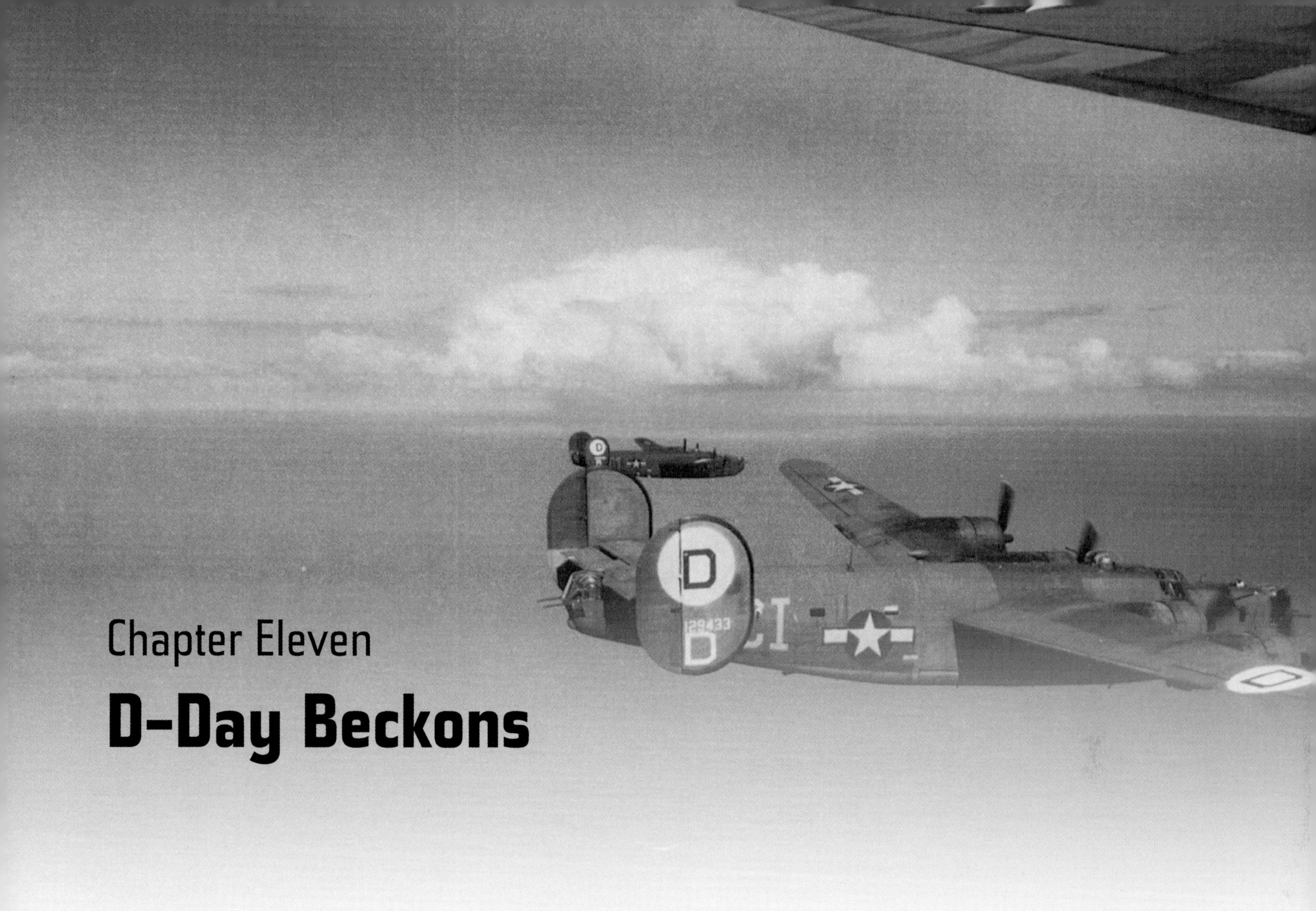

Chapter Eleven

D-Day Beckons

Comment

March 1944 had witnessed some of the fiercest daylight aerial battles to date between the 8AF and the Luftwaffe. Bomber losses had continued to be heavy, but had shown a steady advance towards a regular sustainable loss ratio. This situation was primarily due to the 8th Fighter Command pilots' equally accelerating and effective encroachment upon their *Jagdwaffe* adversaries' hitherto almost unrestricted ability to bring often overwhelming forces to bear upon the B-17 and B-24 formations. The month of April would see the German fighter pilots being placed evermore on the tactical back foot; the loss of numerous *Experten* (Aces) in combat, coupled to reductions in the length of training schedules for potential fighter pilots would be key factors resulting in the aerial initiative swinging towards the Allied air forces in an ultimately permanent manner.

Bruising Long Haul

This advance towards regular air supremacy was not apparent during April, at least not as far as the bomber crews were concerned. The *Jagdwaffe* would still be able to inflict painful losses, albeit at irregular intervals, while the increasing numbers of flak batteries would ultimately replace the fighter as the bombers' main adversary. Ludwigshafen, in SW Germany, was listed for 1 April, with the 2BD sending three CBWs. However, adverse weather conditions allied to poor navigation standards not only caused the Primary to remain inviolate, but resulted in assaults on the Swiss city of Schaffhausen, an action that later saw the U.S. government paying reparations.

Adding to the frustration of only bombing various Targets of Opportunity by just over half the Force of 195 dispatched, was the loss of twelve crews over enemy territory, plus three crashes in southern England. The 2nd and 14th CBWs shared the MIA figure equally; the 448BG had a particularly bad experience in suffering the highest loss figure of bombers (four), as well as losing its CO in the process.

The group was flying Lead for both the Division and 20CBW; up front in 41-28763/YO: A—a 389BG PFF B-24H—was Col. James M. Thompson (Group CO) and Lt. Alan Teague with his Hethel-based crew. After confronting very poor visibility over France, an optional "recall" signal from 8th AFHQ was declined and the formations proceeded on. The 446BG, flying High Group, became detached from the Wing and headed back home, but the other two groups kept on course. A protracted period of time spent over the target area with no bombing conducted and a strong headwind on the return route left the twenty-one bombers still holding in formation dangerously short of fuel. As it was, no less than four crews would run out while still over enemy territory.

This 445BG Consolidated B-24J bears a hydraulically-operated Motor Products A6B nose turret. A small L-shaped pitot mast located below **Grim Reaper**'s artwork displaces the large horn-pattern units borne by D, H, and J Models to date. The masking of the rear fuselage by the massive fins has merited the repetition on that surface of the aircraft letter and squadron reference (S+) that could otherwise be rendered invisible.

B-24D-165-CO 42-72866 was a 565BS bomber (seen earlier in her combat career) that eventually had the squadron code EE applied before mid-March 1944. This addition to **Jackass Male** was not enjoyed for long, because on 1 April, she became one of three Hethel losses, along with eight on Lt. William Knowles's (POW) team during a mission to Ludwigshafen.

One was the Thompson/Teague B-24, but their machine was not the first to falter. Lt. Harrison Meller lost one engine on 42-110087/IG: as the formation was between Paris and the Pas de Calais and soon decided to ring the bail out bell, as his fuel gauges were virtually registering zero. All the crew jumped, but Sgt. William A. Warren's parachute failed to open, while the pilot's pack only operated when he was dangerously close to the ground. On the other hand, four crewmembers managed to evade capture.

Lt. Teague faced the same situation and took the same action, but remained on board with a view to crash landing his charge. Col. Thompson had originally vacated his seat and moved into the fuselage, but then reappeared to briefly resume his position. The bomber was not too far above French soil when the Col. told Teague he was going to jump—a decision that had tragic consequences, since he was subsequently found dead with his parachute either not deployed or alternately deployed, but at too marginal a height to take full effect.

Teague crash landed in good order, but, after vacating the immediate scene, he realized he had made no effort to destroy the specialist PFF equipment. Unfortunately, he was spotted by a German patrol before he could re-enter the B-24 and was arrested. On the other hand, although the Germans came across the equipment, they did not immediately remove it. Two guards were assigned to the B-24, but several days later they were reportedly overwhelmed by three members of Teague's crew who had gained access to the Resistance and returned to the site in order to destroy the equipment!

Fuel shortage was the cause of the other two crews failing to return to Seething. **Crud Wagon** (42-52098/ CT:), in Lt. Charles Knorr's hands, was abandoned over the Pas de Calais. However, some of the crew were still on board when a fighter attack made up their minds to get out. All but one landed close to St. Pol and were rounded up; Lt. Charles McBride (B) was more fortunate in being picked up by the Resistance, signaling the start of a five-month successful bid to evade capture until the area was liberated. The fourth B-24 to suffer fuel shortage was 42-100109 **Eastern Queen**, which bore Lt. Kenneth Weaver's crew. Parachute failure was the cause of Sgt. Harvey Dickey's death, but all his colleagues landed safely to face a POW camp.

A fifth Group bomber nearly made it back to England—42-100356/IG: L. **Black Widow**. Progressive engine failure left just one motor functioning as the B-24J headed out from the NE French coast at minimum altitude. The enemy coast was just 15 miles behind when Lt. Jack Black was compelled to lower his failing bomber into the sea; both he and Lt. Joe Pomfret (CP) received deep head gashes when impacting with the cockpit frame due to the absence of shoulder harness fittings. All crewmembers survived the impact, which apparently left their bomber relatively intact, but a major obstacle to full salvation lay in the fact that the life raft hatches had jammed.

With no hesitation, and while his colleagues clung desperately to the airframe, T/Sgt. Eugene Dworaczyk (ROG) went back inside the partially submerged fuselage and managed to release the dinghies, an act of raw courage that subsequently won him the Soldier's Medal. Meanwhile, Lt. Pomfret, who could not swim and who had been further injured when thrown out of the cockpit by the "ditching" impact, was being supported by Lt. Peter Werment (N); sadly, the frigid water soon affected the navigator's limbs to the extent he could not hold onto Pomfret without risking going under himself and had to let go, whereupon the copilot sank before any further assistance from other crewmembers could reach him. The nine survivors gratefully climbed into their rafts, unaware that it would be almost two days before rescue would occur. During this period, T/Sgt. Charles Nissen's (Eng.) condition deteriorated to a fatal level. The dinghies drifted steadily across the English Channel to within sight of the English coast before a fishing boat spotted them and hauled the eight airmen out of their cramped and dangerously exposed rubber "perches."

Two Hardwick crews were lost with a sole survivor out of nineteen. Nobody emerged alive from 42-40983/GO: **Judith Lynn**, in Lt. Joseph M Roznos' charge, after flak brought it down near Rheims. On the way home, a single survivor emerged from Lt. Edward L. Robbins's crew on 42-100248/GO: P after the B-24J piled in at an airfield at Rheims during what was reportedly a failed crash landing bid. A third group bomber (42-99943/YM: R), having suffered battle damage, crashed at Rochester.

2CBW Fortunes

Seven crews were culled from the 2CBW, shared between Hethel and Tibenham. However, the 389BG MIA figure included Lt. Teague's aircraft, which was a PFF-equipped machine that had flown Lead for the 448BG. Whereas all but Col. Thompson had survived from this bomber, the death toll on the other two Group losses was much more severe at sixteen out of twenty-one. B-24D **Jack-Ass Male** (42-72866/EE: Q) had consumed eight on Lt. William H. Knowles's (POW) team, with the B-24 crashing near St. Pol; the other two survivors were in 42-99977/HP: P, flown by Lt. Sidney W. Eline, who was one of the eight casualties.

Lt. Thomas J. Madden's (POW) 42-109825/WV: caught fire on the port wing following a flak strike and the ten-man crew jumped clear before their bomber crashed near Ypres, in Belgium; Lt. Erling M. Dawes (CP) alone evaded capture. Lt. Joseph A. Gfelner's (KIA) 42-110046/RN: was homeward bound, but was then attacked by fighters; at least five of the crew bailed out, but only half the ten on board survived the crash south of Balingen. Lt. William Lafferty (Evaded) guided his 42-110029/RN: M homeward, but he did not get further than the Laon region in NE France when a bail out was called for; of the ten airmen, no less than seven made it into the hands of the Resistance. Less fortunate were six members on Lt. Phil C. Dana's (KIA) team, after 41-29463 / WV: V came down near Long Stratton on return.

A three-day lapse in operations for the 8AF ended on the 5th, although only the 2BD was involved in three-Group strength. The bid to bomb *No-Ball* sites at St. Pol/ Siracourt was largely thwarted by heavy cloud patterns. An even smaller percentage of bombs struck a similar Primary at Watten the next day, when the Division was again the sole participant, having dispatched five Groups, of which one twelve-plane formation delivered its load; continuing cloud cover was the cause of the mass "abortions." (The sub-force that bombed was equipped with the British *G-H* blind bombing equipment and involved individual crews from the participating Groups.) These easy-paced if frustrating runs would abruptly fade into the memory for the participants when they were alerted 48 hours later for the latest deep penetration run into Germany.

Brunswick Blues

Aviation industry plants in Brunswick were the focus of attack on the 8th. The city was the epicenter associated with a particularly vicious defensive response to the 8AF bombers' incursions. Today would enhance that reputation in a very bloody way in general for the Division and specifically for the 44BG element. The group was flying both 14CBW and Division Lead, an "honor" that would be paid for with just over one-third of the day's final casualty figure and the worst MIA total on any mission flown out of Shipdham.

The Division's progress towards its Primary target was relatively calm until the lead formations were over-flying the distinctive shape of the Duemmersee, when "peace and quiet went to Hell," at least as far as the 44BG records are concerned. In fact, the initial encounters with the *Jagdwaffe* occurred further on after the 14CBW alone failed in its briefed intention of making a triangular course change from North of Brunswick, culminating in a westerly bomb run; the Primary was missed and Targets of Opportunity were being sought when the unequal air battle erupted. A mass of fighters from one of the three *Gefechtsverbaende* all unluckily homed in upon the 2BD from twelve o'clock to deliver devastating attacks. The Wing's specific attackers came from the ranks of JG3 and *Sturmstaffel 1*, who descended upon the group and its Wendling co-formation.

Lt. Pino (CP), on Lt. Wahler's 42-52293/NB: G **Judy's Buggy**, recalled the effect of the attacker's gunfire assuming the form of winking light bulbs. No. 3 and 4 engines were struck with immediate disablement of the former and ultimate failure after "bombs away" of the other. The pilots then had to apply full rudder and trim tab adjustments against the asymmetric drag caused by this power imbalance, but managed to withstand the tremendous physical pressure on their lower torsos as far as the airfield at Beccles.

Prior to landing, five crewmembers elected to bail out, including Sgt. Joseph M. Meskinis (TG), who had survived the demolishment of his turret. Salvation turned to tragedy for him, since he was found dead with his heated suit cord instead of his ripcord in his hand. Before landing, the flaps had to be manually pumped down, since the hydraulic pump normally used was within the now-defunct No. 3 engine, but all passed off well for the five airmen still on board, two of whom had received wounds of a magnitude thought to have prevented a safe bail out on their part.

The group's martyrdom was to be spread among all four squadrons, with the 66BS least affected in this respect. This was no consolation for Lt. William M. Richardson's team on 42-99996/

The semi-clad figure alongside the aircraft name is seen on a 458BG "original" (B-24H-10-CF/41-29295/Z5: K), whose Emerson turret and straight camouflage separation lines are features of Consolidated, Fort Worth airframes. She lasted until the Tutow mission on 9 April, when fighters brought her down, three on Lt. Walter J. Raiter's (POW) crew dying in the process.

QK: I, none of whom survived the bomber's violent demise over Salzwedel. The 67BS surrendered two B-24s, one of which (42-110083/NB: X) piled into the ground near Langenhagen, which was to be the "Target of Opportunity" for the Group, as both Primary and Secondary targets were denied access thanks to heavy smoke screens. Sgt. Archie M. Thomas (WG) was the sole survivor on Lt. Robert A. Mayes's crew and he only managed to scramble clear scant seconds before the B-24's final impact. Lt. George J. Thom had been experiencing difficulty in holding position with 42-7767/NB: C, according to Lt. Gerald G. Gille (N), who was one mission behind his 506BS crew and today had volunteered to fly with this crew. The bomber was isolated at the point of attack and fell further away from the Group as fighter gunfire rendered it helpless. The bail out order was finally given and all ten airmen descended safely, leaving their charge to crash within Hannover's city boundaries.

There was a grim arithmetic progression of 1-2-3 relative to squadron number progression, because the 68BS gave up a trio of bombers with thirteen of the thirty crewmembers killed. Lt. William B. Altemus was flying 42-110020/WQ: Z and according to T/Sgt. Lanning C. Baker (Eng.), the effect of the strikes was that the fuselage caught fire in the bomb bay, with the flames shooting forward towards the flight deck. Baker promptly opened the cockpit roof hatch, which had the desired effect of ducting the worst of the fire out into the slipstream, but still left him badly burned around the head. He lost consciousness for a few seconds, but on recovering he snapped on his parachute pack and exited via the front starboard bomb bay door space that had been forced open by some unknown means. Only Lt. Eugene A. Phelan (CP) and two others got clear out of the eleven airmen on board.

Both in-board engines were knocked out on 42-99987/WQ: S **Pizz and Moan** and S/Sgt. Raymond H. McKenna (Eng.) and Lt. Warren H. Barry were killed; the other nine crewmembers managed to bail out safely. The third loss involved Lt. Raymond H. Townsend's 42-109822/ WQ: O. **Townsend's Terrible Ten.** On a previous mission, the crew had been fortunate to survive the jettisoning and explosion of the load when they were at far too low an altitude to safely carry out the action. The good fortune experienced then now deserted five among the ten on board. The first of three separate attacks knocked the bomber out of formation, as well as disabling an engine, while the second assault just as the pilots regained formation reduced power to well below 50%. The now wallowing and steadily descending B-24 was ripe for more punishment that duly arrived. Lt. Paul A. Jones (N) had his helmet blown off and thought he had been blinded because he could not open his eyes; in fact, blood had sealed his eyelids, which he thankfully was able to quickly pry open. He assisted T/Sgt. Walker K. Nealon (Enlisted bombardier) to clip on his pack and bail out via the nose wheel aperture. The Sgt.'s pack had been inadvertently donned upside down and in his dazed state of mind—doubtless caused by a serious head wound—he literally tore the canvas cover off in his bid to deploy the canopy instead of searching for the ripcord that was now on the wrong side! Only three further crewmembers emerged, but the pilot was not among this number.

Although the 506BS absorbed nearly half the losses in aircraft (five), the scale of fatalities (seven) among the fifty crewmembers was low, if tragic for the individuals concerned. Lt. Ernest A. Herzing's 42-110023/GJ: T **Rubber Check** was thoroughly shot up, leaving Nos. 1 and 2 smoking and No. 3 set ablaze. Momentary hesitation between the pilots regarding what next to do ended with a decision to "get the Hell outa' here!" An exit via the bomb bay was made more hazardous by the fact the open doors were swinging wildly in the slipstream. In spite of this, all ten airmen reached the ground as imminent "Kriegies."

Similar corporate good fortune was realized by Lt. Robert H. Marx's ten on 41-29153/ GJ: Z **Greenwich**. Flak had already damaged the bomber, knocking out No. 3 engine prior to "bombs away." Then a spin developed following release of its load, a motion that was only arrested after several thousand feet of altitude was surrendered. T/Sgt. Robert C. Franklin (Eng.) threw the hydraulic switch by way of gaining the necessary pressure to activate the flaps and the bomb bay doors, so providing a firm level flight platform for a bail out. Time was of the essence, especially when the pilot and Lt. Vernie R. Brockman (CP) called up to say there were scant seconds to go before control of the B-24 would be lost. The gallant action of these three airmen happily ended up positively for all ten, who got out and down near Herford. The third crew to be totally spared was led by Lt. Jack M. Winn, who was one mission ahead of his crew—at two! Flying behind the deputy Lead bomber, 42-100423.GJ: A. had both port engines set on fire and soon after was abandoned by all on board.

Lt. Guy W. Johnson's 42-73506/GJ: X remained structurally intact until after "bombs away," but scarcely had Lt. Robert J. Bauman (N) reached for his log book to record the fact when flak struck home. He was badly burnt by flames that erupted around his compartment, but prior to bailing out he ensured Lt. Charles L. Wiest's (B) safe exit from the nose turret by opening its doors. (The absence of an internal emergency release handle would have otherwise trapped the bombardier in this position.) As distance was lost with the formation, all ten airmen took to their parachutes but only nine remained alive after landing. Lt. Leroy M. Williamson (CP) had heard small arms fire as he was almost down; then, as he divested himself of his parachute, he heard Lt. Johnson shouting to the effect that he was giving up and for his captors to desist from shooting, followed by an immediate burst of firing that killed the pilot.

The squadron's MIA tally was completed by Lt. Dallas L. Sprinkle's 42-109827/GJ: Q, flying in the rear of the formation and shot up by the fighters around the IP. Cannon shells smashed into the upper fuselage, puncturing the fuel cross feed pipes and oxygen lines. The resultant fierce fire was further fed by the air sluicing in via the waist windows. The bail out signal was given, but only S/Sgts. Charles Winn (ROG) and Jack B. Freeman (TG) and one waist gunner got clear before the bomber exploded. Amazingly, the pilot survived being blasted out of the cockpit and opened his parachute, but none of the other six were so lucky. S/Sgt. Charles L. Radu (Eng.) probably got as far as donning his parachute pack prior to the B-24's disintegration, since he was found lying in the vicinity of the crash site with an undeployed parachute.

Capt. Walter Stewart holds one side of the platter, along with an ARC representative believed to be Helen McDonald. The cake is part of the farewell ceremony not only for the tour-expired Stewart, but behind the party is another "veteran" in the form of **Bomerang**—with 53 missions the first 2BD B-24 to break the half-century mission mark—that the officer soon will fly Stateside for a War Bond tour.

A 328BS contemporary of **Naughty Nan** (seen in Chapter ten), **Able Mabel** is snapped heading for Bourges, France, on 4 April. This B-24J-130-CO departed Group ranks three months prior to **Nan**; a projected mission to V-1 sites in the Pas de Calais ended with Lt. Robert W. Brown (POW) baling out his crew near Bruges, only seven of whom deployed their parachutes in time.

Sterile Errol's still-smoking fuselage/wing junction is being promptly attended to by Hardwick's Fire Section; a "Hot Papa" clad in an asbestos suit is walking under the wing. The B-24J-105-CO is 42-109810/AG: F, and damage was severe enough to merit salvage action; the date of the mission from which she returned is unclear, however.

Lt. Wind (506BS), upon return from his first mission as a supernumerary pilot a day or so previous, told his crew: "There was nothing to it. We just flew there, dropped our bombs and came home." His second, and the crew's first mission today, brutally disillusioned him on this matter! Cannon shells knocked out No. 2 engine and a flak burst shattered Plexiglas panels that cast fragments into his face and hands. No. 3 and 4 engines' oil tanks were riddled with holes. After joining the Shipdham circuit and entering into his landing run, a B-24 ahead ground looped and blocked the runway. Two engines were by now "red lined" and liable to fail, so a desperate switch of direction was made towards the cross runway. After making contact, a punctured main gear wheel caused the B-24 to slew off the runway before its momentum was spent, but the crew got out intact apart from the pilot. However, a different ordeal was awaiting Lt. Wind over the ensuing 24 hours, as bureaucracy raised its ever-frustrating head.

The two other Wing MIA losses were borne by the 392BG. Lt. Tievo E. Eleranto's 42-110061/DC: W+ was reported at debriefing as blowing up with no parachutes seen, but in fact it was successfully abandoned by all ten crewmembers after suffering fatal damage between the IP and the target; the B-24 crashed SW of Wunstorf. In stark contrast, just one gunner out of Lt. James W. Dickson's eleven-man team on 42-7599 (formerly CI: B but now EC; B) **Mac's Sack III** survived after the bomber was brought down by fighters prior to the bomb run; the crash site was 10 miles SW of Uelsen. A third group casualty was 42-73505/DC: S+ **Fairy Belle**. Oil pressure failure in two engines just in from the enemy coast forced a turn-back. Steadily lowering altitude despite jettisoning of bomb load and excess equipment saw the bomber barely gain solid ground near the coastal village Sidestrand, where an emergency crash landing was made by Lt. Thomas L. Anderson; he was one of five fatalities out of ten on board after the B-24 caught fire.

Spreading the Cost

The 14CBW's costly experience was partially matched by two of the other three Wings, who each gave up seven crews. The 458BG suffered the least within both the Division and the 96CBW, losing a single B-24. Lt. Edward Sievers was flying 42-52392/J4: O. **Wabbit Twacks**, which progressed as far as the target before being fatally damaged either before or after the bomb run was completed. All ten airmen bailed out safely to land several miles from the target, their B-24's crash site being Immekath, NE of Langenhagen. The B-24 had been parked on a dispersal close to Wood Farm, where a Ms. Anne Wooten lived; she recalled the great sadness when she realized the crews were MIA; this illustrated the growing bond many civilians living around the USAAF airfields were indulging in with their Transatlantic "cousins."

The 466BG, in contrast, almost doubled its casualty figure to date (seven, of which four were confirmed or reported losses due to collision) by coming back six light. Lt. Allan H. Strom's 41-29422/T9: J. **Rebel Yell** was one of three 784BS losses; near the IP, one engine was disabled and fire caught hold of a wing, leaving the nine survivors little option but to jump. A second squadron B-24 was downed by fighters between the IP and target (42-52516/T9; P. **Virgin Sturgeon**, flown by Lt. Harry E. Sturdevant). The resultant mid-air explosion killed the pilot and seven others, the two survivors having the good fortune to be blown clear. The third squadron casualty was 42-52596/T9: R, which was thoroughly shot up before coming down near Diepolhz; Lt. Robert E. Bryans (P) was one of four survivors.

The 786BS lost two, beginning with 42-52480/U8: K, which was on the way home when the latest fighter assault inflicted fatal damage. Lt. John T. Fouts and Lt. William F. Gray finally brought off a crash landing near Bassum, out of which nine crewmembers emerged alive, Lt. Orlie A. Hatfield (B) having already died. Fire enveloped the port wing on 42-52610/U8: D **The Madame** following strikes over the target. Further fighter attacks resulted in the aircraft coming down near Lembruch, minus only four of the ten-man crew led by Lt.

The first Assembly ships operated by 2BD Groups were B-24D veterans retired from combat. **Fearless Freddie** was formerly **Eager Beaver** of the 93BG. Now with all armament deleted and her airframe finished overall in International Orange, she stands ready for her new function. Transfer to the 446BG occurred on 24 February 1944.

S/Sgt. De Sales Glover strikes a pose at his waist gun hatch. He was very mature physically for his age, sixteen years! This salient fact, leading to his "grounding" and Stateside dispatch, was only established after he had flown at least six missions; whether he ever received the Air Medal for his operational participation with the 458BG has never been confirmed.

Kenneth K. Messenger (KIA). The final group loss involved 41-29365/6L: J bearing Lt. Daniel B. Harris's crew; the crash site was close to Fallersleben, but by then all but one out of ten crewmembers were floating down to captivity.

The same casualty rate borne by the 96CBW was experienced by the 453BG, and was not the last time this group would be struck so hard; in addition, nearly a 70% fatality rate would be experienced, although this unfortunate factor was tragically not atypical among B-24 crews. The 732BS lost two crews with 41-28650/E3: peeling off under fighter assault prior to the IP; Lt. James K. Bingaman (P) was the sole fatality out of twelve on board, while his body was never recovered, having presumably been totally consumed in the bomber's demise. The fellow squadron B-24 42-52185/E3:, with Lt. Joe E. Dejarnette and crew, was supposedly brought down near Salzwedel, but since no physical evidence has yet come to light, the likelihood is that the aircraft got back out over the North Sea but came down in its anonymous waters.

A second pair of crews from the 735BS were lost, beginning with 42-64453/H6:, out of which only S/Sgt. Ralph Fordyce (Eng.) got out alive before the aircraft plunged into the ground NW of Salzwedel. Its partner in misfortune was 41-29571/H6:; Lt. Jack J. Dixon's mount left the pilot and six out of the other nine free to jump clear near Jagen. The 733BS airmen declared MIA were unfortunate, in that just five out of twenty survived. Four of these were on 42-52180/F8**: Lil Eight Ball**, which sustained a flak burst on the nose that almost certainly killed all "up front," since it was the four airmen from Lt. Fred G. Brady's crew in the rear section who bailed out. Lt. August V. Bergman, flying 42-64464/F8:, was one of nine fatalities when fighters downed the bomber at Wistedt. The group's punishment across its entire structure was completed when 42-110076/E8:, flown by Lt. Robert R. Swigert (KIA), was another fighter casualty that came down at Tylsen to leave a single survivor out of ten.

20CBW

The single 93BG loss was credited to Oblt. Karl-Heinz Willius, an *Experte* from 2/JG26, who, having secured his 48th *abschuess,* was then almost immediately downed by a P-47. Lt. Joseph A. Buland, Jr.'s B-24/42-73495/AG: came down on Dutch soil adjoining the Ijsselmeer, as did Willius's Fw190. The *Jagdwaffe* pilot's aircraft, with his body still inside, was unearthed during land reclamation work in 1967. Six of the nine American airmen were more fortunate in surviving their bomber's downing. Bungay lost two crews,

Jamaica? A 466BG aircraft is lifting off from the runway at Attlebridge. Her landing gear is already being retracted in order to ensure a swift transition to a clean aerodynamic outline. Take-off was one of the most hazardous stages of a flight, in what were bulky and unwieldy aerofoils, regardless of whether light or heavily laden.

Gens. Leon Johnson (left) and Ted Timberlake are almost certainly photographed after both were promoted from their former Colonelcies, when they held command of the 44th and 93rd BGs; their uprating was linked with their switch to command of the 14th and 20th CBWs.

beginning with 42-7620/ RT: M **The Princess**; during run-in to the target flak struck home and inflicted a scale of damage that finally persuaded Lt. George C. Kougias to bail his crew out, only seven of whom survived. Then, 42-679/FL: O **The Beast** received a mix of flak and fighter damage that caused all on Lt. Percy H. Schopfer's team (P) to vacate their aircraft, which crashed at Osterlinde. Schopfer was supposedly killed by small arms fire, but this matter was never resolved.

Bureaucracy - U.S. Style

Lt. Wind's physical condition following his eventful return from Brunswick to Shipdham was sufficient for Dr. Allison (506BS Flight Surgeon) to recommend his transfer to a nearby military hospital. However, six hours elapsed before his condition was cleared; during this period the doctor attending to him appeared more interested in lecturing a fellow practitioner about his technique. Here was the first of several 'administrative' hurdles the pilot would face over the ensuing 24 hours.

He was assigned to an otherwise empty ward, where what he said was a "hard-nosed nurse" threw him a pair of pajamas and ordered him to take a shower before allotting him a bed. The garment was found to be too small, but when the issue was raised the surly response was to point him towards the clothing store for him to sort the problem out. Having done so, he went to bed more than 24 hours after waking up. After six hours, he was peremptorily woken up and ordered to make his bed within 30 minutes, after which he was ordered to search out another bed. Hardly had he settled into his new unit when he was again woken up to be greeted by what transpired to be an unappetizing breakfast!

The next "hurdle" related to the fact that he was not categorized as a "bed" patient and therefore had to seek his meals in the Mess hall; on reaching there, he was informed he had to bring his Mess kit. The mordant expression now uttered by what was a thoroughly frustrated "inmate" shook the staff into issuing him with the necessary equipment! He had arrived at the hospital while still wearing his flight suit, and because he could not return to the ward until 1900 hours, sought to gain access to the Officers Club to pass away the time, only to be told that he could only enter when wearing a Class A uniform.

This last bureaucratic "hurdle" proved to be the last straw. Consequently, when his face bandages were removed next day he was informed his release was dependent upon paperwork whose completion could take anything up to two weeks, so he decided upon instant action. Within 24 hours, two of his crew arrived with an ambulance into which he scrambled; what he said to the surly nurse who said he could not depart without the necessary medical documents was never recorded, but surely it was plainly, if bluntly, pitched!

Continuing the Strategic Brief

The 8AF's strategic brief would extend regularly over the remainder of April, this in spite of the dictates of the Transportation Plan. Nine out of fourteen missions would reflect the basic trend, beginning on the 9th. Aviation production sources were targeted, with the 2BD going to Tutow. Whereas the Division had taken the vast bulk of the casualties on the 8th, a more even MIA distribution would see 14 B-24s lost out of 32 bombers, of which half would gain neutral sanctuary.

All ten groups were dispatched, but only 126 out of 246 crews attacked either the Primary, Secondary, or Targets of Opportunity; adverse weather was responsible for many of the "abortive" sorties. The mission commenced badly for two crews from separate Wings. Lt. Glenn Reece's 42-99982/RR: H. **Might of the Eighth** was reportedly run into by Wendling's 41-29485/EC:, flown by Lt. Hubert F. Morefield, while assembling in thick overcast conditions. Of the eleven Hethel airmen, only Capt. John Driscoll (Gp. Armament Officer) and S/Sgt. Harvey Dionne fought clear of the centrifugal forces to parachute down; eight on board the other B-24 were consumed in their mount's destruction, the bombers impacting near Bintree and Twyford, some ten miles NE of the 392BG airfield. Lt. Morefield, along with Lt. Kenneth F. Kaufman (N) alone survived from the 392BG B-24. (An RAF observer in nearby Foulsham's control tower stated that a single bomber approached at right angles to the formation in which the other was included prior to the collision.)

The 96CBW had lost seven crews 24 hours previous and now added a further six between the two groups. Twelve 458BG crews "aborted," and a fragmented formation pattern that only began to pull together over Denmark left the group open to particular fighter attention that duly arrived near Kiel. Lt. Walter E. Mangerich's 41-28667/7V: F **That's Jayhawker** was already down to three engines over Denmark and began to lose distance. The bomb load was jettisoned and a heading for Sweden taken up by the seemingly doomed B-24; in fact, the bomber made it safely there. **Batchelor's Paradise** (42-52432/J3: P) was badly shot up in the course of two fighter passes, with total failure of both starboard engines and partial power loss on No. 1; hydraulic and electrical systems were adversely affected, as was rudder control. This scale of damage probably impelled Lt. Byron Logie to also head northwards for Sweden, but if so, it failed over the Danish island of Seeland, when a bail out of the six surviving crew took place, the bomber crashing in the town of Venslav. Logie and two others managed to evade capture and not only gained Swedish territory, but were back in Britain around the month's end!

The group's two other losses were initiated between the IP and the target. First, the Lead bomber (41-29295/Z5: K **Bomb Totin' Mama**, bearing Lt. Walter J. Raiter's team on their 13th mission) went down to half power thanks to fighter gunfire, whereupon the bombs were jettisoned and a turn was made for home. A reprieve from further aerial assault extended over the next hour, although altitude was being steadily lost. Then, just as the pilot had sent S/Sgt. James A. Goins (ROG) back to inform the gunners of this decision, a single fighter assault followed quickly by two more sealed the bomber's fate. The burning aircraft disintegrated with Raiter still on board, along with two dead colleagues; in the lottery that was aerial combat, the pilot was blasted out intact and was able to deploy his parachute to join the seven airmen already floating down.

The terminal condition for 42-52423/J3: R only began to show after "bombs away," when previous-incurred damage kicked in to leave the bomber straggling. Again, the aircraft remained free of the *Jagdwaffe* pilots' attention until approaching Osnabrueck. In similar fashion to **Mama's** fate, one or more fighters intervened to set their prey alight in the bomb bay. All ten airmen exited but Lt. Joseph M. Stroup, who had to be assisted out of the top hatch thanks to serious leg wounds, subsequently died in unknown circumstances, as did T/Sgt. Tommy Glass (Eng.).

Attlebridge's 42-52555/2U: G+ **Ol' Tom Cat**, bearing Lt. Clinton H. Caverne's crew, just disappeared on the way out, and since no trace of bomber or its human content subsequently came to light, it was almost certain that the sea had claimed another victim. The fate of 42-52569/U8: N- **Lovely Lady** was established after Lt. Albert J. Taft pulled out to starboard of the 466BG formation. Fire took hold and the Danish island of Lolland was where the B-24 came down, close to Rodbyhavn, on the southern coastline, minus seven of the ten-man crew.

2CBW

All three 2CBW Groups lost crews, but only one went down over hostile territory, the others diverting into Sweden. The unfortunate exception was Hethel's B-24D/ 42-63961/EE: T **Zoomin' Zombie**, with Capt. Don Westerbake (566BS Ops. Officer) on board. The circumstances of its demise are unclear, but the MACR makes reference to the bomber describing a full circle and momentarily trailing the Group formation, during which time six parachutes blossomed out; it then went into a spin and crashed. However, all but S/Sgt. Guy G. De La Riviere (TG) did get clear.

Ringaby received the two Old Buckenham crews, beginning with 42-52240/H6: in Lt. Keith O. Hamby's hands; fighter damage was of a scale to merit his action. The other squadron machine following this course was Lt. Mark B. Neary's 42-52244/H6: **Black Jed**, which had left the group over the target; the reason for the pilot's action was unclear, but the ten crewmembers joined the same number from Hamby's team in being interned. Lt. Charles E. Rowland, flying 42-7627/WV: **BTO**, adopted the neutral option, albeit for reasons unknown, joining the 453BG personnel at Ringaby along with his nine crewmembers.

14CBW

The 44BG was one of the groups afflicted by "aborting" aircraft, but those remaining in the formation bombed the Primary. Lt. Hiram G. Palmer was flying 42-72858/WQ: U **Pistol Packin' Mama**, but the crew's final destination would be Sweden instead of Shipdham. Cannon shells had badly damaged the starboard wing's center section and the twisted metal's exposure to the slipstream induced an irreversible drag that could not be countered, even on full power. The decision was finally taken to head the now isolated B-24 northwards; the protracted distance was safely completed despite several sightings of fighters, none of whom closed to firing range. A Flight of Italian

Reggiane 2001 fighters flown by the Swedes picked up the bomber as it approached the mainland and escorted it to a landing at Malmo. A potential problem intruding upon a safe landing arose when the nose wheel would not deploy. Palmer had four crew in the back to act as a counter-weight until the aircraft's momentum was reduced enough for the nose to strike the grass surface; the "ploughing" action cast earth into the bomb bay, but the airframe remained intact and ten more internees were delivered whole and unharmed.

The 392BG also lost one B-24 (42-52097/DC: O+) in the hands of Lt. Robert H. Griggs. The bomber was reported being under heavy fighter assault but was not seen to crash; no trace of the machine nor its human contents ever came to light, so the Baltic Sea around the Peenemunde region most likely became a repository for both.

20CBW

The sole MIA losses within the 20CBW both came from Seething, although two further B-24s were "written off" following landing crashes. The 448BG had been forced to scatter during Assembly thanks to another CBW formation that crossed their path, but reassembly was made. However, in the end the group abandoned the mission, although seven crews continued on, having not rejoined the group, but linking up with other units. Lt. Vincent Liedka in **Piccadilly Pete** (42-52118/CT:) suffered fighter-inflicted damage over the Baltic Sea that damaged a wing and punctured fuel cells. The risk of running out of fuel impelled the crew to head up to Sweden, where a landing was made at Bulltofta. Another crew heading out in **The Impatient Virgin** was led by Lt. Kent Moseley. Similar damage to fuel reserves on 42-110042/CT: decided the pilots to follow Lt. Liedka's example and an unimpeded course northward also ended up at Bulltofta.

Wendling lost a second B-24 on return, one of three 2BD aircraft declared "salvage." Lt. Charles L. Neff's shot up 42-52593/CI: B ran off the runway end at an RAF airfield into which it was diverted. Seething's 42-110069/EI:, in Lt. Joseph C. Liebich's hands and bearing its full bomb load, also skidded off the runway end, while lining up problems with the similarly-laden 42-110079/CT: B flown by Capt. James D. Conrad culminated with the B-24's landing gear collapsing after the bomber slewed off onto the grass and ran over a ditch. All thirty airmen involved came through intact.

The aircraft industry and airfields in France and the Low Countries took center stage (10th), with both categories allotted each Division. The latest unit to join the 2BD (467BG) was aloft for the first time, along with nine of the other ten Division units; the Rackheath group's appearance brought the 96CBW up to full three-Group strength and left the twin-unit 14CBW as the sole incomplete entity among the four B-24 Wings. Actual MIA losses were minimal at one out of 217 crews gaining mission "credit." The sole casualty suffered came from the 389BG (42-99992/HP: Z **Black Jackie/Flak Magnet**). Lt. Charles Nanco's charge was already detached from the formation when it was assailed by up to twelve Fw190s; a wing was set on fire before the bomber exploded, throwing the pilot up through the roof but leaving him intact and able to open his parachute. Only two other crewmembers out of ten shared Nanco's luck, while the pilot was the sole member to evade capture. (It is possible that the heavy armored pilots' seats fitted in many B-24s probably protected Nanco from the main explosive blast that generally directed itself in an upward manner, but even so, he was extremely fortunate to avoid a lethal impact with the cockpit frame.)

Oscherleben Blues

Oschersleben, with its major FW production plant, was a target synonymous with high losses for the 8AF on all of the three previous sorties. Today (11th) it was selected, along with Bernberg's similar facilities, for assault by the Division, while the other Divisions struck aviation industrial resources within Germany. By the day's end, the overall loss scale for the 8AF reached 64—a figure that although painful when set against the numbers of crew dispatched here (over 900) would have constituted a disaster just several months previous, when overall bomber strength was notably smaller. The 2BD was least affected at twelve among its 274 dispatched crews, with the cost almost equally shared between the four CBWs.

2CBW

The 389BG suffered a trio of losses for the second time in ten days to provide the 2CBW's entire MIA contingent. Mission No. 13 was on hand for Lt. Louis J. Jweid and crew, but Fate went against them. Post mission reports said that on the way in, 42-73498/RR: G lost its No. 2 engine to attacks from six o'clock, whereupon it drifted back; the bomb load was salvoed and the B-24J was last seen shortly before the target was reached as it fell away and down into the clouds; all but S/Sgt. Ed Hunnefeld, who died after landing, ended up as POWs.

Kansas City Kitty (42-100817/RR: F) lost five of its crew, including Lt. Jack L. Wyatt (P). The formation was in between Bielefeld and Hameln when strikes badly damaged the starboard wing around No. 2 engine. Course was still held as the B-24 fell behind and sustained for the bomb run, even as far as "friendly soil" in terms of Nazi-occupied Europe; Sgt. Ed Mims (Eng.) temporarily became the fortunate exception among the six survivors, since he evaded capture, although he was subsequently apprehended.

The day's casualties were completed by Lt. John Downey's 42-109798/EE: X, who survived along with six of his crew. A fighter pass south of Hameln knocked out the tail turret and shattered the top turret Plexiglas, fortunately without killing or injuring the Engineer. This B-24 also fell back, but did complete

A Danish photographer has captured a real moment of drama, as several fellow citizens at Venslev assist T/Sgt. Thomas R. Murphy out of his parachute harness. He had bailed out of Lt. Logie's 42-52432/J3: P (458BG) and was now unknowingly at the initial stage of evading capture by reaching Sweden within the month, as did his pilot and one other. Date was 9 April 1944.

This B-24H-10-CF/41-29273/J4: Z/Q was a 458BG "original" whose visible mission tally would not extend much beyond the number seen here. The Hamm mission on 22 April saw her downed by fighters from II/JG1 after ironically living up to her title to become a straggler ready to be picked off; Lt. George N. Spaven, Jr. (P) was the sole fatality.

the bomb run, although No. 2 engine was ablaze and No. 3 badly damaged; it finally faded away into the clouds. The pilots brought off a crash landing SE of Vreden when T/Sgt. Orville E. Beck (Eng.) became one of the three fatalities after he was crushed by the top turret frame.

14CBW

The 14CBW contributed one-third of today's MIA statistic. Shipdham's latest loss involved 42-7522/GJ: S **Southern Comfort**. The bomb bay door tracks on Lt. John D. Money's aircraft were reportedly frozen partially or totally, but this matter became academic after a flak strike in this area started a fire within the bay. Only three of the ten crewmembers would escape alive. S/Sgt. Eugene W. N. Roop (TG) took his pack and clipped it onto Sgt. Donald L. Young's (WG) harness, as the latter had suffered incapacitating burns to his hands—an act of sacrificial gallantry, since Roop would be one of the seven fatalities. Lt. Money was lucky to escape from the cockpit, which was wreathed in flames. A tortuous exit was made via a kicked-out side window, and even then, the pilot was lucky to suffer no more than being temporarily knocked out by marginal contact with a propeller tip on No. 3 engine.

Three further Wing losses were borne by the 392BG. Lt. Thomas F. McNichol, flying Lead in 42-52754/DC:, "aborted" the mission not long after crossing in due to supercharger problems. This was the last seen of the bomber, which almost certainly descended into the North Sea with fatal consequences for all eleven airmen. On 4 January, McNichol had brought back the body of S/Sgt. McPherson (G), killed during the mission; now his colleagues were united with him in eternal rest. **Nighttime Nellie** (42-52654/GC: J-Bar), flown by Lt. Walter B. Sherwood, suffered the "friendly fire" fate, being taken down by bombs from a fellow B-24; the MACR indicates that the port wing erupted in a tremendous explosion and the aircraft swung over onto its back to tumble to destruction close to Halberstadt airfield—only two out of the ten airmen escaped. The third loss occurred in the target area and involved 42-109835/CI: H, which incurred fighter-inflicted damage; two engines were fired and the landing gear descended. Lt. George P. Callaghan (CP) was the sole member failing to respond to Lt. Edward J. Conneran's order to jump, his body being discovered within the wreckage near Koethen.

20CBW

The first of two Bungay losses involved 42-99942/FL: E. **Brown Noser** (or **Knowser**), flown by Lt. Kermit A. Fuchs, which was observed to lose position and several thousand feet in height before levelling off. There was no obvious reason for this action, but sight of the straggler was ultimately lost. In the event, the B-24 came down at Lohne, close to Vechta, and only Lt. Philip R. Westcott (B) emerged alive.

Lt. Sterling Tuck had charge of 42-7572/HN: M **WereWolf/Princess O'Rourke**, but progress towards the target was halted by a flak strike over the Duemmersee that set No. 2 engine on fire. Attempts to shut off the fuel supply and "feather" the propeller failed, and as the bomber began to falter and drop away up to six parachutes were later recorded. All on board jumped clear to be rounded up and taken to a gaol in Wagenfeld, where their spirits cannot have been lifted when the sound of the returning bomber stream was heard soon after. Worse still was the

The aftermath of the "Night of the Intruders" debacle over several 2BD bases is caught at Hethel on 23 April. Lt. Edward W. Foley's crippled B-24J-145-CO /44-40655/HP: Z slewed off the runway—barely missing the control tower, as seen by the wheel marks—before slamming into a radar shack that was totally demolished; two airmen in occupation tragically lost their lives in the incident.

A more comprehensive view of Foley's bomber confirms the massive airframe's almost total consumption by the fire that ensued from the impact; it is amazing that all crewmembers survived, although several had to be hauled out by ground personnel. One was Capt. John Driscoll (Group Gunnery Officer), who would receive the Airman's Medal for his actions.

"duty" imposed upon them by their guards. Loaded onto a truck holding blood-stained stretchers, they were driven to a B-24 crash site and told to pick up various body parts. The burned out bomber's frame with three crewmembers on the flight deck still in position was angled upwards, giving the impression that a crash landing had been attempted.

96CBW

Two-thirds of the thirty 466BG personnel manning the group's three MIA bombers would not see the day through. The region around Diepholz provided the crash sites for two B-24s, with 41-29423/U8: and all but one on Lt. William C. Foushee's crew killed after the bomber spun in at Renzel. Then, 42-52582/U8: E made its terminal descent at Stroehem to bear nine of the ten-man crew led by Capt. B. B. Skaggs (KIA) to their deaths. The final victim of what were sustained fighter attacks was taken down as the IP loomed up. Lt. Thaddeus W. Tedrowe called for a bail out from 41-29353/2U: F, but although none of the ten crew were injured only eight jumped clear, the remaining duo being found within the wreckage at Deilmission, SW of Hildesheim. The 467BG's first loss was incurred today when on its return 42-52531/Q2: **Devil's Hostess** piled in at Sutton, north of Rackheath, striking a farmhouse in the process and killing Lt. Jack Skinner and six of his crew.

Strategic Priorities Maintained

The planned mission to Zwickau and Oschersleben (12th) was the first of four sorties up to 19 April falling into the strategic category, with a single tactical mission (17th) involving five B-24s bombing *No-Ball* sites under PFF guidance. The entire day's effort that involved the B-17 Divisions heading for separate targets was finally abandoned in the face of deteriorating weather conditions, with the 2BD getting as far as the German borders.

Five crews, all from Tibenham, were missing from the group formation on return; all were victims of fighter attacks initiated by elements of II and III/ JG26, as well as two *Staffeln* from JG2, with the action occurring over central Belgium, judging by the *Jagdwaffe* pilots' reports. The most unlucky in terms of death was Lt. Benjamin L. Love's (KIA) crew on 42-100203/IS:. The pilot was killed during a head-on fighter attack and fell over the controls, but the mortal blow was arguably self-administered thanks to the B-24 drifting into the path of several fragmentation bombs released from another bomber, one of which set the nose area ablaze.

Gen. Doolittle is photographed pinning the Airman's Medal on Capt. Driscoll as they stand alongside the burnt-out airframe. This was the second time in thirteen days that the Capt. had faced injury or death. On 9 April, he was participating in a mission on Lt. Reese's B-24J-35-CO/42-99982RR: H+ **Might of the Eighth** when it collided with a 392BG bomber; he and one of the ten-man crew alone managed to bail out safely.

The resultant spinning motion left just Lt. Robert Ripps (CP) not only able to bail out, but also beginning a successful six-month evasion effort thanks to the Dutch Resistance.

Lt. Samuel G. Schleichkorn (P) was one of a further five Americans emulating Lt. Ripps's luck on 41-29118/RN: **Nine Yanks and a Jerk**. Successive loss of three engines allied with shot-up systems between Liege and Louvain culminated with nine out of ten bailing out (one of whom suffered parachute failure), with the B-24 piling in west of Louvain, along with the tenth crewmember.

The air battle, being over Nazi-occupied soil, was to create no less than eleven more evaders out of the thirty airmen on the remaining three losses. Lt. Joseph Pavelka, flying 42-7601/WV:, had steered his charge back from around Koblenz with one engine and the bomb bay set on fire. By the time the group were assailed by JG26, the situation was bad enough for the bail out bell to be rung, to which all ten crew reacted, their bomber exploding in mid-air and depositing its remains NE of Namur; the pilot was one of three escaping captivity. The last two MIA crews each ended up with four evaders. Lt. Herbert W. Schultz (P) on 42-110021/IS: + at least reached a *Stalag* along with five others before the B-24 fell SW of Bastogne. Two of these "Kriegies" enjoyed a 16-day period of freedom prior to being captured. The pilot on the final MIA aircraft 42-109807/MK: -bar (Lt. John B. Anderson) was one of the two unlucky exceptions not enjoying evasion or even "Kriegydom" after he reportedly attempted what was a failed forced landing near Florennes.

The emphasis for the 8AF on the remaining three missions was the Nazi aviation industry. During this period, the 2BD lost a total of eight crews MIA out of 734 dispatched. On the 13th, Oberpfaffenhofen's facilities and Lechfeld's experimental airfield absorbed over 500 tons of bombs and incendiaries at a cost of six B24s shared between five groups; half this number made it to Switzerland, however. Rackheath's 42-52535/6A: **Katy** was badly shot-up by flak over the target and was last seen with the port wing ablaze on an apparent heading for Switzerland; it never arrived there and Lt. E. Calouri (P) was one of three fatalities out of the ten-man team, the others becoming POWs.

A duo of crews failed to land back at Tibenham. Lt. Jack Farmer (POW), flying 41-29132 /RN: **Tenovus**, got all but one of the crew out safely—of which six evaded capture—after fighters set the bomber on fire over Luxembourg, leaving the aircraft to crash at Aleweier. The sole casualty was F/O Leo A. Carey (B), who was thought to have impacted with the tail. Lt. John E. Frisch's crew on 42-110048/WV: gained no reprieve after flak impacted with the bomb bay, causing the aircraft to break in two, with the remnants falling at Argelsried, on the SW edge of Munich.

Shipdham's sole loss involved one falling into the internment category. Lt. Rockford Griffith had brought off a spectacular crash landing on 18 November, along with Lt. Grono. Now overheating engines on the outward leg proved incapable of being controlled; the resultant high fuel consumption thanks to the drag of the extended cowl flaps and placing of the fuel mixture levers into the "full rich" position persuaded the pilots that the chances of regaining Shipdham were poor. They turned south after "bombs away," but lost No. 2 through low oil pressure along the way. On reaching Switzerland, they were met by several bursts of Swiss flak, but managed to reach Duebendorf and land 42-100330/NB: L in good order.

The 466BG's 42-52567/6L:, flown by Lt. Norman C. Flynn, lost its No. 2 engine, but was equally successful in gaining neutral soil at Duebendorf. The final internment candidate came from the 453BG and involved 41-28629/F8: P, with Lt. Robert J. Dooley's crew. A combination of fuel shortage, oil loss on No. 2 engine, and oxygen system failure impelled Dooley to head towards Switzerland; the B-24H was also shot at and in this case slightly damaged by Swiss flak guns, an act that probably caused two crewmembers to bail out; nothing further intruded to prevent a smooth landing, however.

There now ensued a four-day period where the "heavies" remained ground-bound. Adverse weather would seem to be the primary reason for this inactivity, especially when given the still-urgent need to hammer both the Nazi industrial infrastructure as well as their transportation network within France and the Low Countries as demanded under the terms of the Transportation Plan. Normal service in respect of the strategic operations was again taken up (18th), with the enemy's aviation industry again focused upon. The Arado plants at Brandenburg and Rathenow, just west of Berlin, were the 2BD's targets, with the 96CBW alone going to the former location. Unfortunately, this sub-unit's bomb run was frustrated by cloud and Targets of Opportunity were sought out at the cost of one crew.

Horsham's **Wurf'less** (42-52382/7V: I) never reached Brandenburg, having

The chaos caused among the returning 2BD formation by a mere handful of KG51 Me410s is demonstrated here at Seething. Three of the four B-24s that ended up in this shambles are (front to back) B-24H-15-CF/41-29575 **The Ruth E K**, B-24H-1-DT/41-28585 **Ice Cold Katie**, and B-24H-5-CF/41-29240 **Tondelayo**. The flanking aircraft are from the 714BS.

A view from the rear of the intermingled trio of B-24s demonstrates the full extent of the destruction wrought upon the B-24 in the center, **Ice Cold Katie** (713BS). The fractured fuselage and almost total excision of the tail section renders her fit only for salvage whereas the other two bombers were brought back into service. Unbelievably, no deaths or even serious injuries were borne by the crews.

stalled out thanks to prop-wash; Lt. George W. Schuman, having arrested the resultant spinning motion, then temporarily linked up with another Group, but the decision was finally taken to "abort" and the bomb load jettisoned. Luck remained with the crew as far as Oldenburg, when two intercepting Fw190s made short work of their prey, which was inadvertently "bellied in"; soon after, a P-47 strafed the B-24H, probably causing some or all of the seven fatalities ultimately borne by the ten-man crew.

The sole other Division MIA casualty came out of Wendling's ranks, being 42-52704/ DC: P+ **Son of Satan**, flown by Lt. Dexter Tiefenthal. Flak was the executioner, the strikes turning the B-24 on its back to finally impact west of Brandenburg, along with six of its ten-man team, the pilot being one of the four exceptions. Elsewhere this day, a PFF-guided mission by twelve B-24s split between three Groups attacked V-1 sites at Watten, in the Pas de Calais, the second such small-scale effort to this location in 12 days.

The pressure on aviation facilities was kept up (19th) with plants east of the Ruehr struck, although the 2BD and 3BD were actually allotted operational airfields. Paderborn and Guetersloh were squarely struck by nearly three-quarters of the 249 B-24s dispatched and a welcome bonus was the return of all crews. Not so fortunate was a single 448BG crew, when the Group participated in yet another PFF-guided foray against Watten's V-1 sites. **Maid of Orleans II** (41-29565/IO:) was struck squarely by flak on the bomb run and set on fire; the Group having completed the bomb run and headed back, Lt. Roy Davis dived out of formation with a view to extinguishing the fire, but shortly after the bomber exploded out over the English Channel. ASR launches dispatched to the area picked up one survivor and one body.

The still-latent threat of Germany's V-1 and V-2 missiles was much more fully addressed the next day, with over 800 B-17s and B-24s assaulting sites in the Pas de Calais;. The reputed "milk run" nature of such missions again proved no consolation for the nine MIA crews, a total that was four more than had been borne on the much more extended run into Germany 24 hours previous. The 2BD's quota was two, with Seething losing a second crew in 24 hours. Flak administered the death blow to 42-72981/IG: **Fascinating Lady**, in Lt. Bill Martin's hands. Two crewmembers in the nose compartment—where the strike occurred—were killed immediately and the others bailed out after fire caught an inexorable hold as the bomber, having dropped out of formation, was heading homeward. Flak dealt a terminal blow to the 445BG's 42-109921/MK: -Bar. Lt. Layne Rogers (KIA) stood little chance when the tail section was excised and the B-24 tumbled to destruction south of St. Omer airfield; Lt. Howard H. Kelley (N) was very lucky to survive, being ejected bare seconds before the crash, unlike his nine colleagues, since centrifugal forces held them firmly in place all the way down to the final and fatal impact.

Nocturnal Nightmare (22 April)

Although 8AF bomber crews had received a modicum of training in nocturnal flying, they were never tasked with flying combat missions in this manner, other than on leaflet dropping flights or OSS-directed sorties to assist the Resistance Movement, both activities being allotted to specific units. The mission to Hamm's marshalling yards on 22 April was dispatched in the late afternoon and its duration guaranteed that the formations would not return until darkness had shrouded East Anglia. In this manner was unknowingly sown the seeds of a sharp rebuff specifically affecting the 2BD.

The key transportation link was heavily punished by nearly 800 B-17s and B-24s, with a third coming from

Capt. Alvin D Skaggs is seen examining the burnt-out wreckage of his regular mount **Vadie Raye** (B-24J-50-CO/42-73497/IO:). The aircraft was set on fire by a combination of Me410 "intruder" and (allegedly) ground gunners on 22 April 1944, and was finally crash landed at Seething; two crewmembers had already bailed out, while the other eight got clear from the now-blazing aircraft.

the 2BD's ranks that included all eleven Groups. The MIA cost to the Division was six out of an 8AF total of fourteen, but double this number of B-24s would be shot down or wrecked over England. The actual mission losses were spread between the CBWs, with single casualties for all but the 2CBW, who lost three.

Hethel's 42-63963/HP: X **Round Trip Ticket** was to belie her optimistic title. While skirting the Ruehr on the inward route, the No. 4 engine was flak-afflicted and the bomber assumed a steady downward circle to starboard as several parachutes blossomed out. However, Capt. Willard Stotter, with Lt./Col. Paul T. Burton acting as Command Pilot, managed to keep the crippled aircraft aloft until over Dutch soil, when they and one remaining crewmember vacated their charge. Two crews were lost from the 2CBW on either side of the target. Lt. Edward W. Sadlon (POW) was in charge of 42-50325/RN:, which was downed by flak near Neuss, leaving one dead out of ten on board. Lt. Francis C. Sneed (POW) was bringing 41-29306/IS: + back under escort under diminishing power; the bid failed near Tournai, where all but one got out and down safely. However, S/Sgt. Robert M. Varty (ROG) was reportedly killed either by the SS or SD authorities.

The No. 4 engine on 42-52603/GC: J-bar was set ablaze shortly after bombing and several parachutes were seen to deploy at this point, followed by others as the 392BG headed back. The bomber's martyrdom proved surprisingly extended, even though the fire steadily spread out over the wing. Capt. Wyeth C. Everhart (Command Pilot) and Lt. Gordon L. Hammond gamely got her as far as the Belgian/French border region before those still on board among the 12-man crew abandoned the aircraft after the outer wing separated; the B-24's aerial disintegration cast the remnants down close to Oostkeerke. (Ironically Everhart, on what was to have been his final mission, had been told by Maj. Keilman (579BG CO) to go with and instruct Hammond, whom the Major was "grooming" as a Lead pilot. Also on board as an observer was Maj. Robert L. Cox, Operations Officer for the recently-arrived 489BG.)

Lt. George N. Spaven's 458BG crew had survived a nasty crash landing on 8 March, when their B-24 ran out of fuel while in Watton's circuit. Now the 753BS airmen's combat tour was terminated after flak badly damaged **Flak Magnet** (41-2927/ J4: Q). The B-24 limped homewards, but two firing passes by Maj. Heinz Baer—an *Experte* with 200 "kills"—sealed the cripple's fate. Sadly, the second fusillade left Spaven lolling in his seat, either badly injured or dead, and he went down with the disintegrating aircraft, the sole casualty among the ten on board.

The Foxes are in the Hen House

As the bomber stream turned for home in the gathering evening gloom, the crews had no idea that elements of II/KG51 operating the twin-engine Me410 from Soesterberg, in Holland, were aloft and tracking them. The 2BD, bringing up the rear of the stream, was the closest element to its Luftwaffe adversaries and would bear the brunt of the impending punishment to be handed out by what was actually a very small force. Of the four Wings, only the 14CBW would remain inviolate from assault.

Hethel's Tithe

The 389BG had provided PFF crews for the Division and had also led the 2CBW, albeit with mixed navigational and bombing results. The village of Cantley lies approximately twelve miles northeast of Hethel, and one of its youthful occupants, who was a very knowledgeable aircraft recognition enthusiast, was enthralled by the ghostly aerial procession. Then, his keen eyes picked out the hostile shape of what he correctly identified as an Me410, which was maneuvering below and ahead of one B-24. It was now that the *schraege-Musik* technique used by German night fighters against RAF Bomber Command was emulated by the Luftwaffe crew; in this case, the side fuselage mounted MG131 machine guns in their flexible barbettes were angled up and to the rear as the gunner sprayed his prey's underside with deadly effect. Fire caught hold as the bomber began to spiral in a deceptively gentle manner and parachute packs spewed forth their silken canopies before one wing detached, trapping those of the eleven-man crew still aboard. Lt. Wilkerson and four crewmembers survived the demise of 42-119915/EE: -Z, but others were discovered dead with unopened packs, or in one case impaled on a tree. The crash site was alongside the Norwich-Great Yarmouth line, but this had no adverse effect upon rail traffic movements.

Hethel was currently being visited by General Hodges (CG, 2BD) and Ted Timberlake (CG, 2CBW), both officers having taken up station upon the control tower roof. A collapsed nose wheel on Lt. Rubich's bomber caused the main runway to be blocked by this B-24, but Flying Control moved swiftly and efficiently to put runway 17 into emergency operation—an act that was to unconsciously place the Generals' safety at risk within the next few minutes. Lts. Foley and Muir (CP) were piloting 44-40085/HP: Z on the downwind leg when their charge was similarly selected for instant destruction.

The No. 2 engine was set ablaze and worse still, the damaged engine throttle linkage jammed the engines into the high RPM position, while the brakes were rendered inoperable. The latter deficiency would normally have left the pilots facing an overshoot at the runway end. This was a risky enough option, but the problem was exacerbated for both crew and control tower personnel moments after the bomber settled down on the runway.

The inexorable leftward drag caused by the deflated tire forced the now errant aircraft into a seeming collision course with the tower structure. Fortunately (for all but two unsuspecting ground staff), the curved path traced by EE: Z- cleared the building by a safe but still uncomfortable distance. However, its momentum was still far from spent when it impacted with the radar technician's workshop, demolishing it and expunging the lives of its two occupants in the process.

Fire caught hold of the rear fuselage and it seemed there would be few if any survivors among the crew. Capt. Driscoll (Gunnery Officer) led the way in gaining access to the forward fuselage, where he dragged out several inert figures, as did other rescuers. Amazingly, all ten airmen survived and the very next day, Driscoll received the Airman's Medal from General Doolittle while standing by the remnants of the burned out B-24.

Old Buckenham's Share

The 453BG, based at Old Buckenham, was part of the 2CBW, which had encountered navigation problems during target approach. This in turn resulted in the Group formation fragmenting into three sections: two linking up with the 389th and 445th BGs to bomb Hamm, while the third elected to retain its loads and only released over Koblenz on the return leg. No combat losses were incurred during the mission.

On board 42-64490/H6: U **Cee Gee II**, the tail gunner (S/Sgt. Ralph V. McClure) remembered the advice of an RAF Lancaster contemporary and scanned downwards in an arc as the sea passed unseen below, hoping not to sight the outline of a "bogy," but ready to react by firing first in an attempt to scare it away should the need arise. The close-packed formation with all navigation lights exposed was yet another cause for concern, since it was more likely to attract hostile attention.

Suddenly, he caught a glimpse of a shadowy outline at the 8 o'clock low position and called on T/Sgt. John F McKinney (LW) to join in with his single flexible machine gun. Scarcely had the .5 weapons thrown out their chains of heavy caliber bullets when a return hail of cannon and machine gun fire lanced into the fuselage and port wing to set No. 2 engine ablaze. Both gunners were knocked unconscious, but McClure quickly recovered. After establishing that his fellow gunner was at least alive, he scurried forward to inform Lt. James S. Munsey (P) of the fire.

Still some distance away from land, those crewmembers physically capable of bailing out nevertheless resisted Lt. Munsey's call for them to do so. Meanwhile the fire, fed by the ruptured inner-port wing fuel tanks, was steadily eating its way into the cockpit area, but Munsey and Lt. Robert O. Crall (CP) still gallantly held to their task. The B-24 was describing an inexorable downward path as the vague outline of the Suffolk coastline slipped underneath; it was then what McClure and Sgt. Norman V. Brown (BT) was certain were fuel tanks exploding ejected them and the still-unconscious Sgt. McKinney out through the rear hatch.

Both pilots stood no chance, as their charge apparently inverted and bare seconds later smacked into entombing marshland near Reydon. Three other crewmembers shared their fate, although all actually got out beforehand; one landed in the sea and drowned, while the other two, one of which was McKinney, struck the ground with their parachute packs still intact. The following 13 July, Lt. Munsey was granted the (posthumous) DSC for "his selfless devotion to duty in staying at his post to ensure all the crew had exited."

Seething's Woes

The 448BG suffered upwards of half the losses sustained during KG51's intrusions. The first casualty was Lt. Pitt's 42-52608/, flying off Lt. A. D. Skagg's right wing; a vertical spear line of tracer bullets or shells suddenly penetrated the belly of the bomber, which erupted in flames and it descended rapidly into the sea, along with its ten-man crew, none of whom survived the incident. (The reprieve from death granted T/Sgt. Ernest Robinson after he alone survived his B-24's "ditching" on the 19th had extended a mere 72 hours.)

Seething's troubles aloft were quadrupled during the evening's lethal "activities." First, **Repulser** (41-28843/ IO:), flown by Lt. Pulcipher, was crossing in over Southwold when observers on the ground watched with a mix of frustration and horror as cannon and machine gun fire ignited the starboard wing root. In a matter of seconds, the B-24 rolled helplessly to one side and as it descended the entire wing detached; the truncated remains ended up strewn across the marshes near Kessingland, a bare mile inland from the North Sea.

The second crew by contrast were extremely fortunate, in that they all survived. Once again, witnesses watched what turned out to be Lt. Alspaugh's 42-94744/IO: **Peggy Jo** absorbing punishment. The bomber was describing a U-turn over the coast prior to making the landing approach when the Me410 struck, leaving No. 3 engine wreathed in fire and the bomber in a violent downward motion. All ten airmen safely evacuated their doomed charge, which struck a railway embankment close to

A Ford-built B-24H sweeps majestically across Wendling sometime in April 1944, passing over **Silver Streak** (NMF B-24H-25-FO/42-95040/DC: O) in the process. The latter machine was the first non-camoflaged example assigned to the 392BG and proved to be more fortunate than many of its contemporaries, since it returned Stateside after VE-Day.

Worlingham, although once again, none of the debris impeded train movements.

Vadie Raye (42-73497/IO:), flown by Lt. A. D. Skaggs, had an engine set on fire and was also ablaze inside the fuselage. The B-24 faltered under partial power loss and several crewmembers bailed out. On reaching Seething and landing, Skaggs deliberately swerved his charge off the runway in order to avoid any possibility of blocking the runway. The now errant bomber finally slewed to a halt on its belly and the fire spread relentlessly, eventually reducing the fuselage to molten metal; thankfully, all those still on board got clear.

One further 448BG bomber would be "written off" Group records, although not thanks to the Luftwaffe. **Sky Queen** (42-110026/), flown by Capt. Lamberton, ran off the runway end and the B-24 became stranded after its huge main undercarriage wheels sank into the ground. Then, Lt. Williams touched down in **Ruth E. K Allah Hassid** (41-29575/EI: K-square) and slithered to a similar mired-in halt, but almost a full wing span away from **Sky Queen**. In the meantime, Lt. Apple in **Ice Cold Katie** (41-28595/IG: D-circle) had delayed his landing until the current situation became more stabilized. Finally, after several circuits were completed but with the runway lights still extinguished, Apple used the reflected light from the burning hulk of **Vadie Raye** as a marker and managed to find the runway.

It was only when he flicked on the landing lights that his horrified gaze took in the sight of the two other bombers perched at the far end. Realizing that his bomber's forward momentum could never be halted in time to avoid a collision, he solved the potentially disastrous problem by guiding his charge into the space between the aircraft, although he excised both outer wing sections in so doing. Scarcely had the B-24 come to a halt and the crew exited when another B-24 rolled into sight; this was **Tondelayo** (41-29240/IG: C-circle), piloted by Lt. Barak. This time, the errant B-24 smacked its right wing into **Ice Cold Katie**, shearing off the tops of the fins and rudders, as well as breaking its companion bomber's back just behind the wing roots, leaving it a candidate for "Category E" treatment.

Bringing up the Rear

It was the 96CBW that was the final sub-force over Hamm; so far, just one 458BG crew had been culled from its ranks during the mission, but matters would now take a decided turn for the worse, both in respect of this Group and the 467th BG. Horsham St. Faith is located on the northern outskirts of Norwich, and the Group was scant miles distant to the southeast when the "intruders" struck twice in quick succession. Lt. Teague G. Harris, piloting 42-52353/J, noted how Lt. Stilson's bomber received punishment almost simultaneously with that handed out to his own aircraft, a situation suggesting two "intruders" were present, although he later asserted that ground fire was also observed. He and Lt. Robert T. Couch struggled to retain control of their bomber as it sagged out of the sky and finally crashed heavily at Lakenham. Harris was more fortunate than his copilot and five others, since he was dragged out of the wreckage alive, albeit suffering a fractured spine that only healed after many months.

Lt. Charles W. Stilson's 42-100357/Z5: D was in equally deep distress with No. 3 and 4 engines ablaze, while No. 2 finally went out of control as the Horsham runway was tantalizingly looming up. Its bid to remain airborne finally failing, the bomber was crash landed in a field. The B-24's high wing configuration and weak bomb bay center beam duly exposed its oft-repeated structural failure in such circumstances; the impact with the soil induced a double fuselage fracture just behind the cockpit and ahead of the waist gun positions, with the forward and rear segments canting off to one side. Among the civilian rescuers who hauled the four survivors out, including Stilson, were a husband and wife who ironically were close friends of Lt. Robert T. Couch, Lt. Harris's dead copilot. Two crewmembers were already dead, while a third expired later in hospital. The remaining four crewmembers had already taken to their parachutes.

One of two Seething-based bombers diverting into Switzerland on 26 April was B-24H-1-DT **Rum Runner**, assigned to the 713BS. She was bearing Lt. Robert E. Lehman's crew; the sagging fuselage is probably due to the bomb load still being in place, as confirmed by the Swiss. The reportedly minimal structural damage saw the aircraft utilized by the authorities as a transport.

The burned out wreckage of **Rum Runner**'s squadron contemporary that also sought this neutral haven still leaves enough evidence of its 448BG origin upon the outer fins. The crew, led by Lt. Henry H. Schroeder, landed at Payerne on three engines, but **Commando** overshot with fire catching hold following heavy structural damage.

Rackheath Misfortunes

The 458BG's travails were equalled by its companion unit, the 467BG. While still some 20 miles to the south of Rackheath, Lt. Roden's 42-52536/X7: K, which was leading one element, had its tail section literally sawn off by cannon fire; it plunged into a wood at Withersdale, southwest of Beccles, where the blazing aeronautical carcass formed a funeral pyre for all ten of its occupants.

Lt. Stalie C. Reid had returned to the ranks of the 466BG and once over land he guided the B-24 out of his "adopted" Group and took up a course for Rackheath. His solo appearance over the airfield circuit resulted in his intervention adversely affecting the landing approach being made by Lt. Newhouse, who cursed his fellow pilot roundly. Almost immediately he was notified by one of his crew regarding the presence of a "Messerschmitt" sidling in behind what he later asserted was Reid's 42-52445/4Z: D. The report turned out to be tragically accurate, since tracers now reached out to grasp the B-24's left wing in a fiery embrace; four gunners in the rear of the doomed bomber managed to scramble out, but one suffered a failure of his parachute harness and fell to his death. In spite of the terminal damage suffered, the bomber must have staggered on for several minutes before finally succumbing, since its crash site was at Barsham, some 15 miles southeast of the airfield.

April Run-down

Forty-eight hours elapsed before the 2BD again launched its crews to airfields at Gablingen and Leipheim; the four losses out of the 230 B-24s dispatched was low compared to the 1BD's equivalent 10% figure. Wendling's ranks were shorn of two crews lost on either side of the target. The first victim was 41-28688/EC: Q, with Lt. Travis W. Griffen's crew. Two engines went "out" in succession, after which a heading for Switzerland was taken up. A third engine began to fail according to crewmembers, and all ten took to their parachutes near Freiburg before the B-24 piled in at Freudenberg. However, although S/Sgt. Harold A. Bryant (Eng.) was seen to bail out, he did not survive, as did Sgt. Eugene M. Gallup (BT).

A worse casualty rate was realized on Lt. Carl F. Ellinger's 44-40105/GC: B-bar. The formation was tracking homeward over Belgium when a flak concentration near Chievres opened up. A shell impacted with the fuselage behind the wings and split it apart. Fire took hold of the front section, while the other section went into a spin. Sgt. Merle J. Hasenfratz (TG), along with two other crewmembers, was tossed around as his section whirled aimlessly downward, but finally managed to haul himself out into space to become the sole survivor out of ten. Lt. Franklin C. Kendziora had lost No. 1 and 2 engines to fighter strikes over Belgium, which had also started fires in the bomb bay. On approach to the region around Liege, the 445BG's 42-110062 /WV: - was evacuated and none too soon—the bomber exploded almost immediately after the last member bailed out, with the fragments raining down at Huy-sur-Meuse.

The sole internment candidate from the 2BD out of fourteen in all belonged to the 448BG. The loss of an engine on the way in created the almost inevitable penalty of increased fuel consumption, as power was advanced on the other three engines in order to maintain position. As Strasbourg was being bypassed, Lt. John A. McCune eased 42-110098/IO: M-diamond **Flying SAC** out of formation and banked away to starboard for the relatively short run to Switzerland that ended successfully at Duebendorf—the first of three Group bombers to seek Swiss refuge within 24 hours.

Mannheim lies on the east bank of the Rhine, opposite Ludwigshafen, and its marshalling yard complex came to the 2BD's attention (25th). The 44BG was not present thanks to a bout of food poisoning among the personnel; this reduction in strength mattered naught, since cloud conditions over the Primary saw all but seven crews releasing thereon—an extremely poor return, even with just five crews MIA. Mannheim lies some 150 miles north of Switzerland, but the rather protracted run across hostile soil did not prevent three among the loss figure from heading in that direction and reaching their goal.

Seething's allocation was two, beginning with 41-28602/E-circle **Commando**. The day previous, Lt. Henry Schroeder had returned on three engines, but a repeat performance was not deemed feasible thanks to power loss early on to No. 2 and strong headwinds barring the passage home. The possibility of running out of fuel in these circumstances was countered by taking up a course for neutral territory. A steady loss of altitude still left the B-24 with sufficient altitude to cross the Swiss border, but disaster struck, at least in technical terms, upon landing at Payerne; the bomber overshot the runway, smashing through a fence and some trees that excised the wings. Fire then caught hold, but all on board managed to scramble clear of their potential "crematorium."

The other 448BG crew to head south was led by Lt. Robert E. Lehmann, whose four-engine experience was reportedly established prior to Pearl Harbor with Pan American Airlines. Following a safe landing at Duebendorf—one that was nevertheless fraught with risk due to the 5,000lb bomb load still hanging in the racks—examination of the airframe on 41-28583/IG: F-circle **Rum Runner** revealed no obvious damage and a fuel residue, suggesting that the crew could have made it back to England. Both crews had seemingly lost contact with the Group formation after it had headed back; there was no obvious reason why the bomb load had been retained on Lehmann's aircraft, however.

The third interned crew came from the 453BG, and the bomber concerned (42-64496/H6: X+) had been casting up a number of electrical problems that had Lt. Louis Scherzer "aborting" one mission. A switch to the Secondary while on the bomb run resulted in the engine RPM level shooting up by nearly one-fifth, with the pilots unable to bring this down to normal cruise setting even when operating the auxiliary power unit (APU). The Engineer's opinion that the increased fuel consumption would not suffice until back across the North Sea or English Channel made up Scherzer's mind to "go south." Duebendorf received its latest "visitor," but the bomber's career was not quite over; soon afterwards, she took to the air and subsequently featured in a Swiss propaganda film outlining the "tough" stance the Swiss fighter pilots purportedly took against such intruders into their National air-space!

One of the two aircraft lost over enemy soil was the 458BG's 42-52335/Z5: R. **Admirable Little Character** in Lt. John H. Comb's hands. The Group was currently experiencing a rate of aircraft "abortions" that was far from satisfactory, and the Mannheim run added to the problem when the original 29-strong formation was cut back to 21. Comb's B-24 had completed both the outward leg of the mission and was still in formation as the Group was over eastern France, near Rheims. It was then that a sudden, slashing attack by one of several fighters landed lethal strikes that caused the bomber to rear up and flop over into a spin, with one rudder falling off. Up to four parachutes were reported as the spiralling machine headed down for a final impact ESE of Vitry-Le-Francois.

In fact, no less than eight of the ten-man crew reportedly got out; tragically, Lt. Charles C. Bieber (B) suffered parachute failure and S/Sgt. Richard O. McCarthy (TG) was cruelly denied his life after he precipitately pulled his ripcord on exiting and was dragged to his death when the canopy fouled one wing. In contrast, Combs was one of two survivors among the six so blessed who ended up in a *Stalag*. A flak strike set the bomb bay on 42-95019/F8: T+ on fire as the 453BG was bypassing Paris. Lt. Elmer B. Crocket wasted no time in bailing out the crew before the doomed machine fell away to impact near Puiseux, the second casualty to be borne by the 2CBW.

A duo of missions flown on 26/27 April briefly reflected minimal MIA loss rates for the 8AF, totalling six crews overall. In addition, the 27th witnessed a "double header" pattern. However, the first day's run proved totally "abortive" for the 2BD. A planned assault upon either Paderborn or Gutersloh (at least two Group accounts list the latter location) did not proceed; again, the reason was ascribed either to adverse weather or the absence of PFF-equipped B-24s. Next day, V-1 sites were focused upon and hammered by nearly 500 crews. The Division's single loss out of four on the day's first sortie was incurred by the 44BG. Lt. Carey's 41-29467/NB: X received a lethal strike that tore off the starboard wing, thereby inducing a tight spinning action quickly followed by violent disintegration; Sgts. Ray Shirley (Eng.) and Paul A. Chagron (ROG) somehow managed to clear the doomed bomber, unlike their eight colleagues. Two French marshalling yards constituted the second mission, which was completed without any MIA casualties. However, one 392BG crew was lost over England on return, while the 446BG lost no less than three crews: two during Assembly and a third on return.

Berlin Strikes Back—Again

The second Berlin mission in April was launched on the 29th and resulted in a severe 10% MIA factor among the 616 crews given mission "credit" out of 679 dispatched. On this occasion, the *Sturmgruppen* method of assault cut a swathe through the 3BD ranks (28), but a scarcely lower total (26) was borne by the B-24 formations and extracted from among all four CBWs.

On 29 April, Lt. Richard J. Hruby's entire crew was fated to be one of the very few B-24 teams to buck the tragic trend of partial or total loss of life on board a "ditching" 2BD bomber. The pilots put B-24H-15-CF/41-29513/GJ: Z down safely; they are seen with Royal Naval personnel from the vessel reported as a minesweeper (in many cases a converted trawler fishing boat) that picked up the 44BG airmen.

The Division was bringing up the rear of the bomber stream; progress as far as the Duemmersee appears to have been relatively undisturbed before matters first turned sour when the 354FG engaged up to 75 enemy fighters. Two Bf109s swept through the 2CBW to strike 41-28676/YO: C, bearing L/Col. Bob Sears (Command Pilot from the 453BG) and Capt. Joseph Higgins and crew, and set it on fire. Although the last sight of the bomber saw it going down in a disintegrating state with no parachutes seen, both pilots and all but three other crewmembers survived.

Then, at a point north of Hannover, a pack of fighters loomed up in front of the 14CBW and started in upon the two groups, with the 392BG's eighteen-strong force destined to lose six B-24s over Europe and two over England. Lt. Fred J. Kane (B) on 42-100100/EC: T **Double Trouble**, flown by Lt. Gerald C. Rogers, had scarcely called in the "twelve o'clock" angle attack when a cannon shell killed him and demolished the nose turret. A bail out was called for as the B-24 began to falter from the punishment and its surviving occupants took to their parachutes; the crash site was due north of Hannover. The pilot was still MIA on VE-Day, and it was 1947 before his body was found in woodland with an unopened parachute pack.

Strikes upon 42-110062/CI: A, in Lt. Leo E. Ofenstein's hands, probably induced a swing to starboard that resulted in a collision with Lt. William T. Kamenitsa's 42-100371/CI: F. The element Lead B-24 was worse affected, with the tail section being chopped off, but although a spin quickly developed, half the crew got clear before the truncated remains piled in near Marklendorf. Kamenitsa retained control of his machine, despite losing a sizeable portion of the port wing, and finally managed to crash land on flat ground near Meitze, not far from its companion in fate. Even then, luck was on most of the crew's side, because the B-24 careened over a ditch and the entire nose section was ripped off in the process, killing Lts. John C. Caulfield (N) and Gene A. Miler (B), while the pilot was rendered unconscious; a further fatality involved Sgt. Joseph R. Trivison (ROG). Also downed during the assault was 42-100105/EC: T, flown by Lt. Robert R. Bishop, which fell out and came down at an undisclosed site with the loss of all on board; even if anyone survived the impact, they would have been killed when part of the bomb load exploded, blowing the airframe apart.

The 96CBW was also bypassing Hannover when a 467BG crew was culled by the fighters; 41-28749/Q2: N, being flown by Lt. Frank P. Prokop, had the pilot and only two other survivors out of the ten on board. This was the first of six Wing losses today, but the *Jagdwaffe* attackers appear from this point to have left the Division's ranks intact as it headed eastward. A far worse situation would exist, however, as the assaults were resumed, first by Berlin's flak batteries and then added to by fighters during the return leg.

Flak's Contribution

Flak over *Big B* was as extensive and concentrated as ever, leaving its mark upon a number of B-24s. Two of those so stricken came from Rackheath's now 25-strong formation. Lt. John P. Gavin's 41-28730/Q2: A **Blond Bomber** was badly damaged, but the pilots cleared Berlin and held course for home as far as a point near Hannover, then all control was lost. Only Gavin and three of his crew survived as POWs. The other group casualty was 42-52506/X7: M, in Lt. William F. Moore's charge, with Maj. Robert L. Salzarulo (788BS CO) acting as Command Pilot. Once again, the crippled bomber limped westwards as far as Holland before the eleven-man crew bailed out. Six of them, including Gavin, evaded capture, but tragically the pilot remained MIA after WWII, his death a mystery, although his corpse was reportedly found and is now interred at Margraten.

The Toll Mounts

The tally of losses as the target was left behind was a statistically tolerable one, but the defenders were destined to cut deeper into the Division's formations, with the 448BG leading the way. However, the fighters did not make their presence again felt until the distinctive Duemmersee waters began to loom up. The Seething fliers were viciously assailed and the first of six crews to taste the seeds of defeat were manning 42-7683/EI: **Sweet Sioux**. Lt. William Rogers's bomber was pounded unmercifully until it became an untenable aerial platform, whereupon the ten airmen successfully bailed out; unfortunately, the pilot was never seen alive again, being a likely victim of civilian summary justice. Lt. William Ponge, piloting 42-99988/EI: **The Sad Sack**, was later felt to have been killed when a fusillade of fire struck the cockpit and one engine, setting both on fire. The doomed bomber peeled out of formation and began to tumble out of control, a desperate situation that resulted in just three crewmembers scrambling clear.

Yet another victim of possible summary justice was on board 42-52435/IO:, Lt. John W. Cathey's mount. F/O John L. Carlson (B) was uninjured when bailing out, but was unconscious and bleeding from bullet wounds when seen by fellow crewmembers after landing; before expiring, he told them he had been shot by soldiers. (A German report stated he was shot making an escape attempt.) Lt. Max E. Turpin's 41-29523/IG: **Miss Happ** was cut out and dispatched near Minden, while **Chubby Champ** (42-7655/CT:), flown by Lt. James G. Clark, progressed as far as Oldenburg before the latest fighter pass ended with the B-24 tumbling into a spin that saw only half the crew escape the physically-cramping centrifugal forces sufficiently to jump clear; Clark was not among them.

The final Group MIA casualty appears to have been making a desperate but unsuccessful bid to reach Sweden in what was to have been titled **Big Bad Wolf** by Lt. Orland T Howard's crew, an intention that would now be stillborn. However, it was flak that started the rot for 41-29479/. The bomber lost much of its hydraulic system and was ultimately reduced to quarter power by the time the pilots were over-flying Denmark's Poulsker Island. The resultant bail out was successful for all and even better for six, including Howard, who evaded capture for later "delivery" to Sweden.

Much more fortunate in their bid to gain the neutral haven was Lt. Dale R. Morris's team flying in 42-28718/7V: M **Bo**. The 458BG bomber progressed homeward as far as Hannover before eyewitnesses said it lost an engine and went into a spin with several parachutes observed. The latter observation was incorrect, but even so, the chances of making the roughly 200-mile stretch to Sweden seemed hopeless. Nevertheless, luck was definitely on the eleven-man team's side and they won through to land at Ringoby.

Wendling's 42-7510/GC: O. **El Lobo**, in Lt. Bert W. Wyatt's hands, was recorded as flying the inward leg with the 44BG and reaching the target. Dinklage lies roughly between Osnabrueck and Bremen, and was where German eyewitnesses said the stricken bomber emerged from the clouds with both port engines stopped and heavy smoke emerging from the forward fuselage. None of the ten airmen survived the resultant impact, followed by a raging fire that lasted for some considerable time; one was observed to jump out seconds before the crash but without either wearing a parachute or alternately being unable to open it in time, while a second crewmember was later discovered hanging from a tree with his parachute draped on tree branches.

The 392BG finally surrendered its sixth crew, headed by Lt. Fred C. Shere in 41- 28759/ DC: V+, as the Dutch/German border was approached. The bomber was reportedly flak-stricken over Berlin and fell out of formation. Once again, the pilots maintained a homeward course, but when near Nortrupp, south of Cloppenburg, the crew began to jump. Unfortunately, the pilots' chances of survival were cruelly denied when the tail section separated to cast the airframe out of their control; Sgt. Fonzy M. Wilson (ROG) also lost his life.

The 489BG arrived in Britain during April 1944, but unlike other Heavy Bomb Groups was destined to end WWII not in Europe, but back in the States, having returned there the following November. This 845BS B-24H-20-CF is 42-50280 **Rum Dum** displays the all-yellow fin and rudder that was the unit's visual identity within the 2BD after August 1944.

Shipdham Fortunes

Shipdham's share in the 14CBW's punishment occurred mainly on the homeward leg, but left the group three short on return. Lt. Keith Schuyler's crew in 42-100279/NB: I **Tuffey** was on their tenth mission, but a flak barrage after "bombs away" knocked out one engine and crippled a second, whereupon the B-24 inexorably straggled. Fuel levels were felt to be sufficient only as far as the enemy coast, but the westward flight path was maintained as far as central Holland. Then, a group of Fw190s initially engaged in attacking another Group banked away and made an angled approach at Schuyler's aircraft. Nothing daunted, he dived into the pack, all but one of which broke away downwards. The exception unfortunately turned to deliver a fatal burst that set the B-24 ablaze. The pilot's last act after bailing out the others was to bank his charge round on a course back into Germany before vacating his seat!

B-24H-10-FO/42-52121/IG: has suffered a heavy landing that has collapsed the nose wheel. The bomber, known as **Wolfpack**, was declared salvage on 9 September, but whether as a result of this incident remains unclear. Mud was a regular problem on British airfields thanks to the often wet weather patterns.

The B-24 was not an easy aircraft to control, even in level flight. The marginally downward angle of the nearest bomber and the fairly low altitude might suggest the 392BG is heading homeward. On the other hand, the aircraft's flight altitude as seen here was recommended for making the pilots' task as physically bearable as possible.

Lt. Glenn E. Sweigart's 41-29471/WQ: X lost the oil pressure on No. 3, resulting in a loss of altitude only finally steadied at 5,000ft, as well as a weaving forward motion just above stalling speed, but cloud cover initially left the crew safe from assault. Once out in clear sky, the lumbering cripple was focused upon by flak batteries. One close burst hurled Lt. John W. Torucy (N) out through the nose wheel aperture, but his luck was in, since he had previously donned his chest pack. Equally fortunate on abandoning the B-24 was Sweigart, who had neglected to secure his harness leg straps before jumping; it was as well he only had several thousands of feet to descend, and even then he had slipped so far down the harness that there was an imminent danger of hanging himself. Lt. Floyd H. Greene (CP) was the sole other survivor before the aircraft fell to its destruction at Bothfeld, three miles NE of Hannover.

Casualty Round-Off

Four further crews would never make it back. Lt. Weems D. Jones's 42-100360/RT: B. **Luck and Stuff** was another flak-afflicted casualty from the Berlin flak gunners. However, the ailing 446BG B-24H progressed homewards as far as the area around Helmstedt before fighters sealed its fate; seven of the crew got out alive, the other three either going down in their aerial tomb at Ruehen, or in one case discovered dead on the ground. The first of two Old Buckenham losses involved 42-50322/E8:, flown by Lt. Frank R. Tye. Debriefing reports that the bomber went down to fighter attack near the Duemmersee were seemingly contradicted by the total absence of a crash site for the aircraft or disposal of the crew's bodies. It was more likely that Tye got his charge as far as the Ijsselmeer or North Sea, where he and the crew met their anonymous fate.

Attlebridge's MIA contribution of two crews involved firstly 41-29399/T9: **Playboy** (Lt. Franklyn V. Cotner), which made the home stretch as far as Holland, despite having borne heavy flak and fighter damage. S/Sgt. Robert I. Falk (BT) was already dead when his colleagues abandoned the bomber, which came down at Tolplas. Joining it on Dutch soil at Twello was 41-28754/6L: N **Tell me More**, which Lt. C. Hitchcock put down for a smooth crash landing, leaving the ten airmen to clamber out.

"Ditching" Fortunes

Three 2BD crews featured in "ditching" acts from which a gratifyingly high proportion of the thirty-two airmen involved (twenty-six) actually survived, especially when given the B-24's usually poor ability to remain intact in these torrid circumstances.

The first was 41-29513/GJ: Z, piloted by Lt. Richard Hruby. Despite jettisoning all surplus equipment and easing back power, rapidly drying fuel tanks caused by flak damage over Berlin finally resulted in a remarkably smooth transition from air to water. Even so, the fact that one of the life rafts only partially inflated left some crewmembers clinging on; in addition, one crewmember was drifting away when the fortuitous arrival of a Royal Navy minesweeper after some forty minutes saved the day for all ten airmen.

Fortune was less kind to the other two crews, with six of the twenty-two airmen losing their lives. All but one on the 453BG's 42-52301/, flown by Lt. Max A. Davison, came through their immersion. The other five deaths occurred on the 389BG's PFF B-24/41-28784/YO: F, piloted by Lt. Alfred Locke and Col. Ralph S. Bryant (Command Pilot); also on board was T/Sgt. Harold Freeman (ROG), who had completed his combat tour, but volunteered to stand-in for the indisposed normal crewmember. The bomber had led the 2CBW, but became another flak victim that ran out of fuel. This time around, the "ditching" impact split the B-24 behind the wing/fuselage joint.

In spite of this, all twelve crew got themselves out—or in one case was rescued after being trapped—but the threat of exposure from the ever-chilled waters during the airmen's 45-minute immersion ultimately took the lives of Bryant and Lt. Arthur C. Delclisur (B), even though they were picked up alive. Lt. Kenneth O. Reed (N) drowned despite attempts to assist him, while Lt. John D. Bloznelis (PB N) was also lost; both are commemorated on Madingley's "Wall of the Missing." Arguably, the cruellest death was that of T/Sgt. Freeman, who had not needed to participate in the mission. Several of the other survivors suffered injuries, including a broken back for Lt. Errol A. Selfe (CP) and a fractured skull for S/Sgt. Dale Van Blair. Selfe later received the Soldier's Medal for going back into the largely submerged fuselage to rescue the trapped Sgt. Paez (WG), while Lt. Locke was awarded the DFC.

Only Safe When Down and Stopped

To Wendling's loss of six MIA crews were added two more B-24s and eleven airmen over England. Lt. Bernard Fryman's 41-29427/GC: U-bar **Ready, Willing and Able** had sustained serious damage on what (ironically and tragically) was its thirteenth mission. The crippled bomber entered the airfield circuit but then violently disintegrated, bearing all ten airmen to their deaths. Elsewhere, Lt. John W. Reid, IV was bringing home his equally stricken B-24H 42-7546 /DC: P+ **Alfred II**, but having made a landfall near Beccles felt that in view of his charge's parlous state, there was no choice but to bail out his crew. All but one on board safely exited, the pilot proving the sad exception, having probably struck some section of the airframe in his attempt; the abandoned machine piled in at Walcott, Norfolk. Pilot error in not applying the brakes properly was later adjudged to be the reason why 41-29302/7V: P **Nokkish** swerved off the runway at Horsham St. Faith and sheared off the port main landing gear wheel; fortunately, none of Lt. Millard P. Schaff's crew were injured, although their mount was "written off."

Comment

The operational mayhem visited upon the previous day's participants over Berlin was in sharp contrast to April's final Divisional sortie. The latest assault upon the enemy's *No-Ball* facilities saw just fifty-five crews from four Groups striking sites at Siracourt without any cost. April 1944 would be retrospectively established as the final month where the 8AF would suffer a high but not unbearable loss rate; from then on, the ability of the defenses—especially the *Jagdwaffe* element—to create even a temporary stalemate in bombing operations would be relentlessly suppressed and finally smothered.

With Winter having now largely given way to Spring and the ever-lengthening daylight hours providing enhanced visual access to the Continent, the 8AF "heavies" could reach out over the Nazi hinterland to strike its every industrial and military-based corner. However, the dictates of the Transportation Plan were destined to take growing priority during the intervening several months surrounding Operation *Overlord,* the failure of which would have rendered the Combined Bombing Policy largely null and void from the Western Allies' point of view at least.

Chapter Twelve

A Plane a Day has Flown Away

During the course of the Daylight Offensive, the majority of the 38 Bomb Groups serving within the ranks of the VIIIBC/8AF were destined to suffer a number of missions that severely depleted their strength. However, all these units soldiered on until VE-Day, albeit with one notable exception. The Group concerned was the penultimate example to arrive in East Anglia for assignment with the 2BD, the first B-24s touching down at North Pickenham on 18 April. The 492BG's first mission was flown 11 May and the 66th and last on 7 August—in the course of which no less than 52 MIA crews had gone down over the Continent or into the North Sea, with six more being destroyed in "operational" crashes. Two days prior to the final mission, the authorities took the decision to effectively terminate the Group's function in its primary role and redirect part of its personnel strength towards providing special Operations duties at Harrington, in the Midlands, thereby assuming the function previously carried out by the 801BG (P). This chapter concentrates on the short and tragically ill-starred period of its service as a pure Bomb Group.

The almost daily loss of crews in a statistical sense was largely concentrated within no more than three missions that between them excised no less than 34 bombers and their crews. The remaining 63 missions witnessed a loss rate far below 1%, which was more than acceptable and therefore adds a degree of confusion as to why the reallocation order was issued. There were dark suggestions that the Luftwaffe had selected the group for particular attention, and this was probably linked to the issue of natural metal finish (NMF) B-24s that literally made the 492BG stand out within the bomber stream. Rumors are far more easily created than quashed, as the reason for the *Bloody Hundredth* reputation as a "jinx outfit" that is still put forward by many of the personnel from Thorpe Abbotts attests to!

A Deceptive Start

The first four missions were free of combat casualties, but the first "Category E" incident occurred on return to England (11th). The 856BS' 44-40087/5Z:, flown by Lt. Shalvoy, diverted into Rougham (94BG) due to fuel shortage, but crashed as it crossed the airfield threshold. The fuselage was twisted and fractured, with the cockpit section literally strewn around in a manner that suggested few survivors from "up front." Amazingly, only one airman was killed and three of the nine survivors injured, but the incident was an augury of things to come.

Brutal Awakening

On 19 May, Brunswick was scheduled for Divisional attention by all four CBWs at full strength. The assembly procedure initially went well, but alterations in the briefed altitude, as well as the zero hour for the Division Lead Group to depart the English coast at the designated Division Assembly Line (DAL) point provided ample time for the enemy Ground Controllers to first plan and then launch their countermeasures.

A further complication arising from the confusing pattern of delay now arose in slotting each CBW within its planned position in the bomber stream. The 14CBW, of which the 492BG was a part, was scheduled to take the second slot, but was still minus the North Pickenham portion, whose 26 crews, led by two PFF aircraft from the 44BG, had orbited below the undercast layer, having not received the instruction regarding the final 23,000ft DAL altitude. When link-up with the CBW was finally made over the Dutch coast, the crews found that their Low Group slot was totally vacated; one of the two 392BG squadrons that was originally assigned to position itself as the 492BG's High right element had repositioned itself along with the other Wendling sub-force as High-right to the Lead 44BG; this decision arose out of the 492BG still being absent at final CBW Assembly. The still-acolyte group was accordingly on its own and wide open for assault!

Another fly in the operational ointment occurred when the 14CBW over-flew the IP northwest of the target. In itself this was serious enough, but further repercussions would arise in terms of each CBW being able to bomb in orderly fashion. The 25 crews still on hand as the Group formation passed north of Celle were now put to the sword as a formation of Fw190s made a head-on pass. The first B-24 taken down was the Lead bomber, flown by Capt. James L. Lewis (44-40133/9A:) and bearing the squadron Operations and Navigation officers among its 11-man crew; three gunners were the fortunate exceptions that got clear before the bomber's final crash. Lewis's No. 2, Lt. Lloyd H. Herbert, in 42-110153/9A: R was simultaneously dispatched, although what transpired after it disappeared out of sight was never established. Much more fortunate were all but one on Lt. Robert D. Fisher's crew after their 44-40152/9A:, flying as No. 3 in the Lead element, was knocked out of formation. The pilots headed for home, but only progressed as far as Holland before bailing out. Fire took hold on 44-40151/9A:, flown by Lt. Charles C. Pratt, but the pilots held course for the target; all too soon the bail out order had to be given, but only three crewmembers made it out before the bomb load exploded.

The good fortune that had deserted the majority of airmen so far now held for Lt. Wyman Bridges, who had now assumed the squadron Lead. His 44-40157/9H: **Lucky Lass** not only received damage to two engines and an aileron, but furthermore was literally run into by a Bf109 that removed half the starboard fin and rudder, as well as its own wing. The B-24 remained aloft and would get back to be repaired and ultimate return Stateside after VE-Day. Not so its companion squadron machine flown by Lt. Alvin M. Murray (42-110151/9H :); during this series of fighter assaults, two gunners were killed and the bail out order proved too late for all but four of the crew before a violent explosion expunged the lives of the others.

Problems with completing the bomb run for each CBW left the overall Division formation hopelessly split into three segments, with the 2nd and 14th CBWs that had held together for the Rally Point now bereft of the escort cover provided by the 353FG, which had linked up with the 96CBW. The attention of the flak gunners was superseded by a second bout of fighter assaults that handed out more punishment, especially to the 492BG. The unfortunate propensity for exploding that seemed to affect so many B-24s was visited upon 44-40088/9H: **My Dying Ass**, containing Lt. Roger J. Brague's crew. The pilot and two gunners were killed by an Fw190's fusillade and only four airmen—two of whom survived the bomber's disintegration—formed the (initially) lucky group of survivors. A similar proportion of immediate survivors emerged from 44-40065/X4: D+, in Lt. Haywood E. Brantley's hands. Fire took hold on one wing and only the four gunners in the rear fuselage were able to obey the bail out order before the bomber became the latest to

Lt. Hugh A. Shalvoy was returning from the 492BG's first mission on 11 May (Mulhouse in France) when B-24J-145-CO/44-40069/X4: suffered total fuel starvation and crashed close to Rougham, in Suffolk. The shattered forward fuselage section offered little prospect of survival for anybody stationed there, but in fact only the navigator was fatally injured.

A second view, this time of the cockpit area, presents an even starker image of the scale of destruction. Lt. Shalvoy is the airmen stretched out on the ground with several rescuers commencing the initial bid to move him to the waiting ambulance. It was later confirmed he had suffered spinal fractures, but he survived, although whether sufficiently to resume operations is unclear.

That's All Brother (B-24J-145-CO/44-40120), an 859BS bomber, has been caught at the very moment of bomb release; the lower rack of bombs are seen about to clear the base of the bomb bay. This aircraft, unlike nearly sixty of its Group contemporaries (fifty-one MIA and six lost in "operational" crashes), would return Stateside after VE-Day.

disintegrate in mid-air. As it was, one of the four was discovered dead after he had landed.

Lt. Charles W. Arnett was positioned as No.2 to Brague in 44-40171/9H: **The Boomerang.** The aircraft was observed to fall into a slow spiral, with smoke exuding from the No. 2 engine. The spin was happily arrested and the pilots set course for home. A second engine went "out" and the crippled B-24 was finally put down near Tuitjenhorn, on the peninsula separating the Ijsselmeer from the North Sea; nine of the ten airmen walked away alive from their aircraft, Sgt. Uriel Robertson (Eng.) having been killed during the heavy crash landing. The day's savage experience was now completed and a P-38 group's appearance provided the necessary respite from assault. Two of the returning crews diverted into Shipdham and an unnamed airfield. The survival of Lt. Bridges' **Lucky Lass** was regarded as even more miraculous, when upon examination of the starboard main wing spar it was found to have been broken in two by a 20mm shell!

The tragically transient existence of personnel undertaking combat operations was unconsciously echoed by Lt. Bill "Willie" Sparks, an 856BS navigator, in his diary notes covering the day's events:

> Out of our Group of twenty-four planes that were on the mission, eight didn't come back. Fifty per cent at most of the men were all that could have gotten out alive. I saw five of those planes go down and counted the chutes as they came out. It is hard to watch those B-24s go down with the men you know in them. The fellow that was playing cards last night, the one I was talking to at dinner, and a few of them singing old folk songs at the Mess hall after breakfast this morning. The lucky ones are probably in German prison camps tonight...

Sparks's crew might easily have been one of the MIA casualties, as his diary records:

> Over the target, we were flying right behind and about fifty feet lower than the Lead plane. One of the Lead plane's bombs stuck and just as we pulled up into closer formation it fell. This seemed to be a bad day all around, and what happened but the darn thing fell on our No. 3 propeller and engine. Luckily, it was a 100-lb incendiary and didn't go off. It bent the prop and the wing quite a bit; that was the reason for losing the engine.

A Tragic Misinterpretation?

Of the four survivors of Brague's crew who had descended by parachute, three of them, including Sgt. Vincent Kline, had landed close to the village of Lutter. Their stricken B-24's forward section had plunged into a farmhouse owned by a Herr Rabe and set it ablaze. The trio of Americans were swiftly rounded up and brought into Lutter by a group of villagers that included Willi Rieke, a sports coach; he had appointed himself the group leader and ordered the captives to assist in extinguishing the fire. Kline was of German/American descent and had been acting as interpreter, but upon Rieke's making his demand he said something that so angered the latter that he killed the Sgt. by means unknown. Reike's crime did not go unpunished, because in 1948 he was convicted of murder and sentenced to death.

The six missions following the Brunswick debacle brought forth a very welcome run of loss-free operations, other than on 27 May, when the 2BD attacked three marshalling yards between Saarbruecken and Trier with the 14CBW assigned to Saarbruecken. The sole Wing loss out of five Divisional casualties came from North Pickenham, although Lt. Robert P. Daly's crew suffered a better fate than many of their contemporaries. The No. 3 engine went "out" on 44-40102/5Z: as the formation passed the IP, with fuel starvation the cause. Before this situation could be rectified to bring the lagging B-24 back into formation, No. 2 suffered the same fate, in addition to which several fighters loomed up. Amazingly, the lumbering bomber, whose engines were only 75% functioning, not only managed to survive the encounter, but the pilots, having decided to head south for Switzerland (whose border was upwards of 150 miles distant from the target), succeeded in their bid. A further boost for Daly compared to his interned crew was that he subsequently jumped his internment "bail" and was back in England by August.

On the 28th, the Group headed for Zeitz-Troglitz, whose synthetic oil production plant was one of a large number briefed for assault by the 8AF. The 492BG was flying CBW Lead, but a major problem cropped up on the Lead B-24 during the bomb run when Capt. Robert M. Munson discovered the bomb bay doors would not deploy. T/Sgt. John E. Eckstrom (ROG) immediately undertook to edge out onto the bay catwalk and for up to eight minutes succeeded in holding the doors open; the confines of the catwalk did not allow a crewmember to hook up a parachute pack and the ROG's courage in taking the risky action was later recognized by the award of a DFC—but only after he involuntarily exchanged North Pickenham for internment in Sweden on 6 July.

Poelitz—a Forewarning

Next day oil targets, this time at Poelitz, up on the Baltic coast, were again on the operational menu for the 2BD at least, while elements of the 3BD attacked nearby Tutow's aviation industry. Strong *Jagdwaffe* twin-engine forces were assembled roughly between Berlin and the Baltic coast in a manner that would intrude on the approach of the two sub-forces, and by the day's end half the 34 bombers declared MIA from the 8AF would come from their ranks. The B-17s broke off to the NE for their Primary and in doing so missed the main thrust of the enemy fighter force over-flying the Muritzsee that were directly in the 2BD's path. The 14CBW, flying behind the 2CBW Division Lead, found itself in danger of over-flying their fellow Wing and adopted a zigzag flight pattern; unfortunately, the formation was at the furthest extension of one leg when sixty Me410s caught them in this vulnerable status, especially since the assigned 8FC escorts had been drawn off.

The Low squadron absorbed the brunt of the fighter assault, with Lt. John F. Landry's aircraft in the sub-unit's "coffin corner" (No. 6 position) being thoroughly shot up and finally ending up with the port wing set ablaze, although not before the bomb run was completed. Lt. C. Moore (CP) was killed, but the others all bailed out. However, centrifugal forces as the aircraft spun downwards after the port wing became detached prevented the pilot and Sgt. E. Burr (ROG) from getting clear until the doomed bomber (44-40115/9A:) was down at a dangerously low altitude. On being apprehended by a Wehrmacht officer, who demanded to know what their target was, Landry received a pistol whipping for laughing at what he regarded as a superfluous question, given that huge fires and smoke plumes were clearly being cast up from the refinery scant miles from where the duo of airmen had finally descended!

The Group's travails continued as it headed back under heavy fighter assault, with no less than nine bombers sustaining serious damage. Lt. Dave O'Sullivan's B-24 lost two engines and a fire was seen around the radio room as the seemingly doomed bomber peeled away and downwards. Lt. Gaulke's 42-95011/5Z: J had only arrived as a replacement two days previous, but was destined never to regain its North Pickenham dispersal. However, Fate was kind to both bomber and crew after the pilots dropped out of formation, because the subsequent attempt to head north to Sweden proved successful.

Although the formation managed to hold together during the protracted flight across northern Germany and out over the North Sea, it was one more short on reaching base. The 859BS' 44-40154/X4:, flown by Lt. William V. Prewitte, had to be abandoned while still some distance from friendly soil. The crew parachuted down into the sea, which was normally an act of desperation that ended in failure; on this occasion all but one crewmember was fished out of the lethal waters by an RAF ASR Launch. (Tragically, Lt. Prewitte's battle with the sea would be lost during a second watery immersion on 18 August. Now based at Rackheath, he was flying 42-50580/, which had also been transferred from the 492BG. The B-24J was struck by "friendly fire" while participating in a practice mission and crashed into the North Sea.)

The initial absence of four crews was reduced to three when Lt. O'Sullivan's shot-up bomber finally joined the airfield circuit, albeit minus his navigator, who had bailed out during the initial attack. Worse still was the absence of navigation maps, while the destruction of both dinghies rendered any thought of "ditching" extremely ill advised. Somehow, and despite being almost down to half power, the heading taken up brought the highly vulnerable straggler clear of enemy territory and ultimately back to East Anglia.

Deceptive Lull

The final two May missions were similarly loss free in terms of aircraft, and with a single example so were the subsequent sixteen. The unfortunate exception occurred during the strike on Avord airfield in France (4 June) and was not even due to enemy action. Lt. R. Sachtlaben's 42-95160/5Z: S stalled out while forming up and spun to its destruction near Garveston, killing all ten crewmembers. The crash site was barely two miles east of Shipdham, whose fire crews were dispatched to the scene. The airmen were dousing the flames when one of the fragmentation bombs from among the B-24's load exploded; Sgts. Monroe A. Atchley and Ted R. Bunalski were killed outright

A shamrock outline around a female's head is applied to B-24J-150-CO/44-40157. The confident mood of the bomber's title was to extend up to VE-Day. Having survived its time at North Pickenham, the bomber was transferred to the 93BG.

A sound percentage of the 51 bombers declared MIA from the 492BG actually remained intact, although operationally "neutered" after diverting into neutral soil. A Swedish guard stands by **Sknappy** (B-24J-145-CO/44-40142/5Z:) following Lt. Seitzinger's decision to take this course of action on the disastrous mission to Poelitz on 20 June 1944, an action paralleled by four further Group crews.

and the others thrown to the ground by the concussion. The two Sergeants were posthumously awarded the Soldier's Medal while four others received the Bronze Star.

Lt. Wesley R. Williams, an 859BS Bombardier, kept a diary that on 11 June commented on the use of 2,000-lb bombs:

> We had never carried 2000-lb GPs before. They took special bomb racks. Why do I suspect that these were still in Cosmoline? Pray note that these racks had to be bolted into special stations in the bomb bay. Also note that an aircraft which is being used tends to have its airframe warped a little (although most of ours were never around long enough to have a problem is this area), so the holes probably didn't match the racks and *vice versa*. Then, assuming you got the rack bolted in place and the electrics connected, the ordnance chaps had to load real live 2000-lb bombs and drop them on big canvas pads on our parking hardstands. Got to make sure they work, of course, then you've got to load 'em again and install the fuses before take-off at dawn. The ordnance guys looked pinch-faced for a long time after that. But we hearties took off into the blue and dropped those big bombs all over France. I watched four of them go into a fair-sized lake and raise a gorgeous plume of spray. I assumed that someone had seen a Panzer division hiding in the pond/lake.

Wesley's pithy style of expression as shown here is a key feature of his diary notes.

The M34/2,000-lb bomb was the largest general purpose bomb in the USAAF's arsenal that could be carried internally by the B-17 and B-24. Apparently, the ballistics of this weapon were imperfect, in that there was a tendency for it to tumble and in so doing impact other than directly onto the target. Early research also threw up the disappointing fact that a sizeable proportion of USAAF bombs were not exploding; a primary cause of failure was felt to be that the fuse arming mechanisms were freezing up. Attempts to limit this critically deleterious effect by inserting the fuses as late as possible were to meet with only limited success right up to VE-Day.

By 17 June, the Group had flown 27 missions and lost just fifteen crews MIA, so constituting a satisfactory return in crude operational terms. The ensuing seven missions would noticeably alter this balance to a virtually one-to-one equation. The downturn commenced on 15 June, with a run to bomb a railroad bridge at La Frilliere. During the approach, a single pass on the formation was made by Fw190s, one of whose number landed crippling strikes upon the No. 4 engine, as well as damaging No. 3 on 42-95132/9A: G, flown by Lt. David P. McMurray. The salvoing of the bomb load did not prevent the bomber dropping out and a course was taken up for the Allied lines in Normandy. All ten airmen bailed out over an Ally-occupied zone, although the pilot had a job to successfully trim his aircraft to fly "hands off" prior to exiting; Lt. Farrell (N) had the ill luck of breaking his ankle. Compared to Farrell, the "lucky nine" were unknowingly living on borrowed time that would swallow them up a mere 22 days later; the navigator's original misfortune proved to be his salvation, because he was still recovering from his injury on 7 July.

French airfields at Melun and Tours were struck without loss (17th), but next day, the thirty-three-strong force dispatched to Bremerhaven returned two short, both victims of flak. However, the good fortune enjoyed by Lt. Donald Miller's team in winning through to Sweden on board 44-40159/X4:

Battling Boop was not matched by all but two gunners on 44-40053/X4: A **Sweat'er Girl**, flown by Lt. Carl B. Roads, Jr. The damaged B-24 limped back almost to within sight of the English coast before the pilots, after ordering a bail out, were probably forced to execute a "ditching" maneuver that failed for them; Sgts. Morton E. David (WG) and Gerald A. Polzin (NG) were doubly fortunate to emerge alive and escape death from exposure, because they were immersed in the rough seas for some 90 minutes before an ASR launch arrived. A return to French targets by a reduced formation of eleven crews passed off uneventfully (19th), but the roof was about to fall again on the Group, as two in every five crews from the thirty-five teams attending Briefing early next morning were destined to experience.

Poelitz's Huge Tithe

The 492BG's experience over Poelitz on 29 May had resulted in three crews declared MIA and a fourth barely making it back to North Pickenham. Today's return mission (20 June) would see this sad statistic totally eclipsed in terms of casualties, as well as bringing the Group its greatest rebuff during its relatively short operational function within the 2BD. However, the latest exposure to the *Jagdwaffe* assaults would come about through unfortunate operational circumstances, rather than any lapse on the part of the Group itself.

Thirty-five crews were rostered for the mission and would fly level with but echeloned left to the Lead 44BG, with the 14CBW as Division Lead. The outward route traversed the Baltic as far as Ruegen Island before angling SE, until the target lay directly west, when the final bomb run approach would commence. All proceeded in deceptive calm, although the B-24 piloted by Lt. Velarde (856BS) "aborted" the mission prior to reaching Ruegen. Despite being dangerously isolated, the bomber made it back to England—unknowingly the sole participating squadron aircraft destined to do so.

The single escort Group on hand at this point (339FG) was hardly adequate to cover the bomber stream's 2nd and 14th CBW elements. This support potential was then totally dissipated when *Jagdwaffe* formations engaged the P-51s, permitting the Me410s of ZG26 up from Koenigsberg free rein in attacking the 492BG in particular. No less than 19 crews would taste the bitter seeds of defeat, of which fourteen were from the 492BG. However, at least five crews would gain salvation in neutral Sweden, along with fourteen other Division contemporaries out of a total of 34 declared MIA.

The cannon shell and rocket barrage continued for upwards of 30 minutes, with the unyielding Baltic waters absorbing five B-24s as the group bypassed Ruegen Island, north of Peenemunde—all but one from the luckless 856BS. Worse still was the crew survival rate, which shockingly stood at nil on board 44-40128/5Z: I (Lt. Franklin D Abbott, Jr.); 44-40161/5Z: O (Lt. Richard C. Kaufman); 42-110143/5Z: **Little Lulu** (Lt. Eugene H. Hadden); and 44-40143/5Z: L (Lt. John R. Curtis). Lt. Goodridge, in 44-40169/9A: I **Bottle Baby** (858BS), was the sole survivor out of the forty-eight airmen concerned.

Four further B-24s were lost either in the sea or over enemy territory, and although the crew survival rate was much enhanced, it still amounted to just eighteen out of forty. Lt. George B. Faucher (POW) lost three on 42-110152/5Z:, while seven, including Capt. Peter Val Preda (P), exited successfully from 44-40163/5Z: P. Lt. George C. McKoy (P) was one of eight fatalities on a third squadron aircraft (44-40150/5Z: H. **Ruptured Duck**), while just three airmen emerged alive from Lt. Roscoe E. Harris, Jr.'s (KIA) stricken 44-

One of the three companion bombers to **Sknappy** succeeding in landing at Bulltofta, Sweden, was B-24J-145-CO/44-40103/9A: M **Say When**. The 858BS aircraft was in the hands of Lt. Malcolm M. Heber's crew. Damage incurred in the target area decided the pilots to head north in their ultimately successful bid to avoid captivity or worse.

This B-24J-145-CO from the 859BS bears a mix of a black Division circle and the diagonal band confirming its assignment within the 14CBW on the fins. This bomber transferred on 12 August to the 467BG, with whom as X7: K it flew missions until 17 February 1945; then, none on Lt. Leon F. Porter's crew survived her loss in the North Sea during what ironically was a mission "recall."

Switzerland similarly accommodated several North Pickenham crews. B-24J-55-CF/44-10496/X4: Q+ was one of two winning through to Duebendorf after becoming separated from the Group in adverse weather conditions. The crew was led by Lt. William H. Wessom.

The other Swiss internee gained from North Pickenham ranks on the same day (21 July 1944) was B-24J-155-CO/44-40290/9H: R-bar. The bomber's nose wheel has collapsed, leaving the nose underside crumpled, but the crew emerged intact, if also rather shaken.

40227/5Z: Q **Four Beers Doc**, so increasing the squadron's loss figure to eight. The pilots had reportedly held their bomber steady to permit a bail out before it fell away into the Baltic.

The relative proximity of Sweden was a natural lure for no less than five crews, of which four made successful landings, while a fifth was abandoned over land by its pilot, who by then was the sole occupant. Lt. Joe L. Harris was group Lead in 44-40136/9H: I **Silver Witch**, but was nearly bombed out of the sky as his B-24 wallowed under three-quarters power with a "windmilling" propeller on No. 4 and finally fell back out of formation. A fuel mist spray from punctured feed lines filled the fuselage while the navigator, thinking his bomber was doomed, had bailed out. The pilots took course northwards while the Engineer finally released the single bomb that had jammed in its rack. A landing approach to Bulltofta airfield was successful, although one main wheel blew out; the B-24 stopped before its path intersected with the landing approach of a Swedish airliner! Three other group bombers followed Harris's example, being Lt. Elvern P. Seitzinger in 44-40142/5Z: K **Sknappy**; Lt. Heber flying the 858BS' 44-40103/9A: M **Say When**; and Lt. Robert C. Liggett's 44-40106/9H: F, which appears to have been the only one among this trio to get over the target and bomb.

The fifth group bomber heading for Sweden had already divested itself of all but the pilot when still over the Baltic; this action was taken due to the parlous state of Lt. Nicholas B. Kehoe's 44-40112/5Z: G, which included a fire in the fuselage. Sadly, all but two of the ten airmen concerned drowned or perished from exposure, the two exceptions being fished out by boat. For his part, the 856BS pilot, after trimming his charge and engaging the auto-pilot, managed to go back to extinguish the flames before regaining control. However, the bomber's condition was obviously deemed too critical to risk a landing, since Kehoe elected to bail out once neutral landfall had been made.

"Jinx" Misnomer?

Mission No. 34 for the 492BG had brought the MIA loss-factor borne so far to almost exactly one B-24 per mission (33), as well as striking savagely at the morale of the surviving combat personnel and their ground support contemporaries. On the other hand, there was no real reason to place the unit's reputation in a "jinx outfit" category similar to that "enjoyed" by the 100BG. As it was, the ensuing ten missions saw just a single crew added to the casualty figure, during which time two of the targets were locations deep inside Germany and one was on its western fringe. The single loss occurred on 23 June, when the French airfield at Laon/Athies was chosen for attack.

The Group was tracking back home close to Brussels when a flak shell struck the starboard wing on 41-29470/5Z:, flown by Lt. John D. Monroe (KIA); fire caught hold and initiated an explosion that separated the sub-unit from the fuselage. The resultant spinning motion caused the fuselage to break in two, providing a fortunate and involuntary exit point for the two survivors, S/Sgts. David F. McClenny (Eng.) and Lee

Hampton (ROG). The wreckage descended into Watermael-Boltstorf, a city suburb. In September 1994—the exact 50th Anniversary of Belgium's Liberation from Nazi tyranny—a beautiful memorial to the crew was erected by the community and McGlenny and his wife Edith were invited to the dedication ceremony. This was the second MIA B-24 that should have carried Capt. Geitz (group Chaplain), but he had hitherto been forced to cancel both flights—he took the hint and desisted from all further efforts to "hitch a ride"!

July was four days old before the group took off on its latest mission to bomb a French airfield at Beaumont-le-Roger, which ended well for the twenty out of 27 crews dispatched making bomb runs. Not so 48 hours later, when Kiel's submarine yards were targeted. The flak batteries took out the No. 1 engine on Capt. Robert M. Munson's 44-40195/9A: **Boulder Buff** just as the bomb loads were released; somehow the descending turn to port that then developed saw the bomber emerge unscathed from contact with the rain of missiles. As it was, their abrupt isolation from the formation coupled to a slow but inexorable rate of descent, even after pulling back into level flight, persuaded the pilot to head northeast for Sweden. Once again, luck was on the crew's side and an unimpeded passage to and safe landing at Bulltofta was effected. Similar fortune attended all but two on board a second squadron bomber flown by Lt. Curtis A. Abernethy (44-40064), which ended up "ditched," the survivors being fished out by the ASR Service. Three crews MIA over eleven missions was a logistically satisfactory state of affairs for the authorities at least, but Nemesis was again lurking in the wings for the third and final time as the crews went to bed on the 6th.

Martyrdom over Bernberg

Bernberg SW of Berlin, was one of a clutch of locations in the region housing key aircraft production facilities and was allotted to the 14CBW on 7 July. In the case of the 492BG, two squadrons flying Lead and Low positions had been allocated to the CBW's High Group, while the 44BG, instead of being staggered to the left of the 392BG flying Lead, would instead fly in a trail position; the 492BG elements within the CBW therefore appeared more than adequately boxed-in against any fighter opposition. This cosy situation became unstuck as target approach was on hand, however.

The 14CBW was the third Wing in the Divisional stream and was reportedly bereft of almost all its allotted escort cover, according to German radio transmissions that in turn were being monitored by specialist B-24s on hand. As the IP was reached, the rear cover hitherto provided by the 44BG totally disappeared when that Group took evasive action to starboard to avoid collision with encroaching B-24s from the Wings up ahead that had already bombed. This left the 492BG exposed to attack from six o'clock by a huge formation of Fw190A-8s from IV (*Sturm*) JG3 that now swamped the North Pickenham formation. Disaster on the scale of 20 June was looming with the Low squadron the first to suffer.

Capt. Ernest E. Pelkey's crew in 44-40086/9A: and Lt. D McMurray's flying 44-40145 /9A: were promptly dispatched, with nobody surviving the violent demise of these 858BS aircraft, the former B-24 being taken down by Ltn. Hagenah. The Lead B-24 flown by Lt. Bernard N. Harding (POW) was 44-40110/X4:, out of which all twelve crew emerged alive; sadly, one among their number was killed by civilians, who also beat up most of the others.

The 859BS suffered the loss of at least five further B-24s during the vicious air battle that extended on both sides of the target. All but the nose and tail gunners got clear from 44-40153 /X4:, flown by Lt. Robert H. Jacks, while Lt. Roland E. Steneman also survived the loss of his 44-40156/X4: K+, along with two out of the other nine on board. The other two pilots were not so fortunate, as they were killed: Lt. Elmer J. Smiley piloting 44-40050/X4: **Super Wolf** and Lt. Donald M. Kilpatrick, Jr. in 44-40132/X4: J+ **I'll Be Around**. The latter B-24's executioner was Uffz. Schafer, whose gunfire had killed two crewmembers, with two others going down with the bomber. The remainder successfully bailed out, but the pilot was reportedly killed by rifle fire while still in mid-air.

Replacement aircraft were the mounts for four more MIA crews, starting with Lt. Ernest L. Watson in 42-95005/ and Lt. Clayton J. Newman in 42-95177/. Both pilots were killed, as was Lt. Alfred A. Bocksberger in 42-50370/. The sole airplane commander to survive as a POW was Lt. Frank Haag flying 42-95230.

Frank's brother George was also serving with another Group squadron and both were "original" personnel. Now the latter could only watch helplessly as 42-95230/ began to absorb what was ultimately fatal punishment. Both copilot and ROG were killed as fire caught hold in the bomb bay. Lt. Ralph R. Golovan (N) was very fortunate to survive. He was standing on the nose wheel doors— that on a B-24J open inwards, but open outwards on the B-24H, the Haag-piloted machine coming from the latter production type. Having taken off his flak vest in order to maneuver more freely before going to assist the nose gunner in his jammed turret, the Lieutenant illogically but very fortuitously reached for his parachute pack. Just then, the bombardier hit the emergency release for the doors prior to bailing out himself, whereupon Golovan was precipitated out into mid-air! His luck would still hold, since his grasp on the parachute pack was not affected by the air blast, although he only managed to attach one hook to his harness before deploying the canopy.

The 453BG was part of the 2CBW flying ahead of the 14CBW and briefed to attack Halle, almost due south of Bernberg. Both Wings made their target approach from the SW, but the Bernberg force was upwards of ten minutes late in making its approach. Therefore, when the 492BG reached its Initial Point, the

The original Martin top turret design remained a standard fitting until the summer of 1944. Then the introduction of a more sophisticated gunsight demanded a marginally higher and re-contoured Plexiglas outline; what was the Company's A3D modified unit became known as the "High hat." Two holes in the circular frame vent the gun gas residue.

An oil refinery at Hamburg casts up a massive black cloud from blast-ruptured facilities as the 492BG heads for home during what was to be the Group's penultimate mission on 6 August 1944. Lt. Carl W. Ruthenbeck pilots B-24J-1-DT/42-51258/5Z: N. The formation is being pecked at by the flak gunners, with two bursts seen below the 856BS bomber.

2CBW, which included the 453BG, had already bombed and was swinging to the south on a course that should have been parallel to and east of the 14CBW, but which instead intersected with the 14CBW's formations, as they were roughly halfway to the target! The scene was set for a particularly tragic incident that was self inflicted.

Lt. John L. Cary was flying 42-110091/X4:—a group "original" B-24J with 29 missions already recorded—which was No. 2 in the group Lead element. The oncoming 453BG was also under fighter attack at this point, and as the two formations angled almost head-on to each other, the 453BG deputy Lead bomber was set on fire in the starboard wing and veered directly towards the 492BG Lead element. Violent evasive action did not spare Cary's machine nor the 453BG B-24 as their wings impacted, excising 42-110091's wing in the process before the entire airframe disintegrated; only Cary's navigator would survive from both crews.

This last loss ensured that 110 North Pickenham crewmembers had been violently removed from Group records. Mission No. 46 was to prove the third and final occasion on which the 492BG would shed aircraft and crews in copious quantity, even if the virtual one-to-one relationship of missions to losses (46 to 45) was still being maintained. On the other hand, one calendar month from today would witness the Group's final mission as a strategic bombing entity.

Running Down the Clock

The remainder of July operations for the Group now reverted to a more than acceptable loss pattern in relation to missions flown. This was even more gratifying when considering that nine of the thirteen missions were to strategic targets spread across Germany, even if five of the seven MIA crews lost during this period arose from launching these longer-ranged forays that invited prolonged fighter and flak opposition. The first assault on a German target occurred 11 July, when the first of two consecutive daily missions went out to Munich, deep in SE Germany. Of the sixteen Division losses, two were from the 492BG, out of a total of five crews diverting into Switzerland. Flak disabled three out of the eight engines split between Lt. John C. Tracey's 44-40168/9H: -Bar and Lt. S. Platinski's 42-95196, but both pilots safely traversed the stretch from the target to Duebendorf airfield, although the former bomber suffered a collapsed nose wheel.

The next day's return to Munich added one more crew to the loss list. Lt. Herschel Smith, flying 44-40130 (859BS), lost his ball turret gunner, who was trapped and burned to death in his turret following a fire in the waist section. Smith's attempts to emulate his fellow airmen off yesterday's run were thwarted by fighters who desisted from downing their prey, but instead reportedly provided a compulsory "escort" southwards as far as the Swiss/Italian border region, where the North Pickenham crew was "persuaded" to land at Ghedi. This action seemed contradictory, given the distance from the target zone to Ghedi is over 200 miles. In fact, solid cloud cover foiled the pilots' attempts to establish their position until breaking into the clear near Ghedi, when the Luftwaffe effected their ever-unwelcome interception and compulsory "guidance"!

A similar two-day mission sequence to Saarbruecken left the Group formations intact, but a return to tactical targets in France ironically reversed this positive situation to some degree. Flak so damaged Lt. S. Seger's 42-95215 that he was forced to abandon the bomber over the Normandy beachhead with one member on what was an acolyte team losing his life thanks to a failed parachute. A second crew being "blooded" in combat was led by Lt. M. Vowinkle, who made a creditable crash landing on an Allied airstrip, with his charge pulling half power and with a fire under the flight deck—moreover, with ten bombs still on board. His efforts later resulted in the award of a DFC.

The next three daily runs were all to German targets, the latter seeing the 2BD heading back into SE Germany, with an industrial plant at Oberpfaffenhofen allotted to the 14CBW. By the day's end, twenty-two Division crews were gone, including six getting through to Switzerland. Two among this latter figure were from the 492BG, but the circumstances affecting what were replacement teams taking this action were unclear, although both apparently lost contact with the formation when encountering heavy cloud on the way in. The pilots concerned were Lts. William M. Walker flying 44-40290 and William H. Wesson in 44-10496. The remaining four July missions, split equally between strategic and tactical operations, passed off without further loss. The latter mission to Ludwigshafen (31st) for once involved a positive milestone for the Group, since it involved the first crew to complete a combat tour. This was Lt. "Dashing" Dave O'Sullivan's team, whose luck had held true, none more so than during the mission to Poelitz on 29 May, when they had to make a solo return flight in their badly damaged B-24. Gen. Johnson (CG, 14 CBW) was on hand to congratulate the crew and later join in the celebration.

Abrupt *Finis*

As August was entered, the persistent rumors regarding a move away from North Pickenham that had spanned several weeks began to gather pace towards a conclusion. Daily missions were flown other than on the 2nd, with a "double header" launched on the 4th, albeit a single-figure number (5) for the strike against a V-1 site in NE France. Two of the 23 crews heading out the same day for Kiel must have later wished they had been rostered for the short-range mission, because they never came home. Both were "rookie" teams led by Lts. Harold Both, Jr. in 44-40135 and Lt. Lawrence C. Ives flying 42-50770; a measure of comfort was that all twenty crewmembers ended up surviving their aircraft's loss.

Extremes of Fortune

The completion of their combat tour by the O'Sullivan crew had initiated a sequence of five further tour completions inside four days. First was Capt. D. Mack (3rd), followed by Lt. R. Menweg next day. Then, between the 5th and 6th, Lts. R. Scott's, J. Skorupan's, and Wilfred L. Hamilton's teams joined the band of "happy warriors" within the Group's ranks. However, misfortune was hovering in the wings on the latter date and unfortunately would arise in a self-inflicted manner.

The B-24s were coming in from a mission to Hamburg (6th), with Lt. Richard W. Fleming's 42-50719/X4; O+ in some distress; in front of him—while both B-24s were on final approach—was 44-40146/ 5Z: M, flown by Lt. Pitzenbarger. The damaged bomber was deemed to be closing dangerously in upon the 856BS machine from above, so Pitzenbarger was instructed to "abort" his landing run. However, his action in pulling up steeply not only induced the bomber to falter and stall out, but Fleming's reaction to Pitzenbarger's maneuver caused him to similarly pull up sharply, thereby also stalling out his aircraft. Both machines slammed into the ground, with Fleming's bomber breaking up and erupting in flames to kill all but one crewmember. The other B-24 also broke up upon impact, but the survival/fatality proportion was diametrically opposite at nine to one.

And so Death had unknowingly struck for the last time among the North Pickenham fliers off what was their penultimate strategic bombing mission. Tactical targets predominated on the 7th, with no Divisional MIA casualties, but as the twelve crews dispatched but failing to bomb their cloud-covered

Col. Eugene Snavely (492BG CO), in a full Olive-drab uniform, is seated seventh from the right, along with a large cadre of Senior and middle-ranking officers. The date is recorded as 6 August, just 24 hours following the official declaration of the Group's disbandment. Col. Snavely would go on to command the 44BG.

No crews were lost over Europe during the Group's penultimate mission, but a tragic accident in the landing circuit claimed two B-24s and half of their occupants. Lt. Pitzenbarger's shattered 44-40148 /5Z: M literally fell out of the sky following a collision with Lt. Fleming's bomber; amazingly, only one of the crew was killed, compared to the single survivor among ten on the Fleming-crewed B-24.

Primary landed back, the group personnel were already aware over the previous 48 hours that a major reorganization—or more accurately, a breaking-up of the unit's structure—was on hand. The short-lived and tragic odyssey for the 492BG was accordingly at an end.

Reflections

Only two Bombardment Groups out of the large number assigned to the 8USAAF during the course of WWII would subsequently be removed from its strength in this primary role. One was the 489BG, whose appearance in British skies only extended from May to November 1944; the unit was then redeployed to the Pacific Theater of Operations, where its crews still functioned in their primary duty of bombing. The 492BG was the other group withdrawn, but unlike the 489BG, its redeployment (or rather its practical disbandment) witnessed a partial switch to the more passive if no less vital role of a courier unit—in this instance, the delivery of agents and their backup equipment to support the Resistance Movement in Occupied Europe.

In practice, only one squadron's aircraft and personnel (856BS) was destined to currently make the transfer to Harrington, from where the 801(P) 36th and 406BS' personnel had been conducting these clandestine operations to date. The 857BS was ordered to dispatch its B-24s and their crews to a number of other Groups within the 2BD, with the ground personnel transferring to the 490BG (a 3AD unit). The 859BS combat and ground crews transferred to the 467BG, where they became the kernel for that group's 788BS. The 858BS had already been transferred out on 21 June.

"Missing in Action" No More

Lt. McMurray's crew had been one of the casualties of the 7 July Bernberg mission. Their exact fate had never been fully determined in over half a century following the end of WWII. Indeed, many within the 492BG senior ranks were of the opinion that the airmen had progressed home as far as the North Sea before their B-24 succumbed to its damaged condition and descended there.

The efforts of the American authorities to trace as many as possible of the 78,000 MIA personnel from WWII had borne fruit in many cases prior to 2003. A major player in this function was the U.S. Army Central Identification Laboratory, whose attention on 7 July 1944 was directed towards the town of Westeregeln, which had been the epicenter for a number of B-24 crashes off the Bernberg strike. A suspected crash site indicated by a Herr Schwartz, who had conducted his own "dig" that wielded results, was more comprehensively excavated. The search revealed human body parts and supporting evidence, such as dog tags and personal effects; the initial result was that six of the nine crewmembers were identified as members of McMurray's ill-starred team. However, a total of eight separate human remains appear to have been finally confirmed. Three of these were traced to named crewmembers who received burials in specific State locations; the other five were buried at Arlington, along with artifacts traced to all nine on board the B-24. (S/Sgt. Cotey was identified by his dog tag and ring only, so the Arlington headstone makes reference to all nine airmen's names.)

Chapter Thirteen

Focus on Normandy

Applying the Pressure

The pace of 8AF operations during May 1944 was highly intensive, with 23 of the 31 days involving bomber operations. On the other hand, as far as the 2BD's participation was concerned, there was an apparent three-way split in mission categories. Tactical and strategic missions totaled eight and nine day's effort, respectively; the remaining seven involved assaulting V-1 sites in France. The latter sources, unlike the aforementioned missions, would remain primarily latent until after D-Day, while the rain of missiles directed toward SE England, with London as the epicenter from 13 June onward, would not have any direct effect upon Operation *Overlord*. On the other hand, the negative psychological, if not material effect upon the British population within SE England could not be totally discounted.

The month's activities were focused upon the Pas de Calais, with its plethora of V-1 sites, but saw barely one-quarter of the dispatched crews penetrating the cloud cover over the region to strike their targets. A second mission to marshalling yards in France and Belgium yielded better results, with none of the three MIA crews coming out of Divisional ranks. Next day, separate attacks in single CBW strength led by PFF bombers of the 93BG mounted the latest V-1 site assaults, with the 12th and 2nd CBWs the involved sub-units. None of the 231 crews sent out to Brunswick (4th) ever reached there, since a general "recall" was issued in the face of ever-looming cloud formations. The accent on CBW-strength forays against V-1 sites was resumed over the ensuing two days. It was the 96CBW's turn to carry out the latest PFF-led sortie against sites at Sottovast, on the Cherbourg Peninsula (5th), while three Groups went out to Siracourt (6th).

The 458BG's flak-damaged **Spare Parts** (41-28706/J4: F), in Lt. Evert R. Thompson's hands, lost all engine power shortly after crossing over the English coast on return from Sottovast. A crash landing site near Odiham, in Hampshire, appeared suitable, but although the initial impact was smooth, contact with what was probably a tree stump ripped the lower fuselage apart and buckled the frame, trapping some of the crew. The No. 3 engine had burst into flames and only five of the nine crewmembers ultimately survived, despite the valiant efforts of Lt. Walter F. Landers (CP), who was aided by a civilian to get everyone out.

The nil loss rate in MIA crews to date during May was almost sustained next day, when Muenster and Osnabrueck were targeted by the full Division. The 2CBW was seemingly part of the sub-force attacking Osnabrueck and the 389BG arrived back one crew short. Lt. Bernard J. Schott's ROG had radioed in the coordinates for the imminent "ditching" location for their 42-100422/EE: Y **Swee'pea**. The subsequent entry into the sea either killed some or all of

A sunlit Seething dispersal during the early summer of 1944 contains the frame of B-24H-5-CF/42-52606/CI: A **Hello Natural II**, whose predecessor was now a Swedish internee. Her time with the 448BG spanned just over four months before she was declared "salvage" on 21 July. This shot was probably taken later in her operational career, judging by the bomb log under the cockpit window.

the seven airmen so affected; Schott and Lt. Hugh Mayher (CP), along with T/Sgt. Daniel J. Brock (B) were extremely fortunate to survive almost two hours' immersion, supported only by their "Mae Wests" before the summoned ASR launch arrived. As it was, Brock died on the way back due either from his severe injuries or to exposure; Lt. Myron Lloyd (N) had been on his 48th mission.

The "Reaper's" Return

The 2BD had suffered greatly over Brunswick a full calendar month previous, and its defenders would exact a toll (8th) that was barely a third compared to the 30 crews downed from the April mission. This diminished statistic was of no comfort to the 453BG airmen, since no less than eight of the eleven MIA teams came from their ranks.

Target approach NW of Brunswick was being completed when 42-52298/E3: **Choo Choo Baby** absorbed punishment from a fighter that killed two crewmembers; Lt. Richard T. Witten followed the seven survivors out into mid-air, leaving his charge to plunge into the ground west of Celle. Lt. Ray R. Keith's (POW) 42-52147/E3: was hacked from the sky around the same stage, its final descent being north of Nienberg at Hassbergen, along with six out of the ten on board. Lt. Fred V. Parker, in control of 41-28745/F8:, was one of eight fatalities after flak dealt a terminal blow that brought the bomber down several miles south of Brunswick, with the navigator and one gunner in the rear section being the fortunate survivors.

The bomb run was completed and a turn for home in progress when a series of persistent fighter attacks commenced that ripped into the Group's ranks in shocking succession. Lt. John B. Mackay's 42-94806/H6: had No. 3 engine shot completely off and the controls were jammed. The bail out order was given, to which only three, including Mackay, succeeded in completing before a spin developed; nobody else survived the crash at Wolfenbuettel, due south of Brunswick. Another crew downed at this stage appears to have been that of Lt. Thomas J. Stilbert, Jr. in 42-52169/E8: - **Lucky Penny**. One engine was set on fire and the flames swiftly spread into the fuselage. Eight of the eleven airmen got out alive before an explosion ripped the aircraft apart NE of Goslar.

Almost immediately 42-50278/E8:, flown by Capt. John W. Banks, made contact with a fellow squadron B-24 (42-110025/E8: in Lt. Dean H. Hart's (POW) hands). Only Banks and T/Sgt. Harry K. Gates (Eng.) escaped the loss of their B-24, which crashed scant miles SW of the target. Seven airmen were consumed in the other bomber's demise; however, its crash site was some 20 to 30 miles further west outside Hameln, indicating that temporary control must have been maintained before its total failure resulted in disaster. Hameln was the epicenter for the final loss involving 42-50327/H6:, which blew up with the shattered airframe strewn over the ground and into the river Weser at Tuendern, on Hameln's southern outskirts. Lt. Endicott R. Lovell, Jr. was united in eternity with six of his colleagues, leaving two survivors to face a *Stalag*.

On the return leg, the first of two Tibenham B-24s (42-94957/MK:) was taken down by fighters to crash at Vienenburg, along with all ten on Lt. William M. Peters's crew. The vagaries of combat by contrast spared all ten of Lt. John C. Burnett's (POW) team on 42-95051 /WV: after it came down near Meidenthal.

The sole MIA loss suffered by other than the 2CBW was from the 467BG, whose three squadrons, dispatching thirty crews in all were, unusually separately assigned to form up with the other 96CBW Groups and the 392BG. Fighter attacks initiated just after the bomb run was completed finally took down 42-52477/X7: E.; Lt. Charles D Harrison's bomber was observed to turn over and go down, the pilot becoming one of six fatalities out of ten airmen on board. Another group B-24 (42-52542/4Z: + **Stinger**) had two engines disabled and suffered heavy damage to the radio and electrical systems and landing gear. Nevertheless, Lt. Thomas H. Murphy maintained control, and having gained friendly soil, bailed out the crew before carrying off a forced landing at Watton with only one landing gear wheel lowered. The scale of damage merited "Category E" treatment for the aircraft.

Stinger was just one of four B-24s involved in "operational" crashes off Brunswick. Another CBW companion

USAAF uniform variations are evident here. Gens. Timberlake (right) and Hodges wear jacket-top outfits, with the former all Olive drab in texture. Hodges, Doolittle, and Spaatz have the more regular mix of Olive drab tops and Pinks trousers, although Hodges's tunic lacks a belt. The latter two officers have donned blouses as opposed to jackets. The occasion was the Distinguished Unit Citation (DUC) ceremony at Hethel on 9 May 1944.

Col. Jack W. Wood, who was the original CO of the 389BG and who flew the Ploesti mission the previous 1 August, stands on the left of a lineup of personnel being presented to Gen. Spaatz. The casual position of the men's arms while at attention contrasts sharply with the "thumbs aligned with the trouser seam" action of their British ally.

B-24 was already a shattered wreck at Frettenham, scant miles from Horsham St. Faith's perimeter. One engine failed on takeoff and Lt. Paul E. Kingsley's frantic attempt to remain airborne in 42-52404/Z5: Q **Belle of Boston** failed when one wing struck a tree; the pilot and four of the other eight airmen did not survive the subsequent disintegration, but the fortuitous failure of the bombs to explode contributed to there being any survivors at all. Single B-24s from Old Buckenham and Attlebridge completed the figure. Lt. Catlin bailed out his crew to leave battle-damaged 42-52176/F8: N **Valkyrie** to come down at Morningthorpe. A fighter strike created a raging fire within 41-28743/2U: H **Eastern Front's** forward fuselage, resulting in what turned out to be the precipitate bail out by two Enlisted men; fortunately, the flames were extinguished by another crewmember and the return flight ended with a crash landing at Rivenhall.

Next day, airfields and marshalling yards scattered around the Franco/Belgian and Franco/Luxembourg borders received a thorough pasting from all three Divisions at minimal cost, although the four B-24 crews out of six MIA in all would not have agreed. The second Hethel crew to "ditch" within 48 hours enjoyed no more success than Lt. Schott's crew. The English Channel coastline was tantalizingly close when Lt. John Shepherd was finally forced to ease his damaged charge (41-29451/HP: R) into the sea. Only Lt. George Huck (N) and S/Sgt. John Busch (WG) survived the occasion; however, the fact that parachutes were seen emerging before the final action indicates that the unfortunate individuals concerned perished through drowning or exposure. Busch was hospitalized with pneumonia but recovered.

While over Liege marshalling yards, flak struck home on the 448BG deputy Lead bomber. The impact between No. 3 and 4 engines set fuel from punctured tanks alight and Capt. Robert T. Lambertson quickly assessed his bomber's situation as terminal; he rang the bail out bell and all on board, including Maj. Ronald V. Kramer (Command Pilot), jumped before 42-100287/IG **Margaret/Busted Flush** disintegrated to spread its remains near Tongeron. One gunner suffered a parachute collapse, but all other crewmembers survived as POWs.

Single losses were also borne by the 453BG and 466BG. Half of Lt. Ed J. Perro's (POW) ten-man crew on 42-52186/H6:O were killed either by gunfire from their Fw190 executioner or in the violent mid-air explosion close to Arendonk. The Attlebridge casualty also came down on Belgian soil west of Antwerp, another fighter victim; fire took hold on 42-52584/6L: F **Worry Bird II**, after which it descended in a spin, killing Lt. Warren M. Wallender (P) and five of the nine others on board in the process.

There should have been a fifth MIA loss from Shipdham over St. Trond airfield. The load of 100-lb M-47 incendiaries was falling out in a close train when the Lead weapon exploded to set off a series of sympathetic blasts tracking upwards almost into the bomb bay of 42-100110/ WQ: P **Northern Lass**, flown by Lt. Arnold V. Larson. The impact detached No. 4's propeller and knocked out the intercom system. The crewmember sent aft to check-up discovered his five colleagues from the 28-mission team had gone, all having clearly assumed the B-24 was doomed. Nothing daunted, the pilots held for home in their now isolated and half-crewless bomber and succeeded in their endeavor by landing at Attlebridge; next day, the B-24J was declared "Salvage."

The dislocation of the enemy marshalling yard system was allocated solely to the 2BD and two B-24 groups

There are several tons of non-aerodynamic pressure applied upon the wings of B-24D-65-CO/42-40506 **Fightin' Sam** from the presence of around sixty airmen viewing the DUC ceremony at Hethel on 9 May 1944. The veteran bomber assigned to the 566BS was one of at least two Ploesti survivors lined up for the occasion.

Red Ass (B-24H-25-FO/42-95203) presents a sharp and pleasing image for the photographer as she heads out on a mission to Bielefeld, Germany. The photo angle confirms the need for any fuselage-applied aircraft letter to be repeated upon the fin, since the former is totally obscured. This bomber finally returned Stateside with the 446BG.

of the 3BD on the 11th; in addition, the strikes were aimed at locations in SE France extending towards the Swiss borders. Over two-thirds of the 364 crews mainly struck their Primaries, with the residue picking out Targets of Opportunity. The cost was single crews lost from four Division Groups, three from the 96CBW. The proximity of Switzerland to the Wing's assigned target of Epinal caused Lt. Stuart Goldsmith to direct his 41-28738/Z5: O **Meat around the Corner** that way. The B-24H had suffered pre-target oil pressure problems on No. 3, followed by a "windmilling" propeller; this negative combination now stood against a guaranteed return home before running out of fuel. The bomber crossed the border safely and was put down near Jagenstorf. Goldsmith, along with Lt. Ritter, later escaped into France disguised as a woman, both men linking up with the Resistance.

Rackheath's 42-50354/Q2: N **Messie Bessie**, with Lt. William T. Shoup's crew, was just heading for the Rally Point when the Engineer reported damage to the B-24H; the nature and extent was unclear, but it was sufficient for the pilots to take up the same heading as Goldsmith and make a landing at Geneva/Cointrin, although not before encountering ground fire that proved thankfully ineffectual as they circled for the landing.

These two crews were fortunate compared to the other two sharing their MIA fate and for whom capture was the least of their problems. The 44BG had been heading for Mulhouse but ended up over Orleans/Bricy airfield and Belfort's marshalling yards. A sharp assault by Bf109s over the former location saw one descend upon 42-94999/GJ: B-bar to riddle the starboard wing and fuselage and set No. 2 engine ablaze. Fortunately, all ten crew led by Lt. James H. Walsh jumped clear, leaving the B-24H to impact near Patay, NW of Orleans. S/Sgt. Joseph O.

Peloquin (Eng.) suffered ripcord failure, but was fortunate enough to tear open the pack and feed the pilot parachute out into the slipstream; the canopy's deployment was barely sufficient to halt Peloquin's precipitate plunge towards a terminal conclusion, depositing its human bundle safely on the ground bare seconds later! (An added bonus was his successful evasion attempt that was emulated by Sgt. Richards (WG) and Lt. Walsh.) Lt. John C. McDonald, flying 41-28664/2U: P+ **Chant of Venice/ Merchant of Venice**, reportedly radioed that he was diverting into Switzerland, but nothing more of the 466BG bomber or its eleven-man crew was ever destined to come to light and both remain on the MIA list.

Oil Strike

The search for very vulnerable products with which the Nazis were prosecuting WWII had by this stage of the conflict settled upon oil as the key component in thwarting Hitler's bid to even sustain his sadly-deluded nation's bid for European domination, let alone advance its progress towards that end. Gen. Spaatz has been credited as the leading figure in putting forward the idea; it is ironic that as early as 1940, the RAF's "Supremo" Sir Charles Portal had advanced the same basic argument, although not treating oil targets at the total expense of other target categories, such as transport. The RAF had neither the aircraft nor the heavy bomb capacity with which to home in upon oil-related sources, and even more limiting was Bomber Command's ability to even get within striking distance, let alone unleash its bomb loads accurately in 1940. By May 1944, the advent of regular daylight bombardment coupled with the ability to strike using massive forces of bombers had granted an immeasurably greater degree of feasibility to the project.

What was to be the 8AF's first direct assault upon Germany's oil industry on 12 May had already been initiated by its companion Italian-based force by around one month. In early April, the 15AF had resumed its assault upon the massive Rumanian complex at Ploesti, scene of the bloody "success" visited upon the attackers the previous 1 August. Whereas Ploesti was the enemy's major source of natural oil, along with a smaller complex at Brasov, in Rumania, the 8AF's attacks would be directed against a welter of synthetic oil plants, there being no natural oil resources within Germany itself. (Ploesti and Brasow's product was crude in nature and accordingly unsuited to the refined variation necessary for aircraft engines that the synthetic plants produced.) Between them, the twin arms of America's strategic bombing force would seek to cut off the product that literally assisted the overall Nazi war machine to flow along in its nefarious manner.

The six Primaries for nearly 900 B-17s and B-24s were paired off, with one such grouping allocated to each Division—in the 2BD's case, this was Zeitz and Boehlen. Five were located in eastern Germany and one (Brux) in Czechoslovakia. The "deep penetration" nature of this and subsequent missions, coupled with the enemy's swift awareness of the need to defend these highly vulnerable locations, would dwell on the average American airman's mind whenever he was dispatched therein.

The 3BD was almost wholly responsible for the overall 46 loss factor, with the 45CBW alone surrendering 27 crews to strong fighter attacks out of a final Division figure of 41. The other two Divisions remained almost inviolate to loss by comparison, and only three B-24s failed to return—a cosy equation that would alter violently at any point up to VE-Day. Lt. Lewis I. Vance's 67BS crew did not return to Shipdham after flak caught the then-straggling 42-100042 /NB: J on the return leg from Zeitz; all but F/O Ed Davidowitz (B) exited the burning bomber safely.

The 389BG PFF team led by Lt. Baldwin C. Avery, which had transferred from Tibenham after 15 missions, had seen their 41-28715/YO: I—flying as the 466BG deputy Lead—have its No. 4 engine fired by cannon shells. The homeward course was still maintained until near Koblenz, when the area's flak batteries scored their latest success by excising part or all of one wing; all 13 crewmembers thankfully failed to share their mount's fate, however. The final Divisional loss was borne by the 93BG's 42-73503/YM: Y **Marion**; flak strikes induced a tight starboard circle that was never corrected by Lt. Warren O. Van Winkle, who was the sole fatality out of the ten-man crew prior to the aircraft coming down NE of Eisenach.

Two more B-24s ended up as "Category E" this day. Hardwick's 42-64437/AG: B, in the hands of Lt. Thomas F. Condon, arrived back over RAF Woodbridge's emergency facility with only two engines functioning. All power was then lost during landing approach, and although the bomber crashed and broke up short of the runway end, all of the crew survived, though one man was trapped for several hours before being extracted. The 453BG's 41-29447/ came down at Forncett, in Norfolk, reportedly due to fuel exhaustion; details of the crew and their fate are still not on hand.

Gen. James Hodges (CG, 2BD) is photographed with Gen. Doolittle outside the main entrance to his HQ at Ketteringham Hall, close to Wymondham. He was later replaced in August 1944 by Gen. Bill Kepner, the reason reportedly being linked with the "friendly fire" incidents on 24/25 July incurred during Operation **Cobra**.

The 445BG Assembly ship bore large black and orange bands across its airframe; an additional aid to proper Group link-up was the flashing lights mounted on the fuselage with a white "L" background that flashed this Group letter. The normal practice of deleting the first number within the serial has lapsed here, as seen on the fin surface.

L/Col. Leon R. Vance (Deputy CO of the 489BG) smiles broadly as he holds his daughter Sharon. The B-24H-15-FO bearing her name is 42-94759, its full title being **The Sharon D**. The picture was taken prior to the Group's overseas deployment. Vance would win a CMH for his gallantry on 5 June, only to be MIA along with others on board the Med Evac C-54 transporting them back to the USA.

The strategic aspect of operations was to be granted priority up to the 19th, when tactical considerations would largely hold sway for the remainder of the month. The participants in the previous day's extended run must have echoed the expression "My achin' back!" when they gazed upon the Briefing maps on the 13th and saw the ribbon reaching up to Tutow, near Stettin, on the Baltic coast. Once again, the Division's ranks were even less affected by enemy assaults, with only one Attlebridge crew out of 228 striking the aircraft plant Primary failing to return. Fighter-inflicted strikes fired the No. 1 engine on Lt. Russell T. Swain's 41-29391/6L: M **Little Lulu**, followed shortly after by the bomber exploding, with the remains falling SE of Neumuenster. Swain and Lt. John F. Hardy, Jr. (CP) were miraculously thrown clear, unlike their eight companions, who perished to a man. A welcome albeit temporary return to the Pas de Calais by the 2nd and 14th CBWs under Hardwick-based PFF crew guidance struck V-1 sites at Siracourt without loss (15th).

The latest strategic thrust (19th) saw the B-17s sent to Berlin and the 2BD to Brunswick, with that city's air industrial plants as the Primary. This time round all three Divisions roughly shared in the loss factor, with the 2AD's figure of twelve the highest. Two-thirds of this in turn came from the ranks of the ultimately disbanded 492BG. (This was the third successive run to the city over which a specific 2BD group had suffered heavily: the 44BG with eleven on 8 April and the 453BG with eight on 8 May.) In addition, a trio of B-24s did not regain their Wendling dispersals, along with a single 448BG aircraft.

Lt. Charles L. Felsenthal's crew in 41-29474/GC: M-bar all forfeited their lives after fighter strikes caused the bomber to blow up north of Wernigerode. Gevensleben, SE of Brunswick, claimed the bodies of a second crew flying in 42-95060/EC: R, headed by Lt. Robert J. Lang, after the bomber spun in, having suffered terminal damage from a fighter. The third loss was 41-29129 / CI: A, flown by Lt. Donald D. Prell (KIA), downed by fighter attacks over the target with a total of five parachutes seen before the ship went into a dive. A German ground report confirmed the aircraft was shot down at 1315 hours, 19 May, at Abbenrode, north of Bad Harzburg, by a Me109 fighter, and that casualties found at the crash site were buried at the Abbenrode village cemetery on 20 May at 1600 hours. Two of the eight dead could not be identified due to the burned condition of their bodies. These German reports also noted the capture of Lt. Hervey E. Stetson (N) and Sgt. Albert J. Riley (WG) on the same day at 1320 hours in the village of Stapelburg, some five minutes after their plane had been shot down.

Lt. Stetson rendered an informative MACR account on his fellow crewmembers. Lt. Prell was alive at that moment, having just spoken to him about two minutes prior before the interphone system went out; he knew of only one other member who did manage to bail out, this being S/Sgt. Riley. In regard to the mission tactics followed at and over the target of Brunswick, Lt. Stetson also gave a rather detailed account of what actually took place:

> I feel that our Wing's activity was rather odd. We were to bomb Brunswick and to follow this course [a rough diagram reflected a route in just north of the target city, then a turn directly of ninety degrees to a south heading for the briefed bomb run, followed then by a turn westerly to egress the target area]. Instead, our Wing made a 360 degree turn over the city after we had dropped our bombs and made another bomb run [rough diagram shows this 360° turn by the formation to the right back over the city complex to re-intercept the original bomb run course of 180 degrees over the briefed target]. This unexplained extra run resulted in our loss, and because our fighter support had gone on with the remainder of the 2BD, we were easy prey for approximately 250 fighters.

Lt. Lester Martin (standing in the center) and his crew are posed in front of their B-24H-25-FO/42-95183/J4: U. The bomber had originally served with the 753BS and would end up with the 754BS. On 27 May 1944, **Briney Marlin** was involved in a mid-air collision during Assembly that should have proved fatal, but for the pilots' skill.

The full extent of the damage to **Briney Marlin** arising from the incident that bent the starboard outer wing downwards is seen here. The first-class performance by Martin and Lt. Francis Thompson (CP) not only saw the B-24 brought back under control, but brought back for a proper landing; Martin later received the DFC.

> I imagine our Wing suffered heavy losses through this mishandling of the situation by our Leader.

The Seething loss involved 42-52638/EI:, in the hands of Lt. Robert C. Silver, Jr. The fatal punishment handed out by the *Jagdwaffe* pilots finally brought the bomber down at Helmstedt. Both pilots, along with one gunner, comprised one-third of the crew who were granted the gift of life.

A trio of daily missions then ensued without any MIA or "operational" losses. A six-group run to bomb Rheims' marshalling yards and airfield (20th) was followed by successive sorties to V-1 sites at Siracourt, with respective forces of 110 and 96 B-24s dispatched, both attacks delivered under PFF guidance. The growing tendency to have the 3BD groups operating in concert with the 2BD was displayed (23rd) when the full Division strength was sent out against French airfields at the cost of a single Bungay crew.

The loss over Orleans/Bricy airfield was very unfortunate, as it was self-inflicted. The bomb doors on Bungay's 42-7583/ **Wee Willie** became detached, one of which impacted with the tail section, sending the other bomber into a terminal spin resulting in none of Lt. James C. Blackwood's crew escaping alive. A second B-24 from the 458BG had gone down during Assembly due to a mid-air collision with a 351BG B-17; none of Lt. Kenneth C. Barton's crew flying 42-110172/Z5: D as group deputy Lead got clear from their mount's truncated remains that impacted at Hoxne. This mission was followed by another cost-free run to bomb airfields around Paris.

The 2BD ranged the furthest afield down to Belfort and Mulhouse, adjoining the Swiss border (25th), and came home light two crews out of 208 gaining mission "credit." Lt. Frank J. Tomer's 42-94962/NB: I had first been observed in a steep dive with one propeller "feathered" and a second engine smoking before finally dropping out of sight on a heading that would take it to Switzerland. In fact, a homeward heading was actually taken up, but lumbering along at medium altitude, the isolated bomber was an easy target for flak as it was progressing west of Paris. Only the three gunners in the rear fuselage bailed out, their seven hapless Shipdham colleagues going in with the bomber.

The other MIA crew came from the 446BG, being Lt. Eugene T. Winn's 41-29140/HN: C **Banger**. Engine problems over Luxembourg forced the pilots to "abort," but an encounter with flak batteries at Brussels reduced power further. An inexorable loss of altitude caused a bail out order to be made near St. Nikolaas, with half the ten-man crew evading capture while the B-24 came down further NW at Waasmunster. The day's operations also involved small sub-forces from all three Divisions bombing heavy gun batteries at Fecamp and St. Valery-en-Caux, on France's Channel coast; this was a process the 2BD would repeat at St. Valery within 24 hours and reflected another aspect of the evermore intensive preparations for *Overlord*.

On the 27th, it was the 2BD alone that was wholly tasked with taking out targets clearly in the tactical category, the B-17 Divisions dividing their effort between tactical and strategic locations. Three marshalling yards in the Saarbruecken region were focused upon by the full Divisional strength, with all receiving a fair to heavy measure of punishment. The loss of four crews from the force was ameliorated when two took up a successful southward course for neutral soil. Hethel lost two crews, led by Lts. Loren Reid and Ed Leininger. The former team were in 42-94951/HP: and the other was in 42-95091/HP:. Whereas Reid lost four among his nine, eight of the ten on Lieninger's B-24H bailed out successfully; both pilots were among the survivors.

The Cat's (Ass)/42-94946/7V: R was one of 22 Horsham St. Faith aircraft

Top: The Briefing room at Metfield is filling up as the 491BG crews assigned to what will be the Group's first mission prepare to challenge the Third Reich's still potent defenses, an action to be duplicated 186 times. Col. Carl T. Goldenburg sits in a ruminative mood in the center foreground.

Left: Lt. Norman Siegal's frighteningly youthful features are evident as he receives the DFC following his tour completion on 5 June 1944. The 466BG bombardier's oversize flight suit may not be due to any error in issue size; rather, it may well be that its owner has lost a good degree of weight during his time on operations, thanks to the physical and mental stresses involved in the extremely hazardous act of combat flying.

bombing Neunkirchen. Lt. James E. Nedrow lost No. 4 engine minutes prior to bombing and the decision was taken to go south, an act that ended successfully at Payerne airfield; Lt. Bernard O. Wilson was not present at this point, having bailed out over enemy soil. (This was the second time the crew had landed in neutral territory; during the transit flight to England they had ended up in Spanish Morroco on 5 February.) A North Pickenham crew led by Lt. Bob Daly in 44-40102 /5Z: F was a fellow internee. Loss of one engine followed soon after by a second forced the diversion action upon the pilots, who finally pulled off a landing at Geneva-Cointrin.

Horsham was actually short two bombers by the day's end thanks to that constant bugbear arising during Assembly—collision. **Briney Marlin** (42-95183/J4: O) was run into by 42-95159/J3: P **Rough Riders II**. The buckled starboard wing tip and outer aileron on **Briney** initially promised serious if not lethal control problems for Lester Martin, but both he and Lt. Francis S. Thompson (CP) managed to halt the spin into which their B-24 had been peremptorily thrust and headed back to Horsham, where a safe if scary landing was made. Not so Lt. Howard J. Lobo's aircraft, which plunged into the sea just off the Norfolk coast. Joining this crew in death were Sgts. Chester R. Calstrum (normally Engineer on Vogel's crew) and Wilbert Abshire (normally tail gunner on Lt. Mattson's crew). Both had responded promptly to the bail out bell rung immediately after Martin's bomber began to spin but it was then cancelled. Tragically, even a short delay in so reacting might have saved their lives, since they almost certainly would have been over solid ground instead of the North Sea. A further irony is that both, having just a few missions left to complete their tour, had elected to fly in order to provide experienced backup to the otherwise "rookie" crew assigned to Martin.

Strategic Considerations Again

The original strategic brief handed to the 8AF was destined to occupy three of the final four days in May, despite the Transportation Plan's priority. However, this apparent contradiction in the "heavies"' operational deployment did not mean that attention was in any way slackening off regarding the ever-looming advent of Operation *Overlord*. The medium bomber and fighter-bomber resources of the 9AF and the RAF's Tactical air Force (2TAF), along with elements of the 8FC were ensuring that the punishment administered to the Germans' communications network was being continued, despite the temporary absence of the "Big Friends."

The synthetic oil industry was on the target menu on the 28th for over 1,300 crews, of which some one-third—almost wholly from the 1BD and 3BD—would not gain mission "credit." Merseburg/Leuna and Zeitz/Troglitz were assigned to the full 2BD, with the latter target largely focused upon. The cost in crude terms was again gratifyingly minimal at three, considering the extended time over enemy soil.

Lt. Jack Eley's crew in 42-110074/HP: P **Satan's Mate** (389BG) were only on their third mission and experienced progressive engine failure

This B-24H-30-FO/42-51474/EE: U has the addition of **D-Day** to its original name **Patches**. On 6 June 1944, during its first mission, the bomb bay was thoroughly riddled by the premature explosion of a fragmentation bomb at "bombs away." A major repair effort brought her back to operational status, which was when the additional wording was added in.

on the return leg that culminated in a drastic loss of height and a bail out order as the French coast was just left behind. Seven crewmembers jumped for their lives and landed in the waters, which claimed all but T/Sgts. Jim Tennant (ROG) and Howard Crepp (Eng.). The latter airman managed to clamber into a fortunately available dinghy, whereas Tennant was totally immersed, with his "Mae West" his sole dangerously fragile support. In addition, the Walrus amphibian responding fully two hours after sightings by Allied fighter pilots of the men's plight were radioed had to land in what was understood to be an area strewn with mines! The Sergeants were picked up, but Lt. Eley ended up a POW, having banked his charge back in over the coast before jumping along with Lt. Walter L. Tucker (CP), who lost his life through in unstated circumstances.

One of the other two MIA bombers progressed no further than the Duemmersee region, where flak disabled the No. 2 engine on Shipdham's 42-110045/GJ: K **The Banana Barge** and Lt. Irving S. Gurman decided to turn back. Shortly after, he advised the crew to bail out; all nine landed safely, but Sgt. Eino J. Wiitala (NG) was shot and wounded in the back by a farmer, an act that was fortunately not fatal. Tibenhan's 42-50346/RN: did complete the bomb run, but was then fatally crippled by flak and abandoned south of Merseberg; all but one on Lt. John W. Campbell's crew ended up as POWs, the exception (Sgt. Roy M. Warpler, ROG) being shot after landing.

Another Baltic Rebuff

Next day, it was only the joint B-24 strength of the 2nd and 3rd BDs that took on oil-related facilities at Poelitz on the Baltic, although a sizeable proportion of the 443-strong force was directed against an aircraft depot at nearby Tutow. The Luftwaffe was up in some force to challenge the formation's onrush and cull some if not all of the 34 crews failing to clear this operational hurdle. However, the scale of this negative total borne by the 2BD would again be somewhat ameliorated by the beckoning presence of Sweden, into which six B-24s, along with one B-17, would divert.

The main enemy fighter thrusts seem to have directed at the 14CBW, with a 2-3-4 loss scale borne by the 44BG, 492BG, and 392BG, respectively. The *Muritzsee* (Lake Muritz) was below as one of the estimated 50-strong pack of Fw190s shot up Lt. Frank L. Foy's 42-73500/WQ: F. The loss of No. 4 engine and damage to the controls persuaded the pilots to reverse course for home, a seemingly doomed enterprise in the circumstances; the B-24 remained inviolate from further hostile attention, but after tracking back for 30 minutes, the decision was taken to turn northward in what was a successful bid to reach Sweden, where a landing was made at Soeve, near Gothenburg.

Fighter gunfire from an Me410 also damaged 42-63962/GJ:W-bar **Princ-Ess** (previously applied more pungently as **Princ-Ass**!). The "original" B-24D was bearing the equally experienced crew of Lt. Ralph Golobuck, but now the disabling of No. 1 engine with a propeller that refused to "feather" placed an inordinate physical strain on the pilots. Fuel flowing from punctured tanks was the likely catalyst in deciding a turn to starboard out over the Baltic. An encounter with a group of fighters unbelievably resulted in their over-flying the crippled and seemingly easy prey and the course that ended at Bulltofta was duly made without further hindrance. (The *Jagdwaffe* pilots were almost certainly out of ammunition, there appearing to be no other logical explanation for what transpired.)

The survival of all crewmembers on the 44BG internee aircraft was in almost stunning contrast to those borne by the four Wendling crews, who suffered almost a 75% death rate out of the forty individuals concerned. Lawrence E. Larson's team on 42-95243/DC: A+ fell out north of the *Mueritzsee* and finally piled in near Kittendorf. Seven of the crew were found in or near the wreckage, but the fate of the other three was arguably more cruel; all had bailed out safely, but were shot "attempting to escape," according to the Home Guard and Police submitted reports. The village of Gueltz, north of Altentreptow and some 20 miles east of Kittendorf, was where Lt. Ace W. Tyler's 42-95136/CI: A came to earth, having been hacked down by fighter gunfire. Only Lt. Earl F. Bassett (N) bailed out after fire swept through the nose section and the B-24 sharply inverted, trapping some or all of the other nine crewmembers, none of whom reached the ground alive.

Lt. Gilbert O. Eisermann did not complete the bomb run in 42-52604/ EC: Y, his heavily damaged charge having forced him to ring the bail out bell just short of the target. The B-24 was reported at debriefing as having suffered damage to one wing as the formation was on the bomb run. Altwarp was where the bomber came down minus all ten airmen. Lt. Clarence E. Fothergill was fortunate to only sustain a broken arm following a beating by civilians, while S/Sgt. Edward B. Coleman had the later misfortune to lose his life during the prolonged forced march in early 1945 that was suffered, and in numerous cases such as here not survived, by those airmen unfortunate enough to be incarcerated in *Stalag-Luft IV*. All on 42-95045/CI: H were lost during what appears to have been the return leg, according to the crash time; the site was NE of Wismar at Tuezen, and all ten on Lt. Clarence E. Stolze's team were discovered in the wreckage, with flak gunners being credited with its destruction. (The experiences of the North Pickenham crews failing to return, as well as the Group's tragic history are comprehensively covered in chapter Twelve.)

Single losses were suffered by four Groups from the 2nd and 96th CBWs. Hethel's 42-94973/RR: F, flown by Lt. John Forsyth, joined the two other 2BD bombers in Sweden (Bulltofta), where another eleven internees were logged by the authorities, as did Lt. Edwin R. Peterson's Tibenham mount 42-110065/ RN:, which landed at Ringoby. Elsewhere, the 96CBW suffered a tithe of two crews, one coming from Rackheath's ranks. On the return leg near Greifswald, 41-29450/4Z: sustained two flak strikes in the starboard wing. Lt. Ernest Beasley (CP) recalled that the pilot Lt. Rufus B. Stephens turned pale and became inert as the B-24 went into a tight spiralling attitude. Two gunners bailed out before the bomber was stabilized temporarily, by which time the stricken wing and tail surface were swept by fire. Beasley ordered a bail out, to which all but the pilot and S/Sgt. Charles L. Peacock (Eng.) responded. The two original parachutists also perished in the cold Baltic waters. Attlebridge's 42-52570/ U8: A- **Sack Happy/Throbbing Monster**, in the hands of Lt. Adolph Komer, having been damaged by flak and then fighters, was finally crash landed at Schleswig-Land airfield, where all ten crew were apprehended.

The penultimate May mission saw full Division participation in the blitzing of two airfields and one aircraft depot around Oldenburg. All three targets were hammered at no cost. Back in England, nineteen combat crews as yet untried in combat were participating in a practice mission of the recently-arrived 489BG based at Halesworth. Observers on the ground noted how the formation was none too good and the situation tragically deteriorated when two bombers collided to deposit themselves at Tivetshall; none of Lt. Thomas E. Jones's eight-man team on 41-29546/S4:, nor the nine souls on board 42-98868/4R: in Lt. John C. Hall, Jr.'s control advanced any further on the road to tour completion.

Mother Nature made her latest and ever-unwelcome intervention on the 31st, as far as the 1st and 2nd BD crews were concerned. The weather conditions over France and Belgium were poor enough for less than one-fifth of the dispatched B-17 force to seek out its Primary; in the case of the 2BD, none of the main 491-strong force attained any result (Primary or otherwise), while a small-scale assault upon a railroad bridge at Beaumont-sur-Oise by 458BG bombers releasing specialist AZON weapons achieved nothing concrete. The single "operational" loss involved 42-99983/JU: E. **Merle Lee II**. Almost immediately after take-off, the B-24 began to oscillate and dip up and down, a situation that F/O Lewis B. Bibb and Lt. George A. Andrews found impossible to fully correct; thankfully, sufficient

Lili Marlene's pristine condition is emphasized by the sunlight as she rolls along the perimeter track past Shipdham's control tower. The B-24H-25-FO is 42-95260 (68BS), and was to fly combat until 29 December. On that day, Lt. Bledsoe "aborted" the mission with engine problems; he was unable to line-up properly and while rejoining the circuit, the aircraft stalled with part of the bomb load erupting when it struck the ground to leave no survivors.

A mailed fist clutching a weapon mounted within a shield provides the artistic backing for **Rage in Heaven**, a B-24J-150-CO (44-40165) assigned to the 491BG. Following retirement from combat and reassignment as the Group's second Assembly ship, the natural metal finish (NMF) was exchanged for close-packed green stripes on the wing surfaces and fuselage between the wings and stabilizers.

altitude was attained for all ten airmen to jump and soon after, the Bungay-based bomber came down NE of Norwich at Hickling, on the coast.

June 1944 – Liberation's Kindly Light

What would be the decisive month for the Allied military in establishing an initial and ultimately firm grasp upon the Western element of the Nazis' ill-gotten European "empire" commenced with regular tactical operations in mind: the mass of B-17s and B-24s sent to bomb over sixty V-1 sites on the morning of 2 June delivered 2,500 tons of bombs. In the evening, considerably smaller forces assaulted French railroad and airfield targets. In the case of the 2BD, only the 95CBW, comprising the 489BG on only its second mission and the equally "greenhorn" 491BG making its first mission, were sent to Bretigny, due south of Paris. Less than one-fifth of the participating 77 crews bombed the Primary; in sharp response, the defenses brought down five B-24s, with a sixth flak-stricken machine being abandoned over East Anglia.

The original day's activity for the 491BG was to have been the latest practice mission. This was "scrubbed" in the late morning, and two hours later, the revised Briefing map displayed a ribbon that extended not to an English source, but to the French airfield—school was over and things were very much for real! The immediate consequence was that mission planning was a hurried affair, with bomb loading being particularly hindered by the current absence of electrical bomb hoists. The 36 crews taking off also experienced difficulty in achieving the Assembly stage—an operational factor that would plague the inaugural series of missions, but by the month's end would see the situation totally reversed, with the Metfield-based Group leading the 2BD in sound formation flying, numbers of aircraft dispatched, bomb tonnage dropped, etc.

The planned course was for the Wing to approach Bretigny from west of Paris, then to swing in an arc around the southern and eastern city fringes before heading back. In the event, only one squadron from the 489BG released its loads on the Primary, while the 491BG's 854BS, totalling fourteen B-24s, released on what was identified as Bretigny in the hazy conditions, but was later confirmed as Villeneuve, within Paris's boundaries. Any recriminations at bombing a target within a Nazi-occupied country surrounded by built up areas were laid aside when strike photos confirmed that all bombs had landed within the airfield. The remainder of the Wing retained their bombs for the Secondary at Creil, but a further negative course alteration now led to the Wing traversing the center of the French capital!

The punishment was handed out by flak and commenced over Bretigny, with the afflicted bomber being the 491BG's sole casualty (42-95310/3Q: W, with Lt. William J. Evan's crew). In quick succession, shells blew No. 1 engine clear away and crippled No. 2, as well as removing part of one rudder, but the pilots retained enough control to trail the formation northwards as far as clearing the capital's northern fringe, although a steady loss of altitude occurred. The pilots finally called for a bail out, although by then their charge was only several thousand feet up. The chances of all ten making a secure bail out were tragically limited when the parachute borne by Lt. Malcolm Blue (N) failed and Sgt. Raymond G. LeMay (TG) was shot dead by ground fire while descending. Beaumont-sur-Oise became the aircraft's final resting place; ironically, the crash site was the local airfield, with the stricken B-24 unconsciously adding to the destruction already visited upon this source by a B-17 formation. (Evans was fortunate to get out after his parachute pack opened inside the bomber, but he successfully gathered the lines and cleared out via the bomb bay.)

The 489BG's 42-94933/8R: +D **Stubby Gal II** lost both port engines and sustained fuselage damage. The stricken bomber succumbed northeast of Creil, upon which 47 crews had unloaded. All but one on Lt. Charles C. Bouchard's team bailed out safely. Three further 489BG crews were taken out by flak, two of which finally came down around the Dieppe region. The impact of a shell on 42-94832/T4: H's starboard wing around No. 3 engine induced an explosion that in turn was sufficient to tear the complete aerofoil off; the resultant violent gyrations of the dismembered airframe clearly held all ten of Lt. Peter M. J. Fierro's crew in place up to the crash near Neufchatel-en-Bray.

The other flak-stricken Group machine came down at Port d'Ancourt, several miles east of the seaport. This was 42-94864/8R: +U **Stinky**, which absorbed the strike or strikes on the way back. Fire erupted in the forward and center fuselage area and only four of the ten airmen exited safely, although Lt. James T. Behout was not among this fortunate number. The final MIA loss at least did not involve any fatalities, while six of Lt. Elvin W. Cross's (POW) ten-man crew evaded capture. Both starboard engines were disabled, but Cross and F/O Paul E. Bartlett (evaded) still managed to bring off an emergency landing south of Roguemont, after which they set the B24 on fire.

Flak damage appears to have been of a scale sufficient for the abandonment of 42-94793 /S4: U **Jeane** by Lt. Elmo A. Coker on return to East Anglia. The ten airmen all bailed out successfully near Chipping Ongar; the absence of a crash site for the aircraft seems to confirm that the pilot's final act of heading it out towards the sea where it could crash clear of land appears to have borne fruit. Four crews and five B-24s short of its second mission was a hard blow for the Halesworth personnel to accommodate; however, the ensuing 106 missions before the unit returned Stateside would witness an immeasurably more acceptable MIA crew figure of 25 —other than for the individuals involved, of course!

The scantily-clad native-American wielding a bow and arrow with a more lethal title to the small deer is seen on B-24J-80-CO/42-100190/RR: J, serving with the 389BG. Lt. Bob Roeder's crew took the bomber to Poelitz on 20 June 1944, but the "feathered" No. 3 engine seen in the second picture was part of the serious battle damage that ended up with a northern diversion into Sweden.

Run-down to Invasion

The operational clock was by now rapidly running down towards the launch of *Overlord*. Next day (3rd), nine Division Groups added their weight to a PFF-directed assault largely upon coastal defenses in the Pas de Calais region—the latest move in a bid to convince the enemy's High Command and especially Hitler that the planned landings would indeed occur here. A double strike repeated next day against the same region and target categories surprisingly involved smaller forces on each strike, although the overall figure for both missions equalled that of the 3rd. However, to these sorties was added a third mission directed against railroad bridges by the B-17 Groups concerned, while the 2BD sent six groups to bomb airfields around Paris. No MIA casualties were incurred. However, several "operational" losses spoiled this ever-welcome statistic.

Flak damage to 42-100261/GC: A **Sweet Chariot** during the outward leg to bomb St. Avord airfield forced Lt. Harry A. White to "abort"; once over friendly territory, the nine crewmembers abandoned their 392BG B-24J. Unfortunately, the aircraft did not immediately descend, but when it did near Sleaford, in Lincolnshire, it scythed through one side of a house prior to skidding some distance and disintegrating; fortunately the house occupants were not affected. No such luck came the way of Lt. Clifford R. Galley and his nine colleagues during Assembly out of Halesworth. Their fully-laden 44-40206/3Q: F **Sack Rat** stalled out following a steep turn as the pilots endeavored to get into proper formation position; the spin that ensued was never corrected and Galley's previous combat experience with another Group proved fruitless to prevent the crash on the Suffolk coast. A 492BG crew was also lost during Assembly.

Medal of Honor

L/Col. Leon R. Vance, Jr. was Deputy CO of the 489BG and on 5 June was assigned as Command Pilot for the 95CBW; he would fly in one of Shipdham's PFF aircraft (41-28690/QK: B+ **Missouri Sue**), which would lead the group that in turn was leading the Wing. The briefed target was gun batteries at Wimereaux, close to Boulogne, but faulty PFF equipment forced a second bomb run that unfortunately was conducted without altering altitude or speed—circumstances granting the flak gunners a better chance of "zeroing in" on the formations.

Just prior to "bombs away," a devastating shell strike around the cockpit killed Capt. Louis A. Mazure (P) and virtually severed one of the Colonel's feet. Hydraulic and oil systems were disabled, radio compartment destroyed, and the starboard rudder and elevator shredded. The bombs were still on board as Lt. Earl L. Carper (CP) cut off power to the engines and held the bomber in a shallow glide across the Channel. Lt. Bernard W. Bail (Radar navigator) applied a tourniquet to Vance's leg and subsequently ordered the crew to jump once the English coast was crossed, but Vance alone did not take up this obvious option.

What then transpired is a matter for conjecture, but it is thought that the Colonel believed that one badly-injured crewmember was still on board, whereupon he took up control of the B-24 in a bid to "ditch" the machine and provide a chance for their survival. A crash landing would have been a better option, but the area being overflown might not have provided a suitable site. The "ditching" was brought off close to Broadstairs, in the Thames Estuary, but as the airframe was settled down into the water it either disintegrated on impact or collapsed due to one of the bombs exploding. Either way, it was amazing that Vance survived the incident; after making a fruitless search for the suspected trapped personnel, he was picked up by a boat while striking out for the shore! His actions subsequently saw him awarded the sole Congressional Medal of Honor (CMH)

Princess Konocti's largely uneventful and intact landing in Sweden was not copied in the case of Lt. Wesley A. Schafer's B-24J-1-FO/42-50586/GC: U-bar. The starboard main wing and stabilizer/fin structures were ripped off and the nose section badly crumpled in a field near Kjortshog, fortunately without serious injury to all nine crewmembers.

granted to a 2BD member while flying from a British airfield during WWII. How tragic, having come through these horrendous events, that the Medical Evacuation C-54 transporting him back to the States in late July was fated to go missing over the Atlantic.

"See the Front o' Battle lour. . . ."

The foregoing heading is taken from the first verse of "Scots Wha Hae," the poem by Roberts Burns that commemorates Robert the Bruce's rallying cry to his troops on the eve of the Battle of Bannockburn in 1314—the critical fight against English hegemony whose success led to Scotland's independence six years later. Now, on the eve of 5 June 1944, the expression held no less import for the looming hope of freedom from oppression and fear yearned for throughout Western Europe over four years. Even as the last elements of the 8AF were settling down on their airfields, tens of thousands of Allied sailors and soldiers were already embarking on the "Great Crusade" to be commenced on the Normandy beaches next morning.

A general alert was in full force by early evening that in some cases barred unfortunate civilians still on bases from leaving the airfields in question, as well as airmen previously anticipating a Pass. The B-17s and B-24s were amassed in loaded condition as usual, but the numbers involved were way ahead of any total dispatched on a mission—no less than 1,800, in fact. The awakening of the combat crews in the dead of night was nothing unusual, but their reaction as the Briefing maps were exposed was probably summed up by an anonymous airman who said, "This is what we were sent over here two years ago to do!" Another combat crewmember at Metfield provided a more detailed account:

> We were wakened at 0330 and found a state of confusion in the Briefing room, with MPs checking everybody and a guard at the Briefing map posted to stop peekers. Then Col. Goldenburg (Group CO) walked briskly up to the platform and the room fell really quiet as he stood silent for a complete minute—tired, unshaven, with clothes seemingly slept in. We loved him, and when he spoke his affection for "his boys" was uncontrolled. "Gentlemen, this is a day you will be able to tell your children and grandchildren about—D-Day! Time is short, so all I can say is good luck, and give 'em Hell!" He stepped down and walked out, a tired man with lines of responsibility etched on his face.

The launching of such a mass of bombers in the dark merited an extended, and to many crewmembers a pointless series of course maneuvers over central England. The intention was for the bombers to pound the German heavy gun batteries opposing the Allied armada of transports and warships shortly before the initial troop landings.

The B-24's bomb load capacity was a maximum of 8,000lbs, but in this case the B-24s of the 467BG are bearing twelve 500-lb weapons, as instanced by the six pairs just released by B-24H-25-FO 42-95273/Q2: I from the 790BS. She was an ex-445BG bomber that served from mid-May until 4 December, when a taxiing collision at Rackheath rendered her fit only for salvage.

The travails of B-24 waist gunners while operating their guns out of the hitherto unglazed apertures were evident, with frostbite a real and constant threat. **War Bride** (B-24H-20-FO/42-94924/S4: D of the 489BG) was part of the first batch of the Consolidated design to be factory fitted with glazed panels, whose presence provided a solid measure of relief from air blast for the gunners.

The three Divisions would advance in parallel streams across the breadth of the five beachheads, with the 2BD granted the honor of opening the aerial assault. The four Division CBWs, once formed up, would fly a roughly parallel course west, then northwest and finally take up a converging SW course that would bring them together SE of Worcester. This heading would alter to due south as the Channel coast east of the Isle of Wight was overflown. The Division's primary target was around St. Laurent-sur-Mer and Colleville-sur-Mer, on the western side of the overall landings zone, with the other Divisions taking out the briefed targets within the central and eastern zones.

All went well with the gigantic Assembly process, despite the enhanced risk of mid-air collisions in the dark skies and blacked-out landscape below, and the three bomber streams bored on relentlessly. However, any sense of pleasure at witnessing one of history's key events unfolding was to be totally thwarted. Instead of a clear view of the targets being smothered in bomb bursts, the crews encountered an almost solid undercast that in turn merited the bomb loads being aimed blindly. Worse still, as was retrospectively established, the vast bulk of the bombs overshot the allotted targets, brought about by the fear of under-shooting and creating "friendly fire" situations among the first wave of troops—this despite the fact that upwards of 30 minutes were briefed to, and indeed did, extend between the bombing assault and the landings. A further limitation would have risen even had accurate bombing been achieved; almost 50% of the 839 crews briefed did not bomb, while a similar although smaller deficiency (around 30%) occurred among the B-17 ranks.

Rough Debut

A typical example of ground crew dedication occurred at Hethel following D-Day operations, when 42-50474/EE: U returned from her inaugural mission shot full of holes, with the region around the bomb bay as well as the wings particularly affected; a malfunction of some sort had detonated some of the fragmentation bomb load at "bombs away," and it was the crew's very good fortune that the result, bad as it was, did not eliminate the bomber altogether. Sgt. Bill Curry was an airplane mechanic from the 463rd Sub-Depot and recalls what happened after the battered B-24 was hauled into a hangar, where a veritable swarm of mechanics, electricians, and sheet metal specialists descended upon the airframe:

> The initial task involved the leaking fuel tanks, which were normally self-sealing but normally failed to do so, especially when given the degree of damage inflicted here. The remaining fuel residue had to be drained through the manifolds before each of the eighteen tank cells could be extracted. However, this was none too easy; bear in mind that each tank normally expanded to a five-foot dimension but only after being forced and folded via a two-foot gap! (The 300 gallons of high octane fuel was deposited into the sewers.)
>
> The damaged tanks were removed and the replacements duly installed, but only after much physical effort was extended. All the time sparks were flying around as the sheet metal workers worked their drills in fitting numerous patches to the fuselage—it was truly a mercy that we didn't blow ourselves right out of the picture! (As it so happened, the wings were liberally riddled underneath, but the upper surfaces had been unaffected). We returned the bomber to combat status in good time and she went on to fly many successful missions—is it any wonder she was christened **D-Day Patches**?"

In fact, the aircraft survived combat operations right through until VE-Day, but ironically was "written off" two days

This "beheaded" 491BG B-24H-25-FO/42-95191/V2: T+ has lost its navigator and bombardier to a flak strike during a mission to Fleury, France. The bomber also sustained progressive power loss on the return flight and was finally crash landed on the SE Channel coast; seven crewmembers on Lt. Charles Stevens's crew survived, but a further two became fatalities thanks to bailing out too low.

Lt. Leo Mower's B-24J-145-CO/44-40093 from Attlebridge has suffered a crushed nose section after toppling into a ground depression at Bulltofta airfield's perimeter. Pilots had diverted following engine and fuel loss while heading for Berlin on 21 June 1944. All eight crewmembers survived the experience and were duly interned.

later, following what was probably a heavy landing or overshoot that included the nose wheel being torn off.

The virtually total absence of the *Jagdwaffe* on 6 June was appreciated, but this did not guarantee a clean casualty slate. During the first mission Assembly, Hethel's 44-40247/YO: **Shoot Fritz, You've Had It** was bare minutes into its flight when it faltered and finally fell to earth at Trimingham, killing all ten on Capt. Marcus V. Courtney's crew. (Although part of the bomb load exploded, not all of the remaining examples were discovered at the time. In 1996, a tractor driver was ploughing a field where the crash occurred when he made abrupt contact with a missile that fortunately remained inert until a Bomb Disposal team ultimately arrived on the scene!)

Many Groups flew between three and four missions on *D-Day*, with the subsequent sorties involving attacks on communications links or hammering the defenses around the key city of Caen, close to the eastern fringe of the landing zone. The use of PFF in most of the attacks further increased the sense of anti-climax among the bomber crews. However restricted their supporting effort might have been, the psychological if not material effect of their assaults upon the Germans must have left its mark. The initial, albeit tentative dent in the enemy's Western shield had been achieved; now the bomber crews would play their part in restricting German reinforcements intended to bolster the Wehrmacht and SS defenses against Allied expansion of the beachheads.

Tightening the Tactical Stranglehold

The emphasis for the USAAF "heavies" for the remainder of June would, apart from several notable exceptions, be firmly directed towards the tactical aspect of operations. Argentan and Lisieux, located south and west of Caen on two of several link roads to that city, was assigned the Division, along with one other location on L'aigle, where a Group of minor roads merged (7th). Next day, a joint 2/3BD force of over 500 crews set out for targets spread in an arc between LeMans, Angers, and Nantes, over 100 miles south of the *D-Day* beaches. Just one 2BD bomber was downed today. Lt. James Q. Ogden's 42-109830/FL: **Daisy Mae Scraggs** was assailed by one or more of the fighters comprising the *Jagdwaffe's* belated and very staccato response to the Invasion. The Group's coastal target was below the western base of the Cherbourg Peninsula and after fire took hold with the bomber then down to half power, the bail out order was given. All but one of the ten jumped clear but only five survived, the others drowning.

Two further B-24s were salvaged, beginning with the total loss of the 491BG's 42-110169/T8: N **Lucky Penny**, which sadly belied its positive title. The fourth landing attempt by Lt. Fletcher E. Sharp in what was a heavily-laden aircraft with one engine "out" ended with a fatal stall and crash for all nine airmen. Seething's 42-110026/IG: I **Sky Queen** was more fortunate after Capt. James P. Sullivan "aborted" and flew out over the coast to jettison his load; the explosion of two dangerously volatile fragmentation bombs close below the B-24 badly damaged the airframe and adversely affected the landing gear's deployment. Diversion to the Emergency Airfield of RAF Woodbridge was carried off in order and all ten airmen emerged shaken but alive, although one Segeant received a leg wound.

This was the 446BG's second loss in 24 hours. **Nature's Nymphe** (42-51116/HN: H) was climbing up during the Assembly stage of the mission when Lt. Robert Zeller apparently lost control and the B-24H entered into a terminal spin that ended at Rumburgh, about ten miles SSE of Bungay. Of the twelve-man crew, just four somehow effected an escape from the normally restraining centrifugal forces.

The enemy was granted a 24-hour respite from attack before normal service was resumed (10th) on what was the first daily operation for the ensuing eight days. In this period, just 37 crews out of the near-eight thousand individual sorties were declared MIA, of which seven came from Division ranks. Seething's 44-40107/EI: F sustained a flak strike immediately after "bombs away" over Evreux/Fauville airfield that snapped the fuselage in two. Lt. Raymond S. Towles (P) went down with four other crewmembers, while a sixth, S/Sgt. Earl L. Taylor (BT), having suffered severe burns, later succumbed in a French hospital. A 446BG crew was forced to bail out of 42-7659/HN: L **Brown Knowser** near Metfield, during which one crewmember on Lt. Dana L. Jones's team suffered parachute failure.

Next day, the flak gunners at Creil airfield scored their second success against the 491BG by knocking out both port engines on 42-95301/T8:, with fire taking hold on No. 1. Lt. Warren C. Moore managed to head for home despite the degree of punishment, but failed by a matter of miles to reach English soil, being forced to "ditch" in the Channel after a third engine acted up. In the lottery between death and survival affecting all such incidents, only Moore and four of the other nine were fished out either by boat or an ASR Walrus RAF amphibian. Assembly problems were still plaguing the group, especially since no *Judas Goat* B-24 was yet on hand. The arrival of **Little Gramper**, with its overall yellow airframe spotted with red spots, saw the next day's mission utilizing the bomber's visual services, after which matters quickly resolved themselves on this basic but vital aspect of operations.

The drip feed of losses continued (12th), with two 20CBW crews failing to return. Flak's malign influence was felt by the latest 446BG casualty (42-94859/HN: F in Lt. Wilbur H. Turner's hands) shortly after bombing Rennes/Ploermel airfield. A subsequent fighter pass added to the damage, and as fire took hold a bail out was ordered; the B-24's exploding in mid-air reportedly only resulted in two deaths within the airframe, but three further airmen died either through parachute failure or ground fire. Turner was one of four evaders out of the remaining five crewmembers. **Squat N' Droppit**'s (41-28710/CT: P) crew of nine, led by Lt. William J. Bailey, almost earned a complete reprieve from death or capture. Their B-24 suffered similar flak and fighter punishment as its Bungay contemporary—in this instance fire in the bomb bay, No. 3 engine disabled, and one vertical stabilizer shot away—before it was abandoned to crash near Bonnemain. The cruel exception to survival was Sgt. Kenneth A. Zierdt (ROG), whose parachute collapsed close to the ground. Lt. Ben Isgrig (B) was fortunate to escape being killed by a marauding Bf109, whose apparent strafing pass on the helpless airman was thwarted by several P-51s of the 352FG. On return, a Tibenham bomber (42-110037/IS: B) was destroyed in an attempted landing at a 3BD airfield that killed two of Lt. William R. Kraham's crew.

A five-Group force went over next day to attack airfields and bridges in western France, but ended up seeking out Targets of Opportunity at a cost of two crews from Hardwick. Lt. John R. Hoffman's 42-95153/AG: G drooped into a spiralling action, the assumed victim of a flak strike, to crash north of the U-boat base at Lorient, killing the pilot and all but two of his crew. A fellow-squadron bomber (42110104/AG: M) was still bearing its bomb load that impacted under the effect of flak shells. How anybody on Lt. Albert B. Cool's team survived the horrendous blast that tore the airframe apart just confirms the extreme luck some airmen experienced in aerial combat; in this case, Sgts. Tom C. Sornsin (WG) and John R. Rudy (TG) not only survived their bomber's loss, but added to their good fortune by evading capture.

The following three daily missions proved to be free of MIA casualties, although a 492BG crew was forced to bail out over the Normandy beachhead and a 392BG bomber was "written off" at Eye (490BG) on the 15th. Lt. Harry A. White lost Sgt. John W. Wehunt (TG), whose turret was shattered, and suffered further heavy cannon shell damage around the left waist gun position during a fighter attack on 42-95025/GC: P. Sgt. John F. Braccioforte (LW) bailed out, but the pilots held course for England. The 491BG also bore a "Category E" casualty on the15[th] (44-40124/T8: C **Uninvited**). The flak strike wounded Sgt. Leondis O'Bryant (G) in one eye which was subsequently removed. In spite of this, the Sergeant, having found the Engineer and ROG lying unconscious and bereft of their oxygen masks, secured these back on their faces and remained with his colleagues until they revived. Lt. William L. Stokley's flapless and brakeless charge ran off the Metfield runway end despite the use of parachutes attached to the waist gun mounts, but no further injuries were suffered among the crew. O'Bryant's action was one of countless thousands that never received recognition, but were symptomatic of the deep bond between combat crewmembers, even in the face of personal adversity.

The final tactical mission in the current daily sequence was launched on 17 June against a number of French airfields. In the case of the 2BD, five Primaries were struck by what was almost a full-strength Division force whose ranks were surprisingly limited to an average of 12 bombers. The period since *D-Day* had resulted in the German reaction to that key event being well blunted in terms of even adequate reinforcements reaching the Front, while the Luftwaffe's ability to contest the Allied air cover was equally inhibited. As the bomber crews settled down on their airfields, there was no indication that a temporary lull in their tactical involvement was being initiated at 8AFHQ.

Oil Strikes Resumed

Gen. Spaatz's initiative against Germany's synthetic oil resources was given its latest expression on 18 June, with a full-scale 8AF assault by nearly 1,400 bombers. For whatever reason, the 2BD was basically directed towards striking at *Luftwaffe* control centers in NW Germany, with the 95CBW excluded from its ranks. Over 90% of the B-17s and B-24s gained mission "credit," although the majority bombed Secondary or Target of Opportunity locations. The cost was small at eleven overall, four of these B-24s. The maligned 492BG lost two, with single losses from two other groups adding to the toll. The 448BG's 42-51119/EI:, flown by Lt. Leland L. Beckman, was part of the sub-force bombing Fassberg's control center. Flak struck home, and as the afflicted bomber struggled to bypass Hamburg the crew began to jump; only Sgt. Dan A. Wais out of the ten crewmembers failed to survive before the bomber piled in NW of Hamburg.

Horsham's contribution involved 41-28733/Z5: P. **Rhapsody in Junk**, which went to Neumuenster. Flak again struck home during the bomb run and the bombs were salvoed. When last seen, Lt. Henry H. Northrop's stricken machine was heading northward, but it never reached further than Barup-Holz, on the border with Denmark. Again, there was just one fatality out of the ten on board; Sgt. Harold J. Flaugher (Eng.) had to be persuaded to jump and his death was suspected, although never confirmed, as having been at the hands of civilians.

It was back to short-range missions the next day, although these guaranteed no security from risk, as a single Hardwick crew discovered. The flak concentrations in the Pas de Calais were intense and left their mark on 42-110081/GO: A **Able Mabel**, flown by Lt. Robert W. Brown. Fire caught hold of No. 4 engine as the pilots attempted to head back, followed by a second engine igniting; a bail out order was issued that all ten crewmembers responded to, only seven of which came through alive before the B-24 came down near Bruges, in Belgium.

Back to the Baltic

The accent on oil targets was resumed next day, with the 2BD heading up to the Baltic to apply the latest blow to Poelitz. The extended range of the mission promised an equally extended response from the *Jagdwaffe,* especially its twin-engine element. The 14CBW was to feel the particular impact of the defenses, losing nineteen of the 34 Division crews declared MIA, although twenty among the overall number would seek refuge in Sweden.

Awaiting the advance of the 2BD around the *Muritzsee* region were the Bf109s of I and II/JG300 and I and II/ZG26's Me410s. The single 8FC unit accompanying the Division at this stage was incapable of affording comprehensive cover, although its pilots pounced upon III/JG26 after it had engaged part of the 492BG, downing a sizeable number of the Bf109s. This, however, left the way open for the Me410s to engage the North Pickenham Group in particular in an unfettered manner—at least until the relief force of P-51s turned up to exact a belated revenge upon the Luftwaffe "twins" to the tune of twelve—two less than the number of 492BG bombers joining the MIA list.

Although the *Jagdwaffe* was handing out much of the punishment to the 14CBW, three of the four Wendling losses were ascribed to flak damage which in all three cases did not turn out to be fatal. Instead, Lts. Charles H. Bell, Wesley A. Schafer, and William M. Forsythe took their B-24s (42-50343/DC: C+ **Tondelayo**, 42-50586/GC: U, and 42-95135/GC: D, respectively) up into Sweden, where 27 airmen in all were duly interned. The fourth MIA crew in 42-51125/DC: F+ had seen their B-24 assailed by fighters and flak, with the bomber dropping down after "bombs away" and nearly going out of control. The same northerly route was then taken up, but just as Swedish soil passed below the aircraft began to spin, and of the ten-man crew of Lt. Leander Page, Jr. only eight reached the ground alive. The sole Shipdham loss also featured an interned crew: the nine-man team of Lt. Richard I. Keller, whose 42-94892/WQ: U **Battlin' Baby** had sustained a flak strike that disabled the engine turbo-supercharger controls, an absolutely vital requirement for sustaining high-altitude flight. This, along with fuel shortage was one of the twin factors in making the diversion.

Spreading the Cost

The remaining losses were shared equally between the 2nd and 20th CBWs, with the 389BG's strength reduced by six, a figure that included a PFF B-24 flying deputy Lead for the 448BG. The initial pair of crews was downed in a cruelly self-imposed manner, namely mid-air collision. The Group was tracking on the outbound leg and bypassing Kiel when 42-95144/EE:, flown by Lt. Herschel R. Chappell, was cast aside by the concussion of a flak shell. Its wayward motion was repeated by 42-100351/EE: and the resultant collision cut the tail section off Chappell's bomber. The spinning main airframe became a tomb for other than Sgt. Jacob G. Heilich (BT).

Lt. William Power's charge lost a propeller, but although trailing a stream of fuel seemed to be holding a gliding attitude; this soon changed into a spin, and although five parachutes were later reported, only the pilot and Lt. Oscar Boudreaux (CP) got down safely—even then they were fortunate after landing in the Baltic waters to be fished out by a Danish-manned boat. Lt. Felix Keeton, flying in the Lead squadron, retained a horrifying image of the incident in his mind; this was the sight of the tail turret from Chappell's bomber hurtling past his B-24 with the occupant seemingly staring straight at him.

A measure of comfort regarding the other three direct losses was that all joined the internee list. Target flak adversely affected the fuel reserves on 41-28787/YO: P, impelling Capt. Jerrold M. Vivian to lead his ten fellow-airmen north. A similar situation faced Lt. Ralph P. Leslie as he headed 42-100146/HP: U **Mistah Chick** homeward, in addition to which No. 3 engine was "out"

Daisy Mae Scraggs, a character from the Lil' Abner cartoon series, has her title applied in what appears to be a daisy chain pattern. The 446BG bomber was a J-105-CO airframe (42-109830/FL: G) that came down on the French coast after being assaulted by fighters 48 hours after D-Day; Lt. James Ogden (POW) was one of five survivors from among the ten crew.

The native-American "Thunderbird" design from the Arizona region of the USA featured on several 8AF aircraft, including this example on a 491BG B-24J-150-CO. The aircraft is 44-40238/3Q: Y, which is part of a formation heading out across a sky filled with cloud tendrils that permit a partial view of the ground.

and No. 4 faltering, so he took the same neutral-bound course. Finally, Lt. Bob W. Roeder's diversion in 42-100190/RR: J. **Princess Konocti** increased the Group's internee representation to thirty-two. A very different fate awaited Hethel's sixth MIA bomber today...

Aiding the Enemy - Unwillingly

The B-24 in question was 41-28779/YO: A, flown by Lt. Tom Purcell with Maj. Chester B. Hackett—formerly a Group member but currently the 715BS CO at Seething—as Command Pilot. As the 448BG was banking south from the IP, Hackett raised the question of the altitude at which the target should be traversed with Col. Mason (Group CO). He suggested this should be pitched at a different level to the preceding formations, which were shrouded in the flak barrage being cast up, but this suggestion was not acted upon.

Directly following "bombs away," the deputy Lead bomber sustained several strikes that seriously limited its chances of getting back. Ten of the thirteen-strong crew took up the option to bail out, but Lt. Milton L. Rosas (CP) died soon after sustaining serious wounds. Hackett headed for the bomb bay to jump, but there he encountered Lt. Garland East (B) searching for a replacement pack, since his had been shredded by an exploding oxygen bottle and he was unable to find Rosas's pack.

Hackett told East to follow him back to the cockpit and the B-24 was put into a glide after reducing power in order to reduce the risk of an explosion from leaking tanks whose content was drenching the bomb bay. On the way down, two Bf109s made a pass but thankfully did not land any strikes before reportedly being challenged by P-51s. A flat stretch of ground west of Stettin was selected and a wheels-down approach carried out; contact with an unseen ditch tore the nose wheel off, but the B-24 remained in a level attitude and ground to a halt. All secret equipment was destroyed before local civilians arrived to apprehend the two airmen.

The crew's flying days were done, but this was not the case for their bomber. With the nose wheel replaced, the "star and bar" insignia gave way to the *Hakenkreuz* (swastika) and other Luftwaffe markings. Assignment to *Kampfgeschwader* 200 saw her being used in clandestine operations up to 6 April 1945. Then "friendly fire" forced an emergency landing between Wackersleben and Fuerstenfeldbrueck, during which the nose wheel again failed. Although repairs were made, the restricted space in which to attempt a take-off ended up with the aircraft being "torched."

A single loss was borne by the 453BG, but at least the result was not a disaster for either 42-94850/H6: **Becky** or the eleven men headed by Lt. Donald F. Kolb. Battle damage resulted in the Old Buckenham B-24H bringing off a safe crossing of the Baltic for a landing at Sweden's Bulltofta airfield.

20CBW

All three groups within the 20CBW shared the eight losses almost equally. A duo from the 93BG tasted the bitter seeds of failure, beginning with 42-95039/AG: N, which succumbed to a flak strike on its starboard wing; a spin developed and Lt. Edward J. Woodward (P) was one of six fatalities, along with Lt. Harry M. Purdy (CP), even though both bailed out. An arguably crueller fate awaited five crewmembers on 42-95030/GO: T **Take it Easy**. Target flak crippled both starboard engines and with formation contact lost a heading for Sweden was adopted. The landing approach at Bulltofta was proceeding in order almost to the runway threshold, but then matters went drastically wrong. The B-24 went out of control, smashing into the ground and catching fire. Lts. Elwyn H. Shaw (P) and Cark G. Heskamp (CP) were so badly injured that they soon succumbed. A third airman was trapped in the aircraft and could not be freed. One of the remaining two fatalities was already badly wounded from flak fragments, while the other was killed outright in this tragic culmination to the mission.

Although the CBW MIA toll reached eight, there were no further human casualties, nor did any of the six B-24s end up wrecks, although flak damage was the primary reason for their diversion. Instead, Sweden's neutral territory gave a welcome to all. Bungay surrendered 42-52733/FL: **Jiggs** (Lt. Harry E. Grafton); 42-94765/HN: D (Lt. Franklin C. Douglas); and 42-51213/FL: (Lt. Paul J. Pincus). The trio of 448BG casualties consisted of 42-51079/CT: **Carol Marie** (Lt. Aldrich A. Drahos); 42-95013/EI: N **Sweet Sioux** (Lt. Robert P. Nimmo); and 42-95200/CT: (Lt. Raymond A. Wermeyer). Altogether, 58 airmen were manning these aircraft that all landed at Bulltofta.

No "Milk Run" Missions

With the V-1 Offensive already in progress for seven days, the emphasis on interdicting the "doodlebug" facilities in the Pas de Calais and to a lesser extent the Cherbourg Peninsula gathered pace. Nearly 600 crews were involved in two separate strikes within the former region, nearly all of whom were from the 2BD. A single loss was recorded during each mission, of which the first was the 445BG's 42-95098/MK: E. Two strikes on the fuselage and one on the starboard inner wing were swiftly followed by a total disintegration that nevertheless left six out of Lt. Charles L. Thornton's crew alive.

The second mission was conducted during the evening, during which a 489BG crew in Capt. Leroy G. Madsen's charge paid the price when the formations apparently strayed too close to the French port of Dunkirk on the way home. The flak concentrations within this area were heavy and no quarter was given, with 42-94834/S4: G sustaining hits on the port wing and fuselage that culminated in a separation of the tail section and depositing of the bomber into the sea. (This maritime crash site out from Nieuwpoort, in Belgium, which lies close to Oostduinkerke—both locations about 15 miles east of Dunkirk—suggests the flak gunners were probably based at the Belgian coastal town.)

Two further Division bombers were "written off" on return from these short-range runs, the first being the 466BG's 42-94929/U8: S, which bore two dead crewmembers back to a crash landing at a 9USAAF airfield; a third airman was reportedly killed during this act carried out by Lt. Howard A. Fisher. An even more dramatic return was made by Lt. Charles Stevens after his 42-95191/T8: suffered the complete and surgically-clean excision of its forward nose section, which killed Lts. William F. Week (B) and Harold R. Meng (N) instantly. With two engines disabled, the pilots barely made it to the coast at Littlestone-on-Sea, west of Dover, where a successful crash landing was made; unfortunately, two Enlisted men bailed out but fatally delayed opening their parachutes.

Mid-Summer's Day Mayhem

Berlin was in line for its eleventh sizeable bombardment by the 8AF (21st), but the prospect was not looked upon with other than trepidation by the 1,071 crews mustered for the assault. The flak concentrations around and within *Big B* were sufficient on their own to inflict a solid degree of punishment; by the day's end, a good proportion of the 45 MIA crews would feel their lethal effect, which would be added to by several *Jagdwaffe* units.

2CBW

In the case of the 2BD, ten out of the twelve participating Groups would contribute to the overall figure of nineteen B-24s failing to return. The worst affected was the 389BG, with the same figure (six) it had borne 24 hours before. The specific target for the Division was the Daimler-Benz plant at Genshagen, outside Berlin's southern fringe. The Hethel formation was approaching the IP when the so-far undisturbed passage to the target went to pieces, as a pack of Me410s from an unidentified ZG descended upon the bombers.

"Runaway" propellers were a constant danger to aircraft, with the ever-present risk that a detachment from the shaft could dispatch the whirling buzz saw into the fuselage with potentially fatal effect. **Jerilyne Sue** (B-24H-15-FO/42-52499/6A: J) lost No. 1 engine's propeller and suffered bomb bay damage sometime between mid-May and 19 June 1944, when she was salvaged following a collapsed landing gear that day.

The crewmember's body being lifted out of the cockpit hatch by a colleague and a Medic is T/Sgt. Chauncey W. Freeman (Eng.) on 42-95037/GC: M **Call Me Later**. He was mortally injured during the mission to Magdeburg and is certainly dead, as a separate photo showing his blanket-shrouded body confirms. Lt. Roy Miller (P) was wounded, while the B-24H-25-FO was damaged to the extent of being "written off."

Fighting' Sam II (42-52579/RR: M), in Lt. Patterson's hands, suffered heavy damage, including the No. 4 set on fire and No. 2 knocked out. Further hits set the port wing ablaze and the crew was ordered out. T/Sgt. Harrison A. Dodd (Eng.) had been wounded and was assisted with his pack; sadly, his parachute only partially deployed and he died on impact. Sgt. George M. Edgar (ROG) was the other fatality. S/Sgt. Don Serradell (RW) was fortunate to escape being killed by civilians, his rescuer being a German officer. The crash site for the plunging B-24 was directly on Berlin-Johannistal airfield, and the bomber's final defiant action was destined to create sufficient damage that hindered flight operations.

The carnage among the Group's ranks spread rapidly over a matter of a few minutes. **Nuff Sed** (42-109794/EE: S) caught fire up front and Lt. Bob J. McAuliffe (P) became one of six fatalities out of ten on board. The bomber came down at Teltow, scant miles north of the target, where it was joined in death by 42-95122/HP: **The Magic Carpet**, a good luck title that failed three of Lt. Carl E. Hartquist's (POW) crew; one of the trio was Lt. Charles M. Preis (B), who had been tackling the blaze when a second fighter pass landed hits that probably killed him.

Two more crews came down around the target area. A fighter/flak combination culminated with Lt. George J. Schukar's 42-50371/HP: breaking apart and descending NW of Luckenwalde, about 20 miles south of the Primary, but eight of the ten crewmembers survived. The worst casualty rate occurred on 42-95145/RR:, flown by Lt. Willis B. Core (KIA). This was another B-24 that broke up under the impact of fighter gunfire, but this time only Tom C. Jarbeaux (ROG) escaped a terminal fate.

The final loss involved a prolonged agony for 42-95044/HP:. Eyewitness statements indicated two crewmembers were seen bailing out over Berlin's southern fringes with just one pack deploying. The dying B-24 became separated from the formation, but staggered on nearly 100 miles until close to Burg-bei-Magdeburg, where it began to fade out of the sky. In fact, nine or all of the crew were still on board, although S/Sgt. Harold E. Borgens (TG), F/O John J. Mulcahy (B), and Lt. Albert P. O'Steen (P) were fated to die; O'Steen had been severely injured and had to be assisted to bail out, but never managed to pull his ripcord, while Borgens also suffered parachute failure. (Mulcahy was probably one of those airmen recorded as jumping over the capital.)

The 2CBW's punishment was spread among its three sub-units, albeit in smaller scale of bomber losses, but not of personnel, since 14 of the 20 airmen lost their lives. The homeward route was well under way when the flak-damaged 42-50329/RN: O was intercepted and finished off by an M410 over Denmark's Baltic coastline. Seven of the eleven-man crew bailed out, but most if not all ended up within the total of nine fatalities on Lt. Richard R. Plant's crew, he being the sole officer-ranked survivor, along with S/Sgt. Francis DePaul (TG).

The other 445BG casualty was 42-95130/RN: P, which was within 20 minutes' flight time of friendly shores when Lt. Joseph D. Salisbury was forced into ditching his bomber; the rough sea surface clearly contributed to the airframe's fracturing in two, with one officer and four Enlisted men failing to get clear or dying of exposure. T/Sgt. George H. Ruby managed to launch one lift raft into which he, Salisbury, and the other two officers scrambled; even then, they were fortunate to be picked up after floating around for almost 24 hours. The 453BG left 41-28591 /H6: N behind as a shattered pile of wreckage within Berlin, although none of Lt. Melvin H. Williams's ten-man team shared its fate.

20CBW

Hardwick's 42-109816/YM: N **War Goddess** was also heading back when a fuel leak was reported as the formation was approaching the Baltic coastline. The possibility of ending up "ditching" should all reserves be exhausted probably impelled Lt. Martin Barkan into electing to bank away in the direction of Sweden, where the B-24 bearing nine airmen made landfall and a landing at Bulltofta. They were joined by a fellow Wing crew from the 448BG led by Lt. Roland G. Fox and his nine colleagues in 42-95089/EI: E. **Dual Sack**; the reason behind this decision is not clear. Their fate was almost diametrically opposite that of the Bungay crew headed by Lt. John D. Nicholson. Their damaged 41-29124/JU: K **Connie** left the formation near Terschelling, in the Friesian Island chain, and was reportedly taken out by flak while the pilots were attempting a crash landing; only Sgt. Peter A. Bausano (RW) emerged alive from the violently-concluded incident.

An even crueller end to the mission for seven Wing airmen involved the 448BG crew on 42-95186/CT:, flown by Lt. Cleve J. Howell (POW). The B-24 was on half power and failing when all nine crew bailed out NW of Schwerin to float down safely. The lease on life for all but Howell and F/O Bob J. Branizza (CP) was brutally terminated next day, following round-up by the authorities. The *Sicherheitspolitzei* (Security Police, an SS sub-organization) shot dead all seven on the grounds that the airmen were "attempting to escape." Only two bodies were recovered after WWII, but action was taken against the alleged perpetrators, six of whom were hanged. The third Seething loss was 42-95075/IO:, which came down 10 miles NE of the target, a victim of flak; Lt. Jack L. Mercer (P) was one of five survivors out of ten.

96CBW

Two 96CBW bombers were fated to join the internment rota within Sweden, the first being Attlebridge's 44-40093/U8: N **Lovely Lady's Avenger**, flown by Lt. Leo L. Mower. It is unclear whether the loss of two engines and copious fuel leakage occurred on target approach or withdrawal, but either way, the bomber left the formation and headed towards Sweden. The defenses were avoided and final arrival over Bulltofta was achieved. However, the actual landing was of a forced nature that resulted in notable damage to the airframe, although the reduced crew of eight walked away unscathed. (This team bore no bombardier or ball turret gunner.)

As with Lt. Howell's crew from Bungay, so one of the two Rackheath losses involved an even more savage conclusion for Lt. E. Helton's crew, which entered the "War Crime" category when subsequently investigated. Flak damage was incurred over Berlin that set an engine on fire and caused 42-252497/Q2; **Osage Express** to fall out and down, but under seeming control. The 790BS bomber faded out of sight and finally crashed near Klink, bordering the *Muritzsee* (Lake Muritz). It appears that all nine crewmembers were captured, but on arrival at the town of Waren, seven were turned over to the *Sicherheitspolizei*, who summarily executed them. Helton and Lt. R. J. Ludka (B) ended up in the hands of SS Police Commissioner Stempel, who dealt out similar "treatment." Postwar exhumation and removal to St. Avold's U.S. Military Cemetery for all but Helton and Ludka—their bodies remaining missing to this day—confirmed upon autopsy that they had all been shot in the head. The U.S. authorities' investigation resulted in the prosecution of the regional *Gauleiter* upon whose orders the murders were instituted and Friederich Hildebrandt paid for his actions with his life.

The other 467BG crew could not have experienced a more diverse fate. Their B-24H/42-52525/6A: **Six Bits** was in the formation as it was passing north of the Elbe estuary when Lt. Edward F. Rudowski indicated his fuel reserves were too low to guarantee a safe return to base; course was accordingly taken for Sweden, which was successfully achieved with a landing at Bulltofta, where another nine airmen began their internment.

14CBW

This Wing came home just two short, beginning with Wendling's 42-110027/DC: E+, which had suffered damage from flak and fighters, but headed back as far as the region around Oldenburg; this was where a crash landing was finally carried off successfully by Lt. Hans G. Belitz, from which the nine airmen stepped out intact. Eight crewmembers were captured almost immediately, but the ninth was at liberty for thirteen days before being apprehended in northern Holland.

Lt. Norman E. Howe's 44BG crew were fourteen-mission veterans in 42-100411/NB: E, and the flak burst prior to "bombs away" that caused damage to No. 2 engine and a loss of altitude was quickly corrected, after which a heading for Sweden was taken up. Sadly, the bid was thwarted within minutes of clearing Berlin's northern fringe when several Bf109s intercepted the isolated bomber and dispatched it to crash north of Feldberg. After S/Sgt. William L. McConnaughhay (Eng.) bailed out, he was briefly confused as to why his parachute was not deploying, but all was revealed when he looked down—his left hand was holding tight to the ripcord! Once on the ground, he ran over to a tree-shrouded pond and waded in, thereby avoiding detection. His action was the start of a twelve-day sojourn, as he walked north in the hope of making it to Sweden, but sadly he was finally apprehended. At least he and seven other crewmembers ended up as POWs, whereas Lt. Gordon W. Henderson (CP) never turned up and remains MIA to this day.

The Divisional MIA total was added to by three "write-offs," two occurring during Assembly. Only two crewmembers out of ten on Lt. John C. Wunder's 42-95161/T9: S emerged alive when the Attlebridge-based B-24 seemed to stall out while overshooting the airfield on its initial landing attempt.

The name of this 491BG B-24J-145-CO is **Uninvited**, an ironically appropriate name in these circumstances. On 13 June 1944, the brake- and flap-less aircraft was brought in for a landing at Metfield by Lt. W. Stokely. The arresting effect of deployed parachutes attached to the waist guns was not sufficient to halt the onward progress off the runway and into a field; one crewmember was injured from among its number and the bomber was subsequently salvaged.

Line-up of 2BD Senior Staff at Ketteringham Hall around April 1944. Back row (L-R) are Cols. F. Dent (44BG), M. R. Arnold (389BG), J. Brogger (446BG), J. Isbell (458BG), J. Thompson (448BG), L. Fiegel (93BG), A. Shower (467BG), I. Rendle (392BG), and R. Potts (453BG). Seated are: Col.Wood (CG, 2CBW), B/Gen. Timberlake (CG, 20CBW), M/Gen. Hodges (CG, 2BD), B/Gen. Johnson (CG, 14CBW), and Col. Gerry Mason (HQ).

A 445BG bomber (41-29483/MK:) flown by Lt. Harry C. King piled onto the airfield surface after "aborting" the mission, but this time nobody was killed or seriously injured. A second Tibenham crew led by Lt. Richard P. Morris in 42-73501/MK: R lost nine of its eleven-man complement when the bomber came down in Norfolk on the return leg.

Tactical Operations Dominate Again

A wholesale return to tactical operations now occurred for the rest of June, apart from a 1BD thrust at oil targets (24th) and a full-scale 8AF mission with the same strategic theme (29th). A range of marshalling yards, airfields, and bridges spread across NW France were interdicted on the 22nd, with no B-24 losses incurred over enemy territory. However, the 489BG's 42-94826 /4R: G **Johnny Reb** lost most of its controls to flak, but was brought back as far as the approach to the English Channel coast when the bail out signal was given, reportedly not by Lt. William B. Montgomery (P), but by F/O John C. Crowther (CP), neither of whom survived the incident. One other crewmember was lost, but the other seven crewmembers were fortunate enough to float down onto land.

The Division was involved in two missions next day, the first being a joint assault upon V-1 sites with the 1BD that was cost-free. Later in the day, a joint attack with the 3BD on four airfields in eastern France yielded up a tithe of seven MIA crews, all but two from the 2BD. The 392BG headed for Laon/Athies, whose flak defenses took out three B-24s, two of whom came down close to the target. The first was 42-50338/EC: Q, flown by Lt. Charles C. McCarthy (one of five evaders), with two fatalities incurred among the remaining four airmen—this despite all on board managing to jump. Lt. Warren T. Whittlemore's 42-95027/DC: E+ flopped onto its back and deposited itself north of Laon; this time five of the eleven airmen paid the supreme price, one of whom later died in hospital from severe wounds. The final flak-afflicted casualty managed to hold station until approaching the French coast near Dunkirk—a fiercely-defended port—over which Lt. Neil R. Larson (KIA) strayed; the second baptism of fire gave no quarter to 42-50287/DC: V+, which crashed to leave four out of its ten occupants alive.

Single crews from the 492BG and 453BG completed the loss tally. Juvincourt was attacked by the 2CBW; Old Buckenham's 41-28619/E3: J **Begin the Beguine**, in Lt. John H. G. Raiser's (POW) hands, was another flak victim that entered into a spin before breaking up and crashing near Flushing, on the Scheldt estuary, a fate shared by all but three of the nine airmen on board. This crew appears to have been well off course, since Flushing is anything up to 80 miles and almost due north of the target area.

More Milk-run Myths

"Double header" missions were launched next day, in which the Division participated. The first involved two complete CBWs and the 93rd and 446th BGs striking French airfields. Dreux, SW of Paris, was a Target of Opportunity for the reduced-size 20CBW, which had a 93BG crew culled from its ranks. Capt. Norman A. Roggenkamp (P) was one of five out of eleven crewmembers killed after 42-100294/GO: B **Victory Belle** sustained flak strikes while on the bomb run; the bomb load was deliberately or accidentally jettisoned and the crew began to bail out, one of whose parachutes was set alight by burning debris before the machine fell to earth south of the target.

The evening sortie was against electrical facilities and V-1 sites. The 448BG was involved with the latter-listed target category and lost one crew, led by Lt. Elwyn R. Palmerton. His 42-95022/IG: was another flak victim that fell out of formation and was approaching the French coast south of Boulogne when it developed a spinning action; fortunately, all nine crew managed to jump clear into captivity. Oostduinkerke, on the Belgian coast, was where the 453BG's 42-95233/E3: G came to earth in the course of a mission to bomb an electrical plant at Lens, along with all but one member of Capt. George L. Baatz, Jr.'s (KIA) team, flak again being the executioner.

Another "double header" went out on the 25th, which took out five 2BD crews on the evening mission to bomb airfields in and around Paris. Target approach appears to have been from the SE, judging by the crash sites for one of the two 489BG losses. Verrieres-le-Buisson lies close to Villacoublay and formed the last resting place for **SNAFU** (42-94909/8R: +V), whose fuselage interior was ignited by shell impact. Lt. James W. Blackburn joined five of his crew in death as his bomber disintegrated on the way down. A second pre-target loss involved Metfield's 44-40129/V2: F+, whose fuselage was split in two by a strike, leaving no survivors among Lt. Marvin W. Butler's crew.

The rest of the sixty-three bombers of the 95CBW tracked over Villacoublay with a Hethel PFF bomber as deputy Lead. This contained Capt. Titus M. Fern's crew, with Lt. Montee R. Baker (489BG Asst. Ops. Officer) also on board. The bomb run was just behind the formations when a flak strike excised part of 41-28793/YO: J's port wing. The dramatic aerodynamic imbalance thrust the B-24 out of control and took all but three of the twelve crewmembers to their deaths near Dreux. The final casualty cleared the target area, but progressed no further back than SE of Rouen; the flak-crippled 42-95249/S4: U **Teaser** finally gave up the struggle, but was bereft of Lt. J. D. Coffman's team when it crashed east of Les Andelys.

The 466BG's single MIA contribution occurred during the attack on Bretigny and the B-24 in question did not complete its bomb run. Instead, 41-29371/U8: H **The Crippled Bitch** went out of control immediately following the flak strike or strikes; only a single officer and three Enlisted men on Lt. Oscar A. Weeklund's (KIA) crew succeeded in having their lives spared.

The cold-blooded courage of many citizens in Nazi-occupied Europe to conceal Allied evaders is recorded here. Lts. Charles B. Armour (2nd from right) and Don Blodgett (left) were the pilots on 42-51095/Z5: Q, which descended over Holland on 29 June. They are seen at a property in Zele, Belgium, where they remained until the British Army liberated the region. Discovery by the enemy would have resulted in summary execution or transportation to a concentration camp for their guardians.

During the course of three multiple fighter assaults upon the 392BG, S/Sgt. John W. Wehunt (TG), on 42-95025/GC: P-bar, was killed outright. The shattered turret top attests to this ever-grim fact. Date was 15 June 1944. The badly shot up B-24 diverted into Eye (490BG), where it was rendered "Category E" two days later.

Five further B-24s were "written off," including three from Halesworth. F/O Walter E. Saubert's take-off attempt ended with a runway overshoot in 42-94760/4R: K that resulted in two dead crewmembers. Worse still was the death sentence meted out to all but two on 42-94874/R4: S after Lt. Edward L. Hamilton "aborted" the mission. The B-24H was in its landing approach when it banked sharply to port, the resultant crash igniting the airframe and setting off the bomb load. Two airmen, one severely injured, somehow survived the incident. The last "write off" involved 42-94924/T4: D- **War Bride**, which suffered an excised main landing gear after swerving off the runway on its return, leaving the crew intact.

Woodbridge Emergency airfield received Hethel's **Big Time Operator** (421-28796/YO: C), which had jettisoned its bomb load after being temporarily set on fire and turned back; only eight on Lt. Ken R. Kleinshrot's crew were still present, two gunners having jumped following the incident. Elsewhere, a wheels-up landing back at Bungay was carried off successfully by Capt. Laning in his flak-damaged 42-95175/RT: H.

Normal service was resumed after a weather-interrupted 26th, when nine Groups, including four 2BD units, attempted to plaster supply and storage sites for the V-1s in the Pas de Calais. Adverse weather forced a search for Targets of Opportunity and adding to the frustration was the loss of five crews, all from the 2BD, including a trio from Seething.

Creil airfield, north of Paris, would gain the dubious reputation of being one of the most-bombed bases in France, but its defenders would continue to exact a toll, as on this occasion. One definite victim was **Red Sox** (42-50344/EI: H), which was struck on the port wing. Sgt. Robert Slack (TG) suffered a snagged parachute on the tail and was dragged to his death, while Lt. Lawrence Carney (B) was reportedly killed by ground fire. Lt. Peter D. McVean (P) was one of four evaders out of the other eight. The bomber was recorded as being turned for home, but crashed about ten miles due east of the target. The cause of the other two crews' demise would remain a mystery, since none of the twenty airmen survived, nor were their bodies ever found. These teams, led by Lt. Harold C. Turpin in 41-29004/EI: and Lt. Seymour Jarel in 42-50369/IG:, most likely were consumed by the waters of the English Channel or North Sea.

The Creil gunners recorded two more confirmed successes, one of these being 42-95280 /MK: D, which was bracketed and set on fire just after "bombs away." Lt. Clifton G. Miller (Evaded) barely had time to call for a bail out before his 445BG charge disintegrated, with the remnants falling scant miles west of the target. Four airmen did not survive, while four of the other six gained access to the local Resistance Movement.

Shipdham's sole MIA loss occurred as the formation was on the bomb run when the flight deck of 41-29496/GJ: Q **Ram it Dammit** was struck, almost certainly resulting in the deaths of Lt. Bernie K. Scudday (P), two other officers, and the Engineer and ROG. Lt. Raymond A. McCormack recalled the pilot, yelling over the intercom to the G-H Lead bomber to alter altitude, otherwise the flak batteries would zero-in, but to no avail. The navigator and S/Sgt. Carl W. Tepe (NT) scrambled out through the nose wheel doors, with the latter only able to attach his pack in mid-air; S/Sgt. Coyle J. Acuff (WG) was blown out, and was equally fortunate to be able to clip on his pack on the way down to become the sole other survivor.

Two further Shipdham B-24s were "written off" on return, beginning with flak and fighter-affected 42-50339/GJ:

C. **Feudin' Wagon**. A jammed nose wheel was being attended to by T/Sgt. Santo Romeo, but he was still there when the crash landing at Kingsnorth airfield forced the unit back up, crushing the airman in the process. His was the sole fatality among Lt. James Tucker's veteran 27-mission crew. Lt. John R. Anderson's 42-110082/WQ: O **Wendy W** was similarly on half power, as well as non-functioning hydraulics thanks to flak strikes when the B-24 diverted into Manston's emergency airfield; this time round all nine airmen walked away safely.

Only one target source on 28 June was located in Germany, and that was Saarbruecken's marshalling yard complex, which was allocated to nine 2BD groups and accordingly hammered by 90% of the dispatched force. The single loss involved the 389BG's 42-95056/EE: Z, flown by Lt. Lloyd Saari. The bomber, which had lost an engine en route, was judged unlikely to regain Allied lines or England, so it was turned southward for what transpired as a successful bid to enter Switzerland. The airfield at Payerne duly accepted its latest ten internees, with Sgt. Carl D. McDonald (TG) reportedly later escaping into France.

The crucial events of June 1944 were now drawing to a close on the Normandy Front, but the penultimate monthly mission emphasized the basic strategic brief for the 8AF's full-scale assault upon German aviation industrial capacity, as well as a tilt at its synthetic oil capacity. The formerly listed source was granted to the 2BD and three B-24 units from the 3BD, with five Primaries struck SW of Berlin at a cost of nine crews out of more than 400 gaining mission "credit."

The specter of mid-air collision was raised within the 44BG's ranks as it over-flew its Magdeburg target. The bomb loads had barely been released when a flak hit cast Lt. Howard K. Landahl's (KIA) 42-51181/GJ: K-bar **Cape Cod Special** off to the right. S/Sgt. Rinaldo had his tail turret Plexiglas shattered as he was thrown against the fuselage, but he had barely regained his feet when a second impact (naturally assumed by him to be a second flak strike) floored him again. The No. 2 B-24 to Landahl's bomber was 41-28829/GJ: H-bar **My Ever Lovin' Gal**, which had also sustained one or more flak hits. Lt. Gerald S. Westcott (KIA) dispatched a crewmember to inspect the bomb bay, which was now found to be liberally sprayed with fluid from punctured hydraulic lines.

Hardly had S/Sgt. Walter V. Lawrence (LW) returned from his inspection than a huge explosion occurred that literally threw him out into mid-air. Which aircraft collided with the other was never clarified, but the effect was for GJ: H-Bar to violently disintegrate and descend between Magdeburg and Burg, to the NE of the city that also received GJ: K's airframe. Lt. Thomas C. Conzoner (B) to Lt. Landahl averred that the other B-24 was blown apart by the flak and parts of the wreckage fatally landed on their aircraft. Other reports were that the starboard wing on GJ: K-bar impacted with Westcott's aircraft just behind the cockpit. Whatever the facts, two crews were now removed from Group strength. Of the nine survivors out of nineteen airmen, only three on Landahl's bomber and six on the other ended up POWs.

Two other Groups suffered a duo of losses, beginning with the 448BG, whose first casualty was incurred over Bernberg as the bomb run was being completed. Flak hits on the forward and central fuselage clinically dispatched 42-50300/IG: to a fiery death, judging by the charred bodies found within the wreckage; all ten of Lt. William A. Warke's crew were killed. The lottery of aerial combat provided a diametrically opposite fate for the second ten-man crew led by Lt. Glenn F. Jones. Their 42-95326/CT: P. **Shoo Shoo Baby** had developed engine problems that left the B-24H straggling and finally making a wheels-down landing in a Dutch field at Middenbeemster; the port main landing gear folded, but all on board survived after the B-24 slewed to a halt with its airframe in an otherwise intact condition.

The 96CBW was allotted the aircraft plant at Aschersleben and came home light three crews, two from the 458BG. Lt. Robert H. Hannaman was a 23-mission veteran who was in the left seat on 42-95008/J3: R **Able Mabel** with the acolyte second-mission crew of Lt. William P. Perkinson, who was in the right seat. The bomber got to the target, but was then seen to drift back, albeit with no discernible damage until it disappeared. This bomber had suffered engine problems and steadily lost altitude; having progressed as far as a point between Oldenburg and the Dutch border, Hannaman felt he was left with no option but to order a bail out, which all ten airmen successfully negotiated. Sgt. Bruce T. Bean (TG) spilled his parachute in the fuselage but gathered it together and jumped. Then:

> Suddenly, the plane was gone as I floated down in peace. A patchwork quilt appeared below that became more detailed, with a fence "coming up" towards me that I just avoided by pulling on the canopy leads. I was close to a house, so I pulled off my flying boots and put on my English walking shoes. Earl Smith (ROG) had previously kidded me about walking out of Germany—sadly, this was a short-lived hope, as a soldier ran up shouting "Haende Hoch!" All nine of us were soon rounded up and taken by lorry to a nearby base, where after attempted interrogation we were placed in separate rooms. Later on, an unsatisfactory bowl of soup was provided before we were marched to a railroad station, where we were given loaves of black bread prior to boarding. One bite was enough for us to chuck them away, but later we regretted our reaction and would have eaten them, had we realized how long we would wait for our next "meal"! Arrival at *Dulag-Luft* and separate interrogation later led to my release into a compound.

Bruce's comment regarding the crew's initial experience of German-provided food would gain further strength once in a POW camp, where the average "Kriegie" quickly learned to eat and drink all and anything provided him by his captors—hunger and thirst knows no bounds in such basic circumstances!

Stark tragedy awaited a Dutch farmer, his wife, and daughter as 42-51095/Z5: Q **Shoo Shoo Baby** was being abandoned by Lt. Charles B. Armour's crew. The straggling bomber had suffered flak strikes and punctured fuel tanks, and all ten crewmembers not only bailed out in sound order, but no less than eight would evade immediate capture, of which half would remain free until the liberation of Belgium and southern Holland. As it was, the bail out was effected over Central Holland, but the pilot-less B-24 flew southwest until it came down near Kieldrecht. Tragically, it impacted with buildings on a farm owned by the Staes family, all three above-listed individuals being consumed by the aircraft's crash and instant explosion.

Flak in the Aschersleben area took out 42-110187/6A: **Belle of the East** as the formation was heading for the Rally point. The 467BG bomber was observed with flames shooting through the fuselage as it lost altitude, followed shortly after by the tail section separating; further disintegration of the wing sections occurred and the burning remains impacted near Calbe. The sole survivor out of nine was the pilot, Lt. William H. Counts, who ascribed his good fortune to being thrown clear.

The final Division casualty came out of the ranks of the 489BG as the 95CBW took on the synthetic oil complex at Boehlen. Although one engine on 41-28832/S4: -R **Heaven Can Wait** was set on fire in the target area and a second disabled, Lt. Robert E. Cole grittily wended a solo path homeward to reach Eastern Holland, at which point the uphill struggle ended with an emergency landing near Ursem, where the ten-man crew was apprehended.

Three 14CBW bombers became "Category E" candidates, with one fatality out of the 31 airmen concerned. Shipdham's 41-28767/QK: L+ was crash landed at Covehithe due to fuel shortage by Capt. Charles B. Handwright. **Call me Later** (42-95035/GC: S), which had suffered flak damage, was also crash landed near Wendling by Lt. Norman J. Hunt. The sole fatality on board Lt. Roy L. Miller's 42-95037/GC: M **Sally Ann** was T/Sgt. Chauncey W. Freeman (Eng.), who had been mortally wounded by flak; the crash landing in this case occurred at Frettenham, in Norfolk. A single fatality also occurred on board the 446BG's 44-40104/RT: C. **Wistful Vista**, which lost its ball turret, along with S/Sgt. Julian F. Ludwick, as well as suffering further fuselage damage. Although landed safely back at Bungay by Lt. Benjamin F. Inman along with the other nine mission survivors, the B-24J was subsequently declared "salvage."

Jagdwaffe Woes

By June 1944, the depredations wrought upon the *Jagdwaffe,* both in the air, but also on the ground, thanks to increased strafing of airfields by 8AF fighters who had discharged their primary escort function then heading downwards on the way home was one factor in the reduced figure of operational fighters, averaging barely 400 overall between *Reichsverteidigung* needs and the current threat of Allied territorial advancement in Normandy—this out of a practical strength of 900, which in turn was 20% down on the end-of-March equivalent total. This operational deterioration in quantitative terms was never to be reversed as the Allied Bombing Campaign maintained its full momentum. Burgeoning restrictions in fuel availability, especially from May 1944, would result in the previous supply norm of 60-80,000 tons per month never again being remotely attainable; no more than 25/30% of this requirement would be realized once the Oil Campaign got under way and would further decrease to 10% by early autumn.

The qualitative aspect of *Jagdwaffe* operations had been similarly affected over the past year. Pilot training Programs had by mid-1944 been reduced to 1) Basic Training - 52 hours and 2) Fighter School - 111 hours. This figure of 163 hours, usually established over eight months, was barely half the previous norm, both in terms of hours of instruction and time that extended up to two years. Blind flying and gunnery training aspects were particularly reduced, an ironic situation for fighter pilots at this stage of WWII.

Chapter Fourteen

A Stranglehold on Oil and Transportation

As July 1944 commenced, the Allies' hold on the Normandy bridgehead was guaranteed, but nevertheless was demonstrating a wearying pace of advance through the small fields regularly contained within steep-sided roads and lanes that were features of the "Bocage" landscape that accordingly suited the requirements of the German defenders in thwarting any attempt at mobility on their opponents' behalf. In contrast, the situation in the skies above the soldiers displayed a continuing domination by the Anglo-American Air Forces, with the *Jagdwaffe* units unable to do more than put up a steadily diminishing resistance. As it transpired, the first two 8AF missions were directed at the current threat to SE England from the V-1 barrage. The first sortie to the Pas de Calais was largely "aborted" thanks to adverse weather, but over 300 B-17s and B-24s got through (2nd) to pound a number of sites.

The frustratingly poor summer weather patterns forced a total 24-hour delay, while the 1BD element on Independence Day saw less than 20% of its 300-strong force attaining their targets. Not so the B-24 Groups from the other two Divisions, who struck five Primaries—all airfields north or northwest of Paris—at no MIA cost. However, only 27 of the 28 Shipdham crews arrived back at base. The exception was 42-100412/QK: WQ: V. **V for Victory**, which was by then laying wrecked in a field south of London. On the way out, Lt. Schaefer had experienced problems with No. 2 engine and turned back. The situation then deteriorated to the extent that a safe landing was not considered feasible and a bail out was called for, which passed off uneventfully for the crew.

The continuing attention on tactical operations for the USAAF "heavies" (5th) involved a somewhat expanded geographic range, with several Dutch and Belgian airfields included in a cluster of targets that also included several V-1 sites. This was another cost-free mission for the Division that would be ruefully reflected upon in the ensuing days of mid-July, as a more balanced tactical/strategic operational pattern emerged; the return to deep-penetration runs would raise the survival stakes even in the face of what was developing into a seriously reduced *Reichsverteidigung* force thanks to the westward diversion of many of its *Gruppen* to contest the Allied forces in Normandy.

The 2BD dispatched separate forces to attack V-1 sites and shipyard facilities at Kiel. A total of three crews from the latter mission were taken out, all from the 14CBW. The luckless 492BG contributed two, with the third a Wendling team in 42-95041/EC: D.

Lt. Elwin E. Clapper's bomber was No. 2 in the squadron Lead element and had called up on the return flight to say he was going to ditch, having lost fuel

The friendly coast of England, with the town of Gorleston to starboard, slips by a pair of 467BG bombers. **Valiant Lady** (B-24H-15-CF/41-29408/Q2: C was to end up salvaged on 15 October 1944. **Tangerine**, also an H-15-CF airframe, switched from the 788BS during May and flew operations until diverting into a Continental airfield on 14 November, there to be also declared "salvage."

A 93BG aircraft curves gracefully to port as it peels away from the camera. The B-24H-25-FO/42-95043 is named **Lindie**, but any name and/or artwork are mounted on the port side. The ball turret aperture appears to be welded, but the shaded underside prevents a definite confirmation. This aircraft crashed into the Thames Estuary while returning from a tactical strike on 1 August 1944.

from two flak-punctured tanks. Following the crippled aircraft's departure from the Group ranks, the Group deputy Lead crew was instructed to follow in his tracks in order to establish where the "ditching" occurred. No further visual contact was made and the ever-tragic result was nine more names on a postwar "Wall of the Missing."

Sturmgruppe Debut

The first of four full-scale strategic strikes over the ensuing week was sent out as the latest attempt to dismantle the Nazis' synthetic oil industry, as well as their aircraft production facilities. The 14CBW was allotted the Junkers plant at Bernburg and would pay the bulk of the Division's price with 20 out of the 28 MIA crew total. For the 492BG, the day's cost would reach the second-highest figure (twelve) from among the Group's three missions on which they would experience such a human and material martyrdom. The Group was left exposed within the Wing and was latched upon by by Hptm. Wilhelm Moritz's IV (*Sturm*) JG3, the first *Sturmgruppe* to commence full-scale operations. Neither were the other two Groups spared, although the punishment was on a somewhat reduced scale, albeit no less painful.

Wendling Woes

Lt. Leo Ruvolis, Jr. was piloting 42-95229 /GC: R-bar **Rap 'Em Pappy**, whose team had 21 missions under its belt. The 492BG was reportedly heading home when a fighter pass upon the High squadron that was a coopted Wendling element ended with the B-24's No. 3 propeller windmilling, No. 4 disabled, and the landing gear beginning to droop down. The bomber appeared to be under control, but in the event, it crashed at Rhoden, NE of Osterwieck. The pilot, along with Lt. Carl F. Wunderlin (CP) and F/O Randell S. Mayer (N), exited via the nose wheel hatch on account of the bomb doors being jammed; fighter attacks were still being delivered at this point. S/Sgt. James A. Garvey (ROG) was one of two crewmembers whose badly charred bodies were found in or close to the wreckage, while T/Sgt. John C. Cowley (Eng.) subsequently died in hospital from his injuries. Lt. Wunderlin also died in uncertain circumstances. (The recorded time of the crash at 0920 is the earliest for any of the 392BG losses and indicates the Group was actually target-bound.)

Today's run was to prove costly, both for the 579BS and its veteran crews. Lt. Harold W. Prouse's (POW) crew were in 42-52160/GC: K-Bar **Ski Nose**, but their progress was brutally arrested during the bomb run when fire erupted thanks to fighter strikes. The bomber fell out of formation in an almost vertical dive for several thousand feet before exploding. The pilot later reported that two Enlisted men got clear around 5,000ft, while he was even more fortunate to survive both the aircraft disintegration and pulling his ripcord when less than 1,000ft up. S/Sgt. Lowell I. Qwick had been wounded, and although surviving the incident subsequently died in Obermassfeld hospital from a combination of burns and pneumonia on 3 August 1944. The B-24's shattered airframe deposited itself right on the Bernberg airfield perimeter.

Two losses occurred very close to each other shortly after clearing the target area. Lt. Raymond L. Pounds (POW) led his crew in 42-110028 GC: Z-bar, a 27-mission veteran B-24. He described how a fighter pass right after "bombs away" ruptured bomb bay fuel lines that immediately ignited the released liquid. Scarcely had the bail out order been issued when an explosion threw him out of his seat as the bomber tilted sharply, a maneuver that fortuitously left him by the now-exposed top hatch, via which he promptly exited. Five other crewmembers got clear, leaving their charge to erupt into the ground at 0935 near Egeln, SW of Magdeburg, but there was no reprieve from death for the remaining three airmen on board. The other simultaneously timed crash around Egeln involved Lt. William M. Milliken in 42-52517/GC: U-bar and his crew. The precise circumstances of its fate were undetermined, although it too was under fighter attack when it exploded, blowing Lt. Robert W. Darnall (CP) out into mid-air to become the sole survivor. However he, Milliken, and Sgt. George F. Stella, Jr. (ROG) were attempting to open the jammed bomb bay doors at that point, making it clear that the bail out signal had been given.

The group's punishment continued on the return leg with one more crew downed.

Lt. George E. Jones and his crew's 30th mission in 42-94772/GC: J-bar was to be celebrated not by a Stateside return, but with one tragic exception an arrival in a *Stalag*. The persistent fighter assaults finally caught up with their B-24 as the Duemmersee was looming up. By then, the pilot had called for a bail out that eight of the airmen carried out. The ninth, a Lt. John E. Faas (CP), "froze" at the prospect of leaping into space and could not be persuaded to jump by Lt. Jones, even as flames gained hold of the fuselage. The result was that his body was discovered close to the wreckage north of Wagenfeld and two of his colleagues were forced to bury him.

Shipdham's Share

The 44BG absorbed its share of the punishment being handed out not only by the Fw190A-8s from Moritz's *Gruppe*, but also by 2/JG51, whose normal duty was to act as high escort for the Fw190, but who on this occasion joined in the assaults due to there being no P-51s or P-47s on hand. Lt. Steinke's 42-110035/WQ: Y **Any Gum Chum?** lost its No. 4 engine and was seen to bank steeply to starboard before falling away. Only two crewmembers survived, one of whom—Lt. Duane E. Mitchell (N), on his 29th mission—believed he owed his life to Lt. Hybarger (B) pushing him out through the nose wheel doors, which he had been unable to open. On landing, he suffered a broken leg and was paralyzed below the waist, the latter injury leading to three months in traction.

A second 68BS bomber (42-99966/WQ: W. **Full House**) was hit during the initial fighter assault and lost a good proportion of power, but held position until over the Dutch/German border near Ommen, when fire caught hold. Lt. Ted L. Weaver (P) and crew were on their 23rd mission, and although all ten survived their parachute descent, only nine subsequently remained alive. The exception was Lt. Walter B. Shambarger (CP), who was stabbed to death by a Dutch Nazi; Weaver, on the other hand, was the sole member to succeed in evading capture.

Lt. James A. Wilson was a replacement for his crew's original pilot Lt. Morrison, who had finished up already; they had arrived during February and were another 68BS combat-seasoned team, but their experience availed them naught, as fighter strikes over the target caused 42-100170/WQ: G **Patsy Ann II** to begin trailing the group on three-quarters power. The straggling B-24 was further set upon, with fire erupting in the bomb bay and rudder controls knocked out that probably induced a spin. Relative luck was on the side of all but S/Sgt. Dominic P. Yocco (ROG), who perished, his more fortunate colleagues swelling the Allied "Kriegy" ranks.

A relatively climactic phenomenon—a sun-lit English sky—greets two 68BS aircraft at Shipdham. B-24J-65-CF 44-10553/C (foreground) was to be crash landed in France on 28 December 1944. The other bomber is a J-1-FO machine (42-50660/A) that served the Group a mere nineteen days longer; it was flak-stricken and abandoned by its crew over SE France on 16 January.

2CBW Misfortunes

The Wing was assigned to a refinery at Halle, but diverted to an airfield (Secondary), since the Primary was obscured. Then S/Sgt. Dan Raymond (WG), on Lt. Hall's 566BS crew, recalled:

> Suddenly Sgt. Goodwin (TG) called up: "Here comes something and it is coming straight at us!" The "something" was an estimated 50 to 70 Fw190s and Bf109s that delivered a series of assaults. To our right, I saw Lt. Kissling's 42-50374/RR: K struck by shells on the starboard wing that caught fire between the engines. All the crew jumped and right after the last man, the bomber sagged away into a spin.

Three of Lt. James L. Kissling's crew suffered tragic deaths: S/Sgt. Merkle (G) landed on high-tension cables, while Lt. Santomiery (CP) and Sgt. Hamrick (Eng.) were recorded as "shot while trying to escape"—often a euphemistic expression for summary justice. Of the ten members on Lt. Ernest Bevan's crew in 41-28824/RR: O. **Sack Warmer**, only Lt. Frank Dawson (B) and S/Sgt.

The comprehensive and superbly-maintained plant life at Ketteringham Hall provides a welcome break from the strain of command for Gen. Hodges. Here he selects grapes from within one of the greenhouses while accompanied by one of the gardeners, "Charlie" (no surname recorded).

William Chastain were granted the gift of life. Three further crews were culled from the Group ranks, beginning with Capt. William P. Bates (P) and Capt. Walter Beckett (Mission pilot), along with eleven more airmen in 42-51144/YO: A; Beckett was one of just four survivors. A 50% casualty rate was borne by Lt. Ralph S. Baney's (POW) crew on 42-95029/HP: L and Lt. John V. McGee, Jr. was the sole officer survivor on board 42-50617/RR: Z **The Wolf Patrol**. A single Tibenham crew completed the loss roster for the Wing.

Horsham's deputy Lead crew was led by Lt. Lincoln A. Larson (KIA) in 42-100362 /Z5: A, formerly **Sweet Lorraine** but now **Boomerang**—a title that would now fail both bomber and crew. A "runaway" propeller on No. 1 engine that could not be corrected occurred during the bomb run, so the Lead pilot was informed the errant B-24 was dropping out and turning back after jettisoning its bomb load. The requested escort cover turned up in the form of two P-47s, but by the time the trio was approaching the Ems estuary, the ever-lowering altitude coupled with more flak interference made it clear the bomber was doomed. Bail out commenced, but when the survivors were later assembled, the original eleven-strong team was down to six. The 489BG returned light one B-24, being 41-29533/8R: **Little Iodine**; the flak-afflicted bomber ended up in a watery North Sea grave, along with all nine on Lt. Bryan W. Woollen, Jr.'s team.

Munich Mission-Trilogy

A single tactical mission (8th) saw the Division's share almost totally nullified by adverse weather, after which the B-24s remained ground-bound for 48 hours. Munich, in SE Germany, was a key industrial city, whose distance from East Anglia promised a very tiring experience for the 8AF crews. Three consecutive daily runs (11/13 July) would be launched. On the first occasion, the city center and Reim airfield was assigned to a full-strength 2BD, but the anticipated visual conditions had deteriorated to an extent that *H-2X* guidance was required. In addition, although only 20 crews were lost, 85% involved Divisional personnel, and only the 95CBW out of the five Wings remained immune from MIA casualties. However, the relative proximity of Switzerland meant that five crews did successfully divert there to at least reduce the human cost.

14CBW

The loss scale (six) within the 14CBW was equally shared out between the three Groups. Both Wendling bombers ended up in Switzerland, and the account of a member on Lt. Seigvart J. Robertson's crew (flying 42-51106/CI: A) is worthy of full quotation. According to T/Sgt. Michel (ROG):

> Sig [pilot 1/Lt Robertson] rang the bail out bell twice. First, when we were leaving the target area and could not keep up with the formation, even with full power on #1 and #2 engines, but with #3 cutting in and out and overheating and #4 windmilling like crazy. That's when we as a crew decided that after what we had helped do to Munich and with 10/10 cloud cover beneath us, so we had no idea into what we might be jumping into, that Robertson, Willis (Dumbo...his nickname), and Landry could somehow keep us in the air. At that point, four P-51s answered our call for fighter cover because we had fallen far behind the formation and were just a sitting duck for any German fighters that might have seen us. Our heading was toward Switzerland and the Alps, which were sticking up through the cloud cover.
>
> When Lt. Richard "Pete" Peterson, the Lead pilot in that covey of four P-51s, turned his **Hurry Home Honey** and the other three planes north, saying that they weren't allowed to get any closer to Swiss air space, we saw

By the summer of 1944, as the 8AF regularly expended its operations into Central Europe, evermore crippled bombers sought the sanctuary of Switzerland. On 12 July **Miss Fortune** (a B-24H-15-FO and a 467BG "original") suffered serious fuel loss that impelled Lt. Richard E. Evans to divert there and carry out a landing at Duebendorf.

The lateral view for B-24 pilots was extremely restricted compared to the B-17, hence the crewmember sitting on the escape hatch and guiding the two men at the controls. **Fat Stuff II** is B-24H-2-FO/42-7591, which diverted into Switzerland on 12 July when being flown by Lt. George Wilson's crew, a safe landing being made near Altenrhein—in a swampy field!

the first hole in the cloud cover since we had left England. Sig took the plane down through that opening, only to have the flak guns of Friedrichshafen give us a terrific barrage, and he headed the plane out over the Boden Zee, only to have the Swiss start shooting at us. Dumbo lowered the wheels, the recognized signal that we were finished and were trying to come down, but he didn't tell the fellows still in the nose of the plane that he was going to do it.

When the nose wheel dropped out, so did John Gates, our Navigator. He managed to catch himself by his elbows and work his way back into the plane, but accidentally popped his chest pack parachute during his frantic but successful effort to get back inside the plane. At the same time this was happening, Sig was ringing the bail out bell a second time and telling us that parachuting into the Boden Zee was a better option than riding the plane down. Gates in no uncertain terms made it clear that he didn't have a parachute, so we decided again we were in it together and nine men with eight parachutes meant that we'd ride it down and take our chances. It worked.

The B-24 was crash landed at Altenrhein and all nine airmen taken to Adelboden; Lt. Chester W. Drake later escaped into France and was back in the States sometime during the following winter.

Lt. George L. Bridson, flying 42-95033/EC: X **Silver Chief**, made a similar successful diversion. Lt. James Green (CP) recalled that as the bombs dropped, they caught a direct hit in No. 1 engine. From 24,000 feet, they went right down through the following formation, whose airplanes scattered in a desperate attempt to avoid collisions. The B-24 was finally pulled out of the dive and levelled off at 18,000 feet, and an interphone check revealed that everyone was all right. Engineer Ashcraft then reported that they were losing fuel from the left wing tanks. On three engines they could not keep up with the formation and were soon alone. To make matters worse the radios slowly faded out, so they could not call for help or even talk to each other.

After several minutes of agonizing, Bridson turned the aircraft toward Switzerland. A hole in the solid undercast appeared just in the nick of time and they could see both water and land. Lt. Ralph L. White (N) assured the pilots they were over the western end of Lake Constance and the small grass airfield they had been briefed about would be at the eastern end of the lake on the Austrian border. They circled down through the clouds, only to be met by anti-aircraft fire. Luckily, it stopped before the plane or crew were hit, but as they approached the landing field, it became apparent that it was too short. According to Green:

> With full flaps and power off, we nipped the fence at the edge of the field and touched down. It was instantly obvious that we were about to end up in Austria unless we could stop, and soon. George yelled for help on the controls to raise the nose wheel and then slam it down with enough force to collapse the gear and let the nose of the plane dig into the soft ground. This we did, but it took two or three tries before the gear finally broke. The nose started plowing a furrow and slowing us almost to a stop, but not before the forward part of the nose section ended up just across the border into Austria!

Shipdham surrendered its two crews on the way back. The first was 41-28776/QK: E+, bearing Lt. Louis E. Zweig and Maj. James D. Conrad (Command Pilot) at the head of the 448BG and which had suffered punctured fuel tanks. The engines began to falter near Lille, and

The date is 15 July 1944 at Metfield, current home for the 491BG; the unconscious precursor of a nuclear weapon's mushroom plume ascends from the airfield bomb dump. A sizeable tonnage of bombs was consumed in the blast, although the death toll among the armorers was surprisingly limited.

although a bail out was issued only four of the twelve-man crew jumped before the bomber spun in; the pilots, along with Lt. John L. Quail (N), evaded capture, but Sgt. Milton Mollen (Radar Op.) suffered a broken leg and was captured. **Flak Alley II** (41-29544/ WQ: T) suffered oil pressure failure on No. 4, with a similar failure on No. 2 and loss of No. 3 as it was over the enemy coast. The inevitability of "ditching" was faced by Lt. Alfred D. Bonnet (Rtd.) and this occurred some 40 miles from the English coast. The B-24's structural frailty displayed itself once again, with the fuselage fracturing behind the cockpit and further back; those up front, apart from the pilot, were trapped and drowned when the nose section immediately sunk like a stone, and only he and the four airmen in the rear emerged alive to be subsequently fished out by ASR Launch. The CBW's misery was added to by a MIA duo of 492BG crews.

2CBW

Five crews were also culled from the 2CBW. Hethel's 41-28713/YO: G was Lead or deputy Lead in Lt. Ralph Woodward's hands with Capt. Andy Boreske as Command Pilot. Munich's flak gunners punctured a fuel tank and the B-24 began to straggle. A pair of P-38s provided cover, but could do nothing to prevent further flak damage on the Franco/Belgian border near Lille. All thirteen airmen "hit the silk," but Lt. Felbinger's (N) parachute folded. Old Buckenham's single casualty involved 42-52201/ **Battle Package**.

The remaining trio of MIA casualties were incurred by the 445BG, two of which demonstrated the cruelly random nature of combat operations. No reprieve for any of Lt. Philip A. Fry's nine-man crew came their way when 42-50334/WV: was taken down, whereas all nine on board 42-94773/ MK: Q-bar **Our Gal Sal**, led by Lt. Jack Webber, got out alive after force landing in a Belgian field; one (Sgt. James M. Wagner, TG) initially evaded capture, but while being moved through Brussels by the Resistance was betrayed and placed in St. Gilles prison; he then effected a second escape on the train transporting him to Germany and remained free until the British 2nd Army arrived to liberate the city! The third loss involved 42-7571/IS: +, which had problems with two engines en route to the target, a situation further worsened by flak damage that caused one to be switched off. The reputed absence of a navigator could have been fatal for the attempted diversion's success, but the roughly 30-minute flight passed off in order, although the overshoot at Duebendorf led to a collapsed nose-wheel on Lt. Robert A. Gallup's aircraft.

The fact that three of the propellers on Seething's B-24H-10-DT/41-28711 are "feathered" indicates how fortunate Lt. James F. Beaver and crew were to safely attain the Swiss airfield at Duebendorf on 21 July 1944. The bomber overshot the runway, an action that ripped off the nose wheel, but this was of little concern for the airmen on board **Little Sheppard**.

If the crew on **Little Sheppard** felt that they rode their luck, then **Ginny Gal**'s 389BG team must have blessed theirs. The other B-24's airframe was intact, in contrast to the severe fracturing borne by B-24H-25-FO/42-9577/EE: I's fuselage after it overshot into a gun emplacement at Duebendorf. The bomber had landed on half power following the loss of both outboard engines, but Lt. Kay R. Caldwell's crew emerged unscathed.

20CBW

The Bungay-based Group added two B-24s and crews to the MIA tally, the first of which was 42-94994/ **Dissipated Duck**. The flak-afflicted bomber was turned in the direction of Switzerland, but finally came down over enemy territory; all ten bailed out, but the pilot was recorded as being fatally wounded when fired at by German troops. The reverse casualty rate was borne by the crew on 42-95266/ **Heinie Hunter**, which exhausted its fuel reserves while still over the North Sea. The resultant "ditching" attempt at least partially succeeded for five crewmembers that were observed floating in the sea, but sadly only one among this number finally emerged alive.

96CBW

The first of the two Horsham crews lost did not even reach the enemy coast; **Lorelei** (Lt. Gibson's 41-29300/J4: M) tragically lived up to her namesake who, according to German mythology, had lured sailors to their deaths on rocks within the river Rhine. The bomber disappeared in the prolonged overcast at Assembly and was never seen again, so the North Sea had clearly served the same lethal function. A cruel dilemma faced Sgt. Charles E. Stenard on 42-100341/J4: A. **Satan's Mate**. The B-24 was losing the bulk of its engine power as the formation was approaching Belgian territory. On responding to the bail out order, the Sergeant discovered his harness had ring-pattern hooks for his pack, but the pack he had picked up featured snap hook fittings. His frantic search for a compatible pack never succeeded and his body was probably the one recorded by the Germans found within the bomber. The bail out was over the Scheldt Estuary, and since only two bodies in all out of the five fatalities were ever found, the estuarial depths appear to hold the other three airman's remains.

Rackheath also lost two aircraft and one MIA crew. **Tailwind** (41-29368/6A: J-bar) nearly cleared the French coast before crashing at Sangatte thanks to previously-incurred flak and fighter damage; Lt. James F. Underwood (P) and two others went down with their bomber, but the other seven airmen bailed out. **Ruth Marie** (41-28695/ Q2: K) was also punished, but reached as far as a landing approach to Hardwick (93BG). Matters went drastically wrong at this crucial point, with fuel-starved engines inducing a wavering flight pattern; the bomber finally appeared to over-correct, with the port wing dipping sharply and causing the machine to cartwheel and break up, barely missing the control tower, but impacting with the chemical supply structure in the process. Surprisingly, only two of Lt. Edwin B. Lackens's crew were killed, although all but one of the other eight received serious injuries.

Munich Again

The second of the three daily runs to Munich (12th) was also the last for the 2BD. Once again, the Division's ranks absorbed the bulk of punishment, with exactly half the 24 MIA figure. This time, all five CBWs shared the casualty list, the most affected being the 20th and 96th CBWs with four each. A second consecutive duo of crews failed to come back to Horsham St. Faith, although no fatalities among the nineteen airmen involved were incurred. Lt. Herbert Hopkins, guiding 42-95096/Z5: U **Bombs Away**, was seen to bank to port as the target was fading out of sight after informing the Lead B-24 that No. 3's failure coupled to a critical fuel situation impelled him to head for Switzerland, where Swiss MS-406 fighters "escorted" the cripple into Payerne, one of six Divisional crews succeeding in reaching this neutral haven. Fuel shortage on 42-100365/7V: B was also cited as the prime reason for Lt. Charles W. Quirk's action in finally bailing out his crew near Brussels. All nine combat-experienced airmen floated down: three into captivity and six featuring in successful evasion attempts. Their charge crashed at Harveng, close to Mons.

The same loss factor in B-24s (two) also affected the 467BG as on the day before, but this time both crews appeared on the MIA list. The "graduate" flak gunners at the target commenced the demise of 42-52512/ 6A: L-Bar **Baff'ling Brat** during the bomb run. Lt. Fred R. Sullivan swung south for Switzerland, but his effort ended over Austrian territory with a bail out that saw one crewmember presumed drowned and his body never recovered. Prior to the mission, Lt. Lyle Pritchard had made the usual crack to a fellow-graduate Lt. Richard E. Evans: "Where are you going today?" The reply was "Switzerland," a response that might have caused raised eyebrows by the day's end, since that was where **Miss Fortune** (42-52559 /4Z: R+) ended up! (The two pilots had regularly indulged in the aforementioned banter whenever a mission occurred that involved flying in the vicinity of Sweden or Switzerland.) In fact, the B-24 had suffered engine problems on Nos. 2 and 4 and the successful bid ended at Duebendorf airfield.

20CBW

The 446BG bore one of the four Wing losses when 42-52598 **Guess Who's Here** was downed, along with the pilot Lt. Herbert Culp; the other nine crewmembers ended up as "Kriegies," but one among their number had the misfortune to lose his life in the course of a forced march during the final weeks of WWII.

Two of the three Seething crews added to the internment total. Sgt. Rocky Starek (WG), on 42-7591/ **Fat Stuff II**, recalled:

> We dropped out of formation after being crippled by flak. A P-51 appeared and held station for a little while. He called up to ask if Lt. George Wilson (P) could make Italy and received a negative answer. Lt. R. J. Ginn (N) was then asked to lay out a course for Switzerland, since the pilots had established that our fuel would only suffice as far as Belgium, and the P-51 disappeared. On nearing the Swiss border, we saw a group of Germans firing flares with a Red Cross laid out, as if to entice us to land; Wilson decided to fly on and we finally landed in a field near Altenrhein, in Switzerland.

The other Group internee featured 42-94735/ **Bim Bam Bola**, which had lost No. 3 engine to flak. Lt. Billie C. Blanton headed south, and when he reached the *Bodensee* he ordered a bail out. The pilot and three others out of the nine on board were fortunate, in that they drifted down onto neutral soil, while the others found themselves descending on hostile territory. This relative degree of fortune totally deserted Lt. Michael Kuchwara's team on 42-110044/ **Sleepless Knights**, although all but one reached the ground alive, having vacated the flak-stricken B-24 bare seconds before it exploded over the city; the exception was T/Sgt. Calvin C. Crumbley (Eng.), whose canopy was ignited by burning wreckage.

The final pair of interned B-24s commenced with the 389BG's 41-28948/EE: K, in the hands of Lt. Tom P. Vann. No. 3 and 4 engines were successively disabled just prior to and during the bomb run. Once off the bomb run, the B-24 could not hold the formation altitude and a quick vote saw the crippled bomber turning for Switzerland; this crew also saw the enticing "neutral territory" display of flares and flags by the Germans while maneuvering to land at Basel. Payerne accepted the 491BG's 52-51113/3Q: T, which had suffered oil pressure failure

A somewhat abbreviated whale mouth design is seen on B-24J-130-CO/42-110072/AG: L. The collapse of the starboard main landing gear has resulted in a mangled No. 4 propeller after it impacted with the ground. This incident occurred on 1 August 1944, and although no other evidence of damage is discernible, it was severe enough for salvage action to be taken two days later.

Wendling's **American Beauty**, whose NMF finish shows the "ripple" surface on the B-24's bomb bay doors is B-24H-30-FO/42-95293/EC: H. In the right background is a P-47 whose war-weary initials WW can just be discerned on the fin's white band, and which serves the Group as a monitor ship. In the right foreground is a High Intensity/Low Visibility (HI/LV) "Barton" runway light.

on two engines near Stuttgart, and having inevitably lost altitude and formation security was turned towards neutral soil, an endeavor that saw Lt. Gordon W. McDonald's crew ending up as Swiss "guests." Elsewhere, the latest 492BG casualty was the sole 14CBW contribution and Old Buckenham surrendered 42-110089/, in the hands of Lt. Warren D. Freed (KIA).

Two bombers were "written off" on return. The 448BG's 42-50475/, flown by Lt. Richard Moody and bearing Sgt. Bill Gamble with a serious leg wound, was already on half power when the other two engines failed and a hasty crash landing was achieved near Hardwick; Gamble was rushed to hospital, but his leg was subsequently amputated. A 491st replacement crew led by Lt. Max R. Shea came down close to Chediston, with the pilot and four others losing their lives on 44-40200/. The crash site bordered on Halesworth, the 489BG's base.

Railroad "Busting"

Munich's third daily battering (13th) was left to the B-17 Divisions, although once again, weather conditions thwarted any attempt at visual bombing. The 2BD was dispatched on a shorter run to Saarbruecken, close to the Belgian border, where its marshalling yard facilities were given their latest punishment by over 80% of the 366 briefed crews. Seething's 42-94989/ had No. 3 engine destroyed by flak, with another losing power. The protracted distance over hostile airspace needed to reach Switzerland did not deter Lt. Dale Grubb making what turned out to be a successful run for his crew, at least. Fire had taken hold on an engine for some time before crossing into neutral ground, but the bail out of all nine crewmembers was achieved before the B-24 exploded over Batterkinden. Although only one B-24 was declared MIA, three more were involved in crashes during take-off and Assembly, with two more lost on return.

Wendling lost one B-24 and two crewmembers from a second during the mission's initial period. Lt. Norman J. Hunt was flying 42-95103/GC: V-Bar **Berlin Bitch**. During formation Assembly over the U.K., the bomber experienced severe icing conditions and subsequently spun in at Wrangle Common, Lincolnshire. The sole survivor, S/Sgt. Osment (LW), provided these details:

> Takeoff was at 5:30 a.m., in rain and heavy overcast. We had icing conditions for a while, but the ice left and the aircraft resumed normal flight. A few minutes later, however, the ice reappeared, and this time the propellers ran away and the aircraft was out of control. At this time I attempted to leave through the waist window, but was caught half in and half out and was semi-conscious from striking the side of the aircraft. A few seconds later I was thrown clear, pulled the ripcord, then lost consciousness. I regained consciousness on the ground. I remember talking to two children and members of the British Home Guard. I was placed on an ironing board and transported to an RAF hospital. I later learned that no one else survived the crash.

The bombs aboard the aircraft did not explode, giving the local authorities many anxious moments, as the crashed aircraft burned fiercely. Finally, however, the fire died out, the bombs were disposed of, and the crash site bulldozed in.

The acid comment regarding the Davis Wing's inadequacy when icing conditions were encountered was that "it could not hold enough ice to put in a Martini glass," and this insidious factor displayed itself on the second 392BG bomber so affected, although not lethally, for it or other than two of the nine crewmembers. **YMCA Flying Service II** (42-50558/GC: C-bar) contained Lt. Harry A. White's crew on their 30th mission. While climbing up for Assembly, the B-24 encountered icing conditions that caused the aircraft to stall out and enter a spin that was only arrested after the bail out bell was rung—an act to which Lts. William I. Forde (N) and Harry J. Green (B) responded. Unfortunately, the formation was over the Wash, a large water stretch between Lincolnshire and Norfolk, and the upshot was that both men's bodies were subsequently recovered from the water over the next few days. Had they not reacted so promptly, they would have got back to Wendling, to which their B-24 now returned. The "operational" loss list was completed by the 489BG, which lost all nine airmen on one B-24 during take

The 466BG's Assembly ship, with its bizarrely effective red zigzag pattern, has just delivered the Glenn Miller Band to Steeple Morden (355FG) on 18 August 1944. The B-24D-20-CO bears the code letters for the 748BS, but never flew combat missions with the Attlebridge-based Group. Note how the full year of production allocation (41) is not included within the serial on the inner fin.

The NMF finish on the B-24 was the perfect background for unit and national markings display, as demonstrated in this superb view of the 467BG's **Perils of Pauline** over the North Sea. The B-24H-25-FO served in the 790BS from 24 May until 5 August, when it was MIA on a Brunswick mission; seven on Lt. David E. Love's crew shared her fate.

Four incendiary clusters are following a Group of bombs that have been salvoed from the 491BG's B-24J-145-CO/44-40123/3Q: A **She Devil**. The mixture of such weaponry had the intention for the bombs to blow holes in structures and thereby enable the incendiary element to gain a purchase inside.

off, while a second bailed out of their damaged bomber on return.

"Big Bang"

The 2BD did not operate next day, nor did any of the "heavies" on the 15th. Saarbruecken was attacked on the 16th by other than the 491BG; the absence of the Halesworth-based unit was mandatory, thanks to a horrendous event the day previous involving the bomb dump, which literally "grounded" the Group. The relative peace of the countryside was brutally shattered by a series of sympathetic explosions within the weapons storage area. Five B-24s were "written off" during this cataclysm, which reportedly consumed well over 1,000 tons of explosives and incendiaries. It would be the 21st before the airfield was again declared operational.

Human casualties were amazingly light, with five personnel (none from the Group) literally eviscerated. Trucks had been delivering their bomb loads, and it was assumed that the regular practice of unloading by backing each lorry and slamming on the brakes, which literally threw the bombs off, was being indulged. In the past, the explosive content was inert in the absence of fuses, even when so subjected. However, the introduction of RDX, a much more volatile explosive type, had created a situation where fuse insertion was *not* deemed absolutely necessary to induce an explosion, hence the likely reason for a bomb so cast off to initiate the tragedy.

A marshalling yard theme, along with a number of bridges, were targeted, without loss by a combined 2BD/3BD force (17th), and the next day, direct ground support was provided, with several Primaries located close to the city of Caen, in the British/Canadian sector, being assaulted. A desperate attempt to "ditch" 41-29350/2U: + **Spare Parts** off the French coast by Lt. Edward F. Kaspshak following severe flak damage to the hydraulic and control systems failed for him and three of the other nine crewmembers. Clear weather on the 19th promised a good strike against German-based targets, with almost the entire B-17 strength committed, along with ten B-24 groups. A Division Primary was Leipheim airfield, NW of Munich, but barely 15% of the dispatched force released their loads there, while Targets of Opportunity attracted another 20%. This success rate compared poorly with the other Divisions, whose "mission credit" percentage was between 80 and 90%.

Hethel's 42-100281/RR: D **Naughty Norma** provided the single MIA statistic. The 50-mission veteran bomber was being flown by Lt. Dave Deeter's acolyte crew. The bomb run completed, the Lead bombardier closed the bomb doors and then illogically operated the rack salvo lever—without checking to see if any "hung up" bombs were still on board! The single weapon still in place knocked off a bomb bay door as it punched its way out and away, whereupon the shattered remnant impacted with **Norma's** No. 3 engine. The crippled B-24 banked away south, Deeter having decided to head for Switzerland, but this goal was never achieved, as loss of power impelled a bail out while still over German soil.

Great Theory—Practical Near Disaster

Visual "bomb on Leader" aids normally consisted of smoke flares released from the Lead B-24's bomb bay and/or indicator lights below that aircraft's tail turret. At Shipdham, a third variation was experimented with by the 464th Sub-Depot, but this had a potentially lethal conclusion for both the selected bomber, along with T/Sgt. Wolbarst (Senior NCO, bomb sight and autopilot maintenance) and a team headed by S/Sgts. Piela and Goucher (armorers).

Four Verey pistols with cut-down barrels were fitted to a foot-square plate. The firing mechanism involved two

The 8AF's offensive against Germany's synthetic oil industry was to steadily grind it down; the defenses conversely took a steady toll on the attackers. The propensity for the B-24 to catch fire when fuselage fuel feed pipes were punctured is displayed here, with an anonymous bomber exuding a solid mass of flames over Merseburg on 15 August; few if any crewmembers will survive the conflagration.

Three Wendling bombers, one of which is camouflaged, are releasing their loads of what appear to be low-caliber (300lb) bombs; these were often used on airfields, for instance. A smoke marker is partially seen at the bottom of the photo. DC; D+ is a B-24J-1-FO named **We'll Get By**; at top right is B-24H-15-CF /41-28875/DC: H+ **Heavenly Body**.

modified bomb rack releases, which when cocked with a powerful spring and activated electrically would activate the actuating arms that in turn would strike the pistols' firing pins. The selected 68BS bomber had a slot cut in its roof and the plate was then riveted to a longitudinal stringer, with the pistol barrels marginally protruding outside. Wolbarst's feeling that this arrangement was too flimsy brought a tart response from Piela, to the effect that he would not tell Wolbarst how to fix a bomb sight! The armorers strung wire back from the intervalometer to the flare tray's location in the waist and the pistols were loaded and cocked. So far, so good, in theory at least.

When all was ready, Wolbarst, who was up in the nose, began the test. There came a loud bang, followed by a crash of rending metal and hammering on the fuselage mixed up with blood-curdling yells from St. Goucher, who was already outside. Smoke and ricocheting balls of fire filled the interior. It transpired that the weapons' recoil effect had pushed the barrels back inside, where the discharge had occurred; a further effect was that a large section of the surrounding top fuselage was ripped, but all the rapidly-approaching fire truck crew had to do was pour foam onto the smouldering remains. (The control tower had received previous notification of the experiment.) A further unpleasant result from the incident affected those members of the Piela/Goucher team standing out on the wings; they began to suffer intermittent shock effect from their electrical equipment, thanks to conductivity being created by the rain-spattered surfaces!

St. Wolbarst's final recollection from the evening's events was that matters could have been even worse, had even one flare landed in an ammunition box; this was due to the fact that the B-24 was fully bombed and fuelled up, and its likely detonation would have left no survivors. Had this occurred, the fact that the planned mission was subsequently "scrubbed" would have proved all the more tragic.

Clinical Execution

Another deep penetration mission went out next day, with the B-24s getting through to two of the briefed Primaries: Gotha's aircraft industry and an airfield at Erfurt. This time round the "credit" percentage was somewhat increased, but was still moderate at around 40%.

The quality of the German heavy-caliber flak guns was rightly respected,

A beautifully detailed if also risqué piece of artwork decorates the starboard frame of B-24H-15-CF 41-29383/6A: F, based at Rackheath. This bomber served with the 789BS from 11 April until 11 September 1944, before disappearing from Group records.

The angle at which this B-24J-145-CO presents itself to the camera enhances its overall appearance. In mid-1944, a Directive was issued regarding the optional removal of the ball turret, which in this instance has been applied to 44-40242/6X: L **The Hard Way** of the 491BG. Some Groups carried out a comprehensive deletion, with the 445BG rueing their action during the cataclysmic air battle on 27 September.

indeed feared by the Allied bomber crews, and the manner in which the single MIA loss this day was brought about provides a good example of their lethal "art." The 458BG failed to reach its Primary at Eisenach and had split its overall effort between three Targets of Opportunity, with the latter source at Koblenz, where the ultimate failure of the B-24 in question to regain Horsham St. Faith was initiated. Lt. James L. Monohan headed a crew with an average mission tally of eighteen in 42-95117/7V: M **You Can't Take it with You**. Down below in Koblenz were the railway-mounted flak batteries of *3* to *6 Flakabteilung 418* possessing 105- and 128-mm guns, the latter capable of dispatching its shells up to 35,000ft. The formation was established as flying at 24,000ft and the *Kommando-geraet 40* and *Flugmalsi 43* sets provided the precise visual and firing coordinates. *Gruppen* (salvo patterns of fire) were indulged in over some four minutes, with the three 105mm-equipped batteries comprising fourteen individual weapons firing 294 shells per minute. Monohan's bomber sustained a strike on No. 3 engine, but although briefly losing altitude and trailing smoke, it was brought back up and pressed on to the obvious frustration of the gunners below.

In fact, the sentence of execution was only delayed by 20 minutes when the formation was between Aachen and Liege, thanks to a second flak ambuscade from *1* to *4 Schwer-Flakabteilung*, based at Hasselt and equipped with twenty-four 88mm rifles. The now-reduced altitude of 18,000ft was confirmed and the sky around the starboard flank of the formation became speckled with hundreds of bursts, as an individual firing rate of nearly 30 shells per minute over two minutes was sustained. The No. 2 engine on 7V: M exploded and the B-24 commenced a wayward downward path that culminated NW of Hasselt; all nine crewmembers successfully bailed out around 11,000ft, but parachute failure cost S/Sgt. Kenneth S Kenyon (NT) his life. On the other hand, four of the survivors managed to gain access to Belgian Resistance sources.

Oberpfaffenhofen Cull

A clutch of various industrial targets in SE Germany were laid on for the 21st, with the Division assigned Oberpfaffenhofen and Neuraubing, near Munich. The city was to become a Target of Opportunity, while the two Primaries received marginal attention from the 433 bombers dispatched. This mediocre return was more than balanced out by the loss of 22 MIA crews, although one-third became internees. Nine of the losses affected the 14CBW, with the 44BG, 392BG, and 492BG suffering a 4-3-2 relative failure, although four featured within the internee figure.

Two of the Shipdham B-24s came down in enemy territory, both 506BS machines. **Southern Comfort II** (42-95142/GJ: K-Bar) suffered fire in one wing, as well as losing an engine and having part of a stabilizer blown off. The bid for Switzerland was soon realized as doomed, so Lt. Allen bailed out the crew, of which S/Sgt. Kempowicz (ROG) became the sole fatality thanks to parachute failure; the Sergeant had been at Pearl Harbor on 7 December 1941 and had also been involved in a mid-air collision during training, so today's incident was a sad case of "third time unlucky." Fighter-inflicted damage also induced Lt. Butler to consider a southward course, but once again the bid was unsuccessful, although all ten airmen did reach the ground alive from 42-95142/GJ: K-Bar **Cape Cod Special**.

Wendling's three absent crews all joined the 506BS duo on enemy soil. The 579BS surrendered 42-50433/GC: Q-bar, bearing Lt. Richard J. Carey's crew on what was their 7th mission.

Fighter-inflicted damage during the bomb run subsequently caused a departure from the formation SW of Munich and the final crash near Starnberg ended with two dead crewmembers still on board and one of the seven parachutists suffering canopy failure after abandoning the now-burning B-24. The other squadron loss involved 42-52435/GC: P-bar, which was also shot up both by flak and fighters and went down at about the same time. Sgt. Herbert L. Tubbs (TG), on Lt. John F. Menard's team, although last seen donning his pack after bail out was ordered, did not survive, the sole casualty among nine on board; he had sustained injuries from his turret's shattered Plexiglas, but did not seem to be badly injured. The final loss (42-94907/CI: U) witnessed an exact survivor/fatality ratio of 1/8, the lucky exception being S/Sgt. Harrison A. Cuzick (ROG). The bomber descended into the waters of the Ammersee, east of Landsberg, and five of the crew led by Lt. Henry F. Telken were disinterred from the fuselage when it was recovered by the U.S. Army in 1947; the pilot was one of the remaining three bodies found locally and buried at the time of the crash. Cuzick's foot injury, caused by a bullet, resulted in the amputation of five toes, a relatively small price to pay for living through the incident.

The 491BG suffered a quartet of crews failing to return. **Lucky Buck** (42-110158/3Q: I) had its No. 1 engine set on fire, but Lt. Walter Kales managed to evade further fighter assaults by diving down to 12,000ft through the clouds and setting course for the long haul home. After some 45 minutes, the fire, far from being extinguished, had reached a stage where the nacelle and surrounding area were glowing red, while vibration from the engine's "windmilling" propeller was shaking the airframe. Lt. Larry Walker (CP) spilled his canopy after the "bail out" order was given, but managed to gather it up and exit along with Kales at a perilously low altitude, with all nine airmen reaching the ground safely.

Flak knocked out No. 2 engine on 41-28987/, flown by Lt. Earl W. Newton, and even though the bomb load was jettisoned, the B-24 lost pace with the Group. Switzerland became the alternative destination, but it was never reached, especially after No. 3 went "out." A third engine went "out" at the point of bail out, leaving the pilot with what he later described as "a heavy glider"; as it was, only Sgt. John R. Miller (Eng.) failed to survive.

One of the other two casualties did make a successful bid for neutral soil. The saddest individual loss was Lt. Sig Liebfeld, who brought his badly-battered 42-51218 almost home before having to abandon the bomber over the coast. He alone out of the ten airmen did not survive, as he drowned; his gallantry was later recognized through a posthumous Silver Star. Halesworth added one further crew to the 95CBW MIA tally.

A total of eight MIA crews came out of the ranks of the 2nd and 20th CBWs. Of the three 2CBW losses, one involved a 389BG aircraft heading into Switzerland, while the other two came from Old Buckenham; a mid-air collision over the target between 42-95171/ **Diana Mite** and 41-29259/ **Our Baby** resulted in both B-24s going down. The 446BG records declared this mission "a bad day," the heavy cloud patterns causing the Primary to be abandoned in favor of Targets of Opportunity, during which three B-24s were downed. Capt. Eric H. Sherman's 42-100315 **Quivering Box** had two engines knocked out by flak and the final crash left just the pilot and two of his ten-man crew alive. **Maximum Effort** (42-95188) lost two crewmembers after flak administered

This Shipdham B-24H-5-CF 41-29208 transferred in from Seething and flew combat operations between December 1943 and February 1944. The deletion of top and (reportedly) ball turrets was accompanied by the fitting of lights to assist in pre-dawn Group Assembly. The modified nose incorporates a Bell power boost unit drawn from a B-26. The second shot provides a detailed sight of the adaptation. This bomber returned Stateside in March 1945.

A game of volleyball is being conducted by the ground personnel of the 458BG, with one of the RAF "C Type" hangars at Horsham St. Faith as a background; the airman on the right hand side of the net is deftly flicking the ball with a high backhanded motion.

The Falcon was based at Attlebridge and featured a distinctive color pattern around the upper section of the forward fuselage that supplemented the swooping bird as seen here. The B-24H-25-FO was 42-95248/2U:, and she lasted on operations until a crash landing near Shipdham on 8 January rendered her fit only for salvage.

a fatal blow to the bomber and just a single survivor out of ten emerged from 42-51257, which had suffered engine failure, followed by terminal flak strikes. The other Wing losses involved single machines from the 93BG and 448BG, although the latter B-24 did progress as far as Switzerland.

Internee "Harvest"

No less than eight B-24s—all but one from the 2BD—diverted into Switzerland, beginning with a pair from Shipdham. **Channel Hopper** (42-95226/GJ: C-bar) absorbed flak strikes after "bombs away" that led to jammed bomb doors and hydraulic system failure. The former situation was regarded with trepidation by F/O Donald F. Tofte, since it could indicate a hostile intention to the Swiss gunners; on the other hand, the gap acted as a necessary vent for the fuel streaming from punctured tanks. All went well, however, with Swiss fighters picking up the cripple and taking it into Duebendorf, although an overshoot collapsed the nose wheel. A lack of navigation maps for the Swiss area on 42-110049/WQ: A, when coupled to a solid cloud base over northern Switzerland, finally forced Lt. John R. Anderson to bail out the crew from his flak-crippled bomber. S/Sgt. Leo J. Hoffman (LW) suffered parachute failure and his death preyed upon Lt. James A. Hewlett's (N) mind—he felt that had he had the necessary maps, an airfield might have been found upon which to make a landing that would have prevented his colleague's tragic demise.

The North Pickenham duo of internees commenced with 44-40290/, which experienced problems with both starboard engines, leading to excessive fuel consumption and a decision to head for Switzerland, where Lt. William M. Walker put his charge down at Duebendorf. It was followed in by the day's last involuntary "arrival" in the form of 44-10496/X4: Q+, and what was only the second mission for Lt. William H. Wesson's crew. One engine had been knocked out and oil pressure on a second totally lost thanks to flak hits, while fire had momentarily erupted in the bomb bay but was swiftly extinguished. This B-24 also made an uneventful landing at Duebendorf.

Hethel's tithe of one B-24 involved **Ginny Gal** (42-95077/EE: I), flown by Lt. Kay Caldwell. The bomber had suffered overheating in both outboard engines and the intention to bomb the Saarbruecken marshalling yards changed to a run for Switzerland. Although this was successful, the crew were fortunate to escape injury or death; the overshoot on landing resulted in the nose compartment being smashed up after impact with a flak site. Seething's single contribution was Lt. James Beaver's **Little Sheppard** (41-28711) , which ended up with two engines off and propellers "feathered"; the landing at Duebendorf ended with an "overshoot" that still left the landing gear intact. The fourth Metfield MIA crew did make a successful bid for neutral soil after having No. 2 engine set on fire shortly after bombing. Lt. Stanley V. Scott was in charge of 42-95218/3X:, and having been escorted to the Swiss/German border region by P-38s ended up landing at Duebendorf—but not before Swiss gunners opened up with a fortunately inaccurate barrage!

A second 448BG crew completed the mission—but not in England. The loss of both port-side engines on **Dead End Kids** 42-94992) did not prevent completion of the bomb run, but then a course was initially taken up for Switzerland. However, a quick change of plan saw Lt. Melvin Alspaugh's crew making an even more daunting decision—to fly upwards of 400 miles to the Allied lines in Italy. Despite the absence of maps and radio incompatibility with MTO stations, the lengthy flight encountered no opposition

Following the dissolution of the 492BG in early August 1944, the 491BG transferred from Metfield to North Pickenham. The Group's reluctance to adopt their perceived "jinxed" predecessor's black diagonal fin stripe was tacitly acknowledged by retention of the white/green band seen here. A Group bomber is gently orbiting the airfield with twelve dispersed bombers in sight.

and "Sunny Italy" served as the airmen's domicile for upwards of two weeks. The pilot later received Commendations for his action from Gens. Spaatz (CG, USSTAF) and Kepner (CG, 2BD).

Breakout

A momentous advance in the Normandy Land Campaign was looming up as the month drew to a close. The American-held western sector was where a primary breakout of 1st Army armor, with supporting infantry and artillery units, was to be launched. An essential precondition for this was the USAAF heavy and medium bombers would be used to literally blast away the German defenses south of St. Lo, thereby allowing the ground forces to surge south into Brittany, as well as swinging round to the east.

The first day of operation *Cobra* activity in the air was the 24th. Over the previous 48 hours, the bulk of the "heavies" had remained idle at their airfields; the use of a proportion to carry out *G-H* guided assaults on several French airfields (23rd) had resulted in nil losses for the 2BD, at least. Now, as the 24th dawned, a massive force of nearly 1,600 B-17s and B-24s were mustered for the assault upon the German 7th Army positions. In the event, only about one-third of the number sent out actually bombed due to ground haze conditions that bore the risk of the bomb loads falling into the American front lines, which were very close to the briefed bomb line. Even so, some fatal casualties were incurred thanks to "short bombing" incidents. Losses were very light at one B-17 and two B-24s, one of the latter coming from the ranks of the 489BG.

A marginally greater force was dispatched next day, which saw immeasurably more severe punishment visited upon the enemy positions, but also with an even more tragic "own goal" within the American lines. This time round the bombers' approach was parallel to the front lines, but in spite of this adjustment to the previous day's bomb runs, which had been made at right angles to the front lines, a greater scale of self-inflicted tragedy now occurred, when just over 100 soldiers, including Gen. Leslie McNair, were killed and several hundred wounded by bomb loads going astray. Four B-24s were lost, one of which was the 445BG's 42-95192/RN:, flown by Lt. Ben W. Long, who was one of three POW survivors out of nine on board. **Miss Shirley** (42-50478/HP: T) was another flak victim whose crew, led by Lt. Frank Schwerin (POW), was split between six POWs, three evaders, and one fatality (Lt. Werner H. Floyd (CP). The second Hethel loss was 42-95026/HP: I **Yankee Rebel**, with a similar split in individual fortune; Lt. Roe (P) was one of five evaders, while T/Sgt. Bill Owings (Eng.) was the sole fatality among the rest of the crew. Finally, the 489BG surrendered 42-94852, flown by Lt. John J. Slein; only Lt. Harold J. Morse (CP) escaped alive from among the ten on board.

The pace of operations over 26/28 July was much reduced, with the 2BD only participating on the latter date, when V-1 sites were hit by six Groups. Then it was back to the strategic brief for the penultimate and final month's strikes. Oil refineries were up for assault on the 9th, in the Division's case the facility at Bremen/Oslebshausen. No direct MIA casualties were incurred by the force of over 470, but two 44BG bombers were "written off" during Assembly. As the Group was crossing out over Cromer, Lt. Bernard J. Eberhardt, Jr.'s 42-95309/NB: V was No. 3 in the squadron's second element, while Lt. William F. Green, flying 42-109820/NB: N, was No. 3 in the Low left element. A left hand turn saw the latter element slide under the Eberhardt element, while his bomber suddenly drooped downwards. The resultant impact of Eberhardt's No. 2 propeller with the other B-24's rear fuselage literally sawed that section off and cast NB: N into an uncontrollable spin; NB: V. went into a flat spin and also headed down towards the ever-hungry North Sea, which swallowed up its twin prey, along with all but one of the nineteen airmen. S/Sgt. Alva F. Favors (Eng.), on Eberhardt's bomber, had anticipated the collision and snapped on his pack, but was still fortunate to escape the terminal clutch of centrifugal forces and get clear.

Munich was selected on the 31st for the B-17 Divisions, while the 2D went to Ludwigshafen in full strength; by the day's end, just six crews out of 486 did not settle back onto their airfields. Three came from the ranks of the 489BG, two of which were involved in a mid-air collision. Two-thirds of Lt. Wallace J. Bishop's crew, including himself, did not survive the loss of 41-28818/4R: V, which crashed at Dudweiler, near Saarbruecken, while Lt. Frank A. Palmer managed to end up a POW after his **Lethal Linda** (42-94776/T4:) was taken down, the reported cause being a mid-air collision.

Hethel's 41-28778/YO: N bore Maj. Andy Low (453BG Operations Officer, acting as Mission Pilot) and Lt. Bob Lamb's crew. Flak set the PFF aircraft's bomb bay and starboard wing on fire and it dropped down to starboard, with at least four parachutists reported at debriefing. The pilots had attempted to extinguish the flames by diving, but this failed and the resultant bail out order saw all but two crewmembers out of thirteen surviving. The 446BG lost **Hula Wahine II** (42-52467), along with three crewmembers.

The 458BG suffered its latest casualty on the way in, when 42-95116/Z5: V **Junior** failed to reach adult "status." A flak shell impacted with the nose section and the bomb load began to spill out after the B-24 canted sharply to one side, then entered a spinning motion that ended with a crash on the river Rhine's right bank at Mannheim. This was Lt. Rudolf A. Naumann and his crew's fifth mission, but the granting of continued life only came the way of the pilot and three of his nine colleagues.

High Summer Acceleration (August 1944)

The pace of 8AF bomber operations over the first eighteen days of August witnessed a daily deployment, with tactical missions only just inching ahead of those falling into the "strategic" category during the period. The initial impetus of the Normandy breakout on the Allies' western flank was being maintained by the U.S. Army, with Gen. Patton's armored columns setting the pace. Meanwhile, the British/Canadian forces on the eastern flank of the bridgehead were also advancing, albeit at a more staccato rate—not very surprising, given the presence of the bulk of the German armor and artillery in this sector of their overall defensive front.

French airfields and bridges were pounded (1st) and a double header next day involved the 2BD attacking V-1 sites on the second mission. The single MIA loss suffered by the 453BG on the first day did not, as ever, reflect the overall casualty rate. Three further B-24s crashed or crash landed on the 1st, with four more similarly affected next day. A double header (3rd) involved the 1BD going further afield to attack German marshalling yards, while the other two Divisions dispatched reduced-scale forces to tactical targets on the first occasion; adverse weather prevented the B-24s from striking their Primaries, so Targets of Opportunity were struck, albeit by just one-third of the dispatched numbers. The second day's foray continued the tactical pressure, with assaults upon V-1 sites, the Division being involved in both activities. This time round five bombers were "written off" in all, of which only one was lost over enemy territory: Metfield's 44-40241/, flown by Lt. Marshall W. Field being the B-24 in question, with flak the executioner.

A range of targets falling into the aircraft and oil production industries located in northern Germany were visited on the 4th, with the 2BD allotted four Primaries between Kiel and Rostock, on the Baltic. The extended time over the Nazi hinterland indicated a strong defensive response, but the overall 8AF loss of sixteen crews among the 1,186 completing their missions proved very acceptable, in crude statistical terms. Two of the four

The weather conditions over East Anglia are remarkably clear, and Assembly for the 446BG among other Groups aloft today should present little problem. The bomber in the foreground is 42-50814, a B-24J-5-FO serving with the 706BS whose aircraft letter changed to F; it survived the conflict and returned Stateside.

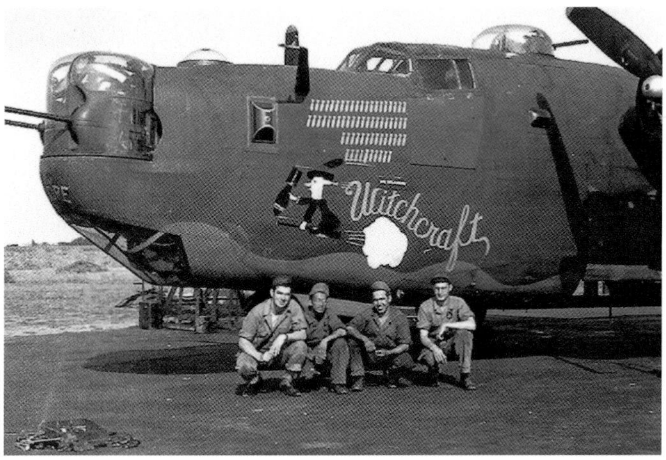

This B-24H-15-FO was a 467BG "original" that was to grow into a Group legend. It was to become the charge of M/Sgt. Joe Ramirez and crew and would amass a staggering total of 130 missions with no recorded "aborts." She is seen here with some 86 mission "bombs" recorded, and her entire combat career was with the 790BS while bearing the aircraft letter M.

Division losses involved the 20CBW, beginning with Bungay's 41-29137, which was part of the sub-force attacking a torpedo production plant at Kiel; the bomber was flak-stricken and went down, along with three of her ten-man crew. The Low left squadron Lead for the 448BG was Lt. Briola's 42-50648, which was adjudged to be too flak-damaged to risk the homeward flight and was turned towards and successfully gained access to Sweden's neutral soil. A duo of North Pickenham crews completed the loss register. Later in the day, a small force of B-24s under G-H guidance from the 93BG assaulted V-1 sites and gun batteries in the Pas de Calais without loss.

Brunswick's Tithe

Six aero-production plants based in, and in one case near Brunswick were the Division's targets next day; the bulk of the Full Division force of 452 bombers struck all the Primaries, but left seven B-24s behind either on the Continent, or in three instances under the North Sea. The MIA casualties affected four of the five CBWs, the 14CBW alone returning unscathed.

The 96CBW surrendered three B-24s, including a pair from the 467BG. The formation was just departing the target area when flak struck home against the veteran 41-29363/6A: B, in Lt. Willard A. Langenfeld's hands; all ten crewmembers bailed out, but only the pilots and one Enlisted man made it through to a *Stalag*, the others assumed to have died at the hands of the German military or civilian population. The second MIA crew were on board 42-95162/4Z: U **Perils of Pauline**, which had dropped out of formation with heavy flak damage. A bail out order was finally given, but the bomber's entry into a spin probably trapped seven of the nine-man crew, since only Lt. David E. Love (P) and one other airman reached the ground alive.

The other two losses over land affected the 389th and 446th BGs. Lt. Everett R. Schieven's crew were on their 28th mission, but the Grim Reaper applied his scythe to seven of the ten airmen after 42-95184/HP: P was taken down by flak; the pilot was one of the fortunate trio to escape with his life. Lt. John C. Clausing and crew had arrived at Bungay in late April and commenced operations the following month. By early August, two from among this team were flying with other crews, while one had completed his combat tour. Today, the crew were part of the force of 85 heading for Fallersleben, one of six Primaries assigned the 2BD. Target flak knocked out No. 2 engine and ruptured the fuel system, leaving **Carolyn Sue** (42-95190/) a straggler and ripe for fighter attention. This arrived in the shape of a Bf109, whose gunfire crippled No. 3, set the starboard wing on fire, and killed Sgts. Joseph Russell (ROG) and Seymour Schonmaker (BT). One of the waist gunners was so badly wounded in one leg that it was later amputated, but he joined the other eight in making a parachute descent.

"Ditching" Variations

The vagaries ever attendant with "ditching" any aircraft, let alone a design as structurally "fragile" as the B-24, were demonstrated today; as events transpired, the survival rate on two of the three B-24s put down in the North Sea was gratifyingly high. All ten of Lt. Morgan C. Higham's crew manning Halesworth's 42-94829/T4: J **Bomb Baby** got out alive, and Lt. James B. Prevost nearly bucked the same odds, losing one crewmember in the process. The apparently undamaged bomber began to manifest engine problems after departing the enemy coastline, which culminated in the loss of 50% power on his ironically-titled **Tailwind** (41-29359/J3: J); worse still was the discovery that only 100 gallons of fuel remained with 40 miles to go to the English coast. The decision to "ditch" the 458BG bomber became mandatory when the remaining two engines "quit." The resultant impact with the sea caused the still-intact airframe to stop in a nose-down attitude, but only Lt. Allen Boorse, Jr. (CP) failed to emerge; the prompt arrival of an ASR vessel ensured that exposure to the generally swift-numbing North Sea waters would not claim any of the nine survivors.

No such total or majority of good fortune came the way of the remaining "ditching" candidate. Lt. Donald Ginevan set course for home in the 448BG's **Lonesome Lou** (41-29465/), but the bid to bring his flak-damaged charge back safely ended in disaster for he and all but two of his crew after the attempt failed; the ASR vessels that plucked the survivors out also provided the same service for the 489BG crew, whose "ditching" location was coincidentally close by.

The Higham crew's total survival is all the more amazing, because the term "ditching" is a clear misnomer in their case—in fact, they all bailed out. In the case of at least four crewmembers, the spot where they descended was right in the path of a Royal Navy MTB, which having been part of a force heading for the Dutch coast, had been ordered back to port after suffering partial engine failure! The pilot's survival was equally miraculous; he was immersed for up to two hours and a fog bank was fast closing in when the same MTB appeared to pick him up. Four of the other five were fished out by vessels likely responding to the "Mayday" containing details of the B-24's position. The tenth was Lt. Davis (B), whose fate was nearly sealed when the parachute canopy settled over him and he was forced to cut himself free. Even then, his partially inflated "Mae West" was rapidly failing when a fishing boat very fortuitously appeared.

Hamburg's Tithe

A clutch of five oil refinery sites in and around Hamburg, along with Kiel Naval Base appeared on next day's Briefing maps, when the full Divisional strength was again mustered; all the Primaries were duly assaulted at a similar MIA cost to Brunswick (8), which was again spread among four of the five CBWs. The 96CBW surrendered a consecutive daily trio of crews, of which two were

The rangy figure of Jimmy Stewart is caught on camera as he is talking to a newly-returned combat crewmember at Hethel. Far from being a "celluloid warrior" like one or two of his Hollywood contemporaries, he completed at least twenty missions and ended up a Lt/Col. and Chief of Staff within the 2AD HQ hierarchy.

Ms. "Birdie" Schmidt, an American Red Cross staff member at Wendling, with three ground crew stands by the very fine artwork devoted to her. It is applied to B-24H-25-CF/42-50387/CI: T, which was destined to complete 62 missions up to 15 February 1945. On that date Lt. Gene R. Hubbartt's aircraft developed engines problems that culminated with all nine bailing out into fairly short-term captivity.

from Rackheath's ranks. The Wing's specific target was the Rhenania/Ossag plant, but the flak gunners took out 41-29421/ 4Z: P+ **Wallowing Wilbert** on the bomb run; following a direct strike on the starboard wing the aircraft disintegrated and only three on Lt. George J. Kotraba's (KIA) team survived.

The "bombs away" signal was scant seconds distant when flak strikes mortally damaged 41-29373/6A: **The Monster/Flak Magnet** (another tragically-titled bomber); this time round all but one on Lt. Damian J. Murray's crew bailed out safely. An individual tragedy also affected Lt. Charles E. White's team; 42-95224/Q2: C **Lonely Heart** returned to base without Lt. Roy L. Doole (CP), who had fallen from the bomb bay while the formation was over the North Sea on the outward leg.

Horsham St. Faith's Lead crew, led by Lt. Tom Hancock, was supplemented by Capt. John E. Chamberlain (Asst. Group Ops. Officer); their mount was 42-100433/J3; B **Big Dick, Hard to Hit**—yet another inappropriately-named bomber. This B-24 was taken out by flak almost simultaneously with its 467BG contemporary. Chamberlain recollected fire breaking out; then, just as he released his seat belt to gain a more detailed sight, the bomber flipped over, throwing him onto the flight deck along with Hancock. The latter got up and tried to open the escape hatch, while Chamberlain felt himself propelled toward the burning bomb bay and almost immediately passed out, coming to in mid-air and pulling his ripcord. Nearing the ground, he sighted Hancock wading out of a pond, hands above his head, but being shot at by a group of Germans. Fire was also directed at John as he came down, but neither officer was hit, to become the sole survivors out of twelve on board.

A second unit suffering double losses was the 448BG. Flak struck home on 42-51104/, and the scale of damage was sufficient for Lt. Mauro Selva Della to ring the bail out bell. Lt. Mike Halpern (CP) suffered a failed parachute and was very fortunate to pull open the cover, especially since the life saving equipment was in the form of a backpack; his descent was not helped by ground fire, which punctured his "Mae West" and damaged the canopy, but surprisingly left him uninjured; he descended into the sea, but was soon hauled out. Lt. Huntingdon Gruening's 41-28945/ **No Nothing** was similarly assailed and heavily damaged by the flak gunners; he turned his bomber northwards towards Sweden, where the B-24 was subsequently set down at Sovde, doubling up Seething's contribution to the 8AF's Northern internee list within the last 48 hours.

The 44BG's Lt. James P. McKenna (KIA) was flying deputy Lead for the 492BG in 42-95561/QK: I+, but was momentarily forced out of position in order to avoid a collision. The downward angle was quickly corrected, but before position could be resumed a tracking flak pattern struck home. Fire caught hold in the bomb bay, but even so, Lt. Tucker (Pilotage Navigator) bailed out through the compartment, being one of two surviving officers out of six; conversely, only one of the six Enlisted men failed to get out.

Wendling's casualty was 42-50604/ DC: B+, flown by Lt. James H. Beatty, which left the formation over the target after suffering flak damage. The bomber progressed no further homewards than Stade, west of Hamburg, when the bail out signal was given. Eight airmen got out and down alive, but Sgt. Earl J. Berquist (ROG), although last seen alive around the bomb bay, became the ever-sad exception. Halesworth provided the eighth MIA statistic when 42-94945/T4: **Cover Girl**, flown by Lt. Mark T. Osborne and Lt. Jack R. Kennedy (CP), was taken out; both pilots survived as POWs. The day's casualties included two 492BG crews who collided while on final approach at North Pickenham.

An easier-paced run in duration (7th) involved tactical support, when fuel dumps and bridges in France and Belgium were targeted with no MIA Divisional cost—but this was no consolation for eight Rackheath airmen on board the still bomb-laden 42-52565/6A: K-bar in Lt. Harold R. Chilver's hands, as the formation returned from bombing an oil storage depot in Ghent, Belgium. The No. 1 engine propeller was "feathered" and a fatal stall developed while the B-24 was in the landing circuit. The crash, just east of the airfield at Salhouse, killed the pilot and seven of his eight-man crew, St. Ray L. Finch (G) being miraculously thrown clear.

Tactical/strategic See-Saw

The ensuing week of 8AF operations saw a see-saw pattern of tactical and strategic-oriented missions. A joint 2nd/3rd BD force headed across the Channel (8th) to blitz four French airfields, as well as adding the latest counter-thrust to the V-1 offensive by bombing the launch sites. To the single MIA loss borne by the 44BG was added a second bomber destroyed after "aborting" the mission; both belonged to the 506BS. Lt. Komasinski and crew were on their seventh mission, but Fate was to deal out a generous card for all ten airmen. A "runaway" propeller on No. 2 engine as the formation headed for La Perthe airfield was followed by a second engine going "out," and when last seen a third engine was reported as being on fire. The autopilot on 42-100415/GJ: Y-bar **My Peach** was finally applied and all the crew bailed out successfully—not only that, but nine of them evaded capture. Pilots landing back with a failed engine were constantly adjured never to dip into a turn with the affected motor or motors on the lowered wing. For whatever reason, when Lt. Myron G. Jacobs, having "aborted" in 42-50328/GJ: D **Pregnant Peg/Flying Log**, did so while in the airfield circuit, the result was a stall and explosive impact with the ground that nobody survived.

Lt. John McClane, a 68BS navigator, recalled that it was probably this crash site that he ventured upon, and what he witnessed would still appal him decades after. The pilots were still strapped into their seats, but their limbs were burned to stumps and body frames rendered charcoal black. Attempts to pull one of them free ended with the torso literally falling apart "like an over-done roast," in John's words. An intact glove picked up was hastily dropped when John realized it contained a hand. Finally, as he walked around the site, one of the bomb disposal team said: "Look what you are standing on, Governor" (the team was British)—this was the top of a skull cleanly cut off at the hairline! Here was an oft-repeated example of the "Clean Air War" that many soldiers or sailors of all nationalities imagined aerial combat to be.

The intended "deep penetration" run to a ball bearings plant at Stuttgart/Sindelfingen next day was thwarted by increasingly banked cloud patterns that forced a "recall" signal for the Division, but not before a high percentage had unloaded on the Secondary choice of Saarbruecken's already sorely-battered marshalling yards on the way back. Three of the four MIA crews came out of the 96CBW, two from the 466BG. Capt. Harry P. McGregor was in charge of one Attlebridge casualty (42-95268/2U: K+). The formation was heading homeward when a flak strike set No. 3 engine ablaze, followed swiftly by the starboard wing separating to cast the bomber into a spin; the pilot and nine of the ten-man crew lost their lives in the gyrating aircraft descent near Puttlingen. Lt. Ernest A. Keyes' flak-afflicted 41-29374 eased down and out of formation and ended up being put down on Dutch soil outside Rotterdam, an action that led to two deaths, including the pilot, out of ten.

The third loss involved the 458BG's **Heavenly Body** (41-28942/Z5: U), with Lt. Evert R. Thompson and crew. Flak had reportedly damaged the B-24 some time prior to its final disappearance around Saarbruecken, upon which its load was released; all nine airmen got out safely and the lack of a definite crash site supported the evidence that a mid-air explosion had widely scattered the airframe's remnants. The 445BG's 42-78483/MK: A-bar, bearing Lt. William L. Howell's crew, had suffered battle damage and finally crashed; the pilot and three other airmen were killed, two ended up as POWs, and three evaded capture. A second Tibenham bomber crash landed at Theberton on return, but delivered its crew to a safe conclusion.

Six B-24 groups, all but one from the 2BD, provided the sole heavy bomber activity (10th) when a mix of fuel dumps and bridges SE of Paris were targeted. A 448BG crew led by Lt. Parmley Ferrie, flying in 41-28648, were fortunate to regain Allied lines at Caen after the bomber suffered flak damage during target approach; the crew abandoned their charge and floated down safely, although one airman broke a leg. Three CBWs went out 24 hours later to attack marshalling yards and fuel damps located in Strasbourg and Saarbruecken and came back three light.

The 453BG casualty was 42-110089/F8, flown by Lt. Warren D. Freed, which nearly made it home, but was "ditched" scant miles short of North Foreland; unfortunately, only three crewmembers emerged alive from the incident. Metfield's 44-10492/, flown by Lt. Charles H. Christian, took a flak strike that removed No. 4 engine propeller and soon forced the switching off and "feathering" of No. 3. Height and speed was steadily lost. However, although reports at debriefing spoke of nine "objects" dropping away from the B-24, it turned out not to be the crew, and in fact the bomber was landed safely, albeit in enemy-held territory, with the pilot at least evading capture. The remaining crew was a 489BG team in 42-94785/T4: N **Struggle Buggy**, flown by Lt. Maynard W. Kisinger. Flak strikes that disabled two engines and punctured fuel tanks would seem to have made the decision to head from Saarbruecken to Switzerland a highly problematical one; however, the German defenses were breached and the ailing B-24 finally put down at Duebendorf.

The drip feed of MIA losses was sustained on the 12th, when four airfields in eastern France were targeted and reached by virtually all the 276 crews dispatched. The 466BG had its ranks reduced by two crews for the second time in 72 hours; one of these was 41-29413/6L: T-bar **Our Baby**, which was "ditched" 40 miles off the Dutch coast, with seven crewmembers getting through the ever-fraught experience alive. They were joined by a 506BS crew from Shipdham led by Lt. Thomas J. McGuire (KIA). On the way back from Juvincourt airfield, he called in to say he was short of fuel and turning back. The bomber (42-110024/GJ; P-bar **Ole Cock**) finally came down near Pont L'Eveque, in between Le Havre and Caen, to leave seven survivors, two of whom not only avoided incarceration in a *Stalag*, but were freed by advancing British/Canadian troops before the month's end.

Support Duties

The full Divisional strength was out on the 13th to provide ground support for the Anglo-American troops, which took the form of striking at highway "bottlenecks" and coastal batteries. Less than 20 of the 466-strong force failed to strike their targets, but once again there was a small but painful tithe to be yielded in the form of five MIA crews spread equally between five Groups. Shipdham lost its second B-24 within 24 hours as the Wing attacked roads between Le Havre and Rouen. The 506BS' 42-95150/GJ: B-bar **Passion Pit** was zeroed-in upon by flak during the protracted bomb run, resulting in two engines being disabled and fire catching hold in the fuselage. Lt. Miliken's crew all exited their doomed mount which subsequently blew apart. The crew were on their third-last mission prior to reaching their revised target of 33, but unknown to them was that this requirement had been reduced by one—after they took off! The pilot was captured, but unlike his crew did later escape from the lorry that was transporting them eastwards, albeit during the night; after wandering for four days he ran into a Canadian Army unit.

One of two 96CBW losses involved the 467BG's 42-52530/4Z: J+ **Bugs Bunny**, which was hit by flak in the bomb bay and starboard wing as the bomb run was progressing. The inevitable weakening of the airframe in these circumstances saw the bomber split in two, followed by the nose section spinning and then disintegrating. Lts. Charles J. Leyes (P) and Myles E. Coolidge (CP) were thrown clear and even then, the former airman was fortunate enough to hang onto his still unclipped pack and attach it before pulling the ripcord. Their fortune was not shared by the remaining eight crewmembers. The other casualty came from the 466BG. Flak struck home on 42-52529/U8: B **Sullys Saloon/Wild Princess**, which came down at Orival, leaving Lt. Dick S. Wollstein and two others dead, three facing captivity, and four evading capture.

Metfield's latest casualty was 42-50572/, which was bearing a 30-mission crew led by Lt. Herbert G. Rock. Flak struck home over Le Havre, bringing the B-24 down in flames, but all the crew evacuated safely, while the pilot was at least one of the team who evaded capture. (By this stage of the Normandy Campaign, the Allied ground advance was rapidly approaching the area around Le Havre, thereby enhancing a speedy return to freedom for any combat crew fortunate enough to evade capture.) Today's loss list was completed by a crew from Hardwick. The final day of this week's varying operations witnessed death and destruction within the Division ranks, displaying a sadly brief absence, as nearly 400 crews headed out to attack several airfields in France.

A Welcome Operational Break?

The current daily involvement of the 8AF bombers was to extend over three of the ensuing four days before Mother Nature intervened with a five-day spell of adverse weather conditions that effectively grounded the B-17s and B-24s. Whether the combat crews welcomed this was debatable; set against the immediate relaxation from strain at the thought of completing missions was the fact that their combat tours were being held in abeyance and their enforced "grounding" only prolonged this primary factor's (hopefully) successful conclusion.

This short operational spell commenced badly for the 466BG, which sustained all four Divisional MIA losses (15th) when attacking one of four airfields in western Germany, during which the *Jagdwaffe* was quite active for the first time in weeks. The Group was tracking between Meppel and the eastern fringe of the Ijsselmeer in Holland when some 20 Bf109s from III/JG53 *Pik As* and II/JG5 *Eismeer* struck. The casualty list involved four B-24s, beginning with 41-29449/U8: **True Love**, flown by Lt. John Archer, which was reported as exploding in mid-air with the fragments falling near Steenwijk, which now became an epicenter for the relatively brief but frenetic air combat. **Lady Lightning** 42-52597T9: M was in Lt. John Suchio's hands; the pilot and two of his colleagues did not survive the final impact between Wepserveen and Nijensleek.

Also taken down was 41-28932/6L: E **Ramblin' Wreck**, in Lt. Robert L. Harrington's charge, and 42-95127, flown by Lt. Verdun W. Monroe. The former machine descended near Giethoorn, while Nijetrijne/Friesland formed the last resting place for

This B-24H-15-FO assigned to the 392BG is 42-50433/GC: Q-bar; the bomber presents a superb image against a stratus cloud layer, a weather condition that if repeated over the target will provide the basis for a sound bombing strike. This aircraft was lost on 21 July 1944, when three on Lt. Richard J. Carey's nine-man crew were killed during a mission to Oberpfaffenhofen.

The transfer of the 491BG into the 14CBW to replace the disbanded 492BG did not result in the Metfield-based Group changing its green/white tail markings for that of the black diagonal band pattern borne by its predecessor. Although the Z Group letter was taken on board, it has been reversed in this picture taken on 24 August 1944.

Munroe's bomber. Harrington and one other crewmember ended up in the hands of the Steenwijk-based Resistance to begin a prolonged but successful eight-month stay until northern Holland was liberated.

The B-24s ventured deeper into Germany next day to bomb aviation and oil-related sources in the Magdeburg area. The Grim Reaper reappeared to hack down seven crews, one of which was a 489BG bomber taken out by "friendly" bombs from another Group machine. The 2CBW lost four crews in all. Lt. Yoders was one of seven fatalities after flak brought down 42-109795/HP: Q over Dessau. Tibenham's 42-51098/RN: _ claimed the lives of all nine on Lt. Joe Gustella's team, while Capt. Thurston Carlisle and all but one of his eight colleagues tasted the bitter and fatal seeds of defeat in 42-52447/RN: _. Lt. Milton A. Stanchfield was one of four from Old Buckenham who did not survive the downing by flak of 42-10138/F8: +. Single losses were borne by the other three CBWs. (The 95CBW had been disbanded two days previous, with the 489BG and 491BG reassigned to the 20th and 14th CBWs, respectively.)

The 448BG contingent was flying High right slot within the 93BG's formation and lost 42-50459/**St. Louis Woman** over Magdeburg; none of the ten-man crew led by Lt. John Buxton appeared to stand much chance of escaping from the flames that engulfed the fuselage and both wings, but Cpl. Leo Stephens (TG) alone achieved this goal. Fortune was equally cruel to all ten of Lt. G. H. Miller's crew flying in Rackheath's 42-50481/X7: I; the flak strike split the B-24 in two and the personnel were either ejected without their packs or pinned down within their aerial tomb by centrifugal forces. This was only one of two Group losses today. Finally, the solitary 20CBW loss emerged from the ranks of the 489BG.

The Perils of Practice

Lt. William V. Prewitte was a combat-experienced pilot at Rackheath, whose operational expertise had actually been honed while serving with the recently-disbanded 492BG. During his time at North Pickenham, he had survived bailing out into the North Sea. Now, on 16 August, he was participating in a Group practice sortie in 42-50580/X7:, which was also a transfer from his former Group. What should have been a mundane flight verging on the boring was destined to be tragically transformed in an instant.

The trigger switch for one of the top turret guns on 41-28981/4Z: V+ **Wolves Inc.** fused, causing the weapon to discharge itself, despite the gunner's desperate bid to twist the ammunition belt. The spray of bullets lanced into Prewitte's B-24J at the starboard wing/fuselage junction and set the bomber on fire. The bulk of the crew were believed to have jumped before their mount began to inexorably descend, finally breaking up and exploding just above the sea—no place for a parachute descent any time of the year.

The ASR Service was contacted as some of the formation circled the crash site. It was gratifying in these circumstances, as the eventual arrival of a launch found some of the submersed airmen still alive to be fished out, but only five out of eleven gained this salvation and Prewitte was not among them—the ever-cruel North Sea had won out the second time round in his case. The incident also stressed the harsh fact that danger lurked every moment one was close to or on board what was an ever-volatile piece of aerial hardware.

Enforced Operational Pause

The penultimate mission before the mid-month weather break that again caused operations to cease (17th) was itself a virtual "washout" thanks to the conditions aloft; only ten B-24s actually took off, none of whom discharged their loads over the assigned French bridge.

Clear weather next day saw the Division dispatching ten Groups, with nearly all the 256 assigned crews unloading on four airfields between Nancy and Metz. Unknowingly ahead of the personnel lay five days of operational inactivity, but this prospect was never to be savored by four on Lt. Roger L. Leister's crew. Fuel starvation when scant miles distant from Rackheath led to 42-50439/X7: J **Broad and High** making a heavy crash landing at Kirby Bedon that resulted in the fuselage fracturing behind the wings. To the four deaths were added three seriously injured airmen from the five survivors. (Aircraft and crew had both transferred from the disbanded 492BG.)

Much more fortunate were the 458BG crews on 44-40281/J4: Q **A Dog's Life** and the deputy Lead B-24 after prop wash forced the listed machine to lift up and strike its companion; not only did both aircraft survive the impact, but the deputy Lead machine completed the bomb run despite a badly-mangled port wing section; **A Dog's Life**'s crew were thwarted in their attempt to bomb, and having jettisoned the load headed back to a landing at RAF Manston, the southernmost Emergency Landing Airfield of three on England's east coast. A second Group bomber 42-95316/J3: N **Princess Pat** lost two engines to flak and diverted into an Allied fighter strip in France.

Normal Service Resumed

The five-day spell of inactivity, although welcomed by the combat crews, would not necessarily have brought equal respite for the ground crews. Instead, here was an opportunity to bring each unit's combat-ready complement of aircraft up to the maximum possible level. The results of their endeavors seems clear, in that the number of rostered aircraft on hand (1,319) when operations resumed on the 24th was way above the figures for the several missions flown up to the 18th—anything up to 40%, in fact.

Nearly one-third of this figure (433) was provided by the 2BD, which was dispatched to bomb aircraft production plants at Brunswick and Hannover, as well as Misburg's synthetic oil facilities. (The latter target would loom large and tragically negative within the 491BG's ranks the following November.) As with the B-17 sub-forces, almost all the 2BD crew gained access to their Primaries at a cost of five out of the overall 8AF total of 26 crews failing to return.

The flak barrage over Langenhagen cost the 44BG its first assigned Natural-Metal-Finish (NMF) B-24, 44-40098/WQ: B **Lone Ranger**. The No. 4 engine on Lt. Arthur H. Dittmar's bomber was knocked out and the fuselage set on fire. All on board vacated the doomed machine, but the pilot and Sgt. Gasperetti (RW) were never to get as far as a *Stalag*, being lined up and shot by a civilian mob. Hethel's single MIA statistic presented a happier picture for Lt. Horace van Heusen's crew on 42-50649/EE: I. The bomber was last seen easing out of the Brunswick-bound formation as it crossed in south of Cuxhaven. The next confirmation of the airmen's fate was from a Swedish source, the B-24 having successfully diverted in that country's direction.

Solo Group losses were recorded for the remaining casualties, beginning with Seething's contribution, which expired over the Group's Brunswick/Waggum target. Lt. Douglas Morse's 42-95812/IO: was the aircraft in question, with the pilot and three of the other nine losing their lives. The 20CBW also lost **Pistol Packin' Bomma II** (42-51278), which received a direct flak hit shortly after "bombs away"; nine of the Bungay-based crew were killed, and only Lts. Ralph E. Maier (P) and Lester Trump (CP) got out alive to become POWs.

Lts. Emanuel Silver (P) and Myron G. Smith (CP) on 42-99949/GO: were seriously injured by flak fragments. The latter airman's neck injury was initially judged to be mortal, but the sub-zero temperature proved his savior, since it cauterized the wound. Meanwhile, Lt. Charles Blackwell (B) took over the controls on the 93BG aircraft and guided it back to an emergency landing on an RAF airfield, where Smith was whisked away for hospitalization. The bombardier was later awarded the DFC for his actions.

Murder Most Foul

The final downed B-24 belonged to the 491BG and the circumstances in which six of Lt. Norman J. Rogers's crew lost their lives provides a gruesome example of Nazi "summary justice." The Group's target was Langenhagen, over which a flak strike on 42-1100107/6X: **Wham Bam**'s starboard wing resulted in smoke streaming from No. 1 engine; the crippled bomber was last seen dropping down and the impression was that the crew had an even chance of survival. As it was, all on board safely abandoned their charge and landed on the ground, where they were soon rounded up for what should have been the start of their Kriegy existence...but not so for six among their ranks.

Ruesselsheim is an industrial city just south of Frankfurt and almost 200 miles distant from Hannover. The eight airmen had been transported as far as here, and for whatever reason were being escorted on foot through the city streets when a crowd of civilians assembled and initially began to harangue them verbally. Matters then turned violent, as bricks and similar items were pitched against them. The party only had two guards on hand, one of whom advised them to start running, since he and his companion felt unable to hold their fellow citizens at bay. A chase began that culminated in the airmen being cornered.

Over the next few minutes, Lt. Rogers and his companions were assailed by a rain of heavy objects that ended with the angry mob satisfied all life had been expunged; the bodies were then dumped in a nearby cemetery. As it was, two of the crew were still alive and after the scene had been vacated by the mob they made good their escape and had the good fortune to end up in official hands for standard process and ultimate transfer to a *Stalag*. After the war, a number of the perpetrators were arraigned before a U.S. military court with several sentenced to death and the others given varied prison terms.

Continued Operational Switch

The 24th signalled a four-day sequence of strategic category missions. Next day, the Division combat personnel faced an extended run to the Baltic region to assault aircraft component plants, while a small force made a separate mission to chemical production sources in Belgium and France. The same loss scale (five) was borne off the initial mission, during which nearly all the 435 crews gained "credit." Rostock's Heinkel aero-engine factory was attacked by 35 Group bombers, but the 446BG formation landed back two light. **Happy Go Lucky** (42-52772/) crashed into the North Sea, killing all ten on Lt. Fred Minck's crew; it was assumed that the B-24 suffered engine failure, according to Group records.

A second bomber (42-51086/ RT:) went down over enemy territory, killing four out of the eleven-man team, including Lt. John W. Simon (P), the others being taken prisoner. Also noted was the end of a proud record for **Ronnie** (41-29144/FL: P), which had to date flown 79 missions without "aborting." The reason for turning back today was adjudged to have been down to engine problems. Named for a crewmember (Sgt. Ronnie Gannon) who contracted polio and died during Stateside training, the bomber would successfully advance to the 119-mission mark by the end of hostilities.

The 458BG headed for Luebeck, but reached the target area one short. The Island of Sylt, level with the western Danish/German border, threw up a flak barrage that landed strikes on the starboard wing of 42-110184/J3: F **Gwen**. The resultant fire that blossomed forth and spread itself into the fuselage caused Lt. Francis H. Morris to tip his bomber into a dive in a vain attempt at extinguishing the flames, so the bail out order was given. Most of the crew were observed to jump before a spin developed that swiftly culminated in the bomber's disintegration and crash SW of Leck. The six survivors out of the nine-man team noted that as their lorry passed by the crash site the next day, they observed three bodies strewn around, but naturally could not confirm these were their unlucky fellow airmen. Single losses by the 453BG and 489BG completed the loss record.

The grim 1-2-3 daily sequence of MIA crews from Bungay was realized on the 26th, when the 20CBW alone went after chemical production plants at Ludwingshafen. The chemical plant was hit in spite of intense, accurate flak, but only by less than half the 109-strong force; the flak gunners in turn knocked down three Group B-24s. Lt. William Nunn, in charge of 42-95626, was one of three fatalities after flak downed the B-24; five of the other seven crewmembers were captured, with the other duo evading capture.

Another unnamed plane—42-50318/, flown by Lt. Dean Peppmaier (POW)—received a direct flak hit and also came down in Holland; three members were killed, five others taken prisoner, and two evaded capture—a coincidental range of fates also experienced by the Nunn-led crew. The third victim was **Ginger** (41-29177), which did not progress so far west, having crashed near Saarbruecken; two of the ten-man crew led by Lt. Ralph V. Schaffer were killed; however, four of the immediate survivors were reportedly shot by SS Auxiliary Police the day after.

The other four CBW losses belonged to the 448BG, with the Lead and High squadrons bearing the punishment. **Lady Margaret** (42-95134/) was blown out of the sky, the fuselage splitting in twain and the starboard wing being wrenched off. The remnants plunged to earth at Ruchheim, west of the target, along with six of the crew, but Lt. Francis Botkin (P) and three of his colleagues survived being thrown clear and drifting down under their parachutes. Almost immediately 42-50788, in Lt. Frank Bastian's charge, absorbed severe flak damage and quickly inverted a maneuver that the pilots managed to correct and take up a course for home. This hope was ultimately thwarted as the B-24's condition deteriorated, but all seven airmen still on board not only managed to bail out, but ended up getting back into Allied hands. The other two crewmembers had bailed out over Ludwigshafen.

The first of the two High squadron MIA aircraft involved 41-28924/, which had the starboard wing fold up when struck by a shell between No. 3 and 4 engines; only Lt. Clifford Unwin (CP) scrambled clear as fire enveloped the savagely tumbling airframe, with Lt. Ed Postemsky (P) sharing his colleagues' fate after the B-24 came down near Mannheim. The formation was heading for the Rally Point when the flak gunners gained yet another victim. Lt. Bill Stonebraker's 42-50443/ broke in two, but amazingly all ten airmen bailed out, although three were fortunate to escape the wrath of civilians before military or police officials took charge. The other Division sub-force of 220 bombers suffered no MIA casualties after attacking oil-related targets around the Dutch/German border.

Month End Retrenchment

Berlin should have received its latest hammering (27th), but solid cloud patterns over southern Denmark, which provided the entry point into Germany, ensured that the formations responded to the "recall" orders. Adverse weather conditions next day held the "heavies" on the ground and also spelled the end of large-scale operations for the month. The final August run for the 2BD was short-range in nature, as well as involving eight Groups with a surprisingly low average of 18 crews. The bombing of V-1 sites in the Pas de Calais went off without loss.

Chapter Fifteen

Strategic Priorities Regained

The Allied armies' advances at the beginning of September were still seemingly unstoppable, as their German adversaries retreated in a hasty and uncoordinated manner. On the 3rd, the British army liberated Brussels, while to the south, the American units were equally well-ensconced within the regions around the Franco/German borders. The need for the RAF/USAAF "heavies" to continue functioning in a regular tactical role were now fast receding, this duty once more comprehensively evolving to the 9th USAAF's and RAF's 2nd Tactical Air Force (TAF). During September, there would be a handful of occasions when tactical operations would call on the 8AF's services, however.

Adverse weather was still proving to be a stumbling block, with operations occurring on just four of the first eight days in the month, one of which involved a "recall" (1st) when Ludwigshafen was the intended target. The 2BD was not called upon on the 3rd, when gun batteries around Brest were hammered, but next morning, 218 crews attended briefing for what would arguably be the Division's most-assigned target type—marshalling yards, in this instance at Karlsruhe.

Two Hethel crews would not join in the debriefing sessions today, with their B-24s resting on French-occupied and Swiss soil and 42-50511/YO: P the more unfortunate aircraft. On board with Lt. Frazee's crew was Capt. Paul Anderson (564BS Ordnance). Anderson was a fellow-townsman of Capt. Ed Appel (Command Pilot), who was scheduled to complete his 30th and final mission today and did so—but not in a positive manner. Flak knocked out two engines and cut rudder cables, leaving the bomber floundering; within ten minutes the crew had jumped, but two of the eleven experienced parachute failure.

Capt. Appel managed to get into friendly French hands after wandering around for ten days, but it was three months before he finally returned to duty; no such good fortune attended Anderson. (Amazingly, after converting to fighters, Appel managed a second successful evasion attempt following his P-47's downing during a strafing run on 16 April 1945.) Lt. John Fanelli and crew on board 42-95205/RR: F **The Lonesome Polecat** were luckier, in that the decision to point their damaged aircraft's nose towards Switzerland culminated uneventfully with a landing at Duebendorf.

The staccato mission pattern was retained over the ensuing three days, with the bombers "grounded" until the 8th, when the Division returned to Karlsruhe's marshalling yards. This time around over 80% of the 300 briefed crews went over the Primary and returned four short. Hethel's 42-94822/EE:, in Lt. L. B. Mabe's hands, was a casualty, although all but one crewmember bailed out safely. Lt. Don

P. Woods's crew were on their fifth mission in 42-52607/DC: V+, but after suffering flak damage over the target, the loss of No. 2 engine seemed to have precipitated a crisis that the pilots found increasingly difficult to handle as the bomber began to spin. This action was momentarily arrested around 13,000ft, at which point PVT Anthony P. Palumbo (Eng.) and one of the other two survivors got out. S/Sgt. Clyde K. Yeates only recovered consciousness fully ten days later in a German hospital, having no knowledge of how he had escaped the B-24, which had re-entered into a spin, with his "blacking out" at this stage. The bail outs occurred near Nancy, in France, and Palumbo alone was fortunate enough to evade capture until U.S. troops liberated the region. The 453BG's Lt. Beecher was forced to "ditch" 42-110085/; he survived the ever-hazardous action, but four of his seven-man crew were not so lucky. Two other Group crews diverted into French airfields thanks to flak damage. A 466BG crew completed the MIA losses.

The marshalling yard theme recurred over the next two days, beginning with a Divisional strike against facilities at Mainz. The 491BG got off to a bad start when 44-10489/ faltered and piled-in two miles south of the airfield; two engines caught fire and the crash landing that Lt. Warzcak (P) managed to carry out saw only he and two others squeezing out of a gap torn in the forward fuselage before the load of incendiaries erupted, expunging the lives of all other crewmembers.

Rough Riders (41-29342/J3: S) was a 458BG "original" B-24H brought over by Lt. Vogel, but today's run was her combat "swan song." Lt. Paul Stoneburner experienced problems with both in-board engines, culminating in No. 2 failing permanently around the IP and followed shortly by No. 3 going "out." On half power and with a "windmilling" No. 2 propeller, a solo heading west was adopted and the bomb load jettisoned. An irresistible altitude loss finally forced a bail out SW of Trier and close to the border with Luxembourg—a factor that enabled seven of the nine crewmembers to cross over and successfully seek assistance from the civilian population of that Nazi-repressed landmass.

The looming supply crisis for the Allied armies as September commenced saw the 2BD diverted into supplying fuel. This lineup of B-24s catches three bombers during a delivery flight to one of three French airfields designated as supply points. The Division circle on the 93BG representative has been moved further out on the wing. The other two bombers are from the 467BG (left) and 446BG.

Lt. Louis M. Stephens's crew were combat tested with 20 missions completed when they took off today. That experience counted for little after flak strikes set 42-52548/EC: S **Jaw-Ja Boy** on fire; the 45-mission veteran bomber fell away and down and had descended several thousand feet when the tail section became detached. The crash site at Diedenbergen was where the authorities discovered nine of the eleven-man team; only the two pilots managed to bail out from the gyrating airframe and they ended up being hospitalized, albeit with non-life-threatening injuries. The 489BG bore the remaining crew loss; Capt. Tom M. Plese's (KIA) eleven-man crew were manning 42-50897/S4; C-bar, along with Maj. William Blum (448BG) as Mission Pilot, but the PFF bomber that was flying Lead for the 448BG progressed no further than the target, where it was peremptorily hacked from the sky; a flak burst in the bomb bay blew the tail section off and the truncated remains descended at Bauscheim.

No Easy Missions

Two marshalling yards at Ulm and Heilbronn absorbed nearly all the Division's tonnage from the 388 B-24s dispatched next day, but these were Secondary targets, the Primary of Mainz remaining inviolate for the time being. **Rough Buddy** (42-95390/), from Bungay, was the sole MIA loss, along with all but one of the ten crewmembers.

Magdeburg's oil production facilities and an engineering plant at Hannover were briefed on the 11th, but barely half the 396 dispatched B-24s struck the four Primaries. Even more sobering was the presence for the first time in weeks of sizeable *Jagdwaffe* formations that added their weight to the taking down of forty B-17s and B-24s. This figure, even if this constituted just 4% of the

The carriage of fuel to France was a particularly hazardous and occasionally lethal duty, as Lt. Herbert H. Humke's scratch crew tragically discovered on 20 September. The 755BS aircraft (B-24H-1-FO/42-7516/J3: K) was barely airborne from Horsham St. Faith when it slammed into the ground at Hellesdon; the entire crew, along with a British housewife, were consumed in the resultant explosion.

Fords Folly has added ten missions to the tally seen in the picture entered in chapter thirteen. The reason for the delivery of a bottle of spirits is unclear, but its enjoyment would soon be lost in the gloom of the bomber's loss. On 11 September, 42-7466/EC: N was taken out by fighters, with only two Enlisted men from Lt. Charles R. Rudd's crew surviving as POWs.

overall 8AF force, was a salutary reminder that the Nazi Fighter Command had not yet totally expended its efforts to resist the Allied airmen's inroads upon the Nazi industrial and military structure. (Two B-17 units were the victims of *Sturmgruppen* assaults, losing nineteen crews between them.)

The ten B-24s failing to return were spread between four Groups, two of whom operated within the 20CBW. One of the two Seething losses involved an incident currently known in modern military parlance as "friendly fire." As the formation bypassed Koblenz, flak had disabled Lt. Richard Vogel's 42-95138/ **No Love, No Nothing** to the extent that it forced the pilots to reverse course for home. The bomber was closing the eastern fringe of the Ijsselmeer when its course intersected with a P-51 from the 361FG. The collision was severe enough for Lt. J. H. Loughheed to be fatally trapped in his fighter's cockpit; in contrast, all ten airmen on the B-24 bailed out, but only nine reached the ground alive, of which four enjoyed the additional bonus of evading their would-be captors. The bomber thumped into the ground at Dalfsen. Koblenz' flak batteries claimed the second Group victim when 44-10505/ **Gung Ho** succumbed, along with five of F/O Albert Lewis's team. (Debriefing reports talked of the fighter assaults commencing after this point, but having no material effect upon the Group formation.) Three crews also reportedly failed to return to Hardwick, one of which was 42-100338/ YM: **Return Engagement**; flak took the bomber down to her demise at Vechtel, leaving all nine on Lt. Fred E. Rylee's crew as the Group's latest "Kreigy" candidates.

The worst-affected unit in terms of MIA losses (four) was the 392BG, one of which featured a "ditching." Fighter assaults were responsible for at least two of the other losses, beginning with **Ford's Folly** (42-7466/EC: N), in Lt. Charles R. Rudd's hands, which was destined never to complete its latest mission, having at least 46 to its credit. Cannon shells ignited No. 3 engine, with the flames spreading rapidly onto the fuselage; descent in a shallow dive for a short period was followed by a spinning action that brought the bomber down close to Allendorf, north of Giessen. Two Enlisted men were the sole survivors out of ten, one man being killed in his turret and the others almost certainly trapped by centrifugal forces induced by the aircraft's spiralling motion. The crew had been on their 13th mission, and the ill luck associated with this number had sadly been realized. **Pleasure Bent** (42-50358.EC: Q) was the other fighter victim. Strikes on the nose section tore the cockpit frame apart and almost certainly killed Lts. Harold E. Jones and Anthony F Sicora, while the stabilizers were badly damaged and fire erupted in the fuselage. The final crash site SE of Marburg was where all five of the dead crewmembers were found, the other four taking the first steps towards captivity. Lt. Frank W. Haines guided 42-50593/GC: R-bar **Lady Diana** as far as the target at Hannover, but severe flak damage finally ensured that the bail out order was given, all nine on board getting out safely.

"Ditching" Account

The 579BS' 42-52615/GC: D-bar, flown by F/O Edmund J. White, ended up in the North Sea, and what transpired during the return flight is well illustrated by Lt. William S. Long (N):

> Over the target, the flak was heavy and intense—our ship received many hits—lots in the nose, though no one was injured from the flak. Alex (Lt. Richard W. Alexander, Bombardier) and I huddled together in the nose and prayed. Bombed at 23,000ft. Such flak. The

Operation **Market Garden**, launched on 17 September, envisaged the use of B-24s to drop supplies to the two U.S. Airborne Divisions protecting the corridor up which the British XXX Corps would push its armor columns to link up with the British 1st Airborne Division at Arnhem. These 491BG bombers are practising for the low-level drops scheduled for 18 September.

The 2BD Groups from the 14th and 20th CBWs have been allotted the duty of supply, as instanced by a picture of two 855BS aircraft from the 491BG. The Continental landscape is deceptively passive, but once over the drop zones, the hostile intention of the defenders will become apparent; an aircraft shot down from this minimal altitude will leave little chance of survival for itself and its crew.

sky was black with it! Reports later were that the German fighters put up their greatest opposition in a long time to meet us. Forty-seven bombers were lost in all.

Here is our damage up to the target area: No. 1 turbo regulator shot away; No. 3 shot out and streaming oil, burning also; Interphone shot out; and bomb sight damaged. On leaving the target, we left the formation and feathered No. 4, but No. 3 couldn't be feathered at the time. Picked up a P-47 escort and made it back to the Zuider Zee ok. Got there at about 14,000ft. Avoided flak fairly well. Had a huge hole in the left wing. No. 3 had two cylinders shot out. Damage was very complete, but we still had hopes of making it back to base.

At Dutch territory between Zuider Zee and the North Sea, Whitey called us to bail out, but changed the order. We decided to try to cross the North Sea. We began lightening the ship, throwing out all loose equipment. Someone threw out the waist window and it struck on the right horizontal tail plane, causing more drag. Whitey and Jim (Lt. J. M. Whalen) had trouble controlling the ship and gave orders to clear the nose and prepare for ditching. Such a feeling realizing that we were going to have to land in the Channel—yet all crewmembers remained calm.

Our P-47 escort arranged with the Air Sea Rescue to meet us; Rescue sent launches out every 15 miles on a heading of 90 degrees from Gt. Yarmouth. Thirty miles out from Yarmouth we hit the water—ship almost completely out of control—climbing, descending, banking, etc. Sea calm and sunny—very good conditions. At 2:45 p.m. we hit the water at 105MPH, skidding to the right with a terrific crash. The bottom half of the plane was ripped off from the bomb bays to the camera hatch. The tail turret and tail was torn completely off. As soon as we hit, the plane evidently nosed down and the rear went up into the air. Everything was very confusing, but most of us managed to get out. Whalen pushed his way out of the nose up through the canopy and White followed him. The top turret dropped and Hayden escaped through the hole where it was. Eight of us were picked up within 15 minutes, but only three got into the life raft.

The plane sank in fifteen minutes. Lt. Orville W. Shelton (Pilotage Navigator) went down on what was his 30th mission. Tough luck. Probably got out of the plane but couldn't keep up, as did T/St. Robert W. McAllaster (ROG). The rest of the crew was alright, but looking forward to a long stay in the hospital. We were picked up by Air Sea Rescue launch and taken to the Naval Hospital in Gt. Yarmouth. From there we went to Morley Hall for further treatment. The Navigator's shoulder was out for 11 hours—most painful. Lt. White did a perfect job—should get the DFC. No more missions for at least one month.

The survival of such a high percentage in personnel illustrates the vagaries attendant upon the act of "ditching," especially when considering the extent of airframe disintegration realized on this occasion.

There could have been two further Group losses, beginning with 41-29131/CI: K **Flying Home**, which was damaged by fighter gunfire. Lts. John I. Meehan and Harry V. Carey managed to stay with the formation and their aptly-titled B-24, flying its 87th mission, duly delivered the crew back to

Wendling; only eight airmen were still on board, since Sgt. William L. Altschaft had bailed out over Germany, having believed the bomber to be doomed. This aircraft was transferred in November to the 466BG. Lt. H. B. McClellan's 42-94764/EC: N **Bad Penny** was assailed by several Bf109s whose fire forced the bomber out of formation, as well as killing Cpl. Robert C. Tollok (TG) and injuring two other Enlisted men. A second pass was fortunately survived and the B-24 duly returned from its 61st (and unknowingly its final) mission. The next day it was "written off" at Manston after crashing during a non-operational flight.

A third victim of Koblenz's flak strength was the 458BG's 42-50314/7V: L **ETO Playhouse**, which knocked out No. 1 engine, whereupon Lt. Thomas H. Horgan's bomber lost distance and height. The area around Westerburg, some 25 miles NE of Koblenz, was where the nine-man crew descended by parachute; their aircraft in contrast flew on to oblivion somewhere under the North Sea's trackless wastes, German reports from the Island of Sylt, off the Danish/German border, having indicated its sighting roughly one hour after being abandoned!

Comment

The 392nd's mission teletype reported the following:

> Most of the enemy aircraft were camouflaged with light-colored bellies and dark on top. A few were noted to be painted olive drab, and some had black and white stripes on their wings to simulate P-51s. Most of the attacks were from level or below, and in general from the tail. Enemy aircraft attacked singly or in small groups of 2-4 echeloned up, or queued up in a line; the enemy aircraft sat high above our formation and queued up for about five minutes before attacking. Attack occurred at a time when we were temporarily without fighter cover. When called, escort came to our assistance.

This incident illustrates the fact that overall, continuous escort cover of the USAAF "heavies" was never capable of being fulfilled and that the bombers would always be faced with the possibility of isolation and parallel exposure to unopposed *Jagdwaffe* assaults.

Ditching Report

The report concerning the "ditching" of Lt. White's 392BG bomber as submitted to HQ2BD contained several pertinent comments; the difference in recommended procedure as opposed to what the crew carried out were as follows:

> The ROG's actual position was in the forward waist, whereas the recommended location was back against the copilot's armor plate... where armor plate has been replaced by armored chairs...(then) strapped to in his seat, head covered and resting on his table. As regards the copilot, he did not "ditch" using his Sutton (seat) harness; recommended procedure is for the pilots to use their harnesses and lock their seats forward. Also none of the crew wore their steel helmets as recommended. As regards jettisoning action; one waist window when jettisoned went through its opening, striking and damaging the horizontal stabilizer. Greater care would have avoided this type of damage

The allotted drop zone for the 14CBW has been reached and parachutes are deploying from the 44BG contingent. Opposition to these activities will prove to be not too fierce, but even so, seven B-24s will be culled from among the overall Force in the process. The low-level altitude provided little chance of survival, other than when able to crash land, and even this option held no guarantee of avoiding injury or death.

The 93BG was at the head of the 20CBW contingent on 18 September. This photo angle demonstrates the close, ground-hugging nature of the operation; even so, any encounter with flak would almost certainly end in favor of the ground-based gunners. The low-flying aspect of operations is emphasized by the aircraft shadows.

The Report's final comments were as follows:

> It should also be noted that both casualties occurred in the forward "ditching" belt, which was unnecessarily overloaded. Certain 2BD instructors say that each belt is designed to hold three men, but to place more than this number against a single belt is to risk its breaking. [The Group seems to have been pointing out that only two members had been in this belt and that one had (ostensibly) perished there, since the other casualty had drowned outside the aircraft.]

In view of the several criticisms so far raised, the concluding remarks were still rather generous:

> Except for the ROG being out of position, the mistakes noted were not disastrous. The crew were well trained and performed their assigned duties. The pilot in particular effected a reasonably good landing under adverse conditions, and he and the copilot performed an outstanding feat.

The assault upon Germany's synthetic oil plants and storage depots was resumed over the ensuing 48 hours. On the 12th, eight Division groups dispatched 241 bombers between them, of which two-thirds struck the Primaries at Misburg, Hemmingstedt, and Kiel. A return to a "drip feed" of losses occurred, with three of the four crews declared MIA belonging to the 14CBW as its units tracked over Misburg. The 491BG surrendered two, one of which was 44-40170 **Lamsy Divey**, flown by Lt. Sparrow; the loss of both inboard engines and a drop out of formation sadly soon culminated in a spin developing, out of which one crewmember managed to escape and deploy his parachute. Within a minute, **Pappy's Persuader** (44-40144), in Lt. Eckard's hands, suffered the same scale of damage and also dropped out, but all on board successfully got away before the B-24 finally went out of control.

The flak gunners added the 392BG's 42-50758/DC: W+ **YMCA Flying Service II** to their target tally. Two engines were knocked out and the B-24 was last reported low down as the formation tracked southward from the target. When control of the bomber became untenable, eight of the 20-mission veteran crew headed by Lt. John F. Buechler bailed out and were captured. The ninth, T/St. Joe P. Cooper (ROG), did not survive; MACR reports of his being shot on the ground were made by two crewmembers, one of whom spoke German enough to understand that his captors were confirming the fact. (Cooper's body was found at the crash site close to Niederkaufungen, on Kassel's eastern boundary.) The 2CBW's Lt. Kenneth F. Webster (POW), in charge of 42-95247/WV: _, lost four of his 445BG crew in the course of the bomber's loss to either flak or fighters over Holland. This MIA casualty was the last for just over two weeks, after which events during the Kassel mission on the 27th would literally tear the Tibenham-based Group asunder.

Schwabish-Hall airfield and a munitions depot at Ulm were two of the three Primaries laid out for 342 crews next day, but just over half achieved their goal, the rest returning without unloading. Once again, the same MIA figure of four was recorded, and for the second day running, two Metfield-based B-24s were included. **Ain't Bluffin**'s (44-40246) challenge was sadly called out when flak disabled No. 2 engine and the bomber sagged down to port; unfortunately, its port wing tip impacted with the fuselage of 44-40234 **Time's A'Wastin**. The former bomber, flown by Lt. John D. Kenney (POW), now

Seven crews were MIA on 18 September, and this 467BG B-24H-15-CF—a Group "original"— may well have been another. The No. 1 propeller has struck the forward fuselage and the pilots were fortunate to keep 41-29348 aloft to make a landing at Woodbridge Emergency Airfield in Suffolk. Salvage action was declared next day. Note the last three of her serial applied to the nose section

A collection of "Meat wagons," along with heavy rescue and support vehicles, sit on one side of Shipdham's control tower as a string of B-24s waddle their way along the perimeter track, their noses dipping and rising as the brakes are applied and released. The ground-hugging aircraft fuselages are clearly emphasized here in this summer of 1944 shot.

The radar pod on this B-24J-10-FO 42-51691/V2: P+ from the 491BG is fully deployed. The bomber bears the "Z" wing marking for the unit's disbanded predecessor (492BG), but retains the green/white tail marking in preference to the diagonal black band borne by the latter ill-starred unit; this anomaly was allowed to continue until early 1945, when the black band was applied.

A pair of 755BS bombers holds a sound formation with the photographer's aircraft. The nearest B-24 machine is a B-24J-5-FO/42-50864 named **Jolly Roger**, fated to fall on 14 October with Lt. Bill Klusmeyer's (POW) crew. **Ten Gun Dottie** (B-24J-65-CF 44-10602/J3: A/P) transferred to the 753BS in March 1945 and changed its aircraft letter to E; it is believed to have survived the conflict.

The distinctive figures of Gen. Peck (CG, 14CBW, on the left) and Col. Luther Fairbanks (CO, 466BG) are pictured on return from a mission. Officers above the rank of full Colonel were not usually encouraged to fly and risk capture, since many were privilege to highly-classified secrets that could be forced from them, especially given the extremely autocratic methods of Nazi security staff!

failed to respond to the pilots' efforts at stabilization, but six airmen, including Sgt. Martin Leibenhaut, with a staggering total of 76 missions, did manage to deploy their parachutes. The impact damage to Lt. R. C. Wilson's aircraft saw the other 491BG bomber's wing tearing back through the fuselage and ripping off the tail section. The aerodynamically beheaded machine plunged vertically for some distance before disintegrating. Both pilots and the navigator, who were hitherto pinned down in positions, now miraculously found themselves out in mid-air and free to pull their ripcords, but their companions were not so lucky.

Lt. Dean M. Mills was flying 42-95111/F8: +, which was flak-stricken; the 453BG bomber, trailing a banner of flame, veered left and down, nearly taking Capt. Alve's B-24 with it in the process. The pilot was not one of the three survivors subsequently confirmed. Wendling's latest loss involved 42-50279/GC: J, which also received ultimately fatal flak damage. When last seen, it was in a steep dive with No. 3 engine on fire, but seemingly still under a measure of control. By then, the bomb bay was a mass of flames and up to six parachutes recorded. In the event, there were only four survivors out of ten following the aircraft's demise at Rudesheim on the Rhine, the pilot Lt. Albert E. Joynt being among the fatalities. (The diving action was a last resort effort to blow out the fire, according to Lt. Edward J. Taylor, the copilot.)

Market-Garden Variation

Unbeknownst to the Division's crews, as they now enjoyed an enforced break from operations thanks to another 72-hour spell of bad weather, was the Plan originally put forward by Field Marshall Montgomery that if successful would see the Allied Armies ensconced firmly on the east bank of the river Rhine and

Jamaica? (from the 466BG) has been forced to divert into an airfield in Normandy. She is a B-24H-10-DT/41-28746 that will end her combat career in a violent manner; on 25 September, she will explode following a crash during a "Trucking" mission to supply fuel to the Allied armies in their quest to harry the enemy back to, if not beyond, the Rhine.

Dusty's Double Trouble/Gypsy Queen has arrived in her dispersal and the Crew Chief has just signalled for the pilots to halt their charge. B-24H-25-DT/42-51179 bears the abbreviated anti-dazzle panel and bombardier's Plexiglas frame layout that are features on all H-variant airframes. It completed 98 missions by VE-Day, having transferred to the 754 (Z5) in October 1944.

by extension would allow a large-scale advance into the Nazi hinterland that hopefully would lead to a German surrender. Operation *Market-Garden* set out the twin intentions of (a) capturing key bridges between Eindhoven and Arnhem, in central Holland—the latter spanning the Lower Rhine—and (b) having the British 30 Corps drive its armored and support columns up the route that would be secured by the U.S. 82nd and 101st Airborne, other than at Arnhem, which was allotted to the British 1st Airborne.

The need to provide supporting equipment to the lightly-armed paratroopers before the region they were dropped over was properly secured by ground-based forces was of paramount importance, and the decision was taken to dispatch elements of the 2BD in carrying out the function at points along the projected "corridor." The roomier fuselage of the B-24 compared to the B-17 was probably a central reason in making this choice; in addition to the large bomb bay, many B-24s had a second ready-made release aperture, namely the ball turret hatch, which was now redundant following removal of the bulky and speed-sapping unit when in the lowered position.

The airborne-led operation commenced on the 17th, but only the B-17s were utilized in bombing defensive positions bordering the "corridor" route. Meanwhile, the B-24 crews were carrying out a low-level practice mission over East Anglia. Next morning, the six Groups comprising the 14th and 20th CBWs were rostered for the supply mission. The briefed drop zones were spread between Eindhoven and Nijmegen, and an average of 31 crews dispatched, each B-24 carrying approximately three tons of supplies. The outward route around 1,500ft would drop to a ground-hugging altitude over the drop zones. The pilots were then advised to climb up into the predicted low cloud strata after releasing their loads; the overall flight plan provided an enhanced prospect of the equipment landing in friendly hands, but equally there was far greater exposure to enemy ground fire.

The 392BG's contribution totalled forty B-24s, with the Wing heading out for drop zone "N." Ground fire was encountered as soon as the formation breached the Dutch coast at Walcheren and steadily increased in intensity that reached a peak between the IP and drop zone. Damage was suffered by a number of B-24s, including Lt. Wade P. Sewell's

Col. Albert Shower waves to the photographer as he taxies the 467BG's "hack" P-47. The bulky fighter was used by the CO to monitor Group formations, a vital aspect of operations that he forcibly impressed upon his pilots, at least verbally! Shower was also the sole 2BD Commander to serve in that capacity with his Group for the entire length of its WWII service in Britain.

Briney Marlin served with three of the 458BG's sub-units during her extended operational career of 100 completed missions. The airman on the right is Rick Rokicki, who recalled flying in her when she returned to operations, having survived a mid-air collision on 27 May 1944. Rick has long been Vice President of the 458BG Association, as well as serving with the 2AD Association.

42-50673 / GC: K-bar, whose bomb doors were found to be jammed. The pilot ordered as much of the supply equipment to be kicked out via the ball turret aperture. The homeward leg was barely entered when No. 4 engine burst into flames. Sewell pulled the bomber up to around 1,000ft after giving the bail out order; of the nine-man crew, plus one Dropmaster and a "passenger," four were killed or died from their injuries, two became POWs, and Sewell ended up as one of five evaders.

The "passenger" in question was a Cpl. Nevin A. Johnson, who had recently been given sanction to transfer to a Paratroop Regiment. In fact, he was technically a stowaway, having not been given permission to fly today and would be recorded as AWOL; how he obtained the flight clothing was a mystery. His death was particularly tragic, since he bailed out safely but broke his leg on landing; the fact that he came down right in the battle zone ensured his extended isolation and he was adjudged to have bled to death before he was found.

No Feathered Injun (42-94886/ GC: N-bar) got through to the drop zone, but Lt. James A. Gerow subsequently called up to say that with both inboard engines casting up problems, he was altering course to the southwest in an attempt to reach Allied-occupied territory, as he was not prepared to risk a direct North Sea crossing. Progress towards this goal was abruptly terminated when less than 15 minutes flight time from Brussels, ground fire set the central fuselage ablaze. All but one of the ten on board bailed out, although one (T/Sgt. Eugene J. Kieras (Eng.)) lost his life; unable to find his pack, he went out "piggy-back" with Sgt. Benjamin E. Brink (WG), only to be cast off in mid-air by the tremendous force of the parachute's deployment. In addition, Pvt. Edward Yensho's (Dropmaster) corpse was found within the aircraft's wreckage.

North Pickenham's Fortunes

The 491BG provided two formations: one to lead the 14CBW to drop zone "W" and the other to head for drop zone "A." According to group records:

> The formations entered Europe at 1,100 feet, which was very close to the optimum range of the German ground fire. Although rated "meager to moderate" in the overall mission report, this small arms fire accounted for six aircraft (none from the 491st) between the coast and the target. The squadrons, flying in trail at 30-second intervals, dropped to 600 feet at the IP and 250 feet or less over the target. Each aircraft carried a Dropmaster from one of the Airborne units, and these men supervised the actual dumping of the supplies from the bomb bays and ball turret wells. The accuracy was exceptional, with very few bundles falling outside the assigned areas.
>
> Coming off the targets the formation was still intact, although small arms fire had killed one crewman and injured several others. The gunners found few targets, for the enemy was using very little tracer ammunition and the crews had been briefed to fire only on enemy troops or gun positions definitely engaging them. The majority of the pilots, having decided to ignore the order to climb, came out on the deck all the way. This proved a wise move, for the 491st suffered less battle damage than the other Groups that took the higher road home. Still it was bad enough....
>
> Shortly after leaving the drop area, the lead plane of the "A" force [Capt. James K. Hunter's 44-40210] caught a burst of flak in the right wing section. With only

The inherently grave weakness of the B-24's structure in attempting crash landings is shown here. On 10 November 1944, Lt. Keith Forrest's 445BG flak-damaged B-24J-1-DT/42-51250 returned from Hanau, but the attempt ended up with the bomber a shattered wreck, with the fuselage fractured severely in the front and rear. The extent of personnel casualties is unknown.

Col. Albert Shower (467 BG CO) shakes the hand of an anonymous crewmember who has completed his combat tour. **Tender Comrade**, whose female figure is frustratingly inhibited by the slab armor plate, is B-24H-15-CF/41-29369 from the 791BS; she served within the Group for five months up to 11 September, after which time she no longer appears on the unit records.

seconds to work, Hunter, one of the best Group pilots, picked his spot and started to bring the Liberator in on its belly. At less than 50 feet, however, the No. 3 engine burst into flames, the right wing dropped, and it was still too low when the plane hit. Hunter actually pulled the plane into the air again, but by then there was no more room; he and eight others were killed when the B-24 struck trees and farm buildings. One casualty was Capt. Mitchell, who had won the trip—and lost his life—on the flip of a coin.

Miraculously, one man did survive; S/Sgt. Frank DiPalma recollected:

> I was discovered leaving the plane by some Fransican brothers, and later treated by several doctors; my mind is blank from the time we hit until the 28th of September.

Sgt. DiPalma was hidden by his benefactors in a Catholic church until the British Army liberated the town of Udenhout:

> Lt. Edward L. Schmitt's 44-40414 lost an engine, but the pilots nursed it to an Allied airfield in Belgium; the plane was "written off," but nobody was hurt. Matters seemed grim at North Pick, when only 33 returned out of the 41 that had left. However, the reports began coming in about an hour later. Stahl had crash landed at Watton with very little port stabilizer. Bridges was down at Woodbridge with heavy battle damage; so were Ostrander and Meglish. Schamahorn and his crew were there too, although nobody knew why any of them was alive. The left gear of their Liberator collapsed on landing and the aircraft wound up on its back and burning. The final score was an improbable and heartening one aircraft MIA, but nobody wanted to do it again right away.

Baggy Maggie (42-100416/YM:) was one of two Hardwick losses, but its final demise at Castelre, in Holland, was matched by just one on Lt. Harry M. Lewin's nine-man crew. A tenth airman on board was PFC James Bolton, described in the MACR as a "passenger"—a journey he would never forget, since it ended in a *Stalag*, rather than his billet back at Hardwick!

Heaven Can Wait (42-94786/S4: P+) was one of two 489BG losses; half of the ten airmen under Lt. Claude T. Lovelace's (KIA) command failed to survive the bomber's final crash at Hummersum, close to Germany's border with Holland. The other Group loss involved 42-94900 **Rum Runner**, which was reportedly brought down at Groesbeek. One fatality involved T/Sgt. Donald C. Brian (Eng.), who had already finished his combat tour, but who had volunteered for the mission, cruelly losing out in the process.

Staccato Operational Pattern

The initially flawed and ultimately failed actions surrounding *Market-Garden* would carry on for a further seven days before its conclusion, but with no further involvement of the 2BD. It was to be 48 hours before the Division's crews were alerted for the first of seven missions up to the month end, the intervening three days seeing the bombers "grounded" by the frustratingly variable autumnal weather. Koblenz and its marshalling yard complex were briefed, but the bulk of the 179 crews dispatched bombed the Primary at the cost of two bombers listed MIA. More destruction might have been done by the 392BG, but for an unfortunate incident; shortly after passing the IP, the Lead squadron's bomb load went down without any involvement of the bombardier. This flaw in the "bombing on Leader" principle was accordingly exposed when all other bombardiers in the sub-unit also released, some 27 tons of bombs and incendiaries impacting 20 miles short of the target. The Group's failure proved to be total when the other squadron found the MPI cloud-covered and subsequently jettisoned its loads.

The Wendling Group returned one light, with Lt. Joe Shelley's 41-29002/ EC: T the bomber in question. Fuel was seen seeping out of the starboard wing before the Dutch coast was crossed, but the pilots kept on course, despite falling back and switching off No. 4 engine. The target was reached and a heading for home taken up for a short period; the situation then deteriorated to the extent that a bail out was ordered. All nine airmen vacated their mount, which piled in at Euskirchen, west of Bonn, with one member saying he emerged scant hundreds of feet from the ground. Unfortunately, Shelley and two others lost their lives, reportedly by civilian "summary justice," although this was never verified. The other MIA loss involved the 93BG's 42-94969/ **Big Noise II**; a second bomber (42-99949/ GO: I **Naughty Nan**, which had returned from the 24 August mission with the bombardier flying it, both pilots having been incapacitated by injury) now diverted into a Continental airfield. Whatever scale of damage it had suffered was sufficient for salvage action to be recommended on 14 November.

Kassel lies 100 miles east of the Ruehr, and the possibility of sustained opposition was accordingly increased. On the 22nd, the Henschel armored vehicle plant was pounded by all of the 208 2BD crews spread between nine Groups who moreover came home with no losses. It was now that the latest weather break made its presence felt over the intervening period up to the 25th. At Tibenham, the third loss-free mission had just been flown, a pattern that would last for two further missions before the return run to Kassel, a name that was to be tragically woven into the unit's history.

"Truckin"

The almost headlong pace of the Allied ground advance out of its formerly constraining Normandy region had by early September created the counterproductive fact that essential supplies with which to sustain the momentum were having to be brought forward over ever-increasing distances. None of the French seaports along the Channel coastline were either in working order or alternately were still in the hands of German garrison forces. The British/Canadian forces had captured the massive Belgian seaport of Antwerp, but did not immediately clear the banks of the Scheldt estuary, which led from the North Sea to the city. One of the most vital commodities required for continued progress was fuel; the Allied armored units forming the spearhead of the overall advance were particularly dependent upon regular quantities being on hand.

A perceived method with which to at least alleviate the burgeoning crisis was the use of aircraft with which to ferry quantities over to the Continent. The B-24 was adjudged to be the better design with which to carry out the duty and the 96CBW was withdrawn from operations towards the end of the second week in September and the bombers adapted to the revised function. At Horsham St. Faith, for example, the B-24s were fitted out to accommodate a total of 3,530 gallons in all. This was distributed between 2,000 and 450 gallons in the main and auxiliary tanks, 915 gallons in separate tanks placed in the bomb bay, and 165 gallons in fighter drop tanks secured in the waist.

Three airfields at Lille, St. Dizier, and Clastres, near St. Quentin, were selected, all being on the approach to, or in the former case right on the French/Belgian

If this 491BG B-24J-150-CO touches down at its present off-balanced angle, then it will create a bumpy landing for the crew and not live up to its **Grease Ball** title. On 26 November 44-40172, bearing Lt. Robert W. Simons's crew, would be one of fifteen bombers shot out of the sky during a mission to Misburg; only three crewmembers would survive its loss.

Shack Time, from the 753BS, flies in the company of two 754th and a single 752nd squadron B-24. The absence of rubber deicing "boots" on the leading edges confirms this bomber is from the first Consolidated production batch to be equipped with thermal deicing equipment.

This B-24D originally completed her combat operations with the 389BG as **Little Gramper**. Following retirement from front line duties, she was transferred to the 491BG to become its first Assembly ship. The overall airframe surface, other than the fins, was yellow; this was interspersed with red circles incorporating irregular light patterns and red streaks on the engine cowlings.

border. Initial problems with an inadequate pace of pumping out the fuel from the bombers was due to the equipment on hand. Col. Isbell (Group CO) recalled that portable gas-powered pump units had been placed on each "original" B-24 prior to leaving the States; these were stored away on arrival in England, but now their location was tracked down and they were dispatched over to France. Between the 12th and 30th, the Group flew over 400 individual sorties, in the course of which over 700,000 galls were delivered.

The volatile nature of these cargoes was a key factor in the loss of at least two bombers and their hapless crews. Horsham lost 42-7516/J3: K **Gator** on the 20th. The veteran aircraft, bearing Lt. Herbert H. Humke and five of his crew, who were yet to fly their first combat mission, failed immediately after take off. The fireball that resulted cost the lives of all on board, along with a housewife in one of the properties that absorbed the B-24's impact. Five days later, 41-28746/2U: O+ **Jamaica?** from the 466BG joined **Gator** in total incineration along with its equally hapless crew while heading over to France.

A second 458BG crew was lost on the 24th, but the cause was reportedly put down to a case of misidentification. The sole survivor from Lt. George J. Koehn's team heard someone say: "The damn fools are firing at us!" as the flight back to Norfolk was in progress. Sgt. Bill Hudson ended up a POW, so there was a strong possibility that the bomber actually strayed off course and intruded upon enemy-held soil that included the still-occupied ports of Calais or Dunkirk.

Back "On the Rails"

It was a case of "back to that 'ol marshalling yard" theme when operations resumed on the 25th. Koblenz was again on the Briefing maps and over 670 tons of bombs and incendiaries rained down on the city's transport facilities; in addition, none of the 257 crews gaining mission "credit" was lost. Next day, the sorely-tested yards at Hamm were targeted and hammered by 274 bomb loads, but the Grim Reaper claimed three bombers: two from the 29-strong Bungay formation. Lt. John E. Mullery, in charge of 42-50477/ **Temptation**, got himself and his ten-man crew clear of their doomed B-24, albeit ending up as POWs. Lt. Thomas H. Gill (P) was not personally so fortunate, since he lost his life, along with one of the eleven airmen on board 42-100347/; the bail out action took place over or close enough to German-occupied territory for four of the survivors to evade capture.

The 14CBW was leading the Division with the 491BG as Lead Group. Lt. Francis E. Fuhr's 44-10500/ had a flak shell explode just ahead of it with no immediate effect. Fragments of shell casing probably penetrated the fuel tank between No. 1 and 2 engines, because shortly after its contents began to siphon out into the slipstream, followed quickly by its ignition. Before the pilots could take action to douse the flames by diving the B-24, the wing snapped off at this burning juncture and the aircraft went into a flat spiral that then developed into a spin. S/Sgt. Earl Alleman (WG) was fortunate enough to make his exit via a hatch by grasping its edge and hauling himself out into mid-air, while T/Sgt. Edward G. Pearce (Eng.) became the second of only four crewmembers to escape alive, the pilot being one of the fatalities.

The particularly horrendous punishment handed out to the 445BG during the mission to Kassel on 27 September is mentioned in passing here; the authors feel that the disaster in which no less than 25 crews remained in enemy territory is deserving of a separate account. As it was, just one other MIA loss was sustained out of the 280 other crews who bombed the Primary or Target of Opportunity. The unlucky team was on board the 491BG's quaintly-named (and grammatically incorrect as presented) 42-110186/3Q: B **Le Simulacre Renegat - L'esprit des Ceux Que Nous Animlous**. Flak at the Belgian port of Ostend on the way in ensured that Lt. Harold S. Lew's crew had little option to abandon their fatally crippled B-24. However, twenty combat crewmembers on board two 489BG bombers would never survive the day; a mid-air collision on return to England saw both B-24s plummet into the ground near Walberswick, killing all their hapless occupants.

September was closed off on the 30th, when 560 tons was released by 206 bombers onto the sorely-tried marshalling yards of Hamm; once again, the MIA cost was minimal, albeit not for the crew concerned. Lt. Arthur S. Ledford's 44-10531/QK: R+ **My Sad Ass** lost No. 1 engine to flak, while No. 3 caught fire just after "bombs away"; S/Sgt. Henry P. Starr (TG) was the sole fatality, having been killed at his post. Two of the survivors were fortunate to emerge alive: Lts. James N. Tomblin (N) and Richard W. Pascal (B) were struggling with the nose wheel doors when the by-now blazing bomber exploded, throwing them out into mid-air. All other crewmembers had bailed out before their aircraft's comprehensive disintegration occurred.

October 1944 - Hard Pounding Ahead

The bright hopes of an end to the conflict by the year end, or even penetration of the Nazi hinterland by the Anglo-American ground forces thanks to forging the Rhine's formidable waters at Arnhem, in Holland, had disappeared with the failure of Operation *Market-Garden*. That very desirable goal would now await the onset of the following late-Winter period, when three separate bridgeheads would be established within sixteen days in March. In the meantime, the strategic Bomber Commands, as well as their Tactical contemporaries, would maintain the pressure on the enemy's manufacturing and transport structures, with the 2BD pursuing the latter entity as demonstrated on the 2nd.

Hamm's marshalling yards received their latest in a lengthy series of hammerings from the Allied bomber fleets; the near-90% of crews gaining mission "credit" released 700 tons of explosives and incendiaries on the Primary and returned just two short. The 491BG's latest loss involved 42-95104/, which was last seen going down with two smoking engines. The reports of parachutes emerging from the B-24 proved to be false, because the crew led by Lt. Dan W. Means (KIA) seemingly chose to ride their charge down to an attempted crash landing that only two of the nine airmen survived. There was a particularly tragic outcome for the pilot on 42-95252/E8:. He was Lt. James Emerson, who had completed his combat tour, and having married an Englishwoman, was awaiting the necessary clearance papers for her to accompany him back home to the States. What was his 39th mission ended fatally for him after the flak-stricken Old Buckenham B-24 burst into flames and broke in two over the target.

The onset of autumnal weather patterns, with their propensity for partial or total obscuring of the ground meant that the bomber crews were forced into making regular use of *H2X*, *Oboe*, *G-H*, and other blind bombing equipment. However, the 2BD, unlike its two contemporaries, was spared this inhibiting factor in bombing accuracy on the next two October missions. Clear visibility over Gaggenau and Speyerdorf's airfield (3rd) allowed for precise bombing by 250 crews, all of whom returned, along with 70 more diverting to Secondary or Target of Opportunity locations. A similar loss-free outcome arose 48 hours later, when a marshalling yard and two airfields NE of the Ruehr were hammered by the Division's crews.

Hamburg's defensive network might have been expected to exact a cost in

The undulating and rough surface of the Beccles marshes in Norfolk have given no quarter to the 489BG's 42-94857 **Lonesome Polecat** in this early October picture. The B-24H-20-FO's fuselage has fractured directly behind the wing trailing edges, while the nose section is thoroughly mangled underneath. The tail colors are an apparent puzzling mix of green at the base with the rest in yellow, to which the Group switched during August.

Sand Bomb Special (B-24H-25-FO 42-95124) has come to a safe but undignified halt following a burst main wheel. The bomber, currently serving with the 67BS, would switch to the 66BS as QK: P+, but a mere five days after today's incident she would lose two engines and be abandoned near Freiburg by Lt. Rogers's (POW) crew, with two out of the ten losing their lives.

The 491BG's **Little Beaver** (44-40194, in the foreground) is seen in the company of the camouflaged **Johnny Come Lately** 42-110154/V2: (both Consolidated-produced bombers) flying off her port wing. The presence of the circle Z Group marking confirms the picture was taken following the insignia's adoption from the disbanded 492BG.

bombers and crew next day (6th), when an oil refinery at Harburg, a munitions dump, and an aircraft production plant were targeted. The former Primary alone had to be attacked using PFF methods; it is somewhat ironic that the sole loss of a 489BG bomber was experienced here, since the flak gunners were literally firing "blind"! However, the Division was again spared attention from fighter attacks, unlike the 3BD's experience over Berlin, which cost it most or all of its sixteen MIA crews, half from the 94BG. Today was the first of twelve further daily missions to be launched by the Division before the month end, with a double header occurring on the 14th.

For the first time in some weeks, almost the entire strength of the 8AF was directed at the Nazis' oil production industry; the exception was the attack upon the Hentschel armor production plant in Kassel (7th), which attracted the briefed attention of nearly half of the 2BD. Once again, the major losses, amounting to 40 crews overall, were borne by the B-17 Divisions, with the 2BD's share limited to four, three-quarters coming from the 14CBW's ranks.

Shipdham's 506BS had borne the brunt of the Group's casualties in recent weeks and now added to this dismal tally by two. Lt. Still's crew had narrowly escaped disaster on their first mission, when 44-40167/GJ: Y-Bar **Sierra Blanco** snagged a fence on take off. Now the same bomber had already lost half its power and was straggling when flak impacted, setting the bomb bay ablaze; two-thirds of the nine-man team got clear, but three Enlisted men were found in the wreckage. Its companion in misfortune was 42-50589/GJ: A-Bar **Lakanookie**, from which all but one on Lt. Salfren's crew bailed out, one of whom suffered parachute failure. This B-24 had also been straggling with engine problems before it too became the flak gunners' victim.

The 392BG was over the Primary when flak again struck, this time at 42-94966/EC: E **Madame Shoo Shoo**. No. 3 engine caught fire and the B-24 then began a gentle canting motion to port that soon developed into a sharp dive. About halfway to the ground the engine fire must have initiated an explosion that severed the wing; in spite of the resultant tumbling motion, six of Lt. Robert H. Johnson's crew ended up alive under their parachutes, a seventh reportedly suffering a failed parachute, while three airmen never got out. The crash site was NW of Roesebeck. The final Division loss involved a crew from the 489BG.

The ensuing 96 hours witnessed a single Division sortie, but even this foray by 384 crews ended up with the Secondary (Koblenz's marshalling yards) absorbing nearly all the bomb loads at the cost of a single MIA crew from Hardwick, along with a 445BG aircraft "written off" at Manston and a 392BG bomber crash landed at West Bradenham on return. Lt. Walter W. "Buck" Sanders's 42-95168 had three engines fired up by flak, whereupon he dived his charge in a vain attempt to blow out the flames. S/Sgt. Paul O. Bergman recalled that after levelling off the bail out order was given. He followed the pilot and probably the copilot down into the bomb bay, ready to jump—whereupon the now uncontrolled B-24 developed a flat-spinning angle that threw the trio around helplessly. Just when it seemed their fate was sealed, the bomber amazingly levelled off to allow all three to jump. As it transpired, Bergman was fortunate enough to deploy his chute bare seconds before slamming into the ground, but his fellow parachutists were not so fortunate; in fact, only four crewmembers in all escaped with their lives. (The doomed B-24's involuntary act of stabilization highlighted the element of chance affecting all combat personnel during a mission.) On the 12th, the Secondary of Osnabrueck's marshalling yards was pounded by 267 bombers, at the cost of two B-24s.

Concentration on Cologne

Cologne's massive industrial complex had received regular treatment from the Allied bombers throughout WWII, and now four massive assaults between the 14th and 18th by the entire 8AF were duly delivered. The first concentrated upon the city's various marshalling yard complexes, with the 2BD heading for Gremberg and Eifelter. Over 80% of the

Division struck their Primaries with G-H assistance and returned three crews light. Lt. Thomas G. Crenshaw's 42-95195/EC: M was fatally crippled by flak over the target and with three engines on fire briefly staggered homeward before canting earthward to crash near Much, on the eastern outskirts of the city. By then, all nine airmen were descending by parachute, two of whom evaded capture for twelve days.

The 96CBW gave up the other two crews. Lt. Bill Klusmeyer had been briefed as Group deputy Lead in 42-50864/J3: B **Jolly Roger**, but then assumed Lead when the designated B-24 "aborted." The signal for "bombs away" was just being uttered when the persistent flak barrage finally caught up with the bomber and dispatched it. All on board got out and Lt. Ernest Sands (B) managed to evade capture for seven days, having travelled 100 miles in so doing. Upon apprehension, his captor made clear his intention to shoot him, but a fellow police officer dissuaded his colleague; even then Sands, having been "advised" to run for it, was fortunate to survive a barrage of stones, fruit, and vegetables before finally being taken into custody.

Rackheath's 42-52507/6A: N-bar **Miss Judy** joined her Horsham fellow machine in Fate. An engine fire followed by heavy vibration at some stage of the mission ended up with Lt. Donald J. Hudson ringing the bail out bell; he alone out of the nine on board did not survive and his demise was reportedly due to being shot while still attached to his parachute, which had "hung up" in a tree.

Düsseldorf lies not far distant from Cologne and possessed two synthetic oil refineries at Monheim and Reisholz. Although the main Division effort was redirected at the Secondary—Gereon marshalling yards in the latter city (15th)—the 2CBW got through to its assigned Reisholz Primary. The visual conditions encountered there had a downside, since the flak batteries had equally good visual sighting of their pedestrian-paced prey. As it was, just two 389BG crews fully felt their sting, one of them lethally. **Maggie's Drawers** (42-50760/RR: M), in Lt. Hanzlick's charge, along with 42-50739/HP: Z ended up straggling, but held course for home in close company. Flak en route caused Hanzlick to swerve in a left-hand curve before linking up again with his straight-course companion. Hardly had he settled back into position when another battery's shell pattern landed a lethal strike between No. 3 and 4 engines; the wing structure immediately gave way and as fire took hold of the airframe, its downward path resulted in progressive disintegration. Even so, the pilot and seven of the crew fought their way clear to parachute into enemy hands, unlike T/Sgt. Richard Ellwart (Eng.) and S/Sgt. Eugene Kalinowski (TG), who forfeited their lives. **Ole Buckshot**'s crew managed to survive their now solo run and get back to Hethel.

The third of the four full-scale assaults on Cologne went out on the 17th. The briefed Division target—a chemical plant at Leverkusen—remained inviolate, and recourse was had by nearly all of the 453 crews to bombing Kalk and Gereon marshalling yards as Targets of Opportunity. The devotion to duty of an Old Buckenham Enlisted man ensured the Group came back in total. Lt. Lofton's B-24 sustained flak strikes that punctured two fuel tanks, as well as damaging the port landing gear and disabling the nose turret. T/Sgt. Edwards (Eng.) immediately acted to vent the fuel vapor by opening the nose wheel doors and other hatches. The 21,000-ft altitude and dispensing with an oxygen mask did not prevent the Sergeant from first ripping up all available fabric and upholstery before moving to the bomb bay; he then lay on the catwalk and stuffed as much of the material into the tank holes as would at least slow down the fuel loss. By the time the front lines were below the bomber was down to half power and its meager 1,500ft altitude provided an easy target for enemy ground fire. The B-24 managed to clear the area and fly onward until a third engine faltered, at which stage the pilot rang the bail out bell and all on board safely evacuated. Edwards was subsequently recommended for the Silver Star.

The fourth and final Cologne-orientated mission (18th) witnessed in the case of the 2BD a surprisingly small force of five Groups dispatching an

Lady Geraldine, a B-24J-60-CF 44-10524/WQ: J, arrived at Shipdham during the autumn of 1944. She is seen through the glazed waist window of a fellow Group bomber; she bears the underside Plexiglas blisters housing the "Carpet" aerials, which was part of the equipment designed to frustrate the efforts of the flak gunners' gun-laying system.

The personnel of the 458BG were well favored compared to other 2BD Groups, as they were assigned to an RAF "Permanent" airfield with superior work and living quarters. In additions, sports facilities were equally well provided, in this case with a tennis court that is currently accommodating a doubles match.

A B-24J-FO belonging to the 845BS has crossed the airfield threshold at Halesworth and is set to bring off a sound landing. The all-yellow tail surface replaced the original green/white/green vertical sections on 489BG aircraft during August 1944. The Group's tenure of service with the 8AF ended in late November, when it redeployed to the States in readiness for Pacific operations.

average of 24 crews. Even then, barely half reached either the chemical plant Primary at Leverkusen briefed the day before or struck a Target of Opportunity at Nippes marshalling yard complex. Four Groups came home intact, but not the 44BG, which sustained three MIA bombers, two of which were "self inflicted" through that constant bane of formation flying—collision.

Col. John Turnbull (a member of the 1936 Olympic lacrosse team and transferee from the 492BG) was Command Pilot with Lt. Bakalo's crew on 41-28944/NB: D **Flying Jinny**. The return flight was in progress and a solid cloud bank over Belgium was being torturously negotiated when the B-24J was recorded by S/Sgt. Encimer (RW) as shuddering and canting sharply left, whereupon the throttles were pulled back. Col. Turnbull was heard to say "Center the Needle!" and barely had the gunner clipped on his pack when the bomber flipped onto its back and fell to its destruction SW of Ghent. Encimer suffered a broken arm as he was thrown around, but still managed along with S/Sgt. Scott to force his way out; they would be the sole survivors out of twelve, and Scott would require a blood transfusion due to his scale of injury. The Colonel was reported to have also been found alive, but he apparently succumbed two days later.

The loss of Lt. Dayball's 42-50381/ WQ: D, which similarly plummeted to earth near Ghent, killing all on board, was later ascribed to the B-24 running into **Flying Ginny**. Encimer had noted a bomber behind and to the right with apparent steering problems just as the formation entered the cloud bank, but whether this was Dayball's aircraft could never be confirmed.

Lt. Ed Lehnhausen was a brother of Bob, a Group "original" now holding Major rank. Today he was piloting 42-50596/WQ: O, but the bomber became detached from the formation and never returned. It appears that the B-24's errant course took it over the heavily-defended island of Walcheren, whose flak gunners promptly zeroed in to blow the aircraft's tail assembly completely off; nobody escaped the terminal effect of centrifugal force.

Germany's armored vehicle production was taken on (19th) by the 1BD and 2BD, but both Primaries—Gustavsburg in the case of the B-24 force—remained largely inviolate; the vast bulk of the B-24s unloaded upon nearby Mainz's marshalling yards. Single casualties were borne by three Groups, with the 489BG losing two. Flak polished off 42-95047/ F8: + in Lt. Lloyd C. Carter's (POW) hands. Hethel's MIA crew in 42-50842/HP: J **Betsy II** included two close friends, Lts. Ken Simmons (B) and Terrell Hollis (N), both of whom were among the seven survivors from their B-24's destruction. They landed in the same field and were immediately surrounded by civilians wielding heavy implements. One was equipped with a hammer with which he administered "summary justice" to Lt. Hollis; the Lt. was knocked to the ground and his skull smashed in by a single blow to leave an everlasting, horrific image in Ken's mind.

The completion of a combat tour that by now stretched to 35 missions was still fraught with risk at any stage; the Grim Reaper's scythe was poised to strike at any point and in any malign manner possible. To date, the 446BG crew led by 29-year-old Lt. Martin J. Mullane (known as "Pappy") had completed 33 of the mandatory mission figure and today they were going out on the penultimate run towards tour completion. Their B-24, 42-50681/ **Slightly Dangerous**, was mortally wounded by the flak gunners bare seconds after releasing its bombs.

Mullane was either mortally wounded or unable to get to an exit point as the doomed B-24 began its wayward path towards the ground, but the other nine airmen managed to fight their way out and deploy their parachutes. However, what should have been the beginning of a positive albeit shadowy existence as a POW was cruelly denied in the case of Sgts. Willard Perry (Eng.) and Hoover Baucom (ROG). They both encountered the unbridled wrath of the civilian population who, as with the 389BG victims, dealt out their form of summary justice on the hapless duo.

Comment

The staccato pace of missions already recorded up to 19 October (13) slowed even further for the remainder of the month, with only five being flown, of which four involved the Division. Up to the 19th, the overall MIA loss factor (112) was barely 1% of the roughly 12,000 completed sorties, of which around 70% had been borne by the B-17 Divisions. These positive statistics reinforced the general feeling that the *Jagdwaffe's* ability to even blunt the Allied Air Forces' largely punishing incursions, let alone reverse the situation, had been pushed firmly into the background.

However, the lurking threat of the *Sturmgruppen*, whose malign influence had been demonstrated over Kassel in September was a reminder that the German fighter pilots still posed a challenge, however irregular and dissipated that might be expressed. Flak in contrast had never been—and moreover was never to become—other than a frighteningly unpredictable "deterrent" in physical and psychological terms. The range of targets might be beginning to shrink as the Allied land armies pressed in upon the Third Reich, but this was not the case in terms of ground defense resources; there were ever-greater flak concentrations, particularly around key industrial facilities, such as synthetic oil refineries.

The aforementioned missions involved a variety of target categories, beginning with Hamm's sorely-tested marshalling yards (22nd), Neumuenster airfield and Scholven/Buer's oil refinery (25th), the Minden/Mittelland canal and a refinery at Bottrop/Welheim (26th), and culminating on the 30th with twin thrusts at refineries within the Hamburg/Harburg conurbation. The first three runs proved cost-free, but a pair of crews failed to come home on the latter occasion.

The 44BG's intention to strike its Harburg target was thwarted by units of the preceding CBW and its crew ended up releasing either on the Secondary or the town of Uetersen, west of Hamburg. Lt. Bentcliff's veteran crew was on board 424-10523/GJ: T, flying as the High right squadron's Lead. The heavy weather front encountered on the way over and during the bomb run was recalled by Sgt. Fuller (Eng.). The bomb run was scarcely over when slipstream turbulence from an errant bomber that cut across its path threw his bomber over onto its back and into a terminal spinning motion. Fuller was one of three Enlisted men who cheated death this day; tragically, Lt. Barefoot (PN) had flown the mission in order to complete his combat tour.

The 458BG was similarly thwarted from bombing Harburg, and to add to this basically negative result came back one crew light. **Bomb-Ah-Dear** (42-100431/J4: B) was a Group "original" being flown by Lt. William H. Curland, but whether fighters or flak were responsible for this loss remains unclear. It is sufficient to record that a bail out order was being responded to when the tail section snapped off; the resultant uncontrolled gyration of the shortened airframe almost certainly trapped the pilot, along with F/O Grover M. Long (N), T/Sgt. James C. Butler (Eng.), and Sgt. Victor C. Drahos (TG).

November 1944

Oil-related targets dominated the first three November missions, and although the 2BD suffered nil MIA casualties on the 1st, two *Sturmgruppen* forces tore through the 91st and 457th BGs on the 2nd to highlight this specific menace. Castrop/Rauxel's facility was attacked by seven Division Groups on this mission, with a single 453BG crew going down, but the contrast between the men's combat experience and their B-24 could hardly be greater. **El Flako** (42-64469/E3: I) was a 77-mission veteran compared to Lt. Isaksen's team flying their first. A flak strike blew the bomber's fuselage in half and all on board shared in her brutal crucifixion.

Hannover/Misburg was selected on the 4th, when six Groups dispatched 222 crews in all—almost double the average unit strength sent out on the 2nd. This time around the defenses claimed three crews: two from the 20CBW and one from the 14CBW. The latter machine was 42-95293/EC: H **American Beauty**, which was later reported as going down in the target area trailing flames from one engine. One survivor recalled that the bail out order had been given, but when the German authorities inspected the wreckage they discovered no fewer than five corpses; Lt. Hayden H. Clifford (P) was one of four POWs.

The indifferent to poor weather conditions were forcing the regular use of blind bombing equipment, and with it a further degradation in the avowed principle of precision bombardment, but at least a majority of the Primaries were being assaulted, albeit with variable degrees of destruction. The Division escaped almost unscathed during the ensuing six missions between the 5th and 11th, when marshalling yards and oil refineries formed the bulk of the targets; the exception occurred on the 9th, when tactical locations around Metz were plastered with a view to aiding the advance of Gen. Patton's 3rd Army, an intention that was not realized until several more weeks ensued.

The trickle of losses during this week of intensive operations commenced on the 6th, when two targets were assigned. The 448BG was an element of the sub-force heading for the Minden/Mittelland Canal, a key transport conduit. The formation was bypassing Muenster on the way in when a flak shell ignited the No. 2 engine on 42-50820/, flown by Lt. Frank Genarlsky. The motor was switched off and part of the bomb load jettisoned after the bomber reversed course. However, it remained aloft only for several minutes before coming down at Billerbeck; the remaining bomb load exploded, expunging the lives of any crewmembers who might have survived the heavy crash landing. The North Sea was the likely tomb for Lt. Maynard M. Ungerer's nine-man crew on the 10th. **Snooper** (42-52571/Q2: D) was last seen on the return leg from bombing Hanau/Langendiebach airfield with its No. 2 propeller "feathered" when SW of Brussels. Finally, a 453BG crew was MIA from a run to Bottrop oil refinery (11th). Lt. John H. Friedhaber (734BS) was one fatality after his 42-95167 **Never Mrs** was observed disappearing into the undercast.

Just one mission was flown by the Division over the next eight days, but the overall involvement of the 8AF in bombing tactical targets ahead of the U.S. 1st Army resulted in a "nil" MIA figure. This positive scenario was repeated on the 20th, but not so 24 hours later, when no less than six B-24s were stricken off Division records. Hamburg's oil refinery resources were duly hammered by 359 bombers, but four Groups registered losses over Europe. Seething's latest casualty was one victim of the ferocious flak barrage thrown up by Germany's second-largest industrial city. **Little Joe** (41-28925/) was culled, along with all but one on Lt. Joe Bowers's (KIA) team. Another shell that fortunately penetrated the fuselage of 41-28958/ but did not explode until it had exited nevertheless severed the rudder cables and started a small fire; Sgt. Louis Owens (Eng), in addition to extinguishing the flames, also managed to re-splice the cables so that Lt. Elliot Sidey could regain a measure of control and bring his charge back to base. **Satans Little Sister** (42-95180RT: N-Bar) from Bungay consumed seven of the nine-man crew in the course of her demise; in stark contrast, Lts. John Quinn (P) and Melbourne Simmons (CP) not only parachuted safely, but got into Resistance hands. One of the other two losses involved an Old Buckenham crew who won through to Sweden; the B-24 in question was Lt. Kaylor C. Whitehead's 41-29005/E8:, which had lost an engine over the target.

The specter of mid-air collision had already caught up with two Hethel crews as the Group assembled. The Lead B-24/44-10513/RR: O **Earthquake McGoon/Sweet Pea** was in Lt. Rhine's hands, while Lt. Ralph Jacobson (566BS) would be his No. 2. Jacobson reached Group-forming altitude ahead of Rhine; off to the former pilot's bomber was 42-50452/RR: D, flown by Lt. Brookes. When Rhine arrived, he initially pulled left of Brookes before reversing his course. The next recollection Jacobson had was of a solid "thump" sound; on looking to the left, his shocked gaze absorbed the sight of the Rhine-flown B-24's outer starboard wing panel hurtling off into space, followed almost immediately by the bomber slumping into a tight spin.

Meanwhile, Brookes's B-24, which was the other "participant" in the collision, was seen to adopt a shallow diving attitude. This provided a sadly deceptive impression that the pilots were still in control, because the B-24's port wing suddenly detached, and only Brookes and Lt. Bill Martin (B) managed to fight their way out. S/Sgt. Pete Ferdinand (ROG) to Lt. Rhine proved to be the only other survivor between the twenty airmen manning the two B-24s. Sgt. Ferdinand would repeat his parachute experience on Christmas Day.

Martyrdom over Misburg

The 25 November mission to Bingen's marshalling yards evolved as another cost-free run for the 254 crews involved. Among the Division's ranks was the 491BG, whose last MIA casualty had been incurred on 2 October; since then, fully 26 missions had been flown without loss. The 31 crews rousted out of bed for an 0530 Briefing next morning must have felt that the way matters were going by now there was at worst a marginal threat to life and limb being presented by the German defenses. Before the day was out that confident mood would have been fully displaced by the realization that the enemy would go down fighting and take every opportunity to savagely punish the American crews in the process.

Take off and Assembly had been completed by 0900 and the three squadrons headed out. However, one B-24 quickly "aborted" with fuel problems and a second developed radio malfunction that impelled the pilots to follow the same course of action. Whatever frustration these airmen must have felt at suffering this current block to their tour completion, they would arguably appreciate their good fortune at not being present within the formation.

The distinctive Duemmersee geographic reference was over-flown and the IP at Wittingen, NE of Misburg, had been reached—from where the formations would bank right and bomb on a reverse course—when the sense of security from assault began to dissipate. A huge fighter formation was sighted to the southeast that did not attack, but hovered around in an almost casual manner. Unfortunately, the P-51 and P-47 escorts took the bait and totally rushed off to engage their adversaries.

L/Col. Parmele, as Air Commander, now had to make a choice between carrying out the normal "in trail" bombing pattern, thereby splitting the bombers' defensive integrity during the bomb run, or maintain the formation's integrity, an action that would reduce the chances of a truly accurate strike. He chose the former method and the three squadrons broke up into the standard sequence of Lead, Low, and High. Even this action might not have been too critical in defensive requirement, had not matters gone further wrong. Accidental contact with the bomb release toggle in the Low squadron's Lead B-24 saw its load spill out, to be followed by the other nine bombers. With no requirement to risk a flak barrage over the target in these circumstances, the squadron's CO decided to pull away left and head for the Rally Point; this in turn left a sizeable gap between the other two sub-units. Thus was the scene unknowingly set for disaster.

The unprotected Group's run-up suddenly became free of flak interference. This puzzling but welcome anomaly had barely been taken in by the crews when the reason for its cessation became shockingly evident—a

Weather conditions over East Anglia on 16 November 1944 forced a diversion for the 448BG. The slippery runway surface at RAF Lissett, on the Yorkshire coast, caused 42-50759 **Shady Lady** to skid off and end up with its nose section thoroughly mangled by the ploughed-up soil; six days later, the B-24J-1-FO (the last airframe in this production batch) was deemed fit only for salvage.

Sturmgruppe force mainly comprised of Fw190s and later estimated at around 100 zoomed in from behind to literally swamp the group's High squadron. The carnage really began on the fighters' second pass, with the B-24s flown by Lts. Charles W. Stevens (41-29 464/T8: Y) and Daniel C. Budd (KIA) 42 -100167/ T8: Q **Firebird** becoming the first casualties. Stevens, who had not flown since crash landing on 20 June, recalled T/Sgt. Joseph L. Boyer (Eng.) yelling: "They're coming in again!" before a 20mm shell killed him; seconds later, the B-24 exploded to blow the pilot out into mid-air.

The bomb run was barely completed when five more crews were culled; those led by Lt. Warren Moore (POW) in 44-40205/T8: G **The Moose** and Capt. Wayne E. Stewart (squadron Lead, KIA), flying 42-5153/T8: F **Idiots Delight**, appears to have gone first. Moore's No. 2 engine and the bomb bay were set on fire and the intercom and hydraulic system disabled during the initial pass. Lt. Ross S. Houston (N) fought frantically but in vain to free Lt. George K. Patten (B) from the nose turret that had jammed to one side. The bomber began to tumble after several explosions occurred in the rear and Houston was forced to leave his fellow-airman to his cruel fate; the navigator was one of five crewmembers to reach the ground alive after taking to his parachute. The Stewart crew had been flying their 30th mission, but the same number of survivors as on Lt. Moore's aircraft remained alive to savor the doubtful pleasures of a *Stalag*.

The hapless duo were followed by Lts. John P. Hite (KIA) in 41-28884/T8: X **Problem Child**; Lt. Robert E. Cloughley (POW) piloting 44–44212/ T8: I; and Lt. Charles J. Eklund's (POW) 44-10534/ T8: B. The demise of the first two listed B-24s, along with Lt. Budd's, must have been violent, since only four of the 28 airmen involved escaped with their lives. The sub-unit's almost total excision from group strength culminated when Lts. David N. Bennett (KIA) in 44-44073/ T8: B **Ark Angel** and Ralph J. Butler (POW), piloting 44-10485/T8: K, made a desperate bid to link up with the Lead squadron, one that only the former-led crew was very fortunate to achieve. However, the reprieve was temporary, because the heavily-damaged bomber, with the top-turret blasted off and a large hole in the starboard wing, gradually fell behind and was losing altitude when last seen. What then transpired remains unknown, but nobody survived the B-24's loss. In this manner did the 853BS cease to exist as part of the day's Group strength.

Their voracious appetite almost fully satiated in respect of the High squadron but not the Group, the enemy force now switched to the fully isolated Low squadron. Lt. James J. Wynn (KIA) and crew went down in 42-95007/6X: S+ almost immediately after the left element Lead 42-51253/6X: R-, in Lt. Warczak's (KIA) charge, was summarily hacked from the sky. The gunners were fighting back as ferociously as possible, but their adversaries' weight of gunfire bit further into the squadron's ranks. Lt. Matthew Vukovich did not survive the loss of his 44-40108/6X: A+, as did anybody else on board the viciously-spinning bomber. **Hare Power** (44-40117/6X: J+), flown by Lt. Floyd I. Weitz, who ended up as a POW, fell away with the bomb bay ablaze and came down at Deckbergen. Lt. Robert W. Simon's 44-40172/6X: H- **Grease Ball** suffered a fusillade of gunfire that killed two gunners, disabled communications, and set the bomb bay on fire; the pilot was one of only three survivors escaping the clutches of the tumbling machine.

A particularly tragic situation arose on 44-40271/6X: K- **House Of Rumor**. Lt. Harry W. Sonning (B), on going through the fuselage to check that all had received the bail out order from the now-burning B-24, found that three Enlisted men were completely ignoring the order. An explosion blew the Lieutenant out into mid-air, but the three gunners went in with the bomber. All were uninjured, so it is likely they "froze" at the thought of leaping into what was a noisy and challenging unknown void. The group martyrdom was concluded with Lt. Lenning's -610/6X: I-. The B-24 had suffered shattered bomb bay doors during bomb release, but the battered machine managed to directly survive the aerial slaughter and stagger on as far as Belgium, where the crew abandoned their mount.

Whereas the other two squadrons had been overwhelmed, the same fate was not suffered by the Lead sub-unit, although it too was engaged by the enemy force. Its 100% survival rate was in part due to the belated arrived of escort fighters. However, the first eight P-51s to turn up belonged to the 2nd Weather Scouting Force, which was led by a former 458BG pilot, Capt. Bob Whitlow! This miniscule unit waded into the attackers until further reinforcements arrived, after which the hunters swiftly became the hunted. The nine-strong Lead squadron, along with the pitifully few survivors from the other two squadrons (four of the 854BS), linked up and wended their now depressing way home.

Aftermath

It had happened regularly in the past and would recur in the future, albeit with diminishing frequency for the ground personnel concerned. The men belonging to the 853BS scanned the formation that was maneuvering in the airfield circuit. Those with binoculars could confirm that none of their squadron's aircraft were present, but all assumed that these would be part of a separate formation. But no such formation loomed up as the B-24s above broke off and landed. One airman recorded his reaction, clearly echoed by all:

> Today, nine crews took off with an ETR of 1600 hours. Minutes after that time, one and a half squadrons appeared; none of our ships were present, so we waited for a second formation. The clock moved on up to 30 minutes... It initially never occurred to us that our ships had gone down. Gradually, after we constantly checked with the tower we realized such a thing could happen...that maybe it had happened. We made ourselves believe the aircraft had come down in France or Belgium, or at least that some of them would return... but after interrogation hope died.

The immediate debriefing reports indicated the number of parachutes seen coming from the High squadron as over 90%, while a revised estimate still suggested between 50% and 75% of the crewmembers had emerged safely. Sadly, an almost reverse percentage of fatalities (at least 50 out of the 84 individuals concerned) would be realized, with the rest sitting out the conflict in captivity. The overall group "butcher's bill" was 90 dead and 52 POWs. Misburg had firmly put the cap upon any optimism at the base regarding a dwindling and/or ineffective resistance to Allied aerial incursions over the Third Reich.

The total MIA cost today was further extended to 21, the 2CBW being the source, with the 445BG losing five and the 389BG a single B-24. The latter casualty was 44-10579/RR: D **Pugnacious Princess Pat**, flown by Lt. Robert Hicks. The flak burst excised most if not all of one wing to cast the airframe into a sharp canting angle in that direction. In these circumstances, it was a wonder that anyone, let alone four of the ten-man crew, got out alive, the pilot being among this very fortunate number. Lt. Daniel W. Snow and crew survived the loss of their Tibenham-based B-24/42-50756/RN: J, which reportedly fell to earth near Hameln, although two crewmembers were recorded as being apprehended more than 40 miles west of this location. Lt. Clarence W. Harris, flying 42-51549/RN:, got his nine-man crew safely out of his doomed bomber to join their fellow squadron colleagues in captivity.

The trio of missions closing off November saw the Division indulging in its seeming "priority" target category—marshalling yards on two occasions—with railroad viaducts cropping up as a variation on the third (29th). The weather conditions on the first two missions dictated wholesale use of PFF equipment, but conversely, overall 8AF losses amounted to just one crew; unfortunately for the Division, it was a Tibenham-based team. Next day, the B-17 Divisions lost 28 crews between them while attacking oil refineries, while the 2BD came home three light, two of which belonged to the 446BG. Lt. John V. Colson (P) was to be the sole survivor out of eleven on 42-51272/RT: T, and even then his salvation was almost miraculous, since he was blown out after a flak shell split the airframe in two. The disintegrating B-24 shed its debris directly into the path of 42-51115/RT: Z; one crewmember was killed by these lethal remnants and a second who was among the nine bailing out subsequently died on the ground from unknown causes. The other lost bomber added to the already sizeable MIA total borne by the 445BG.

Chapter Sixteen

Martyrdom at Kassel

Preamble

In the course of the USAAF's Daylight Bombing Offensive, there were to be regular occasions where a specific Group was destined to suffer severe depredations from the German defensive system, with the *Jagdwaffe* pilots administering a sizeable proportion of the punishment. There were eight such missions from which the "Bloody Hundredth" earned its dubious reputation as a "jinx" outfit, while a number of its fellow units could recall between a single and several instances of heavy losses. The initial period of operations up to early 1944 had seen the bombers ranging well beyond regular fighter cover and therefore ripe for this treatment, which cast heavily-armed fighters against their less maneuverable and therefore more vulnerable adversaries. The equally heavy armament of the B-17s and B-24s was not sufficient in itself to guarantee immunity from the *Jagdwaffe's* lethal punching power. Even when regular escort cover was on hand from 1944 onwards, the advent of fighter packs that culminated in the formation of the dreaded *Sturmgruppen* seeking to exploit gaps in that cover virtually ensured that an isolated Group formation could expect to bear a swinging degree of loss when so encountered.

However, the majority of these ever-traumatic actions involved a protracted period of time between the first and final casualty being incurred. This was the case for the Tibenham-based 445BG on 24 February 1944, when thirteen B-24s were hacked from its ranks. On the other hand, what was to transpire during the mission to Kassel on 27 September would far exceed either this previous experience, or indeed and arguably all of the other instances of heavy losses by any other Group. First of all, the percentage loss factor would prove to be way ahead of any other Group's experience when dispatching a formation of today's scale. (The 100BG's second thrashing over Muenster on 8 October 1943 had cost it twelve of the thirteen-strong formation, but this initial figure was barely one-third of the 445BG's strength of 38 initially heading for Kassel.) In addition, the vast bulk of the execution dealt out by the three *Sturmgruppen* involved in the slaughter was to span less than ten minutes from initiation to completion.

Mission Background

Certain targets, with Berlin, Hamburg, and Merseburg as prime examples, did elicit a heightened degree of tension among the airmen. Kassel, on the other hand, probably did not fall into that category, although it was a regularly briefed target, with its huge Hentschel armored vehicle production plant a central focus of attention. The 2CBW, along with the 14th and 20th Wings, was part of a ten-Group force; the other two Divisions were at full strength and briefed to attack the Merseburg/Leuna and Magdeburg/Rothensee oil refineries. The combat crewmembers gathered in the Tibenham Briefing room were under no illusions regarding even a guarantee of survival from today's impending mission, let alone of gaining permanent salvation by completing their tours. They naturally had no inkling of the scale of individual and corporate disaster looming up. Fully 112 among their number would not see another dawn, including all aboard Lt. Seed's B-24, all but two on Lt. Mowat's team, and a single survivor out of Lt. Bolin's nine-man crew—all from the 703BS, whose ranks would be further thinned by 28 hapless souls for a final "tally" of fifty-two. The other three squadrons would share the remaining sixty fatalities. A further 98 airmen were unknowingly facing the twilight world of "Kriegydom."

Lt. Bob Tims (N) recorded a detailed account of the mission from its very inception. He remembered the artificially-barbed remarks flowing between his crew during breakfast that were especially directed at Lts. John French (P) and Bob Cochran (CP), who were scheduled to fly their final mission—"One way or the other," as the former acidly stated. Also included in the conversation was Lt. Malcolm McGregor, bombardier to Lt. Sollien. After two aborted missions, "Mac," who had been acquainted with the French crew since phase training in Boise, Idaho, was also due to complete his combat tour. Fate would be kind to all three, albeit in a harsher and protracted manner as regards "Mac." At Briefing Tims whispered to Lt. Cochran: "I'd hate to meet the Luftwaffe on your last mission," a remark that would surely come back to haunt both in the hours ahead.

The weather conditions in central Germany at least were expected to be adverse enough to merit the use of PFF equipment with which to direct the bomb loads onto the Primary. An added risk where heavy under or overcast conditions if encountered lay in the chances of a Group becoming detached from the bomber stream—a factor that was to arise today, and in doing so probably if not definitely sowed the seeds for the largest-scale disaster to affect an individual 8AF unit during WWII.

The 2CBW was to be positioned in the middle of the 2BD stream, with the 445BG assigned as Lead Group for the Wing; Maj. Don W. McCoy (700BS CO) was appointed Air Commander and joined Capt. John H. Chilton's crew in 42-51541/RN:. Lt. Cloys V. Johnson was the DR Navigator upon whose judgement the mission's success for both the Group and Wing primarily depended. Deputy Lead was 42-51547, piloted by Capt. Wilber Uebelhoeur, with Capt. James Graham as Deputy A/C. Take off from Tibenham and the subsequent Group Assembly proceeded without any hitches, other than Lt. Rene Schneider's 44-40250, which slashed a tire and failed to launch. The 2CBW was also successfully assembled and duly slotted into the bomber stream.

Setting Out

The thirty-eight B-24s that had formed up were split into four squadron dispositions, with the normal Lead, Low-left, and High-right sub-units supplemented by a Slot sub-unit. In addition, a fifth sub-unit provided by the 453BG was allocated to what was recorded as 2CBW/2A, with Hethel and Old Buckenham linking up their resources to form the 2CBW/2B. (The subsequent divergent action of the 453BG element within the 2A formation in remaining with the 2BD main stream would add to the post-mission confusion regarding the Tibenham-based airmen's fatally-wayward conduct.)

The overall strength of the 445BG was to be further diluted by three "aborts" during the inward stage: 42-94939/MK:

This 445BG B-24J-95-CO has suffered the collapse of its port main landing gear after overshooting the runway at Tibenham on 16 September. The 703BS bomber is 42-100343, which bears a shark mouth design on its nose and has already seen ample operational service, judging by her oil- and dirt-stained wings.

On 14 July 1944, B-24H-20-FO **Lonesome Louis** diverted into Beccles airfield with this recorded result. Her serial number on the fin is short of the year of production procurement (42). The aircraft letter applied in yellow on the fuselage is repeated on the fin for clearer identification. Glazed windows are fitted to the waist hatches and a "chaff" chute is mounted below the letter K.

A plan view of an anonymous Tibenham-based B-24 is taken with an almost solid cloud undercast, a condition that eliminated any prospect of sound bombing accuracy. The aerodynamic quality of the Davis Wing is evident at this angle, but not so the relatively clumsy fuselage outline.

S-Bar **Heavenly Body** (Lt. Wilbur Williams) and 42-94921/MK: B-Bar **Tahelenbak** (Lt. Don McClelland) relinquished their positions within the Slot squadron, along with Lt. Keith Frost's 44-40294/MK: C-Bar **Slossie**. No specific reason for their actions arose in respect of other than the McClelland-piloted bomber, which suffered the loss of one engine to flak.

The briefed outward route was for a course that tracked the formations in over Holland's Ijsselmeer, then turned to starboard to thread in between Munster and Hamm and the northern fringe of the Ruehr before straightening out until reaching the IP some 60 miles NW of the target. A comprehensive fighter cover was to be on hand, provided by P-47s and P-51s. In the case of the Leading elements of the 2BD, the duty was assigned to the 355FG, led by Col. Everett Stewart. Also on hand was the 361FG, whose subsequent actions, however belatedly exercised, would bring succor to what was to be the bare remnants of the 445BG formation.

The predicted persistent undercast and resultant absence of ground references with which to further confirm the formation was on course naturally cast an extra responsibility upon Johnson in maintaining an accurate Air Plot. On the other hand, the Wing's central position within the Division stream should have provided some degree of visual contact with the Lead CBW, especially in the case of the 445BG.

Jagdwaffe Response

Gen. Schmid's constant dilemma in marshalling his depleted fighter resources was that there was little or no guarantee of bringing his pilots into effective contact with more than a proportion of the by-now regularly dispersed elements of the 8AF bomber stream. Regarding today's mission, a comprehensive and well-researched history of the *Reichsverteidigung* indicates that he (correctly) regarded the primary threat as being directed towards the German oil industry and ordered the dispatch of around 120 fighters in total, all provided by *Sturmgruppen* units: IV (*Sturm*) JG3, II (*Sturm*) JG2, and II (*Sturm*) JG300. These heavily-armed and armored Fw190s would have a high escort provided by *Stab* and I/JG300, whose more maneuverable Bf109s were needed to ward off any 8FC counterattacks that might descend upon their less nimble and accordingly more vulnerable bomber destroyer contemporaries.

Confused Approach

Lt. Tims remembered the mounting confusion within the crew during the bomb run stage:

> Although a degree of break in the cloud cover occurred over Holland, it then vanished totally for the remainder of the inward leg. The bomb run was in progress when I checked my watch, whose hands indicated the Group was beyond their ETA for bombing, assuming my calculations were correct. It was then that Sgt. Schwartz (TG) called up to say he could see smoke marker trails behind and to the southwest as well as flak, thereby increasing the feeling that the 445BG was out of station with the 2BD stream. Sgt. Greenly (NG) said he believed we had passed up Kassel and they must be bombing back of us. I replied that I thought so; my navigation showed we were several minutes east—which could have been wrong, however, since I did not have a visual fix position. Almost at once, Lt. Cochran confirmed the Lead B24 had released its load, whereupon I hit the toggle switch. Still no flak was encountered. As we turned for home, I kidded the pilots that they should be ashamed to finish up on a mission with no flak encountered! Cochran responded by saying: "Well, I feel kinda bad about this, so we'll just have to fly another one tomorrow!" Within a minute or so, the flak threat would become an almost welcome alternative to what was to evolve with shocking force.

Armageddon Awaits Lt. Bob Tims

Bob Tims remembers the Group had just turned westwards when he glanced back. Then:

The picture's caption gives 8 March 1944 as the incident date, but tree foliage confirms this as inaccurate. In fact, on 14 July 1944, **Fearless Fosdick** made a wheels-down emergency landing in a cornfield near Newmarket on 1 August. B-24H-15-CF/41-29604/WV: Y remained intact, something that might not have occurred had she been "bellied in," given the propensity for the fuselage to collapse when bearing the stress of impact.

Tahelenbak has seemingly incurred a noticeable degree of damage to her lower fuselage that has merited the NMF replacement panel directly behind the bombardier's Plexiglas. This B-24H-20-FO/ 42-94921 successfully lived up to her defiant title, serving with two Tibenham squadrons and returning Stateside in May 1945.

What I saw froze me to the bone—a bee swarm of fighters. Recognition was sickening—a large radial engine and spinner and a slender tapered fuselage. Fw190s! As I pressed my switch, Schwartz despairingly shouted: "Fighters! 6 o'clock! Hundreds of them!" I tried to call out the attackers' positions, but this proved futile, as they just swarmed all over us. Someone called out to Greenly (NG): "Coming past at 9 o'clock—get him! Now!" Then mingled calls: "Three more at 9. Oh Jesus!"... "I got one!" [This from Sgt. Jim Coman (WG)] .. "Watch that one coming under us!"

Parson's B24 [This was probably Lt. Jim Schaen's 44-10511/WV: C, with S/Sgt. Dick Parsons (WG) on board] suddenly blossomed into bright red flame before kicking over and down; Carrow's ship [42-110022/IS: F+ **Patches**], behind him trying to fight off the angry bees, trailed tell-tale smoke from its bowels; one man dropped through the rear hatch before the ship fell like a broken child's toy, leafing and spinning from 23,000ft.

There were nauseating thumps on our ship and the No. 2 caught fire before the flames died. "Where are our fighters! Oh Christ!" Then Schwartz yelled: "Keep the intercom clear so I can call em' coming in!" Cochran shouted: "Watch that S.O.B on your side, French—he's almost in formation," with French replying: "I can't move over, Doc; Bruce [Lt. Bill Bruce flying 42-95128/IS: R+ **Bonnie Vee**] is on fire and running into us!" I witnessed flames extending from Bruce's cockpit to the tail, the aluminium skin curling and baking brown under the murderous assaults. Never a chance! I glimpsed a waist gunner fighting his window to escape while dying his hot death.

Up front, the Group Lead ship had been shattered. A complete prop came sailing back; from somewhere a body and a single flying boot. Then our ship lurched as if stricken to the core. With this came the knowledge of utter giving up to us all. Death was more certain than can ever be again. There was no conscious fear, the heat of action having burnt it out to leave a residue of utter abandonment. I only waited and hoped to be spared pain...

No. 3 was apparently "feathered," after which the airframe's trembling eased and we seemed to fly almost smoothly on two. [A broken propeller blade on No. 3 had adversely affected the damaged right rudder thanks to the turbulent airflow thus created, so switching off had at least removed this aerodynamic hindrance!] We had not noticed the attacks had slackened, with no Fws streaking in to finish what they had started. I saw only four B24s far up ahead and above in formation. Then someone called out: "Oh Christ, here comes four more at 9 o'clock!" strangling the infant hope just born. Oh God, to tease us, just to snatch survival away! Greenly almost immediately called out: "Look, Look—straight ahead and high! P-38s! P-38s!" He could find no other words, but his utterances were pregnant with wild joy. Then I saw them, Hope riding in on twin-winged angels and Promise reborn after seeming to be dashed!

"Waist to crew—the bandits are gone into the clouds away from the P-38s!" called out Greenly again, as the fighters, having driven away their adversaries, wheeled around to assume their primary escort function. We had survived the immediate attention of the enemy, but still faced a long and uncertain struggle to at least regain friendly soil within the Continent..."

Jack Mercer

The first indication Lt. Jackson Mercer, flying 42-51549/RN: G off Lt. Isom's port wing in the Low left squadron, had that the Group was under assault was contained within the following account:

> There we were at 26,000ft, somewhere south of the target, which I naturally thought had been Kassel, and flying above a 9/10 overcast with the time 1006 hours—and then "boom!" Isom's B24 was our element Lead and his officer complement with whom we shared our hut were good friends. Suddenly, Sgt. Harry Lied (TG) called up to say: "Bandits, ten to twelve across at 6 o'clock level." I alerted the crew, but was interrupted by Leid adding: "They're firing—looks like their wings are on fire—they're closing fast" before his voice was cut off. The damaged intercom system now meant I had no idea what was happening; all I could see was the sky filled with bursts like flak, so I concentrated on keeping the B24 aloft.
>
> The controls went slack and No. 2 began to run rough while oxygen pressure dropped. It was impossible to hold close position with Isom and I was forced to engage the auto-pilot and increase engine RPM and boost. Our radio system was also disabled, but Paul Pouliot (CP) was initially unaware of this and grew increasingly red-faced, as he naturally failed to gain any response from our fighters via their channels.
>
> The enemy fighters' approach appears to have been both from behind and below, the latter indicating they were aware that our B24s had dispensed with the ball turrets in order to gain better handling characteristics. However, the overwhelming number of fighters would probably have been too much even with these turrets in place.
>
> I began to sense the catastrophe now taking place. Our formation location provided a view of the others, although my concentration was basically on formatting with Isom. Planes on fire or blowing up... parachutes cascading from damaged B24s....smoke from 20mm bursts....but the most eerie sight was of two complete sets of propellers corkscrewing ahead of their aircraft but maintaining temporary formation before falling into a horizontal attitude as they lost speed to float downwards." [Their violent detachment was probably due to the pilots ramming the throttles "to the wall" before increasing the RPMs sufficiently and shearing off the propeller shafts in the process]

"Slaughter Alley"

A veritable clutch of nineteen crash sites were to be established within a roughly 20-30 mile arc west of Eisenach, the first of which was well to the northwest of that town and just east of Eschwege. The B-24 concerned was 41-29542/WV: A, flown by Lt. Howard Jones, who lost three out of ten crewmembers, with the bomber impacting at Doringsdorf. Creuzberg, due north of Eisenach, was where 42-51355/RN: K, bearing Lt. Roy Bolin's crew, descended with Sgt. Orland Schooley (TG) the sole survivor out of nine—surprisingly so, given his extreme exposure to the firepower of the encroaching *Sturmgruppen* force. Some six miles separated this initial casualty from where 42-50340/WV: B descended at Archfeld, along with Lt. Herbert Potts and four of the other eight airmen. Nesselroeden, which was close by, was the last resting place for 42-51287/WV: Y.

Herleshausen and Launchroeden, immediately south of Nesselroeden, received the carcasses of four bombers, three at the latter location. **Fort Worth Maid** 42-50321/WV: V spread itself

A 700BS B-24 that appears to be a Ford-built J-Model, judging by the anti-dazzle panel's position, forms a background to several crewmembers. The horizontal white fin band is confined to the fin, suggesting the rudder is a replacement fitting, and a similar layout applies to the B-24 in the left background.

Skippers Clipper appears to be fully laden for a mission by the pronounced degree of dihedral displayed by the wings. The Group practice of applying the aircraft letter in yellow as well as in smaller proportion to the squadron codes is clearly demonstrated. This B-24H-20-FO/42-95000 was a 701BS aircraft.

The aerial version of a "summary execution" is grimly portrayed in this picture. What is almost certainly a flak strike has excised the port wing of a B-24 from just beyond the No. 1 engine. The aircraft is already canting to port and centrifugal force build-up is pressing inexorably upon the crew; they will be very fortunate to escape its clutches and bail out from their airborne "tomb."

along with half of Lt. Carl Sollien's (POW) crew. There were only six out of 27 airmen who survived their aircrafts' demise at Lauchroeden, with the nine-man teams of Lts. Edgar Walther in 44-10490/MK: Z-Bar **Jane** and Andrew Seeds piloting **42-110073**/WV: Q totally wiped out; the fortunate six all came from 42-10497/IS: P+, whose pilot (Lt. Ralph Pearson) was among this number. Another pair of casualties was inflicted near Gestungen, SW of Lauchroeden. The first was 44-10511/WV: C, bearing Lt. Jim Schaen's crew. (A detailed account by Lt. Collar (B) is recorded further on in this chapter.) Its companion in death was 42-100308/WV: Q **Our Gal**, from which just one-third of Lt. Lesley Warman's crew got out and down alive, the pilot being one of the fatalities.

A second pair of B-24s found their final resting place several miles NW of where the foregoing duo crashed, namely Richelsdorf. These were 42-95128/IS: R+ **Bonnie Vee**, flown by Lt. William Bruce—one of only two survivors out of nine—and 42-95078/IS: C+, in Lt. Robert Hansen's charge; the fatality percentage was the same as for the Warman crew, with the pilot added into this statistic.

The slaughter proceeded apace, six more bombers being downed within a rough circle with Netteshausen as its epicenter. Ulfen, Lindenau, and Breitau form a triangle NW of Nentershausen. The recurring figure of one-third of survivors among nine featured in the loss of Lt. Don Brent's (KIA) 42-50324/WV: S **Eileen** close to the first-named location. **Clay Pigeon** (41-29579/RN: N) consumed four of the nine-man crew, including Lt. Oliver Elder, as she piled in at Lindenau. The best survival rate among this trio—eight out of ten—occurred on board 42-51342/RN: I **Fridget Bridget**, and for once Lt. Joe Johnson (P) was not one of the fatalities.

The overall loss factor at this stage was largely completed west and south of Nentershausen. Hoenebach, due south of there, was where 42-51532/RN: P **Hot Rock** came to earth bearing Lt. Bill Mowat and six of his eight colleagues to their deaths in the process. Iba, the apex of a triangle formed with the two aforementioned locations, received the shattered remains of Lt. Rapheal Carrow's 42-110022/IS: F+ **Patches**; the pilot and four out of his eight-man team fought their way out and parachuted to safety—or as safe as one could feel when descending into the autocratic world of the Third Reich. The penultimate loss in "Slaughter Alley" seems to have been **Ole Baldy** (42-94863/MK: T-Bar), flown by Lt. William Golden; he was to prove the unfortunate exception among his crew, since all of them defeated the Grim Reaper's attempt to claim their bodies. The bomber crash site near Cornberg was none too distant from that of **Patches**.

The final loss around this stage of the withdrawal leg ironically appears to have also been the one crashing the closest to Kassel; Lt. Fromm's 42-52080/RN: U ended its operational career south of Hessisch Lichtenau-Reichenbach, scant miles distant from what was to have been the Primary. Lt. Edward Gibbs (CP) was the sole fatality out of the nine on board.

Down on Enemy Soil

The following series of personal accounts of the one-sided action provide a sound image to the reader of the trauma faced this day, and by extension in the months of imprisonment that lay ahead.

Lt. Carrow

The first indication of attack for Lt. Carrow was a glimpse of the B-24 to his right catching fire and parachutes starting to appear, followed by the shock of strikes on his own bomber 42-110022/700BS **Patches**. The bomber lost two engines, and on glancing back into the fuselage he was greeted by the sight of a raging fire, probably caused when gunfire ignited the fumes gathering from punctured fuel lines. Lt. Newell Brainard (CP) was already gone when Carrow initially attempted to get out of his seat, but the combination of his heavy clothing and flak suit made it difficult for him to release his seatbelt. By the time he achieved this vital act, the aircraft had begun to disintegrate and he was able to get to the nearest aperture to bail out. (One of his flying boots came off, but he was able to re-shoe himself once down on the ground, thanks to having tied a pair of walking shoes to his harness straps!) The pilot was one of only three survivors out of nine; although Lt. Brainard also reached the ground alive, a lethal fate awaited him within hours at the hands of a labor camp administrator and his staff.

Lt. Collar

Lt. George Collar was Lt. Jim Schaen's bombardier on 44-10511/WV: C and was manning the nose turret when the initial assault erupted. What he described as a cluster of small flak bursts "the size of basketballs" appeared to the sides and front of his B-24; in fact, these were almost certainly 20mm cannon shells with time fuses issuing from the Fw190 gun barrels. The bomber shuddered and jolted as it was struck, and bare seconds later a Fw190 shot by extremely close overhead; when Collar attempted to operate his turret nothing happened, probably due to the hydraulic system having failed. His next impression was the unpleasantness of glancing left to see the wing sprouting smoke and flame. The doomed B-24 was duly abandoned by all three surviving officers and Sgt. George Eppley (Eng.) before it plunged to destruction at Gerstungen, yet another location in the approximate vicinity of Eisenach.

Lt. Bill Bruce

Lt. Bill Bruce's **Bonnie Vee** (42-95128/IS: R+) finally descended to its destruction close to Richelsdorf, roughly fourteen miles west of Eisenach, by which stage only he and T/Sgt. Peter Popovich (ROG) were alive. The pilot later reported:

> There had been confusion as to the proper target, but after the bomb run we dropped 500ft and headed for home, with only flak to contend with. Soon after we sighted what was felt to be our escorts, but there were so many they had to be the enemy. It was unbelievable how they just sat back and below us to shoot the Hell out of us. I saw at least seven ships (B24s and fighters) go down in flames, while I wondered where in Hell were our fighters?
>
> Our ship had two engines on fire and the interior was a shambles; the gunners kept firing but ended up wounded or dead, and I finally knew the end was near once our power was down to a single engine. I gave the bail out order and asked Lt. John Willet (CP) to unbuckle my seat belt, but as he stood up a cannon shell killed him instantly. The right wing was sheered off when a fighter struck it, followed by the other wing detaching and finally the fuselage disintegrated, throwing me clear, but in great pain. I delayed pulling the ripcord because 1) I thought my clothing was on fire, 2) I thought I might be shot-up, and 3) I was rather groggy.
>
> I finally opened the chute but landed in a large tree, draped around its branches. My B24 had crashed into a wood, setting it on fire, and I heard much yelling and screaming. Having got down, I crawled painfully along and finally reached a farmhouse, where a man and two women brought me inside. They tried to wash my face and gave me milk that I could not swallow. Then a young boy, maybe 10 or 12, rushed in brandishing a rifle, which the man knocked out of his hands, upon which he ran out again and brought back seven armed soldiers. I was searched for weapons by the officer in charge before a cart turned up, into which I was loaded. On passing through a village the civilians hit, cursed, and spat on me, but I survived to be incarcerated in a barn, although the mob persisted in beating on the walls and casting stones through the windows.

A 712BS B-24 has made it back to Seething, but is very fortunate to have done so, given the extent of the damage to its tail turret. The partially-mangled turret frame dangling to one side provides little prospect for its occupant to have even escaped serious injury, let alone death; on the other hand, the unpredictable effect of blast was sometimes (but not often) directed away from the crewmember involved.

Clay Pigeon's semi-recumbent figure displays her shapely form on the starboard nose of 41-29579/RN: N. This bomber, along with **Bonnie Vee**, would fall to the enemy during the Kassel mission. Of the nine-man crew, four, including Lt. Oliver Elder (P), would be killed.

Maria-Lupine served with the 701BS at Tibenham. The B-24J-1-FO (42-50701/MK: E) flew to Kassel on 27 September 1944, and unlike so many that failed to run the **Sturmgruppe** gauntlet, she would win through at the hands of Lt. Don Smith and his crew.

Although relatively few B-24Ls joined the 8AF, many were fitted with a lightweight rear turret incorporating a hand-held control mechanism. The guns were mounted into a U-pattern swivel frame, with the entire turret frame resembling a cupola snugly fitted into the rear fuselage skin.

Bill's injuries included a broken pelvis and a badly damaged shoulder, while the doctors at Obermassfeld hospital said he would never walk again, nor use his right arm properly. (On return Stateside he was found to have also broken his neck!) He had at least survived the mission for future delivery to *Stalag Luft 3*, as well as the local populace's "summary justice," unlike a number of his colleagues this day.

Lt. Weinstein

Lt. Ira Weinstein was a PFF bombardier with no regular crew and with the Jewish festival Yom Kippur being today was excused from flying the mission. He decided to do so anyway, in order to accelerate his combat tour, and finally got permission against the advice of his CO. He joined Lt. Myron Donald's crew in 42-51287/WV: Y. This B-24 was among the first clutch of victims, judging by the final crash site at Nesselroeden, close to Eisenach's NW boundary. The pilot—whose fate was particularly cruel—the Engineer, and the three gunners at the rear did not survive, unlike Ira and the remaining three crewmembers.

Ira was not trained as a gunner, but when trouble erupted he took up the vacant nose turret in true *ad hoc* fashion. He was blasting away when the doors opened and he was pulled out by Lt. Smith (N)—only then becoming aware that the bomber was doomed. His normal chest pack was being re-stowed back at Tibenham, so he was fortunately wearing a backpack. However, his progress out was sharply halted when a strap caught the bomb sight; with great difficulty he pulled himself back in, despite the increasing centrifugal forces accruing from the B-24 flat spin motion, before disengaging the strap and falling away.

His descent ended on a hillside, which was his second lucky break. A parachutist later established as his pilot, Lt. Myron Donald, landed in the adjoining valley, but having suffered fractures to both feet was rendered helpless; while lying there, several farmers with pitchforks appeared and killed him with their implements; after dusk fell, Ira went down and removed his dog tags.

Ira had lost his flying boots after jumping, but during the 48 hours he was still free before the physical drain on his system finally impelled him to surrender, he improvised a pair of "moccasins" using sections of his flight suit, along with wires from the heated suit to bind them together; the double pair of socks he habitually wore provided an extra degree of insulation. After being apprehended and brought in front of what he regarded as the *Commandant* of the unit, it was ironic that his sparse knowledge of Yiddish could have got him killed. He interpreted the CO's final statement to the guard as: "Take him out and shoot him."

In fact, he had apparently said: "Take him out and get him shoes!," the respective words having a similar pronunciation. When duly taken out, he was marched across the compound with a gate at the end. Thinking his fate was sealed and imagining he would be shot in the back, he decided to make a run for it upon reaching the gate. Happily, halfway there the guard indicated to him to turn towards a building they were passing, from where he was issued his replacement footwear. As Ira later wryly stated: "That was the nearest I came to being shot that day, either during the battle or otherwise!"

In common with other captured personnel, he had been ordered to collect equipment from the various wrecks and recalled toting two .5 machine guns out of his own B-24, a task that in retrospect seemed extremely difficult in terms of physical effort, but which raised no problem then. Much less pleasant was having to remove the bodies of his former fellow airmen, their corpses having been dreadfully roasted in the conflagration of their airborne coffin.

The Punishment Continues

Some accounts regarding the Kassel mission indicate that the final MIA figure of 25 was incurred within a matter of several minutes. Great as the loss scale was between Eisenach and Bad Hersfeld, it did not fully equate with the foregoing figure. However, three of the remaining six destined to be lost over enemy soil went down as the formation skirted by the latter location. The furthest back appears to have been 42-50383/WV: X **King Kong**, which crashed near Braunhausen, close to **Ole Baldy's** site; Lt. James Baynham was one of five survivors out of the nine airmen on board. Friedlos is just NE of Bad Hersfeld, and it was there that the Group Lead (B-24 42-51541/RN: H) fatally descended. Both Maj. McCoy and Capt. Chilton went in with the bomber, while three of the other eleven also forfeited their lives at some stage of the brief air battle. Finally, 42-50961/WV: W came down at Grebenau, roughly fourteen miles SW of Bad Hersfeld; Lt. Virgil Chima (CP), on Lt. Reginald Miner's team, was one of two fatalities among the twelve on board.

The final trio of MIA crews held course westward, albeit in varying states of distress, until approaching Giessen, still east of the Rhine. It was close to there that **Texas Rose** (41-28922/MK: Q-Bar) finally faltered and crashed to earth while still bearing two gunners on Lt. Palmer Bruland's crew, the other seven having cleared the doomed bomber. It was not long after the shattered remnants of the Group traversed the Rhine, only to see two more aircraft go down. **Mairzy Doats** (42-109789/RN: A), flown by Lt. Edward Hautman, came down several miles west of Koblenz, along with the pilot and two gunners. Lt. Donald Reynolds's charge 42-50579/MK: R-Bar **Little Audrey** was abandoned around the same time to crash eleven miles from the city's SW fringe; this time round he and six of the other eight managed to parachute into captivity.

Return Leg Fortunes

The proud ranks of the Group's 35-strong formation that had completed the outward stage of the mission were now reduced to a motley collection of ten B-24s as the Rhine was passing below, not all of whom would attain their Tibenham dispersals, either today or in the future. Three among the number would furthermore not even retrace their steps across the North Sea, being already in particularly high degrees of distress. Lt. Raymond Heitz had charge of 42-95210/IS: U+, which reached as far as Brussels before having to be crash landed; eight of the crew walked clear of the bomber, but the ninth—Sgt. Louis Ochevsky (WG)—was either already dead from his wounds or failed to survive the final incident. Lt. William Hunter progressed closer to the Continental fringe by attaining the area around Lille, in NE France, before carrying out his forced landing; this time round all eleven airmen, including Sgt. Thomas Spera (Photographer), emerged unscathed, but the "supernumerary's" experience of combat must have left him with an abiding wish never to go aloft again!

The third of these cripples was in the hands of Lts. French and Cochren, who along with their crew were flying their final mission, and the following account of what transpired was provided by their Navigator. Lt. French urgently asked Lt. Tims how far they were from Allied territory, especially since the ailing 42-50784/IS: D+ was by now down to 18,000ft and still descending. The answer was that a course to Belgium-liberated soil would encompass roughly 90 minutes flight time, given that they were heading into the wind. The fuel flow from fractured bomb bay pipes was an added problem, both in terms of fire hazard and dwindling reserves. Finally, Tims had to estimate his course, since not only were the ASI panel and Gee-Box destroyed, but the magnetic compass was also "dead."

The still-solid cloud cover allowed for no error in deciding when to actually break out with a guarantee of finding friendly territory below. Around the estimated ETA, a measure of negative benefit accrued when a non-persistent flak barrage was encountered, so Lt. French held position. Then a break in the clouds allowed the navigator to confirm they were near Koblenz, having identified the city's siting on the Rhine/Mosel river confluence.

Power had been restored to No. 3 and a search for an airfield initiated on reaching the Allied lines—one that was a "blind guess" in nature, since maps of Belgium and Northern France had been inadvertently thrown out during efforts to lighten the bomber. A radio fix led to the pilots heading for the region around St. Quentin and Rheims, in France, which possessed a number of airfields, at which time a P-47 field (Metz/Frescaty) finally loomed up. The refusal of the nose wheel to deploy promised a hazardous landing, but the Grim Reaper thankfully withheld his scythe and the bomber scraped to a tail-high halt. On emerging from the thoroughly shot-riddled airframe, they adjured those airfield personnel arriving on the scene to stay well clear on account of the fuel fumes.

Later, while drinking at the chateau forming the Officers' quarters, the crew surmised on what was the scale of loss to the Group. Lt. Tims recalled seeing a total of four B-24s in the immediate aftermath of the air battle. French opined that at least 50% of the crews had probably gone down, but even this swinging loss factor would fall short of the final figure, As it was, Bob, before toasting both pilots on completing their tour, said he was particularly glad he was now able to retract his previous "unfortunate" comment about both finishing the tour on an "easy" mission!

More Formation Pruning

The handful of B-24s (seven) crossing out over the sea by now constituted exactly 20% of the original attacking force, and two among the figure would seek salvation at the RAF's emergency airfield at Manston, in Kent. Lt. William Dewey, piloting 42-50855/MK: A-Bar, was one of this duo; the degree of damage suffered by his B-24 is unclear, but it must have been sufficient for him to take this course of action, although the nine airmen on board at least remained free of serious injury. A full account of what occasioned the other crew led by Lt. Jackson Mercer to follow suit is presented here; Lt. Mercer's B-24J 42-51549 /RN: G had survived the brutal few minutes of the *Sturmgruppen* assault, but the overall situation for his B-24 and crew was still critical:

> Once certain the attack was over, I had Paul and Sgt. Ken Kribs (Eng.) check the crew, as well as assess damage, while I at least kept sight of Isom's B24, our duo being the sole squadron aircraft still on hand. Both reported that the crew was "shook up" but unhurt. Damage was severe—no radio, hydraulic pressure, nor rudder controls, while a major leak in the fuel transfer valves up in the bomb bay had Kribs opening the bomb bay doors slightly to vent fumes. The fuel loss was serious, so I had Lt. Milt Fandler (N) work out a direct course for the Emergency Field at Manston. Not only did it have a 12,000-ft runway, but the revised course would take us quicker over friendly soil.
>
> I then eased downwards, since our oxygen situation was increasingly critical, but did so in "steps" of 500ft, in order not to use too much fuel; No. 2 was kept running, since I wanted maximum power should an emergency arise, although I did reduce its RPMs to reduce the vibration caused by its rough performance. After fully two hours, Milt made swimming gestures through his astrodome—we were over the sea, with a 3,500-ft altitude. Not long after the wonderful sight of Manston appeared.
>
> Kribs cranked down the main landing gear and kicked out the nose wheel, but no green light indicating gear lock-down showed up, so the crew prepared for a possible crash landing. On approach, Paul worked the auto-pilot rudder control to assist in lining up and we touched down smoothly, albeit at an excessive speed, since our flaps were inoperable. We even had sufficient pressure in the brake accumulators to set the brakes one more time. We were home!
>
> We later found out that the damage report covered six pages and contained over 300 items, with replacements for the No. 2 engine, left fin and rudder, elevator, and bomb bay doors, while a 20mm shell was found in the No. 2 fuel tank. We remained overnight while awaiting transportation back to base.

This picture of a 445BG sub-formation joining the circuit at Tibenham would attract no particular attention from those on the ground, provided there were little or no gaps in the overall Group formation. On 27 September, just one-third of the number seen here would appear overhead; the natural impression they were only part of the Group strength would have soon given way to absolute shock when the facts of the disaster became known.

"Nearly, but not quite"

Sgt. John Cadden was Lt. Stanley Krivik's ROG on board 42-100331/702BS **Percy**, which lost one engine during the air battle and suffered oil pressure drop in a second, as well as hydraulic system failure. Cadden's first indication of trouble was hearing the waist gunners calling out the fighters when the initial assault wave came in, followed by the sound of bullets striking the fuselage. The pilot then ordered Cadden to go back and open the bomb bay doors, but did not give any reason for this; he was doing so when he lost consciousness, and on regaining his senses found himself in the nose compartment; his helmet and oxygen mask were gone, so he was fortunate not to have inadvertently fallen out of the half-exposed bomb bay nor suffered the lethal effect of anoxia. The portable oxygen bottle was still in his possession, so he was able to recover from his naturally befuddled mental state. His steel helmet had lost one of its flexible ear flaps and was deeply scored on that side, so it is clear he would have been seriously injured or even killed by whatever caused the damage.

He returned to complete the opening process, only to find all power was gone, whereupon the task of protracted manual cranking had to be carried out. This achieved, he reported his success to Krivik. The bomber's steady descent made it unlikely that the North Sea could be safely crossed, so a heading for Brussels was assumed—and Krivik ordered Cadden to close the bomb bay doors! The solid undercast prevented any indication of where the B-24 was, and when the cloud cover was broken through it must have shocked the pilots that water instead of solid ground lay below. The decision to head westward over what was later confirmed as the North Sea at their now perilous 2,000-ft altitude while Cadden called for ASR support thankfully culminated with no need for its use, as the East Anglian coastline finally loomed up, whereupon a heading for Tibenham was taken up.

The hydraulic system was "out," so the landing gear had to be hand-cranked into position, an onerous duty that was barely completed by Sgt. Bugalecki (Eng.) when the B-24 was seemingly about to be set down. However, an overshoot had to be made since the runway was blocked by several trucks. The attempt to initiate a pull-up for a second circuit failed and the B-24 nosed down onto the ground. The hard impact, combined with the inherent frailty of the B-24 airframe in these circumstances, thoroughly wrecked the overall structure, including the fuselage, which split in two.

Cadden, along with Lt. Trotto (CP) and Sgt. Bugalecki, was pulled out of the aircraft by Lt. Krivik, all three injured airmen ending up in hospital. Of the nine crewmembers, only Lt. Daniel Dale (N) failed to survive the crash landing. This was the second crash landing for the Krivik crew after their bomber ran out of fuel on mission return and had to be put down in a cornfield; the scale of damage resulted in "salvage" on that occasion. Unbeknownst to them was that only four more crews would come home today, one of which would be fortunate to make a safe landing.

"Where's the others? ...."

The three B-24s that swung into Tibenham's circuit were the Group deputy Lead 42-51547/IS: E+, flown by Capt. Graham; 42-50710/MK: E-Bar **Marie Lupine**, in Lt. Donald Smith's hands; and finally 42-50811/RN: E **Patty Girl**, with Lt. Cecil Isom at the controls. The miniscule scale of the force probably raised no reaction among the manifold observers on the ground, other than the other elements of the Group were either following or alternatively had diverted into airfields on the Continent. They would be disabused of such logical conclusions within the ensuing hour or so as news of the holocaust was spread around Tibenham.

The fourth B-24 was Lt. Paul Swofford's 42-51105/MK: O-Bar **Sweetest Rose of Texas**. The bomber had lost No. 2 engine as well as external radio functions, while the hydraulic system was also crippled. In order to sustain its formation position without "feathering" the propeller, extra power had to be applied to the other three motors in a manner that normally wore them out. This fate was miraculously avoided until the formation was almost clear of enemy soil. Then the errant engine's propeller was "feathered" and power reduced to normal level, after which the pilots took up a separate homeward course.

Arrival at Tibenham involved the manual lowering of landing gear and flaps, but the inability to talk to the tower, from which red warning flares were being liberally dispensed, "warning off" the unidentified bomber, had Swofford urgently calling for these landing aids to be swiftly retracted, as he finally decided to overshoot. The tasks completed he pulled away, and after taking his time to circle headed in for his landing bid, which this time was aimed at the runway in use; the bomber was halted at the very end, although finally veering off to port due to asymmetric power thrust. (The warning flares were likely fired because Swofford's initial approach had him coming in on one of the short runways that was not in current use due to the wind angle. Also, the radio failure meant the personnel had no inkling of the emergency situation facing the B-24 and crew.)

Lt. French's Ex-crew

A Group's departure and return were arguably the main breaks in the monotony for the ground support. So it was that at 1230, the Tibenham personnel raised their eyes to the east. The ground crews were at their dispersals; Intelligence staff at their desks; Flight Surgeons in the "meat wagons" out on the perimeter; and Red Cross girls ready with hot coffee and doughnuts, all ready and awaiting the ever-wisecracking horde.

On Dispersal 7, four former members from Lt. French's crew waited to congratulate him and Lt. Cochran. "They're overdue; it's 1245," said Moynihan. "Not the first time it has happened," replied Havard, as O'Kelly and Winard chatted with the Crew Chief. Then O'Kelly said: "Here come some, I think," as three ships appeared and swung around, wasting no time in breaking into the circuit. "Wonder where the rest are?" worried Moynihan. "The formation has probably broken up to let down through the undercast," laughed Winard.

Scarcely had he spoken when the first news of the aerial holocaust reached them. Maj. Graham had answered the control tower staff's query tersely: "We were hit by fighters...practically wiped out...two wounded on board." When the Controller expressed his consternation and disbelief, Graham added: "This is all, I guess; one made it back but crashed near the field—not sure who it is (Lt. Krivik in 42-100331/WV: U)."

The four men on Dispersal 7 were hearing about, but not really comprehending the tragedy and left reluctantly to gather at their squadron's area. Perhaps a returning crewmember had witnessed chutes coming from French's B-24, or maybe the crew made it to a French or Belgian airfield? Their hopes appeared dashed when they got through to Maj. Graham and asked him. He replied: "Yes, I saw him better than anyone else. He was alongside and burning all the way back from the cockpit. He didn't have a chance! I never saw a soul bail out before their ship kicked over."

This confusion with another B-24 would remain uncorrected for some time, but had to currently be accepted. Lt. Switzler (B) flatly refused to accept the situation and furthermore refused to let a Sergeant—and later a Lieutenant—who came to collect French's and Cochran's effects do so, brandishing a revolver in the latter individual's case! His faith was rewarded when the radio message sent by Sgt. Fiske (ROG) confirming the aircraft's landing in France was received. Tragically, for all too many of his colleagues, similar positive news of their fellow airmen's fate would never materialize.

Aftermath

The postmortem remarks attributed to Lt. Mercer were probably echoed by other surviving colleagues:

> It was only when we returned to Tibenham that we were appraised of the mission's gory details, including the fact that we had bombed 30 miles NE of the Primary, close to Goettingen. All these terrible losses because the Lead navigators and bombardiers apparently misread their radar scopes. Their errors placed our return route virtually over at least five German fighter bases in the region around Eisenach. (As postwar research would confirm, the latter observation bore some relevance to the assertion, but at the time, the fact of the already-assembled *Jagdwaffe* force was naturally not on hand. However, Erfurt-Bindersleben was occupied by II (*Sturm*) JG300 in September, with IV (Sturm) JG3 fairly close by at Alperstedt, both airfields being in the vicinity of where the air battle erupted.)

Lt. Frank W. Federici was the Navigator on Jim Williams's crew, which was (fortunately) not called upon for today's mission, and he later recalled:

> As a Lead crew, we flew many practice missions to maintain top proficiency. On the day of September 27, 1944, to Kassel, we flew a Colonel up to Aberdeen, Scotland. When we returned to Tibenham, we noticed that a lot of aircraft were not in their parking places, which was strange, since the mission should have returned to base already. We landed and I walked over to our ground Crew Chief and asked, "Where are all the ships?" He answered with, "We have been wiped out, sir." I replied, "That's *not* funny, Sergeant." He replied, "Honest to God, sir," and started to cry. I felt badly and placed my arm on his shoulder and apologized to him.
>
> We eventually went to our hut, which accommodated officers of four crews (four per crew), or a total of sixteen men. Our hut was empty when we walked in because the other three crews had been shot down over Germany, near Kassel. We were shocked at the great loss of men, but also very angry at the enemy. The next day, our base put up ten aircraft that flew with another Group and went back to Kassel with 1000-lb bombs. All returned safely. Results were very good. It was amazing how fast replacement crews came to our base—within ten days our hut was full again.

"Summary Treatment" Justice

Some of the 445BG airmen who reached the ground alive never reached the security of a POW camp, having suffered "summary treatment" by the Germans. One of five among this figure was Lt. Newton Brainard, Lt. Carrow's copilot. He was officially declared MIA until 1947, when his hitherto-unidentified corpse was disinterred at St. Avold Cemetery and confirmation was established by dental records. His bandaged head, concealing two gunshot wounds, set in train an investigation culminating in a U.S. Military trial on 5 February 1948. Six Germans were arraigned and accused of murdering the five airmen, including Lt. John Cargill (N) and Hector Scala (B) on Lt. Baynham's crew, all five deaths having occurred either in one of two slave labor camps at Nettershausen and Suess.

Brainard had suffered a head injury that was attended to and bandaged by a nurse, who in turn was sent for by a mother of a family who had reached him after he landed. For whatever reason, instead of being handed over to the military, the chief of a slave labor camp at Nettershausen or Suess took him away. He was then reportedly shot by a Herr Eggert, who was executed for this and other crimes. Of the six accused, Joseph Ehlen claimed he was not guilty of the actual shooting, although he was

Bonnie Vee has returned safely from a mission, but not without sustaining the loss of a sizeable proportion of her port rudder. The B-24H-25-FO/42-95128 survived combat until 27 September, when she was one of the mass of 445BG bombers taken down during the infamous Kassel mission; only two on Lt. William Bruce's crew survived her fiery demise.

present at the scene, Eggert having claimed that he did the shooting. However, the U.S. Court adjudged Ehlen guilty by association, as was deemed August Viehl. The four others involved in the incidents received prison sentences of between four and six years, but one (Paul Winkler) was sentenced *in absentia*, since he had already been executed for another war crime.

From Confrontation to Compassion

One of the abiding contradictions arising from any conflict is how the sometimes extreme feelings about one's adversaries existing during that feral activity can so often ultimately turn to a basic bond of understanding on each side of the former and seemingly unbridgeable divide. Perhaps it is based on the feeling that individuals are primarily pawns in the hands of the political and/or military structures that impelled them towards opposing one another; when linked to the basic sense of individual survival, the result can be reconciliation and even genuine friendship.

Walter Hassenpflug was a 12-year-old *Hitlerjugend* (Hitler Youth) member living in Bad Hersfeld. On 28 September, he and his HJ colleagues were dispatched to collect 8AF propaganda leaflets, and in the course of their search they came across Lt. Frank Bertram (N), of Lt. Reginald Miner's downed B-24. One boy could speak English and confirmed the airman was injured, after which the boys took him to the town. Walter managed to establish his name and that he was from California before parting company.

The following 21 November, Walter was the sole survivor when an 8AF unit bombed the town, killing his parents and leaving him with serious injuries. His immediate reaction on leaving hospital was to hate anything relating to Americans and he suffered recurring nightmares centered on bombing raids that extended long into adulthood.

On the other hand, the presence of U.S. Occupation troops gradually weaned him from his feral WWII attitudes towards that nation's citizens to a tolerant and finally friendly disposition towards them. In particular, he wanted to trace the injured airman and question him on the mission, as well as his background. Fully six decades passed before he and Frank Bertram were finally face to face in a Bad Hersfeld restaurant, and within a matter of minutes an inseparable friendship was established.

The Kassel Mission Memorial near Freidlos stands in an artificial woodland clearing that was caused by the explosive descent of the Lead B-24. One of those involved with its creation was Walter, but some friends queried his motive, asking: "Why are you doing this and why do you care about them—they killed your parents and put you through Hell, didn't they?" His response was to say there should be no taboos concerning wars—you have to talk about what happened, what we did to them and *vice versa*. "We know we started WWII, but balancing out things against each other doesn't get you anywhere. Therefore, that is why I want the memorial as a symbol of reconciliation."

The Memorial was dedicated on 27 September 2004, in the presence of both sets of veterans and their families, and contains three separate obelisks. One each are dedicated to the American and German aircrew killed in the air battle. The centrally-aligned one is devoted to *all* victims of conflict and in essence confirms the fact that no nation wins a war unconditionally or unscathed—the material and human cost is probably less in the victor's case, but still leaves corporate and especially individual scars upon the physique and minds of millions of those caught up in such conflicts.

Chapter Seventeen

Last Rites

Battling the Elements

The pace of 8AF operations as the first full month of the 1944/45 winter arose would display a contrast between the first three weeks and the remaining period. Mother Nature would be in a particularly perverse mood, and this factor in turn would tend to restrict the number of missions up to the 22rd; from then on, the "heavies" would be able to progress over the Third Reich on a daily basis.

The first monthly run to Bingen's marshalling yards brought a sharp reminder to the Division in particular that the defenders could still pack a punch; whereas the 1BD lost none of the 140 crews gaining mission credit out of 153 dispatched, no less than eleven out of 143—representing around an 8% factor—would never see their bases again. As with the 26 November debacle, today's losses would be primarily attributable to the *Jagdwaffe's* depredations, with the 14CBW largely involved.

Wendling had dispatched nine-strong elements of the 577BS and 578BS to respectively fly Low and High positions off the 44BG. The mission proceeded in order as far as the IP, when a massive cloud bank was encountered that caused the 577BS to become scattered, although the bomb run was still carried through; the 578BS in contrast encountered no similar problem. The former sub-unit was still loosely assembled as it headed for the Rally Point, when the Luftwaffe intervened to the tune of some 50 Fw190s. The ensuing and unequal air battle was destined to last around 15 minutes, as the bombers headed on a NW course. By its conclusion, no less than six crews would be gone.

All but one of the losses appear to have occurred in a roughly triangular region between 20 and 30 miles southwest of the target. Stipshausen, at the western tip of the triangle, collected the remains of two B-24s, one of which was 42-50323/DC: D+ **Heaven can Wait**, which exploded in mid-air and deposited the corpses of Lt. Edward J. Cieply's nine-man crew within its scattered remnants. The other casualty was 42-94961/DC: Z+ **Alfred IV**; Lt. William F. Davis lost T/Sgt. Charles W. Crabbe (killed at his post), while Lt. Charles E. Astleford, although bailing out with the other seven on board, did not survive, having been shot after landing, a probable *Terrorflieger* victim.

The same area was the likely crash site for 42-95012/DC: U+: **Trips Daily**, since it lay between Stipshausen and Kirn /Hunsruck to the east. The badly shot-up bomber's bail out bell had been rung by Lt. Walter C. Buass, but his seat had jammed and had to be released by his copilot, Lt. Charles H. Pedrotta; both then made their way to the bomb bay, where the pilot collapsed and all his companion's efforts to get him out of the tumbling B-24 proved fruitless. Scarcely had Pedrotta jumped when the bomber exploded, but he and five of the nine on board did get down alive. (Buass

A duo of 491BG B-24s are transiting a stretch of sky dotted with patches of "cotton wool" clouds. The Group was allowed to retain its green/white fin and rudder markings, as opposed to adopting the black diagonal stripes of its North Pickenham predecessor, the 492BG. That transfer from North Pickenham is confirmed by the "Circle-Z" insignia on the starboard wing that was a feature on 492BG aircraft.

The Crew Chief on the right signals that all is in order for the pilots to taxi out of their dispersal. The 505BS bomber is B-24LHO-5-FO/44-49322, whose GJ code letters are lightly outlined for greater clarity. The anti-dazzle panel on Ford-built B-24s was generally terminated at the top of the scalloped nose panel joint, as seen here.

had previously complained to Pedrotta about his heart, but resisted suggestions that he inform the Medical staff; if correct, the condition had now caused him to suffer a fatal collapse.)

The squadron's 42-94867/DC: A+ had barely completed the bomb run when it was assailed and thoroughly shot-up, with six of the nine airmen either killed or rendered incapable of bailing out. The dying bomber staggered on as far as Kellenbach, about ten miles west of Stipshausen, before it exploded. By then, Lt. Glenn R. Billingsly (P) was almost certainly dead, having probably been killed during the second fighter pass, according to Lt. William B. Pettigrew (B), who was one of three survivors.

Sgt. Ray. Janinski (NT) provided an account of 42-51207/DC: A+'s fate:

> I was throwing out "chaff," and following the bomb run we entered a haze that enclosed us for about two minutes. Upon emerging from this blanket, the call "enemy fighters" was made. On this first pass, Sgt. Hiatt H. Kearns (WG) was hit in the stomach; his flak suit's three bottom buttons were undone, so when he stood up to fire his body was exposed to the 20mm strike, which tore a hole in his stomach. Fire broke out in the bomb bay and command deck, and I heard Sgt. Paul W. Haney (ROG), who was talking to the pilot, begin to say "There is a fire..." when he stopped, I believe due to his being hit. Just as the fighters commenced their second pass the pilot said: "This is it fellows—bail out." I waited until Sgt. John C. Prendergast (TG) got out and held the escape hatch open, but I jumped first. [Prendergast did not survive.] I saw nobody else jump nor saw any parachutes; my last impression was that fire was sweeping the fuselage from the bomb bays forward.

Sargenroth is roughly ten miles NE of Stipshausen, and this was where the B-24 descended, along with the bodies of Lt. Eugene L. Comeau and six of his eight-man team, with S/Sgt. Harold L. Krause (WG) being the other survivor.

The battered remnants of the 577BS had not long progressed in a northwesterly direction when its strength was further diluted by one, although the B-24 in question (42-50785/DC: N+) had already become separated from the formation. The single survivor was Sgt. Charles L. Williams, who recalled that he abandoned the battered bomber; Capt. Howard D. Watkins and the remaining seven on board shared their aircraft's violent demise at Klotton, on the River Mosel SW of Koblenz.

The duo of casualties borne by Shipdham involved one crew that was flying Lead for the 577BS. Lt. Herbert L. Bayliss's (KIA) 42-50766/GJ: D-bar was set on fire under the flight deck, whereupon T/Sgt. Robert L. Moore, realizing the situation was terminal, reached up to open the cockpit roof hatch before descending towards the bomb bay. The B-24 suddenly flipped onto its back, casting T/Sgt. Joseph B. Dosmann (ROG) out through the hatch, but he was fortunate, in that he had already snapped on his pack. The three other officers managed to scramble clear, but Moore and the other four Enlisted men never made it out.

The other MIA crew were in 42-50805/WQ: T and had found their bomber out on its own after maneuvering to avoid a collision and accordingly ripe for individual treatment from the fighters. The bomb bay on Lt. John C. Hobbs's (KIA) bomber was set ablaze

It is a case of "All hands to the tiller"—or shovels, in this instance—following a heavy snowfall at a B-24 airfield believed to be Seething. The need to provide some definition to the perimeter track as well as clear a path out of each dispersal was paramount to safe aircraft movement; the protracted and back-breaking effort would hardly be appreciated by the "volunteers," but at least they would be kept warm by the duty.

and S/Sgt. Don W. Montre (Eng.), although severely burned, managed to attach his pack and get as far as the bomb bay prior to passing out. Coming-to in mid-air, he pulled the ripcord but was still fortunate to escape serious injury or even death; a large hole in the canopy saw him descending at a very fast rate, and it was only a large tree on which his parachute snagged that saved him. On return to the States, he had to have facial and hand skin grafts.

The travails of the 14CBW were thus complete, but three other crews would add to the Divisional loss factor. Hethel's 42-50366/YO: was culled, along with Lt. Ralph Kley and three crewmembers. A far worse fatality rate (100%) attended the loss of 42-95105/**She's Mine** and 42-51100/**Tiger** flying out of Bungay; a total of 21 crewmembers were involved and indeed, over the ensuing ten days, the same fatality rate would affect two further 446BG crews.

The ensuing four Divisional missions flown up to the 10th passed off almost loss free, the exception being two days after Bingen. Shipdham's third monthly casualty on the run to marshalling yards at Bebra involved 42-95124/QK: P+ **Sand Bomb Special**, whose demise was later attributed to technical failure. Oil began to stream from both port engines and the power was finally switched off. The swiftly-isolated B-24 turned for home, but a call for fighter assistance from Lt. Rogers's gradually descending charge was wrongly sent out on the ASR channel. A single fighter did appear, but only for a short period. Although a direct westerly course was assumed as the direction for France, in fact, the B-24 began to meander off to the southwest. When its capacity to remain aloft appeared terminal the bail out order was given (the fact that *Jagdwaffe* elements were appearing undoubtedly hastened this course of action). The eight airmen taking to their parachutes descended close to Freiburg, in the *Schwarzwald* (Black Forest), and S/Sgt. Mike Harkovich (LW), along with Lt. Alexander B. Moir (CP) were fortunate to be rescued by soldiers from an enraged group of civilians who had administered a potentially life threatening beating. Lt. John McCracken (N) and Sgt. Spier (NT) did not survive the B-24's loss.

The onset of winter over northern Europe normally dictated the use of PFF techniques, but the season spanning 1944/45 almost saw the death knell of precision bombardment, since visual target sighting was to become very much the exception thanks to particularly severe and prolonged conditions. At least the following three monthly missions flown by the 2BD resulted in a nil MIA figure, followed by a marginal downturn in fortune commencing on the 11th, when Hanau's marshalling yards and the Maximiliansau railroad bridge were struck by the full Division.

Five crews were lost: two each from the 491BG and 445BG and a single 446BG team. In the former case, there was no debriefing report on either B-24's fate, only that Lt. Fandell, flying 44-40232, and Lt. Meyers in 41-28820/**Four-Five-Time** had disappeared at some stage; Group Assembly had been a shambles, with only six of the 43 forming up, seventeen others tacking onto other units, and twenty "aborting." (The formerly listed crew was later reported as crash landing near Verdun, in France.) Bungay's loss involved flak-stricken 42-110093/JU: **Black Magic**, with none of the eleven airmen on Lt. William D. Getmen's crew surviving their aircraft's destruction near Longuyon, France.

One of the Tibenham casualties was self inflicted through a mid-air collision. In this instance, none of Lt. Henry C. Lewis's nine-man crew survived the contact in 42-50453/MK:, which reportedly bore the tragic title **The Grim Reaper**; the afflicted aircraft crashed at Zinswiller, in Alsace Province. The other bomber (42-95291/RN:) escaped relatively intact and was subsequently landed.

A similar drip feed of loss (three) occurred next day, when Hanau's yards again formed the Primary for the bulk of the 378 crews sent out. The 445BG suffered its latest casualty, as did the 389th and 446th BGs. Hethel's 42-50662/EE: V-bar, flown by Lt. Myron Kagan, was observed to cant sharply to port twice during the bomb run; shortly after "bombs away" and with its starboard wing now wreathed in flames, the B-24J had its tail section detach, followed by the main section exploding. The

The winter weather patterns experienced over Western Europe in 1944/45 were among the worst for several decades and the 446BG's **Dragon Lady** is one of numerous 8AF bombers to lose out to the elements, in this case on 8 January. The B-24H-30-FO is 42-95306/RT: S and the crash location is recorded as Duxford, home of the 78FG.

maelstrom of fire and disintegrating metal provided little grounds for survival and only Lt. Lester Baker (B) of the nine aboard escaped alive. Bungay gave up its contribution to the North Sea on the way out when a further eleven Group personnel were lost in the attempted "ditching" of 42-95178 **Wedding Belle** off the Suffolk coast.

Precision Bombing Vicissitudes

On 5 January, the 453BG completed its 200th mission an exact eleven calendar months after commencing combat operations. The Group records contain a breakdown of the visibility or otherwise during the bomb runs as follows:

Visual .... 94 missions
H2X assisted .... 49 missions
Gee-H assisted .... 43 missions
Aborted................ 14 missions

These figures demonstrate the need for technical backup for the bombardiers in the face of the variable weather conditions encountered over northern Europe during the offensive. That the Group records show such a sound percentage falling into the "visual" category is a positive aspect of operations. Assuming this is an average experience for any Group, the fact remains that more than half the missions were conducted under electronic guidance and demonstrates how the original intention to pinpoint military or economic locations without materially affecting civilian property was steadily eroded from late 1943 onward.

This in no way infers a deliberate switch to "area bombing," a gibe that some postwar critics tend to throw at the RAF's parallel assault upon the enemy. The limitations of *H2X* and its electronic contemporaries simply ensured that the bomb spread could not be guaranteed to limit itself to the selected Primary. WWII was a total war, whether or not the apologists for the Allied Bombing Policy wish to ignore that basic but brutal fact.

"Bravery?—No Way!"

Lt. Ken "Deacon" Jones and his crew were fortunate to survive on 11 December after four flak shells sent their B-24 yawing wildly before falling into an apparent fatal spin. The bomber was halfway towards the ground before it was pulled out so heavily that the pilots almost blacked out. No. 2 engine was "dead," and although No. 1 was running out of control, a switch to that power plant resurrected the vacuum controls for the instruments covering the artificial horizon and directional compass—especially vital items with a solid undercast on hand! It was very fortunate that No. 1 engine's performance did not completely fail, as a terminal situation would surely have occurred; instead, it held up, thus allowing the aircraft to finally gain friendly shores.

After the war, Ken's comment regarding this mission ran so:

> I read a piece on our perceived bravery, stating it was a pity the beautiful girls could not observe how brave we were over Germany. The truth was that if the No. 1 engine had failed we were likely to augur-in and never see any girls, beautiful or not. We were apprehensive, rather than brave in combat. Bravery was learning to eat the Mess hall food or taking a cold shower outside in the winter!

Hitler's Gamble in the West

The general impression among the Allied High Command as the year end loomed was that the German armies on the Western Front were in as much of a terminal decline as their comrades in the air. Their Anglo-American adversaries, although currently held in check as much by the weather conditions as the defenders' resources, were anticipating that as winter turned into spring, their forward progress into the Reich's heartland would prove irresistible.

Any sense that a counteroffensive could be initiated, let alone cause serious inroads into the Allied lines, was being dismissed. However Hitler, the inveterate military and political gambler, had this very idea in mind. *Wehrmacht* and SS units in formidable strength had been mustered for weeks in the Ardennes region—the very zone that battle-weary U.S. elements had been transferred to, along with the

The overall effects of completing around 100 missions over Europe clearly reveal themselves upon **Home Breaker**, a B-24H-15-FO operating out of Bungay. The inner wing surface scarring on 42-52612/RT: L is probably intensified by the regular presence of the mechanics and their heavy boots during maintenance activities. The starboard dinghy hatch appears to be a replacement.

A somewhat dispersed 466BG sub-formation includes a B-24 with its H2X pod lowered. The virtually clear sky conditions would appear to render the BTO equipment redundant; however, conditions ahead of the formation could be noticeably reduced in visibility terms, given the perverse weather conditions ever liable to exist over the Continent.

recently-arrived 106th Infantry Division.

The steadily deteriorating weather conditions experienced up to the 16th now culminated in cloud and fog conditions over the Ardennes that totally cloaked the German armor and infantry from aerial interference for upwards of a week. The ability of the 8AF "heavies" to carry out any missions had already been blunted since the 12th, with only the B-17 Divisions going out on the 15th and 16th, while only the 3BD completed the run on the latter date, and then with barely half the dispatched force. The 2BD's first foray for six days (18th) resulted in total frustration, with cloud formations forcing a "recall."

Next day, tactical targets immediately behind the enemy front in Luxembourg were briefed for what was a surprisingly small force; these, along with a Secondary marshalling yard at Ehrang, were struck, although the accuracy factor even with the assistance of G-H could not have been high. One B-24 was absent from its Bungay dispersal today, its remains strewn on Belgian soil near Brussels. Lt. George H. Alter's battle-damaged 44-10622/RT: E had to be abandoned, although the nine-man crew effected a safe bail out.

The Germans had made dangerous inroads into this U.S.-held sector of the Allied front, although their delayed occupation of St. Vith allied to a total failure to capture the key town of Bastogne—a hub for several main roads—proved to be the initial "nails in the coffin" for their attempt to drive through to the key port of Antwerp and simultaneously split the Anglo-American forces. Nor was Mother Nature going to continue to provide the cloak of fog forever, which first started to peel back on the 23rd. Visual conditions were still variable, both over East Anglia and the Continent this day, although the 1BD did achieve visual sighting of its Primary; PFF methods had to be resorted to by the other Divisions, but at least losses were restricted to a single B-17. And then occurred the breakthrough longed for by both U.S. soldiers and airmen, as Hitler's minions were literally exposed to daily comprehensive counterattack up to the year end.

Christmas Eve "Present"

The high-pressure front moving in from the Atlantic on the 23rd had encompassed southern Britain and the western Continent by the time Christmas Eve's dawn light began to seep into the shroud of darkness. Every available B-17 and B-24 in 8AF strength, including several

The second picture, with the deep snow covering now totally gone, reveals the full extent of the damage. The pilots, having found their aircraft veering towards the control tower, applied left rudder. The result was that the landing gear collapsed, the propellers snapped off, and the fuselage fractured directly behind the cockpit; all on board got out in sound order, however.

Pleasant Surprise's artwork is recorded on the nose of B-24J-1-DT/42-51186/EC: J-bar. On 10 January 1945, Lt. J. C. Clarke "aborted" the mission, but was unable to locate Wendling thanks to heavy snow and cloud conditions. He finally got down at Seething, but the bomber was wrecked in the process.

The vagaries of air currents, especially in cross-wind conditions, presented a particular hazard during landing and take-off. The crabbing action adopted by the pilots on board B-24J-140-CO 44-40140 /X7: N **Alice** is to counter the wind, which is at odds with the runway direction. The former 492BG aircraft completed the conflict with the 467BG and returned home in May 1945.

Assembly ships, were mustered for the mission; the official figure for dispatched aircraft was 2,048, constituting by far the greatest single mission force destined to be launched. The 2BD element of the figure was 634, of which all but a small handful struck their 14 allotted targets.

As the daylight was fast fading into dusk, all but two B-24s came back. Seething lost 42-50799/ **Patrick Dempsey**, which caught fire in its starboard wing thanks to flak; Lt. L. C. Barneycastle's bid to extinguish the flames by diving swiftly came to naught when the fuel tanks exploded and ripped the airframe apart; he was killed, along with all but three of his crew.

An equally tragic fate affected all but three airmen on 42-109812/7V: V, which held Lt. Charlie Giesen's 23-mission crew. The pilot had previously expressed a view that he was "burned out" and consequently a danger to his crew. Now, having returned from a rest home, their B-24 was tucked in behind the Group Lead as the 458BG negotiated its bomb run over Schoenecken's marshalling yards. Scarcely had bombs been released when a flak shell burst under Giesen's bomber; split seconds later, having nosed gently out of formation, eyewitnesses were shocked to see the tail section totally detach itself, leaving the truncated airframe to droop to the right in an ever-

EC: /42-95040 is about to make perfect three-point contact with its Wendling runway, but normal procedure was for a nose-high angle to be adopted. The 14CBW horizontal band is only applied to the rudder, which appears to be a replacement unit. The three numbers borne on the nose are normally a repeat of the serial sequence, but represent some other matter in this instance.

The Falcon, a 466BG veteran bomber, encountered problems on return from a mission on 8 January 1945. An intended diversion into Shipdham went awry at some stage and the B-24H-25-FO/42-95248 /2U: ended up in an ice-covered pond, with particularly heavy damage to the starboard wing.

tighter spiral. Given this normally terminal situation, it was a miracle that any of the ten-strong crew got out. Indeed, Lt. John E. Thompson (CP) "came to" in mid-air under his deployed canopy, having probably been blown out by the explosion that was his last previous aural recollection. He later reported that Giesen had also got out of his seat, but unlike him had not survived.

No Let-up for Christmas Celebrations

The cloudless and freezing conditions rendered the 1BD's airfields blanketed-out by fog, which meant that Groups were forced to divert into the other two Divisions' bases, the 381BG's Ridgewell location seemingly the exception to this restriction. In spite of this logistical pile-up, the 2nd and 3rd BDs still managed to launch on Christmas Day, albeit with reduced forces. Hethel dispatched 25 crews, but any prospect of celebrating Christmas must have been dampened with the return of only 22 B-24s. Flak units around a communications center at Wahlen damaged 42-95028/EE: L **The Daddy's Rabbit**, forcing it out of formation. A course for home under escort cover was set, but all too soon one engine failed, followed by a flak spin developing; Lt. Marion Hutchens (P) and four of the eight others on board ended up dead, the others becoming POWs.

Jagdwaffe intervention was responsible for the other two losses, beginning with Lt. Raymond E. Price's 42-50612/EE: R **King Size**. One crewmember was T/Sgt. Pete Ferdinard (ROG), who had already survived a mid-air collision on 21 November. Now his bid to escape from the mortally-damaged bomber by jumping on the normally flimsy bomb bay doors, which had a weight tolerance of just 100lbs, came to naught. He hastily clambered back up and forward into the nose compartment before exiting via the nose wheel aperture. As he floated down, he could hear the snickering of bullets that fortunately missed before he slammed into the snow-covered ground—just within the U.S. lines. Lts Price, O'Rourke (CP), and John R. Tideman (N) remained on board in order to attempt a crash landing, but the B-24 exploded in mid-air; the pilot later received a posthumous Silver Star. Lt. Oral C. Chippeaux (POW) was observed to dive down in his 42-100372/EE: X **Old Glory** with fighters in pursuit, but having descended to around 10,000ft, the B-24 then entered a spiral and exploded. A 50/50 split in fatalities and POWs resulted among the ten-man crew.

Lt. Walter R. Kunkel had bailed out and managed to guide his parachute down to a landing among a group of GIs. The Germans had infiltrated English-speaking troops at the start of the "Battle of the Bulge," so the U.S. authorities had ordered their personnel to quiz anybody under suspicion. A favorite tactic was to ask sporting questions and Walter was duly asked: "Who won the World Series?" However, not every American was either versed in the subject nor in this instance could provide a knowledgeable response. The latter circumstance applied to Walter and he snapped out: "How the Hell do I know—I was on the boat coming over at the time. It was probably the Dodgers!" This highly-qualified reply fortunately tipped the scales of doubt regarding his "friendly" status and he was duly passed down the lines en route to Hethel. A far greater degree of fortune would come his way on 7 April, when he would survive a mid-air collision deliberately engineered by a *Sonderkommando* Bf109.

Weather conditions on the 26th had again deteriorated to the extent that less than 200 crews spread between the 2nd and 3rd BDs went out. Twenty-four hours later, a noticeable increase in overall 8AF numbers (641), of which 182 were provided by the Division, sallied forth in the face of a particularly lethal freezing fog condition, which caused the 453BG to cancel take-off after one B-24 piled in. The crash involved a PFF crew led by Lt. Brown (732BS). His progress off the salt-covered runway and into the air was minimal and he was heard to say: "I cannot keep her up—we have had it" before the B-24 slammed into the ground, the tail section separating. S/Sgts Marvin C. Mackey and Tommy F. Dickson leapt out of their waist gun hatches and rushed over to the tail turret, where they extracted S/Sgt. Earle W. Richmont after beating out the flames licking at his body. Ammunition was "cooking off" as the trio made for a ditch, and no sooner had they reached its dubious shelter when the bomb load erupted, killing all still on board.

Over at Bungay, 42-50330/HN: R **Umbriago** also crashed shortly after take-off, but this forced no similar inhibition upon Group Assembly; Lt. Jerome Andrews (P) was the sole fatality after the nose section was badly mangled. He had to be chopped out of the wreckage, but later succumbed in hospital. However, the Group's travails today would extend to three further crews. The North Sea was no place for a "ditching" at any time, let alone in the depths of winter, as all but Lt. Wallace Malone (piloting 42-50491) and two of his nine fellow crewmen discovered, this action of last resort having been forced upon the crew by engine problems. Then 42-51312, one of eighteen bombers releasing on a railroad junction at Enkenbach, suffered flak strikes that culminated in all on board bailing out over the front lines. The wind condition probably played its part in ensuring only four out of the ten airmen drifted down on the Allied side. Finally,

Sgt. Edward J. Garcia was a member of Lt. Herbert C. Hopkins's crew; on 12 July 1944, their B-24H-25-FO/42-95096/5Z: U **Bombs Away** diverted into Switzerland due to fuel shortage and engine problems. Ed is seen here flanked by two fellow internees in pleasant, albeit snow-covered surroundings. All three wear a mix of uniform and civilian clothing.

This close-up view of a 446BG B-24 on the bomb run during a February 1945 mission unconsciously highlights the fact that it was all too easy for a lower-stacked aircraft to be affected by bombs from aircraft above should the former stray out of position. The bomb load appears to consist of 1,000lb weapons, of which the B-24 could accommodate eight.

The relatively clean surfaces presented by B-24J-1-DT/42-51282 tend to suggest she has not seen a great deal of combat operations. The practice of repeating the last three serial numbers in large-scale manner is well illustrated, as is the abbreviated anti-dazzle panel that was a Douglas, Tulsa (DT) feature on its NMF B-24 airframes.

An engine run-up is in progress at Seething, with **Umbreago** (B-24J-1-FO/42-50678) the bomber concerned. It was lost in particularly tragic circumstances on 15 February, when a life raft hatch detached on take-off and its cord jammed an elevator. Lts. Schroeder and Roonda got the crew out, but went in with the bomber near Attlebridge after it finally went out of control before they could jump.

The correct procedure for landing a B-24 is demonstrated by the pilots of B-24H-20-FO/42-94986/X7: R. The nose will be held up for as long as possible to enable the maximum braking effect provided by the extended flaps. The pilot's already poor forward vision is further reduced during the action, so they will have to ensure a straight course down the runway is made. Aircraft is **Three Star (III Special)**, an ex-492BG machine that survived the conflict.

42-52747/JU: L **Shoo Shoo Baby**, having suffered severe damage to one or more of its engines, staggered as far as Belgian territory, over which the crew parachuted to safety.

A return to four-figure numbers of briefed crews first occurred on the 28th, when a string of marshalling yards and railroad bridges were targeted. The mission commenced badly for the 44BG when Lt. Bledsoe "aborted" in 42-95260/WQ: P **Lilli Marlene** following the failure of No. 2 engine. His attempt at landing failed, but as he maneuvered to complete a second circuit, a second engine's failure initiated a stall and heavy impact with the ground; even then, some of the crew might have survived had not part of the bomb load exploded.

This was the first of three 14CBW losses with a second Shipdham crew involved. Capt. Gus Konstand's 44-10582/WQ: D, a G-H ship leading the 491BG, absorbed two flak hits during the bomb run. The B-24 faltered and fell out of formation, but maintained flight for some two minutes before abruptly breaking in two. Sgt. Davis recalled how the first strike ignited a box of flares while the second threw him over. Having donned his pack, he was moving back to assist S/Sgt. Stepanovic (TG) out of his turret. His next recollection was of falling through the air, presumably having been cast out by the fuselage fracturing where he was positioned. Four more from among the twelve-man specialist team survived, but Konstand was not among this figure. The pilot had transferred over from the "jinxed" 492BG when it was disbanded, but Fortune, having seen him safely through at North Pickenham, finally deserted him.

The ever-pernicious flak barrage also caught up with Wendling's 42-50623/EC: B **Idiots Delight** just short of Kaiserlautern's marshalling yards, firing No. 2 engine and the bomb bay. Lt. Robert E. Baetz's (KIA) aircraft sagged downward under apparent control for two minutes before No. 4 engine also caught fire; shortly after, the crippled machine disintegrated to cast its remains close to Muenchweiler. An interesting but sad feature of this crew's composition as stated in the relevant MACR was that S/Sgt. Gunther Schamburg was on board as a voice interpreter, his duty being to tune into the enemy's airborne radio system. The Sergeant was among the eight fatalities suffered out of the ten participants.

The German advance into Luxembourg that had created a bulge—providing the battle with its postwar title—was by now clearly on its heels. This was not only due to the depredations wrought upon his forces by the 8th and 9th AF, but was also due to Gen. Patton's ability to turn his 3rd U.S. Army units northwards, pinching off the southern side of the "bulge" and culminating in the relief of Bastogne. Hitler's gamble had failed, although it would be well into January before his forces would be pushed right back to their 16 December starting lines.

Bad Day at Rackheath

The battering of the enemy's support system of railroad communications in particular was again hammered on the 29th, when the bulk of the 2BD suffered a single MIA statistic from Rackheath, However, this Group suffered an additional attrition rate similar to Bungay the day previous, primarily thanks to the weather conditions. A constant danger to aircraft during WWII was the build-up of ice, particularly on wing and stabilizer surfaces, which dangerously and often lethally impeded their ability to get and/or remain airborne. This was never more so than during take-off, with what was already a fully-laden bomber.

Shortly before mission launch, the visibility at Rackheath became so marginal that a request for mission cancellation was first communicated to the Wing HQ and then 2BDHQ. Both sources issued a firm refusal, leaving Col. Shower (Group CO) with no option but to proceed. The first B-24 lifted off safely with L/Col. A L. Wallace (Command Pilot) soon signalling that the blanked-out area below would create a particular take-off hazard, at least for acolyte crews, but the mission proceeded, sowing the seeds for a tragedy.

Lt. David W. Foster cracked open the throttles on 42-51572/Q2: W and was almost immediately swallowed up in the gloom. Within a minute, the sound of emergency power being fed to the engines was followed by a cracking noise. Nothing daunted, 42-95115/Q2: T **Topper II** lumbered down the runway to be followed by two more crews. However, the second one, flown by Lt. Russell E. Scott, was barely into its run when a loud explosion was heard. An immediate halt to the take-off sequence was issued while senior staff sped off to the far end of the runway. What they found was a scene of destruction involving not one but two B-24s close to the railroad line.

It appears that the cracking sound was caused by Foster's bomber striking trees just off the runway end and making a heavy crash landing. However, the tragedy lay not in this element of the incident, since the B-24 had not exploded and some or all of the crew were most probably alive and extricating themselves from the aircraft. **Topper II** had suffered a similar fate in striking the tress and had likewise crash landed—but its impetus was not spent when it ran into its companion. The resultant violent contact induced an explosion that expunged the lives of all ten on Lt. Kurt E. Schellhas's crew in **Topper II**. It was something of a mercy that there were any survivors (five) from the same number on the other bomber, although two bore serious injuries; both pilots, along with three Enlisted men, constituted the unlucky element. (It is not clear what actually caused the explosion, but the fact there were survivors provided a strong indication that most or all of the combined bomb loads did not "cook off," otherwise the possibility of anybody emerging alive would have been very problematical.)

All was not well with two of the three airborne aircraft. Lt. Scott's 44-10607/6A: C had also clipped the tree line after nosing down under the effect of prop wash and what transpired was recounted by S/Sgt. Charles W. Cox (Eng.):

> Three bombs fell out of the left rear bomb bay, ripping off the door in so doing. Visibility was nil, but we succeeded in gaining the formation. We attempted to contact base for instructions but in vain. Then contact was made with the Group Leader, who advised us to jettison and return. We did so, but Rackheath was socked in, so we first headed to Horsham St. Faith. This was also socked in, so we took up a course for Attlebridge, which was open. All went well with the landing until the nose wheel made contact, at which time the left landing gear snapped off, smashing into the stabilizer. We slid leftwards and ground to a halt on the runway intersection, barely missing a civilian steam roller.

The crew were uninjured, but their B-24, having also suffered damage to No. 2 and 4 engines, was deemed fit only for salvage.

The Lead B-24 had not escaped damage that was also tree-inflicted, since its landing gear was the worse for wear. Lt. John F. Moffette,flying 42-94881/6A: N-bar, was finally advised to bail out the crew before pointing the B-24 eastwards and out to a watery grave in the North Sea. All went well with this course of action. The remaining 21 crews briefed to bomb Prum's marshalling yards only achieved a G-H assisted strike rated as "poor," so the

A group of ground crew, along with several white-helmeted MPs, are gathered round the starboard wing of 42-52390/DC:. A mobile crane is preparing to raise the wing, while a second party of ground personnel are perched rather precariously on the port wing as a counter balance. The incident occurred on 15 February 1945, and the B-24H-30-FO was returned to combat operations.

The distinct odor of burning rubber would assail the nostrils of the photographer after this 392BG B-24H-25-FO/42-95223 **Little Lulu** carried out what was a rather sharp contact with the Wendling runway surface. The bomber flew operations up to 15 January 1945, when it was declared MIA.

This 446BG B-24H-1-CF bears the name of Sgt. Ronnie Gannon, who contracted and died of a medical condition during Stateside training. His airborne legacy is snapped at the point of bomb release; note the impressive 110-mission tally on the armor sheet and the NMF bomb door.

The five airmen sharing a joke alongside **Ronnie**'s fuselage are most likely her ground crew. The camouflage paintwork is inevitably scarred, but the bomber would repay the dedication of both her ground support personnel and the combat crews by making it through to VE-Day. The navigator's blister Plexiglas was originally a cockpit sliding panel.

mood at base that evening must have ranged from reflective to depressed and probably remained so over the ensuing 24 hours.

Fortunate "Failure"

Among the five railroad bridges allocated to the 2BD (30th), was the Ludendorff structure spanning the Rhine north of Koblenz. The pencil-thin image of this target type, especially when viewed from normal 8AF bombing altitude, guaranteed a high rate of failure in landing the bomb loads even approximately, let alone accurately. The 2CBW appears to have been assigned the bridge and the bomb run was conducted with the assistance of G-H. A hole in the cloud cover permitted a visual sighting as the bomb run was progressing, but the Lead bombardier had no real chance to take advantage of this and the resultant drop ended in failure—of a sort.

In fact, this was not the last time the bridge would be targeted and missed. The pattern of failure would switch to success on 9 March 1945, but would involve the 9th U.S. Armored Division, rather than the USAAF. The structure's still-intact status worked in the Allies' favor that day, since it provided a springboard for what was the initial penetration of the Nazi hinterland sheltering behind the mighty fluid barrier.

The 8AF's primary concentration on tactical targets over the past week or so was now shared with strategic issues on Old Year's Day 1944. The 1BD went after oil-related targets around Hamburg and paid a sharp price, with only 27 out of 501 crews gaining mission "credit." Meanwhile, the 2BD continued its current brief of bridge busting using G-H; no MIA losses were suffered, but three B-24s either force landed on the Continent or crash landed in England. Two came out of Wendling's ranks and both were fortunate to survive the sudden slashing fighter attack that descended upon the Low squadron as it sought a Target of Opportunity. Sgt. Dick Esenwein (RWG), on Lt. Alex Majesky's 906/DC:, recalled:

> While trying to bomb a bridge, three of our engines were shot out after 36 fighters attacked. I was in the bomb bay at the time, trying to release the bombs with a screwdriver. It seemed like the Fourth of July, with cannon shells going off. On returning to the waist,

I found Sgt. Seymour Adelman (WG) wounded and Sgt. Joe F. Martin (TG) with glass in his eyes. I told Martin to keep moving his guns to let the Germans know we were still alive before calling Sgt. Melvin A. Ivey (ROG) to bring morphine. I injected Aldelman's leg with it, but it went "crunch"—it was frozen. We were very lucky to find an old field near Rheims that housed a Field Hospital, to which I took Adelman, and Sgt. Francis "Pat" Patton (Eng.) took Joe. Pat and I were later asked if we wanted Purple Hearts for the scratches we had suffered, but we said no—in my case because I knew Dad would get notice of it before I could explain the situation in a letter. Little did I know that it was worth five points towards my discharge!

On 3 February 1945, B-24L-5-FO/44-49279 took off on a practice flight, but shortly afterwards, the 564BS machine was a crumpled wreck in a field at Fundentall, having suffered engine failure. The fuselage has literally been ground into the soil; the fate of the airmen involved is not clear, but most if not all of those on board would have been fortunate to survive.

The other affected crew on 44-10528/CI: F, flown by Lt. Willis C. Blakeley, was doubly lucky to survive. Having managed to avoid being shot down, the B-24 was brought back to Wendling and was making its landing approach when another aircraft cut across its path. The pilot pulled up and commenced a second circuit. Suddenly, all power was lost and the bomber slumped nose down. At the last moment its errant and potentially lethal path was corrected. However, the still-heavy contact with a field at Beetley twisted the fuselage to the left and ground its lower section down as well as snapping off the tail; none of the nine airmen were injured, despite the severe scale of damage.

January 1945

News Year's Day for the now redesignated 8AF Air Divisions saw the 2AD alone continuing to hammer the communications system behind the enemy's steadily shrinking Ardennes Front, with the B-17s striking at oil-related targets. All but the 448BG participated in striking at railroad bridges north and west of Koblenz. The weather conditions were a probable factor in the take-off crashes borne by three Groups—all the more ironic, since just one of the 273 crews in mission completion went down. The extremely strong headwind encountered by the 96CBW at least provided the flak gunners with a prolonged period in which to pitch their barrage. Sure enough, 42-50614/X7: A **Massachusetts Gal**, in Lt. Arthur M. Holter's (POW) hands, sustained a devastating strike up front that killed Capt. John W. Smith (N) and Lt. Charles A. Fiedler (B). Four further crewmembers out of eight lost their lives as their B-24 fell to earth near Andernach.

Back at Old Buckenham, the ground personnel were clearing up the crash scene that had tragically claimed nine lives, including that of Lt. A. C. Judd (P), out of eleven on board the Group Lead B-24. The bomber had refused to lift off the runway and finally slithered into two parked B-24s; the latter machines were reportedly little damaged. **The Big Drip** (41-29524) gave no quarter to any among its ten occupants when it suffered a similar fate at Bungay.

Over at Wendling, only 23 of the 27 dispatched crews returned to England, the remaining four having come down on the Continent. In the case of Lt. Roger Brandt's 41-29560/DC:, his bomber's absence was to prove permanent. The aircraft had steadily lost power due to fuel shortage and when the last motor failed at 1,000ft, a crash landing had to be hastily initiated onto a conveniently-sited airstrip, an action that left all nine airmen alive but the B-24 fit only for salvage. Battle damage to 42-51268/EC: F resulted in a similar course of action by Lt. Phillip W. Kaiser, but once again, all nine airmen either bailed out or walked away unscathed, other than Sgt. Brown (ROG), who was slightly hurt.

Pyrrhic Victory

Several 467BG crews among others diverting into Brussels-Evere gazed upon a scene of widespread destruction

This B-24M is one of a number allotted to the 482BG and equipped with AN/APN7 "Eagle" ground scanning radar housed in a horizontal aerofoil placed directly ahead of the bomb bay. The rear turret is a lightweight SACT.A6C applied to all M models and featuring an extra vision panel in the lower center of the turret frame.

A closer view of the "Eagle" cover shows how it is attached to the fuselage. Equipment was linked to the bombsight and provided an enhanced image compared to H-2X screen returns. On the other hand, pilots at Shipdham, to which this aircraft (44-42263) was transferred on 30 April, reported that stability on take-off and landing was uncertain and full attention had to be paid to controlling the aircraft during these ever-critical stages of flight.

within the dozens of aircraft scattered across its surface. What they witnessed was the aftermath of a mass Luftwaffe assault upon Allied airfields in Holland and Belgian under the codename *Bodenplatte* (base plate). Several hundred fighters had approached at minimum altitude in the dawn light and descended upon their allotted targets with a view to inflicting major damage upon the mainly RAF units stationed along this sector of the Front. True, a three-figure number of aircraft had been destroyed or badly damaged, but the attacks had generally not been well coordinated by those pilots managing to avoid being downed by their own flak gunners, who had apparently not all been briefed on the Operation and opened up upon their fellow airmen! The final cost to the Luftwaffe far outweighed any equivalent logistical disability suffered by the Allied Air Forces. As for any effect the assaults might have on the Bombing Offensive, the vast bulk of the "heavies" remained in virtual security from aerial assault on their British bases; *Bodenplatte*, far from benefitting the Germans, simply depleted the *Jagdwaffe* of many of its combat-experienced pilots still on hand and thereby accelerated the pace of failure for the *Reichsverteidigung*'s overall structure.

"Operational" Mishaps

The four missions launched between the 2nd and 6th, with marshalling yards, railroad bridges, and communications centers the target categories, led to no MIA losses, although PFF methods for bombing had to be used in the face of the perverse weather conditions. This cosy scenario was marred as ever by the occasional "operational" incident, as evidenced at North Pickenham on the 5th. **Rage in Heaven** (44-40165) was the yellow/green-striped Assembly Ship; it rumbled down the snow-shrouded runway, but shortly after take-off something went wrong and it crashed, killing all on board. The second B-24 followed, but it was barely airborne before it too descended to a terminal fate just off the runway end. Two more bombers did manage to get safely aloft, at which point the mission was abandoned. On return, a 466BG aircraft crash landed near its airfield.

Next day, 41-29575/ **Ruth E. K**, a veteran machine that had survived the multi-collision scenario at Seething the previous 22 April, turned back over the sea after suffering engine malfunction. An inexorable descent ensued even after the bomb load was jettisoned. Lt. Sampson, sighting solid ground through a gap in the undercast, ordered the crew out before pointing his B-24 back out to sea. When his turn came the aircraft had cleared the coastline, so he circled before jumping clear, albeit at a perilously low altitude. A combination of technical failure and Mother Nature had once more combined to thin the 8AF ranks without any enemy intervention.

Maintaining Tactical Pressure

The ensuing four missions up to the 13th continued to involve the 8AF in the duty of harrying the German retreat from the Ardennes by striking at their communications. A total of 23 crews from the 3,410 gaining mission credit were added to the MIA list. The weather conditions were still marginal enough to merit the wholesale use of various PFF aids. The Division share of the foregoing loss figure was just two, but was not appreciated at Seething, from where the crews had departed.

Flak caught up with the Group over Achern (7th) as it turned for home to fatally cripple 42-94972/**Daisy Mae**. The 81-mission veteran B-24 struggled homeward, but finally succumbed over French soil, killing all of Lt. Paul O'Neil's crew. Similarly afflicted was 42-51349, flown by Lt. Francis Piliere, but this time around the pilots reached the safety of a French airfield; next day, they flew on to Seething, but without their B-24, which was declared fit only for salvage due to the damage scale. The following two missions did not add to the MIA figure, but two B-24s were involved in crash landings on the 10th.

"Blind" Luck

One of these "operational" casualties involved the 392BG, whose original 28-crew total was whittled down to 19 making Assembly thanks to the appalling snow and icing conditions. The deputy Lead was Lt. John C. Clarke and crew, who were flying a "spare" (42-51186/EC: C), since their regular B-24 was unavailable. Problems with start-up saw them take-off after the other crews instead of being No. 2 in sequence. All went well until they were closing with the formation, when according to the copilot, Lt. Oak Mackey:

> No. 3 over-speeded, probably due to congealed oil trying to pass through the propeller governor—serious, as this could junk the engine or cause the prop to detach. Power was shut off, but when the "feathering" button was pushed in it popped out again, for it is its own circuit breaker. T/Sgt. F. C. Brunett (Eng.) pushed and held the button in, causing the secondary circuit breaker to pop open, which he then held down with his other hand—a risky action, as it could cause the "feathering" oil pump or its wiring to catch fire. Thankfully, the prop blades finally "feathered" and engine rotation halted.
>
> We turned back and dropped our bombs "safe" into the sea, but as we headed for base No. 2 "ran away," and although we shut it down without difficulty, our aircraft began to drop down, especially with an almost full fuel load on board. An immediate bail out option was rejected in favor of making it to Wendling. However, south of Norwich a break in the undercast allowed sight of an airfield (Seething). Having made all landing checks, lowered the gear and flaps, and assumed a runway line-up, the canopy iced-up due to our descending through a temperature inversion!
>
> We were committed to landing, and as I peered through a small space on the side window I saw we were almost down and that men were running fast; I assumed they were clearing a building in our direct path. Without thinking, full left rudder was applied which slewed the B-24 left and caused the gear and No. 1 and 4 propellers to snap off when we touched down. The fuselage broke behind the cockpit (a common experience in crash landings) and the nose tilted up. This expanded the side window frame, through which I scrambled. I then ran to the waist window to check if anybody was there, but on continuing round the tail, I found everyone else assembled without a scratch. We now realized we had missed hitting the control tower by some 100 feet. An ambulance pulled up and when an airman brought out a bottle of 100-proof rye, we took our "medicine" like men!

This incident, one of all-too-many arising during the course of the Offensive, illustrates the fact that luck played a prominent part in individual and corporate survival, especially in what here was literally a "blind landing" scenario.

Operational Retrenchment

The Division had to date participated in every monthly mission, but this pace would noticeably shrink over the rest of January. The first of nine such sorties went out on the 13th, when a full Divisional effort against railroad targets saw virtually all the 276 crews dispatched come back one short from Seething, although a further five crews were absent out of 32 taking off. Capt. Ed Wall's 42-50661 provided the MIA statistic thanks to flak strikes at Saarbruecken; only one crewmember failed to get down alive. Of the other five crews, four diverted into airfields abroad. The fifth was 42-50745/ **Flexible Flier**, which staggered back with serious flak damage; its condition by then was regarded as incapable of allowing a safe landing, so Lt. Harold Soldan ordered a bail out near Stowmarket, with all floating down safely. However, their B-24 headed west as far as Sarrat, north of London, before piling in. In all, this was a rather unsatisfactory manner in which to complete the Group's 200th mission, but it was the 13th after all!

Landing and take-off were regular sources for "operational" disaster and the latest victim was the ironically-named **Lassie Come Home** (44-40283/J4: I) from the 458BG. Lt. Stanley E. Diehl was carefully guiding the B-24J in on landing approach, being currently on three engines. Then all went wrong when a second engine on the same wing went "out." The drastic power loss caused the machine to falter and witnesses on the ground heard the remaining two engines' noise rise in desperate cadence as the pilots vainly tried to stabilize the bomber's flight before **Lassie** suddenly snapped into an inverted roll and smashed into the garden of one of a terrace of houses.

Eight of the nine-man crew were killed, along with two children; even so, it was a miracle that the two properties adjacent to the crash site were only slightly damaged. A 389BG tour-expired veteran who could count Ploesti among his missions was visiting his fiancée, who was living in one of the houses. T/Sgt. Earl Zimmerman rushed out to the crash scene and assisted in pulling two still-living crewmembers from the fuselage. He would surely reflect upon this incident as the one bringing him the closest to eternity during his entire tour of duty!

The third of five consecutive daily missions (15th) involved a reduced four-Group force that had recourse to bombing its Secondary marshalling yard, along with several Targets of Opportunity. The sole casualty out of 120 bombers was another 448BG machine that was fortunate to crash

The basic inability of the B-24 airframe to even remain aloft, let alone fly a protracted home leg after suffering this degree of damage, was thwarted on 16 February; bombs from another B-24 sheered off most of the port stabilizer and fin on 42-96031/CI: P. Having regained friendly shores, Lt. Novik bailed out his 392BG crew; his charge immediately went out of control as he attempted to leave the cockpit, and it was only the subsequent airframe's disintegration that threw him out to deploy his parachute!

land on a Belgian beach after reversing course and running out of fuel as the Continental coastline appeared; this was 44-40224/ **Sky Lark**, in Lt. Herschel Hausman's hands. Next day, another B-24 was removed from Group inventory as the bomb run was in progress. **Unholy Virgin** (42-95544), flying Low squadron Lead, took a flak strike, causing Lt. Wesley Issacson to call his bombardier and tell him to jettison—an act that unfortunately was acted upon by the other sub-unit aircraft. The damaged bomber was finally abandoned SE of the city. A second B-24 (41-28819/**Rosie's Rivets**) had its fuel tanks thoroughly riddled by flak and got as far as Lille, France, where it was successfully "bellied in." A third 20CBW crew went down over Germany (42-51275/YM: from Hardwick). The flak-crippled B-24 steadily descended to around 5,000ft before spinning in, along with six out of Lt. Donald A. Hastreiter's (POW) team.

Thirty Out—None Back at Wendling

Weather conditions for the return flight on the 16th were so marginal over East Anglia that over half the force diverted into Continental airfields. The 14CBW in particular suffered a total of seven aircraft "written off," primarily thanks to a combination of flak and fuel shortage.

The 392BG had dispatched 30 crews, but by the time the IP was reached five had "aborted." The Primary was "blanketed out," so a switch to three Targets of Opportunity was made. The flak gunners contributed to the resultant failure of five crews to get back home, beginning with 42-51121/EC: U **Jays Poolhall**, with Lt. Robert E. Vicker's team. During the bomb run, two engines were observed either "out" or smoking, while the B-24's errant path nearly led it under the bombs from the Lead bomber. When last seen it was steadily flying under P-51 escort and was recorded at debriefing as MIA. In the event, having suffered further punishment around Frankfurt and with a third engine on fire all jumped clear near Metz, France. Two airmen on Lt. Novik's crew were killed during a bail out near St. Maur, when 42-50489/GC: G ran out of fuel.

Two of the other three "write offs" involved crash landings on the Continent: 480/CI: B and 4250813/DC: V, flown respectively by Lts. Meehan and William J. Clower. The latter B-24, with one engine "out," ended up in a field at Luneville; the crew was congratulating the pilots when fire was observed, causing a hasty evacuation. (The flames must have been quickly extinguished, since photographic evidence shows a basically intact airframe, other than a smashed top turret Plexiglas and a collapsed left landing gear.) Lt. Stoddard made it back to England in 345/DC: D, but was ordered to divert further north, since Wendling was "socked out"; a switch to Woodbridge Emergency airfield was made in view of extreme fuel shortage, but when this was found to be similarly unavailable the decision was made to bail out. Although the B-24 was set on a due east course, it somehow reversed course and ultimately ploughed into rising ground north of London, fortunately with no effect on property or human life! All the remaining Group aircraft had diverted into Continental bases, so the total absence of any at the anticipated ETA must have sent shivers of apprehension through the ground staff until the situation was clarified.

Shipdham's casualty list commenced with Capt. Testa's 42-50725/WQ: M, also bearing Col. Snavely (CO) as Command Pilot. Flak had set No. 2 engine on fire, but although this fortunately went out, further loss of power and a second flak strike that caused the loss of the port wing's fuel content culminated in a bail out where the German, French, and Luxembourg borders conjoin. Fortunately, all crewmembers came down on friendly soil.

Lt. Lindsay followed his Wendling contemporary's initial luck in getting back to England, but finding no airfield visually available was similarly forced to bail out his crew from 42-110095/WQ: G **Hellsadroppin** near Norwich; the bid to direct the bomber out over the sea seemingly worked on this occasion.

A Lead 458BG bomber, 42-50954/J3: E, stricken by flak and set on fire, did not prevent Capt. John W. Moran from completing the bomb run. The flames went out, but the manifold problems, including a fuel tank blown out of the wing and an inability to "feather" one engine, with the adjacent power plant revving-up, boded ill for the chances of regaining friendly soil. Amazingly, an almost two-hour sojourn brought the ailing B-24 back to a point estimated to be over Allied territory, at which stage the almost dry tanks induced an engine shut-down. The glide was held while all jumped out; sadly, two out of those on board suffered parachute failure.

No "Milk Runs" to Hamburg

Hamburg was rightly feared for its comprehensive flak defenses, and the latest 8AF sortie (17th) by twelve groups spread between the 2nd and 3rd ADs had its price in aircraft and crews, with four each from the Divisions. An element of fortune lay in the fact that four crews did win through to Sweden, however. The 2AD force averaged only 12 B-24s per unit, of which all but six struck the Primary of Harburg's Rhenania oil refinery.

A trio of flak bursts surrounded 41-28963/7V: T, bearing Lt. Roger T. Hicks and crew, knocking out No. 1 engine, which was quickly "feathered," and causing fuel to siphon from a tank; worse still was a bomb bay fire. The B-24 banked to the right in what appeared to be a doomed bid to head north, a bid whose success was further compromised by Hicks stating that his fuel reserves could only last less than one hour. The absence of a map extending up to Sweden forced a guess at course direction, finally settled upon as 25 degrees. The rate of descent was materially lessened with the jettisoning of the ball turret, and although two enemy aircraft were sighted at one point, they ignored the cripple. The fuel tanks were registering minimal figures when land was sighted that turned out to be the neutral country's area around Falkenburg. It was here that all bailed out successfully as the B-24's engines abruptly coughed and spluttered to a halt.

The B-24's aerodynamically advanced wing structure cast up its inherent weakness whenever it encountered any sort of a solid flak strike. On this occasion, the 491BG was 14CBW Lead with Capt. Dean B. Strain, a Group "original" pilot flying the Lead bomber (42-5148). During the bomb run, a shell struck the port wing between the engines and the result was the almost complete excision of the flight surface. The resultant vicious spin held the twelve-man team in position until its final fiery impact; the aircraft's descent was recorded on several strike cameras.

Personal "Luck of the Draw"

Joining the 458BG crew in internment was one of a duo of Hardwick crews declared MIA. The Group was Division Lead, with 42-51523/RE; V, flown by Capt. Harry Gruener, and bearing Maj. John Floore as Command Pilot up front as deputy Lead. The Lead B-24 "aborted" the bomb run and Gruener took over; Maj. Floore in turn vacated the right seat in favor of Lt. John F. Harrington (CP). Seconds short of "bombs away," a flak shell burst alongside the starboard nose section to cripple both engines on that side; even worse was the severe head injury suffered by the copilot.

Gruener turned northward, but his original intention to reach Danish soil over which the crew would jump was cancelled on the basis that Harrington was unlikely to survive the experience. The 12-man crew finally reached Malmo, where a crash landing was made and Harington was rushed to hospital. Unfortunately, the nature of his injury resulted in his death 72 hours later. His fate again highlighted the luck (in Floore's case) or ill fortune (for Harrington) that was a salient feature of combat flying.

Up Against the Elements

Only four more January missions were to come the Division's way out of nine, while the entire 8AF remained ground-bound between the 24th and 27th, doubtless due to the disobliging winter weather. There were no MIA losses on the 21st, but three B-24s were involved in incidents, with all landing on the Continent. The 458BG's 42-95165/7V: L. **Cookie** was one of these, having lost two engines and suffering a forced landing in a French field that extensively damaged the nose; Lt. Ralph O. Hoffman's team flew back home without their B-24, which was declared salvage eight days later.

A full week elapsed before the B-24s were launched, this time against oil facilities at Kaiserstuhl and Gneisenau. Near 90% of the 225 crews bombed either Primary or alternative targets at a cost of seven. Two of the losses were initiated by the constant bane of formation flying—collision—although the flak gunners contributed to the disaster. A shell hit one wing on **Lady Eve** (42-95164/DC: P), flown by Lt. James R. Dodd, which promptly rolled over and struck 42-50868/DC: X in Lt. William H. Schuster's hands, severing most or all of his B-24's wing that was so affected. Both bombers fell away and down before being seen to explode. The reports of up to four parachutes were half correct, because Sgt. John J. Muka and Cpl. Maclovia Olivas (WGs) did reach the ground alive; Muka broke both legs and ended up in traction at a hospital in Ludenscheid, from where he was liberated in mid-April, while Olivas was unconscious for nearly 48 hours.

A third 14CBW aircraft was MIA with two more salvaged, all from Shipdham. **Corky** (42-51101/WQ: H) received a direct flak hit in the bomb bay during the bomb run and just three parachutes emerged before Lt. Corwine's aircraft blew up, with only the pilot and T/Sgt. Colosimo (ROG) actually surviving. Lt. Perrault's 44-10542/GJ: G+, although suffering progressive engine failure that included the third motor so affected catching fire, did make it to an airfield at Brussels, but power loss forced a wheels-down landing in a field short of the runway end. Finally, Lt. Muldoon ordered his crew out while circling Brussels/Melsbroek airfield in 42-52618/GJ: V+ **Chief Wapello**. A trio of Hardwick crews and one from Hethel completed the MIA tally. One of the former unit's losses involved 42-78486/ GO:, which came down close to Haamstede, on the Dutch Island of Schouwen, leaving all ten on Lt. Joseph J. Rosacker's crew facing captivity. **Miss America** (42-50558/RR:C) was the 389BG victim, with half of Lt. Berthelson's (POW) crew failing to survive their bomber's loss—all the more sad, since they were five missions short of tour completion.

The final monthly mission was launched on the 29th, but nearly all the 357 crews unloaded upon marshalling yards at Muenster or the notorious marshalling yard complex at Hamm, NE of the Ruehr—both Secondary choices. The latter target was being overflown by the 2CBW following "bombs away" when flak struck home against Hethel's 44-40476/RR: and split the fuselage in two; the forward section dipped vertically downwards, while the tail section assumed a more leisurely floating descent. As it was, only S/Sgt. John O'Neill survived, having probably been cast out from his waist gun position; Lt. Statton (P) and his seven colleagues were not to enjoy such good fortune.

Deadly Natural Hazard

Ice was a particular hazard to aircraft especially during take-off, no more so than when the situation was created by other aircraft. On 28 January the slush-covered Shipdham runway was being traversed by the veteran 42-50349/WQ: F **Flak Magnet** when it encountered the spray thrown back by a preceding B-24. The almost instant ice-accretion that resulted robbed the wings of vital lift-capability and resulted in the aircraft literally falling out of the sky when barely two miles off the airfield at Whinburgh. Sgt. Scott (Eng.) was fatally crushed by the top turret, dying in hospital one week later; otherwise all the crew emerged safely from the now-burning bomber.

February 1945 - Magdeburg's "Jinx" Status

Berlin was once again back on the menu for 3 February, albeit only for the B-17 sub-forces. A key target of equal importance was allotted the 2AD, namely the Magdeburg/ Rothensee oil refinery. Strangely, less than 30% of the 434 crews dispatched struck the Primary, despite clear conditions, while almost double this percentage had recourse to striking the city's marshalling yards—and required PFF assistance to do so! At least the cost was marginal (two), although not to the crews concerned. For the third mission in a row a Hethel B-24 was downed, with the 566BS involved in all instances. **Delectable Doris** (42-50551/RR: R) had been named for Lt. Bill Graaf's wife. He had survived his combat tour, but now a flak strike that excised the entire nose section ensured his original aircraft's demise. Lt. John Merrill (CP) and Sgt. Bill Weidman (WG) somehow escaped from the terminal descent that consumed Lt. Robert W. Bonner (P) and all other crewmembers.

A return to the same briefed Primary (6th) was even less productive, since the adjacent marshalling yards absorbed the loads of 418 out of 434 B-24s, while the butcher's bill was set at just two MIA aircraft, one each from Hardwick and Attlebridge. The 93BG loss involved Lt. Howard E. Jennings' (POW) 42-50505/ AG: E. **Little Gee/Gremlins Roost**, which exploded in mid-air over Akersloot with the loss of two out of the nine crewmembers. Two of the survivors were momentarily taken away for concealment by two young Dutchmen (Wim Woesterberg and Louw Beumer), but the party was unluckily intercepted by the Germans. Whether or not the airmen witnessed their would-be rescuers' fate of being summarily shot on the spot was unclear; if they did, both would have had no illusion of the peremptory treatment being comprehensively handed out by the Nazi regime and the reason why they and their colleagues were "over there" striving to free Occupied Europe from such malign influences. A third B-24 was lost during Assembly, believed due to the unseen but malign effect of prop wash. Lt. Roy F. Flatt was piloting 44-10515/E8:, but the heavily-loaded 453BG bomber stood no chance of survival for itself or its human cargo when it tumbled to earth.

The Third Reich's industrial infrastructure was steadily declining, but the defensive priority accorded target categories such as synthetic oil production ensured a hot reception for the pedestrian-paced B-17s and B-24s. A recalled mission (8th) for the entire 8AF was followed next day by each Division dispatching two sub-forces, with oil the focus for the larger formations. Ten 2AD groups went out, with the smaller force successfully reaching its railroad viaduct Primary at Bielefeld, albeit with no positive result from G-H support but also without loss. Once again, Magdeburg/Rothensee's oil refinery remained inviolate from all but ten out of 288 crews gaining mission credit, the vast majority again diverting to the marshalling yard Secondary with *H2X* assistance.

Three Groups left a tithe of one crew behind, starting with Wendling's **The Philly Folly** (41-28841/DC: Z+), bearing Lt. Burton L. Wade and crew on their first and tragically last mission. Heading home over the North Sea, eyewitnesses saw the B-24 reverse course, presumably for reasons of fuel shortage. Nothing further was found of the B-24, but the drifting ashore on the Dutch coast of four bodies out of the nine-man crew was ample proof that the sea had claimed yet another victim. Two further aircraft landed on the Continent due to either fuel shortage or battle damage.

The 491BG lost 42-51267/ **Miss Francia**, which was finally abandoned

The 93BG's 42-51191/AG: H **Carioca Bev** (a B-24H-20-FO) has returned from a mission with at least one casualty on board. The cluttered interior, coupled with the B-24's horizontal and low-slung "ground sit," made stretcher extraction difficult, if not hazardous for the affected crewmembers. Departure via the waist windows as seen here provided an awkward handling act for the Medics.

This 578BS aircraft nearly made it to the culmination of the 8AF's bombing campaign. On 14 April, 42-50446/EC: R **Jay's Poolhall** lost power to both port engines during take-off. The resultant crash just off the airfield killed all but one crewmember in Lt. Charles M. Warren's complement in the incident, with the survivor, Sgt. Kight, dying several weeks later.

successfully in terms of evading capture by all but two on Lt. Kenneth A. Rowe's crew. A "prepare to bail out" bell signal, normally requiring a swift push on the button, went wrong when the button jammed; this was misinterpreted by the navigator and tail gunner, who assumed it to be the full "bail out" signal, whereupon they jumped—over still-occupied Dutch territory!

A 453BG bomber flown by Lt. E. R. Jochens (42-52472/E3:) suffered the progressive loss of three engines and had to be put down in the North Sea with the coastline at Great Yarmouth tantalizingly in sight; the result was that the pilot and five out of the other eight on board survived the experience. The group's travails today were added to by a collision over Old Buckenham involving the 734BS crews led by Lt. Rollins and Lt. Glass; the former-crewed B-24 crashed, bearing its eleven-man content to their deaths.

An oil depot at Dulmen was plastered by a reduced-scale force of 124 (11th), following which the crews stood idle for two days before again being briefed (14th) for Magdeburg / Rothenssee's still-intact refinery complex—and intact it remained, thanks to being "socked in." The much-punished city marshalling yards received 340 bomb loads, one of which was released by Lt. Weiss's 44-40109/RR: H. The 566BS had lost four B-24s over the last sixteen days and now suffered a fifth. The No. 4 engine was set on fire as the 389BG turned for the Rally Point and the pilot called for escort cover; when last seen, the fire appeared to be out but the bomber was slowly descending. It later transpired that of the ten-man team, two were killed and the others bailed out into captivity.

Success—At Last

By this point in February, the Division crews involved in the previous four failed attempts at striking their Magdeburg Primary must have groaned in frustration when Rothensee's oil refinery appeared on the Briefing screens on the 15th. The weather forecast quality for the overall mission must have cast doubts upon gaining a visual sighting of the target, but in fact, it was only the 2AD out of the three sub-structures that was reportedly destined to enjoy this undoubted bonus—at least as far as the 353 bombardiers were concerned. Only one crew was posted MIA, but this marginally negative situation was marred by two "operational" incidents, one involving fatalities.

The 392BG records clearly contradict the foregoing statement regarding target clarity, since they state that bombing was conducted using *H2X*—in addition to which P-47s were going to go in ahead to drop smoke markers. To the frustration of not confirming bombing accuracy was added the loss of a crew led by Lt. Gene A. Hubbartt flying in 42-50387/CI: T **Birdie Schmidt ARC**, which was making its 63rd mission. Mechanical problems that saw a very late take-off had steadily built up to the point where the bombs had to be jettisoned between the IP and target. The loss of two engines to target flak inevitably resulted in a steady height loss that culminated with the nine airmen bailing out into captivity near Mulhausen.

The mission had commenced badly for the 448BG with an unfortunate incident involving 42-50678/ **Umbreogo**. The B-24 was barely airborne when the starboard life raft hatch opened; the raft was ejected and its tethering rope tangled with and jammed the horizontal stabilizer. A succession of shallow dives and upward surges evolved, but Lts. Harlyn Schroeder and Delwin Roorda still managed to retain basic control, intending to head the B-24 out towards the sea prior to jettisoning the bombs. All too soon the handling became increasingly problematical following an order to bail out. Finally, with Sgt. Vetterneck (Eng.) volunteering to remain and handle the throttles, the pilots unstrapped, with all three intending to rush for the exits. The Sergeant went first, but he was barely out before witnessing the tail section snapping off; his gallant companions stood no chance as the truncated airframe entered into a spin and smashed into the soil near Attlebridge.

On return, Hethel's 42-50548/RR: L **Leter Rip** was commencing its landing approach when all four engines suffered fuel starvation. The B-24 careened into a convenient field, but not before its starboard outer wing smashed into a house's outbuildings directly in the bomber's path. The impact tore off the section, fortunately without either affecting any of the property's inhabitants or casting the B-24 into a fatal crash angle; all the crew emerged unscathed, at least physically!

The extremely bad weather conditions extending throughout this winter were destined to once again force the 8AF crews into a mass diversion away from their bases onto either Continental airfields or the equivalent facilities in Western England (16th). Most of the 362 B-24s struck their Primaries, but the trickle of MIA casualties continued with a single 467BG bomber. **Super Wolf** (42-95080/Q2: V) was the aircraft in question. Lt. John D Mulligan's charge had safely negotiated the bomb run, but flak struck on the return leg to inflict a damage scale that forced a bail out near Valthe, Holland; of the ten airmen all but one—Sgt. Walter E. Sise (Eng.), who suffered parachute failure—ended up as POWs.

A recalled mission (17th) cost the 453rd and 467th BGs single crews, with fourteen among their number being lost in the North Sea, while three airmen on a 466BG bomber were killed on English soil during a third incident. This was followed two days later by a successful trio of Primary strikes spread between Siegen and Kassel, once again at a single MIA cost. The 389BG's latest blood debt was paid during the 2CBW assault upon a munitions plant at Jungenthal; however, 42-95088/HP: X **Stinky/ Wynn, Our Little Lady** never even reached the Primary. Instrument failure over Holland was called in by Lt. Mercer, after which nothing was known about the crew's failure to return. Only later was confirmation received that eight were POWs, with the ninth (S/Sgt. Tzolog Aaronian, ROG) killed. Next day witnessed a totally thwarted effort to attack Nuremberg, with Mother Nature providing the reason, although the formations reached Belgium before being recalled.

Clarion

The bad weather conditions notwithstanding, the 8AF "heavies" would now go aloft virtually daily until the end of February and extending to 5 March. Nuremberg's reprieve on the 20th was short-lived, as it was assaulted without loss next day. A 24-hour operational gap was closed up on the 22nd, when Operation *Clarion* was launched. This entailed a comprehensive two-day assault upon Germany's transportation infrastructure; anything that could be construed as "transport" was to be bombed or strafed—even horse and carts were fair game for the latter type of attention, while bombing altitudes for the B-17s and B-24s were significantly reduced in cases where flak defenses over a specific target were deemed marginal or nonexistent.

Just short of 2,800 individual crews gained mission credit between 22 and 23 February at a cost of two MIA, one of which was from the 2AD; added to this were three more B-24s involved in "operational" crashes, with a 93BG aircraft diverting to a Continental airfield (23rd). The single MIA casualty on the 22nd came from the 392BG, which headed for Nordhausen's marshalling yards, but largely ended up striking similar facilities at Northeim with poor results. Flak was meager but sufficient to cripple Lt. Joseph R. Walker's 42-95241/EC: G **Jolly Duck**. The final sight of the now-straggling bomber was with its No. 3 engine "feathered" and easing south along the Dutch coast with a view to reaching Allied territory. That bid failed at Zoeterwoude when, despite the landing gear down as a surrender indication, the enemy guns opened up; the ensuing forced landing involved the loss of the landing gear and the nose section breaking off and twisting to one side. One sprained ankle was the surprisingly small crew casualty figure arising out of the incident. All nine airmen split up into two groups of four and five; the former party ran into the Germans, but the other got into Resistance hands, including S/Sgt. John E. McCormick (WG).

The bomber's final resting place was right alongside a farm, and this fact led to a tragedy four days later. Following examination of a 542 (RAF) Squadron fighter's picture of what was interpreted as an intact aircraft whose technical equipment could benefit enemy intelligence circles, several of the unit's Spitfires were directed to the site and made three strafing runs upon the bomber. Unfortunately, the hail of gunfire killed the farmer, Martinus Janson—one of the local Resistance group who had sheltered the five evading airmen—as well as four other individuals that included two children. (The events surrounding this American airman's tragic fate on 29 April, as well as the heart-warming postwar remembrance of the Dutch people of what occurred that day will form a separate addendum account at the end of the book.)

The second *Clarion* mission was in its final homeward stage when another tragedy in the form of a mid-air collision struck the 458BG. Lt. Russell J. Bechtel's six-month veteran crew flying 42-50449/J4: W **Heavenly Hideaway** and 41-29596/Z5: R **Hells Angels**, in Lt. Daniel F. Hunt's hands, came together in fatal embrace as the Group was separating into squadron sequence for landing. The latter B-24's starboard outer wing sliced off part of the other bomber's port fin before itself separating. Bechtel's machine tipped into a near vertical dive, while its companion banked sharply to starboard to also commence an inexorable descent.

All nine on Bechtel's crew died in their B-24's violent demise at Skeyton, but three from Lt. Hunt's team somehow escaped the same fate by bailing or being cast out before **Hells Angels** spread herself in a Norfolk field at Felmingham, two miles further north. Losses in these circumstances were arguably more upsetting to combat crews than those incurred during combat, since no enemy hand had intervened.

Comment

The second day of *Clarion* involved all but two bomb Groups, although this time round barely 30% of the 28 reported targets were in the Primary category, compared to almost half of the 41 recorded at debriefing on the 22nd. In addition, all of the latter grouping fell into the "Target of Opportunity" rather than "Secondary" category. This in turn indicated a desire on the part of the 8AF authorities to punish the collective will of the enemy population as opposed to striking at their nation's ability to militarily or industrially sustain the conflict. (A postwar TV documentary centered on *Clarion* would suggest that the Operation's conduct was verging on the edge of psychological warfare, or to put it more bluntly "terror bombing," and was therefore a basic negation of the avowed aim of pursuing a policy of precision bombardment.)

Daily Pressure Applied

All three Divisions were employed daily for the remainder of February, striking at a range of target categories from oil to communications. The minimal MIA figures of thirteen out of more than 5,000 completed individual sorties were shared out, with three allotted the 2AD. To these were added several "operational" losses, beginning on the 24th when a 445BG bomber went in on take-off, killing four of its crew. To this Tibenham loss was added the sole pair of MIA crews lost off the mission to Halle's marshalling yards on the 27th, while the only other MIA casualty came from Hardwick (24th). This was Capt. Gene L. Maddocks's Lead bomber 42-51495, which turned back with flak damage and progressed only as far as the edge of Holland's Ijsselmeer before being abandoned by its twelve occupants. The pilot was the exception to being captured; he wandered for several days until, on the verge of exhaustion, he approached a canal barge whose fortunately pro-Ally occupants contacted the local Resistance cell.

One further crew did not return on the 26th, but their temporary "residence" was on Allied soil—east of Berlin. By now, the Russian Armies were almost within audible distance of the Reich capital and were therefore a very handy source for any crippled American aircraft to be directed towards. Lt. Frank M. Jenson's 42-50680/T8: was observed to "feather" No. 3 engine and drop out of formation while adopting a 90 degree course. The steadily descending B-24 was abandoned when the pilot (correctly) assumed he was over Russian-occupied territory. Once reassembled, the 491BG crew were taken to Odessa, from where they made a protracted ship and aircraft-based journey back to North Pickenham. Belgian soil accommodated the wreckage of 41-29500/WV: R. **Ramblin' Wreck**, which had to finally be successfully abandoned by its crew.

Chapter Eighteen

Nailing Down the Coffin

Comment

As March 1945 was entered, there was a clear sense that the Third Reich was in its death throes. That eminently desirable situation notwithstanding, none of the Western political or military hierarchy could be certain that the outcome would be a totally favorable one. The Germans were still showing no signs of reacting to the call for an unconditional surrender. The last barrier to Anglo-American advancement on the ground, the Rhine River, had yet to be breached. The Soviet forces were well into eastern Germany and driving forward towards Berlin, but that factor could create a postwar problem for the West, should its armies remain rooted on the Rhine's western shores. Joseph Stalin's record on democratic conduct did not promise any great prospect for a return to democratic governmental structures in the territories either occupied by his country since 1939, nor for those lands already "liberated" over the past several months, or likely to be so afflicted prior to the conflict's conclusion.

The *Jagdwaffe*'s strength in the skies over central Europe was generally limited to a mix of *Sturmgruppen* tactics and the use of advanced designs, with the Me262 jet-propelled fighter and the rocket-powered Me163 to the fore. In the former case, Willi Messerschmitt's superlative creation was thankfully available only in relatively small numbers, while the Jumo 004 engines demonstrated very short lifespans in terms of serviceability. All the same, its presence left the bomber crews with a justified feeling of great vulnerability should the formations encounter what the Germans had named *Sturmvogel* (Stormbird).

The Diminishing Cost

The Division's inaugural mission for the month passed off loss-free, but next day (2nd) occurred the latest albeit small-scale reminder that the defenses were "alive and kicking"; ironically, one of the three 2AD losses out of fourteen overall was self-inflicted, while the nature of close formation flying contributed to the incident. For some reason, the gunners on a 392BG bomber decided to test fire their weapons when already well on the way to the Magdeburg/Rothensee oil refinery. The misdirected fire of at least one gunner struck Lt. Willis G. Blackney's 42-51302/CI: N, which eased down and out of formation near the Duemmersee and finally crashed NE of Osnabrueck. The pilot was one of five fatalities, all being discovered in or close to the wreckage; the other five, including Sgt. Herbert M. Halpern, flying as a German interpreter of enemy radio transmissions, ended up as POWs.

A duo of enemy-inflicted casualties came from the 96CBW, one each from Attlebridge (42-51273/2U:) and

Rackheath. The 467BG's 42-51171/Q2: P **Eli Swof Jr.** suffered the successive loss of two engines to a combination of flak and fighters. Fire caught hold on Lt. Alvah D. Reid's bomber and four crewmembers bailed out, one of whose parachutes caught fire; he was soon united in death by the pilot and the remaining four airmen who perished in their B-24H's demise close to Dorsten.

The constant specter of mid-air collision caught up with the 448BG next day when it lost two of the four MIA aircraft, the other duo coming from Tibenham. Magdeburg/Rothensee was again the Primary and the *Jagdwaffe* was up in numbers that included the Me262, two of which swept from head-on into the Seething formation just as the IP was looming. Fire smashed into 42-51247/ **Feuden' Rebel**, deputy Lead for the Low squadron and in Lt. James Guynes's hands. A partial loss of power induced a yawing action to the left that led it to inadvertently make lethal contact with 42-50463/ **Gung Ho II**, despite Lt. Irving Smarinsky's (KIA) frantic bid to maneuver out of the way. His B-24 had its tail section severed, while the other bomber flopped over onto its back. Two airmen cheated death on **Gung Ho II**, as did the pilot and Sgt. Don Schleicher, despite the mid-air disintegration of **Feuden Rebel**; however, Lt. Guynes's lease on life lasted less than one month before he died in hospital from his wounds.

The daily run of missions for the entire 8AF continued with one exception (6th) up to the 12th. The mission launched on the 4th had unfortunate overtones for two Division Groups. The allotted target or targets were in that southern German zone with Switzerland, but the real problem arose when, with the Primaries blanketed out, the force sought out Targets of Opportunity. In the case of elements from the 392BG and 466BG, the crews concerned attacked what was described as facilities in Freiburg; in fact, the Groups, in delivering their bombs, had strayed well south and flown over neutral territory as far as Zurich and Basel. Today's transgression was not the sole such incident to bedevil Swiss/U.S. relations during WWII. All but one B-24 returned home, although the exception nearly made it. Rackheath's second loss in three days was 41-28961/6A: V, which had to be put down in the sea by Lt. George W. Mills within sight of Cromer. This ever-unpredictable action tragically ended in failure for all eight airmen.

The next three missions up to the 8th did not add to the Division's MIA figure, but this proved to be of no consolation to a 389BG crew on the 7th. Lt. Dale Williams lifted 42-51343/YO: K **Shazam** off the Hethel runway, but bare minutes later the B-24, along with its crew, was smashed into the ground at Costessey, west of Norwich. The cause of the crash was suspected as having been due to ice accretion, causing the heavily-laden aircraft to go out of control. The villagers later put up a plaque in their church to the airmen, who in their view "had given their today for the locals' tomorrow."

The winter weather conditions so far in March had shown little sign of relenting visually, so *H2X*, *G-H*, and *Micro-X* assistance were largely called upon in striking targets. On the other hand, the same solid cloud patterns probably inhibited *Jagdwaffe* operations to some degree, although predicted flak continued to make for an uncomfortable and occasionally lethal passage between the IP and the relative target. The four missions after the 8th threw up just a single B-24 loss over Muenster's marshalling yards (9th). The 389BG's 44-49382/YO: T, flown by Lt. Bill Hunter (KIA), with eleven other airmen on board, was struck by one or two shells during the bomb run. It drooped into a spin, but had barely rotated twice when a complete wing tore away, followed by a brutally swift disintegration of the remaining airframe; reports of up to six parachutes was not equalled by the same survival rate, since only two airmen ended up alive. (Muenster would claim another Group crew exactly two weeks later.)

The pace of operations slowed temporarily in mid-March, with none flown on the 13th or 16th, after which daily service was resumed up to the month's end. A different target category presented itself to the Division on the 15th, with a major Wehrmacht HQ at Zossen, near Berlin, selected for assault. Over 300 bombers got through to blitz the location, but one returning crew literally fell short of East Anglian shores. Problems with the fuel transfer system ensured that Lt. John B. Kelly had no option but to ease 42-50659/CI: D into the sea about 20 minute's flight time from the coast. The 68-mission veteran B-24 surprisingly acted like a lady and not only remained basically intact, but stayed afloat for nearly ten minutes. This positive scenario was tragically degraded when difficulty arose in extracting the dinghies. Although this was finally achieved, only five of the nine airmen managed to clamber into one or the other; their colleagues, although wearing Mae Wests, drifted helplessly away. The ASR launch that arrived after several hours only succeeded in locating Sgt. Stanley J. Poremba (WG) from among this group, and by then he had expired from exposure to the frigid North Sea.

Soviet Sanctuary

A return to Muenster's marshalling yards (17th) left the Division's ranks unscathed. Then, 24 hours later came a briefing for the 8AF's latest lunge at Berlin, which for the second successive occasion called upon the 2AD to supplement the efforts of its B-17 contemporaries. Strangely, the B-24s were only being included for the third time out of the previous eleven missions to the Nazi capital; this would also be their last involvement. Two armored vehicle plants were hammered by 305 B-24s out of 347 dispatched, with the Henningdorf sub-force surrendering one aircraft. However, this was one of no less than eleven bombers that sought refuge behind the Soviet front lines.

Rackheath's 42-50599/4Z: X was a former 466BG B-24JSH equipped for PFF duties and today was flying Lead for one squadron. Flak during the bomb run delivered a shattering blow to the

The mission is "on" and a line of Horsham St. Faith bombers are lined up along the perimeter track. The leading bomber is a B-24J-100-CO (42-100408/J4: I) bearing a garish piece of artwork that exemplifies her title—**The Beast**. Directly behind is B-24H-10-CF/41-29305, although with all four engines stopped it is uncertain if **I'll be Back** will live up to her name by even going!

On 10 March 1945, it was "down tools," as the personnel exchanged overalls or flight equipment for the Class A uniform—willingly or otherwise, given the average airman's distaste for parading in any form. However, this was a special occasion to celebrate the 458BG's completion of its 200th mission; the band leads the marching columns towards the Parade Ground.

forward lower fuselage, and the next thing Lt. Bill R. Chapman realized was that his charge was turning to starboard, having lost more than 3,000ft altitude. Sgt. George E. Fuller (Eng.) stood no chance of survival, as he was blasted out into mid-air through the flak-created hole, while a shell fragment killed Lt. Harold P. Van Tress (DR Navigator) at his post. Attempts to jettison the bomb load failed and with a steady altitude loss and inability to bank left and follow the formation home, the decision was taken to head due east.

A pass by a Bf109 was thankfully survived and three Yak-9Ds then appeared to drive off the fighter—before turning upon the bomber and shooting it up! Having estimated they were over Soviet lines, the bail out order was given and responded to, but Chapman recalled bullets slamming into the fuselage as he hastily made his way out via the bomb bay, but only after confirming Lt. Van Tress was dead.

However, the pilot's particular troubles were mounting, since he was not only shot at by a Yak while drifting down, but also encountered rifle fire from the ground. On landing, he was held at gunpoint, then marched over to two of his colleagues; one of the latter was fortunate that the pistol wielded by a wild-eyed soldier on a horse did not go off after being pointed at him and the trigger depressed several times! Matters ultimately stabilized when they were transferred to a senior officer's post, although at least one hour passed before Chapman succeeded in persuading him that they were American. Lt. Van Tress was buried with full military honors next day and the survivors then began the extended journey back to base.

Berlin initiated a miniature run of single losses on the next two missions. Shipdham dispatched 33 crews to an aircraft assembly plant at Neuberg, in Bavaria, but six B-24s were missing on return, five of which had diverted into Continental airfields. The sixth fell into the MIA category, being 42-51907/QK: B+, flown by Lt. Podojil. It was last seen with two engines "out" as the Allied lines were looming up on the return leg. The straggling B-24 did not make it further than the region around Stuttgart, since two Bf109s appeared and brought it down. Only one officer and two Enlisted men managed to bail out, but S/Sgt. Norbert J. Schmitz (TG) subsequently died following amputation of one severely injured leg. Lt. Bernard W. Bail (N) had previously bailed out of the B-24 on which Col. Leon Vance won his CMH the previous 5 June, but this time he landed in hostile territory. Next day, it was Tibenham's turn to remove one crew from its establishment following an attack on Hemmingstedt's oil refinery facility. The B-24 concerned was 44-48851/MK:.

The daily battering of the enemy's resources extended up to the 26th, but left the 2AD free of further MIA casualties for the next two days before a sortie to marshalling yards and a bridge (23rd) took out three more crews, including two from the 2CBW. The 389BG's contribution involved 44-19510.RR: H **Yankee Doodle Dandy**, which suffered a flak strike on its starboard wing. The section folded up and the tanks ignited in a ball of fire; up to six parachutes were reported, but only four airmen out of twelve on board, including L/Col. Lister, who was acting as Group Air executive, reached the ground alive from what was a wildly gyrating airframe. The ensuing two days of operations would involve the Division in a similar function to Operation *Market-Garden*, but would prove to be a more expensive experience in aircraft and crews.

Varsity—the Background

The Anglo-American forging of the River Rhine under Gen. Montgomery's overall command that bore the foregoing title was to be initiated over 23-24 March. As dawn broke on the 24th, the first of eight separate missions was launched by the 1AD, followed by two more B-17 and one B-24 assaults, all four being directed against enemy airfields. In the meantime, the bulk of the 2AD was being retained for the specifically vital duty of resupplying the Anglo-American parachute units. The nature of these low-level missions left them particularly vulnerable to ground fire, but the more ample bomb bay capacity of the B-24 naturally merited the Consolidated design's utilization in this activity.

The 2AD's Field Order issued on 23 March stated:

> *Varsity* can be considered the most important combined operation since D-Day. It is the supply of assault and airborne forces landed on the German side of the Rhine shortly before our crews drop supplies to them. The magnitude of such an operation makes it essential that for its complete success, the part of each force participating must be made with exactitude. We are committed to drop supplies in the designated places.

The paratrooper units' vulnerability to counterattack could only be assuaged by prompt and accurate delivery of the necessary arms and equipment. The 2nd, 14th, and 20th CBW were assigned the duty, which must have weighed heavily upon the crews' minds, who could have been under little or no illusion that the chances of losing out to the enemy's defensive capability were increased in a manner similar to the previous September's *Market-Garden* missions. The preparations at Wendling were probably symptomatic of what was occurring at the other eight airfields.

The average load was 2 1/2 tons, which would be ejected via a combination of the bomb bay and the ball turret and rear hatch wells, while a loadmaster would be added to each crew complement. The bomb bay-located bundles featured static lines attached to the bomb shackles to ensure the parachutes would deploy properly. A crewmember would have the unpleasant task of retrieving the lines once the drop was made—unpleasant because the bomb bay's narrow confines prevented the wearing of a pack. The warning bell would be used as a signal for bundle release, rather than indicating bail out. Finally, and somewhat contradictorily, gunners were adjured not to open up on ground positions within the drop zone in case these were occupied by their paratrooper colleagues—a situation that made their participation redundant, at least during this key segment of the mission!

Operational Procedure

The missions' briefings entailed several hours, with sandbox models of the drop zones on hand. Each squadron would fly as loosely as possible with the Elements virtually line abreast, but would then close up as much as possible shortly before the allotted drop zone. Two zones were involved roughly four miles apart, one each occupied by the U.S. and British Divisions. Altitude at the IP was to be 500ft, but pilots were warned not to go below 300ft, in order to permit full parachute deployment. Speed was to be no greater than 150 ASI, while the period of release was not to exceed 20 seconds. Once release was made, they were to resist the natural tendency to make a tight 180-degree turn, since this would present the Germans with a plan-view and therefore an easier focus for gunfire. Altitude was not to be regained until the B-24s were back over the Rhine. This was logical in theory, but the experience of some units, particularly those covering the British 6th Airborne zone, was to prove a rather costly one.

Into the Cauldron

The scene of battle that greeted the crews as they finally closed in upon their target areas was one of chaos. The smoke and haze enveloping the overall

The thin-rimmed circle with a yellow background is borne by this 446BG bomber to denote its Lead ship status in a PFF function. The parallel-sided housing for the original British 10-centimeter H2S equipment contrasts with the circular equivalent fitting for aircraft bearing the original American 3-centimeter H2X sets.

Three 506BS bombers are crossing in over the Norfolk coast. In the foreground is 42-50748/GJ: J-bar **Big Headed Kid**, a recent assignment to the 44BG. **Clean Sweep** (42-51351/GJ: P-bar) arrived at Shipdham during August 1944, with 42-95016/GJ: Z-bar **Down de Hatch** received three months previous; all three returned Stateside.

The great reluctance expressed by 491BG personnel to adopt the black diagonal marking adopted by their seemingly "jinxed" 492BG predecessors was indulged in by the continued (but illogical) retention of the green fin/rudder with a white horizontal band. Common sense finally prevailed in early 1945, with the correct marking applied as seen on the 854BS' 44-50532, which bears three "Carpet" Plexiglas covers.

The heavy damage administered to this 392BG bomber's port fin and rudder was inflicted while the H-30-FO assigned to the 578BS was sitting on its Wendling dispersal. A by-now very rare Luftwaffe "intruder" assault over Britain was launched on 20 March, but in this case the damage was reparable and the bomber soldiered on until VE-Day.

combat area only partially concealed the litter of gliders, many badly damaged or completely smashed; numerous structures were on fire and the scurrying figures of soldiers (Allied or enemy?) were everywhere. The combination of restricted visibility and low altitude was likely to present problems in picking out the drop zones. The 14CBW's sub-division of effort involved the 44BG with 27 loads for the U.S. paratroopers, the 491BG heading for the British drop zone with the same number of loads and the 392BG dividing its 26 loads equally between the two locations. The Wing's loss factor that was about to ensue would be nearly 50% of the overall Division tally.

One of the two worst-affected Groups regarding MIA losses (three) was the 491BG; in addition to the material casualties was a dreadful 100% death rate. Lt. James W. Brown's 42-50749 had its No. 3 engine ignited, but he coolly said "Roger" in response to a fellow pilot pointing out the fact; bare seconds later the B-24 erupted in a massive explosion. Lt. Paul Fox's 44-40162 had clearly received fatal damage, since he was observed to pull sharply up with the bomb bay ablaze; before anyone could take advantage of the increased height factor to jump, the bomber rolled over and plunged to the ground. **Green Hornet** (44-40286), in the hands of Lt. Andy T. Wilson, cleared the drop zone, albeit with severe damage; the pilot called up to say he was going to attempt a crash landing once across the Rhine, but the effort culminated with nobody surviving the incident.

Wendling's Lt. James E. Reynolds was copilot to Lt. John R. Hummel on 42-50709/ CI: E and recalled:

> We had encountered some ground fire on approach to the drop zone, but this really intensified at the release point, with 20mm strikes on the airframe. I hollered to Jack that No. 3 engine was on fire, which persisted, although I switched everything off. Jack then said No. 2 was losing pressure, at which point he pulled up to 500ft and called for a bail out, since we could not maintain flight on two engines, especially with our low speed. Jack hollered for me to work the rudder pedals as we prepared to force land, but my next recollection was of our being down and stopped, so I must have been temporarily knocked out.
>
> Blood was running down my face as Jack and I scrambled out through a big hole on my side of the cockpit to find four colleagues standing by the fuselage. Sgt. Elmer Milchak (WG) lay dead on the hatch sill, having been shot either by a sniper or one of a group of German soldiers walking towards the shattered aircraft. We fortunately induced them to stop firing and were taken to a house, where shortly after the tables were turned by the arrival of U.S. paratroopers.

Two further crewmembers—Lt. Bernard L. Knudsen (N) and Cpl. James A. Deaton (ROG), the latter tasked with retrieving the static lines—were killed. Knudsen had definitely bailed out, along with Sgt. Ellis H. Morse (NG), but had not shared the Sergeant's luck at surviving what was at best a marginal parachute descent.

Capt. Ursel Harvell (Photo Officer) was on board a 44BG bomber and shot tragically graphic film footage of both Group losses. One was Lt. Crandell in 42-100314/BN: G+, a thirteen-month veteran machine. The B-24 suddenly reared up and rolled before emulating Lt. Fox's fatal crash out of the 491BG's ranks. The other loss involved 42-50896/GJ: R-bar **Southern Comfort III**, flown by Lt. Chandler. Ground fire hit home upon the B-24 as the torturously-graduated turn for home was in progress. No. 4 engine was seen to be smoking, followed by the bomber striking the ground and momentarily bouncing back aloft; it came down again and the starboard wing tip made the initial contact to cast it into an incipient ground looping motion that ended with the airframe splitting in two. The two survivors out of nine on board (Sgts. DeBlasio and Vance), who had been throwing out supplies in the waist, were thrown out and soon apprehended by some civilians. Vance had suffered a head injury that left him incoherent at times, but their arrival at a hospital in Ahlen lasted barely one week before U.S. soldiers liberated the town.

20CBW Fortunes

The 26 bombers dispatched by the 448BG were assigned to the British drop zone north of Wesel, but one crew accidently released the supplies prior to traversing the Rhine, with two further teams acting upon this misfortune. The remaining 23 ploughed on through the inevitable barrage of ground fire that claimed one immediate victim. **Piccadilly Lilly** had 105 missions behind it, but with the control cables shot out Lt. Hugh McFarland (KIA) was unable to prevent 42-50341 from piling into a ridge and consuming eight of the ten-man crew in the process. Lt. Laurence Lofgren was in charge of 42-50375/ **Queen of Angels**, which succumbed under the weight of gunfire to leave a single survivor out of nine. (The pilot was killed on what was his 26th birthday.) Two further Bungay bombers—42-50545/JU: and 41-28814—suffered six fatalities between them following their being brought down.

2CBW's Tithe

That section of the third sub-force going in to the Wesel drop zone arrived back home short of four crews. One of Hethel's trio of casualties involved Lt. Bloore in 42-50779/EE: J. S/Sgt. John Young (NG) remembered, with no sign of Allied presence at the briefed site, but rather a hostile one whose participants poured up a rain of gunfire, what was almost certainly **Skerby** (44-40245/HP: J) having its No. 2 engine completely excised and reported as sagging down to strike the ground. The

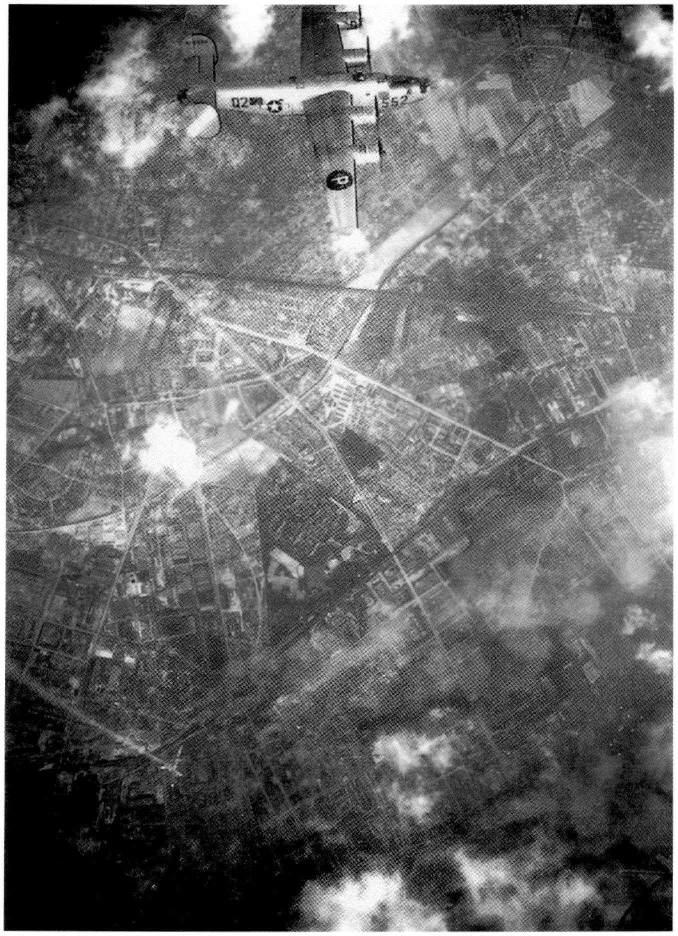

The 8AF fully struck "Big B" nineteen times, but its defenses never failed to claim a tithe of victims. The camera has caught B-24H-15-FO 42-52546 /6A: E. **Southern Clipper** as it descends steeply while trailing a fuel-fed banner of smoke. Its more fortunate 467BG companion is B-24J-60-CF/ 44-10552 /2Q:. The date is 18 March 1945, and it is the third-last occasion the 8AF will assault the Nazi capital.

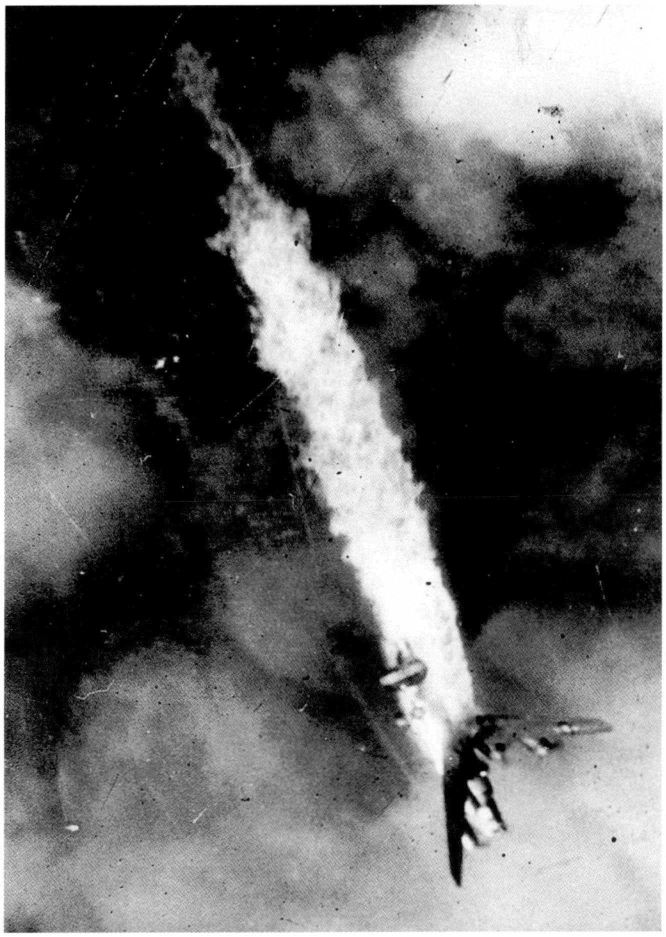

"We live in Fame, go down in Flame" is the penultimate line of the Air Corps Song. This shot of a fire-stricken and disintegrating 389BG bomber tragically fulfils the prophecy inherent in these words. The USAAF Daylight Offensive played a prominent part in hammering the life out of the Nazi industrial and military fabric, albeit at a high cost in aircraft and crews—over 26,000 personnel in the latter case.

closed bomb bay doors indicated release had been made, but in fact the equipment was still on board. Although Lt. Bennett had applied the auto-pilot after giving the bail out order, he was one of only two out of nine to survive; he owed his luck to jumping as the doomed B-24 was crossing over a valley, which provided enough vertical clearance for the pilot's parachute to open. The drop had just been achieved when 42-95240/YO: C **The Old Veteran** failed to live up to its title; none on Lt. Harry Mosher's team came through the huge explosion made by the 113-mission bomber as it impacted with the ground.

Bloore's B-24 was still airborne at this point, although all four engines were displaying a mix of fire, windmilling propeller, and over-revving, with No. 1 "feathered." The dying aircraft finally came down at Sevelen—directly into an ammunition dump, where wings and tail were torn off and the fuselage remnants split open! Three soldiers from the 131st AAA Unit, on seeing the incident, leapt into a Jeep and rushed to the wreck. Seven crewmembers were extracted by them and others before smoke and fire impeded further efforts. Some ammunition was already "cooking off," so rescuers and rescued were hustled away as quickly as possible. However, L/Col. Arthur Arend, Capt. Jim Flynn and T/5 George Rollo, having got the victims into an ambulance, had scarcely gone 100 yards when the dump's contents, estimated at 74 tons, erupted volcanically, leaving a crater some 100yds long, 25yds wide, and 15ft deep! The trio amazingly survived, but several other rescuers, including German civilians, were less fortunate. John Young, who had no recollection of the crash and spent a protracted period in hospital, said of the three soldiers: "I can never thank the fellows enough. They received the Soldier's Medal, but it should have been the CMH." Sadly, only one more on the crew came through alive. The Wing's tribulations today were added to by a single crew from Tibenham.

Aftermath

The nature of the *Varsity* mission ensured that battle damage would not only be sustained by a fair proportion of the bombers, but that a number of those so afflicted would regain Allied territory only at the cost of being "written off." The 448BG's Lead aircraft—**Miss Muff** (42-50902), bearing Col. Westover (Group CO)—was thoroughly shot-up and Capt. Bill Wilhelmi (P) and a waist gunner were injured. The B-24 was eventually crash landed at RAF Manston thanks to its damaged landing gear. A second Group aircraft (42-51504, flown by Lt. Voight) absorbed equally heavy damage that included the loss of the control cables, nose wheel, and hydraulic lines. Level flight was only maintained through use of the auto-pilot and a course taken up that also concluded over Manston. In this case, any landing would have been problematical, not to say lethal, since most of the controls were out of commission, so the bail out order was given. One airman was injured during his jump, but everybody, including L/Col. Heber Thompson, landed safely. However, Fate would cruelly intervene in the case of the 713BS CO the following May. Back at Seething, 42-50772 **Jokers Wild**, with Capt. James Shafter's crew, was involved in a ground collision with Lt. McCluhan's wayward charge, which had swung off the runway after landing and upon impact sheared one stabilizer off its companion bomber.

The 392BG's 41-29476/ **Gashouse Gus**, flown by Lt. Proctor, lost an engine over the drop zone and a second went "out" as the B-24 was heading for the nearest available airstrip. The crew were quickly ordered to assume crash positions and the pilot decided to attempt a wheels-down landing that

The mission to drop supplies to the Parachute Divisions on 24 March did not result in the 2AD units flying over enemy-held territory for more than a short time period. However, the low-level nature of the mission to both ensure an accurate drop and avoid the worst of enemy ground fire ensured that altitude was reduced to a bare minimum, as this shadow of a 392BG aircraft dramatically illustrates.

One of the Group casualties that Capt. Harvall probably caught on his film was 42-50896/GJ: R-bar **Southern Comfort III**. The drop zone at Wesel had just been traversed with the Group turning for home when Lt. Chandler's aircraft was set on fire; it struck the ground and rose up momentarily before the starboard wing impacted to swing it right around; shortly after, the truncated remains exploded, with the sole survivors being two gunners who had previously been thrown clear.

A constant "bogey" associated with 8AF operations was that of mid-air collision. On 25 March 1945, the 392BG lost two B-24s, along with all but four crewmembers during Assembly. The shattered tail section belongs to Lt. Philip W. Kaiser's (KIS) **Pleasant Surprise II**/EC:, which impacted at Burton Lamas. Three of those killed had originally been interned in Sweden on 18 November 1943, but had resumed operations after repatriation and return to Wendling.

A presentation event at the Ford/Willow Run plant in Michigan involves B-24LSH-20-FO/ 44-50250. **School Daze** was purchased with War Bonds bought by the Ford Trades School personnel. She subsequently served with the 467BG as 4Z: E, flying four missions prior to VE-Day.

fortunately came off in an obligingly flat field; Sgt. Denver Kerfoot (ROG) was thrown out and suffered a broken leg, but the others emerged intact. Another "write off" occurred at Wendling when 41-28875 suffered brake failure and overshot; Lt. Campbell McKellar's aircraft was subsequently declared salvage.

Sharp Contrast

The second involvement of the Division in the events of 24 March was to prove a sharp contrast with the short but savage encounter with the ground defenses suffered by the preceding operation. Two airfields at Stormede and Kirtorf were assaulted without any loss by the bulk of the 182 crews dispatched. At the day's closure, the morning mission crews could reflect upon the fact that the Allied paratroopers had been well backed up and were able to play their vital part in fully securing the bridgehead across the Rhine, ready for the inexorable ground advance into the Ruehr and the Nazi hinterland.

Unequal Contest

The ever-lurking menace of jet-propelled technology was destined to catch up with one Group during the mission to attack three oil-related targets the day following *Varsity*. The location at Buecken was assigned among others to the 448BG, and the Briefing Officer unconsciously set the scene for what transpired by referring to the possibility of both conventional and jet-powered fighter interception.

All three Divisions were involved, but the possibility of later adverse weather conditions over East Anglia resulted in a "recall" during Assembly for the B-17 sub-forces only, the 2AD elements having been regarded as too far advanced towards their Primaries to justify similar treatment. Problems in Assembly had left the 713BS portion of the Seething formation assigned Low left dangerously isolated; by the time the IP was reached, it was at least five miles further back and ripe for the summary punishment by a rapidly encroaching *Sturmvogel* formation from JG7.

As it was, the initial assault fell upon the main body of the Group formation. **Tarfu II** (44-40099/), flown by Lt. Joseph Stefan, was riddled with gunfire and exploded almost immediately after the sole survivor, Lt. Gerald Gottlieb (N), bailed out; the crash\ site was at Langenhorst. The 713BS' isolation did not pass unobserved, as the *Jagdwaffe* pilots now swiftly demonstrated. The

Capt. Ursel Harvall is photographed straddling a large camera positioned in the lower fuselage of a 44BG B-24. This airman was the group Photo Officer and accompanied the Shipdham contingent participating in Operation **Varsity**. His series of cine-film sequences caught the tragic conclusion of the mission for two B-24s and their crews.

Lead B-24 had its cockpit area shot up, with Lts. Knute Stalland (P) and Theo Warner (CP) mortally affected. Fire shot back from the port main fuel tanks and the PFF B-24 began to oscillate back and forth before the starboard wing

The relative fragility of an airframe when impacting sharply with soil or water is graphically recorded in this instance. B-24H-25-DT/ 42-51112/H of the 453BG, while attempting a landing on a Continental airfield (31 March 1945), tipped up; the result was an almost total disintegration of the forward fuselage, bringing little chance of survival for the pilots or any other occupants "up front."

The 44BG's B-24H-15-FO 42-52261, a 66BS-assigned bomber, has the landing gear well on the way to full retraction as she heads aloft and out towards Tirstrup, Denmark; the scheduled mission was later "recalled," however. The NMF waist window frame contrasts with the worn camouflage surround. The two "Carpet" blisters are clearly seen.

ripped off. Only a quarter of the twelve-man crew emerged alive from the rapidly-spiralling bomber.

Do Bunny (42-95185/T) was steadily hammered during several passes, and although Lt. Paul Jones called for a bail out, the shot-out intercom prevented its being heard. The pilots then decided to risk a crash landing after the bid to regain Allied lines was rapidly failing in the face of steady power loss. The landing close to Soltau was initially smooth before one wing "dug in" and the fuselage fractured at the rear cockpit seam, slewing it to the left; in such drastic circumstances, it was amazing that no fatalities occurred, although broken legs were borne by two of the four airmen trapped in the nose section. However, a gathering of pitchfork-wielding civilians around the aircraft boded ill for the other crewmembers scrambling out and only the intervention of an SS officer prevented a possible lethal conclusion to the encounter.

P-51 escorts were on hand, but the superior speed of the Me262s was proving to be a handful as the attacks persisted. The fourth Group casualty was 42-50326/ **Eager One**, but Fate was to prove kind to all but the pilots. Lt. Frederick Tod's charge was so badly battered that its demise seemed imminent, but the pilots not only held it aloft, but managed to maintain a northward course towards Sweden. The neutral coastline was reached, but by then the physical strain on the pilots was beginning to tell. The crew bailed out, but almost immediately the bomber developed a spinning motion and crashed into the Baltic, killing Lt. Tod. Several airmen, including Peterson (CP), drifted down into the sea, but the officer drowned despite efforts by two Swedish men to rescue him.

Constant Nemesis

The collision factor—a recurring issue within 8AF ranks—was demonstrated on the 25th. In this instance, two 392BG bombers were involved during Assembly. One of the four survivors—Lt. Harold W. Hutchcroft, Command Pilot to Lt. Clifford O. Markusen in 42-51340/ CI: M—provided a detailed account:

> We were Lead in the Lead squadron's High element. We were in position, but a 578BS B-24 took No. 2 position, which was still vacant. On entering the cloud Markusen took over, but lost sight of the squadron; our No. 2 was still there. The instruments said we were descending, so I told Markusen I would hold altitude and heading while he sought the main formation. I could no longer see our No. 2 in the clouds.
>
> I then heard a thump, and looking out saw our No. 2 banking away with No. 4 engine gone. I reached for the C1 (auto-pilot), which was on and set. Markusen was fighting the controls and I yelled at him to see if he wanted me to turn the C1 on, but he never responded. We entered a right-hand spin and Markusen yelled "bail out," so I rang the bell before starting to get out, but was pinned down by the increasing spin rate. I finally got out of the seat and could see Markusen trying to do the same. I crawled back to the bomb bay and saw Sgt. Paul L. Cain, who was transferring fuel there; I jumped and he followed.
>
> I flipped over several times before pulling the ripcord around 6,000ft and watched a string of bombs that fortunately missed me as they passed. I landed several hundred yards away from the crash site (at Skeyton) with the remaining bomb load going off.

The other victim crew was led by Lt. Kaiser flying in 42-50804/EC: I **Pleasant Surprise**, from which a further two airmen reached the ground alive before the B-24 slammed into the ground at Buxton Lamas. Sixteen American airmen had just added to the 8AF's massive blood debt.

Combat's Cruel Vicissitudes

For Lt. Eddie Maceyra (N), today's mission to Lt. Markusen would have seen him finish his combat tour of 35 missions. A hut colleague, Lt. Tony Marcelli, recalled: "Eddie had invited me to have breakfast, and during it he turned to me said: 'This is my last mission, one way or another'." Indeed, it was his last, but in a cruelly negative manner. In fact, Lt. Hutchcroft said that the Lieutenant, although in a position to do so, had refused to jump until he had first freed Sgt. Elmer R. Hunter from the nose turret. The expression "Greater Love hath no Man than this—That a Man lay down his Life for a Friend" is fully exemplified in the case of Eddie Maceyra.

Four members of Lt. Kaiser's crew - Lt. John W. Ott (N), Lt. John K Parish (B), T/Sgt. Solomon Louizides (ROG), and T/Sgt. Alex R. Slama (Eng.)—had returned to England from Sweden following their bomber's diversion there on 18 November 1943. Their prospects of regaining America's soil with the Conflict in its closing stages should have been almost as secure, but the Grim Reaper's scythe gave no quarter and would continue to do so right up to and even after VE-Day.

Month End Operations

Although four more missions closed off March, it was the 30th before the 2AD was called upon, when U-boat construction yards and port facilities at Wilhelmshaven were targeted by over 99% of the 382 dispatched crews. The defenses failed in their immediate aim of bringing down any B-24s, but probably initiated the damage to 42-10155/ **Heavenly Body** that culminated in a "ditching" of the veteran bomber; when ASR launch facilities reached the reported site only two airmen on Lt. Robert H. Siek's crew had both survived the impact, as well as the icy North Sea waters; this was the final operational casualty for the 491BG.

An armor production plant at Brunswick was next day's Primary, but the Division ended up striking the marshalling yards Secondary at a cost of three out of 371. Hethel's 44-40439/ RR: O **Shady Lady** stood no real chance of survival after the B-24J fell out of formation and was picked out by two Me262s. Their gunfire set both starboard engines on fire, to be followed almost immediately by the wing separating; all nine on Lt. George Crock's team shared the bomber's fiery fate. The other two losses were from the 453BG. The No. 1 engine on Lt. Owens L. Hopper's 44-49972/F8: caught fire as the Dutch coast was being traversed on the outward route; all eleven on board bailed out before the port wing crumpled and the B-24 descended to its destruction. (Several of the parachutes were seen to be drifting down into the sea.) The other casualty involved Lt. Bussell's crew from the 733BS, whose bomber lost two engines following attack by Me262s. The aircraft dropped out at the Duemmersee and the pilot called-in to say he was taking up a heading for Allied-occupied territory, but that was reportedly the last heard of he or his colleagues.

April 1945

The month commenced with a totally weather-aborted mission by the full 8AF intended to strike airfields in Denmark. The "recall" was given as the leading formations were approaching the Danish coast and all but one crew duly responded to reverse course. The exception was an Attlebridge crew in 44-10521/U8: **Laden Maiden**, who

"A sheep in wolf's clothing" is an apt expression for what was originally the 389BG's 41-28779 /YO: A. The bomber was force landed on 20 June 1944, but restored to flying condition and assigned to KG200. On 6 April 1945, an emergency landing was made into a field; although repaired, an inability to get airborne due to a fractured nose wheel during take-off seven days later impelled the crew to destroy their mount.

Hookem Cow sports a total of thirteen bomb symbols. This was a figure heralding tragic consequences for the last mission of B-24H-25-FO 42-95120/Z5: M on 14 April 1945. The bomber was barely off the Horsham St. Faith runway when she faltered and ploughed in at Hainford; the explosion consumed the lives of five out of Lt. David R. Totten's abbreviated seven-man team.

Hookem Cow was lost during the first of two days' concentration on bombing heavy gun installations on the banks of the river Gironde, in SW France, through the medium of Napalm-filled drop tanks. The 467BG's **Piccadilly Commando** (B-24J-65-CF/44-10600) has just commenced release of the adapted "bombs," whose trajectory path was notoriously wayward.

A second picture taken during the Royan mission on 15 April 1945 confirms the extremely poor ballistic characteristics of a drop tank. The streams of these co-opted "missiles" are tumbling in haphazard manner from the 392BG bomb bays; it is likely many will land well clear of the Primary, with possible tragic consequences for the surrounding French countryside and its occupants.

having suffered engine problems took up the geographically shorter heading for Sweden! A further 72 hours passed before the B-24s went aloft again, but the bulk of the crews returned with retained bomb loads. Less than 40% of the dispatched force struck airfields at Parchim, Perleberg, or Wesendorf, while to this disappointing result was added the loss of six bombers.

The 448BG had lost four aircraft on 30 March, and three more would taste the bitter seeds of failure today. **My Buddie** (42-95083) had been fortunate to get back four days previous and luck would again favor it, as two out of a sizeable jet and rocket-propelled *Jagdwaffe* force swooped in upon the Group at the IP. The fearsome firepower posed by the Me262's four 30mm cannon fortunately was not brought to bear upon Sgt. Ed Chu's (TG) bomber, as these assailants shot past from six o'clock, but was demonstrated in full against Lt. Bob Main's 44-50838. The shells lanced into the aircraft's fuselage at the waist and sawed it in twain. A dreadfully graphic picture shows the two sections in an almost vertical attitude with equipment spewing out; although there was no sign of any crewmembers emerging, one was cast out into mid-air to become the sole survivor. However, Sgt. Charles Cupp was doubly fortunate, because on landing and prior to being taken into custody by some soldiers, he was assaulted by a civilian party, one of whom pointed a gun that did not fire.

Miss B-Havn (42-95620), to Sgt. Chu's right, took punishment that knocked out both port engines, one of which caught fire. Lt. James Shafter called for a bail out, but only seven out of eleven airmen responded before the bomber exploded. Lt. Calvin Ellis (B) had gone up on the flight deck for an extinguisher to battle the fire that had taken hold in the nose; on returning there he found his parachute had been consumed by the flames, and so became one of the four fatalities. A third Group B-24 piloted by Capt. John Ray was culled by a combination of flak and fighters. Six of the crew reached the ground alive after vacating their burning and steadily spinning charge. One of the three fatalities was seen to deploy his parachute but did not survive, having either been killed on landing or suffering "summary justice" from military or civilian sources. The air battle proceeded apace, with P-51s frantically intervening to at least hinder the enemy fighter assaults.

The 2CBW suffered the other three MIA losses: two from the 445BG and one from the 389BG. Lt. Ken "Deacon" Jones was a very erudite individual and his description of what happened to the Hethel casualty is summarized here in all its harrowing detail:

> An Me262 approached from the rear and I pulled the squadron in close—why, I do not know—but we were slightly offset to the Lead squadron's right as the Group turned; we awaited the attack. After appearing to cancel his pass on the Lead squadron he dropped his flaps and closed in on our 42-50653/EE: X **E-Rat-I-Cator**. There is no screaming attack followed by a fast breakaway. He eased up behind X and lowered his flaps as the tail gunner spun his turret and lined up without firing. He sits there in disbelief as he and the enemy pilot stare at each other. The gunner seems paralyzed with fear and his last-ever sight is of four orange flashes.
>
> The turret shatters as the pilot touches his rudder, with the top turret and waist gunners unable to respond. Other gunners in the slot or bucket Elements also do not fire, apparently watching in fascination. Damm, I wish I had a squirrel gun. I hear someone scream: "Shoot! Shoot!" X's right stabilizer separates

and sails past as big as a barn door. The cannon shells impact on No. 2, with debris streaming back before the B-24 enters a flat spin, trailing smoke.

The Me262 is so close I can see the mottle camouflage and mud-splattered fuselage. He pops his flaps and dives for the clouds. Like shooting fish in a barrel. I feel nauseated—half anger and half fear –maybe mostly fear that "There go I..."

Ken's account amply highlighted the frightening technical and performance disparity between the German design and the USAAF bombers, with even the best Allied escort in the form of the P-51 being well outpaced, at least in terms of speed, if not dive and climb rate. As for **E-Rat-I-Cator's** crew, most of Lt. Monroe Harris's team did not share his fortune in evacuating the doomed spinning bomber.

Combat Tensions

The extreme mental pressures of combat often resulted in verbal excitement through observing what was happening to other crews, albeit in an understandable but potentially counterproductive manner. When **My Buddie** was safely down at Seething, Lt. Brock called his colleagues together and delivered the following admonishment, as recalled by Eddie Chu (TG):

> He was mad and said in no uncertain terms that we were to stay off the air unless we had vital information to relay. He specifically referred to our referring to Lt. Shafter's plane burning and what he called the blow-by-blow account of the crew bail out. He emphasized that tying up the intercom, especially when being hit by fighters at this point, could have been fatal. He further said that the vivid descriptions of a plane burning when under the stress conditions at this time were uncalled for. We were silent, as the impact of his words became obvious.

The clock was rapidly running down in respect to the Third Reich's demise, but this fact was naturally of little interest to the Allied servicemen. Their adversaries showed little signs of recognizing this salient fact and fought on regardless. In the case of the 8AF, its airmen continued to suffer a drip feed of material and human casualties, as instanced on the 5th and 7th.

In the former case, ten crews out of 1,039 attaining their targets never returned home, half of whom manned individual aircraft within five of the eleven participating B-24 Groups. Regarding the 2AD's efforts, this loss factor was attained out of 192 gaining mission "credit," with two coming from within the 20CBW ranks. The 44BG was part of the force attacking Plauen's marshalling yards, with the bombardiers resorting to *H2X* methods of "blind" bombing. In return, the defenses landed flak strikes on Lt. Brown's 44-40158/ GJ: Q **Tinker Belle** that crippled No. 1 engine. On the way back, the steadily descending B-24 exited the undercast while still over the Ruehr; a second engine was disabled and Sgt. Travis E. Nash (ROG) killed. The remaining eight airmen bailed out, but the pilot subsequently died from a head wound. The operational blood debt at Shipdham was now closed, but the Grim Reaper would still add to his tally within the Group.

The 389BG had lost one crew 24 hours previous and now surrendered a second in the form of Lt. Howard Young's team on board 42-50747/RR:. The pilot had called in to say his B-24 had suffered a fuel leakage, and feeling unable to guarantee reaching friendly soil, he was going to attempt a crash landing; he at least ended up as a POW, although the entire crew's fate was unclear. Elsewhere, Bungay lost 42-

Thousands of USAAF and Allied POWs ended up within the overcrowded confines of Moosberg in late April 1945. The ragbag range of clothing typifies the average "Kriegy's" dress style. Among this group of individuals and wearing a beret is Lt. Ernest Sands (B) to Lt. Klusmeyer (458BG), both having been captured the previous 14 October.

The Daylight Offensive is over and the 467BG's **Witchcraft** is still on hand, compared to so many of her unfortunate contemporaries. Her final "score board" of mission symbols totals 130, but the supreme irony lays in the fact that she too will be reduced to scrap in some U.S. aircraft "boneyard," her deeds along with that of her crews and ground crew who acted on behalf of freedom notwithstanding.

Another veteran B-24 that more than repaid itself in terms of operational success was the 446BG's **Ronnie**. Its mission scoreboard stands at 122 and is a fine as well as posthumous legacy to Sgt. Ronnie Gannon, for whom the bomber was named

The staging of USAAF units back to the USA was initiated and largely completed by the end of May 1945. In this picture, the 44BG's **Linda Lou** is staging through Meeks Field in Greenland. The pristine condition of 42-51508 (assigned to the 506BS) is not surprising, since there are no records of her flying any mission following her arrival at Shipdham.

94941 **Pin Up Girl** to flak, along with four fatalities among its crew, while all nine on Lt. Philip Ross's crew were killed in the demise of the 466BG's 42-51351/2U: + from Attlebridge. A 93BG bomber completed the loss figure when 44-50697/GO: took her nine-man complement led by Lt. James R. Sample to their deaths at Westenschouwen/Haamstede, where another unit B-24 had also descended on 28 January.

Kamikaze—Nazi Style

The Third Reich was going down in a true Wagnerian "Twilight of the Gods" (*Goetterdaemmeurung*) manner, as its dwindling material and human resources were relentlessly throttled by the Allies. In the air, to the latest desperate measure to stem the Soviet advance in particular, Ju88s packed with explosives and guided to targets on the river Oder by manned Bf109s and Fw190s perched on top of the bombers in a weird "piggyback" arrangement were being dispatched. A second desperate measure aimed this time against the Allied bomber formations had distinct overtones with what was currently happening off the island of Okinawa, namely the *Kamikaze* assaults on U.S. and Royal Naval strength. The pilots of the recently established *Sonderkommando Elbe* were given the brief of bringing down the bombers by ramming should their conventional attacking pass fail. On 7 April, the pilots took off to deliver what would retrospectively be recorded as their single recorded sortie. Several hours later the survivors would land back, having taken out upwards of double figures of 8AF B-17s and B-24s; two of these casualties would add to the run of losses borne by the 389BG.

Col. John Herboth had assumed command at Hethel on 4 December 1944, and today was flying as Force Commander for the entire 2AD, along with Capt. Bob Dallas in 44-49254/HP: K. Flying Group deputy Lead was Lt. Walter R. Kunkel in 44-49533/RR: P, with Maj. Tollason in the right-hand seat. The target at Dueneberg was looming up when the *Sonderkommando* formation appeared overhead, having at least partially managed to evade the escort screen. One among their number was *Obergefreiter* (Cpl) Johannes Roesner, whose action with his Bf109 over the next few minutes would expunge the lives of fifteen American airmen and bring torment and heartache to their relatives.

Roesner was reported as initially sweeping in from ahead before reversing course. He then illogically adopted a close-formation location under one B-24 that inhibited gunners from surrounding bombers from firing upon him before zooming up to the left and banking round for a diving run-in upon the Group. The hail of gunfire directed his way had no apparent effect, as the fighter inexorably closed upon the Lead B-24 in a manner akin to a shark homing-in upon a whale.

The impact with the forward section of the starboard fuselage was brutally clinical in taking out the Herboth/Dallas-commanded B-24, but the loss tally was swiftly added to when Lt. Kunkel's aircraft was similarly dispatched after the fighter's momentum carried it into the deputy Lead's path. The Lead bomber adopted a spinning action that took both pilots and all but two of the crew to their deaths. A large gash behind the top turret was suffered by Kunkel's charge, while jammed rudder and elevator cables as the B-24 was cast over onto its back boded ill for the crew's survival prospects. Having failed to pull the aircraft out through use of the ailerons and AFCE equipment, Kunkel issued the bail out order. Both pilots managed to escape, but it was only the airframe's disintegration casting them out into mid-air that acted as their saviour, since the fierce centrifugal forces had previously held them firmly in their seats. None of the other crewmembers enjoyed the same relative good fortune. (It was supremely ironic that Roesner managed to evacuate his disintegrating fighter and parachute to safety.)

Although a total of seventeen 8AF crews were declared MIA, either from normal operational causes or from ramming, only three came out of the 2AD, the third victim being a B-24 from Tibenham (42-94870/WV: _ **Axis Ex-Lax**), from which only three airmen out of ten emerged alive. The 3AD absorbed all of the other casualties; even then, at least one B-17 emerged the winner from, rather than the victim of, a *Sonderkommando* encounter, with the fighter ending up destroyed.

Diminishing Strategic Returns

Marshalling yards and airfields were now becoming the twin main target categories, now that the main industrial sources, such as the Ruehr, were either in Allied hands, or in the case of synthetic oil plants, had their productive capacity worn down to the bone through constant aerial bombardment. Airfields occupied the 2AD's attention over the ensuing three days at a cost of two aircraft, the first of which was a 458BG bomber over Lechfeld (9th). Flak fired-up the No. 2 engine on 42-52457.7V: Q **Final Approach** on what was her 113th sortie. Her title alluded to an ultimately safe return to the USA, instead of which she ended up a pile of debris on enemy soil; one airman out of Lt. Abramowitz's nine-strong crew sadly shared her fate. A second 100-mission veteran from the Group —42-95316/7V: H. **Princess Pat**—was "written off" following a heavy crash landing at a Belgian airfield.

Next day, a much heavier casualty rate was experienced on Lt. William H. Powell, Jr.'s (KIA) 42-51089/, when only three of the 453BG crew survived after a flak strike cut the fuselage in two around the waist windows. A switch to oil and munitions depots at Regensburg (11th) by part of the Division was a variation that saw all participating crews regaining England without loss—but then the Reaper struck at two 446BG teams whose B-24s came together in fatal embrace over Bungay as the Group were circling within the landing pattern; 22 airmen forfeited their lives in this particularly needless manner on board 42-50790 /RT: and 42-51909/.

Today witnessed the 259th and final mission in the ETO for the 453BG, despite the Campaign still being uncompleted. The reason for this action lay in the fact that the Group personnel were now to be dispatched homeward for potential redeployment to the Pacific. However, they would transfer by ship, with their current establishment of B-24s remaining behind and in some cases reassigned to other Groups. By 9 May, all would be in place for the move that saw the men going by train to Southampton to board the USS *Hermitage*.

How Much Longer?

The next mission, occurring after a 72-hour time lapse, saw the 8AF's Divisions heading in a SW direction. One of the French-based German garrisons cut off after D-Day was based around Bordeaux, and today was the first of two daily missions to strike at various strong points, and one that would end in stark tragedy for two Hethel crews; not only would they provide the sole MIA statistics, but their loss would almost certainly arise from a "friendly fire" source.

The Group was tracking in on its bomb run when a B-17 formation was observed approaching almost at right angles and releasing their loads directly over the B-24 formation.

A total of five aircraft received variable degrees of damage, two of which proved fatal. The worst affected was 42-51233/HP: R **The Bigast Boid**, which lost both outer wing sections and the rear fuselage directly behind the wing trailing edges to what were fragmentation bomb strikes. The majority of Lt. Edward H. Bush's team did not survive the incident, while Lt. Andy Anderson (CP) did. However, he had several narrow escapes: 1) he was thrown out following the airframe's disintegration; 2) his ripcord did not work and he had to literally tear the chute pack apart before the canopy deployed; 3) he floated down right into

M/Gen. Bill Kepner is presenting a Deed for a $600,000 (£150,000 in 1945 value!) Trust Fund to the Lord Mayor of Norwich, E. F. Williamson, JP. It relates to the establishment of what will be a "living" legacy in the form of the current 2AD Memorial Library, as opposed to a standard expression of the B-24 airmen's individual and corporate valor and sacrifice through a granite or marble creation, laudable as this might have been.

Two men who know the tribulations of war: Jimmy Stewart and Tom Eaton—the latter a Japanese POW and here Chairman of the 2AD Memorial Trust—are inspecting the rendition of a B-24 painting that was a part of the original 2AD Memorial Library destroyed by fire in 1974. It was completed by Mike Bailey, one of this book's co-authors, and is simply a fine and detailed tribute to the men of the 458BG, and by extension to all who served within the 2AD.

The blurred outline of a 389BG B-24 skimming low over its Hethel airfield is bisected by the base flagpole with "Old Glory" in full display at the peak. The national banner had served as a spiritual focal point for Americans while they and their Allies fought the crusade against Fascism that had consumed far too many lives in its necessary fulfilment.

Two bombers from the 453BG are probably taxiing out for a mission, with **Dumbo** (B-24H-20-DT /41-28943) already turned onto the runway and lined up for take-off. A High intensity/low visibility (HI/LV) runway light is seen in line with **Dumbo**'s fin and rudder.

the center of the target area; and 4) he was rousted from the bomb crater in which he was sheltering by a bayonet-wielding soldier who ignored Andy's frantic signs to take shelter therein and insisted on marching him to a bunker—and all this with the bombs still raining down! No wonder he would later comment: "It is better to kill a man than to frighten him half to death!"

The other Group loss involved 42-50774/HP: P **Stand By**, flown by Lt. Ned Ansell, who was one of three fatalities out of nine; although he bailed out from the battered B-24, the wind direction guided his parachute out over the Atlantic, where he probably died from exposure. His companions in death were thought to have died within the fuselage as a direct result of the bomb strike. One of the survivors was Lt. Robbins (N), who managed to evade capture and reach Allied lines several days later.

To the day's MIA list were added three more crews involved in take-off crashes. The battle-tested **Hookem' Cow** (42-95120/Z5: M) was in the hands of Lt. David R. Totten, with the crew flying their second mission. A heavy mist, along with rain, shrouded Horsham St. Faith as the bombers were departing, but **Hookem' Cow** had barely cleared the airfield when it came down and crashed to kill all but two of the hapless crew. Lt. Rex M. Gibson's team were also on their second mission in 42-100425/7V: O **The Bird**, but they too progressed just two miles before their B-24 piled in at Spixworth; all but Sgt. W. R. Wilks of the seven-man crew (reduced from normal complement level by the exclusion of three gunners) perished in the aircraft's disintegration. However, it was several hours before an independent source informed the Guard House of the incident. Over at Wendling, 42-50446 /EC:R, a 92-mission bomber bearing Lt. Charles W. Warren's eight-man complement—similarly reduced by two gunners—lost all power on its port engines as it lifted off the runway; it staggered on for bare seconds before descending into a field and exploding. Sgt. Donald A. Kight (NT) was thrown clear to become the sole immediate survivor, but his tenure on life lasted barely one month before he succumbed to his injuries.

Closing Off the Account

The second daily hammering administered to strongpoints at Bordeaux/Royan ended cost-free, other than for a 466BG crew involved in a take-off crash that killed two crewmembers. Next day, the Group struck one further B-24 off its establishment following a mid-air collision over Belgium. The No. 3 propeller on Lt. Tom Felber's 44-10591/U8: B excised the port stabilizer on its squadron companion 42-50585/U8: H, in Lt. Paul S. Evans's hands. The latter B-24 was successfully abandoned by its crew despite going into a spin, while the other aircraft landed back at Attlebridge minus the errant airscrew. The latest take-off casualty occurred at Seething, when 44-50572 lost power just after lifting into the air and ground to a halt with the nose section almost at right angles and with its four occupants trapped; Lt. Douglas Torrance (P) and the other three managed to scramble clear. Fire caught hold on the fuel tanks, and although rescuers arriving on the scene tried to free their colleagues, they suffered the trauma of having to evacuate the immediate area before the bomb load went up, but without achieving their humanitarian intention. None of the four crewmembers survived the resultant detonation.

The four succeeding missions up to 20 April also remained free of combat loss for the Division, as the ever-shrinking perimeter of the Nazi empire was relentlessly pounded. What was the penultimate 8AF mission went out on the 21st to strike at targets in SE Germany and across the Austrian border. This time around a single Attlebridge B-24 was the MIA price paid for what ironically was an "aborted" Divisional effort, cloud over Salzberg's marshalling yards being adjudged too restrictive even under PFF guidance. The demise of 42-95592/T9: U **Black Cat** was matched by all but two within Lt. Richard Farrington, Jr.'s eleven-man crew.

The 3AD had now unknowingly flown its final mission, and it was its two contemporaries who on the 25th were briefed to make the final aerial assault upon Hitler's domain—but on Czechoslovakian as well as German and Austrian soil. The 1AD suffered six losses in bombing Pilsen, but the 2AD's passage to bomb marshalling yards at Salzberg, Bad Reichenhall, and Hallstein, as well as an electrical transformer plant at Traunstein passed off without event for the 278 crew involved.

The USAAF's Bombing Offensive was at an end, although its RAF partner would operate in diminishing strength up to the beginning of May. The prospect of living out their lives in security loomed before the young American aviators and their ground support colleagues—but over the ensuing weeks, Fate would cruelly intervene in a number of individual and corporate cases to rob those so affected from realizing that longed-for and precious goal.

All Haste for Home

The crews circling their 2AD airfields on 25 April had little inkling of the fact that the Daylight Offensive's brief was now effectively closed. The fact that the Allied Armies' pincer movement across Germany was virtually closed off, as newspaper maps were divulging, was a solid indication that ever-fewer targets were on hand to be assaulted. However, nothing could be taken for granted that mission "alerts" would not be called over the ensuing twelve days that thankfully culminated in the announcement of unconditional surrender by the Nazi high command on 7 May. Only then could the combat personnel in particular begin to divest themselves of the hitherto-constant pitch of tension associated with combat operations.

Missions were destined to be flown over Germany just prior to and also in the immediate aftermath of that nation's capitulation. These were known as "Trolley Runs," with thousands of ground personnel loaded into the B-24s and taken across the sea to view what was their part in bringing about victory. On 5 May, Lt. George Sanderson lifted off Hethel in 44-10620/YO: G, along with several other B-24s. For whatever reason, he elected to proceed on his own and was still absent when the others returned. It was later that reports of a half-submerged bomber adjoining a wrecked Rhine bridge filtered back to Hethel which finally evolved into the Sanderson-piloted bomber; none of the twenty personnel on board survived the tragic incident.

The continuing conflict in the Pacific was an indication of likely redeployment of selected Groups to that Theater of Operations. Whereas some nine B-17 units were to be retained in Europe for various Occupation duties on the Continent, the superior range capability of the B-24 was a likely reason for the wholesale return Stateside for the 2AD. The 389BG was the first to commence the "home run" on 19 May, and between then and early July, the Division's strength in bombers was regularly dispatched.

A number of post-combat crashes involving fatalities had occurred within the Division's ranks, but tragedy stalked the 389BG in particular, with the ground personnel again featuring in the casualty figure. On 20 May, Lt. O'Brien took off in 44-50688/RR: Q heading for Valley, in Wales. Turbulence at some stage of the relatively short hop cast the B-24 into an uncontrollable gyration that resulted in the tail section and port wing detaching. It was amazing that two of the twenty airmen managed to parachute to safety, but there was no reprieve for the other eighteen on board.

Finis

The Japanese surrender in mid-August ensured that any prospect of the bulk of the 2AD airmen being shipped out to the Pacific to link up with the reconstituted 8AF based on Okinawa was rendered null and void. As for their B-24s, the presence of ever-larger numbers of the B-29, with its superior overall performance, was to render their redeployment equally unnecessary. Demobilization and a return to normal life awaited the personnel over the ensuing months of 1945, but the serried rows of gravestones at Madingley and ultimately within U.S. military cemeteries created in postwar Europe would bear sad witness to the human cost in winning through against Fascist-based extreme intolerance and lust for conquest.

The seven decades since WWII have not dealt fairly with the B-24 *vis-à-vis* its Boeing contemporary. Many historians and broadcasters still tend to pitch the Daylight Offensive as a primarily B-17-led campaign. This irritatingly inaccurate pitch equates with the winning of the Battle of Britain by the Spitfire alone—little mention of the Hurricane's vital participation—while RAF Bomber Command's efforts are presented as owing everything to the Lancaster, as opposed to its Stirling and Halifax contemporaries. In this warped manner is history accordingly reduced to a dangerously simplistic degree.

The survivors of the 2AD formed their own association to parallel that of the 8th Air Force Historic Association. In addition, their memorial in England is unique, in that it is not a mass of marble and steel—laudable as that form of remembrance might be. Instead, it takes the form of a library within Norwich's Forum. Surrounded by models and paintings of B-24s, the public can browse through the manifold rows of books relating to the 8AF and glean a measure of comprehension from their content, both in terms of what was achieved in restoring peace to Europe, as well as the human toll exacted in the process of attaining that precious physical and spiritual goal.

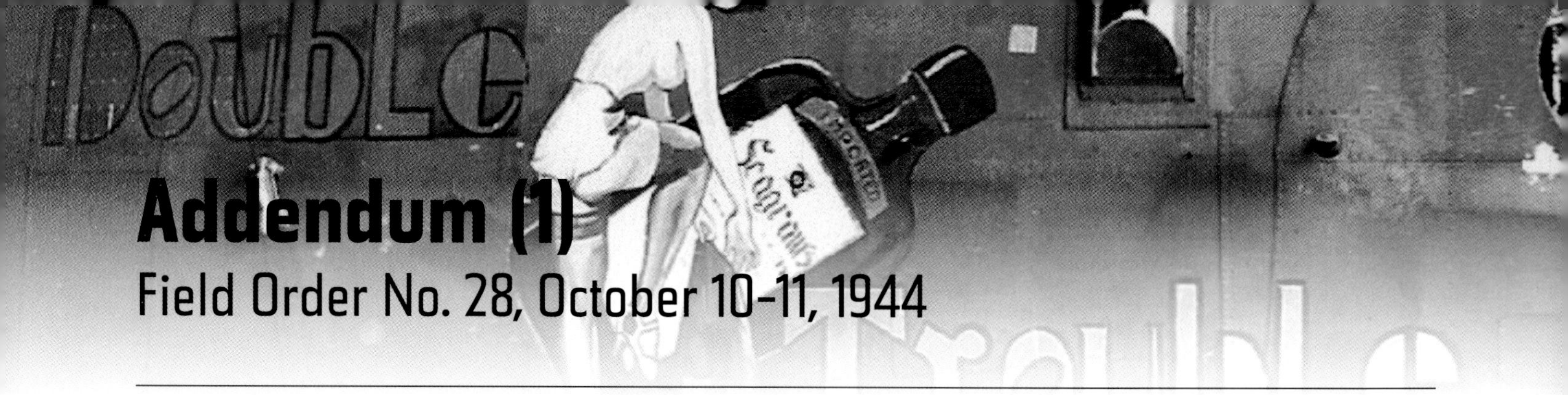

Addendum (1)

Field Order No. 28, October 10-11, 1944

The early-autumn advent of rocket-propelled Me163 fighter assaults upon the 8AF bomber formations, coupled with the initial sorties by the technically-superior Me262 jet turbine design, concentrated the minds of the American High Command as to how effective 8FC countermeasures could be introduced to at least blunt the worst effects of the *Jagdwaffe's* efforts. An exercise involving the 2BD and the 65FW was accordingly set up and executed on 10-11 October 1944.

Field Order No. 28 involved 120 B-24s, whose pilots were tasked with flying the distance between Peterborough and Colchester before retracing the route while being escorted by the 4FG. The RAF had recently introduced the Gloster Meteor jet-propelled fighter into operational service with No. 616 Squadron—commanded by W/Commander McDowell—and four of these were assigned to stand in for the *Jagdwaffe*; their brief was to intercept the formation. Apart from providing the gunners with how to sight upon these "intruders," the primary aim was to discover how best to handle the "assaults," with fighter cover mainly in mind.

Two Meteor flights were launched during the sortie, the first of which intercepted at 1507 to launch two distinctive approaches. A head-on approach from 2,000ft higher altitude was matched by a similar attack from a four o'clock angle, also delivered with the same height advantage. The jets landed and refuelled before taking off at 1632 and intercepting, albeit with only three aircraft; the same attack angle and altitude advantage were indulged in. Once the exercise was completed, critiques were subsequently carried out that day by the attacking and defensive fighter units that also involved the bomber formation Lead pilot.

The recommendations accruing from the exercise were three-fold:

- A close escort was deemed ineffectual due to the Meteor's high speed (although this lesson should have been evident, considering its basic abandonment in dealing with conventional-powered attackers as mooted by Gen. Doolittle).
- The escorts should be at least 5,000 feet above and laterally distant from the bombers in order to provide adequate cover.
- The bomber formation lead elements in particular should have escort cover well above their altitude as a basic defense against head-on attacks.

These recommendations were now to be incorporated into the following day's exercise, after which the flight leader was to render a tactical commander's report on further affiliation exercises. What follows is the resumé as contained in the Wing's Field Order No. 2. The bombers flew between Hethel and Colchester, escorted by four-ship Flights from the 56th, 355th, 361st, and 479th FGs, along with eight from the 4FG. The overall composite squadron was led by Col. Kinnaird (4FG CO). The four Meteors in two elements flew three times and attacked about an average of three times.

The bombers flew in four strung-out boxes, each thirty-strong with the fighters grouped as follows: Red Flight, four 4FG P-51s; Yellow Flight, four 361FG P-51s; White Flight, four 56FG P-51s; Blue Flight, four 479FG P-51s; Green Flight, four 355FG P-51a NS; and Purple Flight, four 4FG P-51s. The recommended altitude and lateral distances mentioned above were flown and 361FG records indicate its Flight was positioned to port of the leading two boxes.

The Meteors made determined head-on, astern, and beam attacks, and on one occasion engaged the escorts. Following the exercise's completion, the 361FG records contain the following observations. The cloud pattern above the bombers provided insufficient height separation as recommended. The jets were observed on three occasions, the first two of which involved passes from 11 and 9 o'clock angles. Attempts to head off the Meteors proved ineffectual, with the attackers cutting through the bombers before they could be engaged. The Flight was level with the bombers when the third attack developed and resulted in an engagement. The P-51s were able to turn into the jets at 240mph, with the leader able to fire; the Meteor was not attacking the bombers, however, and was surprised in a shallow climb while flying at around 220mph; he managed to disengage by diving, but only after providing a good opportunity for the P-51s to "fire" upon him.

These observations were surely of cold comfort to the Americans, and indeed were to be experienced in the months ahead, as the Me262 came to be steadily encountered. An added burden upon both bomber and fighter pilots was that the Me262's overall performance was better than the Meteor, whose top speed, assessed at 415mph, was well over 100 mph less than its *Jagdwaffe* contemporary. The bald truth was that the day of the piston-engine bomber was certainly drawing to a close, while its fighter equivalent was also disadvantaged, albeit to a lesser but still material degree. It was as well that the Luftwaffe design never appeared in more than relatively small numbers and suffered technical problems, particularly in respect of its Jumo engines—factors that would prove to be the 8AF's salvation from having the Offensive severely disrupted, if not rendered moribund.

Addendum (2)

Keeping the Memory Alive

To the populations in Occupied western Europe, the sole indication that liberty from the Nazi yoke would come to pass, however long it might take, was primarily aural. The nocturnal roar of RAF Bomber Command's aircraft and its USAAF contemporaries by day—the latter force sometimes visually present—provided that hope over nearly five years in the case of northern Holland. The Dutch population had witnessed so much of the Allied airmen's progress into and back from the epicenter of the Third Reich's evil spread, given that their territory directly lay on the threshold of Hitler's fiefdom. In the course of the aerial conflict, the often ferocious defenses had consumed thousands of bombers and crews, a sizeable number of whom found their final resting place on Holland's soil or in the Ijsselmeer's waters.

Following the war's conclusion, the American authorities carried out a policy of removing their dead personnel to military cemeteries, but there were a handful of occasions where the individual body in question was permitted to remain at the original internment site. This was the case for a 392BG airman, and the circumstances in which this occurred demonstrate the respect the Dutch, and by extension all those who lived through Occupied Europe's nightmare, continue to demonstrate for those who brought about liberation, albeit at a dreadful cost in life and limb.

S/Sgt. John E. McCormick was originally a waist gunner with Lt. Sturm's crew; the team had operated since August 1944, but on 22 February 1945, John and S/Sgt. John Lingle (WG) were assigned to fly with Lt. Joseph R. Walker in 42-95241/EC: G. Apparent fuel loss through flak damage on return from the target finally forced the pilots to put the B-24 down extremely close to a farm near Zoeterwoude; the impact was hard enough to cause the nose section to end up twisted to one side. As it was, all nine crewmembers survived, but one or two suffered injuries, with an ankle injury to Sgt. Lingle requiring Sgt. Shea's (NT) assistance in extracting him. These two, along with Sgts. Hicks (Eng.) and Nagle (ROG), were quickly rounded up, but John was one of the remaining five who evaded capture.

Four days later, RAF fighters from No. 542 Squadron, acting upon the report submitted by one among their number earlier in the day, arrived on the scene to thoroughly shoot up the bomber. One of the German guards from the party that had examined the bomber, on seeing the fighters, shouted out to several Dutch civilians, including the farm owner, Martinus Jansen, to take cover; unfortunately, the initial strafing pass caught some among their ranks before they could fully react, killing the farmer and one other female adult, as well as a brother and sister in the process. (It was ironic that the German salvage party had previously extracted around 600 gallons of fuel from the B-24's tanks.)

McCormick was taken in hand by the local Resistance group, who took him to a hunting lodge on the river Rotte; when given the option of surrendering to the Germans or becoming active with the group he chose the latter. Over the ensuing two months all progressed well, and in that period he even had contact via letters with two fellow crewmembers secreted in The Hague. Then, on 29 April, with the war virtually concluded, tragedy struck. The hideout was surrounded by a German patrol and in the ensuing fire fight John was fatally injured; several RAF fellow evaders were luckier in either evading capture or in one case being taken POW in circumstances that could have easily led his SS captors to execute him.

The postwar policy of U.S. authorities to bury their war dead in designated military cemeteries would normally have been the case for Sgt. McCormick's corpse. Following his initial internment in the Dutch town of Zoetermeer in October 1945, his father raised the matter of his son's permanent location there, a request that appeared to have been rejected on the grounds that "there was no guarantee of his grave receiving continued attention"—little did the authorities realize the emotive impact upon the Dutch of what his presence meant to them! McCormick Senior firmly pressed the point, stressing that a body's location was not important in comparison with its soul and further pointing out how the Zoeternmeer people, far from erasing his son's memory from their minds, had even erected a memorial to the deceased airman. The final official requirement from the U.S. authorities was that a Dutch agent be appointed by Mr. McCormick to ensure his son's remains were legally held in the nation's custody and permanently retained in Zoetermeer.

The eternal respect that the Dutch and fellow peoples of Nazi-Occupied countries hold for the Forces of Liberation in general and the aircrews in particular is exemplified by this incident. For those who have never suffered the degradation and soiling fear of Occupation, in this case handed out by an extremely autocratic regime and spread over an extended time period, the burgeoning feeling of impending salvation offered by the sight and sound of the Allied bomber streams certainly sustained the nations so affected and still earns an ongoing legacy of gratitude and high respect for the airmen who pushed forward towards victory—a victory achieved at a high human premium among their ranks, but one that restored a relative degree of sanity within the European Continent's political code of conduct.

Addendum (3)

B-24 Armament

The original combat variant within the VIIIBC was the B-24D, which featured a streamlined nose section housing the navigator and bombardier. In contrast to subsequent variations, the armament provision was all manual, in the form of three .5 machine guns, one either side (behind the nose Plexiglas frame on the port side) and one mounted centrally in the frame below the bombardier's sighting panel. The top (Martin) and rear (Consolidated A6A) powered turrets contained twin .5s, there were single machine guns mounted in the waist windows, and finally, a third single gun mounted underneath in the entry/escape hatch. The 44th and 93rd BGs operated this sub-variant.

A later production run of the D variant issued to the 389BG in mid-1943 featured displacement of the underside weapon with a retractable Briggs/Sperry ball turret with twin guns, but this advance in defensive capability was currently being more than offset by the inability to direct an effective weight of fire against the now-regular "twelve o'clock high" attack approach by the *Jagdwaffe* fighters. The central nose gun was mounted too low for it to be even directed towards a level approach angle, let alone be elevated to take on the aforementioned diving approach.

Hasty adaptation of the weapon into the upper Plexiglas frame, with a second gun sometimes added, was often carried out. However, the difficulties incurred in physically manipulating the heavy weapons while also sighting and firing them in the fleeting seconds available before their adversaries were gone became evident. The encumbrance of bulky and heavy flight gear while standing inside the narrow confines of an aerodynamically unstable platform further rendered the duty extremely exhausting for the airmen concerned. In these circumstances, the rosy figures for "kills" submitted at debriefing were to prove a world away from the actual number of fighters even struck, let alone brought down!

The arrival of the fourth 2BD unit (392BG) introduced the H and J variants into ETO combat. These both featured a major change in forward-mounted armament with the introduction of a power turret. The J Models bore the hydraulically operated Consolidated A6A and A6B units (already utilized as the B-24's tail turret), but fitted with aerodynamic fairings to ease airflow effect. The H variant was equipped with the Emerson A-15 turret, which was electrically driven and moreover was superior both in terms of efficiency and internal space for the gunner; it would eventually become standard on all USAAF B-24s.

The extra weight of these turrets, far from having a negative effect upon the design's center of gravity, rather improved the aerial "sit" of the airframes from the previous "nose up" attitude to one slightly angling down. However, there were two negative features, both affecting the two nose compartment occupants: 1) forward visibility was severely limited in comparison with the B-24D's comprehensively glazed nose canopy, and 2) the turret seals intended to shut off the ingress of airflow did not do their job, so the Navigator and Bombardier had to put up with the resultant sub-zero airflow.

By early 1944, the B-24D was gradually disappearing from front-line service, but the continuing demand for B-24s witnessed no less than five production plants involved. Supplies of the preferred Emerson turret could not keep up with production, however. Enter the Motor Products Co., who designed and turned out an improved version of the original Consolidated unit. This was the A6M hydraulically-operated turret, which in the case of San Diego-built airframes was placed in both nose and tail positions; it also became a standard fitting in the tails of most of the other four production companies' airframes.

The lot of the two waist gunners was arguably the worst, with their open window frames feeding in extremely frigid air as they maneuvered their hand-held flexible guns, all the time under threat of frostbite. This dangerous physical situation affected so many among their ranks that it had to be tackled. Fords' Willow Run technical staff came up with the solution; it took the form of a detachable Plexiglas panel that incorporated a swivel mount at its base into which the gun was mounted. B-24s so fitted began to arrive in the ETO during the spring of 1944.

The original Martin top-turret design remained a standard fitting until the summer of 1944. Then the introduction of a more sophisticated gunsight demanded a marginally higher and re-contoured outline; what was the Company's A3D modified unit became known as the "Highhat."

The wresting of air superiority from the *Jagdwaffe* by mid-1944 and the resultant diminution of regular attacks upon the bomber streams encouraged the removal of the ball turret on B-24s; these had proved to be drag-inducing when lowered into the slipstream. However, the decision to take this action was left to the Group COs. In some Groups a compromise was reached, whereby a proportion of bombers retained the turret; these aircraft would then be located among the formation at perceived points of vulnerability to ventral assault.

Between mid-1943 and late 1944, the vast bulk of 2BD B-24s variants steadily displacing the B-24D were H and J variants that differed in detail according to their production source, but two new variants now turned up, albeit in limited numbers. The first was the Ford-built B-24L, many of which were utilized as H2X "Mickey" ships. One major difference was the displacement of a conventional rear turret with a lightweight cupola mounting twin hand-held guns known as a "Stinger Unit." Its presence in turn lightened the tail section and was a likely reason for the model's adaptation as an H2X aircraft, the radar pod taking the place of the ball turret.

The final B-24 variant was the M Model. It was very similar to the L Model, but reverted to the conventional tail turret. However, the Motor Products fitting had been improved by using lighter metal and incorporating a Plexiglas panel in the lower rear-sloping plate. This adaptation was carried out by the Southern Aircraft Co. and (unsurprisingly) bore the initials S.A.C.T.

Unconventional nose armament was to be seen in various forms on some B-24s, an example being the Bell power boost unit normally borne by the B-26 Marauder. They were the result of experiments within some Groups and only extended to a handful of bombers; the 44th, 93rd, and 389th BGs were among the Groups indulging in this field of operations.

Appendix
Listings

Group Markings

2CBW

Group	Squadron	Squadron Letters	Aircraft Call letter
389BG	564BS	YO	none Call letter
	565BS	EE	"bar" before Call letter
	566BS	RR	"+" after Call letter
	567BS	HP	"bar" after Call letter

Introduction of black fin/rudders with vertical white stripes in the center in May 1944 saw the following Call letter indicator changes;:

	564BS	none
	565BS	'bar' above Call letter
	566BS	'+' below Call letter
	567BS	'bar' below Call letter

A Black Group letter "C" in a white circle was originally applied to starboard upper wing and fin/rudder outer surfaces during late 1943, but the latter marking gave way to fin/rudder colors.

445BG	700BS	IS	"+" before/after Call letter
	701BS	MK	"bar" above Call letter
	702BS	WV	"bar" below Call letter
	703BS	RN	none

Introduction of black fin/rudders with horizontal white stripes in May 1944 saw no change in Call letter indicator positioning. (Some 702BS B-24s repeated the aircraft letter on the fuselage.) A Black Group letter "F" on white circle was originally applied to starboard upper wing and fin/rudders, but the latter marking gave way to fin/rudder colors.

453BG	732BS	E3	none
	733BS	F8	'+' after Call letter
	734BS	E8	'bar' after Call letter
	735BS	H6	'bar' below Call letter

This Group also used colored propeller-spinners;

	732BS	white
	733BS	blue
	734BS	red
	735BS	yellow

Introduction of black fin/rudders with diagonal white stripes in May 1944 saw no change in Call letter indicator positioning. A Black Group letter "J" in a white circle was originally applied on starboard upper wing and fin/rudders, but the latter marking gave way to fin/rudder colors.

14 CBW

Group .... Squadron .... Squadron Letters ....Aircraft Call letter
44BG.............................. 66BS........................QK + after Call letter
.... 67BS .... NB ....“bar” below Call letter
.... 68BS........... WQ ....none
.... 506BS......... GJ ....“bar” above Call letter

Introduction of white or silver fin/rudders with black vertical stripes in May 1944 saw no change in Call letter indicator positioning. A Black Group letter “A” in white circle was originally applied on starboard upper wing and fin/rudders, but latter marking gave way to fin/rudder colors.

392BG .... 576BS .... CI ....none
.... 577BS .... DC ....+ after Call letter
.... 578BS .... EC ....“bar” under Call letter
.... 579BS .... GC ....“bar” above Call letter

Introduction of white or silver fin/rudder with black horizontal stripes in May 1944 saw no change in Call letter indicator positioning. Insignia blue Group letter “D” in white circle (colors reversed on NMF aircraft, but with Insignia blue replaced by Black) was originally applied to starboard upper wing and fin/rudders, but latter marking gave way to fin/rudder colors.

492BG .... 856BS......... 5Z............................none
.... 857BS .... 9H ....“bar” above Call letter
.... 858BS......... 9A ....“bar” below Call letter
.... 859BS......... X4 ....+ after Call letter

Group arrived after April 1944, so Call letter indicators were placed on a black diagonal stripe that was applied to silver fin/rudders. Insignia blue Group letter “U” in a white circle (Colors reversed on NMF aircraft, but with Insignia blue replaced by Black) was applied to starboard upper wing. Black circles on fin/rudders of some NMF aircraft were intended to have white letter “U” applied, but introduction of the black diagonal stripe cancelled this out, although circles were not universally deleted.

20CBW

Group .... Squadron .... Squadron Letters ....Aircraft Call letter
93BG.............................. 328BS......................GO
.... 329BS......... RE
.... 330BS......... AG
.... 409BS......... YM

Call letter indicators limited to “bar” above or “bar” below the same Call letter within the Group. No indicators used after yellow fin/rudders with black vertical stripes introduced in May 1944. Black Group letter “B.”

446BG .... 704BS .... FL............................none
.... 705BS .... HN ....“bar” below Call letter
.... 706BS .... RT ....“bar” above Call letter
.... 707BS .... JU ....“bar” above and below Call letter

Introduction of yellow fin/rudders with black horizontal stripe in May 1944 saw the use of the above-listed indicators. Prior to this, minus “bars” had been applied.
Black Group letter “H”

448BG .... 712BS.......... CT ....Triangle-surround to Call letter
.... 713BS.......... IG ....Circle-surround to Call letter
.... 714BS .... EI ....Square-surround to Call letter
.... 715BS.......... IO ....Diamond-surround to Call letter

Introduction of yellow fin/rudders with black diagonal stripes in May 1944. (Group dispensed with Squadron codes in later stage of WWII) Black Group letter “I”

96CBW

Group .... Squadron .... Squadron Letters ....Aircraft Call letter
458BG....... 752 .... 7V............................no specific Squadron indicator
.... 753 .... J4............................no specific Squadron indicator
.... 754 .... Z5............................no specific Squadron indicator
.... 755.............. J3............................no specific Squadron indicator

"Bar" signs behind the aircraft letters used generally but not comprehensively within the Group. Last three of serial number sometimes applied on the nose of the B-24s so marked. Introduction of red fin/rudders with white vertical strip in center in May 1944. Black Group letter "K"

466BG....... 784BS.......... T9............................none
.... 785BS.......... 2U ....+ after Call letter
.... 786BS.......... U8 ....“bar” after Call letter
.... 787BS.......... 6L.............................“bar” below Call letter

Introduction of red fin/rudders with white horizontal strip in center in May 1944. Black Group letter "L"

467BG .... 788BS.......... X7............................none
.... 789BS.......... 6A ....“bar” above Call letter
.... 790BS.......... Q2 ....“bar” below Call letter
.... 791BS .... 4Z............................+ after Call letter

Introduction of red fin/rudders with white diagonal strip in May 1944. Black Group letter "P"

95CBW

Group .... Squadron .... Squadron Letters ....Aircraft Call letter
489BG....... 844BS.......... 4R ....none
.... 845BS.......... T4............................“bar” before or below Call letter
.... 846BS.......... 8R ....+ after Call letter
.... 847BS.......... S4............................“bar” above or after Call letter

Introduction of green fin/rudders with white vertical stripe in center was changed in August to all-yellow fin/rudders when Group transferred to the 20CBW.

Black Group letter "W" in a white circle on starboard-upper wing; no similar marking on fin/rudders.

491BG .... 852BS.......... 3Q ....none
.... 853BS.......... T8............................“bar” before Call letter*
.... 854BS.......... 6X ....“bar” above Call letter*
.... 855BS.......... V2............................+ after Call letter

**(the 853BS also used a "bar" below, and the 854BS a "bar" after" their respective Call letters*

Green fin/rudders with horizontal white stripes were introduced at start of combat operations with the 95CBW. These were retained when the group transferred to the 14CBW to replace the dis-banded 492BG whose group letter was Z. Change only initiated around March 1945.

Then, black Group letter Z" in a white circle (colors reversed on NMF aircraft) applied to starboard-upper wing; no similar marking on fin/rudders.

Photograph Credits

Pat Everson
Tony Fairbairn
Ian Hawkins
Darin Scorza
Paul Wilson
Bob Dance

Thanks also to Andrea and Dale Featherby of Anglia Flight for their photographic expertise in respect of the book"s cover drawing.

Color Gallery

Lucky B-24, lucky airman. **Bomerang** (41-23722) is a veteran 93BG bomber that now sports a half-century of mission symbols. Her pilot here is Capt. Walter Stewart, who having survived his combat tour, which included the Ploesti run, flew the aircraft Stateside in April 1944, where this picture is likely shot.

M/Gen. William Kepner's first post within the 8AF was as the Commanding General of the Organization's Fighter Command. In the summer of 1944, he replaced M/Gen. James Hodges as CG of the 2BD. This picture is taken at Ketteringham Hall, along with two of his Colonel subordinates.

Three American Red Cross women are posed alongside an anonymous B-24. The well-cut and smart nature of their uniforms was typical of the American female Armed Forces and support organizations, such as the ARC, and were surely the envy of their British counterparts – other than the Women's Royal Navy Service (WRNS), whose outfits were of the same quality in cut and appearance!

Satin's Little Sister's artwork takes the form of a nude figure astride a huge bomb. What is B-24H-25-FO /42-95189/RT: N, seen with 21-mission bombs, took the place of **Satans Sister** at Bungay. Her luck finally ran out on 21 November 1944, when she crashed at Eemnes, in Holland.

Kentucky Belle's beautiful female upper torso artwork was confined to the starboard side on 44-40268/RT: H, with the name applied along with its 80-mission bomb log on the port side. This B-24J-150-CO had transferred from the 490BG after that unit changed to the B-17 in the autumn of 1944. The bomber's Crew Chief, Sgt. Albert Krassman, stands alongside his charge.

The range of 2BD Assembly ships included one of the most distinctive color schemes applied to these combat-retired airframes. **Tubarao** (Portugese for "Shark") utilizes green and yellow stripes on the upper wings and rear fuselage, the latter position having the Group letter in a circle. The 491BG aircraft was the third and final example to serve with the Group in this specialist function.

Uncle Sam's pugilistic stance is applied to B-24D-65-CO/42-40506, which has survived 38 missions. Capt. John Driscoll (Group Armaments Officer), standing by the nose, was instrumental in saving personnel from a burning B-24 on 22 April, a feat that earned him the Airman's Medal presented by Lt/Gen. Doolittle next day. The 389BG's **Green Dragon** Assembly ship is in the background.

A 458BG practice formation reveals a single 753BS and two 754BS bombers. J4: V is 44-40006, a B-24J-145-CO bearing the initials **S.O.L.**, standing for "**S... Outa Luck**"! In the lead is **Dorothy Kay Special** (Z5: D/42-50456), a J-401-CF airframe, while 42-95165/Z5: S, a B-24H-25-FO, is the other Element wingman.

This picture is taken in the winter of 1944/45, with the clue to this time period being the red color applied to the curved nose frame on a 329BS B-24J-FO based at Hardwick. The squadron was assigned as the unit's PFF sub-force and the red was a visual indicator of the function. The 20CBW tail marking was particularly outstanding.

A duo of 68BS B-24s from Shipdham are snapped over the flat Norfolk countryside on 1 September 1944. Nearside machine is 44-10553/WQ: C/L, a J-65-CF airframe that was crash landed in France on 28 December. Its companion is 42-110057/WQ: Q, the J-130-CO that lasted a mere eight days more; it crashed off a mission to Mainz and was promptly declared "salvage".

The Beast (42-100408/J4: L) bears a fine rendition of a predatory animal mouth whose distinctive outline is further enhanced by the yellow background and the astrodome "eye". This 753BS machine flew many missions from mid-1944 and won through to VE-Day.

Do Bunny (42-95185), of the 448BG, holds a tight formation with the photographer's aircraft. This 713BS bomber was one of four victims of Me262 assault on 25 March 1945. Lt. Paul Jones managed to make a heavy crash landing near Soltau that left everyone alive, but required the pilot and three of the other eight to be cut free from the crumpled nose section.

Sgt. Clifford Coates is seen working on the regulator fitted to a main supply oxygen tank that will be slotted into position adjacent to its companion units mounted in the B-24's ceiling. The tanks were ever vulnerable to puncture from fighter or flak, apart from which the contents under pressure created a potential explosive mix if a tank was struck squarely.

PFC Lemuel J. Putty is inserting a fuse into one of a group of 100-lb general purpose (GP) bombs at Attlebridge. These were the smallest explosive weapon in the USAAF arsenal and were generally used on large-scale targets; airfields were an example, the intention being to disrupt the overall surface and so hinder the movements of aircraft, particularly in landing and take-off.

With extremely limited hangar space, the bulk of maintenance work on WWII aircraft was conducted outdoors, regardless of all but the very worst of weather conditions. Two mechanics from the 466BG are uncovering a Pratt & Whitney engine that will probably replace the one hanging from a crane in front of the B-24's No. 1 engine nacelle.

"Hurry up and wait" is a reasonable summation of the average ground crews' situation once their charges had been dispatched on a mission. There was often little to do but await the formation's return and hope that all had gone well with the B-24 and crew concerned. These individuals are photographed at Bungay, home for the 446BG.

This view of a post-WWII boneyard for the now-redundant USAAF B-17s and B-24s features several among the former design in relatively intact state in the right background. The pile of metal remnants on the left includes the distinctive red and white fin of a B-24 that had previously been a component of the 466BG.

Here is the culmination of the ground crews' often extended period of "sweating out" the mission. These B-24s coursing over Bungay are holding a sound formation pattern, suggesting the mission has proceeded in order. A dispersed formation by contrast was often the result of a severe and prolonged encounter with the enemy defensive network.

Two B-24s of the 489BG are seen on their dispersals at Halesworth prior to their August 1944 transfer from the 95CBW to the 20CBW. The move merited deletion of the green/white tail markings and substitution of an overall yellow finish. The nearest bomber is B-24H-25-CF/42-50360/8R: +Y **The Ripper**.

The slab-sided fuselage of the B-24 was ready-made for large-scale and detailed artwork. This is the 446BG's 42-9306/RT: S, an H-30-FO airframe. The lady's aerial platform came to an unfortunate end on 9 January 1945, when it crashed at Duxford following take-off from Bungay; no 8AF mission was launched this day to confirm a non-operational flight was in progress.

A mechanic steadying his bicycle alongside a Hardwick-based B-24H-25-CF watches two colleagues working around the No. 2 engine. **Silver Eagle** is 42-50362/YM: J and the yellow cowling front and propeller spinner was a feature on some 409BS aircraft from the summer of 1944 onwards.

The two airmen seen in the original picture of **Silver Eagle** are now engaged in the onerous duty of turning the propellers that weighed in over 400lbs. The duty was deemed necessary prior to engine start in order to clear each engine's nine cylinders of any oil residue.

Spotted Ape was the second Assembly ship of the 458BG, which after serving with the 754BS as 41-28967/Z5: Z was sprayed in the distinctive color scheme seen here. It was "written off" in a crash landing on 9 March 1945; now bereft of its tail section, the truncated remains are fit only for transport to a USAAF scrapyard.

DNIF (Duties Not Including Flying) clearly apply to the character slouching out of a PRO Station, his physical condition doubtless compromised by an encounter with a "lady of the night". Lightweight uniform confirms the picture was taken after B-25J-145-CO/44-40100/3Q: E (491BG) returned home after VE-Day, having enjoyed a relatively trouble-free fate, in contrast to its artwork personality!

B-24J-95-CO "BOOMERANG" (42-100362) 458TH BG

B-24D-24-CO "BUZZIN" BEAR (41-24229) 44TH BG

B-24M-5-FO "FLAMIN' MAMIE" (44-50529) 453RD BG

B-24L-10-FO "FRAN" (44-49582) 466TH BG

B-24H-1-FO "LAZY LOU" (42-7609) 446TH BG

B-24H-15-CF "LIL" PEACH" (41-29375) 467TH BG

B-24J-150-CO "LUCKY LASS" (44-40127) 492ND BG

B-24J-150-CO "MAH AIKIN BACK" (44-40226) 491ST BG

B-24J-55-CO "NAUGHTY NAN" (42-99929) 93RD BG

B-24H-20-FO "OLD BALDY" (42-94863) 445TH BG

B-24J-1-FO "SHADY LADY" (42-50759) 448TH BG

B-24J-55-CF "SHORT SNORTER II" (44-10495) 392ND BG

B-24H-20-FO "TIGERS REVENGE" (42-94816) 489TH BG

B-24D-95-CO "TOUCH OF TEXAS" (42-40751) 389TH BG

Index

Name	Unit	Pages
A		
Aaronian, S/Sgt Tzolog	(ROG) 389BG	264
Abbott, Lt. Franklyn D Jnr.	(P) 492BG	159
Abell, Lt. Peter T	(P) 445BG	107
Abernethy, Lt. Curtis A	(P) 492BG	161
Abramowitz, Lt.	(P) 458BG	279
Abshire, Sgt Wilbert	(TG) 458BG	172
Acuff, S/Sgt Clyde L	(WG) 44BG	1287
Adams, Capt. Howard	(P) 44BG	14, 22, 27, 28
Adams, Lt. N	(N) 93BG	49
Adamson, Lt. John D	(P) 458BG	119
Adelman. Sgt Seymour	(WG) 392BG	257
Ager, Capt. Robert L	(Gunnery Officer) 44BG	91
Aho, Sgt Augustus	(G) 44BG	78
Alachua, Lt. Homer W (P) 453BG	113	
Albert, Lt. Frank L	(P) 44BG	122, 123
Aldridge, Lt. E	(P) 44BG	59
Alexander, Richard W	(B) 392BG	215
Alleman, S/Sgt Earl	(WG) 491BG	224
Allen, Lt.	(P) 44BG	201
Allen, Lt. John H	(CP) 445BG	80
Allen, Lt. Lee V	(P) 446BG	83
Allen, Sgt Richard E	(ROG) 44BG	91
Allison, Dr	Flt/Surgeon 44BG	138
Alschaft, Lt. William A	(P) 392BG	217
Alspaugh, Lt. Melvin L	(P) 448BG	146, 203
Altemus, Lt. William B	(P) 44BG	134
Alter, Lt. George H	(P) 446BG	250
Alve, Capt.	(P) 453BG	219
Anderson, Capt. Paul	(Ordnance Off.) 389BG	213
Anderson, Lt. Andy	(CP) 389BG	279, 280
Anderson, Lt. E	(CP) 44BG	50
Anderson, Lt. Ellsworth F	(P) 392BG	124
Anderson, Lt. John R	(P) 44BG	188, 203
Anderson, Lt. John B	(P) 445BG	142
Anderson, Lt. Russell A	(CP) 453BG	113
Anderson, Lt. Thomas L	(P) 392BG	136
Anderson, Major/Gen. Fred	(Deputy CG) USSTAF	)
Anderson, Maj. William M	(P) 44BG	91
Anderson, Sgt W M	(TG) 389 BG	101
Anderson, T/Sgt Donald E	(ROG) 458BG	119
Andrews, Lt. George A	(CP) 446BG	174
Andrews, Lt. Jerome	(P) 446BG	253
Ansell, Lt. Ned	(P) 389BG	280
Appel, Capt. Ed	(P) 389BG	213
Appert, Maj. Donald A	(P) 392BG	62
Apple, Lt.	(P) 448BG	147
Archer, Lt. John A	(P) 44BG	209
Ardery, Capt. Phil	(P) 389BG	51
Arend, L/Col. Arthur	U S Army	272
Armour, Lt. Charles B	(P) 458BG	187, 189
Arnett, Lt. Charles W	(P) 492BG	156
Arnold, Col. M R	CO, 389BG	185
Arnold, Gen. H. H. 'Hap', CG,	USAAF	10
Asch, Lt. Alfred	(P) 93BG	33, 34
Ashcroft, Sgt	(Eng.) 392BG	194
Ashworth, Sgt Edwin R	(WG) 446BG	83
Astleford, Lt. Charles E	(N) 392BG	246
Atchley, Sgt A	(GC) 44BG	157
Atkinson, Lt. Thomas W	(P) 93BG	65
Austin, Lt. Albert B	(P) 44BG	97
Avery, Lt. Baldwin C	(P) 389BG	169
Avery, Lt. Bernard H	(P) 445BG	82
Ayerst, Lt. Richard C	(CP) 448BG	98
Ayerst, Lt. Richard C	(P) 448BG	68
B		
Baccash, Sgt	(GC) 44BG	61
Baatz, Capt. George L	(P) 453BG	186
Baer, Maj. Heinz	Kommandeur II/ JG1	145
Baetz, Lt. Robert E	(P) 392BG	254
Bail, Lt.	(N) 44BG	268
Bail, Lt. Bernard W	(RN) 489BG	268
Bailey, Mike	458 BG Historian	279
Bailey, Lt. William J	(P) 448BG	180
Bailey, Sgt	(GC) 44BG	61
Bakalo, Lt.	(P) 44BG	228
Baker, Col. Addison,	(Posthumous CMH) CO, 93BG	13, 47, 52, 54, 69
Baker, Lt. Lester	(B) 389BG	278
Baker, Lt. Montee R	(P) 489BG	186
Baker, T/Sgt Lanning C	(Eng.) 44BG	134
Ballard, Lt. Beverley E	(P) 458BG	118
Balsley, S/Sgt L M	(G) 44BG	29
Baney, Lt. Ralph S	(P) 389BG	193
Bank, Lt. Sidney L	(B) 44BG	32
Banks, Capt. John W	(P) 453BG	166
Barefoot, Lt. Charles L	(PN) 44BG	229
Barak, Lt.	(P) 448BG	147
Barkan, Lt. Martin	(P) 93BG	184
Barlow, T/Sgt Archie R	(Eng.) 44BG	92
Barnett, Lt. Joseph C	(P) 392BG	107
Barnett, Lt. Kenneth	(CP) 448BG	114
Barneycastle, Lt. L C	(P) 448BG	251
Barrett, Lt. Kenneth	(CP) 448BG	114
Barry, Lt. Warren H	(P) 44BG	134
Bartlett, F/O Paul W	(CP) 489BG	174
Bartmess, Lt. Thomas E	(N) 44BG	23, 31
Barton, Lt. Kenneth C	(P) 458BG	171
Bassett, Lt. Earl E	(N) 392BG	173
Bastian, Lt. Frank	(P) 448BG	212
Bateman, Lt. W R	(P) 44BG	55
Bates, Capt.	(P) 389BG	193
Baucom, Sgt Hoover	(ROG) 446BG	228
Baum, Lt. Paul F	(P) 44BG	129
Bauman, Lt. Robert J	(N) 44BG	135
Bausano, Sgt Peter A	(WG) 446BG	184
Bayliss, Lt. Herbert L	(P) 44BG	247
Baynham, Lt. James	(P) 445BG	241
Bean, Sgt Bruce T	(TG) 458BG	188, 189
Beasley, Lt. Ernest	(CP) 467BG	174
Beatty.Lt. James H	(P) 392BG	207
Beaver, Lt. James	(P) 448BG	196
Bechtel, Lt. Russell J	(P) 458BG	264, 265
Beck, T/Sgt Orville E	(Eng.) 389BG	141
Becker, Lt. John R	(P) 392BG	87
Beckett, Capt. Walter	(P) 389BG	193
Beckman, Lt. Leland L	(P) 448BG	181
Beecher, Lt.	(P) 458BG	214
Beese, Oblt.	Staffelkapitaen, JG26	90
Behout, Lt. James T	(P) 489BG	175
Belanger, Lt. Alton G		
Belitz, Lt. Hans G	(P) 392BG	185
Bell, Lt. Charles H	(P) 392BG	181
Bell, Lt. Phillip W	(P) 44BG	108
Bennett, Lt.	(P) 389BG	272
Bennett, Lt. David N	(P) 491BG	231
Bentcliff, Lt. Clifford L	(P) 44BG	229
Berger, Lt. R	(P) 392BG	80
Bergman, S/Sgt Paul O	(ROG) 392BG	226
Berquist, Sgt Earl J	(ROG) 392BG	208
Berthelson, Lt. Alvin L	(P) 389BG	262
Beumer, Louw	Dutch citizen	262
Bevan, Lt. Ernest	(P) 389BG	193
Bibb, F/O Lewis B	(P) 446BG	174
Bickerstaff, Lt. Robert B	(P) 453BG	
Bickerstaff, Lt. Robert G	(P) 389BG	70, 99
Bieber, Lt. Charles C	(B) 458BG	149
Billemay, S/Sgt. Larry	(GC) 44BG	102
Billings, Lt. James R	(P) 44BG	26, 81
Billingsly, Lt. Glenn R	(P) 392BG	247
Bingaman, Lt. James K	(P) 453BG	137
Bingham, Lt. Milford O	(P) 392BG	76
Bird, Lt. Luther S	(P) 93BG	79
Bishop, Capt. Robert H	(P) 44BG	31
Bishop, Lt. Robert R	(P) 392BG	150
Bishop, Lt. Wallace J	(P) 489BG	205
Blakely, Sgt Charles W	(WG) 44BG	92
Blakeman, Lt. Warren R	(P) 389BG	101
Blackney, Lt. Willis G	(P) 392BG	266
Black, Lt. Jack	(P) 448BG	132
Blackburn, Lt. James W	(P) 489BG	186
Blackis, Lt. J T	(P) 389BG	55
Blackwell, Lt. Charles	(B) 93BG	211
Blackwood, Lt. James C	(P) 446BG	171
Blaine, Lt. Robert W	(P) 44BG	29
Blakeley, Lt. Willis C	(P) 392BG	257
Blakely, Sgt Charles W	(WG) 44BG	92
Blanton, Lt. Billie C	(P) 448BG	197
Blednick, Lt. Leonard W	(B) 458BG	128
Bledsoe, Lt.	(P) 44BG	174, 254
Bledsoe, Lt. Jesse W	(P) 446BG	254
Blitz, Sgt Aulus L	(WG) 44BG	81
Blodgett, Lt. Don	(CP) 458BG	187
Blomberg, Lt. Robert R	(P) 445BG	106
Bloodworth, T/Sgt Archie J	(Eng.) 453BG	97
Bloore, Lt.	(P) 389BG	271, 272
Bloznelis, Lt. John D	(PN) 389BG	152
Blue, Lt. Malcolm	(N) 491BG	175
Blum, Capt. W	(P) 44BG	81
Blum, Maj. William	(P) 448BG	214
Bocksburger, Lt. Alfred A	(P) 492BG	161
Bogusch, Capt. Jack L	(P) 458BG	117
Bohnet, Lt. Herbert F	(P) 446BG	119
Bohnisch, Lt. Carl A	(P) 44BG	97
Bolick, Lt. Henry P	(P) 392BG	73
Bolin, Lt. James O	(P) 44BG	97
Bolin, Lt. Roy	(P) 445BG	234, 237
Bolton, PFC James	( ) 93BG	222
Bonner, Lt. Robert W	(P) 389BG	262
Bonnet, Lt. Alfred D	(P) 44BG	195
Books, Lt. Dallas O	(P) 392BG	125
Boorse, Lt. Allen	(P) 458BG	206
Boreske, Capt. Andy	(P) 389BG	195
Borgens, S/Sgt Harold E	(TG) 389BG	184
Borris, Htpm.	Kommandeur I/ JG26	90
Bosetti, Lt. Leroy R	(P) 389 BG	70
Both, Lt. Harold Jnr.	(P) 492BG	163
Botkin, Lt. Francis	(P) 448BG	212
Bouchard, Lt. Charles C	(P) 489BG	175
Boudreaux, Lt. Oscar	(CP) 389BG	181
Bowers, Lt. Joe	(P) 448BG	230
Bowman, Capt. John	(P) 93BG	69
Bowman, Lt.	(P) 44BG	76
Boyer, T/Sgt Joseph L	(Eng.) 491BG	231
Braccioforte, Sgt John F	(WG) 392BG	180
Brague, Lt. Roger J	(P) 492BG	155
Brainard, Lt. Newell	(CP) 445BG	238, 239, 244
Braley, Lt. Roy	(P) 389BG	73
Bramhall, Lt. Aaron M	(N) 448BG	120
Brand, Lt. Gilley T	(P) 466BG	128
Brandon, Lt. William H	(P) 44BG	48
Brandt, Lt. Roger	(P) 392BG	257
Branhall, Lt. Aaron	(N) 448BG	120
Branizza, F/O Bob J	(CP) 448BG	184
Brantley, Lt. Haywood E	(P) 492BG	155
Brent, Lt. Don	(P) 445BG	238
Brereton, B/Gen Louis	CG, 9USAAF	44
Brian, T/Sgt Donald L	(Eng.) 489BG	222
Bridges, Lt.	(P) 44BG	31
Bridges, Lt. Richard W	(P) 44BG	59
Bridges, Lt. Wyman	(P) 492BG	155, 156
Bridges, Sgt Charles	(G) 44BG	46, 50
Bridson, Lt. George L	(P) 392BG	194
Bringardner, Lt. John	(P) 448BG	120, 121
Brink, Sgt Benjamin E	(WG) 392BG	221
Briola, Lt.	(P) 44BG	206
Britt, Lt. Richard W	(N) 389BG	51
Brock, Lt.	(P) 448BG	277
Brock, T/Sgt Daniel J	(B) 389BG	166
Brockman, Lt. Vernie R	(CP) 44BG	135
Brogger, Col. J	CO, 446BG	185
Bronstein, Lt. G	(P) 44BG	58
Brookes, Lt.	(P) 389BG	230
Brooks, Maj.	(P) 389BG	51
Brown, Harold	44BG	60
Brown. L/Col. G S	(P) 93BG	47, 49, 52
Brown, Lt.	(P) 44BG	277
Brown, Lt.	(P) 453BG	253
Brown, Lt. Bill	(P) 448BG	114
Brown, Lt. James W	(P) 491BG	270
Brown, Lt. Llewellyn	(P) 93BG	14
Brown, Lt. Marion E	(P) 389BG	106
Brown, Sgt	(ROG) 392BG	257
Brown, Sgt Norman V	(BT) 453BG	146
Brown, Lt. Robert L	(P) 44BG	31
Brown, Lt. Robert W	(P) 392BG	135, 181
Broxton, Lt. Harvey E	(P) 448BG	102, 104
Bruce, Lt. Bill	(P) 445BG	95
Bruce, Lt. William	(P) 445BG	232, 236, 237, 240, 245
Brukand, Lt. Palmer	(P) 445BG	241
Bryan, Sgt Walter F	(WG) 392BG	76
Bryans, Lt. Robert E	(P) 466BG	136
Bryant, Col. Ralph S	(P) 389BG	153
Bryant, S/Sgt Harold A	(Eng.) 392BG	148
Bryl, S/Sgt E B	(TG) 44BG	58
Buass, Lt. Walter C	(P) 392BG	246
Budd, Lt. Daniel C	(P) 491BG	231

Buechenstein, Lt. Joseph L (P) 44BG 108
Buechler, Lt. John F (P) 392BG 218
Bugalecki, Sgt (Eng.) 445BG 243
Buland, Lt. Joseph A (P) 93BG 137
Bunalski, Sgt R (GC) 44BG 157
Bunker, Lt. Walter (P) 44BG 61
Burnett, Lt. John C (P) 445BG 166
Burns, Robert Scottish Poet 177
Burr, Sgt Edward P (ROG) 492BG 157
Burton, L/Col. Paul T (P) 389BG 145
Busch, S/Sgt John (WG) 389BG 167
Bush, Lt. Edward W (P) 389BG 279
Buschman, Lt. John B (P) 392BG 64
Bussell, Lt. (P) 453BG 275
Bussing, Capt. Henry G (P) 445BG 107
Butler, Lt. (P) 44BG 201
Butler, Lt. Marvin W (P) 491BG 186
Butler, Lt. Ralph J (P) 491BG 231
Butler, Lt. Richard (P) 44BG 59, 71
Butler, T/Sgt James (Eng.) 458BG 229
Buxton, Lt. John (P) 448BG 210
Byerman, Sgt Harry E (TG) 93BG 74
Byers, Sgt John F (Eng.) 44BG 81

C
Cadden, Sgt John (ROG) 445BG 243
Cain, Lt. Paul ( ) 392BG 274
Caldwell, Capt. Kenneth H (P) 389BG 51
Caldwell, Lt. (B) 44BG 25
Caldwell, Lt. Kay R (P) 389BG 196, 202
Caldwell, Lt. (B) 44BG 25
Caldwell, Maj. Kenneth H (P) 389BG 88, 91
Callaghen, Lt. George P (P) 392BG 141
Calouri, Lt. E (P) 445BG 143
Calstrum, Sgt Chester R (Eng.) 458BG 172
Cameron, Lt, Bill, (P) 44BG 15, 23, 44, 55
Campbell, Lt. Donald G (B) 392BG 63
Campbell, Lt. John W (P) 445BG 173
Campbell, Lt. Lawson D (CP) 448BG 114
Campbell, Maj. Robert L (P) 448BG 87, 127
Canfield, Lt. Dale K (P) 44BG 23
Cardenas, Lt. Robert L (P) 44BG 124
Carey, F/O Leo A (B) 445BG 143
Carey, Lt. (P) 44BG 149
Carey, Lt. Harry V (CP) 392BG 216
Carey, Lt. Richard J (P) 392BG 210, 210
Carnahan, Lt. James R (P) 93BG 89
Carter, Lt. (CP) 93BG 79
Carter, Lt. Lloyd C (P) 453BG 228
Cary, Lt. John L (P) 492BG 73
Cargile, Lt. Nolan B (P) 44BG 24
Cargill, Lt. John (N) 445BG 244
Carlisle, Capt. Thurston (P) 445BG 210
Carlson, F/O John L (B) 448BG 151
Carlton, Lt. Freelin A (P) 389BG 106
Carney, Lt. Lawrence (B) 448BG 187
Carpenter, Lt. Reginald J (P) 44BG 53, 58
Carper, Lt. Earl L (P) 489BG 176
Carroll, Lt. Robert W (P) 448BG 127
Carrow, Lt. Raphael (P) 445BG 236, 238, 244
Cary, Lt. John L (P) 492BG 162
Case, F/O Rodolph (P) 93BG 108
Cashman, S/Sgt (G) 389BG 73
Cathey, Lt. John W (P) 448BG 151
Catlin, Lt. (P) 453BG 167
Caulfield, Lt. John C (N) 392BG 150
Caverne, Lt. Clinton H (P) 466BG 139
Cavit, Lt. C (CP) 389BG 52
Chagron, Sgt Paul A` (ROG) 44BG 149
Chamberlain, Lt. Alfred C (P) 93BG 121
Chamberlain, Lt. John E (P) 458BG 207
Chandler, Lt. Max E (P) 44BG 270, 272
Chapman, Lt. Bill R (P) 467BG 268
Chappell, Lt. Herschel R (P) 389BG 181
Chase, Lt. Philip J (P) 448BG 83
Chastain, S/Sgt William (TG) 389BG 193
Chilton, Capt. John R (P) 445BG 234, 241
Chippeaux, Lt. Oral C (P) 389BG 252
Christian, Lt. Charles H (P) 491BG 208
Chu, Sgt Ed (TG) 448BG 276, 277
Cieply, Lt. Edward J (P) 392BG 246
Clapper, Lt. Elwyn E (P) 392BG 190
Clark, Lt. James C (P) 448BG 151
Clarke, Lt. J C (P) 392BG 251, 259
Clausing, Lt. John C (P) 446BG 206
Cleary, Lt. John J (N) 44BG 91
Clemmons, Lt. Charles H (CP) 445BG 82
Clifford, Lt. Hayden H (P) 392BG 229
Clifford, Lt. William W (P) 392BG 64
Cline, Lt. Clair W (P) 448BG 104
Clover, Lt. Donald K (P) 392BG 125
Clower, Lt. William J (P) 392BG 260
Cobana, Lt. William E (N) 448BG 87
Cochran, Lt. Bob (CP) 445BG 234, 235, 241, 243
Coffman, Lt. J D (P) 489BG 186
Cofield, Maj. Curtis H (P) 445BG 129
Cohan, George M U S Entertainer 13
Coker, Lt. Elmo A (P) 489BG 174
Colby, Lt. Eldon N (P) 389BG 82
Cole, Lt. Robert E (P) 489BG 189
Cole, Lt. Woodrow W (B) 44BG 91, 92
Coleman, S/Sgt Edward B (TG) 392BG 174
Collar, Lt. George (B) 445BG 236, 238, 239
Colosimo, T/Sgt (ROG) 44BG 261
Colson, Lt. John V (P) 446BG 232
Combs, Lt. John H (P) 45BG 149
Comeau, Lt. Eugene L (P) 392BG 247
Comin, Sgt Jim (WG) 445BG 236
Compton, L/Col. Keith CO, 376BG 36, 47
Condon, Lt. Thomas F (P) 93BG 169
Connelly, Lt. Samuel R (P) 389BG 70
Conneran, Lt. Edward J (P) 392BG 141
Connor, Lt. Tom B (P) 445BG 95
Conrad, Capt. James D (P) 44BG 140, 194
Conrad, Maj. James D (P) 44BG 194
Constable, Lt. John S (P) 445BG 106
Conzoner, Lt. Thomas C (B) 44BG 188
Cookus, Lt. Keith (P) 44BG 86, 91, 109
Cool, Lt. Albert B (P) 93BG 180
Coolidge, Lt. Myles E (P) 467BG 209
Cooper, Lt. Earl T (P) 389BG 88
Cooper, T/Sgt Joe P (ROG) 392BG 218
Core, Lt. Willis R (P) 389BG 184
Corner, Richard ( ) 44BG 60
Corsilli, Sgt Gene (BT) 44BG 108
Corwine, Lt. Maurice D (P) 44BG 261
Cosgrove, Lt. Joseph F (P) 93BG 78
Costain, Lt. Philip M (P) 445BG 107
Cotey, S/Sgt Robert L (TG) 492BG 164
Cotner, Lt. Franklin V (P) 466BG 152
Cotterman, T/Sgt, 44BG 14
Couch, Lt. Robert T (CP) 458BG 147
Counts, Lt. William H (P) 467BG 189
Courtney, Capt. Marcus V (P) 389BG 179
Cowart, Maj. Bill (P) 93BG 37
Cowell, Lt. Dwight W (CP) 448BG 104
Cowley, T/Sgt John C (Eng.) 392BG 191
Cox, Lt. Thomas J (P) 392BG 107
Cox, Maj. Robert L (P) 392BG 145
Cox, Sgt A (Eng.) 93BG
Cox, S/Sgt Charles W (Eng.) 467BG 255
Cox, Sgt Jack (G) 389BG 54, 55
Crabbe, T/Sgt Charles W (Eng.) 392BG 246
Crall, Lt. Robert O (CP) 453BG 146
Cramer, Capt. Thomas R (P) 44BG 25
Crandall, Lt. Leonard J (P) 44BG 270
Crenshaw, Lt. Tom C (P) 392BG 227
Crepeau, Lt. Lawrence T (P) 448BG 68
Crepp, T/Sgt Howard (Eng.) 389BG 173
Cripe, Lt. Hubert (P) 453BG 113, 118
Crock, Lt. George (P) 389BG 275
Crocket, Lt. Elmer B (P) 453BG 149
Crockett, Lt. Elmer B (P) 453BG 119
Cross, Lt. Elvin W (P) 489BG 174
Crowther, F/O John C (CP) 489BG 186
Crumbley, T/Sgt Calvin C (Eng.) 448BG 197
Crump. T/Sgt John W (Eng.) 44BG 25, 27
Cullen, Capt. Arthur V (P) 44BG 25, 26
Culp, Lt. Herbert (P) 446BG 197
Cupp, Sgt Charles E Jnr. (ROG) 448BG 276
Curelli, Lt. R A (P) 44BG 55
Curland, Lt. Bill H (P) 458BG 229
Curry, Sgt Bill (463SD) 389BG 178
Curtis, Lt. James E (P) 448BG 87
Curtis, Lt. John R (P) 492BG 159
Cuzick, S/Sgt Harrison A (ROG) 392BG 202
Cyr, Lt. Joe G (B) 453BG 118

D
Dale, Lt. Daniel (N) 445BG 243
Dallas, Capt. Bob (P) 389BG 278
Dalton, Lt. Gerald M (P) 392BG 124
Daly, Lt. Bob (P) 492BG 120
Daley, Lt. John (P) 448BG 120
Daly. Lt. Robert P (P) 492BG 156, 172
Daly, T/Sgt Herbert B (Eng.) 93BG 40
D'amore, S/Sgt James J (ROG) 389BG 114
Dana, Lt. Phil C (P) 445BG 133
Darlington, Lt. Julius (P) 93BG 52, 53
Darnell, Lt. Robert W (CP) 392BG 192
David, Sgt Morton E (WG) 492BG 159
Davidowitz, F/O Ed (B) 44BG 169
Davis, Lt. (B) 489BG 206
Davis, Lt. Parkman W (P) 93 BG 40
Davis, Lt. Roy (P) 448BG 144
Davis, Lt. William F (P) 392BG 246
Davis, Sgt ( ) 44BG 254
Davis, S/Sgt Ray W (BT) 392BG 124
Davison, Lt. Max A (P) 453BG 152
Dawes, Lt. Esking M (CP) 445BG 133
Dawson, Lt. Frank (B) 389BG 193
Dayball, Lt. (P) 44BG 228
Daywalt, Lt. Harry A (P) 93BG 79
Deaton, Cpl James A (ROG) 392BG 270
Deavonport, Lt. John G, (N) 44BG 23
DeBlasio, Sgt Louis J (WG) 44BG 271
Decker, Lt. Donald R (P) 44BG 101
Deeter, Lt. David (P) 389BG 198
De Kalb, Lt. Lyle E (B) 445BG 116
De Lay, Sgt Harold (WG) 448BG 109
De La Riviere, S/Sgt Guy (TG) 389BG 139
Delclisur, Lt. Arthur C (B) 389BG 153
Della, Lt. Mauro (P) 448BG 207
Denton, Sgt Richard (TG) 446BG 118
DePaul, S/Sgt Francis (TG) 445BG 184
Desmond, Lt. William J (P) 445BG 106
Devers, Gen. Jacob 31, 73
Devinney, Lt. James F (B) 44BG 32, 55
Dewey, Lt. William (P) 445BG 242
Dickey, Sgt Harvey L Jnr. (TG) 448BG 132
Dickson, Lt. James W (P) 392BG 136
Dickson, S/Sgt Tommy F (WG) 453BG 253
Diehl, Lt. John (P) 44BG 12, 24, 25
Diehl, Lt. Stanley E (P) 458BG 259
Dinda, S/Sgt Bernard F (TG) 392BG 125
Dionne, Sgt Harvey (G) 389BG 139
Dipalma, S/Sgt Frank ( ) 491BG 222
Dittmar, Lt. Arthur H (P) 44BG 211
D'More, S/Sgt James J (ROG) 389 BG 114
Dobson, Lt. Edward (P) 44BG 71
Dodd, Lt. James R (P) 392BG 261
Dodd, T/Sgt Harrison A (Eng.) 389BG 184
Donald, Lt. Myron (P) 445BG 240
Donnelly, Lt. Edmund H (N) 44BG 123
Doole, Lt. Roy L (CP) 467BG 207
Dooley, Lt. Robert J (P) 466Bg 143
Doolittle, Lieutenant/Gen J H 'Jimmy' CG, 8AF 84, 85, 93, 142, 143, 146, 167, 169, 282
Doolittle, Sgt L A (GC) 392BG 75, 82
Dosmann, T/Sgt Joseph B (ROG) 44BG 247
Douglas, Lt Frnklin C (P) 446BG 183
D'Oust, Lt. Wallace W (P) 392BG 69
Dout, Lt. Boyd (P) 389 BG 58, 73, 94
Downey, Lt. John (P) 389BG 140
Doyle, Lt. Charles C (CP) 392BG 107
Drahos, Lt. Aldrich A (P) 448BG 183
Drahos, Sgt Victor C (TG) 458BG 183, 229
Drake, Lt. Chester W (B) 392BG 194
Driscoll, Capt. John (Armaments Officer) 389BG 139, 142, 143, 146
Dubard, Lt (P) 44BG 21
Dudziak, Lt. Ted (P) 392BG 72
Dunlevie, Lt. Malcolm W (P) 458BG 128
Dunster, Sgt (ROG) 445BG 107
Dworaczyk, T/Sgt Eugene
Dyer, Lt. Eugene N (P) 44BG 124

E
Eaker, Lieutenant/Gen. Ira A CG, VIII BC 35, 73, 84
Earley, T/Sgt Stanley A (Eng.) 389BG 59
East, Lt. Garland (B) 389BG 183
Eaton, Tom Chairman, 2AD Memorial Trust 279
Eberhardt, Lt. Bernard J (P) 44BG 204
Eckard, Lt. (P) 491BG 218
Eckstrom, T/Sgt John E (ROG) 492BG 157
Eden, Sir Anthony British Foreign Secretary 31
Edgar, Sgt George M (ROG) 389BG 184
Edman, Lt. Lawrence E (P) 448BG 109
Edwards, Capt. Leonard P (Chaplain) 458BG 95
Edwards, Lt. (Eng.) 453BG 227
Edwards, Lt. W (CP) 448BG 127
Eggert, Herr Nazi labor camp Kommandant 244
Ehlen, Herr Joseph Nazi labor camp staff member 244
Ehrmann, Lt. Everett G (P) 453BG 119
Eike, Lt. Lester I (P) 445BG 89
Eisenhower, 5-Star Gen. Dwight D 84
Eisermann, Lt. Gilbert O (P) 392BG 174
Ekhard, Lt. (P) 491BG 231
Elder, Lt. Oliver (P) 445BG 238, 239
Eleranto, Lt. Tievo E (P) 392BG 136
Eley, Lt. Jack (P) 389BG 172
Eline, Lt. Sidney W (P) 389BG 133
Elliot, S/Sgt Richard H (WG) 448BG 127
Ellinger, Lt. Carl F (P) 392BG 148
Ellis, Capt. Frank (P) 389BG 83
Ellis, Lt. Calvin (B) 448BG 276
Ellis, Lt. John D (P) 392BG 120
Ellis, Lt. L N (P) 389BG 52
Ellwart, T/Sgt Richard (Eng.) 389BG 227
Emerson, Lt. James (P) 453BG 225
Encimer, S/Sgt (RW) 44BG 228
Enlow, T/Sgt Elroy R (Eng.) 445BG 107
Ent, B/Gen Uzal Air Commander, 'Tidal Wave' 44, 47
Eppley, Sgt George (Eng.) 445BG 239
Epting, Lt. Jacob (P) 93BG 36
Erhard, Sgt Kenneth L (WG) 44BG 29

Name	Unit	Page
Ernst, T/Sgt Ralph C	(ROG) 44BG	31
Erwin, Lt. Roy B	(P) 44BG	23
Esenwein, Sgt Dick	(WG) 392BG	256
Etheridge, Lt. Harold E	(P) 44BG	108
Evans, Lt. Paul S	(P) 466BG	280
Evans. Lt. Richard E	(P) 467BG	193, 197
Evans, Lt. William J	(P) 489BG	175
Everhart, Capt Wyeth C	(P) 392BG	78, 145
Ewald, M/Sgt George E	(GC) 93BG	86
F		
Faas, Lt. John E	(CP) 392BG	192
Fairbanks, Col. Luther	CO, 466BG	219
Falk, S/Sgt Robert I	(BT) 466BG	152
Fandell, Lt. Harold L	(P) 491BG	248
Fandler, Lt. Milt	(N) 445BG	242
Fanelli, Lt. John	(P) 389BG	213
Farmer, Lt. Jack	(P) 445BG	143
Farrell, Lt.	(N) 492BG	158
Farrington, Lt. Richard	(P) 466BG	280
Faucher, Lt. George B	(P) 492BG	159
Favors, S/Sgt Alva F	(Eng.) 44BG	204
Federici, Lt. Frank W	(N) 445BG	244
Felber, Lt. Tom	(P) 466BG	280
Felbinger, Lt.	(N) 453BG	195
Felsenthal, Lt. Charles L	(P) 392BG	170
Feran, Lt. John E	(P) 392BG	124
Ferdinand, S/Sgt Pete	(ROG) 389BG	252
Ferguson, Lt. C V	(N) 389BG	51
Ferguson, Lt. William F	(P) 448BG	87
Fern, Capt. Titus M	(P) 389BG	186
Feuerstacke, Lt. Thomas A	(P) 392BG	62
Fiedler, Lt. Charles A	(B) 467BG	257
Fiegel, Col. Leland G	CO, 93BG	69, 185
Field, Lt. Marshall W	(P) 491BG	205
Fierro, Lt. James M J	(P) 489BG	175
Fino, Lt. John	(B) 389BG	51
Fippinger, T/Sgt Eugene A	(ROG) 445BG	87
Fish, Lt. George E	(P) 44BG	105, 108, 109
Fisher, Lt. Robert D	(P) 492BG	155
Flatt, Lt. Roy F	(P) 453BG	262
Flaugh, Lt. Harold E	(B) 44BG	105
Flaugher, Sgt Harold J	(Eng.) 458BG	181
Fleenor, Capt. Beattie H	(P) 93BG	37, 40
Fleischmann, Sgt Abel	(ROG) 44BG	81
Fleming, Lt. Richard W	(P) 492BG	163
Fletcher, Lt. Marion E	(P) 389BG	74
Fletcher, Lt. R E	(P) 392BG	75
Floore, Maj. John	(P) 93BG	261
Floyd, Lt. Werner H	(CP) 389BG	204
Flynn, Capt. Jim	U S Army	272
Flynn, Lt. Robert K	(P) 44BG	25, 27
Flynn, Lt. Norman C	(P) 466BG	143
Fogarty, Lt. David N	(P) 392BG	72
Foley, Lt. Edward W	(P) 389BG	142, 145
Ford, Capt. Herrell E	(P) 93BG	80
Ford, Lt. William I	(N) 392BG	198
Forrest, Lt. Keith	(P) 445BG	222
Forsyth, Lt. John	(P) 389BG	174
Forsythe, Lt. William M	(P) 392BG	181
Foster, Lt. David W	(P) 467BG	81
Foster, Lt. Thomas A E	(P) 44BG	81
Fothergill, Lt. Clarence E	(CP) 392BG	174
Foushee, Lt. William C	(P) 466BG	142
Fouts, Lt. V R	(P) 44BG	29
Fowble, Lt. E	(P) 389BG	43, 61
Fox, Lt. Paul T	(P) 491BG	270
Fox, Lt. Roland G	(P) 448BG	184
Foy, Lt. Frank L	(P) 44BG	173
Francis, Kay	U S film actress	22, 23
Franklin, T/Sgt Robert C	(Eng.) 44BG	135
Frascati, Lt. Charles V	(P) 446BG	83
Fravega, Lt. Thomas P	(P) 389BG	52, 74
Fravega, Sgt Anthony	(ROG) 389BG	74
Frawley, Lt. Herbert	(P) 44BG	12
Frazee, Lt.	(P) 389BG	213
Frazier, Lt. Leo O	(N) 44BG	29
Freed, Lt. Warren D	(P) 453BG	198, 208
Freeman, Sgt Jack B	(TG) 44BG	135
Freeman, T/Sgt Chauncey W	(Eng.) 392BG	183, 189
Freeman, T/Sgt Harold	(ROG) 389BG	152, 153
French, Lt. John	(P) 445BG	234, 236, 241, 242, 243
Friedhaber, Lt. John M	(P) 453BG	230
Frische, Lt. John E	(P) 445BG	143
Fromm, Lt. Richard A	(P) 445BG	238
Fry, Lt. Phillip A	(P) 445BG	195
Fryman, Lt. Bernard	(P) 392BG	153
Fuchs, Lt. Kermit A	(P) 446BG	141
Fuerst, Lt. Michael J	(P) 389BG	64
Fuhr, Lt. Francis E	(P) 491BG	224
Fuller, Sgt	(Eng.) 44BG	229
Fuller, Sgt George E	(Eng.) 467BG	268
G		
Gable, Clark	Screen- actor	16
Galland, Hptm 'Wutz', Kommandeur. II/JG26		29
Galley, Lt. Clifford R	(P) 489BG	176
Gallop, Lt. Robert A	(P) 445BG	195
Gallop, Sgt Eugene M	(BT) 392BG	148
Gamble, Sgt Bill	( ) 448BG	198
Gannon, Sgt Ronnie	(G) 446BG	256
Garber, Lt. Marvin W	(P) 446BG	97
Garcia, Sgt Edward J	( ) 458BG	253
Gardner, T/Sgt Dan 'Gluck'	(Eng.) 389BG	71
Garrett, Lt. Robert L	(P) 466BG	128
Garrett, Lt. W J	(P) 44BG	45
Garrett, T/Sgt C E	(Eng.) 44BG	53
Garvey, S/Sgt James A	(ROG) 392BG	191
Gates, Lt. John	(N) 392BG	166, 194
Gasser, Sgt H C	(WG) 44BG	121
Gaulke, Lt. Frederick D	(P) 492 BG	157
Gavin, Lt. John P	(P) 467BG	150
Gefelner, Lt. Joseph A	(P) 445BG	133
Geitz, Chaplain	492BG	161
Gellings, Lt. Ray C	(P) 448BG	81
Genarlsky, Lt. Frank	(P) 448BG	229
Gentry, Capt. Rowland M	(P) 44BG	46, 50
George, Lt. J D	(B) 93BG	89
Geron, Lt. Alva J	(P)	54
Gerow, Lt. James A	(P) 392BG	221
Gerritts, Lt. J F	(CP) 44BG	53
Gerstenburg, Col. Alfred.	Ploesti Defence-Controller	47
Getman. Lt. William D	(P) 446BG	248
Gewehr, Capt. Ralph P	(P) 93BG	69
GFelner, Lt. Joseph A	(P) 445BG	133
Ghormley, Sgt	(ROG) 448BG	109
Gibbs, Lt. Edward	(CP) 445BG	238
Gibson, Lt. Rex M	(P) 458BG	280
Gibson, Lt. Samuel T	(P) 458BG	196
Giesecke, Lt.	(Engineering) 389BG	75
Giesen, Lt. Charles	(P) 458BG	251, 252
Gille, Lt. Gerald G	(N) 44BG	134
Gill, Lt. Thomas H	(P) 446BG	224
Gilow (rank?)	Combat crew 389BG	74
Ginevan, Lt. Donald	(P) 448BG	206
Ginn, Lt. R J	(N) 448BG	197
Glass, Lt.	(P) 453BG	263
Glass, Lt. Albert W	(B) 44BG	24
Glass, S/Sgt Tommy	(Eng.) 458BG	139
Glover, S/Sgt De Sales	(WG) 458BG	137
Gnong, Lt. Harold	(B) 389BG	102, 103
Godwin, T/Sgt H T	(Eng.) 389BG	52
Goins, Sgt James A	(ROG) 458BG	139
Gold, Lt. John C	(P) 389BG	106
Golden, Lt. William	(P) 445BG	238
Goldenburg, Col. Carl T	(CO) 491BG	172, 177
Goldsmith, Lt. Stuart	(P) 458BG	168
Golobuck, Lt. Ralph	(P) 93BG	173
Golovan, Lt. Ralph R	(N) 492BG	161
Gomez, Sgt	(G) 93BG	45
Goodridge, Lt.	(P) 492BG	159
Goodwin, Lt. R K	(P) 392BG	90, 102
Goodwin, Sgt	(TG) 389BG	193
Gorrell, Lt. Kenneth M	(P) 458BG	113
Gotke, Lt.	(N) 44BG	14
Gottlieb, Lt. Gerald	(N) 448BG	273
Goucher, S/Sgt	(GC) 44BG	199, 200
Graff, Lt. Bill	(P) 389BG	262
Grafton, Lt. Harry E	(P) 446BG	183
Graham, Capt. James	(P) 445BG	234, 243, 244
Gray, Lt. William F	(CP) 466BG	136
Gray, Maj. Clyde T	(P) 482BG	95
Grayhosky, Lt.	(CP) 44BG	58
Green, Lt.	(P) 389BG	63
Green, Lt. Harry	(B) 392BG	198
Green, Lt. James	(CP) 392BG	194
Green, Lt. William F	(P) 44BG	204
Green, Sgt Miles S	(WG) 44BG	94
Greene, Lt. Floyd H	(CP) 44BG	152
Greenly, Sgt	(WG) 445BG	235, 236
Greiner, Oblt.	(P) NJG1	117
Gricas, S/Sgt William J	(BT) 453BG	118
Griesel, Lt. Kenneth C	(P) 389BG	117
Greyhosky, Lt.	(P) 44BG	58
Griffen, Lt. Donald G	(P) 466BG	128
Griffen, Lt. Travis W	(P) 392BG	148
Griffith, Lt. Rockford W	(P) 44BG	72, 94, 143
Griggs, Lt. Robert H	(P) 392BG	139
Grono, Lt. Lawrence W	(CP) 44BG	72, 94, 143
Gross, Lt. Morton P	(B) 44BG	29
Grubb, Lt. Dale E	(P) 448BG	198
Gruener, Capt. Harry	(P) 93BG	261
Gruening, Lt. Huntingdon	(P) 448BG	207
Gunn, Lt. James M	(P) 389BG	53
Gurman, Lt. Irving S	(P) 44BG	173
Gustella, Lt. Joe	(P) 445BG	210
Guynes, Lt. James	(P) 445BG	266
Guyton, Lt. Graham G	(P) 448BG	87
H		
Haag, Lt. Frank	(P) 492 BG	161
Haag, Lt. George	(P) 492BG	161
Hackett, Maj. Chester B	(P) 448BG	183
Hadden, Lt. Eugene H	(P) 492BG	159
Haffermehl, Lt. George T	(P) 392BG	125
Hagar, Lt.	(P) 44BG	55
Hagenah, Ltn. Walter	(P) IV (Sturm) JG3	161
Haines, Lt. Frank W	(P) 392BG	215
Hall, Lt.	(P) 389BG	193
Hall, Lt. John C	(P) 489BG	174
Halpern, Lt. Mike	(P) 448BG	207
Halpern, Sgt Herbert M	(GI) 392BG	266
Hamrick, Lt. Herbert	(Eng.) 389BG	193
Handwright, Capt. Charles B	(P) 44BG	189
Hamby, Lt. Keith O	(P) 453BG	139
Hamilton, Lt. Edward L	(P) 489BG	187
Hamilton, Lt. James W	(P) 453BG	128
Hamilton, Lt. Wilfred L	(P) 492BG	163
Hammond, Lt. Gordon L	(P) 392BG	145
Hampton, S/Sgt Lee	(ROG) 492BG	161
Hancock, Lt. Tom	(P) 458BG	207
Haney, Sgt Paul W	(ROG) 392BG	247
Hannaman, Lt. Robert H	(P) 458BG	188
Hansen, Lt. Leroy M	(P) 44BG	70
Hansen, Lt. Robert	(P) 445BG	238
Hanzlich, Lt.	(P) 389BG	227
Harbin, Lt. Foster P	(N) 446BG	128
Harding, Lt. Bernard	(N) 492BG	161
Hardy, Lt. John F Jnr.	(P) 446BG	170
Harkovich, S/Sgt Mike	(WG) 44BG	248
Harleman, Lt. Richard E	(P) 44BG	87, 129
Harms, Lt. Roy C	(P) 93BG	49
Harrington, Lt. Bob L	(P) 466BG	209
Harrington, Lt. John F	(CP) 93BG	261
Harris, Air Chief Marshal Sir Arthur T	C-in-C RAF Bomber Command	130
Harris, Lt. Clarence W	(P) 445BG	232
Harris, Lt. Daniel B	(P) 466BG	136
Harris, Lt. Jack D	(P) 93BG	116
Harris, Lt. John D	(P) 392BG	69
Harris, Lt. Joe L	(P) 492BG	160
Harris, Lt. Melvin C	(WG) 392BG	76
Harris, Lt. Monroe	(P) 389BG	277
Harris, Lt. Roscoe E	(P) 492BG	159
Harris, Lt. Secar J	(P) 93BG	123
Harris, Lt. Teague G	(P) 458BG	147
Harrison, Lt. Charles D	(P) 467BG	166
Hart, Lt. Dean H	(P) 453BG	70
Hart, Lt. W H	(P) 44BG	70
Hartquist, Lt. Carl E	(P) 389 BG	184
Harvall, Capt. Ursel	(Photo Sect. Officer) 44BG	
Harvey, Sgt Arthur	44BG	11
Hasenfratz, Sgt Merle J	(TG) 392BG	148
Hassenpflug, Herr Walter	German civilian	245
Hastreiter, Lt. Donald	(P) 93BG	260
Hatfield, Lt. Orlie A	(B) 466BG	136
Hatton, Lt.	(B) 389BG	112
Hatfield, Lt. Orlie A	(P) 466BG	136
Hausman, Lt. Herschel	(P) 448BG	260
Hautman, Lt. Edward	(P) 445BG	241
Havard (combat crew)	445BG	244
Havens, S/Sgt Leycester D	(TG) 93BG	49
Hawkins, Lt. Thaddeus I	(B) 93BG	40
Haynes, Wiley W	(WG) 44BG	108
Heber, Lt. Malcolm M	(P) 492BG	126, 159, 160
Hebron, Lt. Walter T	(P) 392BG	126
Heilich, Sgt Jacob G	(BT) 389BG	181
Heitmann, Fw	(P) 4/JG26	70
Heitz, Lt. Raymond	(P) 445BG	241
Helder, Lt. Ronald H	(CP) 389 BG	51
Helfer, Lt. Clifton F	(P) 446BG	120
Helton, Lt. E	(P) 467BG	185
Helvey, Lt. V W	(P) 448Bg	104
Heming, Lt. Dwight	(P) 93BG	121
Henderson, Lt. Charles P	(P) 44BG	58
Henderson, Lt. Gordon W	(CP) 44BG	185
Herbert, Lt. Lloyd H	(P) 492BG	155
Herboth, Col. John	CO, 389BG	278
Herzik, Lt. Frank W	(Po 458BG	114
Herzing, Lt. Ernest A	(P) 44BG	134
Heskamp, Lt. Carl G	(CP) 93BG	183
Hesketh, Lt. Donald J	(P) 44BG	81
Hess, Lt. Harold F	(P) 44BG	129
Hess, Lt. Lowell K	(P) 389BG	74, 129
Hestad, Lt. Erling A	(P) 392BG	117
Hetzler, Lt. Harold W	(P) 458BG	128
Hewlett, Lt. James A	(N) 44BG	203
Hickman, Capt. Cleveland H	(P) 93BG	78
Hicks, Lt. Robert	(P) 389BG	232
Hicks, Lt. Roger T	(P) 458BG	261
Hicks, Sgt	(G) 392BG	283
Hicks, Sgt James C	(WG) 448BG	80
Higgins, Capt. Joseph	(P) 389BG	150
Higham, Lt. Morgan C	(P) 489BG	206
Hildebrandt, Friedrich	Nazi Party Gauleiter	185
Hill. Lt. William E	(B) 44BG	31
Hilliard, Lt. Ray L	(P) 44BG	23, 32
Hinton, Lt. FJ	(P) 446BG	97

Hitchcock, Lt. C (P) 466BG 152
Hobbs, Lt. John C (P) 44BG 247
Hobson, Lt. Thomas (P) 44BG 59
Hockensmith, Lt. William A (P) 446BG 109
Hockert, Lt. Reino E (CP) 392BG 64
Hodges, B/Gen. James CG, 2BW/BD 10, 12, 32, 58, 145, 167, 169, 185, 193
Hodges, Lt. Frank R (P) 93BG 40
Hoelke, Lt. Donald R (B) 44BG 91
Hoffman, Lt. John R (P) 93BG 180
Hoffman, Lt. Ralph O (P) 458BG 261
Hoffman, S/Sgt Leo J (WG) 44BG 203
Hollis, Lt. Terrell (N) 389BG 228
Holmes, Lt. Tommy (P) 44BG 31
Hood, T/Sgt James H (Eng.) 448BG 120
Hopkins, Lt. Herbert C (P) 458BG 196, 253
Hopkins, Lt. Thayer (P) 458BG 118
Hopper, Lt. Owens L (P) 453BG 275
Horgan, Lt. Tom H (P) 458BG 217
Horine, Sgt Stanley M (TG) 389BG 53
Horton, Lt. Robert W (P) 389BG 51
Houghtby, Lt. Raymond C (P) 44BG 123
Houle, Lt. Joseph L (P) 44BG 71
Houston, Lt. Rowland B (P) 93BG 49
Howard, Lt. Orland T (P) 448BG 151
Howe, Lt. Norman E (P) 44BG 185
Howell, Lt. Cleve J (P) 448BG 184, 185
Howell, Lt. Malcolm C 'Mac' (P) 44BG 31
Howell, Lt. William L (P) 445BG 208
Howington, Lt. Hartwell R (P) 44BG 91, 92
Hruby, Lt. Richard J (P) 44BG 150, 152
Hubbartt, Lt. Gene A (P) 392BG 207, 263
Huck, Lt. George (N) 389BG 167
Hudson, Lt. Donald J (P) 467BG 227
Hudson, Sgt R E (WG) 448BG 104
Hudson, Sgt William ( ) 458BG 224
Hughes, Lt. Charles E (P) 44BG 53
Hughes, Lt. Lloyd, Posthumous CMH (P) 389BG 48, 51, 54
Hughes, Lt. William D (P) 44BG 31
Hughey, Lt. Edward D (P) 448BG 80
Hull, Lt. Robert L (P) 392BG 87
Humke, Lt. Herbert H (P) 458BG 215, 224
Hunnefeld, S/Sgt Edwin D (WG) 389BG 140
Hummel, Lt. John R (P) 392BG 270
Hunt, Lt. Daniel F (P) 458BG 264, 265
Hunt, Lt. Grady G (P) 93BG 80
Hunt, Lt. Norman J (P) 392BG 189, 198
Hunter, Lt. Bill (P) 389BG 267
Hunter, Lt. C J (P) 392BG 115
Hunter, Lt. William (P) 445BG 241
Hunter, Sgt Elmer R (NT) 392BG 275
Hurlbart, S/Sgt Richard C (TG) 93BG 65
Hurst, Sgt Clifford C (WG) 44BG 70
Hutchcroft, Lt. Harold W (CP) 392BG 274, 275
Hutchens, Lt. Charles R (P) 93BG 66
Hutchens. Lt. Marion (P) 389BG 252
Hybarger, Lt. (B) 44BG 192

I
Ingram, Lt. Richard M (P) 453BG 105
Inman, Lt. Benjamin F (P) 446BG 189
Irwin, Lt. William C (P) 44BG 123
Isaksen, Lt. (P) 453BG 229
Isbell Col. Jim CO, 458BG 103, 185, 224
Isgrig, Lt. Ben (P) 448BG 180
Isom, Lt. Cecil (P) 445BG 237, 242, 243
Issacson, Lt. Wesley (P) 448BG 260
Ives, Lt. Lawrence C (P) 492BG 163
Ivey, Sgt Melvin A (ROG) 392BG 257

J
Jacks, Lt. Robert H (P) 492BG` 161
Jacobs, Cpl A C (GC) 392BG 75
Jacobs, Lt. Myron G (P) 44BG 208
Jacobson, Lt. Ralph (P) 389BG 230
Jacobson, Lt. Sidney G (P) 446BG 79
James. Lt. H (P) 389BG 43
James, Lt. Harold (P) 44BG 53
Janic, Lt. E (P) 489BG 37
Janinski, Sgt Ray (NT) 392BG 247
Jansen, Lt. (P) 44BG 32
Janson, Martinus Dutch civilian 264, 283
Jarbeaux, Sgt Tom C (ROG) 389BG 184
Jarel, Lt. Seymour (P) 448BG 187
Janinski, Sgt Roy (NT) 392BG 247
Jaslovsky, Lt. Julius C (P) 446BG 128
Jeffs, Lt. Robert H (B) 44BG 108
Jennings, Lt. Edward J (P) 446BG 126
Jennings, Lt. Howard E (P) 93BG 262
Jenson, Lt. Frank M (P) 491BG 265
Jerstad, Maj. John, Posthumous CMH
Jewell, Lt. Kenneth G (P) 44BG 114, 120
Jochens, Lt. E R (P) 453BG 263
Johns, Lt. Mervyn T (P) 389BG 107
Johnson, B/Gen. Leon CG, 14CBW 73, 138, 185
Johnson, Col. Leon, CO, 44BG 12, 23, 48, 50, 54, 62
Johnson, B/Gen. Leon CG, 14CBW 73, 138
Johnson, Cpl Nevin A (U S paratrooper) 221
Johnson, L/Col. (P) 392BG 107
Johnson, Lt. Cloys V (N) 445BG 234
Johnson, Lt. Earl T (P) 44BG 71
Johnson, Lt. Guy W (P) 448BG 135
Johnson, Lt. John V (P) 392BG 107
Johnson, Lt. Robert A (P) 93BG 35
Johnson, Lt. Robert H (P) 392BG 226
Johnson, Lt. Rex I (P) 392BG 89, 123, 125
Johnson, Lt. William P (N) 44BG 101
Johnson, T/Sgt T E (Eng.) 392BG 8
Jones, Gwen, ARC member at Hethel 83
Jones, Lt. C E (P) 392BG 102
Jones, Lt. Dana L (P) 446BG 180
Jones, Lt. Fred H (P) 44BG 48, 53
Jones, Lt. George E (P) 392BG 192
Jones, Lt. Glenn (P) 448BG 188
Jones, Lt. Harold E (P) 392BG 215
Jones, Lt. Howard (P) 445BG 237
Jones, Lt. J (P) 458BG 103
Jones, Lt. Ken 'Deacon' (P) 389BG 248, 276
Jones, Lt. Paul (P) 448BG 274
Jones, Lt. Paul A (P) 44BG 134
Jones, Lt. Thomas E (P) 489BG 174
Jones, Lt. Weems D (P) 448BG 152
Jope, Lt. F L (N) 44BG 70
Jordan, Lt. Max R (P) 448BG 82
Joynt, Lt. Albert E (P) 392BG 219
Judd, Lt. Alan C (P) 453BG 257
Judd, Lt. Stephen P (P) 389BG 120
Jweid, Lt. Louis J (P) 389BG 140

K
Kagan, Lt. Myron (P) 389BG 248
Kaiser, Lt. Philip W (P) 392BG 257, 273, 274, 275
Kale, Lt. William A (P) 392BG 117, 126
Kales, Lt. Walter (P) 491BG 202
Kalinowski, S/Sgt Eugene (TG) 389BG
Kamenitsa, Lt. William T (P) 392BG
Kane, Col. John R, CMH CO, 98BG 52
Kane, F/O William P (P) 445BG 82
Kane, Lt. Fred J (B) 392BG 82, 150
Kaspshak, Lt. Edward F (P) 466BG 199
Kaufman, Lt. Kenneth F (P) 392BG 139
Kaufman, Lt. Richard C (P) 492BG 159
Kearns, Sgt Hiatt H (WG) 392BG 247
Kearns, Lt. Louis L (CP) 392BG 69
Keeton, Lt. Felix ( ) 389BG 181
Keeffe, Lt. (CP) 389BG 106
Kees, Sgt Frank J (Eng.) 389BG 50, 51
Kehoe, Lt. Nicholas B (P) 492BG 160
Keilman, Maj. Myron (P) 392BG 145
Keith, Lt. Ray R (P) 453BG 166
Kelleher, Lt. Daniel P (P) 392BG 107
Keller, Lt. Richard I (P) 44BG 181
Kelley, Lt. (N) 44BG 24
Kelley, Lt. Howard H (N) 445BG 144
Kelly, Lt. John B (P) 448BG 267
Kelly, Lt. Stanley D (P) 453BG 127
Kempowicz, S/Sgt (ROG) 44BG 201
Kendall, Lt. Walter H (B) 453BG 119
Kendrick, Lt. John M Jnr. (P) 389BG 120
Kendziora, Lt. Franklin C (P) 445BG
Kennedy, Lt. Jack P (CP) 489BG 208
Kenyon, S/Sgt Kenneth S (NT) 458BG 201
Kepner, Brigadier/Gen. William CG, 8FC 12,
Kepner, Brigadier/Gen. William CG, 2BD 84, 85, 169, 203, 279
Kerfoot, Sgt Denver (ROG) 392BG 273
Kessler, Lt. (P) 44BG 60
Ketchum, Lt. Horace R (P) 93BG 68, 74
Keyes, Lt. Ernest E (P) 466BG 208
Key, Lt. Carroll C (P) 448BG 67
Key, Maj. Algene, (P) 44BG 22, 23
Kight, Sgt Donald A (NT) 392BG 263, 280
Kieras, T/Sgt Eugene J (Eng.) 392BG 221
Kight, Sgt (G) 392BG 263
Kilcheski, Lt. Frank (P) 93BG 72
Kill, Lt. J (CP) 44BG 50
Killian, Lt. Harold J (P) 93BG 95
Kilpatrick, Lt. Donald M (P) 492BG 167
King, Lt. Harry C (P) 445BG 186
King, Lt. James P (CP) 44BG 108
Kingsley, Lt. Paul E (P) 458BG 167
Kinnaird, Col. Claibourne CO 4FG 282
Kiser, Lt. Robert M (P) 445BG 101
Kissinger, Lt. Louis I (N) 44BG 31
Kissinger, Lt. Maynard W (P) 489BG 200
Kissling, Lt. James L (P) 389BG 193
Kittridge, Lt. Abraham J (P) 448BG 81
Klein, Sgt Alfred M (WG) 44BG 92
Klein, Sgt Warren E (WG) 44BG 92, 97
Kleinshrot, Lt. Ken R (P) 389BG 187
Kley, Lt. Ralph (P) 44BG 248
Kline, Sgt Vincent M (BT) 492BG 156
Klug, S/Sgt Lester G (WG) 44BG 29
Klusmeyer, Lt. Bill (P) 458BG 219, 277
Knoke, Oblt. Heinz (P) JG11 28
Knorr, Lt. Charles (P) 448BG 132
Knowles, Lt. William H (P) 389BG 132, 133
Knudsen, Lt. Bernard L (N) 392BG 270
Koch, Fw. (P) 3/JG1 24
Koehn, Lt. George J (P) 458BG 224
Koeppel, Lt. Paul E (P) 453BG 109
Komaninski, Lt. Edward J (P) 44BG 208
Komer, Lt. Adolph (P) 466Bg 174
Konstand, Capt. Gus (P) 44BG 254
Koon, Lt. Loren I (P) 93BG 13, 69
Koontz, Lt. Harold L (CP) 44BG 114, 120
Kotraba, Lt. George J (P) 467BG 113, 207
Kougias, Lt. George C (P) 446BG 138
Kraham, Lt. William R (P) 445BG 180
Kramer, Maj. Ronald V (P) 448BG 167
Krause, S/Sgt Harold L (WG) 392BG 79, 247
Kretzer, T/Sgt Harold (Eng.) 44BG 44
Kreuger, Sgt Victor W (BT) 458BG 118
Kribs, Sgt Ken (Eng.) 445BG 242
Krivik, Lt. Stanley (P) 445BG 243, 244
Kroell, Lt. Carl I (P) 446BG 108
Kuban, Sgt William T (BT) 44BG 72
Kubinsky, Lt. Henry (G) 448BG 104
Kuchwara, Lt. Michael (P) 448BG 197
Kuehler, S/Sgt (GC) 389BG 74
Kunkel, Lt. Walter R (P) 389BG 252, 278
Kunze, Capt. Owen L (P) 93BG 36
Kuroki. T/Sgt Ben (Eng.) 93BG 39, 54
Kurtz, Lt. John H (P) 389BG 112

L
LaCombe, Lt. Raymond J (P) 44BG 125
Lacombe, Lt. Richard L (P) 448BG 124
Lafferty, Lt. William (P) 445BG 133
Lamb, Lt. Bob (P) 453BG 205
Lambert, Lt. Paul J (P) 389BG 80
Lambert, Lt. Paul P (P) 392BG 87
Lamberton, Capt. Robert T (P) 448BG 147, 167
Lamma, Lt. Ralph E (P) 392BG 69
Landahl, Lt. Howard K (P) 44BG 188
Landers, Lt. Walter F (CP) 458BG 165
Landry, (rank?) Combat crew, 392BG 193
Landry, Lt. John F (P) 492BG 157
Lane, Lt. Albert L (P) 453BG 101
Lane, Sgt Harold J (ROG) 448BG 81
Lang, Lt. Robert J (P) 392BG 170
Lange, Hptm. (P) 6/JG26 101
Langenfeld, Lt. Willard A (P) 467BG 206
Laning, Capt. (P) 446BG 187
Larsen, Lt. Lawrence E (P) 392BG 173
Larsen, Lt. Neil R (P) 392BG 186
Larson, Lt. Arnold V (P) 44BG 167
Larson, Lt. Lincoln A (P) 458BG 193
Lasco, Lt. Henry A (P) 44BG 50
Lauren, Lt. Rutledge (P) 389BG 71, 78
Lawrence, S/Sgt Walter V (WG) 44BG 188
League, Lt. Miles R (P) 93BG 65
Ledford, Lt. Arthur S (P) 44BG 225
Lee, Mr. British civilian (44BG) 30
Lee, T/Sgt Al (Eng.) 93BG 41
Lehmann, Lt. Robert E (P) 448BG 148, 149
Lehnhausen, Lt. Robert (P) 44BG 54, 228
Lehnhausen, Lt. Edward C (P) 44BG 228
Leibenhaut, Sgt Martin (G) 491BG 219
Leininger, Lt. Ed (P) 389BG 171
Leister, Lt. Roger L (P) 467BG 211
Le Jeune, T/Sgt E G 389BG 61
LeMay, Sgt Raymond G (TG) 491BG 174
Leseur, Larry CBS Reporter 83
Leslie, Lt. Ralph P (P) 389BG 93, 181
Lew, Lt. Harold S (P) 491BG 225
Lewis, Lt. Henry C (P) 445BG 248
Lewis, Capt. James L (P) 492BG 155
Lewis, F/O Albert (P) 448BG 215
Lewis, Lt. James R (P) 44BG 101
Leyes, Lt. Charles T (P) 467BG 209
Lidgard, Lt. Willard C (CP) 392BG 125
Liebfeld, Lt. Sig (P) 491BG 202
Liebich, Lt. Joseph C (P) 448BG 140
Lied, Sgt Harry (TG) 445BG 237
Liedke, Lt. Vincent` (P) 448BG 140
Lien, Capt. Alvin (P) 445BG 129
Liggett, Lt. Robert C (P) 492BG 160
Lighter, Lt. D C (P) 389BG 55
Lindsay, Lt.
Lingle, Sgt John (WG) 392BG 283
Lister, L/Col. Ralph B (P) 389BG 268
Little, Lt. W H (B) 93BG 49

Name	Unit	Page
Lippert, Lt. Rexford W	(N) 44BG	29
Lloyd, Lt. Myron	(N) 389BG	166
Lloyd, Sgt Ira C	( ) 448BG	104
Lobo, Lt. Howard J	(P) 458BG	172
Locke, Lt. Alfred	(P) 389BG	152, 153
Loebs, Lt. Herbert	(P) 44BG	98
Lofgren, Lt. Lawrence	(P) 448BG	271
Lofton, Lt.	(P) 453BG	227
Logie, Lt. Byron	(P) 458BG	139
Long, F/O Grover M	(N) 458BG	229
Long, Lt. Ben W	(P) 445BG	204
Long, Lt. John B	(P) 44BG	23, 26
Long, Lt. Thomas B	(P) 446BG	78
Long, Lt. William S	(N) 392BG	215
Long, Lt. Worthy A	(P) 93BG	49
Looney, Lt. Alfred J	(P) 445BG	107
Lo Presto, Lt. Henry C	(P) 392BG	78
Lougheed, Lt. J H	(P) 361FG	215
Louizides, T/Sgt Solomon	(ROG) 392BG	275
Love, Lt. Benjamin	(P) 445BG	142
Love, Lt. David E	(P) 467BG	142, 198, 206
Loveday, Lt. William	(P) 93BG	57
Lovell, Lt. Endicott R	(P) 458BG	166
Lovelace, Lt. Claude T	(P) 489BG	222
Low, Maj. Andy	(P) 453BG	205
Lown, Lt. Franklin D	(P) 93BG	39
Lowry, Sgt Richard G	(Eng.) 458BG	123
Lowry, Lt. Walter F	(P) 392BG	129
Lucas, Lt. RobertJ	(P) 44BG	123
Ludka, Lt. Richard Jnr.	(B) 467BG	185
Ludwick, Sgt Julian F	(BT) 446BG	189
Lundstrom, Sgt John V	(WG) 44BG	70
Lundy, Sgt Will	(GC) 44BG	61
Lymburn, Lt. George H	(P) 445BG	117
M		
Mabe, Lt. L B	(P) 389BG	213
Mabee, Sgt Floyd	(G) 93BG	37
Maben, Lt. Jack F	(P) 392BG	124
Maceyra, Lt. Eddie	(N) 392BG	275
Mack, Capt. D	(P) 492BG	163
Mackay, Lt. John B	(P) 453BG	166
Mackey, Lt. Oak	(CP) 392BG	259
Mackey, S/Sgt Marvin C	(WG) 453BG	
Mackinster, Lt. Chester D	(P) 93BG	129
Madden, Lt. Thomas J	(P) 445BG	133
Maddocks, Capt. Gene L	(P) 93BG	265
Madsen, Capt. Leroy G	(P) 445BG	183
Maier, Lt. Ralph E	(P) 446BG	211
Main, Lt. Bob	(P) 448BG	276
Majesky, Lt. Alec	(P) 392BG	256
Makiewicz, Lt. Edward A	(P) 448BG	98
Malavisic, S/Sgt Anthony J	(TG) 392BG	83
Malen, Lt. Fred	(P) 445BG	107
Malone, Lt. Wallace	(P) 446BG	253
Maneval, Lt. Weldon H	(N) 44BG	91
Mangerich, Lt. Walter E	(P) 458BG	139
Mankin, Lt. Charles W	(P) 93BG	112
Manning, Lt. David E	(P) 448BG	80
Marfia, Lt. Frank	(P) 392BG	70
Markusen, Lt. Clifford O	(P) 392BG	274, 275
Martin, Lt. Bill	(P) 448BG	144
Martin, Sgt Joe F	(TG) 392BG	257
Martin, Lt. Lester	(P) 458BG	171, 172
Martin, Lt. Orvis G	(B) 453BG	119
Martin, Lt. Robert A	(P) 448BG	114
Martin, Sgt Joe F	(TG) 392BG	256
Maruszckski, Sgt Frank	(TG) 44BG	44
Marx, Lt. Issac	(P) 392BG	70
Masci, Peter J	(ROG) 44BG	108
Mason, Col. Gerry	2ADHQ	182, 185
Mason, Lt. Harley	(P) 389BG	75
Mathisen, Lt. Gary M	(P) 44BG	91
Matson, Lt. Kenneth M	(P) 44BG	59
Mattson, Lt.	(P) 458BG	172
Mattson, Lt. Carl A	(P) 389BG	88
Mayer, F/O Randell S	(P) 392 BG	191
Mayer, Hptm. Egon	Kommandeur, III/JG2	88
May, Lt. Gordon L	(Eng.) 44BG	108
Mayes, Lt. Robert A	(P) 44BG	134
Mayfair, Mitzi	U S film actress	23
Mayher, Lt. Hugh	(CP) 489BG	166
Mayhew, Sgt Richard A	(TG) 44BG	91
Maynard, Lt. George L	(P) 44BG	93
Maynor, Lt. William M	(P) 448BG	78
Marx, Lt. Robert H	(P) 44BG	134
Mazure, Capt. Louis A	(P) 489BG	176
Meador, Lt.	(N) 389BG	51
Means, Lt. Dan W	(P) 491BG	225
Mechan, Lt. John L	(P) 392BG	216
Meehan, Lt.	(P) 93BG	49
Meek, Lt. Herman J	(P) 453BG	118
Meglish, Lt.	(P) 491BG	222
Melby, Lt. Lawrence F	(P) 445BG	82
Mellor, Lt. Harrison	(P) 448BG	132
Menacker, Lt. Norman	(P) 445BG	121
Menard, Lt. John F	(P) 392 BG	202
Meng, Lt. Harold R	(N) 466BG	183
Menweg, Lt. R	(P) 492BG	163
Mercer, Lt.	(P) 44BG	105
Mercer, Lt. Leo E	(P) 389 BG	264
Mercer, Lt. Jack L	(P) 448BG	184
Mercer, Lt. Jackson	(P) 445BG	236, 242, 244
Merkle, S/Sgt	(G) 389BG	193
Merrill, Lt. John	(CP) 389BG	262
Merriman, Lt. James A	(P) 466BG	120
Meskinis, Sgt Joseph M	(TG) 44BG	133
Messenger, Lt. Kenneth K	(P) 466BG	137
Metcalf, Lt. Earle G	(P) 445BG	97
Meyers, Lt.	(P) 491BG	248
Michel, T/Sgt	(ROG) 392BG	193
Mied, T/Sgt A F	(Eng.) 448BG	114
Mike, T/Sgt Kenneth A	( ) 389 BG	61
Mikoloski, Lt. Edward	(N) 44BG	32
Milchak, Sgt Elmer	(WG) 392BG	270
Miler, Lt. Gene A	(B) 392BG	150
Milillo, Sgt.Antonio G	(ROG) 44Bg	108
Miller, Col. Joseph A	(P) 453BG	127
Miller, F/O Kent	(P) 44BG	80
Miller, Lt. Clifton G	(P) 445BG	187
Miller, Lt. Bert D	(P) 392BG	121
Miller, Lt. Donald	(P) 492BG	158
Miller, Lt. G H	(P) 467BG	210
Miller, Lt. Herman H	(P) 392BG	104
Miller, Sgt John R	(Eng.) 491BG	202
Miller, Lt. Robert E	(P) 44BG	14, 31
Miller, Lt. Roy L	(P) 392BG	189
Miller, Sgt Don C	(TG) 458BG	128
Miller, Sgt John R	(Eng.) 491BG	202
Miller, Sgt Kenneth J	(WG) 389BG	120
Milliken, Lt.	(P) 44BG	209
Milliken, Lt. William H	(P) 392BG	191
Mills, Lt. Dean M	(P) 453BG	219
Mills, Lt. George S W	(P) 467BG	267
Miltner, S/Sgt Robert F	(WG) 448BG	127
Mims, Sgt Ed	(Eng.) 389BG	140
Minck, Lt. Fred	(P) 446BG	212
Miner, Lt. FReginald	(P) 445BG	241, 245
Mitchell, Capt.	(P) 491BG	222
Mitchell, Lt. Duane E	(N) 44BG	192
Mitchell, Lt. Edward R	(P) 44BG	53, 71
Moffette, Lt. John F	(P) 467BG	255
Mogford, Lt. Robert J	P) 466BG	129
Moir, Lt. Alexander B	(CP) 44BG	248
Mollen, Sgt Milton	(RO) 44BG	195
Money, Lt. John D	(P) 44BG	141
Monohan, Lt. James L	(P) 458BG	201
Monroe, Lt. John D	(P) 492BG	160
Monroe, Lt. Verdun W	(P)	209
Montgomery, Field Marshall Sir Bernard Law	36, 219	
Montgomery, Lt. Bill B	(P) 489BG	186
Montre, S/Sgt Don W	(Eng.) 44BG	248
Moody, Lt. Richard	(P) 448BG	198
Mooney, Capt. Robert C	(P) 44BG	53
Moore, Capt. Charles T	(P) 93BG	36
Moore, Lt. C	(P) 492BG	157
Moore, Lt. Warren C	(P) 491BG	231
Moore, Lt. William F	(P) 467BG	150
Moore, Maj. 'Pappy'	(P) 44BG	26, 32
Moore, T/Sgt Robert L	(Eng.) 44BG	247
Moran, Capt. John W	(P) 458BG	261
Morefield, Lt. Hubert F	(P) 392BG	139
Moritz, Hptm. Wilhelm	Kommandeur, IV (Sturm) JG3	190, 192
Morphew, Lt. Orvil S	(P) 392BG	62
Morris, Lt. Dale R	(P) 458BG	151
Morris, Lt. Francis H	(P) 458BG	212
Morris, Lt. Richard P	(P) 445BG	186
Morrison, Lt.	(P) 44BG	192
Morse, Lt. Douglas	(P) 448BG	211
Morse, Sgt Ellis H	(NG) 392BG	270
Moseley, Lt. Kent	(P) 448BG	140
Mosher, Lt. Harry	(P) 389BG	272
Mosser, Lt. Edward J	(P) 467BG	121
Mowat. Lt. Bill	(P) 445BG	232, 237
Mower, Lt. Leo L	(P) 466BG	179, 184
Moynham,	(Combat crew) 445BG	243
Muir, Lt.	(CP) 389BG	146
Muka, Sgtg John J	(WG) 392BG	261
Mulcahy, F/O John J	(B) 389BG	184
Muldoon, Lt.	(P) 344BG	121, 126
Muldoon, Lt. James E	(P) 392BG	121, 126
Mullane, Lt. Martin J	(P) 446BG	228
Mullery, Lt. John M	(P) 446BG	224
Munsey, Lt. James F	(P) 453BG	146
Munson, Capt. Robert M	(P) 492BG	157, 161
Murphy, Capt. John	(P) 93BG	36, 37
Murphy, Lt. Thomas H	(P) 467BG	166
Murphy, T/Sgt Thomas R	(ROG) 458BG	141
Murray, Lt. Alvin A	(P) 492BG	155
Murray, Lt. Damian J	(P) 467BG	207
Murrow, Edward R	CBS Reporter	83
Musselmann, Lt. Everett	(P) 448 BG	121
Must, Lt. John A	(N) 392BG	63
Mc		
McAdams, Sgt Robert C	(G) 44BG	76
McAllaster, Robert W	(ROG) 392BG	216
McArthur, Lt. James B	(P) 389BG	120
McAuliffe, Lt. Bob J	(P) 389BG	184
McBride, Lt. Charles	(B) 448BG	132
McBride, Maj. Ralph J	(P) 93BG	53
McCarthy, Lt. Charles L	(P) 392BG	186
McCarthy, S/Sgt Richard O	(RG) 458BG	149
McClane, Lt. John	(N) 44BG	208
McClellan, Lt. H B	(P) 392BG	217
McClellan, Lt. John L	(N) 389BG	71
McClelland, Lt. Don	(P) 445BG	235
McCluhan, Lt.	(P) 448BG	272
McClure, S/Sgt Ralph V	(TG) 453BG	146
McConnaughhay, S/Sgt William	(Eng.) 44BG	185
McCormack, Capt. John B	(P) 389BG	72
McCormick, Lt. Ray A	(N) 44BG	187
McCormick, S/Sgt John E	(WG) 392BG	264, 283
McCoy, Capt. 'Wild Bill'	(P) 44BG	27, 28
McCoy, Lt. George C	(P) 492BG	159
McCoy, Maj. Don W	(P) 445BG	234, 241
McCracken, Lt. John	(N) 44BG	248
McCue, S/Sgt Miles J	(WG) 44BG	74
McCune, Lt. John A	(P) 448BG	148
McDonald, Helen	ARC (93BG)	135
McDonald, Lt. Gordon	(P) 491BG	198
McDonald, lt. John C	(P) 466BG	169
McDonald, Maj.	(P) 44BG	25
McDonald, Sgt Carl D	(TG) 389BG	188
McFarland, Lt. Hugh	(P) 448BG	271
McFetrich, Lt. Robert L	(P) 466BG	129
McGee, Lt. John V Jnr.	(P) 389BG	193
McGee, S/Sgt. J E	(BT) 392BG	120
McGee, Lt. John V Jnr.	(P) 389BG	193
McGlenny, S/Sgt David F	(Eng.) 492BG	160
McGrady, Sgt Leo V	(G) 44BG	32
McGraw, Lt. John J	(P) 389BG	52
McGregor, Capt. Harry P	(P) 466BG	208
McGuire, Lt. Thomas J	(P) 44BG	209
McKee, Lt. Thomas R	(P) 392BG	83
McKellar, Lt. Campbell	(P) 392BG	273
McKelvey, F/O W M	(P) 93BG	45
McKenna, Lt. James P	(P) 44BG	207
McKenna, S/Sgt Raymond H	(Eng.) 44BG	134
McKinney, T/Sgt John F	(WG) 453BG	146
McKoy, Lt. George C	(P) 492BG	159
McLachlan, Sgt 'Red'	(G) 389BG	63
McMains, Lt. Jesse L	(P) 458BG	117
McMullen, Lt. Don H	(CP) 392BG	106, 125, 126
McMurray, Lt. David P	(P) 492BG	158, 161, 164
McNair, Gen. Leslie	U S Army	204
McNichol, Lt. Thomas F	(P) 44BG	87, 141
McPherson, S/Sgt Albert J	(P) 44BG	87, 141
McVean, Lt. Peter D	(P) 448BG	187
N		
Nading, Lt.	(CP) 389BG	58
Nanco, Lt. Charles	(P) 389BG	140
Nardi, Lt. Richard	(B) 448BG	98
Nagle, Sgt	(G) 392BG	283
Nash, S/Sgt Travis E	(ROG) 44BG	277
Naumann, Lt. Rudolf A	(P) 458BG	205
Neal, Lt. Stanley R	(P) 445BG	101
Nealon, T/Sgt Walter K	(B) 44BG	134
Neary, Lt. Mark B	(P) 453BG	139
Nedrow, Lt. James E	(P) 458BG	172
Neef, Lt. Melvin E	(P) 389BG	51
Neff, Lt. Charles L	(P) 392BG	140
Nelson, Lt. Norman N	(P) 445BG	80
Newhouse, Lt.	(P) 467BG	148
Newman, Lt. Clayton J	(P) 493BG	161
Newton, Lt. Earl W	(P) 491BG	202
Nichols, Sgt Lawrence C	(WG) 445BG	107
Nicholls, Lt. Hollis J	(P) 44BG	124
Nicholson, Lt. John D	(P) 446BG	184
Nicholson, Lt. William P	(P) 392BG	69
Nickerson, Sgt	Joseph (WG) 448BG	104
Nimmo, Lt. Robert P	(P) 448BG	183
Nissen, T/Sgt Charles	(Eng.) 448BG	133
Norquist, Lt. John E	(P) 44BG	93
Norson, Lt.	68BS, 44BG	12
Northrop, Lt. Henry H	(P) 458BG	181
Novik, Lt. Albert	(P) 392BG	260
Nowalk, Lt. Donald R	(P) 389BG	105
Nugent, T/Sgt James R Jnr.	(ROG) 448BG	120
Nunn, Lt. William	(P) 446BG	212
O		
Oakley, Lt. Warren W	(P) 44BG	81
O'Brian, Capt. James E	(P) 44BG	21
O'Brian, Maj. James E	(P) 44BG	24, 30
O'Brien, Lt.	(P) 389BG	281
O'Bryant, Sgt Leondis	(G) 491BG	180
Ochevsky, Sgt Louis	(WG) 445BG	241

Name	Unit	Page
Ofenstein, Lt. Leo E	(P) 392BG	150
Ogden, Lt. James Q	(P) 446BG	179, 182
O'Kelly	(Combat crew) 445BG	244
Oliphant, Lt. Rufus A	(P) 44BG	25
Olivas, Cpl Maclovia	(WG) 392BG	261
Olliffe, Lt. Vic	(P) 93BG	52
Olsen, Lt. Stanley F	(P) 44BG	59
Olsen, Sgt George E	(TG) 44BG	70
O'Neil, Lt. Paul	(P) 448BG	258
O'Neill, Lt. Richard F	(P) 44BG	76
O'Neill, Sgt C D	(G) 44BG	69
O'Niell, S/Sgt John	(WG) 389BG	262
Opitz, Sgt. Gerald	(GC(389BG	79
Oppelt, Lt. Harry J	(B) 448BG	98
Oppenstein, Cpl.	(GC) 392BG	75
Opsata, Lt. Andy	(P) 389B	52
O'Reilly, Lt. Robert J	(P) 389BG	50, 51, 63
O'Rourke, Lt.	(CP) 389BG	252
Osborne, Lt. Mark T	(P) 489BG	208
Osment, S/Sgt	(WG) 392BG	198
O'Steen, Lt. Albert P	(P) 389BG	184
Ostrander, Lt.	(P) 491BG	222
O'Sullivan, Lt. David	(P) 492BG	157
Ott, Lt. John W	(N) 392BG	275
Ottenstein, Cpl.	(GC) 392BG	75
Owen, Lt. Alvin L	(P) 445BG	87, 101
Owens, Sgt Louis	(Eng.) 448BG	230
Owings, T/Sgt Bill	(Eng.) 389BG	204

P

Name	Unit	Page
Packer, Lt. Leon C	(P) 93BG	40
Paez, Sgt	(WG) 389BG	153
Page, Lt. Leander Jnr.	(P) 392BG	87
Paliga, S/Sgt	(Eng.) 44BG	58
Palmer, Lt. Hiram G	(P) 44BG	139, 140
Palmerton, Lt. Elwyn R	(P) 448BG	186
Palumbo, Pvt Anthony P	(Eng.) 392BG	214
Paltz, Lt. Robert E	(P) 446BG	118
Parish, Lt. John K	(B) 392BG	275
Parker, Lt. Fred V	(P) 453BG	166
Parker, Lt. Gordon B	(P) 445Bg	126
Parmele, L/Col.	(P) 491BG	230
Parry, Sgt Alan T	(Eng.) 44BG	32
Parsons, S/Sgt Dick	(WG) 445BG	236
Pascal, Lt. Richard W	(B) 44BG	235
Patten, Lt. George K	(B) 491BG	231
Patten, Sgt Francis 'Pat'	(Eng.) 392BG	256
Patterson, Lt. Edward H	(P) 389BG	184
Patterson, Lt. Joseph B	(P) 392BG	107
Patterson, Lt. Milton A	(P) 445BG	78
Patton, Gen George S	CG, U S 3rd Army	205
Pavelka, Lt. Joseph	(P) 445BG	143
Payne, S/Sgt Charles F	(WG) 392BG	124
Payton, Lt. Joseph B	(P) 392BG	102, 108
Payton, T/Sgt Joseph B	(Eng.) 392BG	108
Peacock, S/Sgt Charles L	(Eng.) 467BG	174
Pearce, T/Sgt Edward E	(Eng.) 491BG	224
Pearson, Lt. Ralph	(P) 445BG	238
Peck, B/Gen Walter	CG 96CBW	103, 219
Pedrotta, Lt. Charles H	(CP) 392BG	246, 247
Pelkey, Capt. Ernest E	(P) 492BG	161
Pellegrino, Sgt	(NT) 389BG	106
Peloquin, S/Sgt Joseph O	(Eng.) 44BG	169
Peppmaier, Lt. Dean	(P) 446BG	212
Perkinson, Lt. William P	(CP) 458BG	188
Perrault, Lt.	(P) 44BG	261
Perro, Lt. Edward J	(P) 453BG	167
Perron, Lt. Gregory H	(P) 389BG	112
Perry, Sgt Willard	(Eng.) 446BG	228
Peters, Lt. Neil J	(P) 458BG	123
Peters, Lt. William M	(P) 445BG	166
Peterson, Lt.	(CP) 448BG	274
Peterson, Lt. Clifford L	(P) 392BG	125
Peterson, Lt. Edward R	(P) 445BG	174
Peterson, Lt. Lynn C	(P) 392BG	125
Peterson, Lt. R E	(P) 44BG	45
Peterson, Lt. Robert C	(N) 44BG	53
Peterson, Lt. Richard 'Pete'	(P) 357FG	193
Pettigrew, Lt. William B	(B) 392BG	247
Pettit, Lt. Richard J	(P) 93BG	96, 121, 122
Peyton, Lt.	(P) 392BG	78
Phelan, Lt. Eugene A	(CP) 44BG	134
Phillips, Capt. F S	(B) 448BG	127
Phillips, Lt. Chester R	(P) 44BG	15
Piliere, Lt. Francis	(P) 448BG	258
Pincus, Lt. Paul J	(P) 446BG	183
Pinder, Lt. Hal H	(P) 44BG	93
Pinkus, Lt. Robert F	(P) 448BG	129
Pino, Lt.	(P) 44BG	133
Pinto, Lt. Prosper F	(P) 466BG	129
Piola, S/Sgt	(GC) 44BG	199, 200
Pippert, Sgt Donald D	(TG) 392BG	77
Pitts, Lt.	(P) 448BG	146
Pitzenbarger, Lt.	(P) 492BG	163
Plant, Lt. Richard R	(P) 445BG	184
Platinski, Lt. Saul	(P) 492BG	162
Plese, Lt. Tom M	(P) 489BG	214
Podojil, Lt. Robert J	(P) 44BG	268
Podolak, Capt. Stanislas T	(P) 389BG	94
Polzin, Sgt Gerald A	(NG) 492BG	159
Pomfret, Lt. Joe	(CP) 44BG	132
Ponge, Lt. William	(P) 448BG	151
Poole, Lt. William A	(N) 44BG	25, 27
Poor, Lt. Albert A	(P) 445BG	67
Popovich, T/Sgt Peter	(ROG) 445BG	239
Poremba, Sgt Stanley J	(G) 392BG	267
Portal, Sir Charles	C-in-C Royal Air Force	169
Porter, Lt. Enoch M	(P) 93BG	47
Porter, Lt. Leon F	(P) 492BG	159
Posey, Col. James T	CO, 44BG	49, 62
Post, Robert Perkins	NYT Correspondent	28
Postemsky, Lt. Ed	(P) 448BG	212
Potts, Lt. Herbert	(P) 445BG	237
Potts, Maj. Ramsey	(P) 93BG	33, 47, 49, 52, 53
Potts, Col. Ramey	CO, 453BG	185
Pounds, Lt. Raymond L	(P) 392BG	191
Power, Lt. William	(P) 389BG	279
Powers, Lt. Frank D	(N) 44BG	81
Pratt, Lt. Charles C	(P) 492BG	155
Preis, Lt. Charles M	(P) 389BG	184
Prell, Lt. Donald D	(P) 392BG	170
Prendergast, Sgt John C	(TG) 392BG	247
Prevost, Lt. James B	(CP) 458BG	206
Prewitte, Lt. William V	(P) 492BG	157
Prewitte, Lt. William V	(P) 467BG	210
Price, Lt. Raymond E	(P) 389BG	252
Price, Maj. Clyde E	(P) 44BG	29
Priller, Maj. 'Pips'	Kommodore JG26	17
Pritchard, Lt. Lyle	(P) 467BG	197
Proctor, Lt.	(P) 392BG	272
Procyszyn, S/Sgt W	(Eng.) 44BG	70
Prokop, Lt. Frank P	(P) 467BG	150
Proteau, Lt. Frank O	(CP) 458BG	116
Prouse, Lt. Harold W	(P) 392BG	191
Pulcipher, Lt.	(P) 448BG	146
Purdy, Lt. Henry M	(CP) 93BG	182
Putty, Sgt Lemuel J	(GC) 466BG	VII

Q

Name	Unit	Page
Quail, Lt. John L	(N) 44BG	195
Quantrell, Lt. C B	(N) 389BG	43
Quinliven, Lt. Robert	(P) 93BG	14
Quinn, Lt. John	(P) 446BG	230
Quirk, Lt. Charles W	(P) 458BG	196
Qwick, S/Sgt Lowell I	(WG) 392BG	191

R

Name	Unit	Page
Rabe, Herr	German civilian	135
Radu, S/Sgt Charles L	(Eng.) 44BG	135
Raiser, Lt. John H C	(P) 453BG	186
Raiter, Lt. Walter J	(P) 458BG	133, 139
Ramirez, M/Sgt Joe	(GC) 467BG	205
Ramsey, Lt. Floyd R	(P) 93BG	69, 71
Rankin, S/Sgt Jack H	(WG) 392BG	124
Raroha, Lt. Richard A	(P) 445BG	123
Raschke, Lt. Walter C	(P) 392BG	124
Ray, Lt. James	(P) 448BG	276
Raye, Martha	U S film actress	22, 23
Raymond, S/Sgt Dan	(WG) 389BG	193
Read, Sgt J J	(Eng.) 93BG	49
Reasoner, Sgt Robert J	(TG) 44BG	59
Reece, Lt. Glenn	(P) 389BG	139
Reed, L. John W	(P) 392BG	93
Reed, Lt. Kenneth O	(P) 389BG	32
Reese, Lt., Glen	(P) 389BG	139
Reeves, Sgt Ray P	(ROG) 44BG	91, 92
Reid, Lt. Alvah D	(P) 467BG	266
Reid, Lt. John W IV	(P) 392BG	153
Reid, Lt. Loren	(P) 389BG	171
Reid, Lt. Stalie C	(P) 467BG	148
Reinhart, Lt. E	(P) 44BG	49
Rendall, Lt. William A	(N) 44BG	81
Rendle, Col. I	CO, 392BG	185
Reynolds, Lt. Andrew M	(P) 93BG	87
Reynolds, Lt. Donald	(P) 445BG	241
Reynolds, Lt. James E	(CP) 392BG	270
Reynolds, Quentin	U S War Reporter	83
Rhine, Lt.	(P) 389BG	230
Rhodes, Lt. John P	(P) 448BG	68
Richards, Sgt	(WG) 44BG	169
Richardson, Lt. David M	(P) 93BG	89
Richardson, Lt. William M	(P) 44BG	133
Richmond, S/Sgt Earle W	( ) 453BG	253
Rieke, Herr Willi	German Civilian	156
Rigby, Lt. Clyde W	(P) 392BG	87
Riggs, Capt. Benjamin F	(P) 93 BG	36
Right, Sgt John P	(ROG) 392B	107
Riley, Sgt Albert J	(WG) 392BG	170
Rinaldo, S/Sgt	(TG) 44BG	188
Ripps, Lt. Robert	(CP) 445BG	143
Ritter, Lt. Ralph T	(B) 458BG	168
Ritter, Lt. Kelly	(P) 93BG	97
Roach, Lt. William A	(P) 44BG	
Roads, Lt. Carl B	(P) 492BG	159
Robbins, Lt.	(N) 389BG	280
Robbins, Lt. Edward L	(P) 93BG	133
Roberts, Lt. Alvis D	(B) 389BG	117
Roberts, Lt. Samuel W	(N) 458BG	118
Robertson, Lt. Seigvart J	(P) 392BG	193
Robert the Bruce	Scottish patriot and Monarch	177
Robinson, Col. Frank H	CO, 44BG	11, 22, 23
Robinson, T/Sgt Ernest	(WG) 448BG	146
Roche, Lt. John	(P) 93BG	35
Rock, Lt. Herbert G	(P) 491BG	209
Rodin, Lt.	(P) 467BG	148
Roe, Lt. William D	(P) 389BG	204
Roeder, Lt. Bob W	(P) 389BG	176,182
Rosener, Ogfr. Johannes Sonderkommando Elbe	(P)	278
Rogers, Lt.	(P) 44BG	225
Rogers, Lt. Charles O	(B) 389BG	71
Rogers, Sgt Fred B	(LWG) 44BG	108
Rogers, Lt. Gerald C	(P) 392BG	116, 150
Rogers, Lt. Guy C	(P) 458BG	116
Rogers, Lt. Layne	(P) 445BG	144
Rogers, Lt. Norman J	(P) 491BG	211
Rogers, Lt. William	(P) 448BG	150
Roggenkamp, Capt. Norman A	(P) 93BG	186
Rogillo, Lt. Douglas S	(P) 392BG	76
Rokicki, Rick	458BG	221
Rollins, Lt.	(P) 453BG	263
Rollo, T/5 George	U S Army	272
Romero, T/Sgt Santo	(Eng.) 44BG	188
Rommel, Erwin	Wehrmacht Gen.	35
Roop, S/Sgt Eugene W N	(TG) 44BG	141
Roorda, Lt.	(CP) 448BG	254, 263
Roosevelt, Pres. Franklin Delano		11
Roper, Capt. Hugh R	(P) 93BG	50
Rosacker, Lt. Joseph J	(P) 93BG	262
Rosas, Lt. Milton L	(CP) 389BG	182
Rosenblatt, Lt. Milton	(CP) 44BG	91, 92
Rosenblatt, Sgt Alvin A	(ROG) 44BG	92
Ross, Lt. Philip	(P) 466BG	278
Ross, Lt. William A	(P) 448BG	114
Roth, Ofw.	(P) 4/JG26BG	29
Rowe, Lt. Kenneth A	(P) 491BG	263
Rowland, Lt. Charles E	(P) 453BG	139
Rudowski, Lt. Edward F	(P) 467BG	185
Roznos, Lt. Joseph M	(P) 93BG	133
Rubich, Lt.	(P) 389BG	145
Ruby, T/Sgt George H	(G) 445BG	184
Rudd, Lt. Charles R	(P) 392BG	215
Rudowski, Lt. Edward F	(P) 467BG	185
Rudy, Sgt John R	(TG) 93BG	180
Russell, Sgt Joseph	(ROG) 446BG	206
Ruthenbeck, Lt. Carl W	(P) 492BG	162
Ruvolis, Lt. Leo Janr.	(P) 392BG	191
Ryan, Lt. James L	(P) 392BG	69
Rylee, Lt. Fred E	(P) 93BG	215

S

Name	Unit	Page
Saari, Lt. Lloyd	(P) 389BG	188
Sachtleben, Lt. R	(P) 492BG	157
Sadlon, Lt. Edward W	(P) 445BG	145
Salfren, Lt.	(P) 446BG	226
Salisbury, Lt. Joseph D	(P) 445BG	184
Salzarulo, Maj. Robert L	(P) 467BG	150
Salyer, Lt. Charles A	(P) 389BG	52
Sample, Lt. James R	(P) 93BG	278
Sampson, Lt.	(P) 448BG	258
Sanders, Lt. Walter W	(P) 392BG	226
Sanderson, Lt. George	(P) 389BG	281
Sands, Lt. Ernest	(B) 458BG	227, 277
Santomiery, Lt. Anthony J	(CP) 44BG	193
Saubert, F/O Walter E	(P) 489BG	187
Saunders, Lt. Oliver J	(P) 445BG	82
Savage, Lt. Charles C	(P) 392BG	126
Sayre, Lt. Fred	(P) 389BG	83
Scala, Lt. Hector	(B) 445BG	244
Scarborough, Lt.	(P) 44BG	93
Scates, Lt. A J	(P) 389BG	45
Schaefer, Lt.	(P) 44BG	190
Schaffer, Lt. Ralph V	(P) 466BG	212
Schaen, Lt. Jim	(P) 445BG	236, 238, 239
Schafer, Lt. Guy L	(P) 446BG	128
Schafer, Lt. Richard F	(P) 389BG	82
Schafer, Lt. Wesley A	(P) 392BG	176, 181
Schafer, Uffz.	(P) IV *(Sturm)* JG3	161
Schaff, Lt. Millard P	(P) 458BG	153
Schaffe, Lt. Ralph V	(P) 446BG	212
Schamahorn, Lt.	(P) 491BG	222
Schamburg, S/Sgt Gunther	(GI) 392BG	254
Scherzer, Lt. Louis	(P) 453BG	149
Schieffellbusch, Lt. Dick L	(N) 44BG	32
Schievin, Lt. Everett R	(P) 389BG	206
Schleicher, Sgt Don	(G) 445BG	267
Schleichkorn, Lt. Samuel G	(P) 445BG	143

Schlossberg, Lt. Marvin E (P) 392BG 108
Schmid, Gen. 'Beppo' CG, 1 Fliegerkorps 113, 235
Schmidt, Ms. 'Birdie' ARC, 392BG 207
Schmitt, Lt. Edward L (P) 491BG 222
Schmitz, S/Sgt Norbert J (TG) 44BG 268
Schneider, Lt. Rene (P) 445BG 234
Schellhas, Lt. Kurt E (P) 467BG 255
Schettler, Sgt W (Eng.) 44BG 50
Schonmaker, Sgt Seymour (BT) 446BG 206
Schooley, Sgt Orland (TG) 445BG 237
Schopfer, Lt. Percy H (P) 446BG 138
Schroeder, Lt. Henry B (P) 448BG 149
Schott, Lt. Bernard J (P) 389BG 165
Shroeder, Lt. Henry H (P) 44BG 148, 149
Schroeder, Sgt Ed (WG) 448BG 98
Schukar, Lt. George J (P) 389BG 184
Schultz, Lt. Herbert W (P) 445BG 143
Schuman, Lt. George W (P) 448BG 90, 144
Schuster, Lt. William H (P) 392BG 261
Schutz, Lt. George C (N) 392BG 76
Schuyler, Lt. Keith (P) 44BG 151
Schwarz, (NG) 445BG 235, 236
Schwartz, Herr German Researcher 164
Schwerin, Lt. Frank (P) 389BG 204
Scott, Lt. R (P) 492BG 163
Scott, Lt. Russell E (P) 467BG 255
Scott, Lt. Stanley V (P) 491BG 203
Scott, Sgt (Eng.) 44BG 262
Scott, S/Sgt (Eng.) 44BG 262
Scrivenor, Lt. Tom (P) 44BG 50
Scudday, Lt. Bernard K (P) 44BG 187
Sears, L/Col. Bob (P) 389BG 97, 150
Seeds, Lt. Andrew G (P) 445BG 238
Sefton, Lt. Gene H (P) 445BG 126
Seger, Lt. S (P) 492BG 162
Seitzinger, Lt. Elvern P (P) 492BG 158, 160
Selfe, Lt. Errol A (P) 389BG 153
Serkland, Lt. Ned (P) 445BG 115
Serpico, Lt. Frank R (N)) 445BG 117
Serradell, Sgt Don (WG) 389BG 184
Sewell, Lt. Wade P (P) 392BG 220, 221
Shafer, Lt. F F (N) 93BG 65
Shafer, Lt. Guy L (P) 446BG 128
Shafter, Capt. James (P) 448BG 272, 276, 277
Shafter, Lt. James (P) 448BG 276, 277
Shalvoy, Lt. (P) 492BG 158, 159, 160
Shamberger, Lt. Walter B (CP) 44BG 192
Shank, Lt. Joseph A (P) 448BG 67
Shannon, Lt. E M (P) 44BG 55
Sharp, Lt. C (B) 448BG 104
Sharp, Lt. Fletcher H (P) 491BG 179
Sharpe, Lt. William G (P) 392BG 125
Shaw, Lt. Elwyn H (P) 93BG 182
Shea, Lt. Max R (P) 489BG 198
Shea, Lt. Paul F (P) 392BG 115
Shea, Sgt (NT) 392BG 283
Shelley, Lt. Joe (P) 392BG 223
Shelton, Lt. Orville W (PN) 392BG 216
Shepherd, Lt. John (P) 389BG 167
Shere, Lt. Fred C (P) 392BG 151
Sheridan, Lt. Charles M (CP) 44BG 108
Sherman, Capt. Eric H (P) 446BG 202
Sherwood, Lt. Walter B (P) 392BG 141
Shirley, Sgt Ray (Eng.) 44BG 149
Shockley, Sgt (GC) 392BG 75
Shoup, Lt. William T (P) 467BG 168
Shower, Col. Albert CO, 467BG 185, 222, 255
Shurtz, Lt. William E (P) 445BG 107
Sibley, Lt. James M (P) 392BG 81
Sicora, Lt. Anthony F (P) 392BG 215
Sidey, Lt. Elliot (P) 448BG 230
Siegal, Lt. Norman (B) 466BG 173
Siek, Lt. Robert H (P) 491BG 275
Sievers, Lt. Edward (P) 458BG 136
Silver, Lt. Emanuel (P) 93BG 211
Silver, Lt. Robert C Jnr. (P) 448BG 171
Simmons, Lt. Ken (B) 389BG 228
Simmons, Lt. Melbourne (P) 446BG 230
Simon, Lt. (CP) 44BG 108
Simon, Lt. John W (P) 446BG 212
Simon, Lt. Robert (P) 491BG 223
Simpson, Capt. Alexander (P) 93BG 17
Sise, Sgt Walter E (Eng.) 467BG 264
Skaggs, Capt. B (P) 448BG 142
Skaggs, Lt. Alvin D (P) 448BG 145, 146, 147
Skalski, Cpl Chester F (TG) 445BG 116
Skinner, Lt. Jack (P) 467BG 142
Skjeie, Lt. David P (P) 445BG 107
Skorupan, Lt. J (P) 492BG 163
Slack, Sgt Robert (TG) 448BG 187
Slama, T/Sgt Alex R (Eng.) 392BG 275
Slankard, Sgt Paul (WG) 93BG 37, 38
Slein, Lt. John R (P) 489BG 204
Slough, Lt. Frank D (P) 44BG 97
Smarinsky, Lt. Irving (P) 445BG 266
Smart, Col. Jacob *'Tidal-Wave'* Planner 42
Smiley, Lt. Elmer E (P) 492BG 161
Smith, Capt. John W (N) 467BG 257
Smith, Lt. (N) 445BG 240
Smith, Lt. Andrew (P) 445BG
Smith, Lt. Brian T (P) 392BG 62
Smith, Lt. Donald (P) 445BG 240, 243
Smith, Lt. Castleton D (N) 448BG 127
Smith Lt. Herschel (P) 492BG 162
Smith, Lt. Joseph M (P) 446BG 79
Smith, Lt. Leighton C (P) 44BG 55
Smith, Lt. Myron G (P) 93BG 211
Smith, Lt. Richard E (P) 392BG 114
Smith, Lt. Royce E (P) 389BG 87, 89
Smith, Lt. Victor I (P) 445BG 87
Smith, Sgt Earl (ROG) 458BG 188
Snavely, Col. Eugene CO, 44/492BG 27, 163
Sneed, Lt. Francis C (P) 445BG 145
Sneddon, Lt. Gomer J (P) 93BG 114
Snow, Lt. Daniel W (P) 445BG 232
Snyder, Lt. Miles (P) 389BG 123
Snyder, Lt. R (CP) 44BG 121, 123
Sobotka, Lt. Frank W (P) 44BG 50
Sofferman, Sgt Abe (Eng.) 44BG 94
Soldan, Lt. Harold (P) 448BG 259
Sollien, Lt. Carl (P) 445BG 234, 237
Songer, T/Sgt Alvin A (Eng.) 446BG 118
Sonning, Lt. Harry W (P) 491BG 231
Sooy, Lt. Bruce L (P) 392BG 125
Sorensen, Lt. W (N) 44BG 50
Sornsin, Sgt Tom C (WG) 93BG 180
Spaatz, Major/Gen. Carl 'Tooey', CG, USSTAF 10, 84, 93, 100, 130, 167, 169, 1980, 203
Sparks, Lt. Willie (N) 492BG 156
Sparrow, Lt. (P) 491BG 218
Spaven, Lt. George N (P) 458BG 120, 144, 145
Spelling, Lt. (CP) 93BG 46
Spier, Sgt Robert J (NT) 44BG 248
Sprinkle, Lt. Dallas L (P) 44BG 135
Stahl, Lt. (P) 491BG 222
Staib, Henry T (N) 44BG 108
Stalland, Lt. Knute (P) 448BG 273
Stamos, Lt. (P) 392BG 63
Stampoulis, Lt. Nick N (P) 93BG 49
Stanchfield, Lt. Milton A (P) 453BG 210
Starek, Sgt Rocky (WG) 448BG 197
Starr, Sgt Henry P (TG) 44BG 225
Starring, Lt. Alfred A (P) 44BG 90, 91
Statton, Lt. Louis T (P) 389BG 262
Stefan, Lt. Joseph (P) 448BG 273
Stein, Lt. William F (P) 93BG 59
Steinke, Lt. (P) 44BG 192
Steinmann, Hptm. Willi Kommandeur I/JG4 49
Steinmann, Sgt William H (TG) 445BG 107
Steinmetz, Lt. Douglas R (P) 392BG 69
Stella, Sgt George F (ROG) 392BG 192
Stempel, Herr SS Police Commissioner 185
Stenard, Sgt Charles A (WG) 458BG 196
Steneman, Lt. Roland E (P) 492BG 161
Stepanovic, S/Sgt (TG) 44BG 254
Stephens, Cpl Leo (TG) 448BG 210
Stephens, Lt. Louis M (P) 392BG 214
Stetson, Lt. Hervey E (N) 392BG 170
Stevens, Lt. Charles (P) 466BG 183
Stevens, Lt. Charles W (P) 491BG 179, 231
Stevens, Lt. Rufus B (P) 467BG 174
Stewart, Col. Everett CO, 355FG 235
Stewart, Capt. Walter (P) 93BG 13, 69, 86, 135
Stewart, Capt. Wayne (P) 491BG 88, 207, 279
Stewart, Lt. James N (P) 392BG 97
Stewart, Maj. James Maitland (P) 445BG 88, 207, 279
Stilbert, Lt. Thomas J (P) 453BG 166
Still, Lt. (P) 44BG 226
Stilson, Lt. Charles W (P) 458BG 147
Stock, Capt. Phillip A (P) 453BG 127
Stoddart, Lt. (P) 392BG 260
Stoddard, Sgt (CG) 44BG 61
Stoffel, Sgt Glenn C (WG) 44BG 78
Stokley, Lt. William L (P) 491BG 180, 185
Stoltz, Lt. Clarence E (P) 392BG 174
Stone, Lt. Robert N (CP) 389BG 77
Stonebraker, Lt. Bill (P) 448BG 212
Stoneburner, Lt. Paul (P) 458BG 214
Stotter, Capt. Willard (P) 389BG 145
Strain, Capt. Dean B (P) 491BG 261
Strom, Lt. Allan H (P) 446BG 136
Stroup, Lt. Joseph M (P) 458BG 139
Stukas, Lt. John (P) 392BG 94
Sturdevant, Lt. Harry E (P) 466BG 136
Sturm, Lt. (P) 392BG 283
Suchio, Lt. John (P) 446BG 209
Suitch, Lt. John J (P) 445BG 107
Sullivan, Capt. James P (P) 448BG 179
Sullivan, Lt. Fred R (P) 467BG 197
Sullivan, Sgt Kenneth E (WG) 44BG 108
Suprenant, Lt. Charles E (P) 446BG 108
Susan, T/Sgt John L (ROG) 44BG 31
Swain, Lt. Russell T (P) 466BG 170
Swanson, Lt. Clark E, (CP) 44BG 23
Swanson, Capt. John W (P) 44BG 32
Swanson, Lt. Sidney D (P) 445BG 106
Sweatt, Sgt Robert (BT) 389BG 88, 91
Swetlik, Sgt William M (G) 44BG 108
Swick, T/Sgt Ray E (ROG) 44BG 122
Swiegart, Lt. Glenn E (P) 492BG 152
Swigert, Lt. Robert K (P) 453BG 137
Swofford, Lt. Paul (P) 445BG 243
Sykes, Lt. William W (N) 93BG 59
Synder, Lt. Miles A (P) 389BG 123
Szabo, Sgt Paul A (TG) 44BG 108

T

Taft, Lt. Albert J (P) 466BG 139
Talbott, Lt. David R (P) 44BG 121
Tannenbaum, Lt. Hal J (P) 93BG 40
Tate, Lt. Joe (P) 93BG 17
Tate, L/Col. Joe (P) 93BG 79
Taylor, Lt. Charles (CP) 44BG 80
Taylor, Lt. Edward F (P) 44BG 74
Taylor, Lt. Edward J (CP) 392BG 219
Taylor, Lt. Roger R (CP) 389BG 82
Taylor, S/Sgt Earl L (BT) 448BG 189
Teague, Lt. Alan (P) 448BG 81, 132, 133
Tedrowe, Lt. Thaddeus W (P) 466BG 142
Teitel, Lt. Abraham (B) 44BG 91
Telford, Lt. George D (P) 44BG 123, 124
Telken, Lt. Henry F (P) 392BG 202
Teltser, Lt. Milton (P) 93BG 52
Tennant, T/Sgt Jim (ROG) 389BG 173
Tepe, S/Sgt Carl W (NT) 44BG 187
Terry, Lt. William J (P) 466BG 128
Testa, Capt. (P) 44BG 260
Thackeray, Lt. Francis J ( ) 389 BG 89
Thom, Lt. George J (P) 44BG 134
Thomas, Lt. J M (P) 93BG 66
Thomas, Sgt Archie M (WG) 44BG 134
Thompson, Col. Heber (P) 448BG 272
Thompson, Col. James E CO 448BG 132, 133
Thompson, Lt. David W (P) 93BG 109
Thompson, Lt. Evert R (P) 458BG 165, 208
Thompson, Lt. Francis S (CP) 458BG 171, 172
Thompson, Lt. John E (CP) 458BG 252
Thornton, Lt. Charles L (P) 445BG 183
Tideman, Lt. John R (N) 389BG 252
Tiefenthal, Lt.Dexter (P) 392BG 127, 144
Timberlake, Maj. Ted CO, 68BS, 44BG 11
Timberlake, Col. Ted CO, 93BG 12, 16, 39, 40, 41
Timberlake, B/Gen. Ted CG, 20CBW 138, 145, 167, 185
Tims, Lt. Bob (N) 445BG 232, 235, 241, 242
Tobin, Lt. Patrick T Jnr. (P) 453BG 117
Tod, Lt. Frederick (P) 448BG 274
Todd, Lt. Edwin J (P) 93BG 82
Tofte, F/O Donald F (P) 44BG 203
Tollason, Lt. (P) 389BG 51
Tollasen, Maj. (P) 389BG 278
Tollok, Cpl Robert C (TG) 392BG 217
Tomblin, Lt. James N (N) 44BG 225
Tomer, Lt. Frank J (P) 44BG 171
Torr, Lt. Francis E (P) 445BG 128
Totten, Lt. David R (P) 458BG 275, 280
Torrance, Lt. Douglas (P) 448BG 280
Towles, Lt. Raymond S (P) 448BG 180
Townsend, Lt. Raymond H (P) 44BG 134
Tracey, Lt. John C (P) 492BG 162
Treichel, Sgt Richard J (ROG) 44BG 91
Trenchard, Sir Hugh 'Boom', Marshal of the RAF 39
Trivison, Sgt Joseph R (ROG) 392BG 150
Trolese, Lt. Alex (P) 44BG 73
Trotto, Lt. (CP) 445BG 243
Trump, Lt. Lester (CP) 446BG 211
Tubbs, Sgt Herbert L (TG) 392BG 202
Tuck, Lt. Sterling (P) 446BG 110, 141
Tucker, Lt. Elbert F (P) 389BG 114
Tucker, Lt. Emmett Z (PN) 44BG 207
Tucker, Lt. James (P) 44BG 188
Tucker, Lt. Walter L (CP) 389BG 173
Turnbull, Col. John (P) 44BG 228
Turner, Capt. Omar A (P) 93BG 98
Turner, Lt. Claude A (P) 93BG 52, 69
Turner, Lt. Wilbur H (P) 448BG 180
Turocy, Lt. John W (P) 44BG 152
Turpin, Lt. Harold (P) 448BG 187
Turpin, Lt. Max E (P) 448BG 151
Tye, Lt. Frank R (P) 453BG 152
Tyler, Lt. Ace W (P) 392BG 173

U

Uebelheuer, Capt. Wilbur (P) 445BG 234
Unangst, Lt. Russell S (B) 93BG 79
Underwood, Lt. James F (P) 467BG 196

Ungerer, Lt. Maynard M (P) 467BG 230
Unwin, Lt. Clifford (CP) 448BG 212
Ursy, Lt. William F (P) 392BG 95
Urban, Lt. James E (P) 448BG 90

V
Val Preda, Capt. Peter (P) 492BG 159
Van Blair, S/Sgt Dale (G) 389BG 153
Vance, L/Col. Leon R (P) 489BG 170, 176, 269
Vance, Lt. Lewis I (P) 44BG 169
Vance, Sgt (TG) 44BG 271
Vance, Sgt Robert T (TG) 44BG 169
Vann, Lt. Tom P (P) 389BG 197
Van Heusen, Lt. Horace (P) 389BG 211
Van Oyen, Sgt Harold D (BT) 44BG 31
Van Tress, Lt. Harold P (N) 467BG 268
Van Winkle, Lt. Warren O (P) 93BG 169
Varty, S/Sgt Robert M (ROG) 445BG 145
Velarde, Lt. (P) 492BG 159
Verberg, Lt. Melvin H (B) 389BG 73
Vetterneck, Sgt (Eng.) 448BG 264
Vickers, Lt. Robert E (P) 392BG 260
Viehl, Herr Nazi Labour camp member 245
Vivian, Lt. Gerald M (P) 389BG 181
Vogel, Lt. Kurt (P) 458BG 214
Vogel, Lt. Richard (P) 448BG 215
Voight, Lt. (P) 448BG 272
Voight, Lt. Robert O (P) 448BG 127
Voskian, Lt. Alfred A (P) 453BG 97
Vowinkle, Lt. M (P) 492BG 163
Vukovich, Lt. Matthew (P) 491BG 231

W
Wade, Lt. Burton L (P) 392BG 262
Wagner, Sgt James M (TG) 445BG 195
Wagner, S/Sgt F Y (G) 392BG 125
Wahler, Lt. (P) 445BG 133
Wahnee, Lt. Myers (P) 448BG 125, 127
Walker, Lt. Larry (CP) 491BG 202
Wall, Lt. Ed (P) 448BG 259
Walla, Sgt Mitchell A (WG) 392BG 107
Wallace, L/Col. A L (P) 467BG 255
Wallace, T/Sgt Frank C (ROG) 392BG 125
Walker, Lt. Joseph R (P) 392BG 264, 283
Walker, Lt. Larry (CP) 491BG 202
Walker, Lt. Robert K (N) 44BG 29
Walker, Lt. William M (P) 492BG 163, 203
Wallace, Lt. C N (B) 389BG 51
Wallace, Sgt Frank C (ROG) 392BG 125
Wallendar, Lt. Warren M (P) 466BG 167
Walls, Capt. Ed (P) 448BG 259
Walsh, Lt. Frank T (N) 392BG 126
Walsh, Lt. H Ben (P) 389BG 45
Walsh, Lt. James H (P) 44BG 168, 169
Walters, Lt. Charles W (P) 93BG 89
Walther, Lt. Edgar (P) 445BG 238
Walzel, Lt. Leland (B) 93BG 116
Wapensky, Sgt Russell A (WG) 44BG
Warczak, Lt. (P) 491BG 214
Warke, Lt. William A (P) 448BG 188
Warman, Lt. Lesley (P) 445BG 238
Warne, Capt. 'Bucky' (P) 44BG 29
Warner, Lt. Theo (CP) 448BG 273
Warnes, Capt. 'Bucky' (P) 44BG 29
Warnock, Lt. Roland D (P) 448BG 108
Warren, Lt. Charles W (P) 392BG 263, 280
Warren, S/Sgt William A (Eng.) 448BG 132
Watkins, Capt. Howard D (P) 392BG 247
Watson, Lt. Ernest L (P) 492BG 161
Waugh, Lt. Colby A (P) 392BG 88
Waxler, S/Sgt Hyman (NT) 93BG 116
Weant, Lt. Baxter W (P) 446BG 72, 76
Weaver, Lt. Kenneth (P) 448BG 132
Weaver, Lt. Ted L (P) 44BG 192
Weaver, Lt. Worden (P) 44BG 192
Webber, Lt. Jack (P) 445BG 195
Webster, Lt. Kenneth F (P) 445BG 218
Week, Lt. William F (B) 446BG 183
Weeklund, Lt. Oscar A (P) 466BG 186
Wehunt, Sgt John W (TG) 392BG 180, 186
Weidman, Sgt Bill (WG) 389BG 262
Weinstein, Lt. Ira (B) 445BG 240, 241
Weiser, Capt. Henry A (B) 44BG 91
Weiss, Lt. (P) 389BG 263
Weitz, Lt. Floyd I (P) 491BG 231
Wenzlaff, Sgt Richard W 107
(ROG) 392BG
Werment, Lt. Peter (N) 448BG 132
Wermeyer, Lt. Raymond A (P) 448BG 183
Wesson, Lt. William H (P) 492BG 160, 163, 202
Westcott, Lt. Gerald S (P) 44BG 188
Westcott, Lt. Philip R (B) 446BG 141
Westerbake, Capt. Don (P) 389BG 139
Westover, Col. CO, 448BG 272
Whalen, Lt. J M (CP) 392BG 216
Whitaker, Lt. Coleman S (P) 44BG 25, 58
White, Lt. Robert K (P) 392 BG 107
White, Lt. Charles E (P) 467BG 206
White, Lt. Claude E (P) 389BG 106
White, Lt. Edmund J (P) 392B 215
White, Lt. H E (CP) 448BG 90
White, Lt. Harry A (P) 392BG 180
White, Lt. Ralph L (N) 392BG 194
White, Lt. Harry A (P) 392BG 176, 198
White, Lt. Robert K (P) 392BG 107
White, Lt. Robert M (P) 93BG 127
Whitehead, Lt. Kaylor C (P) 453BG 230
Whitlock, Capt. Charles A (P) 44BG 55
Whitlow, Capt. Bob 2nd Weather Scouting Force 232
Whittlemore, Lt. Warren T (P) 392BG 186
Whyte, Sgt Jack S (WG) 448BG 98
Wiest, Lt. Charles L (P) 44BG 135
Wiitala, Sgt Eino J (NG) 44BG 173
Wilborn, Lt. Everett W (CP) 44BG 31
Wilhelmi, Capt. Bill (P) 448BG 272
Wilhite, Capt. David L (P) 389BG 88
Wilkerson, Lt. F T (P) 389BG
Wilkinson, Lt. R L (P) 93BG 52
Wilks, Sgt Willie R (G) 458BG 280
Willet, Lt. John (CP) 445BG 239
Williams, Capt. William J (P) 93BG 33
Williams, Lt. (P) 448BG 147
Williams, Lt. Dale (P) 389BG 267
Williams, Lt. Jim (P) 445BG 244
Williams. Lt. Melvyn H (P) 453BG 184
Williams, Lt. Wesley R (P) 492BG 158
Williams, Lt. William F (P) 93BG 38
Williams, Sgt Charles L (TG) 392BG 247
Williamson, Lt. Leroy M (CP) 44BG 135
Williamson, M/Sgt Richard (GC) 44BG 102
Williamson, E F Norwich Lord Mayor 279
Willis (rank?) Combat crew, 392BG 193
Willius, Oblt. Karl-Heinz (P) 2/JG26 137
Wilson, Lt. Andy T (P) 491BG 270
Wilson. Lt. Bernard O (CP) 458BG 172
Wilson, Fonzy M (ROG) 392BG 151
Wilson, Lt. George (P) 448BG 193, 197
Wilson, Lt. James A (P) 448BG 192
Wilson, Lt. R C (P) 491BG 219
Wilson, Sgt Fonzy M (ROG) 392BG 151
Winard, (Combat crew) 445BG
Wind, Lt. (P) 44BG 136, 138
Winger, Lt. George (P) 44BG 50
Winn, Lt. Eugene T (P) 446BG 171
Winn, Lt. Jack M (P) 44BG 135
Winn, S/Sgt Charles (ROG) 44BG 135
Wittala, Sgt Eino J (NG) 44BG 173
Wolbarst, T/Sgt (GC) 44BG 199, 200
Wollstein, Lt. Dick S (P) 466BG 209
Womble, Lt. Hubert K (P) 93BG 49
Wood, Col. Jack W CO, 389BG 43, 167, 185
Woods, Lt. Don P (P) 392BG 214
Woodward, Lt. Edward J (P) 93BG 182
Woodward, Lt. Ralph (P) 389BG 195
Woesterberg, Wim Dutch Resistance civilian 262
Wollstein, Lt. Dick S (P) 466BG 209
Woollen, Lt. Bryan W (P) 489BG 193
Wooten, Ms. Anne British. Civilian 136
Wozniak, Lt. Robert J (P) 389BG 101
Wright, S/Sgt Donald G (TG) 453BG 118
Wunder, Lt. John C (P) 466BG 185
Wunderlin, Lt. Carl F (CP) 392BG 191
Wyatt, Lt. Bert W (P) 392BG 151
Wyatt, Lt. Jack L (P) 389BG 140
Wygonik, T/Sgt Adam C (Eng.) 44BG 32
Wyllie, Sgt (GC) 392BG 75
Wyman, Lt. Elroy F (N) 389BG 102
Wynn, Lt. James J (P) 491BG 231

Y
Yarnell, S/Sgt Robert H (BT) 448BG 104
Yates, Sgt L (G) 93BG 49
Yeager, Maj. William H (P) 389BG 51
Yeates, S/Sgt Clyde K (ROG) 392BG 214
Yensho, Pvt Edward Drop-master 392BG 221
Yerkes, Lt. W L (B) 445BG 87
Yocco, S/Sgt Dominic P (ROG) 44BG 192
Yoders, Lt. (P) 389BG 210
York, Lt. Charles C (P) 448BG 113, 116
Young, Lt. Howard (P) 389BG 278
Young, Sgt Donald (WG) 44BG 141
Young, S/Sgt John (NT) 389BG 271, 272
Yungert, Lt. Walter A (P) 448BG 87

Z
Zeller, Lt. Robert (P) 446BG 179
Zerangue, Sgt Felix A (G) 392BG 107
Zierdt, Sgt Kenneth A (ROG) 448BG 180
Zimmerman, T/Sgt Earl (ROG) 389BG 43, 259
Zweig, Lt. Louis E (P) 44BG 194

Abbreviation Key (USAAF)

(B)	Bombardier
(CG)	Commanding General
C-in-C	Commander in Chief
CO	Commanding Officer
(CP)	Co-pilot
(Eng.)	Engineer/top turret
(G)	Gunner
(GC)	Ground crew
(GI)	German-language Interpreter
(N)	Navigator
(NT)	Nose turret
(P)	Pilot
(PN)	Pilotage navigator
(RO)	Radar-operator
(ROG)	Radio operator/ gunner
(TG)	Tail gunner
(VI)	Voice-interpreter (German-language)
(WG)	Waist gunner

Abbreviations (German Ranks)

Hptm	Hauptmann
Ltn.	Leutnant
Oblt.	Oberleutnent
Ogfr.	Obergefreiter